volume 1

AN AUTOBIOGRAPHY OF

Orville A. Hurt

* introduction by
United States Senator
PAUL SIMON

LACK POLITICS
by DEMPSEY J. TRAVIS

Library of Congress Cataloging-in-Publication Data

Travis, Dempsey J., 1920–
    An Autobiography of Black Politics
    Bibliography: p.
    Includes Index
    1. Afro-Americans—Illinois—Chicago—Politics
and government. 2. Chicago (Ill.)—Politics and
government—1951. 3. Chicago (Ill.)—Race relations.
4. Travis, Dempsey J., 1920–   I. Title
F548.9.N4T73 1987   977.3'1100496073   85-15646
ISBN 0-941484-05-x

This work is dedicated to civil rights workers, both black and white, living and dead, who fought in the struggle to achieve racial parity through the ballot box for All Americans.

Acknowledgments

The writing of a book is a very solitary task. However, this writer had to literally touch bases with thousands of people, both living and dead (through newspapers and books), before putting pencil to paper and writing the first word in the first chapter and the subsequent twenty-four chapters that followed. Therefore, I want to first thank the 362 individuals who took hours out of their busy schedules to permit me to electronically record their political experiences.

The tone of this work would have been different if Mary F. Grady, regional coordinator of community services, United States Department of Commerce, Bureau of Census, had not had blind faith in my belief that George White, Chicago's first town crier and auctioneer was a black man. Prior to contacting Mrs. Grady, I had been told by all of the most highly respected authorities that George White was a white man because there were no indications in the historical reference books that identified him as a black man. However, for reasons unknown to me, I still believed that George White was black. Hence, Mrs. Mary F. Grady, at my request, drove to the Census warehouse which is located west of Chicago, and spent some four hours checking the Chicago 1840 Census Tract. At 4 p.m. on a Thursday afternoon she called me from the warehouse and told me that I was right. She subsequently furnished me with xeroxed copies of documents verifying that George White was a free black man and that he lived in the Second Ward on Chicago's South Side with his wife, two kids and both parents.

Hence, the first chapter in An Autobiography of Black Politics is entitled, "A Man For Sale In Chicago." It was so entitled because George White, a black man, bought a white indentured servant at an auction held on the corner of LaSalle and Randolph in front of the new courthouse.

Authoring a book is a daily writing task in addition to requiring a constant infusion in new research material. Therefore, let me give thanks to those who stuck to the last. Mrs. Ruby Davis, my senior researcher, ran the full four-year course. And without her untiring efforts in unearthing hundreds of documents and thousands of old newspapers and memorabilia, much of the information in this body of work might have never seen the light of day between the covers of a book. Likewise, Dr. Delores Lipscomb, professor of English at Chicago State University and the editor for Urban Research Press has consistently kept me on course. She is truly a dedicated professional. Initially, she came aboard thinking that the editing job would be completed on this current work during her summer vacation. Hence, two years later, we are completing the assignment, and during that period Dr. Lipscomb has never lost her freshness of spirit and her inspirational guidance. Neither of us expected that our modest literary project would grow to giant size. (The original bibliography was over 100 book pages. Therefore, we found it necessary to eliminate 75 percent of the newspaper references at the request of the publisher in order to keep the book size under 700 pages.)

Other persons who have been very helpful in making our work possible were Mrs. Dorothy Lyles, library associate and Mr. Edward Manney, both of the Vivian G. Harsh Collection of Afro-American History and literature at the Carter G. Woodson Regional Library in Chicago, Illinois. Mrs. Sylvia Graber Foley, with the Reference and Research Social Science and History Division of the main branch of the Chicago Public Library and Mr. Lyle Benedict, reference librarian of the Chicago Municipal Reference Library, Chicago City Hall. Thanks also to the Chicago Historical Society for the help of Larry Viskochil, curator of Prints and Photographs, Anne Steinfeldt, assistant curator of Prints and Photographs and Archie Motley, curator of Archives and Manuscripts in assisting me in using both their archival and picture libraries. Last but not least, I want to express my deep appreciation for my wife Moselynne's understanding of my desire to want to ride two career horses at the same time. The stallions respond to the names of writing and real estate.

Dempsey J. Travis
1987

Table of Contents

Introduction by United States Senator Paul Simon

Dempsey Travis is a Jeffersonian type of person with interests in many areas. Many know him as a successful business leader. But my guess is that he will be remembered primarily for his contributions in the field of literature.

This book is a good example. The author tells an important part of history but tells it in a fashion that combines historical accuracy with a great storytelling ability. Unfortunately, most writers of history do not have that skill. The late Alan Nevins of Illinois, one of the finest historians in the history of our country, was one who had that. As I read the manuscript, it reminded me of the Alan Nevins style: direct, interesting, with no excessive flourishes. I like that style.

Dempsey Travis has written a fascinating account of American citizens who have gradually achieved more and more through the political process. I have had the good fortune to know many of the people in the more recent years covered in this book. And even where I have known them, I learned little details I did not know before—that my longtime friend Corneal Davis once lost an election, about Bill Dawson's wooden leg, about a host of small things that are both fascinating and a part of history. From what I know, his account is accurate. But it is much more than accurate. He provides color and a detail that add understanding to this important history.

As you read this account, you come across characters like John "Mushmouth" Johnson, Chicago's first black gambling czar, and other leaders of one variety or another who do not have names quite as fascinating as his but whose exploits are just as intriguing.

The book is also a good illustration of the fact that progress is never achieved easily, nor is the road forward one that is traveled in a straight line.

This history also should remind us that opportunity must be provided to everyone. Those who fought for opportunity for others in some of the difficult days covered by this book can be proud of what they have contributed. Today, there are others besides black Americans who also need opportunity. They include Hispanic Americans, Asian Americans, and women.

Others will write their history.

Dempsey Travis has enriched all of us with this thoughtful, interesting, scholarly book.

Paul Simon
United States Senator

Paul Simon, at the age of 19, began a publishing career at the *Troy* (Ill.) *Tribune* that grew to embrace a chain of fourteen weekly newspapers. At the age of 26, he was elected to the Illinois House of Representatives in 1954. In 1962, he was elected to the Illinois Senate. At the age of 46 he was elected to the U.S. House of Representatives in 1974. And in 1984 he was elected to the U.S. Senate. Mr. Simon has also authored ten books.

Photo Credits

1

"CHECAGOU" (CHICAGO) THE EARLY YEARS

Chicago Tribune Tower rises from the 1779 homesite of Chicago's first citizen, Jean Baptiste Pointe DuSable.

ARTIST'S CONCEPTION OF JEAN-BAPTISTE POINTE DU SABLE

RENDERED FROM A DESCRIPTION IN A BRITISH ARMY REPORT

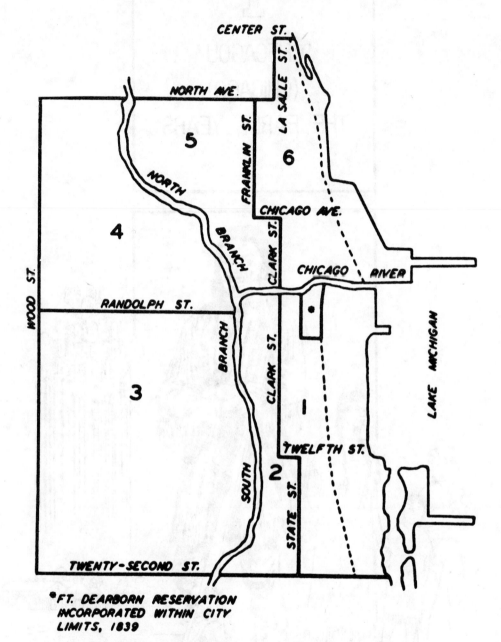

CENTER ST.

NORTH AVE.

5

NORTH BRANCH

FRANKLIN ST.

LA SALLE ST.

6

CHICAGO AVE.

CLARK ST.

4

CHICAGO RIVER

WOOD ST.

RANDOLPH ST.

BRANCH

CLARK ST.

LAKE MICHIGAN

3

1

SOUTH BRANCH

TWELFTH ST.

2

STATE ST.

TWENTY-SECOND ST.

*FT. DEARBORN RESERVATION
INCORPORATED WITHIN CITY
LIMITS, 1839

WARD BOUNDARIES OF CHICAGO, 1837

-------- OLD SHORE LINE

Ward boundaries of Chicago, 1837.

Chapter *I*

A Man is for Sale in Chicago

Zebina Eastman, a tall and slightly-built twenty-seven year old chalk white abolitionist, was standing on the southeast corner of LaSalle and Randolph Streets with his friend, Calvin DeWolf, a young law student, in the law offices of Spring and Goodrich. DeWolf also had co-founded with Eastman, The Western Citizens, an anti-slavery organization. They were waiting to witness the first black slave auction to be held in the city of Chicago. The date was Monday, November 14, 1842. The auction was scheduled to begin at 9:30 A.M. It was 9:50 A.M., and Sheriff Samuel J. Lowe and his Negro prisoner, Edwin Heathcock, had not emerged from the log cabin jail which was located

Left: Calvin DeWolf as an older man in the late 1860s. Right: Zebina Eastman, co-founder of the Abolitionist Movement in Chicago, IL.

on the northwest corner of Randolph and Clark Streets. Auction buyers and spectators were crammed on Randolph Street between Clark and LaSalle tighter than sardines in a can. Everybody was eagerly waiting to witness the historical event.

Zebina Eastman's account of the circumstances leading up to the auction follows. Edwin Heathcock, the inmate who was to be auctioned off, had enjoyed a good reputation as a well-behaved and industrious colored man and an active member of the Chicago Methodist Church. His community status instantly changed after he had a quarrel with a white fellow workman while laboring in the field on the north branch of the Chicago River. The white man retaliated against Edwin's indocile behavior by having him arrested on the grounds that the Negro had entered the state of Illinois without free papers or having posted bond. Heathcock was brought before Justice Lewis C. Kercheval where he refused to say whether he ever had a master or owner, or ever even wanted one.

At 10:05 A.M., Sheriff Lowe walked out of the jail house with Heathcock walking on his right. As they made their way through the crowd in the short walk to the courthouse steps at LaSalle and Randolph, the Chicago wind blew its November breath through the courthouse square, bone chilling cold. Heathcock shuddered as they walked west on Randolph Street from the effect of the brisk Lake Michigan wind or, perhaps, from the fact that he was passing through a mass of unfamiliar white faces implanted with sky blue, cat-gray, and light brown eyes. Being center stage and stared at by a sea of strange colored eyes was an experience unlike any Edwin Heathcock had had in his life.

Judge J. D. Caton, early Chicago leader and magistrate.

William B. Ogden, Chicago's first mayor.

Eastman observed the frightened look on Heathcock's face, turned to DeWolf and said, "I would feel queer if I were being sold by the sheriff instead of my horse, cow or dog." DeWolf shoved his hands deeper into his warm coat pockets and gave Eastman an affirmative nod.

A nod was not enough; hence, Eastman asked DeWolf, a fellow abolitionist, a direct question, "Is this the first slave sale to take place in Chicago?"

DeWolf turned to Eastman with a bright glint in his pale blue eyes and replied:

> Chicago always does justice to her natives. Its first settler was a black man named Jean Baptiste DuSable. DuSable preceded John Kinzie in the settlement of Chicago and is the black root from which all our glory was sprung. Moreover, there was a forerunner for what is taking place here this morning. According to Judge J. D. Caton, a precedent was set in 1837 when a white man was sold in a slave auction on this very same corner. The white man was a vagrant from the State of Maryland, and he was sold as such to a black man by the name of George White who was then the Chicago town crier for auctions and lost children. White still lives in the Second Ward on Market Street with his wife, two children and both of his parents. To my knowledge, George White has always been a free colored person and a good enough Democrat to have been appointed city crier by William B. Ogden shortly after he became the first mayor of Chicago on May 2, 1837. Hence, the auction we are witnessing today is a sequel to an event that took place five years earlier.

Although Eastman appeared comfortable with DeWolf's explanation of the slave auction, Sheriff Lowe's usually tight-lipped English demeanor was showing signs of discomfort because he had been encumbered with an embarrassing circumstance. The sheriff's discomfort was caused by the glum and scowling expressions on the faces of the spectators. Lowe, in the process of carrying out his lawful duties, offered Edwin Heathcock for sale and called for bids. The offer was answered with dead silence. The silent treatment caused Sheriff Lowe's complexion to turn from a cold November beet red to a glowing fireplace ember. Lowe felt called upon to say the following:

> I am only the agent of the law, and this colored man was committed to jail by a sitting judge because he could not prove that he was a free man, nor has any master proved that he was a slave. The law requires that I sell this Negro to pay the expenses for his keep in jail.

No bids came in. The auction went on:

> Here is an able-bodied man; I am required to sell him for a term of service for the best price I can get for him to pay his jail fees. How much am I bid?

An older picture of Mahlon D. Ogden, a younger brother of Mayor William B. Ogden.

Elijah P. Lovejoy, an anti-slavery advocate, who was murdered in Alton, Illinois because of his publishing and organizational efforts for universal freedom.

No bids. Sheriff Lowe looked at the crowd with his arms open as if he were going to hug an obese woman and in a shrill voice said:

> Gentlemen, this is not a pleasant job. Don't blame me, but the law. I am compelled to do it. If I can get no bid for this man, I must return him to jail and continue the sale at another time.

No bids came as a result of Sheriff Lowe's pathetic appeals. Finally, the threat of putting the poor man back in jail caused a spectator with a loud thundering voice standing on the southside of Randolph Street across from the courthouse to shout, "I bid twenty-five cents." It was the voice of Attorney Mahlon B. Ogden, a younger brother of William B. Ogden, the first mayor of Chicago.

Appeals were made by Lowe in the usual manner for an increase of the bid. "Do I hear more? Only twenty-five cents for this able-bodied man, only a quarter?"

No additional bids were made. Since Mr. Ogden refused to raise his bid, the prisoner was sold to him for twenty-five cents. Mr. Mahlon B. Ogden parted the crowd as he walked across Randolph Street and pulled twenty-five cents from his pocket and handed it to Sheriff Lowe in the presence of all the spectators who gave him a loud cheer.

Attorney Ogden then called Edwin Heathcock to him and said: "Edwin I have bought you; I have given a quarter for you; you are my man—my slave! Now, you go where you please."

Heathcock thanked Ogden with a broad smile and gracious bow before walking in short quick steps south on LaSalle Street in the direction of his home on Market Street, which was located in the Second Ward.

Eastman and DeWolfe watched Heathcock until he disappeared in the LaSalle Street early afternoon crowd. They were both pleased with Ogden's act of liberation in the light of the fact that his eldest brother, William B. Ogden, was the vice president of the Chicago Colonization Society, a group that had endorsed the proposition of moving Negroes back to Africa as a solution to the problem.

Zebina Eastman was a professional journalist who became involved in the movement shortly after the murder of publisher, Elijah Lovejoy on November 8, 1837 in Alton, Illinois by a mob of pro-slavery advocates, who were determined that there would be no anti-slavery organizations in Illinois.

The Saloon Building Hall. The structure stood on the southeast corner of Lake and Clark Streets and was erected in 1836. The first meeting to procure a charter for the city of Chicago was held in this building on Monday, January 23, 1837. The Chicago Common Council leased space on the third floor for activities of the city government and for a Municipal Court. Hence, between the years of 1837 and 1842, the Saloon Building functioned as City Hall. The word "saloon" is synonymous with France's "salon," meaning a spacious hall.

Eastman recapped the events that took place in Chicago in January 1838 as a result of the slaughtering of Lovejoy:

> Soon after the murder of Lovejoy, there was a meeting called in Chicago not in sympathy with the cause of abolition but to condemn this assault on the constitutional right of the freedom of the press.

According to Eastman, the brave men who were present at that small meeting in the Saloon Building became prominent afterwards in the anti-slavery movement in Chicago. This was the beginning of the anti-slavery sentiment that became a power in Chicago and distinguished the city throughout the country as one that proved itself a law abiding community by sheltering and protecting the fugitive slaves against arrest.

On January 16, 1840, the same group of noble citizens who met in secret in the small hall in the Saloon Building came out of the closet and held a public meeting in the largest hall in the Saloon Building and became formally known as the Chicago Anti-slavery Society. The president of the group was Henry Smith of the First Presbyterian Church; the secretary was Calvin DeWolf. The organization was also supported by a few individuals who were either Methodist or Baptist. A resolution was adopted for the peaceable abolition of slavery throughout the world and denouncing the "Black Laws" of Illinois specifically.

On December 15, 1840, the *Chicago American* published a petition to the state legislature pleading to remove from Illinois statutes those laws known collectively as the "Black Laws" which prevented Negroes from testifying against whites and which permitted any white man to cause any black man who did not show his papers of freedom to be thrown in jail.

The "Black Laws" was a body of regulations employed to dehumanize the Negro. Section five of the "Black Laws" was extremely severe in that it decreed that any black or mulatto (50% Negro) found in Illinois without a certificate of freedom would be deemed a runaway slave or servant and be committed to the custody of the sheriff. If after a six week incarceration period, the black mulatto could not produce a certificate or give evidence of his freedom, he or she would be sold to the highest bidder. Thus, a black or mulatto would be put on the auction block as a companion to swine, sheep, or cows. The Black Law ignored due process of the law and imprisoned blacks without trial by jury. The only offense necessary for being thrown into prison and subjected to being sold into involuntary servitude was being black or mulatto.

Harassing unknown blacks on the streets of Chicago under the guise of checking their freedom papers was Deputy Sheriff Henry Rhines' favorite pastime. In December 1845, Rhines arrested a Negro who answered to the name of P. C. Jones on a writ issued by the office of Justice Lewis C. Kercheval.

The charge in the writ was that P. C. Jones was not a freeman but a slave because a white man who resided in Missouri charged that Jones was his slave.

The man in Missouri did not have an agent in Chicago to look after his interest in the claim; therefore, the Negro was brought before Justice Kercheval to answer the charge. Zebina Eastman, also an active member of the Chicago Anti-slavery Society, was alerted that another colored man had been apprehended by Rhines while he was at work in the office of the Western Citizens at Sixty-three Lake Street.

Eastman, a journalist and eye witness, described the events of that day:

> The word was in the streets minutes after P. C. Jones was arrested that Rhines 'Got hold of another Nigger', and had him in Justice Kercheval's office.

Eastman recalled that he and Dr. Charles Volney Dyer, accompanied by a score of black friends of the prisoner and quite a number of "respectable" white people, arrived at Justice Kercheval's office where they found him busy making out extradition papers. Dr. Dyer informed the justice that the extradition was being contested.

Attorney James H. Collins was sent for. The rumor that a nigger had been caught spread through the streets. An almost instant crowd of people gathered on the plank-surfaced street and packed the justice's office on the

Dr. Charles Volney Dyer, M.D. He was one of slavery's fiercest opponents. As a physician, he stood at the head of his profession.

John Kinzie in 1804 purchased a home that was originally owned by Chicago's first citizen and landowner, a black man named Jean Baptiste DuSable.

Lake Street in 1843 was the hub of many of Chicago's retail and commercial establishments. It was among the early streets to be blessed by the city fathers with wooden plank walks. In the rainy season mud and gook oozed through the cracks of the planks onto pedestrians' shoes.

second floor of the wooden building on Clark Street. The crowd was very dense in front of the building, blocking up Clark Street from Lake Street to Water Street (Wacker Drive). The little courtroom and the narrow stairwell were stuffed with spectators. Eastman felt that the frame structure was going to cave in and that he would be lost in one common muddle. When Lawyer Collins arrived, he critically examined the papers prepared by Justice Kercheval and found no flaw which would free P. C. Jones.

After meditating several minutes with his eyes closed, Attorney Collins jumped to his feet and yelped out: "This man is charged with being a slave in Missouri now. I deny that slavery exists in Missouri."

The Justice retorted: "Your statement is absurd; everybody knows that slavery exists in Missouri."

"I deny it", protested Attorney Collins as he continued:

And you cannot take as evidence what everybody says; it must be proved before your Honor. Your Honor's court is too high grade to be taking evidence on hearsay. It must be proved by the law itself.

"It must be proved", the Justice agreed and said: "Where is the statute book for Missouri?"

There were no Missouri statutes in the justice's office.

He had to send his messenger to a neighboring law office in search of the Missouri statute books. The crowd grew restless during the long wait for the return of the messenger. Before the messenger returned and during this pause in the process of administering justice, the "Nigger" P. C. Jones rose like a soap bubble and glided over the heads of the throng and down the staircase to the sidewalk. The crowd moved down the stairway to follow and Deputy Sheriff Rhines like Jill, "came tumbling after."

Reaching the sidewalk, Rhines pulled out his pistol, but the pressure of the crowd forced him to point the gun up in the direction of his nose which was not his target. Justice Kercheval, in the meantime, was waiting for the statute and looking out of the window at a frustrated deputy sheriff and an eager and excited crowd of mingling men, wagons, horses and drays. In the midst of the gay carnival-like atmosphere, the Negro was hoisted onto the highest seat of the best carriage on the street while the spare seats were filled with laughing young men. The daring young fellows drove the carriage east on Lake Street while an immense crowd followed, shouting and cheering the rescued and the rescuers.

Eastman wrote in his memoirs that this was the last slavery excitement that he, Zebina Eastman, witnessed under the Black Laws in Chicago, Illinois. However, he was an eye witness to riots and many acts of violence perpetrated against Negroes during the remaining forty plus years of office and life in Chicago. Mr. Eastman died on June 14, 1883.

UNITED STATES OF AMERICA,

STATE OF ILLINOIS, } ss. { To all to whom these Presents may come—GREETING:
Madison County,

Know Ye, That *John Jones* a person of Color, about _twenty seven_ years of age, _past five_ feet _ten_ — inches high, _mulatto_ — complexion,

has exhibited, presented and filed, in the Office of the Clerk of the Circuit Court of the County and State aforesaid, a **CERTIFICATE,** duly authenticated, of **FREEDOM,** as such person of Color, *has a scar over the left eye. Brow a scratch across the cheek bone a scar on the left shin bone foot or to ankle*

Now, therefore, I, **WM. TYLER BROWN,** Clerk of the Circuit Court of Madison County, State of Illinois, **CERTIFY,** That said *John Jones* — — is a FREE PERSON OF COLOR, a resident or citizen of the State of Illinois, and entitled to be respected accordingly, in Person and Property, at all times and places, in the due prosecution of _his_ — Lawful concerns.

In Testimony whereof, I have, to these Presents, signed my name, and affixed the Seal of said Court, at Edwardsville, this *28th* day of *November* in the year of our Lord one thousand eight hundred and forty-four

Wm T Brown Clerk.

John Jones' Certificate of Freedom. Most communities required free Negroes to carry such certificates on their person at all times. Not all of them provided printed forms such as this one, which was issued by the clerk of the Circuit Court of Madison County, state of Illinois.

Chapter *II*

John Jones: A Political Beginning

John Jones was an antebellum love child born in Green County, North Carolina in 1817. His father was a German named Bromfield; his mother was an attractive black woman who answered to the surname of Jones. Jones' mother feared that his father's people were preparing to nullify his status as a free Negro and relegate him to the class of a slave on the Bromfield plantation. Hence, at an early age she apprenticed young Jones to a man named Sheppard who agreed that the youngster should be taught a trade. Sheppard later moved to Tennessee and carried young Jones with him. In Tennessee, he apprenticed Jones to Richard Cleve, a tailor, who lived in Somerville, Fayette County, about fifty miles from Memphis. Richard Cleve gave Jones on-the-job training by hiring him out to various tailors throughout the state of Tennessee. Jones worked for a tailor in Memphis for three years.

It was in Memphis where he met and fell in love with Mary Jane Richardson, the daughter of a Negro blacksmith. The Richardsons moved to Alton, Illinois; Jones followed them north in 1841 after completing his apprentice training. With a little less than one hundred dollars in savings, he proposed to Miss Richardson and subsequently got the blessing of her parents to marry her. Jones stayed in Alton, Illinois for four years and was barely seeking out a living as a young tailor in the pro-slavery climate. Jones had depleted his savings when he decided to move to Chicago, the hotbed of the abolitionist movement.

On the afternoon of March 11, 1845, John Jones, a very light coffee-cream-complexioned Negro and Mary Jane, his mulatto wife, along with their infant daughter, Lavinia, whose skin was very light and nearly white, roared into Chicago aboard a wagon train from Alton, Illinois. The city was split philosophically between the abolitionists and the pro-slavers. Although there were only 140 Negroes out of a total population of 10,280, the pro-slavers feared that

John Jones and his wife, Mary Jane Jones, as they appeared in the late 1860s.

too many free blacks in their midst would mongrelize the white race and also degrade the white labor force.

Jones' physical presence was imposing. He was five-feet-ten inches tall, which was above average height for that period, with very broad shoulders to complement his large head. His oval-shaped face bore a discernible scar over his left eye just above his eyebrow. His penetrating eyes mirrored superior intelligence. Jones had the appearance of a college educated man, but he could not read. He was as articulate as a Philadelphia lawyer, but unable to write. He was a sociable and proud man with a quick smile.

Jones had $3.50 in his pocket when he first planted his feet on the wood plank streets of Chicago. He had to pinch each of the three hundred and fifty pennies to furnish his house. Then he had to pawn his watch to purchase two heating stoves, one for his house, which was a one room cottage located on the northeast corner of Madison Street and Fifth Avenue (Wells Street), and the other for the tiny tailor shop measuring six and a half by thirty-feet, which he opened. The shop was located on the westside of Clark Street near Lake Street where the State of Illinois Building presently stands. At this point, Jones was flat broke in the "Windy City" and had to borrow $2.00 for groceries from C. C. Hansen, a black barber who had a shop located at 250 West Madison Street, just a couple of doors from the Jones' family cottage.

Jones' small well-trained hands and 20/20 eyesight enabled him to build up a thriving tailoring trade among the elite white folk in Chicago within a relatively short period of time. His warm smile and quick wit won him many influential friends. He was most fortunate in that two of the early patrons of his business were very prominent Chicago abolitionists, Attorney Lemanuel C. Paine Freer and Charles Volney Dyer, M.D. Both Freer and Dyer became Jones' faithful friends and remained as such throughout his life time.

L. C. Paine Freer was one of the most revered and highly respected members of the Chicago Bar. Freer taught Jones the fundamentals of reading and writing. During his apprenticeship, Jones became both eager and thirsty for book learning because he recognized its value in maintaining a successful business. During the early years of their friendship, Freer wrote all of Jones' business correspondence and abolitionist protest letters.

Attorney Freer awakened one day to the realization that writing Jones' letters was giving Jones a fish dinner without teaching Jones how to fish. Freer told Jones, without warning, that from that day forward, Jones must learn to read and write for himself. Freer did not desert Jones; he simply sat back, coached and encouraged him to use his excellent mind to acquire this new skill. Freer saw a potential in Jones that Jones was yet to discover, but Jones' most difficult task was learning to read. Jones' writing almost flowed naturally from his reading accomplishments. With Freer's assistance, Jones became an orator and writer of great distinction.

John Jones did not waste his new skills. He put them to work early in a campaign for repeal of the Illinois Black Laws. The Illinois apartheid laws were so restrictive that no more than three blacks were permitted to assemble for dancing unless a white person was present to monitor their activities. These stringent measures stemmed from an obsessive fear by whites of a black insurrection.

Jones became the undisputed business and civil rights leader for blacks in Illinois. As the black leader, Jones was invited by Henry O. Wagoner to address a mass meeting sponsored by the Literary and Debating Society on December 27, 1852. Jones' speech was stirring and well-received by the standing room only crowd.

The loudest applause came when he made the following observations: "The laws of the land are supposed to shield the weak, but Illinois has apparently forgotten that principle of democracy."

He followed that statement with reference to the prohibition of the Negro to defend himself in the courts of law. Jones added, "Poor Shylock, twas true, could not draw one drop of blood in taking his pound, but we, to take an oath, must lose an eight."

Jones was referring to the article in the Black Code in which a person with even one-eighth Negro blood was classified as Negro, and therefore, would be deprived of the privilege of taking an oath in court. Undergirding most of Jones' rhetoric was the fairness test and the need to act like Christians. Although Jones and Frederick Douglass were friends, they differed philosoph-

Free Negro Property Owners In Chicago - 1850

Ward	Name	Age	Property Location	Old Occupation	New Occupation	Value of Real Estate
2	James B. Bower	33	Dennis Lardon's	Hairdresser	Laborer	$ 1,600.00
2	John Jones	34	Lake Street House	Tailor	Same	1,500.00
2	Maria Smith	39	39th & Buffalo Street	not known	not known	1,000.00
3	A. J. Hall	28	North Wells Street near Harrison	Barber	Same	400.00
3	W. Wynder	30	183 West Monroe Street	Cooper	Cook	500.00
4	C. C. Hansen	39	250 West Madison St.	Barber	Same	3,000.00
9	Henry Knight	30	126 Dearborn Street	Livery stable owner	Same	10,000.00

Note: Included among colored property owners were persons of
the following pigmentation:
      African - 100% pure black
      Mulatto - 50% black
      Quadroon - 25% black
      Octoroon - 12.5% black
      Total number of property owners = 7

Source: 1850 U. S. Census Report, and City of
        Chicago Directory, 1850
Graphics: Urban Research Institute

Free Negro property owners in Chicago—1850

Free Negro Property Owners In Chicago - 1860

Ward	Name	Age	Property Location	Old Occupation	New Occupation	Value of Real Estate
1-3	Bonaparte Morgan	36	326 West Clark Street	Grocer	Same	$ 225.00
	Eliza Nox	42	Not Available	Washer Woman	Same	500.00
	Willis Revels	25	9 Buffalo Street	Minister	Same	4,000.00
	James M. Smith	56	161 Jackson	Blacksmith	Same	600.00
	Maria Smith	36	39 Buffalo Street	Washer Woman	Same	2,500.00
	William Smith	50	Edina Pl. South of 12th	Cook	Same	15,000.00
	Edmund Walker	24	224 Buffalo Street	Porter	Same	100.00
	Martha West	25	43 Buffalo Street	Washer Woman	Cook	1,000.00
	Edward Whipple	38	232 Buffalo Street	Waiter	Janitor	250.00
	Thomas Wilson	32	122 Griswald	Waiter	Cook	100.00
	Issac Smith	23	Des Plaines	White Washer	Same	5,000.00
4	Charles Condell	27	162 Wells	Barber	Same	800.00
	Olivere Henson	42	252 Madison	Saloon Keeper	Confectionary	1,500.00
	Henry Taylor	24	253 Buffalo Street	Laborer	Same	2,000.00
5	Joseph Gomer	26	48 Michigan Avenue	Porter	Waiter	500.00
1-3	Issac Ackerson	40	76 Buffalo Street	Omnibus Driver	Baggage Driver	2,500.00
	Joseph Adams	41	137 Buffalo Street	Porter	Sleeping Car Waiter	500.00
	George Alexander	25	168½ Edina Place	Janitor	Laborer	1,000.00
	James Blanks	47	129 Buffalo Street	Janitor	Porter	8,000.00
	William Bailey	32	239 Wells Street	Waiter	Same	800.00
	T. L. Bigelow	67	62 West Harrison	Carpenter	Ship Carpenter	15,000.00
	Henry Bradford	50	139 Buffalo Street	Barber	Same	8,000.00
	Mary Dailey	21	247 Buffalo Street	Washer Woman	Washer Woman	5,000.00
	Louis Douse	30	7 Buffalo Street	Clerk	White Washer	1,000.00
	Jared Gray	48	77½ Clark Street	Wig Maker	Same	1,000.00
	William Harris	34	Richmond House	Waiter	Same	600.00
	Joseph Hadley	26	Not Available	Janitor	Same	800.00
	Carter Jackson	28	218 West Madison Street	Laborer	Porter	100.00
	Lewis Johnson	48	391 Clark Street	Barber	Same	300.00
	William Johnson	19	DuPage County	Waiter	Hairdresser	300.00
	John Jones	44	218 Edina Place	Tailor	Same	17,000.00
	Abraham Logan	50	166 Union	Porter	Same	1,200.00
8-10	John Johnson	42	367 Wells	Whitewasher	Same	$ 1,200.00
	Robert Nelson	32	204 Eric	Whitewasher	Same	11,000.00
	Alfred Richardson	52	180 Maxwell	Laborer	Blacksmith	2,000.00

Note: Included among colored property owners were persons of the following pigmentation:

African - 100% pure black — Mulatto - 50% black

Quadroon - 25% black — Octoroon - 12.5% black

Total number of property owners = 35

Source: 1860 U. S. Census Report, and City of Chicago Directory, 1860

Graphics: Urban Research Institute

Free Negro property owners in Chicago—1860

Frederick Douglass, founder and publisher of the North Star *and spokesman for human rights.*

ically because Douglass would often say, "I would rather meet a wolf than a Christian."

In spite of Jones' efforts, the Illinois Assembly passed an anti-immigration law on February 22, 1855, providing that any person who brought a Negro or mulatto (defined as one having one-half Negro blood), free or slave, into the state would be fined not less than $100.00 or more than $500.00 and imprisoned not more than one year. Any Negro coming into the state of his own volition and remaining ten days would be subject to a fine of $50.00, and if the fine was not paid, the Negro would be sold to any person who would pay it.

The State Anti-immigration Statute of 1853 definitely decreased the flow of blacks and mulattoes who migrated into Illinois between 1853 and 1860. During the seven year period, the percentage of blacks in the Chicago population dropped from 1.1 percent in 1853 to .8 percent in 1860. However, with the enactment of the Federal Confiscation Act, the slaves of the plantation owners were treated as contraband by the Union soldiers and shipped North to points beyond the Mason-Dixon line. Many were sent to Illinois and distributed throughout the state to major cities like Cairo, Springfield and Chicago.

The war between the North and the South along with the ratification of the Thirteenth Amendment by Congress gave John Jones some additional fuel to fight with for the repeal of Illinois' Black Laws. The bravery that the black soldiers displayed against the Confederate army in the Battles of Port Hudson (May 1863), Millikens Bend (June 1863) and Ft. Wagner (July 1863) enhanced the image of blacks among fellow Illinoisans. As a matter of fact, some young, affluent, white, draft-aged men were so impressed with the black warriors' performance on the battle field that they paid to have blacks substitute for them as draftees.

The heroics of the black soldier during the Civil War did not lessen the tension in Chicago between the Irish Democrats and the Lincoln Unionist Republicans. The Shanty Irish, who were at the bottom of the economic ladder, felt threatened by the increased presence of blacks, who were being shipped into Illinois by the Union army. The Irish did not want any black competition in their monopoly of the unskilled labor market. Hence, they started a riot against the Negro dock workers whom they had accused of taking jobs from their immigrant Irish brothers. The labor tension caused the Irish to make a political move that resulted in the Chicago City Council passing the Black School Law of 1863.

The Bridgeport and Slaughterhouse district Irish gave John Jones another cross to bear in his fight against the state of Illinois Black Laws. The Chicago 1863 Black Law Ordinance decreed that all Negro children go to segregated schools. The parents, having been inspired by John Jones' leadership,

Black soldiers were drafted into the Union Army as substitutes for affluent draft age young white boys whose families could afford to pay the authorities to keep their sons out of active service.

disobeyed the ordinance and continued to send their children to the integrated schools in which they were presently enrolled. The school board, under additional pressure from the Irish and others, attempted to split the black community by agreeing to let mulattoes attend school with whites.

John Jones, Joseph Medill, editor of the *Chicago Tribune,* Dr. Charles V. Dyer and Zebina Eastman, along with other abolitionists both black and white, in tandem with the parents of the Negro school children vigorously opposed the blood test prerequisite for entering a Chicago public schoolroom. Their opposition was reflected in a full scale campaign against the Black Laws before both houses of the state legislature, the Chicago City Council and the Chicago Board of Education.

The timing of the Black Laws campaign was on target because President Lincoln signed the constitutional amendment abolishing slavery on January 31, 1865. It was submitted to the twenty-seven states for ratification on February 2, 1865. Illinois, the home of the president, was the first state to ratify the Thirteenth Amendment. On February 7, 1865, Illinois repealed its Black Laws. The blacks in Springfield commemorated the repeal of the Black Laws by firing a sixty-two gun salute. A round was fired for each member of the Senate and the House who voted for the bill. John Jones was signally honored by being selected to ignite a cannon fuse symbolically ending the Black Laws. Chicago and other cities in Illinois with a significant number of blacks had similar celebrations.

Joseph Medill, editor and business manager of the Chicago Tribune *and subsequently mayor of Chicago, following the 1871 fire. He almost single-handedly put Abraham Lincoln in the White House.*

President Abraham Lincoln.

John Jones did not relax with the repeal of the Black Laws. He continued to agitate for Negro suffrage. His efforts did not fall on deaf ears because his friend, Joseph Medill of the *Chicago Tribune,* solicited and gained the support of fellow Republicans at the 1869 Illinois Constitutional Convention in the cause of Negro suffrage. Governor John M. Palmer, in an effort to capture the mood of the 1869 convention, announced that Negroes were now eligible to hold any political office in the state. Within days after the announcement, he appointed Jones the first black notary public in Illinois. To support the governor's pronouncement for black office holders, the Fifteenth Amendment was ratified on March 30, 1870; hence, blacks became eligible to vote in Illinois for the first time on April 5, 1870.

Governor John M. Palmer, 1869–1873.

The following year John Jones' good friend Joseph Medill became the mayor of Chicago. Jones was proposed by the Medill Republicans and accepted by the Democrats as one of the fifteen candidates for the County Board on a bipartisan ticket. Jones was selected to attract the black vote for the Republicans and because he was well-connected and had established himself as a leader with great influence outside of the boundaries of the Second Ward. In addition to being wealthy, he was a distinguished gentleman of color and was given the red carpet treatment by both blacks and whites, Republicans and Democrats. Jones' election to a year term in 1871 marked the inauguration of blacks to elective office in the state of Illinois. Jones' defeat after a three year second term in 1875 marked the end of black representation on the County Board for nineteen years.

The day after John Jones' death on May 22, 1879, the *Chicago Tribune* reported that he had been the most prominent black citizen in the city. No single black until the election of Congressman William L. Dawson on November 3, 1942 has been endowed with the awesome power displayed by John Jones during his thirty-four years in Chicago. Jones' tailoring business on Dearborn and Madison was continued until 1906 by his son-in-law, Lloyd G. Wheeler, the first black to pass the Illinois bar and the grandfather of Lloyd G. Wheeler, III, the current president of the Supreme Liberty Life Insurance Company in Chicago, Illinois. John Jones is buried in Graceland Cemetery where Allan Pinkerton, Dr. C. V. Dyer and other abolitionists lie close to him in death the same as they stood with him in life.

Negro Property Owners In Chicago - 1870

Ward	Name	Age	Property Location	Old Occupation	New Occupation	Value of Real Estate
1	Robert Chatman	22	365 Wells	Porter	Waiter	$ 700.00
	F. B. Grinton	26	24 West Madison	Mailer	Barber	500.00
	Robert Grow	68	44 South Peoria	Janitor	Same	400.00
	John Holmes	40	209 Market	Whitewasher	Same	3,000.00
	Thomas Moore	21	291 Des Plaines	Janitor	Same	1,500.00
	John Smith	36	Adams near Quincy	Restaurateur	Same	100.00
	Charles A. Spruce	32	733 West Lake Street	Janitor	Gardner	300.00
	Stephen Stamps	42	183 Monroe	Saloon Keeper	Same	20,000.00
	Oliver Wenson	60	263 Clark Street	Caterer	Same	10,000.00
	Albert Whiting	26	200 4th Avenue	Mailer	Same	500.00
	Andrew Winslow	25	158 4th Avenue	Porter	Same	500.00
2	George Alexander	40	Loomis Street	Porter	Janitor	6,000.00
	James Blanks	58	89 4th Avenue	Janitor	Same	7,000.00
	Henry Bradford	59	139 4th Avenue	Saloon Keeper	Confection-er	8,000.00
	Allen Dorsey	50	20th & Steward	Laborer	Same	2,000.00
	Oliver J. Jacobs	35	88 4th Avenue	Carpenter	Restaura-teur	10,000.00
	John Jones	54	218 Edina Place	Tailor	Same	100,000.00
2	John Nelson	40	453 South Clinton	Saloon Keeper	Coachman	$ 1,300.00
	Charles Payne	40	835 Clark Street	Porter	Railroad Conductor	1,000.00
	William Randall	51	112 4th Avenue	Cook	Same	1,000.00
	David West	57	43 Buffalo Street	Cook	Same	1,000.00
3	William Alexander	46	212 4th Avenue	Teamster	Drayman	5,000.00
	Charles Anderson	40	331 State Street	Church Sexton	Same	700.00
	John Davis	50	365 Wells	Banker	Teamster	20,000.00
	Dempsey Grant	38	375 Clark Street	Janitor	Porter	4,000.00
	Edward Hawkins	44	Not Available	Porter	Same	4,000.00
	John Henry	43	Not Available	Butcher	Waiter	1,500.00
	Eisse Casher	38	Not Available	House Keeper	Same	50,000.00
	Adelaida Jackson	49	72 Quincy	House Keeper	Same	2,000.00
	John Johnson	42	229 4th Avenue	Laborer	White Washer	4,000.00
	Philip Miles	57	14 Taylor Street	Teamster	Same	4,000.00
	Clara Pane	24	80 Sherman	House Keeper	Same	3,000.00
	Henry Moore	46	196 4th Avenue	Laborer	Porter	3,000.00
3	John Thompson	40	326 South Clark Street	Butcher	Drayman	$ 4,000.00
4	Andrew Adams	24	Not Available	Bell Boy	Same	4,000.00
	Frank Boone	68	365 State Street	Teamster	Room Tender	1,000.00
	George W. Browne	35	129 4th Avenue	Carpenter/Builder	Same	7,000.00
	William Johnson	33	Not Available	Post Office Clerk	Same	1,200.00
	John Young	30	363 Clark Street	Mailer/Cook	Same	5,400.00

Note: Included among colored property owners were persons of the following pigmentation:

African - 100% pure black — Mulatto - 50% black

Quadroon - 25% black — Octoroon - 12.5% black

Total number of property owners = 39

Source: 1870 U. S. Census Report, and City of Chicago Directory, 1870

Graphics: Urban Research Institute

Free Negro property owners in Chicago—1870

John W. E. Thomas was elected to the Illinois House of Representatives in November, 1876. He was the first member of his race to serve in that body.

24

Chapter *III*

Black Vote—Margin of Victory

In 1875, the Democrat and Republican constituents in Chicago were nearly equal. The newly-enfranchised blacks revered the ghost of Abraham Lincoln and consistently voted for the party of the Great Emancipator. The black vote was so predictable that the Republicans found little need to reward blacks for the loyalty that gave the Grand Old Party its margin of victory. Republican tokenism for blacks sufficed. John Jones, the only black elected official in Illinois in the early 1870s, was their original token.

John Jones' defeat for re-election to the County Board in 1875 left the Illinois political cupboard bare of any black representation. Jones went down in an avalanche of Republican defeats that year. Jones' defeat opened the doors of opportunity for a young, twenty-eight year old, energetic black man, John Williams Edinburgh Thomas, who was the secretary of the predominantly white Second Ward Republican Club. John W. E. Thomas was a very light-skinned (octoroon, 12.5% black) man and former Alabamian who resided in what is now downtown Chicago at 198 Fourth Avenue (Federal Street) with his first wife, Maria Reynolds, a high-yellow-complexioned (quadroon, 25% black) lady, from South Carolina. He ran a day school for colored children and an evening school for their parents. His wife conducted a grocery business at the same Fourth Street address. Thomas possessed an education superior to that of the average white man of his day. He had been reared in Mobile, Alabama in the home of a white physician, L. H. McCluskey, who insisted that Thomas be accorded the treatment and education of his sons.

John W. E. Thomas did not limit the teaching activities in his private school to reading, writing and arithmetic. During the day, he taught black children basic education. In the evening, he taught their fathers both reading, writing and an elementary course in political science. Specifically, he wanted his people to understand the cumulative voting system used to elect members of the House of Representatives in the state of Illinois. Each voter was entitled to cast three votes which could be split between three candidates or cast for a single candidate. Thomas' instruction favored that they "plump" or cast all three votes for him. "Plumping" is what Thomas needed to get one leg up in the election process. When a vacancy occurred in the House of Representatives, he was ready to give it his best efforts. Moreover, his secretarial position with the Second Ward Republican Club, in addition to his officeship with the Olivet Baptist Church, put him in the "cat bird's seat" for throwing his hat into the ring as the black Republican token for the office of state representative from the Second Senatorial District.

On Saturday, October 14, 1876, the gentlemen of the all white Third Ward Republican Club were treated to a surprise. The surprise was John W. E. Thomas, the black nominee for the House of Representatives. There had been some dissatisfaction among the club members with the notion of the nomination of a black man for state representative. However, in spite of the turmoil, Thomas was permitted to make a speech before the group. He reviewed his black experience in Alabama and related it to the opportunities for blacks in Illinois. He showed himself thoroughly familiar with the underbelly of politics in both the Democratic South and Republican North. He expressed himself with remarkable clarity and force, maintaining that those who condemned his nomination as unfit were victims of misapprehension, prejudice or both. His

Left: Robert Todd Lincoln, son of the Great Emancipator and spokesman for the Chicago establishment. Right: Lloyd G. Wheeler, son-in-law and business partner of merchant-tailor, John Jones. Wheeler passed the Illinois State Bar in 1869 and became the first black lawyer in the state of Illinois.

speech was frequently interrupted with hearty applause, but this approval appeared neither to elate, disconcert nor swerve him from the political line of his argument. At the end of his speech, John W. E. Thomas received a standing ovation. The Third Ward Republican Club voted solidly to back Thomas in his drive to become the state representative.

The Second Ward Republican Club met on Saturday, November 4, 1876 at Three-fifty-one South Clark Street. It endorsed Thomas at that meeting after hearing him express his great disappointment with the fact that Robert Todd Lincoln, son of the Great Emancipator and chief spokesman for the Municipal Reform Club which represented the Chicago establishment, had strongly opposed him. The Reform Club in the final days before the election permitted Thomas to sneak into the electoral process through the political back door by ignoring him. It endorsed only two candidates, both white. However, under the Illinois cumulative voting system, three candidates would be elected. John Thomas' evening classes on political "plumping" bore fruit because he came in second among the three successful candidates. He received 11,532 votes. The total black population in Chicago in 1876 was less than 7,000, including women and children who were ineligible to vote. Apparently, Thomas received a substantial amount of support from white males.

State Representative John W. E. Thomas was sworn into office in Springfield, Illinois in January 1877 and became the second black elected official in the history of the state. It was a bad year because reconstruction was about to come to a grinding halt, and northern Republicans and southern Democrats had decided to relegate blacks to their pre-reconstruction nonrepresentative positions. The conservative posture of the Republican House during the Thirtieth General Assembly rendered Thomas totally ineffective in championing a black agenda. John W. E. Thomas was tired but undaunted by the lack of progress during his first term. He dispatched the following letter to the Republican leaders on October 8, 1878.

To the Republicans of the Second Senatorial District:

Two years ago, when candidates for the Legislature were being selected by the Republicans of Cook County, I was selected by the Republican Convention in this Second Senatorial District as one of its candidates for the House of Representatives. Urged by large numbers of my fellow colored Republicans in Chicago, who claimed that numbering as they did some twelve hundred to 1,500 voters, they were entitled by every consideration of political fairness to representation in the Legislature, I consented to become a candidate. Many prominent white Republicans, with a heartiness for which I feel most grateful, endorsed my candidacy, and my nomination was secured with little opposition. The majority which I received on election day demonstrated at the polls the fact that the people approved my nomination.

Without egotism I may be permitted to say that it was a proud day for me and for the colored people of the great Republican State of Illinois, when, for the first time, and that in the Centennial year, a colored man took his seat in the Legislature of that State which gave to the world the emancipator of my race, the martyred Lincoln. In that body, where he first became known to the people of this State, where his first utterances in behalf of freedom were heard, in the city where he lived and worked, and within sight almost of his sacred tomb, I, as the representative of a race which under God owe their liberties and everything which men hold dear to them, felt at home.

Deeply impressed by the duties of my new position, and conscious that I was surrounded by friends anxious and fearful lest I should not well discharge those duties, and by open enemies who would watch my course in order to criticize and find justification for the oft-repeated assertion that colored men are not qualified for official position, I conscientiously endeavored by diligent study and earnest thought to prepare myself intelligently and satisfactorily to discharge my duty as a legislator. I may have erred on some occasions; who has not? This I have, however, the proud satisfaction of knowing: *No taint of personal or political dishonesty was ever or can ever truthfully be charged upon me. I was true to myself, true to my state and true to my party.* And I believe that no member of the Legislature of which I was a member can be found, be he Republican or Democrat, who will not say that I have today his respect as a legislator and his esteem as a man.

Left: Ferdinand L. Barnett, brilliant lawyer and newspaper publisher. He married equal rights' activist Ida B. Wells in Chicago in 1895. Right: Major General Benjamin F. Butler of the Union Army, a nineteenth century army integrationist.

I am now a candidate for re-nomination and re-election at your hands. I ask an endorsement of my past conduct. If ought can be truthfully said against me, if it can be shown that I have not done my duty, as well, at least, as the average of my fellow members; if I have been unfaithful in particulars, then let me, without consideration and without pity, be disgraced and discharged from your service at the end of my first term. If such things cannot be truthfully said of me, then, as the sole representative of the colored Republicans of Illinois in its General Assembly, I confidently ask and expect at your hands a re-nomination and re-election. In closing, permit me to say that my own people are solidly with me. It is their battle more than mine. I am in earnest, and they are in earnest in asking that the same consideration which is shown to white Republicans, to Irish and German and Scandinavian Republicans, be shown to colored Republicans.

Respectfully,

J. W. E. Thomas
108 Fourth Avenue

Chicago, Illinois
October 8, 1878

Thomas' plea on behalf of his black constituents fell on deaf ears because the Republican leaders were focusing their attention on such matters as railroads, warehouse regulations, temperance, women's suffrage, and other matters that did not address equal rights for blacks. As a matter of fact, Thomas was ceremonially dumped shortly after he wrote the October letter. The Chicago Republican Party felt that it could function comfortably without the presence of a black token representative in the city and the state. Therefore, it did not slate a black for either the Thirty First (1879–80) or the Thirty Second (1881–82) sessions. Eighteen seventy-nine to 1882 were the last of the lily white years in the Illinois General Assembly.

Thomas was re-elected to the House of Representatives from the Third Senatorial District in 1882. The re-election was prompted by a great deal of restiveness among blacks with overt threats of jettisoning the party of Abraham Lincoln. The Executive Committee of the Colored State Convention met on October 14, 1880 in Bloomington, Illinois and endorsed John A. Oberly, a Democratic candidate for Secretary of State. This independent political action by blacks gave the Republican party a nervous itch while the Democrats beamed like Cheshire cats with restrained optimism.

Democrats in southern Illinois had great hopes in capitalizing on what they thought was an imminent defection by a sizeable number of black voters. They induced Henry Nixon of Jackson County to become a candidate for the

General Assembly. This idea was denounced by Nixon's black neighbors who called him an illiterate, ignorant man who was pushed forward by a Democratic trap.

In October 1883, the United States Supreme Court handed State Representative John W. E. Thomas a cause which magnetically drew a large segment of Illinois black leaders to his side. The court had struck down the 1875 Civil Rights Act as unconstitutional. The Chicago black population was enraged. Lloyd G. Wheeler, the son-in-law of the late John Jones, Ferdinand L. Barnett, the lawyer-publisher, and Reverend Charles Spencer Smith, a Bloomington African Methodist Episcopal Clergyman and a former reconstruction Alabama Legislator, along with twenty-nine other prominent and influential black Republicans were meeting in Springfield, Illinois in a mini-convention when the news about the Supreme Court decision broke in the local newspapers. After a day long battle, the thirty-two men finally agreed to make John W. E. Thomas chairman. The next day before the meeting adjourned, the group adopted a civil rights report in which they accused the Republican Party and the justices of the Supreme Court of breaking the faith with the nation's black folk. They said the decision "robbed them of their civil rights and denied blacks less respect than that accorded to common criminals."

John W. E. Thomas' civil rights' mission was aided by the National Election of 1884. Prominent blacks such as Lloyd Wheeler and Reverend Charles Spencer Smith bolted the Republican Party. They supported the Greenback candidate, the former Major General Benjamin F. Butler, who was considered by some blacks as a consistent friend of the civil rights cause. Butler won his reputation among blacks during the Civil War when he declared slaves "contrabands of war" and emancipated them against Lincoln's policy. General Butler brought down the wrath of both the north and south when he began to treat blacks in New Orleans as social equals by drinking and dining in their homes. Wheeler further buttressed his position for General Butler when he stated: "He was grateful . . . the Negro had been left out of the platforms of both parties, for that was an admission that the Negro was a man and did his own thinking."

On the state ticket Wheeler, Smith, and other blacks of like stripe supported Carter Harrison, the Democratic nominee for governor.

The results of the 1884 election put the fear of God in the State Republican Party. Although the Republicans re-elected Governor Richard J. Oglesby for a third term, Grover Cleveland became the first Democratic president in twenty-four years, and the Congress found one party in control of each house. A solid split between the two houses of Congress made the chances of a national civil rights bill appear nil. Thus, Illinois blacks turned their attention toward getting a State Civil Rights Bill.

Governor Richard J. Oglesby

President Grover Cleveland.

Edward H. Morris, lawyer and state representative.

John G. Jones, lawyer and state representative. He was not related to John Jones.

Dr. James H. Magee, the sole black member of the State Central Committee suggested to fellow delegates at the Illinois Republican Convention in 1884 that State Civil Rights Legislation was important for the following reason: "Democratic baits had been thrown into Republican waters to catch colored fish of African descent. The Civil Rights Bill of Ohio, passed by the Democrats, had caught not only many African fish, but also white whales."

In 1885 black folk in Illinois thought the millennium had begun. On February 3, State Representative Thomas introduced a civil rights bill modeled after an Ohio statute. The House Judiciary recommended its passage, and the bill passed with an overwhelming victory in the House. The bill stated in part: "All persons . . . shall be entitled to the . . . equal privileges of inns, restaurants, eating houses, barber shops, public conveyances on land or water, theaters and all other places of public accommodation and amusement." Violators would be fined $25.00 to $500.00, imprisoned for up to a year, or both. The State Senate sat on the bill, and black leaders predicted that if

Major Franklin A. Denison, civic leader and socialite.

Dr. George Cleveland Hall, physician and civic leader.

the bill failed to pass, every black would be justified in walking out of the political house that Lincoln built. Furthermore, blacks were incensed because Governor Oglesby had not made a single important black appointment. The Senate was awakened on June 3, 1885 by the heat of black rage and passed the House version of the civil rights bill with a handsome margin. Governor Oglesby promptly signed the bill.

Thomas is best remembered as the author of the Civil Rights Bill of 1885. And indeed, there was no legislation passed in the State of Illinois during the nineteenth century that had the psychological impact of that bill on the minds of black folk.

In retrospect, the Civil Rights Bill of 1885 must be seen as cosmetic in that the teeth of the bill were implanted in deteriorating gums that were riddled with a pyorrheric disease. The bill did not fulfill its promise because blacks did not gain access to public accommodation in hotels, theatres, restaurants, barber shops and other public facilities. And seldom were the $25.00 to $500.00 fines enforced. The bill acknowledged a live-in arrangement between the Republican Party and black voters following a fifteen year betrothal.

Black voters in Illinois have John W. E. Thomas to thank for his early pioneering work in voter education. This was a very significant legacy because from his efforts arose a coalition of aspiring young black leaders such as Edward H. Wright, John C. Buckner, Theodore W. Jones, Edward H. Morris, John G. Jones, and Thomas' immediate successor in the House of Representatives, George F. Ecton.

John W. E. Thomas, teacher, politician, and lawyer died at his residence, 3308 South Indiana Avenue, Monday, December 18, 1899. He was survived by his wife Crittie (who joined him in death on February 17, 1943) and five children: Esther, Ethel, Joseph, Logan, and Grace. Among the active pallbearers were Edward H. Wright, Edward H. Morris, J. Gray Lucus and George B. Turner. Among the honorary pallbearers were Judge Orrin M. Carter, Major Franklin A. Denison, Theodore W. Jones, Martin B. Madden, John C. Buckner, and Dr. George C. Hall. Many of John W. E. Thomas' honorary and active pallbearers became powerful political forces on the Chicago scene within twenty years after he was laid to rest in the Oakwood Cemetery.

John "Mushmouth" Johnson, Chicago's first black gambling czar.

Chapter *IV*

Politics: The Mother of Strange Bedfellows

In 1896, there were only two black elected officials in the City of Chicago—Edward "The Iron Master" Wright, Cook County Commissioner and Major John C. Buckner, a member of the Illinois House of Representatives. Both Wright and Buckner were articulate race leaders; however, they did not have the clout of political Irish saloon keepers such as tall, pompadoured, John "Bathhouse" Coughlin or short, pale white, Michael "Hinky Dink" Kenna. Coughlin and Kenna had earned enough political clout through ballot thievery and financial contributions to City Hall to get sidewalks and gutters swept with toothbrushes and streets paved on demand at midnight.

In the absence of black political leaders with clout emerged an alliance between a black saloon keeper and the black church. The first alliance of these strange bedfellows that can be documented was between the Reverend Reverdy C. Ransom, pastor of the Bethel African Methodist Episcopal Church and Robert "Bob" Motts, the dapper dressing, genial gambler and saloon keeper. Bob Motts' saloon and gambling establishment was located on the southwest corner of the 2700 block on State Street. The Bethel A.M.E. Church was located on the northeast corner of the 3000 block on Dearborn Street.

The commonality between Reverend Ransom and "Bob" Motts was their mutual interest in getting the 2600 to 3100 blocks on Dearborn Street paved. Motts had extensive real estate holdings on Dearborn Street, and Reverend Ransom was concerned about his parishioners' inability to get to church on Sunday because of the conditions of the roadway. In 1896, Dearborn Street was paved with round wooden blocks. Many of them had been displaced by use and time while the remaining ones were so loose that vehicular traffic was both rough and bumpy.

The Reverend Reverdy Ransom called on Alderman Addison Ballard in his Second Ward office to discuss the street problem and a possible early solu-

Rev. Reverdy C. Ransom. He founded the Institutional Church and Social Settlement House at 3825 S. Dearborn St. in Chicago on July 24, 1900. The Institutional House became a prototype for the NAACP, the Urban League, and the Colored YMCA & YWCA. Dr. W. E. B. DuBois wrote on August 29, 1935, that Reverend Reverdy C. Ransom's speech in 1906, at the second meeting of the Niagara Movement at Harper's Ferry, did more to inspire the eventual founding of the National Association for the Advancement of Colored People (NAACP) than any other single event.

tion. Alderman Ballard's attitude toward the polished-speaking and properly-attired Reverend Reverdy Ransom was that of a lord talking to his serf. The Reverend Ransom was so enraged by the tone and content of Ballard's conversation that he threatened on the spot to have Ballard voted out of office at the next election. As a matter of fact, Minister Ransom said, "I am going to put you out of office if it's the last thing I do."

The rotund beer-bloated Ballard leaned back in his chair, took a puff on his Dutch Master cigar and replied, "Oh! indeed, the Reverend Ransom is going to put me out of office." He then gave a loud sneering laugh.

Reverend Ransom retorted, "Yes! I will put you out of office if I have to make a speech opposing you under every gas lamp post on Dearborn Street. I will stir up the colored people to such a fever pitch that they will go to the polls in mass and defeat you by a substantial margin."

Reverend Ransom grossly exaggerated the condition of the streets to his parishioners during his sermon the following Sunday. He argued: "Every time undertakers drive to our church with a funeral, they have found Dearborn Street so rough that they have had to open the coffin and turn the corpse's face upward before the families could review the remains of their loved ones."

The congregation's reaction to Reverend Ransom's political sermon was both emotional and positive. The voting membership was ready to take the necessary steps to get Alderman Addison Ballard out of office.

When Robert "Bob" Motts heard about Reverend Ransom's sermon from several of his saloon patrons, he decided to join the church's efforts by putting one thousand dollars in a campaign to help defeat the insensitive white alderman.

The officers of Bethel church objected to an alliance with a reputed hustler, gambler and saloon keeper. Reverend Ransom called a special Wednesday night meeting to calm the water with the deacons and officers of the church.

The minister closed the meeting pointing out that: "Mr. Robert Motts wants what we want and as long as a man is going my way to accomplish the same objectives, I am willing to walk with him. Can I get a witness?"

The response from the deacons and officers was "Amen! Amen!"

The members of Bethel A.M.E. Church and the patrons of "Bob" Motts' saloon walked hand in hand in a political campaign to defeat Alderman Addison Ballard. They were successful in electing another white Alderman, Charles "Candy Man" Gunther, who was grateful to the black people who buttered his bread, and therefore, promptly took the necessary political steps to have the blocks between 2600 and 3100 on Dearborn Street repaved.

Major John C. Buckner, the only black legislator in the Illinois House of Representatives.

Attorney Edward D. Green a member of the House of Representatives, was sponsored by Robert "Bob" Motts.

The Pekin Theater, 2700 S. State St., Chicago, IL. The first legitimate theater owned by blacks in America.

Motts' political sophistication was acquired at the feet of his former boss and tutor, John "Mushmouth" Johnson, Chicago's first black gambling czar. The picturesque Johnson operated one of the largest saloons and gambling houses in downtown Chicago at 464 South State Street from 1890 to 1907. Every two years during the mayoral campaign, Johnson would give $10,000 to the Democrats and $10,000 to the Republicans. Thus, his gambling establishment was protected regardless of the winner. Although "Mushmouth" never became active in the political game, he urged blacks to register and vote in the First Ward where his thriving business was located. Johnson's ability to get out the vote, in addition to his large contribution, made him a political power within his own right. However, he understood coalition politics because when "Hinky Dink" Kenna and "Bathhouse John" Coughlin became the political bosses of the First Ward, Johnson made an alliance with them by contributing to their organization so that he could be protected against police raids. If things got too hot at City Hall and a raid was necessary to satisfy the "do-gooders", he would always get enough advanced warning to put his house in order.

"Hinky Dink" Kenna and "Bath-house John" Coughlin, the political bosses of the First Ward.

Congressman Martin B. Madden. A political leader in the black community from April, 1899 to April 27, 1928, the day he died in Washington, D.C.

"Bob" Motts added a page to "Mushmouth" Johnson's political black book when he started paying his saloon patrons five dollars per day to help the alderman of the Second Ward to register blacks and get them out to vote. Almost two decades before women's suffrage in 1920, Motts enlisted women to work as a troop of door bell ringers for the Second Ward organization. Moreover, his active political involvement enabled him to get some forty black women jobs at City Hall in the Recorders Office long before the Nineteenth Amendment allowed women to cast their first ballot.

Mr. Robert T. Motts, the gentleman gambler, was politically instrumental in getting the brilliant attorney, Edward H. Morris, elected to the Illinois Assembly in 1902. However, in less than twelve months Morris' I.Q. must have dropped dramatically because he naively doubled crossed his sponsor when he introduced a bill to legalize policy (lottery) in the state. Motts was enraged at even the thought of someone encouraging legal competition inside the illicit arena that he found so profitable. Consequently, Motts commenced to pull the political chair from under Morris and instantly started a search for a man to replace him in the 1904 election.

The man selected to take Morris' seat in the House of Representatives was Edward D. Green. Green was a well-to-do bachelor and a very good friend of Daniel M. Jackson and Henry "Teenan" Jones, two gambling buddies of "Bob" Motts. Green served one term in the House and jumped ship to join the Martin B. Madden organization, the new pipeline between the Second Ward and City Hall. Motts' star began an accelerated plummet after he branched into a "for whites only" theater venture on the near northside. He opened the old Columbia Theater at Clark and Division Streets on February 23, 1908 and closed it on May 10, 1908 as a financial flop.

Henry "Teenan" Jones, unlike "Mushmouth" Johnson and "Bob" Motts, was free from gambling raids because he had had a direct wire to the desk of Mayors George B. Swift, Carter H. Harrison II, Edward F. Dunne and Fred A. Busse. Between 1895 and 1910, "Teenan" was the proprietor of two gambling and saloon establishments in predominantly white Hyde Park: the Lakeside Club at 56th and Lake Park Avenue and a saloon and gambling club in the Windermere Hotel at 1642 East 56th Street. Dice, roulette, draw and stud poker games could be played at both the Lakeside and the Windermere. "Teenan" also controlled the gambling operations at several other Hyde Park hotels including the Chicago Beach.

In 1910, "Teenan" Jones was forced to close both the Lakeside and Windermere operations by the Hyde Park Improvement Protective Association headed by Attorney Francis Harper. The objective of the lily white improvement club was to rid Hyde Park of all of its black residents, both sinners and saints. Jones moved his two houses of sin to the broadway of the Black Belt, the

Mayor Carter H. Harrison II.

Mayor George B. Swift.

Mayor Fred A. Busse.

Mayor Edward F. Dunne.

Chicago Beach Hotel, 5050 South Beach Drive.

3000 block on South State Street. The two Hyde Park clubs were renamed Elite #1 and Elite #2. He became an instant power broker in the Second Ward with the blessings of Mayor Carter H. Harrison II because "Bob" Motts had fallen out of favor and was very ill. Motts died in 1911.

In 1911, Mayor Carter H. Harrison II issued an order to close down all gambling houses except those operated by Negroes. He realized that "Jim Crow" restricted the recreational activities in which Negroes could participate; therefore, he felt it would be therapeutic to permit Negroes to shoot craps within the confines of the Black Belt. It was during the period when the ghetto had an exclusive on gambling that whites in large numbers began to visit black owned clubs on South State Street because blacks had the only games in town. Teenan's Elite #1 and Elite #2 became the center of black and tan (white) night life in Chicago. His places featured stars like the great "Jelly Roll" Morton.

The Elite Cafe #2, 3445 S. State Street. Teenan Jones on the extreme right. Second to the right is Jelly Roll Morton. The group is making preparations to celebrate the opening of the New Jazz Club.

Hotel Windermere.

"Dan" Jackson, gambling czar and mortician.

When "Dan" Jackson smelled the aura of success that was being generated by "Teenan" on South State Street, he made several moves. He surrendered his bachelorhood and married Lucy Motts, "Bob's" sister and the sole beneficiary of Motts' estate. The marriage vows between Lucy and Dan were not many days old before "Dan" opened a gambling room in the late "Bob" Motts' Pekin Theater and also expanded the existing gambling room he had in the family undertaking parlor at 2600 block on South State.

Henry "Teenan" Jones' vice empire continued to flourish in spite of the competition from "Dan" Jackson and others until the passage of the Eighteenth Amendment, which prohibited the manufacture, sale, and transportation of intoxicating liquors. (The amendment was ratified by Congress in 1919 and implemented in 1920.) However, "Dan" Jackson began to eclipse "Teenan" Jones as a political power in 1917 after "Teenan" turned state witness against Oscar DePriest, Chicago's first black alderman, and also confessed to being the head of a gambling combine in addition to being the bagman for DePriest.

2

THE YEARS OF THE BLACK POLITICAL BULL DOGS

Oscar DePriest, the first black to be elected alderman in the city of Chicago.

Chapter V

The Earthy DePriest vs the Mighty Wright

Edward H. Wright was a six-foot-two-inch tall, stocky-built man with a black-coffee-without-cream complexion. Oscar DePriest's skin tone was several shades darker than a snow white sheet. His large head was padded with a two inch shock of curly, sandy, brown hair and supported by a six-foot-four inch frame. Both men arrived in Chicago before the turn of the century. Wright planted his size twelve shoes here in 1884 with a traveling bag that included a degree which he had received in 1880 at the age of seventeen from the City College of New York. DePriest detrained with a paint brush and a step ladder in 1893 from Florence, Alabama via Dayton, Ohio. Wright and DePriest were listening to different drummers but destined to make political history in Abe Lincoln's city by the lake.

The energetic Wright started working two jobs shortly after he arrived in the city. During the day, he worked in the Registry Department of the post office. In the evening, he was employed as a stenographer in a real estate firm. The intellect and energy that Wright poured into his job at the post office was brought to the attention of a Republican politician who gave him a position in the County Clerk's Office in 1887. In 1889, he was elevated to bookkeeper and railroad incorporation clerk in the Secretary of State's office in Springfield, Illinois. Wright's Springfield job marked the first time a person of color had held a clerical position in the state government. The elevation to a new job status was given to Wright as a reward for the political astuteness he displayed in helping secure the nomination of Isaac M. Pearson for the Office of Secretary of State during the Republican State Convention of 1888. Wright returned to Chicago from Springfield in 1893 when Pearson left office. Wright's reputation in Springfield enabled him to gain immediate employment in the Office of the City Clerk.

In 1894, at the Republican County Convention, Edward H. Wright showed

Young Ed Wright was hired to work in the state office in Springfield in 1889. He was the first Afro-American to hold a white collar job in the state government.

his political savvy when he withdrew his name from nomination for the Office of County Commissioner in favor of Theodore W. Jones, a better known south-side businessman. Wright recognized that the Republican party was not mentally prepared to tolerate two blacks on the commission. Jones was elected while Wright was rewarded by Jones' backers. They supported Wright for election as clerk of the town of South Chicago in 1895. Edward H. Wright made such an exceptional record for himself and his race as the South Chicago clerk that the nomination for the County Commissioner's office in 1896 was literally handed to him over the encumbered Theodore W. Jones and a field of many well-known and prominent colored Republicans. In addition to Wright's being elected by a handsome majority, he also passed the Illinois Bar. Commissioner Edward H. Wright with his new legal credentials moved into the Cook County Chambers and literally dominated it with his subtle shrewdness and forceful black presence. It was on the Cook County Commission that he first earned the nickname of "Iron Master" because he reacted with a cast iron attitude toward any person or persons who attempted to demean his race.

Edward H. Wright was more politically audacious in the 1890's than New York's Congressman Adam Clayton Powell ever dared to be in the 1950's and 60's. At the same time, Wright generated confidence and respect from both whites and blacks because he wore his political garments with an intellectual black dignity. He also demanded and got both discipline and loyalty from members of the Second Ward Organization. He was known to enforce his demands by placing his size twelve shoes against a disbeliever's rump.

Wright's race consciousness was best exhibited by the bold position he took against the State's Attorney of Cook County shortly after his election to the Board of the Cook County Commissioners in 1896. Wright and Charles S. Deneen made mutual commitments prior to their elections. Deneen told Wright that if Wright supported him in getting elected to the Office of State's Attorney, he would appoint a colored man as an assistant state's attorney. Deneen was elected and took his seat, but Wright's man, Attorney Ferdinand L. Barnett (husband of Ida B. Wells), was not appointed.

Commissioner Edward H. Wright was shrewd enough to recognize that he had only one hold card that he could exercise against the state's attorney once they both took office. Thus, when the appropriation for the state's attorney's office came before Wright, he deliberately made it his hostage.

When Deneen was informed as to why his appropriation was being held up, he allegedly called Wright to his office and in a loud thundering voice exclaimed: "I want you to understand Mr. Wright, that I am all powerful in this office, and you cannot dictate to me."

Theodore W. Jones, county commissioner and successful business executive. He was not related to John Jones or John G. Jones.

To this Wright bristled and looked through Deneen with his large, piercing X-ray eyes and in a slow syrupy and deliberate manner said: "Yes, and I am County Commissioner." Seventy two hours later, Ferdinand L. Barnett became the first colored assistant state's attorney for Cook County, and Deneen's appropriations subsequently passed.

During Wright's second term as County Commissioner, he proved himself to be a master strategist when he was elected president pro tem of the Cook County Board. Wright achieved this feat by polling each member of the board individually, stating that he did not hope to be elected president pro tem while the president of the board was away but that he would appreciate one or two votes as a sign of recognition for his black constituents. There were also two prominent Irish contenders for the chair; however, when the votes were counted, Wright received thirteen votes against the two his contenders cast for themselves.

The Chicago political climate was not ready for an audacious and astute black political leader. Therefore, Edward H. Wright was not renominated to run for a third term on the Cook County Commission. Wright was put into a political green pasture with no grass for the next fifteen years.

Charles S. Deneen served as state's attorney, governor and United States Senator.

Ida B. Wells Barnett, human rights' activist and civic leader.

The Wright leadership void was filled by Oscar DePriest, a man with a totally different style. DePriest was basically a people's person and a huckster. Oscar DePriest, the six foot-four-inch tall, handsome and solidly built quadroon (three-quarters white) was frequently seen walking erectly and very proudly up and down State Street (the stroll), carrying a step ladder and hustling decorating jobs from real estate companies.

DePriest's entry into politics, unlike Wright's, was not based on any philosophical plan. He simply stumbled into the political arena by accident as revealed in the following statement made by DePriest to Harold F. Gosnell, who was a research employee of the Public Works Administration during the early 1930's:

> A friend of mine came by one evening and said, 'Come on go to a meeting with me.' I had nothing to do, so I went. It was a precinct meeting, and they were electing precinct captains. The vote was 20 to 20 for rival candidates, and I saw right away that a deal could be made. So I went to one of the candidates and said: 'Now you're the man who ought to be captain. I'll give you two additional votes if you'll make me secretary.' The man refused. I went to his rival and made the same proposition. He accepted. I was made secretary. I kept at it because it was recreation to me. I always liked a good fight; the chance and the suspense interested me. I never gambled nor played cards so it was fun to me.

DePriest was deadly serious about his fun job as the Second Ward organization's secretary. He was a tireless, high energy performer who knew how to use an opportunity. Oscar DePriest was an excellent organizer and shrewd enough to make himself almost indispensable to John Buckner, a former Illinois legislator and the black political spokesman, in Martin B. Madden's Second Ward political wheel.

Oscar DePriest's ability as an organizer stood out in bold relief and was observed by Congressman Martin B. Madden, who was also the Second Ward Republican Committeeman. Madden needed DePriest's talent to keep the black vote in control, and he rewarded DePriest by engineering his nomination for the County Board at the Republican Cook County Convention in 1904. This shocked the black members of the Second Ward Organization because there were several men such as Attorney Edward H. Wright, Attorney Edward H. Morris, Major John Buckner and E. L. Martini standing in the wings with legislative experience and educational advantages that overshadowed DePriest's. They were all very bright, but none of them had the street smart, organizational ability and the hustler's instinct of DePriest.

The November 10, 1904 edition of the *Chicago Tribune* did not take kindly to Oscar DePriest's nomination. It gave the following account: ". . . .Madden wanted the support of the Negro precinct captains that Oscar controlled. The deal was that in return for their support, Oscar was to be elected Cook County Commissioner. . ."

DePriest's intellectual performance as a member of the Cook County Board was not on par with Ed Wright's. However, he knew how to play the man's game and was renominated in 1906. In 1908, Oscar DePriest's greed overreached his need. He switched sides and was caught on the losing side of a political war between State Senator Samuel Ettelson and Congressman Martin B. Madden, his political benefactors. Although DePriest was successful in getting elected as an alternate delegate to the Republican National Convention of 1908, he was defeated by the Madden and Buckner forces in his desire to return to the Cook County Board. Madden and John Buckner supported a white candidate for DePriest's seat which was not recovered again by a black until 30 years later when Edward M. Sneed was sworn in as a Cook County Commissioner in 1938.

DePriest was put in a political ice box between 1908 and 1915 because of his disloyalty to the Second Ward Organization. During that period, he used his boundless energy to become a full-fledged entrepreneur. In addition to operating a decorating and contracting business, he opened a real estate office at 3434 South State Street where he also operated a successful leasing and brokerage business. His timing was right. The real estate business flourished as a result of the large influx of blacks migrating to the urban north from the rural south in search of jobs in the Chicago stockyards and steel mills.

DePriest became wealthy and independent while in political cold storage. However, he campaigned for the re-election of Congressman Martin B. Madden, a Republican. At the same time, he supported Maclay Hoyne, a white Democratic candidate for alderman. Hoyne ran against DePriest's imaginary black arch rival, Edward H. Wright, who campaigned as an independent Republican in the 1910 election. DePriest also campaigned for Hoyne on the Democratic ticket for state's attorney in 1912.

Edward H. "The Iron Master" Wright's political isolation comforted DePriest because Wright was constantly agitating for black representation and causing white Republicans generally and DePriest specifically feelings of great discomfort during regular Republican Ward meetings.

Oscar DePriest's political behavior toward Wright appeared strange to those who did not know that Oscar was getting his political signals from Madden and quietly preparing to make a bid to become the first black alderman of Chicago. By the summer of 1914, the exiled political maverick had organized and built such a large personal constituency that he was able to present Congressman Madden, the Second Ward Committeeman, with a list of endorsements that included thirty-eight precinct captains, a host of Baptist and Methodist ministers in addition to the signatures of a battalion of saloon keepers, physicians and other professionals.

After viewing all of the prominent names on the DePriest petition, Madden put both arms around Oscar declaring that Oscar was his man for the aldermanic seat. Madden really had no choice in the face of DePriest's genius for rallying people to support his political cause. Oscar DePriest used his own money as opposed to the Republican organization's funds and ran a very effective aldermanic race. He won by a plurality of 10,599 votes in a field of four candidates competing for 21,622 votes. Oscar DePriest's victory put starch in the backbone of every black man and woman in Chicago. Black people stood tall with electrifying pride on Wednesday, April 7, 1915, the day after DePriest was elected. Wherever DePriest appeared in the streets of Chicago's Black Belt, he was followed and surrounded by crowds of black admirers, who literally worshipped the ground he walked on.

Mayor William Hale "Big Bill" Thompson and Mrs. Thompson.

Chapter VI

"Big Bill's" Freedom Train

William Hale "Big Bill" Thompson's freedom train beat the corrupt-laden freight train of Carter Harrison II in the race for mayor on April 15, 1915. Oscar DePriest became Chicago's first black alderman while a passenger on board "Big Bill's" freedom train which consisted of a string of coaches, each packed with riders attracted by the numerous oratorical promises made by "Big Bill" in the heated preelection debates. The riders in the first coach wanted political reform and total liquidation of City Hall aldermanic grafters. Those in the second expected Thompson to fulfill his campaign promises and run all the crooks and prostitutes out of town, while the ones in the third looked for freedom and opportunity in the land of Lincoln. This last coach was the "Jim Crow" car; it was loaded with colored people who enabled "Big Bill" to stump politically in the Black Belt as a reincarnated Abe Lincoln.

"Big Bill" attempted to keep many of the promises he made to colored riders in the third coach. He rewarded them with the appointment of several Second Ward stalwarts. Edward H. Wright of 3144 South Wabash and Louis B. Anderson of 2821 South Wabash were made assistant corporation counsels in the law department at the very respectable salary of five thousand dollars per year. He also named Reverend Archibald J. Carey of 3428 South Vernon as an investigator in the law department at the same high salary. Earlier Carey had been appointed by Mayor Carter Harrison II to the Motion Picture Censorship Board, enabling Carey to act as watchdog against films containing racial insults. Thompson was criticized by his fellow white Republicans and the press for placing three black men in such prominent offices.

"Big Bill" rebutted the critics with the following statement:

> My reasons for making such appointments were threefold: first, because the
> persons appointed were qualified for the positions; second, because in the

name of humanity, it is my duty to do what I can to elevate rather than degrade any class of American citizens; third, because I am obligated to these people for their continued friendship and confidence while I have been in this community.

DePriest, Carey, Wright, and Anderson had all worked extremely hard in getting out the vote in the black section of the Second Ward. Their effort gave Thompson the victory in a very close race. Thompson won the Republican primary by 3,500 votes, and his plurality in the Second Ward was over 6,000. In the general election, he carried the Second and Third Wards by more than two to one.

The gratitude and high esteem that Mayor William "Big Bill" Thompson had for his colored constituents in the Second Ward was reflected in his first official act as Mayor of Chicago. Immediately after Mayor Thompson was sworn in on the afternoon of April 26, 1915, he gaveled the city council to order and called for a resolution from the First Ward. Aldermen, Michael Kenna and John Coughlin answered nay. Alderman Hugh Morris of the Second Ward also said nay. Alderman Oscar DePriest, the first Afro-American to grace this august body, answered yes.

The Council chamber was packed like a can of sardines with wives, children, and parents of the newly-elected aldermen. The chamber smelled and looked like a beautiful flower garden because every aldermanic desk was loaded with huge bouquets of white and red roses. However, there were no persons present that were prouder than the mother, wife, and children of

Attorney Louis B. Anderson, an assistant corporation counsel in the Law Department.

Rev. Archibald J. Carey, an investigator in the Law Department.

Mayor William Hale Thompson being sworn in at 3:02 p.m., April 26, 1915.

Oscar DePriest, the alderman from the Second Ward, the ward credited with greasing the tracks for "Big Bill's" victorious freedom train.

When DePriest rose to read his first resolution, his mother smiled. However, her smile turned into tears when DePriest read the section of the resolution that declared August 23, 1915 a legal holiday in Chicago to celebrate the fiftieth anniversary of the emancipation of the race. (The official celebration of the fiftieth year of the emancipation of the colored people took place at the Exposition Hall in the Coliseum throughout the months of August and September.) Reverend Carey and Robert Jackson were appointed to the State Commission for the Emancipation Exposition prior to Thompson's election by Governor Edward Dunne, a Democrat.

After DePriest finished reading the resolution, the mayor said, "You heard the resolution, if there are no objections, it is passed and I so order." Thus, the first law of the new Republican city council under the new mayor was an ordinance offered by the Honorable Oscar DePriest to celebrate Abraham Lincoln's Emancipation Proclamation.

On Wednesday, September 15, 1915 at 8:15 P.M. sharp, twenty-two thousand blacks gathered in the Coliseum located at 15th and Wabash Avenue to celebrate the half century anniversary of the Emancipation and to hear Mayor William Hale Thompson. The mayor was presented to the cheering crowd of Negroes by one of his most avid black backers, the most Reverend Archibald J. Carey, the flaming orator of the Institutional A.M.E. Church located at 3825 South Dearborn Street.

The Coliseum, located at Fourteenth and Wabash Avenue, was the site of the 50th year celebration of the Emancipation of Colored People, and also the battleground for numerous Republican and Democratic National Conventions.

The Reverend Carey opened his introduction of the mayor with the following statement:

> The colored people ask no favors and sympathy, nor do they ask any return for any support they may give to any cause, political or otherwise. They ask only for what they deserve as American citizens. Whatever Mayor Thompson has done, whatever he will do, it will not be out of sympathy for the descendants of a race once enslaved, but for American citizens who have earned their position. By his appointments, Mayor Thompson is merely recognizing the worth of a people. There are three names which will stand high in American history: Abraham Lincoln, William McKinley and William Hale Thompson.

The crowd jumped to its feet and interrupted the speaker with cheers. Reverend Carey continued:

> William Hale Thompson may not be elected president in 1916, but I am sure he will be in 1920. I helped elect him alderman of the Second Ward in 1900. I helped elect him county commissioner. I helped elect him mayor, and my work will not be completed until I have helped elect him president.

The crowd responded to Carey's remarks with screams, stomping feet, and hands clapping in a wild frenzy.

"I present to you", continued Reverend Carey, as soon as he could make himself heard, "Your friend and my friend, the biggest man in all Chicago, the biggest man in all Illinois, and the best mayor Chicago ever had, William Hale Thompson."

The throng instantly broke into a spontaneous thunderous applause. Twenty-two thousand people strained in unison while standing on their chairs and stretching their necks to make sure they did not miss a single move or utterance that "Big Bill" made.

In an effort to get the cheering crowd to subside, the City Prosecutor, Harry B. Miller, who was sitting next to Mayor Thompson on the dais, jumped to his feet and began waving his arms and motioning to the crowd to stop applauding and sit down. When the cheers abated, City Attorney Miller shouted, "What's the matter with Thompson?"

And the crowd boomed back. "He's all right!"

"Who's all right?" Miller yelled at the crowd.

"Thompson!" roared the twenty-two thousand blacks.

Thompson's droopy eyes were smiling. His huge face became florid as he internally radiated from the jubilation of the crowd. "Big Bill", the six-foot-four-inch gladiator, removed the fat El Producto cigar from his mouth as he lifted his two hundred and sixty pound broad frame from the chair of honor with his long arms stretched out as if he were going to hug the entire cheering crowd. His massive head revolved from side to side in an effort to acknowledge the thunderous greetings from his black constituents. After several minutes, he raised his arms above his head to get order, and then he roared: "Dr. Carey and my friends" . . . the cheers drowned out the next seven minutes of his speech.

After the crowd quieted, he was heard saying:

> I have been presented this evening with the Lord's Prayer embroidered on a silk background and beautifully framed. The work was done by Mrs. Laura Davis, one of your people. That gift will go into the Mayor's Office of the City of Chicago, and it will remain in that office as long as William Hale Thompson is mayor. I hope that I will not need the reminder; but if I do, that token will serve to recall my oath to uphold the laws of Chicago and give a square deal to all.

The audience broke into another round of cheers.

After the cheers subsided, the mayor continued:

> Too much publicity is given the shortcoming and frailties of the colored man, and too little publicity is given his genius and skill. . . It is considered

presumptuous for an individual of your race to aspire to any employment other than menial tasks, and there have been recent instances where even your right to be considered among the laborers in this city has been challenged. . .

Black males had an excessive appetite for Mayor William Hale Thompson's rhetoric because it contained calories that made them feel like whole men; whereas, white America treated most black men as though they were circus freaks, half boys and half men. In the eyes of white workers, native or immigrant, the black man was a boy, though his creditors expected him to be a man. "Big Bill" was consistent in that he treated all blacks like adults and old friends. When they greeted him as "our brother", his face lit up with the pleasantry of a Christmas tree.

"I will protect the weak against the strong," "Big Bill" would often thunder at public meetings in the black community. He meant exactly what he said, and the power of the mayoral position supported his mouthing. He had not been in office a month when he banned the showing in Chicago of the anti-Negro motion picture, *Birth of a Nation.* Secondly, he appointed so many blacks to white collar jobs in the Water Department and the Department of Health that his white colleagues, along with the major print media derisively described City Hall as "Uncle Tom's Cabin." As a matter of fact, "Big Bill" was affectionately thought of as the "Second Abraham Lincoln" in the black community.

The Municipal Voters League was not giving Mayor William Hale Thompson high marks because under espoused "wide-open-town" policy, the joy girls, pimps, pick pockets, and gamblers who were driven out of town during the Carter Harrison II administration returned and integrated their slime into the lives of black families who were locked in the "Black Belt." Thompson made impotent any police officers who attempted to enforce the law against illicit activities in the black community. Thompson's "open city" was a "Garden of Eden" for those weak enough to bite the apple.

All of the Thompson appointees were considered stars in the black "Garden of Eden", but no star shined brighter in the "celestial over the Garden" than that of Alderman Oscar DePriest during Thompson's first administration. There was nothing in the heavens in the spring of 1916 that would indicate that the brightest political star in the black community would plunge to an unfathomable depth by January 1917.

In the summer of 1916, rumors were flying that Oscar DePriest was on the take. As a matter of fact, he made a public denial in late August that he had not accepted a bribe to help open the Panama Cafe on South State Street. The cafe had a very notorious reputation. Although DePriest was not a drinker or a gambler, he was seen in the clubs throughout his political career with gamblers and saloon keepers such as the late "Bob" Motts and "Teenan" Jones.

On January 18, 1917, State's Attorney Maclay Hoyne, a Democrat that DePriest supported in 1912, announced that the Grand Jury had indicted Alderman DePriest, Chief of Police Stephen K. Healey, along with three police lieutenants, a cabaret owner, and several underworld figures for conspiracy to permit gambling dens and houses of joy to operate under an umbrella that was heavily sprinkled with green and yellow tainted dollars. Captain Stephen K. Healey of the Stanton Avenue Police Station on East Thirty-fifth Street and DePriest's old friend Henry "Teenan" Jones, owner of Elite Clubs, signed written confessions and turned state's evidence.

During the trial, a half dozen proprietors of gambling houses testified that their establishments were constantly raided by the police until they paid "Teenan" Jones, who was DePriest's bagman. "Teenan" Jones stated under oath that he paid DePriest $2,500.00 over a four month period and that he also gave some money to Captain Healey in a white sealed envelope while in the Stanton Police Station on East 35th Street. Healey acknowledged while on the witness stand that he had accepted money from Jones and had discussed that fact with Alderman Oscar DePriest.

The lawyers for the defense were Clarence Darrow and Edward H. Morris. DePriest's defense was based on the grounds that the money he had received was not bribe money but campaign contributions. Darrow admonished the jurors not to let racial prejudice cloud their decision. The jury brought in a verdict of "not guilty."

The state's attorney called the action disgraceful and declared that DePriest must stand trial again on one of the six pending indictments. Despite the "not quilty" verdict, DePriest's political career plummeted into an abyss. However, his status as a folk hero remained in orbit in the black community.

Alderman Oscar DePriest posts bond after being charged with bribery in 1917.

Clarence Darrow, one of America's outstanding criminal lawyers.

The Illinois Central Railroad Station located at Twelfth & Michigan was the gateway to the promised land for southern blacks. An elderly southern female migrant walking through the station with hope in her heart.

Chapter *VII*

Black Migration: A Bonanza for Republicans

When President Woodrow Wilson declared war against Germany on April 5, 1917, he pulled the trigger on the starting gun that sent northern industrial headhunters searching for Negro workers in the rural South. Most of these Negroes would be sent to Chicago manufacturers. In fact, the Illinois Central Railroad would not be able to furnish the headhunters from Chicago with enough passenger cars to accommodate all of the southern black laborers needed to man the thousands of jobs in the Chicago stockyards, steel mills, and manufacturing companies. Such jobs were being vacated by 350,000 native Illinois whites who were enlisting in the armed services and several thousand more foreign whites who were deserting America to return to Europe to fight on the side of Germany, Austria, or Turkey. The scarcity of manpower was so critical that headhunters would frequently rent entire trains to express rural black farm workers to the urban North.

The railroad industry had not anticipated such a mass exodus of blacks moving from the South to the North. A poem appearing in an April 1917 edition of the *Chicago Defender* captured the transportation problems of the black labor recruits who were restricted to riding in the coal car because racist laws dictated that only a single "Jim Crow" passenger car per train be made available to black folk. The poem read as follows:

> Some are coming on passenger,
> Some are coming on freight,
> Others will be found walking,
> For none will have time to wait.

Waiting at the end of the journey, in addition to the employers, were the

President Woodrow Wilson.

politicians and the real estate men. Men such as former Republican Alderman Oscar DePriest and Republican State Senator George F. Harding, the white realtor, millionaire-sportsman, and the political boss of the Second Ward and the owner of four hundred parcels of real estate within that ward including the entire 3300 blocks on Rhodes, Vernon, and Cottage Grove benefited both ways. The large influx of blacks arriving at the Illinois Central Railroad's Twelfth Street Station wearing mourning arm bands for the martyred and revered president, Abraham Lincoln, were signs of a political bonanza for the Republican party and money in the bank for the real estate industry. However, there was a suppressed anti-Negro sentiment in both the Democratic and Republican organizations because the enlarged body of blacks was bursting the seams of the segregated Black Belt and spilling over into the adjacent white areas east of State Street between Twenty-second Street and Thirty-ninth Street.

Contrary to the ambivalence of the Republican political establishment, the big industrialists, most of whom were also Republicans needed a large pool of black laborers to work in their plants. Cheap labor was the underbelly of the system; therefore, the northern industrialist won while southern blacks continued to pour into Chicago by the thousands like April rain. It was estimated by the Chicago Urban League that more than fifty thousand black southerners migrated to Chicago in the eighteen months following President Wilson's Declaration of War on April 5, 1917.

The stone gate to the Union Stockyards in Chicago.

A black family of sharecroppers was recruited from the cotton fields of Mississippi by a Northern industrial head-hunter to work in the Union Stockyards in Chicago.

A Mississippi family of sharecroppers shortly after their arrival in Lincoln's city by the lake.

State Senator George F. Harding, millionaire realtor and political boss of the Second Ward.

The expansion of the bulging Black Belt in Chicago could be measured by the bombings of black occupied real estate. Between July 1, 1917 and March 1, 1921, a bombing occurred on an average of once every twenty days. Each bombing militarized countless black minds. Every train load of black arrivals poured additional kerosene on a barn fire of white resistance. The lily white Kenwood and Hyde Park Community Association was determined that blacks would not move east of State Street and contaminate property values. The association called a meeting in October 1918, one door north of the Metropolitan Theater on Forty-sixth and Grand Boulevard, (now Martin Luther King Drive) for the sole purpose of propagandizing that Kenwood and Hyde Park should remain "lily white." At the same time, Frederick H. Bartlett, a major white loop realty firm, had a host of well-dressed salesmen on south side streets passing out hand bills to white home owners in the Douglas, Oakwood, and Kenwood communities which read:

Negroes are coming, Negroes are coming. If you don't sell to us now, you might not get anything.

White folks, suffering from "nigger mania", sold their properties to the Bartlett people at the bargain basement prices of $1,500 to $2,500. Bartlett in turn doubled and sometimes tripled the prices when he resold the houses. He sold to Negroes with down payments as low as $300.00 and with five year balloon mortgages, which meant that the mortgage principle was due and payable at the end of five years. After Bartlett raped the real estate market between Thirty-fifth and Thirty-ninth Streets from South Park to Cottage Grove, he began to build some shoddy frame houses for blacks in the Lilydale area located between Ninety-first and Ninety-fifth Streets, immediately west of what is now the Dan Ryan Expressway.

The Bartlett firm along with the Chicago Real Estate Board played both sides of the street in that they masterminded the use of white restrictive covenants. The Bartlett salesmen would sell property to white folk and tell them that there was a restrictive covenant on the land that would protect them and their children from "niggers" for life. This white veil of protection caused a lot of trauma and drama because many a white family went to bed one night only to awaken the next morning to discover that it had black neighbors.

The competition for housing and jobs intensified the bitterness between the races. The bitterness accelerated to outright brutal hatred by the spring of 1919 when thousands of robust white and black servicemen returned to Lincoln's city by the lake looking for employment and housing.

Clouds of hatred hovered over Chicago from the lake to the stockyards and in the Ashland Avenue area. The clouds became thicker and darker to the

A bomb was thrown into this building occupied by blacks at 3365 S. Indiana Avenue. A six year old child was killed.

The January, 1919 Raymond Elementary School graduation picture of Eugene Williams, the initial riot victim of Chicago's "Blood Red" summer. Williams is the first person on the extreme right in the third row.

The beginning of the Chicago race riot in 1919. Whites and Negroes leave the Twenty-ninth Street Beach after Eugene Williams had been murdered by drowning.

Members of the Chicago Police Department escorting black families from an integrated area to a safety zone in the Black Belt away from hostile whites at 48th and Wentworth Avenue.

Governor Frank O. Lowden called out the National Guard on July 30, 1919, at 10:30 P.M., on the fourth day of the riot.

Attorney William L. Dawson, a crusader for the Republican party.

west of Wentworth, the west boundary of the Black Belt. The racial temperature began to rise. In June 1919, two black stockyard workers were murdered by Back of the Yards' hoodlums before they could reach the safety of the Black Belt. The two senseless killings caused racial fires to smolder, but the fires did not ignite until July 27, 1919, a day of infamy for Chicago because it ushered in one of this country's bloodiest race riots.

On Sunday, July 27, 1919, Eugene Williams, a black youth who had recently graduated from Raymond Grammar School, was stoned to death on a raft because he accidently floated across an imaginary line dividing the Twenty-ninth Street Lake Michigan beach into "white" and "colored" sections. He was the victim of an unwritten agreement that divided the Chicago lakefront by race.

Immediately after the murder of the Williams' boy, a group of black men approached white patrolman Daniel Callahan and asked him to arrest George Stauber, a white, who was seen pelting young Williams with stones until he fell unconscious into the water where he drowned. Officer Callahan did not respond to the black men's request; thus, they commenced to attack him. He enlisted the support of white men and boys on the beach. All hell broke loose. The battle was on. Like a forest fire, it raced faster than time from the beach to the corners of 31st, 35th and State Streets, and from the streets through the beer halls, pool rooms, and from there into the apartments and flats. Within an hour, there were four thousand blacks gathered on the corner of Thirty-fifth and State Streets (then known as The Stroll).

The intensity of the violence that followed for the next four days could not be brought under control by the Chicago Police Department. It took military assistance as well as a thunderstorm and a heavy rain that started Wednesday night, July 30, and lasted throughout Thursday, July 31, to bring the conflict under control. The human cost was the lives of thirty-eight men and boys, including twenty-three blacks. Five-hundred and thirty-seven people were also injured; three-hundred and forty-two of the number were black.

Many of Mayor Thompson's critics maintained that if the mayor had not been playing petty politics and had requested that Governor Frank O. Lowden put the militia on the streets of the city of Chicago at the outbreak of the riot, the death and injury casualties would have been kept to a minimum. The riot had diminished when the troops were called out at 10:30 P.M. on July 30, the fourth day of the blood bath. Because the black troops who had fought in the war and who comprised the Eighth Regiment were not recognized by the political establishment, no blacks were used.

The killing and blood letting of the July 1919 riot did not cause any dimunition in the campaign of the white citizens of the Kenwood and Hyde Park Association to keep blacks confined to the Black Belt. The association's official publication, the *Property Owner's Journal,* seemed to indicate approval of additional drastic steps. In January 1920, the following statement appeared:

> As stated before every colored man who moves into Hyde Park knows that he is damaging his white neighbor's property. Therefore, he is making war on the white man. Consequently, he is not entitled to any consideration and forfeits his right to be employed by the white man. If employers should adopt a rule of refusing to employ Negroes who persist in residing in Hyde Park to damage the white man's property, it would show good results.

In a later issue, the *Journal* exclaimed:

> What a reputation for beauty Chicago would secure if visitors touring the city would not see crowds of insulent, idle Negroes lounging on the south side boulevards and adding ugliness to the floricultural display in the parks, filling the street with old newspaper and tomato containers, and advertising the porosystem for removing the marceled kinks from Negro hair in the windows of the derelict remains of what had once been a clean, respectable residence.

The late Congressman William L. Dawson, who was a young veteran just returning from World War I, digested and regurgitated a great deal of the propaganda of the property owners' association. He also witnessed the blood red summer of 1919. Dawson made the following statement about the activity of Oscar DePriest in the 1919 race riot:

> What great admiration I had for Oscar DePriest as a man who really had 'guts.' I remember seeing him put on a policeman's cap and uniform and drive a patrol wagon into the stockyards to bring out the Negroes who were trapped inside during the riot of 1919. He was respected as a former alderman, and he did what not a single policeman had the courage to do. Again and again he went into the stockyards, bringing Negroes out with him in the patrol wagon until finally he had rescued all of them from the white mob. His courageous action, undertaken at great personal risk, moved me to do something which taught me a lesson and something I rarely have done since. I sat down and wrote Oscar a letter.
>   I told him I thought he had performed a great heroic deed and that I personally wanted to congratulate him. I also told him that he could always depend upon me for support in anything he would undertake in the future and that I was ready to stand beside him. Years later that letter turned up to my embarrassment. Oscar and I were then on the opposite sides of the fence politically, but he remembered that letter and dug it up and used it against me, referring to it in his speeches and waving it before his audiences wherever he went.

Edward H. Wright, the original "ironmaster" of black politics.

Chapter *VIII*

Ed Wright: The "Bull Dog" That Roared

The political tide for Edward H. Wright changed drastically in November 1919 when Louis B. Anderson, a Thompson-Wright backed candidate, defeated Oscar DePriest in the primary in DePriest's third aborted attempt to re-enter the city council as alderman of the Second Ward. Lightning struck twice that winter for Ed Wright because in January 1920, Congressman Martin B. Madden decided that after eight terms in the U.S. House of Representatives, he was comfortable enough in Washington, D.C. to give up the Second Ward committeemanship to a black.

Wright was selected by Thompson and the Regular Second Ward Republican Organization to run for the committeeman's seat. Wright was opposed by Warren B. Douglas, a loquacious and energetic state representative, who was backed by former governor Charles S. Deneen. Wright's political sub-machine ran over Douglas in the committeeman's race like a tractor pressing a tin can in soft tar. Thus, Wright became the first black committeeman in the history of the country.

Edward H. Wright, the new committeeman, and Louis B. Anderson, the alderman of the Second Ward, brought a perfect political balance to the Republican Organization. Wright was symbolic in temperament to storm and oak whereas Anderson was similar to oil and water. Louis B. Anderson was an excellent administrator who kept the machinery of the organization running as smoothly as a 1920 Packard automobile. On the other hand, Wright was a bull dog; he was a gentlemanly head knocker and people motivator. He was known for exercising his size twelve shoe in the rump of a slow moving precinct captain.

Wright's ascension to the Second Ward committeemanship opened doors that gave him an awesome amount of political power, more power than any black man had laid his hands on in the twentieth century. Fortunately for the

Left: State Representative Warren B. Douglas, an independent Republican. Right: Sadie Douglas Waterford Jones, social worker, civic activist, and widow of Warren B. Douglas.

black community, Wright was tough and smart enough to know how to leverage it. His thirty years in Chicago politics had afforded him the opportunity to eavesdrop at the doors of the political powerful. Moreover, Wright knew what his constituents in the Second Ward were entitled to, and he also knew how to use political leverage to get those entitlements.

An early example of how Committeeman Edward H. Wright used his political leverage occurred in a confrontation with Congressman Martin B. Madden about getting blacks in the postal service promoted to supervisory positions. The Phalanx Club, which was composed of a group of black post office workers complained to Ed Wright that it had among its members individuals working at the post office with college degrees with the title of postal clerk but actually working as laborers in overalls on the docks, throwing mail bags into the trucks. Ed Wright had earlier extracted a promise from Congressman Madden to promote a black to the position of supervisor after the election. Sixty days beyond the election, the postmaster told the president of the Phalanx Club that he had not heard anything from Congressman Martin B. Madden about a colored being promoted to supervisor. A delegation from the club which included Corneal Davis, who some years later became a member of the

Illinois House of Representatives, went to Committeeman Wright's office at Thirty-third and Michigan and repeated the postmaster's statement. Wright angrily picked up the phone and called Madden in his Washington office.

Congressman Madden was summoned from the house floor to take Wright's call. Corneal Davis reports he heard the following part of Wright's conversation with Madden:

> Congressman Madden, I have a committee from the Chicago Post Office sitting at my desk. I have talked to you about the condition in that place. I also told you that there were black men down there that were college-trained and with years of service but being relegated to the lot of common laborers. I am damned tired of you making me an embarrassment to my people. We are delivering something like a 25,000 majority to the damn Republican party in my ward. I want a black supervisor in the Chicago Postal System before the damn sun goes down this day. Do you hear me?

Wright then slammed the large black telephone receiver down on the hook. At 3:30 P.M. that afternoon, Dan Hawley, a black man, was sent from the Main Post Office to the Old Armour Postal Station at Thirty-first and Indiana to work as the first black supervisor in the Chicago Postal System.

Another illustration of Wright's use of political leverage was recalled by former State Representative Corneal Davis. When Bernard W. Snow ran for coroner, he came before Wright's Second Ward Republican Organization, and

Left: Governor Len Small. Right: Corneal Davis, a precinct captain in the Edward H. Wright Regular Republican Organization.

asked for its support while promising to make a black man deputy coroner. Wright told Snow that E. M. Cleaves who resided at Thirty-second and Forest Avenue (Prairie) was his choice. "Barney" Snow was elected. Wright sent Cleaves down to see Snow several times about a job as deputy coroner, but Snow refused to see him. Cleaves then reported to Wright that he had not had an audience with Snow. Wright told Cleaves, "I will go down to Snow's office with you this afternoon."

Corneal Davis accompanied Wright and Cleaves to the coroner's office which was located on the fourth floor of the County Building. Cleaves and Davis followed Ed "The Iron Master" Wright into the reception area of Snow's office. Ed Wright told the girl at the reception desk that he wanted to see Barney Snow. The girl went into the inner office and after about five minutes, returned and said: "Mr. Snow will see you in a few minutes. Please have a seat." Ed Wright took his size twelve shoe and with one kick knocked down the four foot gate that separated the waiting room from the secretarial area. Wright then walked directly pass the secretary into Snow's office and said: "This is the man you are going to make deputy coroner now while I am standing here. I am damn tired of your promises." E. M. Cleaves instantly became the first black deputy coroner in Cook County.

Wright's "bulldog" demeanor earned for him both respect and a commitment of solidarity from the colored voters of the Second Ward who saw him as their champion. Ed Wright's leadership ability made him a power to be reckoned with not only at the municipal and county levels but also at the state house. In 1923 Governor Len Small saw Wright and the Second Ward Organization as a vehicle to aid him in his aspiration to serve another term in the governor's mansion in Springfield. Thus, the governor appointed Wright as the first black Illinois commerce commissioner at an annual salary of $7,000.00 per year. The commission was powerful; it had jurisdiction and supervision over all the public utilities in the state of Illinois.

At Wright's suggestions, Governor Small appointed Reverend H. W. Jameson of Peoria County, as inspector in the Department of Registration and Education; Dr. S. A. Ware of Sangamon County, as inspector in the State Department of Health, and Captain Horace G. Burke, of Massac County, as parole agent in the State Department of Public Welfare. These appointments were significant because they were all firsts, made at a time when blacks were not able to eat in restaurants or stay in hotels in either Chicago or Springfield. Wright, indeed, was the right man at the right time because he did not stop with those token appointments. Through Wright's Second Ward Regular Republican Organization, a number of qualified blacks secured highly visible positions through both the electoral and appointment processes.

In 1924, Adelbert H. Roberts, a three term state representative, was

Senator Adelbert H. Roberts, the initial person of color to serve in the upper chamber of the State House.

Attorney Albert B. George, the first black man to be appointed to the bench of the Municipal Court system in Chicago.

nominated and elected the first black senator in the state of Illinois with the support of Wright and George Harding. In the same year, Albert B. George was selected by Wright and subsequently elected to be the first black judge to sit on the bench in the Municipal Court of Chicago. Wright was also instrumental in getting blacks their initial major appointment in the offices of the Sheriff, the United States Attorney, Sanitary District of Chicago, Illinois Free Employment, and the State Department of Public Works and Buildings. In addition to these high profile jobs, he secured numerous minor clerkships in various county and state offices. In reflecting on his accomplishments, Wright stated in the March 12, 1927 edition of the *Chicago Daily News* that "every conspicuous political appointment of a colored man or woman in Chicago and Illinois from the Industrial Commission and Illinois Commerce Commission down was brought about by the Second Ward Republican Organization under my leadership."

Edward H. Wright's indocile attitude and independence upset the white bosses of the Republican party. Thus, they laid plans in the summer of 1926 to destroy his awesome political power by selecting a squeaky clean black who understood how to act colored in the presence of white folk. Wright was acting white. During the fall of twenty-six, he became engaged in a heated quarrel with former Mayor Thompson and Robert E. Crowe over the designation of a committeeman in the First Ward to succeed the late Francis P. Brady.

Mayor William E. Dever (third from the left), appoints Attorney Earl B. Dickerson (second from the right), to the position of assistant corporation counsel in 1923.

Thompson wanted Daniel Scanlon, whom he felt he could trust, to help open the path for his re-election as mayor whereas Wright fought for his good friend, Adolph Marks. The scene was bitter with Thompson accusing Wright of attempting to set up his own kingdom on the South Side. Wright retaliated by threatening to abandon the Republican ship if his man was not selected. Wright left the meeting in a huff while Scanlon was designated committeeman of the First Ward. The white political bosses laughed silently, but gratefully because Wright had stepped on a booby trap that they had not made.

In 1927, Wright put both feet in the political booby trap when he sided with Governor Small who supported the former Commissioner of Public Health, Dr. John Bill Robertson, who ran against Thompson in his re-election bid. Thompson pleaded with Wright to join his team to no avail. Therefore, Thompson and Crowe removed all of Wright's patronage and gave it to the caretaker for corruption in the Second Ward, Dan M. Jackson, the political bagman who collected from policy stations, gambling establishments, pool rooms, and houses of joy. Jackson collected from everybody, but the dead. He even made his brother, Charlie, operator of the Railroad Club at 3448 South Indiana, pay $75.00 per week for protection.

The loss of political patronage knocked Ed Wright down, but not out according to Corneal Davis, a Wright precinct captain. Wright got off the canvass and said to his precinct captains: "I am no political slave, I was chosen by my people in a regular election in 1920, and I do not propose to sell them out to satisfy the whims of the downtown bosses."

The politically-defrocked Wright mounted a spirited campaign with a "rag-tag", political army for Dr. Robertson against Thompson. However, in 1927 the "Second Abraham Lincoln" could not be beaten in the Second Ward. Blacks gave Thompson 91.7 percent of their votes in the Second Ward and 8.3. percent in the Third Ward. Edward "The Iron Master" Wright delivered only 526 votes out of a possible 10,000 for Dr. Robertson, who subsequently withdrew from the race for mayor after the primary. Thompson then steam-rolled over the Democratic incumbent mayor, William E. Dever.

Ironically, after Thompson was re-elected mayor, Len Small and "Big Bill" became lifetime bosom buddies. Shortly after Thompson made his victory statement, Wright sent a carrier pigeon with a message of peace to Thompson's headquarters in the Sherman Hotel. Thompson burned the message and ate the bird. All the members of Wright's "rag-tag" army were invited to come back into the fold, but "Iron Master" Wright and George Harding were declared politically dead.

Two months after Thompson took over the fifth floor for the third time, Wright's health broke. He was confined in Springfield, Illinois at the St. Elizabeth Hospital where "the Iron Master" began a campaign to run for Congress against Martin B. Madden. William L. Dawson and Earl B. Dickerson, both attorneys and friends of Wright's assisted him in circulating 10,000 voting pledge cards. Wright's physical health did not permit him to pursue his objectives; however, Dawson, his young lieutenant did some years later.

Wright was stricken again early in July 1930 and taken to the Mayo Brothers Clinic in Rochester, Minnesota where he passed away at 5:00 A.M. on Wednesday, August 6, 1930. He was funeralized at the Metropolitan Community Church located at 4100 South Parkway on Monday, August 11, at 10:00 A.M. Among the active pallbearers were William L. Dawson, Earl B. Dickerson and Corneal Davis. The "Iron Master", the father of black power politics, was buried in Oakwood Cemetery at 6701 South Cottage. According to Corneal Davis, Wright was lowered into his grave "unwept, unhonored, and unsung."

U. S. Senator H. R. REVELS, of Mississippi. ROBERT C. DE LARGE, M. C. of South Carolina. JEFFERSON H. LONG, M. C., of Georgia.
BENJ. S. TURNER, M. C. of Alabama. JOSIAH T. WALLS, M. C. of Florida. JOSEPH H. RAINY, M.C. of South Carolina. R. BROWN ELLIOT, M. C. of South Carolina.

THE FIRST COLORED SENATOR AND REPRESENTATIVES
IN THE 41ST AND 42ND CONGRESS OF THE UNITED STATES

Picture of the first colored senators and members of the U.S. House of Representatives in the 41st and 42nd Congress of the United States.

Chapter *IX*

A Black Reconstructionist Prophecy Fulfilled

Chicago, the mecca of black politics in the twentieth century, was destined to fulfill in 1929 the 1901 prophecy of George H. White, the last black congressman of the reconstruction period. Representative White standing in the well of the House of Representatives said in his farewell speech of January 29, 1901:

> This, Mr. Chairman, is perhaps the Negro's temporary farewell to the American Congress, but let me say, Phoenix-like, he will rise up some day and come again. These parting words are in behalf of an outraged, heart-broken, bruised and bleeding but God-fearing people, faithful, industrious and loyal people full of potential.

The potential for fulfilling George White's prophecy became a reality in Chicago by the early 1920s because the "Jim Crow" housing pattern had corralled between 75.0 and 89.9 percent of the Negro population in twenty-four census tracts. Ninety-four percent of those tracts were in the Second and Third Wards, and both were in the First Congressional District. In 1922, Richard E. Parker, a weak black congressional candidate, received 2,842 votes out of a total of 17,035 votes. Congressman Martin Barnaby Madden, the white god-father of the Second and Third Wards, beat Taylor by a total of 14,193 votes. However, in 1924, attorney Nathan S. Taylor, a University of Michigan trained lawyer, piled up 40 percent of the 21,054 votes cast in the congressional race and put the fear of a black God in Madden. But it was William L. Dawson, a Fisk University graduate and a Northwestern University trained lawyer, who gave both white and black Republican politicians a religious experience. He garnered 29 percent of the votes as an independent Republican after making a strong ethnic appeal throughout a heated political campaign against Madden who was supported by former Alderman Oscar DePriest. Dawson who had repeatedly preached from political tree stumps throughout the Black Belt proclaimed the following:

> By birth, training and experience, I am better fitted to represent the district at Washington than any of the candidates now in the field. Mr. Madden, the present congressman, does not even live in the district. He is a white man; therefore, for those two reasons, if no others, he can hardly voice the hopes, ideas and sentiments of the majority of the district.

Dawson was on target in his articulations of the black community's desire to want a black congressman, but Oscar DePriest got the call. DePriest, Bishop Archibald J. Carey, Charlie Jackson, and Alderman Louis B. Anderson along with other black political leaders were in Westbaden, Indiana relaxing and taking steam baths after their vigorous primary campaign for the Thompson, Crowe, and Madden ticket. The group had only been in Westbaden a few days when Bishop Carey received a call in the early evening on Friday, April 27, 1928 from Chicago indicating that Congressman Madden had just died in Washington, D.C. Carey immediately went to DePriest who was sitting on the front porch of Waddy's Place where all the black politicians were staying and gave him the news about Madden's death. DePriest reacted by sending tele-

George H. White, last black congressman of the Reconstruction Period.

Left to right: Alderman Louis B. Anderson, Congressman Oscar DePriest and Charlie Jackson.

grams to Dan Jackson of the Third Ward. Daniel Serritella of the First Ward, John Oberta of the Thirteenth, W. S. Finucane of the Eleventh Ward and Mayor Thompson indicating his desire to be selected to replace the late Congressman Madden. DePriest's next move was to jump into his car that night and head straight for Chicago without uttering a mumbling word to either Alderman Louis B. Anderson or Charlie Jackson, who were busily engaged in a serious poker game with other politicians.

The next morning, Oscar DePriest was seated in Thompson's waiting room when the mayor arrived. The mayor invited Oscar into his inner office where he reportedly said: "You know, Oscar, I am with you." DePriest then asked Mayor Thompson whether Committeeman Jackson wanted Alderman Anderson or former State Senator Adelbert H. Roberts of the Second Ward to have the nomination.

Later that day, the mayor asked Jackson his choice for the nomination and Jackson said: "I am with you Mr. Mayor."

The Mayor replied, "Well, I am with Oscar."

On Monday, April 30, 1928, Martin B. Madden was laid to rest on the side of a wind-swept hill at Hinsdale, Illinois, in a cemetery that was not much larger than the grounds surrounding Madden's home, which was less than a half-mile down the road. Madden's heavy bronze casket had not been lowered into the ground twenty-four hours before the five ward committeemen who received DePriest's telegram had unanimously selected Oscar as their choice to replace Mr. Madden, who was nominated in April to make the run in November.

The Republican nomination in the First Congressional District had always been equivalent to being elected. However, that was not the case for the first black nominee. Assistant Attorney General William H. Harrison announced that he would be an independent candidate for Congress against Oscar DePriest. He further stated that he was "against disreputable leadership of the gangster, gambler, grafter type." The law and order white folk were very upset with the possibility of a black man going to Congress. DePriest's congressional campaign was not three months old before he was indicted by a special Grand Jury for "aiding, abetting and inducing" black racketeers to operate gambling houses and disorderly places and "protecting them from the police." The indictment did not satisfy Assistant Attorney General Harrison's people. Thus, they began to propagandize that if DePriest were elected, he could not be seated. They used as an example the recent exclusion of Senator-elect Frank L. Smith. As a last straw, the Harrison people offered to drop the indictment if DePriest would gracefully bow out of the race. Oscar gave them a three word reply: "Go to hell!"

DePriest stumped throughout the Second and Third Wards in the Black Belt proclaiming that he was innocent of all the charges, that he was being persecuted by white folk and that the indictments were simply part of a plot to keep him out of Congress because he was black. He further stated that the indictment was "a nefarious scheme, hatched through the oligarchy of pseudo-Republicans. . ." DePriest with the solid support of the black community won by a very narrow margin because thousands of rock-ribbed white Republicans switched their support to the white Democratic nominee, Harry Baker, the owner of a retail store on the southwest corner of Fifty-first and Indiana. The First Congressional District which had previously given Madden a 14,000 plurality in 1926 gave DePriest a plurality of only 3,800. The total vote was: DePriest, 24,479; Baker, 20,664; and Harrison, 5,861. If Harrison had not siphoned off almost 6,000 white votes as an independent white hope, DePriest would have lost the election to Harry Baker, the perennial white Democratic candidate.

Mrs. Lovelyn Evans, a reporter for the Negro-owned Chicago Whip *newspaper.*

Ruth Hannah McCormick, Illinois Congress-woman at large and widow of the late Senator Medill McCormick of Illinois.

After the election, twelve million blacks across America turned their collective hearts and eyes toward Washington, D.C. with a single question lodged in their minds. Will Oscar DePriest be seated as America's first black congressman from the North? DePriest did not have the answer; however, he felt the heat of the racist political climate and mentally fortified himself with the knowledge that his credentials might be challenged because of his indictment on a charge of graft which was dropped on April 13, 1929, two days before the Seventy-first Congress got underway.

Luckily, Oscar DePriest had a white angel in the person of Ruth Hannah McCormick, Illinois Congresswoman at-large and the widow of the late Senator Medill McCormick of Illinois. Mrs. McCormick felt that the anti-Negro sentiment whirling through white America was the sole factor that stood between DePriest and his rightful seat in the halls of Congress. Hence, she used her long and valuable friendship with Mrs. Alice Roosevelt Longworth, daughter of President Theodore Roosevelt and widow of the late Speaker of the House, Congressman Nicholas Longworth, to intercede on DePriest's behalf. She pleaded with both Alice Longworth and Speaker of the House, Reed, to find a way to open the door to the House of Representatives to let the black man from Chicago be seated.

The day that Oscar DePriest was to be seated, the following observations were made by Mrs. Lovelyn Evans, a reporter for the Negro owned, *Chicago Whip* newspaper. Mrs. Evans said her first mistake was presenting her press card to gain admission to the press section. She was told that a card from a colored weekly could not be honored. She was, therefore, directed to sit in the first floor visitors' gallery with the other spectators. The gallery was packed. The only seat available was between Dean Cook of Howard University and a white woman with a deep southern drawl. The southern white lady looked at Lovelyn Evans, smiled and said: "Do you think that they are going to let that nigger Oscar DePriest take his seat?"

Mrs. Evans gasped and retorted: "I beg your pardon." Lovelyn is a mulatto; the southern woman evidently thought she was white.

Mrs. Jesse DePriest, Oscar's wife and their children were sitting in the row directly in front of Lovelyn Evans but to her left. Mrs. Evans noted:

> Mrs. DePriest appeared to be both disturbed and nervous, but the kids did not look like they were aware of what was about to happen to their father. I was personally sitting on needles and pins.

Lovelyn Evans watched the Speaker of the House, Reed, for a period of about thirty minutes as he rushed around on the House floor buttonholing congressmen of every stripe. A few moments before, the newly-elected con-

President Herbert Hoover.

Mrs. Herbert Hoover.

gressmen had been ushered into the chambers. Reed settled into the speaker's seat in an exhausted posture. Several minutes later, he lifted himself from the chair, strolled to the speaker's lectern and made the following remarks:

> Owing to the complete disorder that was apt to accompany the general practice of administering the oath, I thought that it would be more comport with the dignity and solemnity of this ceremony if I administered the oath to all members at once.

This parliamentary move surprised all the disgruntled dissenters. Oscar DePriest was sworn in with the rest of the newly-elected and re-elected officials before anyone had an opportunity to raise objections. Precedent called for swearing in House members in groups alphabetically by states. Any group that had already been sworn in prior to the Illinois delegates could have challenged DePriest's credentials.

Lovelyn Evans recalled the moments after DePriest was sworn in:

> Everybody breathed a sigh of relief, and a large number of congressmen came over to where Oscar was standing, grabbed his hand and welcomed him to the house. DePriest stood there like a proud lion with a shock of white hair towering over his head. Little Mrs. DePriest was as gentle and quiet as Oscar was strong and forceful.

The white newspaper coverage of DePriest being seated in Congress was very shabby. The print media's concerns were not about the success of the black congressman or how he might represent the aspirations of twelve million black Americans, but how he and his wife's presence might integrate the White House and cause the first lady, Mrs. Herbert Hoover, social embarrassment. To the first lady's credit, she did not exclude Mrs. DePriest from the White House tea welcoming the congressional wives to the Capitol. This social action left a large number of northern and southern solons with gaped mouths.

Congressman Oscar DePriest reacted to the newspaper coverage of the White House tea party with the following statement:

> Mrs. DePriest was not invited to have tea because Mrs. Hoover thought anything of her personally. She was invited because she happened to be the wife of a member of Congress. That is all there was to that.

Tea time for DePriest was short because the country plunged into a deep depression when the stock market crashed on black Thursday, October 24, 1929, exactly five months and nine days after the congressman was sworn into

Big and bulky, Mayor William Hale Thompson makes one of his last campaign speeches.

office. DePriest did not have time to make a legislative record for himself because he was too busy traveling around the country espousing President Herbert Hoover's line about two chickens in every pot and a car in every garage during a period when black folk could not afford to buy neck bones.

DePriest was such a rock-ribbed Republican that he actually believed what he was spewing about Hoover's chicken and car propaganda. How else could he have fought a bill to appropriate twenty-five million dollars for Red Cross-dispensed food and medical relief for the unemployed when there were five million men walking the streets with newspaper-soled shoes and eating out of garbage cans? The congressman was solidly against a federal "dole system" because he thought states and cities should take care of their own poor folk. However, DePriest said in his own defense: "No one, could accuse him, a child of the 'poorest of the poor,' of being unsympathetic to the jobless."

DePriest survived the 1930 Democratic sweep in spite of his economic philosophy because he was thought to be straight on the race question. He appointed Negroes to Annapolis and West Point. He defied the KKK in Alabama and was frequently quoted as saying: "That I am a Negro before I am a Republican." In the eyes of colored people, he was a black folk hero. DePriest's bigger than life pro-black posture made him a winner.

Congressman Oscar DePriest was re-elected to a third term in 1932, again without any difficulty against the Democratic perennial candidate, Harry Baker. DePriest's victory was a monumental political achievement in the wake of Mayor William H. Thompson's defeat and Franklin D. Roosevelt's presidential victory in a Democratic landslide.

DePriest's re-election berth was not soft. The South Side Communist Party accused him of being a hard-hearted capitalist landlord because he evicted unemployed blacks from his South Side flats. DePriest was concerned about the personal accusations and the inroads that the Communist party was making among black Americans who were convinced that fair treatment in the courts for blacks was not in the realm of reality for Negroes under capitalism. DePriest was cognizant of the judicial inequities. He reflected his concern in an address before the House in early May 1933 when he contrasted the court's handling of the nine Scottsboro, Alabama boys accused of raping two white girls of questionable morals with the case of a white naval officer who admitted to having killed a dark-skinned Hawaiian. The naval officer was convicted and given a sentence of one hour. Eight of the Scottsboro nine were convicted and given the death sentence.

DePriest wanted the Fourteenth Amendment revised to assure all Americans equal protection under the law. The congressman ended the observations made that gray afternoon in the halls of Congress with the following statement: "If we had a right to exercise our franchise . . . as the Constitution provides, I would not be the only Negro on this floor."

President Roosevelt's alphabet-labeled, "pump-priming" programs such as the WPA, CCC, and NRA along with dozens of other attracted blacks to the Democratic party's philosophy in large numbers in 1933 and 1934. DePriest was still voting rock-ribbed republicanism against FDR's New Deal programs which were structured to help Chicago's depression riddled Black Belt. The congressman was obviously tone deaf to the rumbling sound of hungry black bellies.

Oscar DePriest was laid back with confidence in the spring of 1934 because Harry Baker, a man who the congressman had beaten three times was renominated to run against the congressman for the fourth time. It was at this point that the scenario changed. Baker died one month after the primary. An unknown Alabama born black lawyer, Arthur W. Mitchell, who had come to Chicago in 1928 via Washington, D.C. and had switched from Republican to Democrat in 1930 was selected by Tom Nash, the Democratic ward committeeman, to replace Baker. Louis B. Anderson, former alderman of the Second Ward, had suggested Mitchell because Mitchell had given the late congressional aspirant a good race in the 1934 spring primary. Mitchell had lost the primary race to Baker by a very narrow margin. The black Republican leaders laughed at Mitchell's selection because they did not think he had a snow-ball's chance in hell of beating DePriest. Before the ground hardened in November 1934, Mitchell, an enthusiastic supporter of President Roosevelt's alphabet program, defeated Oscar DePriest. Mitchell caught lightning in a jug and rode to the halls of Congress on Roosevelt's two-year-old coattails in the 1934 election.

University trained blacks with several degrees found "Jim Crow" standing in front of the hiring gate when they sought employment under President Franklin Delano Roosevelt's National Recovery Act.

Attorney Arthur W. Mitchell who became a Chicagoan via Alabama, New York, and Washington, D.C., was the first black Democrat ever to be elected to the United States House of Representatives.

Anton J. Cermak is shown being sworn in as mayor of Chicago in the city council on April 22, 1931.

Chapter X

The Changing of Chicago's Political Guards

The defeat of William Hale Thompson and the election of Anton Cermak on Tuesday, April 7, 1931 marked the end of a very significant period in the political history of Negroes in the United States. The sixteen years preceding Thompson's defeat represented the golden era of Negro political achievements in Chicago, which was the black political capital of America.

Out of the 1,143,142 votes cast in the general election, Cermak received 667,529 to 475,618 for Thompson, a plurality of 191,916. This was the largest number ever polled in a Chicago mayoralty election. Cermak carried forty-five of the fifty wards. The five wards won by Thompson had a heavy Negro population. Three of the five wards—the Second, Third and Fourth gave him a plurality of 39,291 votes. Eighty-four percent of the Negroes in these wards cast their votes for "Big Bill", the reincarnated Abraham Lincoln as follows:

SECOND WARD

Thompson	16,877
Cermak	3,583

THIRD WARD

Thompson	20,769
Cermak	4,806

FOURTH WARD

Thompson	19,404
Cermak	9,370

Cermak waged a vigorous fight for the colored vote with the aid of colored

Democratic stalwarts such as Attorney Earl B. Dickerson, who had also supported William E. Dever, a successful Democratic candidate for mayor in the
1923 election; Edward "Mike" Sneed, the cheerleader for Al Smith in the 1928
presidential election against Herbert Hoover; Major Adam Patterson; and
Bryant A. Hammond, a real estate man. Cermak was livid because his efforts
along with those of his colored aides were not rewarded. The new mayor had
done more than any previous Democrat to get the Negro vote. In speeches and
in circulars, he pledged that blacks would not only retain their current jobs
but would get more, notably a place on the school board, a position consistently
ignored by Mayor William Hale Thompson. The Democratic rhetoric was not
convincing enough to get the majority of the Negro voters to see the wisdom of
taking their political fresh eggs out of the Republican basket in exchange for
what they suspected were Democratic "painted-hard-boiled-Easter" eggs.
Hard or soft, Cermak was hell-bent on cracking the shells of the anti-
Democratic eggs.

Cermak was so anxious to start destroying the black Republican patronage
army that he took early possession of the mayoralty suite on the fifth floor of
City Hall on Thursday, April 9, 1931, two days after election and thirteen days
before his inauguration. The better part of his first day in office was black
Thursday for Negroes. He discharged almost 3,000 workers, most of them colored people who had been put on temporary payrolls during the Thompson
administration. Cermak was determined to make blacks pay a handsome
price for boycotting the Democratic party and worshipping at the grave of a
president who had been dead for sixty-six years.

The new mayor recognized that the fired black city payrollers were the
small nuts and bolts of the Republican machine compared with the black policy
and gambling overlords who furnished the money that purchased the grease
to make the political machine's wheels roll smoothly under the big political
elephant in the Second, Third and Fourth Wards. Hence, Cermak opened war
on the policy game. Saturday, July 11, 1931 was the date that Judge Samuel
Heller of the Pekin Court at 2700 South State Street issued a search warrant
for Julius Benvinuti of 2900 South LaSalle Street. The police arrested Benvinuti,
the alleged head of a powerful combine organized to control policy on the
South Side, along with several others who were charged with conspiracy to
operate a policy shop, being inmates of a policy station, and with possession of
policy paraphernalia.

On Monday, September 21, 1931, Captain John Stege, Commander of the
Forty-eighth and Wabash Avenue Police Station, arrested George Jones 29,
and his brother McKissick 26, in a raid on a policy wheel drawing at 4803
South Indiana Avenue. The Jones brothers were black millionaires and owners
of the Harlem-Bronx policy wheel which was reputed to be the most lucrative

Left: George Jones, the policy king. Right: McKissick Jones, the policy baron.

operation in the city because it grossed more than $25,000 per day. The brothers were employing over five hundred men and women in the heart of America's worst economic depression.

Mayor Cermak was not satisfied with the speed in which his fight against vice and policy was proceeding. Hence, he instructed Captain Martin Mullen to form a special vice and gambling detail to work under his direct orders. Cermak's first command to Captain Mullen and John Stege was to give the black policy barons and their ilk holy hell. Stege's Forty-eight Street gestapo-like troops arrested an average of two hundred black men and women a day. The prisoners were vertically-mashed into the Wabash Avenue Jail cells like sardines in a can. The inmates were packed so tightly that they could not sit down on the floor.

Cermak's occupation troops employed tactics that harrassed innocent people by randomly stopping their cars under the pretense of searching for policy drawings or other gambling equipment. For example, Miss Petera Hardesty, playground instructor at Forrestville Elementary School, was accosted by a squad of white policemen who forced her car onto the curb on Indiana Avenue near 61st Street and subjected her to questioning, a search, and abusive language.

Al Capone, Chicago crime boss and Captain John Stege, commander of the Forty-eighth and Wabash Avenue Police Station.

William R. "Billy" Skidmore, the clearinghouse between the South Side policy kings and the downtown politicians, is shown checking the roll call of the black owned policy wheels in the shadows of his junkyard at 2840 S. Kedzie.

Like Hitler's storm troopers, the Cermak raiders broke into the homes of black families in the middle of the night and totally disrupted friendly bridge, whist and bingo games. Mrs. Willie Mae Jones, a domestic worker, lived at 5320 South Wabash when her apartment was broken into at 2:00 A.M. When she protested about the intrusion of the police on her small bridge party, one of the officers struck her on the head with the butt of his gun while another pushed his flashlight into the naval area of her stomach. She was handcuffed and hauled off to the Forty-eight Street Station and charged with obstructing the law and disturbing the peace, although the charges were subsequently dropped.

"Drive to the curb" was the command given Dr. S. W. Smith, a prominent black physician on the South Side. Smith was arrested without cause and carried to the police station where the commanding officer told Dr. Smith that the officers were within their rights and that he had no rights that a white man had to recognize. Dr. Smith was denied the opportunity to protest to Commisioner James Allman, but the NAACP filed a civil suit which was later dropped.

The police arrest census for the year 1931 shows that 87 percent of the private homes raided were located within the Black Belt between Twenty-second and Sixty-first Streets from Cottage Grove Avenue to LaSalle Street. The *Chicago Defender's* headlines screamed about the unwarranted invasion of Cermak's police in the black community. Cermak responded: "If blacks switched their allegiance to the Democratic party, the action by his police department would be stopped."

Mayor Anton J. Cermak, the father-in-law of the late Governor Otto Kerner, Jr., was a selective law and order man. He selected blacks along with the Al Capone operatives to put the heat on. He leaned on the Capone mob because it had supplied a substantial amount of money to the Thompson mayoral campaign. And he leaned on blacks because they were Republican junkies. However, William R. "Billy" Skidmore, Cermak's good friend, collected political payoffs for City Hall from Capone's rivals at his junkyard which was located at 2840 South Kedzie. In fact, when black policy barons who came into the Democratic party under Cermak's umbrella used to say: "I am going to see the junkman," it meant they were going to "Billy" Skidmore's place to pay their weekly political dues.

Seated: policy barons Clifford Davis, Ed Jones, and Theodore Roe being congratulated by their lawyers after winning a successful court battle. Standing right to left are the defendants' lawyers, Attorney Aaron Payne and Attorney Joseph Clayton.

Cermak was dextrous in that he clobbered blacks on the head with his right hand and molded them with his left hand into a black appendage of the Second, Third, and Fourth Ward Regular Democratic Organizations. Edward "Mike" Sneed was pivotal to Cermak's plan in the black community because he was the most visible Negro Democratic activist. Sneed had joined the Third Ward Organization in 1928 under Democratic Committeeman Thomas B. Nash. When Tom Nash moved to the Nineteenth Ward in 1930, he nominated Sneed to succeed him as committeeman. Sneed was not able to complete his Democratic transformation program on black folk under Cermak because the mayor was struck by a bullet on February 15, 1933 in Miami, Florida while sitting near president-elect Franklin Delano Roosevelt on the speaker's platform. Giuseppe Zangara, the fanatical assassin, had attempted to take Roosevelt's life. However, a number of political and law enforcement observers have speculated that Zangara was a hit man specifically hired by the syndicate to kill Cermak.

Edward J. Kelly, president of the South Park Board—an entity of the Chicago Park District and a friend of Cermak's dating back to the early days when they both worked for the Sanitary District, was at the race track in Havana, Cuba when he heard about the mayor being shot. He hastened back to Miami by plane and held vigil at Cermak's bedside until he died on March 6, 1933, nineteen days after he had suffered a pistol wound in the stomach. Kelly companioned Cermak's body back to Chicago. Two-hundred and fifty-thousand persons passed the casket of the mayor while the body lay in state in the rotunda of City Hall. For forty-eight hours, there was a continuous stream of silent people of all races who passed from the Washington Street entrance of City Hall to the one on Randolph Street. Each person paused briefly to bid a last farewell to "Tony" Cermak. The funeral held at the Chicago Stadium on west Madison Street was attended by 23,000 people. Thirty-thousand citizens participated in the funeral march which was witnessed by crowds of spectators estimated by the Chicago Police Department to be in excess of 500,000. Some of the colored citizens seen in the line of march were Edward M. Sneed, ward committeeman of the Third Ward, Paul Parks, leader of the Second Ward ex-service men's league of the South Side, Major James Lawson of the Eighth Infantry, and members of the George Giles post of the American legion.

Negro officers were not permitted by the high command of the police department to share in the honor of guarding the remains of Anton Cermak. However, the following blacks were among the honorary pallbearers: A. M. Burroughs, Dave Hawley, Archie Weaver, and Earl B. Dickerson.

Dickerson, who celebrated his 94th birthday on June 22, 1985, remembers Cermak as a very decent man. Dickerson recalls that he was chairman of the Legal Redress Committee of the Chicago branch of the NAACP when he took a delegation down to the mayor to request that the mayor not permit the showing of the movie *Birth of a Nation*. After they finished the session and had reached the outer door of the mayor's reception area, Mayor Cermak said: "Gentlemen, will you excuse Mr. Dickerson for a moment I want to have a word with him." The mayor lead Dickerson back into his inner office and put his foot on the ledge of the window that overlooked LaSalle Street. The mayor remarked: "Dickerson, you have been with the party all these years, and you have never asked for anything. I would like for you to become identified with us now that we have all of these jobs."

Dickerson replied:

> There are two jobs that I would be interested in but the main one is assistant attorney general. However, I would not want that job unless I could participate fully like the other lawyers.

Cermak walked over to his desk, picked up the phone, called Otto Kerner, the attorney general and told him:

> Otto this is Anton, I have in my office a young man, a colored man by the name of Earl B. Dickerson, who has been with us for a long time, and I would like for you to appoint him as an assistant attorney general.

Kerner told Cermak to send Dickerson to 10 North LaSalle. Upon Dickerson's arrival, he was appointed assistant attorney general after a very brief interview. That position was the vehicle that marked the turning point in Dickerson's career. He remained in that office for seven years and resigned when he was elected alderman of the Second Ward in 1939. Otto Kerner permitted him to name his successor who was Attorney Loring B. Moore.

Although Earl Dickerson's present day memories of Cermak are warm, the mayor's casket had not gotten cold from being lowered into the ground on March 10 in the Chicago Bohemian National Cemetery at Bryn Mawr Street and Crawford Avenue before a free for all had broken out among the aldermen who wanted to succeed the late mayor on the fifth floor of City Hall.

The main contenders were three Irishmen: John S. Clark, the council chairman of the Finance Committee, John Duffy, alderman of the 19th Ward which included the highly affluent Beverly Hills, and Dan Ryan, County Commissioner and son of the former president of the County Board with the same name. Patrick A. Nash, the old guard Twenty-eight Ward Committeeman, and Cermak's hand-picked man to chair the Cook County Democratic Organization stood at the palace gate both to give some order to the transition process and to maintain unity and peace in the council. John Clark did not want peace;

One week before the 1932 presidential election, Mayor Cermak poses with presidential candidate Franklin Delano Roosevelt, Mrs. Eleanor Roosevelt, and their son John Roosevelt outside a near northside hotel.

Below: Giuseppe Zangara, Cermak's assassin, in a Miami, Florida jail cell. Zangara was executed March 21, 1933.

Mayor Anton J. Cermak being assisted by his bodyguards after being shot in Miami, Florida, while visiting with Franklin Delano Roosevelt on February 15, 1933.

A large crowd gathers outside City Hall on March 9, 1933, waiting to view Cermak's body.

Above: Pallbearers roll Cermak's casket out of City Hall past honor guards who were standing at full salute.

Right: Cermak's funeral parade marched north on LaSalle Street past City Hall, and west on Randolph Street to the Chicago Stadium at 1800 W. Madison St. where the late mayor was funeralized.

Below: The bier of Mayor Anton J. Cermak rests in the center of the Chicago Stadium, surrounded by honor guards and flowers.

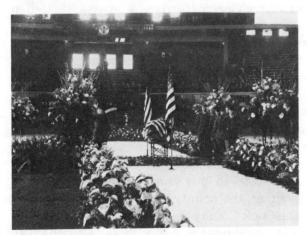

Right: Dignitaries visiting Mayor Anton J. Cermak's grave in the fall of 1933. Second on the left is Mayor Edward J. Kelly, President Franklin Delano Roosevelt, and Mrs. Eleanor Roosevelt. Standing, in the rear to the extreme right is the late Mayor Cermak's son-in-law and young Otto Kerner who became the governor of the state of Illinois.

Attorney General Otto Kerner, father of a son who was later to become governor of Illinois.

Left to right: A. L. Foster, executive director of the Chicago Urban League; Edgar Brown, civil rights' activist; and Mayor Anton J. Cermak. To Cermak's left and to his rear: Jimmy Jones, secretary of the Supreme Liberty Life Insurance Company; Dr. Dudley Turner, president of the NAACP; to his rear is Attorney Earl B. Dickerson, chairman of the NAACP Legal Redress Committee. Directly to Earl B. Dickerson's rear is Robert S. Abbott, publisher of the Chicago Defender; Attorney Joseph Bibbs; Attorney Loring B. Moore; Mr. Harrison, manager of the Grand Theater; unknown.

he wanted the seat because he felt that he was the rightful heir-apparent. History was on Clark's side. When Mayor Carter Harrison was assassinated in 1893, Finance Committee Chairman, George B. Swift automatically assumed the position of mayor pro temp and subsequently was elected on his own merit to serve as a full term mayor from 1895-1897. Another person considered for the mayoral slot outside of the Irish mafia was Jacob Arvey, alderman of the powerful Jewish populated Twenty-fourth Ward. However, most political pundits felt that since Henry Horner, who was also Jewish had just recently been elected governor, that a Jewish mayor at that time would tip the Irishman's political cup to a point that it would runneth over.

On March 12th, two days after Anton Cermak had been funeralized, the Democrats sat down in the Morrison Hotel to lay out a political road map for the party to follow. Robert M. Sweitzer, the county clerk, motioned that Pat Nash's position as titular head of the Cook County Democratic Organization be reaffirmed. The motion was passed unanimously. A few days later, the fifty Chicago committeemen collectively chose Nash to succeed Cermak as their representative on the National Democratic Committee.

The two chairmenships gave Pat Nash enough power to glide into the mayor's chair for the asking. Nash did not want the job because he had reached the advanced age of seventy; he felt a younger man would be better suited for the office. John S. Clark had the right age, the proper credentials, and in addition, he wanted to be the mayor of Chicago with a passion. Pat Nash did not want to appoint Clark or Duffy as an interim replacement in the mayoral seat; therefore, he opted to select a noncompetitive "bland wimp" as acting mayor. Alderman Frank J. Corr of the Seventeenth Ward matched the personality description that Nash wanted for the interim slot. Corr was elected by a council vote of thirty-four to sixteen at a special city council meeting held on Tuesday, March 14, 1933, exactly eight days after Cermak died.

Black political leaders were outraged over Nash's selection of Corr. State Representative William E. King, on the floor of the house, assailed the dictatorial manner in which Corr was made acting mayor. King also described the propaganda surrounding the passing of the "wreck the primary bill"—a bill to by-pass the primary election and handpick Cermak's successor. He further cited the fact that public school teachers were told by the Chicago political establishment that if they lobbied their state representatives to support the bill, their payless paydays would end. The only pay public school employees received between December 1932 and September 1933 had been four weeks of tax warrants in February and two weeks of checks in April. This scheme was intended to add another 30,000 supporters for the bill.

In addition, black and white Republican politicians believed that behind the acting mayor and non-primary scheme was the fear that in an open primary election, "Big Bill" Thompson would be re-elected because under his administration, the teachers, firemen and policemen got their checks on time.

The hope of a William Hale Thompson resurrection died on March 30, 1933 when the Illinois House passed an amendment to section two of the Incorporation of Cities and Villages Act by a margin of 122 to 20 allowing the Chicago City Council to select a new mayor outside as well as within the ranks of the council. The amendment had earlier been approved by the senate by a two-thirds majority vote after its initial introduction by Benjamin Adamowski, Illinois Senate minority leader. The amendment had been engineered in Chicago by Pat Nash. Governor Horner graciously signed the document into law out of his gratitude to Nash for siding with him in a party fight between him and the late Cermak. The road was now clear for Nash to pick his own man for mayor; however, Nash's poker face did not emit even the slightest ray of light on his choice.

At the first council meeting in April following the passage of the section two amendment by the House and Senate, the city council selected five aldermen to go to Hot Springs, Arkansas and come back to Chicago with a recommendation for mayor. The five men chosen were Aldermen Jacob Arvey, Berthold Cronson, Thomas D. Keane, James Quinn, and Thomas Doyle.

Above: Al Horan, Pat Nash, and Governor Henry Horner.

Right: State Representative William E. King, William L. Dawson's nemesis.

Pat Nash and his new mayor, Edward J. Kelly.

After several days of deliberations, the committee wired Pat Nash on April 11, 1933 and asked him to stand for election as the council's nominee to complete the unexpired term of the late mayor Cermak. The wire was signed by all the aldermen on the committee to select a mayor but Berthold Cronson, the Republican.

Nash made the following statement to the press in response to the wire. "I want to say yes, but I don't know," he said. "I want to do what is best for Chicago."

A *Chicago Daily News* reporter retorted: "You are not saying yes or no then?"

"No, I can't say anything", replied Mr. Nash. "I hope we can pick a good man who can handle the job for the best interests of Chicago. I am not going to say now whether I would or would not permit my name to be used."

On Wednesday afternoon, April 12, Jacob Arvey and the other members of the committee returned to Chicago from Hot Springs, Arkansas. Pat Nash hastily called a meeting in his suite at the Morrison Hotel. The following persons were present: Jacob Arvey; Edward J. Kelly, president of the South Park Board; Thomas Courtney; Edward Hughes, secretary of state and Nash's nephew; and Al Horan, municipal court bailiff. Pat told the group that the man who he thought would make a good mayor for Chicago was in the room. He then blurted: "The man is Ed Kelly." Courtney with Nash's permission picked up the phone and called Governor Horner to see if he objected to Kelly. He did not object.

On Wednesday morning, April 13, the aldermen met at the Morrison Hotel to ratify the decision of the caucus. About a half hour after the caucus was called to order, a joint subcommittee of aldermen and committeemen left the main caucus room to deliberate on the suggestion of Chairman Patrick A. Nash that Kelly be the candidate. Within ten minutes, they reported back that they were unanimous in their support for Kelly. In the meantime, Edward J. Kelly was sitting in a room alone on the seventeenth floor of the same hotel awaiting their decision.

Shortly before noon, Police Commissioner James P. Allman sent a detail of forty policemen into the council chambers and the outer corridors to clear that portion of the hall of possible demonstrators from the teachers union or loiterers. The only persons to be admitted to the chambers were hand-picked and given admission tickets by a subcommittee headed by Moe Rosenberg.

Chairman Nash put a vote on the recommendation of the subcommittee, and the caucus adopted it unanimously. "It is the sense of this meeting," Chairman Nash said at the adjournment of the Morrison Hotel meetings, "that we recommend to the city council the election of Edward J. Kelly to be mayor of Chicago to succeed the late Anton J. Cermak and acting Mayor Frank J. Corr."

The aldermen and committeemen hurriedly left the room and rushed down Clark Street to City Hall. The council's chambers were already packed when the announcement was received there of Kelly's selection.

At 2:30 P.M., the council meeting began with Corr surrendering the mayoral chair instantaneously just thirty days after he had taken the seat. Arvey of the Twenty-fourth Ward presented a document that had been signed by thirty-seven aldermen concurring with Nash's recommendation. At 4:15 P.M. on April 13, 1933, the City Clerk, Peter J. Brady administered the oath of office to Edward J. Kelly, president of the South Park board and chief engineer of the Sanitary District as Chicago's new mayor.

In retrospect, the selection of Kelly by Nash made economic sense. Kelly had been a close friend of the Nash family pre-dating his days at the Park Board. In the early years as the head engineer at the Cook County Sanitary District, Ed Kelly had been instrumental in awarding the Nash brothers millions of dollars in sewer contracts which sweetened their relationship. In addition, they were both Irish Catholics which was another prime consideration for moving ahead in Chicago politics.

The Century of Progress Exposition was held on Chicago's lake front in 1933 and 1934.

Chapter *XI*

Edward J. Kelly: The New Deal Mayor

Mayor Edward J. Kelly, a protege of the *Chicago Tribune's* publisher Colonel Robert R. McCormick, reached out to the black community with open arms in a gesture of friendship shortly after being sworn into office. He was more determined than Mayor Anton J. Cermak to bring blacks and other ethnics into the Democratic bloc. Unlike Cermak he saw blacks as a colorful patch in a quilt of political brotherhood.

Mayor Cermak had done an excellent job in creating a multi-ethnic Democratic machine. Kelly, in reaching out for blacks, was determined to enlarge and improve the pattern of that machine. Kelly talked "silk hat" when he was on LaSalle Street or the Gold Coast. However, when he was on the South Side, he talked the language of the common folk. He frequently made references when addressing a Negro audience to the fact that he was their South Side neighbor and that he resided just east of Cottage Grove Avenue at 4821 South Ellis Avenue. Although Mayor Kelly may have talked about being neighborly, blacks were not welcome in his community. In fact, it was dangerous for a black man to venture east of Cottage Grove Avenue on foot in the 1930's and 1940's without being stopped, frisked and in some cases, arrested without cause unless he could prove he worked in the area.

Although Kelly's residence was in an area blanketed with real estate restrictive covenants against Negro occupancy and ownership, his instinctive political philosophy was reflected in a statement that appeared in the April 15, 1933 edition of the *Chicago Defender*. Kelly made the following remark to a query from a *Defender* reporter ten minutes after he had been elected on April 13, 1933: "My pledge is plain, simple justice to all our citizens."

Mayor Kelly was a liberal. He had not been known to exhibit any bigoted behavior toward blacks in his private or public life as the president of the South Park Commission which was headquartered at Fifty-seventh and Cot-

Colonel Robert R. McCormick, publisher of the Chicago Tribune.

tage Grove Avenue in Washington Park on the eastern border of the Black Belt. Moreover, Kelly was instrumental in getting the *Chicago Defender's* "Equal Rights" plank presented and incorporated into the platform of the Democratic party during the national convention which was held in Chicago in June, 1932.

Both Alderman William L. Dawson of the Second Ward and Alderman Robert R. Jackson of the Third Ward were comfortable with Kelly's position on the race question. Although Dawson and Jackson were DePriest Republicans, they voted with forty-five other council members who were in favor of Edward J. Kelly serving out the unexpired term of the late Mayor Anton J. Cermak. Three white Republicans, Arthur G. Lindell of the Ninth Ward, James O. Moreland of the Forty-first Ward, and Oscar P. Nelson of the Forty-sixth Ward were excused from voting.

Kelly had not worn his mayoral hat seventy-two hours when he received the following letter from Attorney Arthur W. Mitchell, a member of the Second Ward's Democratic Organization.

April 15, 1933

Hon. Edward J. Kelly
4821 Ellis Avenue
Chicago, Illinois

Dear Sir:

Because of my desire to have this letter reach you personally, I am taking the liberty to address you at your home. I wish to apologize for this.

You will, perhaps, recall that I wrote you from Washington, D.C., March 11, to which you responded under date of March 23rd. I merely mention this that you may have some idea as to the identity of the writer of this letter.

I am now writing to congratulate you upon your election as mayor of the great city of Chicago. I wish to assure you that the best thinking Negroes of Chicago, regardless of party affiliations, have the highest respect for you and unshaken confidence in your honesty and integrity. Nothing has happened within the Democratic party that has been half so heartening and encouraging to honest and good thinking Negro Democrats for we know that heretofore leaders of the party have given too much recognition to Negro vice-lords and racketeers. With that type of leadership, the Democratic party could never displace the Republican party among the Negroes in wards two and three of this city; but we believe with our leadership the Second and Third Wards will swing to the Democratic party. Again congratulating you upon your fine record as a public servant, your ability, and your promotion to your present office. I am,

Very respectfully yours,

ARTHUR W. MITCHELL

AWM:k

In supporting Mayor Edward J. Kelly, a Franklin Delano Roosevelt New Deal Democrat, Mitchell, Dawson, and Jackson were marching to the rhythmic harmony flowing from the mouths of some of the most eminent black thinkers in twentieth century America. During the 1932 campaign, Dr. W. E. B. DuBois, editor of *The Crisis* magazine said the following about Roosevelt's opponent:

The Negro in the United States today has less opportunity of achievement and less freedom for development than any other American group, and I am unable to see that President Hoover has made any successful effort in increasing our opportunities or our freedom. On the other hand, to single out

Alderman Robert R. Jackson (Third Ward).

Attorney Arthur Mitchell and one of his early campaign volunteers.

two points, his attitude toward the "Lily-White movement of the South and his attitude toward Liberia have both hurt us immeasurably, and these are but two matters of a dozen that I might name. For this reason, I cannot take seriously the platitudes and well-meaning generalizations of the President's last speech.

DuBois' insightful observations were echoed very poetically by the Bishop Reverdy C. Ransom, an African Methodist Episcopal leader and founder in 1900 of the Institutional Church and Social Settlement House at 3828 South Dearborn in Chicago, Illinois. Ransom articulated the following:

It would be a sad commentary upon the intelligence and plain common sense of the Negro voters of this country if they could be either stirred or influenced by the high-sounding platitudes contained in Mr. Hoover's address. Why has Mr. Hoover remained tongue-tied so long? Why has he waited until prostrate upon his political deathbed to give out words of assurance? We would accept them upon their face value if they had been backed by deeds during the nearly four years of his administration. He has had nearly four years to strike a blow on behalf of 'the rights, liberty, justice and equal opportunity' of the colored Americans, but he has remained silent until menaced by the dark shadow of defeat. We are surprised that he has so suddenly lost his stalwart dignity and poise as to act like the traditional drowning man who reached for a straw.

The black families were drowning according to the October, 1933 Unemployment Relief Census. Although Negroes in Chicago constituted only eight percent of the city's available workers, they comprised twenty-two percent of the city's unemployed and thirty-four percent of those on the public relief rolls.

In 1933 industrial employment had been reduced by fifty percent; payrolls were down almost seventy-five percent. Real Estate foreclosures had jumped from 3,148 in 1929 to 15,201 per annum by the spring of 1933. Land value had plummeted from five-billion in 1928 to two billion in January 1933. The Chicago Urban League had reduced its staff to one full-time person, and that was A. L. Foster, the executive secretary. Chicago and the nation had gone from an economic leap forward in January, 1929 to a downhill backward crawl in April, 1933. More than 165 banks had closed their doors within the Chicago metropolitan area. The major banks that were still operating refused to exchange tax warrants issued by the Board of Education to the public school employees for cash because the warrants in the opinion of Chicago bankers had zero collateral value.

In the sixteen weeks between mid-December, 1932 and September, 1933, the school employees received only four weeks in tax warrants in February and two weeks cash payment in April. The April money was not produced until 8,000 teachers marched down Michigan Boulevard from Congress Street to 152 East Monroe Street on April 15 to the City National Bank and Trust Company, the bank where former U.S. Vice President Charles Gates Dawes had been chairman at one time. He was chairman of finance for the Century of Progress (World's Fair), and former president of the Reconstruction Finance Corporation known as the R.F.C. The City National Bank and Trust Company had just received a ninety-million-dollar loan from the R.F.C. (Reconstruction Finance Corporation) which was labeled by Congressman Fiorello LaGuardia of New York as Hoover's "Millionaires' dole" because banks continued to collapse, and small companies were folding like wings on a dead butterfly.

Dr. W. E. B. DuBois, an intellectual liberator

A. L. Foster, executive director of the Chicago Urban League.

Charles Gates Dawes, chairman of finance for the Century of Progress 1933 World's Fair and former vice president of the United States under President Calvin Coolidge.

In the heart of the economic depression of 1933, Chicago school teachers marched on downtown State Street demonstrating against payless paydays specifically, and the Chicago Board of Education generally.

The paraders in the Century of Progress line of march could be followed east along Balbo in the foreground and south along the Inner Drive to Soldier Field, which can be seen directly in front of the eiffel-like tower in the right background.

The Century of Progress Avenue of Flags.

Right: Benito Mussolini of Italy was represented in the Century of Progress Parade by a marching group.

Postmaster General James A. Farley represented President Franklin Delano Roosevelt on the reviewing stand at the opening day of the Chicago World's Fair.

Robert S. Abbott, publisher of the Chicago Defender, *was the only gentleman with an ebony hue who was a member of the World's Fair Board of Commissioners.*

On May 1, 1933, a group from the teachers' volunteer Emergency Committee met with the officers of the five major loop banks and were promised that enough tax warrants would be purchased from the Board of Education to pay the teachers their back salaries within one week. The bankers' promise did not materialize. On the first day of May, the board of education held a special afternoon meeting to clear the way for Henry P. Chandler, head of the sales drive for the board of education, to sell $3,600,000 worth of 1932 tax warrants to pay the school employees part of their September salaries. In the meantime back at City Hall, Mayor Edward J. Kelly was working on a separate scheme that would put $14,000,000 in cash in the hands of the public school employees. His plan was contingent upon both state and congressional legislation that would induce the R.F.C. to accept Chicago's tax warrants directly as collateral for the R.F.C.'s loans to the city. The teachers prevailed by lobbying both the Congress and the General Assembly, and the Kelly plan was ultimately approved.

The salvation of some black female teachers during the payless paydays was their husbands who were employed by the United States Postal Service as clerks at twelve hundred dollars per annum. Federal salaries were not interrupted during the depression; therefore, a post office clerk was considered a better marital catch for black school teachers than a lawyer or physician because of the predictable regularity of the government paychecks. However, some black doctors and attorneys enhanced their economic attractiveness by working full-time at night in the post office and conducting a limited professional practice on the side during the day.

The economy generally and the public school crisis specifically caused Mayor Kelly to quip to Pat Nash within earshot of a *New York Times* reporter: "Maybe it isn't so healthy being World's Fair mayor of Chicago. Two of them have been shot you know." Kelly did not display any apprehension about the possibilities of being the target for a gun in the hand of a disgruntled teacher because in the midst of a huge jubilant crowd, he opened the World's Fair (Century of Progress) with a flourish of activities at 8:30 A.M. on May 27, 1933 that stated that Chicago, the city with the "Big Shoulders," was giving a birthday party. Rocketing and bursting bombs flew through the air above Soldier Field signaling that the Century of Progress (World's Fair) had begun and that the turnstile had revolved for the first customer who had paid the fifty cents admission fee to see Chicago's second World's Fair within forty years. At 10:00 A.M. a parade of 10,000 marched south down Michigan Boulevard from Ohio to Seventh Street. More than 200,000 people lined the east and west side of the street and watched the parade as it snaked down Michigan Boulevard. The boulevard was a veritable garden of color with flags and banners during the parade. The ladies were dressed in their summer finery while the men digested the beauty of their female companions like a side dessert in the holiday atmosphere on a street filled with confetti as the bright sun luminated the buttons and medals on the marchers' uniforms like torches.

The marchers turned east off Michigan Avenue at Seventh Street (Balbo) and marched to the Inner Drive, then south to the Court of Honor (the street between the Field Museum and Soldier Field). They then made a right turn and proceeded through the northeast gate of Soldier Field where they marched before the reviewing stand which was sheltered under a pretty red and white awning. Postmaster General James A. Farley represented President Roosevelt on the reviewing stand. Also present on the dais were Mayor Edward J. Kelly, Governor Henry Horner, Mrs. Potter Palmer, the real estate heiress, and Rufus C. Dawes, president of a Century of Progress.

The first group of marchers to pass before the dignitaries on the reviewing stand were the American Indians, attired in full tribal garments. They marched gravely and out of step with the beat of the drum. A scant dozen of them marched in a straight line facing the flag, and just as gravely they gave their salute to the forty flags of all the nations. Then in alphabetical order came the nationalities in groups led by Major Felix J. Streychmans, the field marshal. They were Assyrians, Austrians, Belgium, the British Brazilians, Canadians, the French and so on. In the line of march were gray-haired Scots in kilts, the Chinese with flowing oriental robes, Hollanders in tiny black flat hats that resembled those worn by monks and wooden shoes which they wore with skill, and flashing señores and señoritas with waving mantillas and wide scarlet skirts. Then came Benito Mussolini's goose-stepping Italian marching group which gave an energetic fascist salute to the nations' flags. As each group passed the reviewing stand to salute the flags, the band played the national anthem of the country represented as aerial bombs spewed up tiny flags of that country. The flags suspended on miniature parachutes floated down through the air toward Lake Michigan. At the same time, huge army bombers escorted by speedy pursuit planes flew in formation over Soldier Field casting a strange shadow of the big war which was to begin December 7, 1941.

All of the World's Fair splendor was taking place in the kernel of a city festered with an army of unemployed men and women, unpaid teachers and a city government that was riddled with corruption. An astute observer with a critical eye and an acid tongue made the following observation, while viewing the tiny memorial cabin and tablet dedicated to Chicago's black founder, Jean Baptiste DuSable, on the grounds of the Century of Progress: "Chicago has accomplished the impossible and ignored the essential."

The Century of Progress was a financial bonanza for some white Chicagoans. Blacks across the board were denied access to even the most menial jobs on the fair grounds. The Urban League under the leadership of

A. L. Foster attempted to get an agreement with the World's Fair Commissioners to permit the league to select Negroes for both white and blue collar positions. The entire job placement assignment was given to a white employment agency; hence, very few blacks were able to escape into any meaningful employment at the 1933 Century of Progress. Although Mayor Edward J. Kelly appointed Robert S. Abbott, publisher of the *Chicago Defender,* to a prestigious position as a World's Fair board commissioner, there was not a single black working as a chair boy at the 1933 Fair, a position James Weldon Johnson, composer of "Lift Every Voice and Sing" (the Negro national anthem), held forty years earlier during the summer of 1893 at Chicago's First World's Fair which was known as the Columbia Exposition. (A chair boy was the pilot of a wheel chair for persons who did not want to walk or who were infirmed.)

Black musicians and singers were the exception to the World's Fair employment rule. Freddie Williams and his orchestras were employed to play at the Jensen Pavilion for the season. However, the Frankie "Half Pint" Jaxon Band only survived the opening night although it too had been hired to play the entire season for Sally Rand, a white fan dancer at the Streets of Paris Pavilion. Jaxon, a black band leader who used a white orchestra for radio work because the musicians' union would not permit blacks to play in the radio studio bands, employed a black orchestra when he performed at theaters and dance halls. When Jaxon's black musicians appeared at the Paris Pavilion to play for the semi-nude Sally Rand, they were given an instant exit notice by the manager according to Dave Young, the current advertising manager of the *Chicago Defender,* who was a member of the Jaxon Orchestra. Lloyd Wheeler, president of the Supreme Life Insurance Company, recalls that Sally Rand came to the Regal Theater on the South Side during her 1933 Century of Progress engagement to do a special show for black Chicagoans because of the racist policies that prohibited blacks from attending shows at many of the pavilions.

Several southern states were unofficially represented at the Century of Progress by Negro gospel groups. The peach state's pride was an excellent choral group known as the Georgia Plantation Singers. Florida boosted the attendance at its pavilion with the very popular Harmony Four. The Melody Mixers were composed of a trio of teenage Chicagoans: Jimmy Jones, Leroy Wimbush, and Eddie Johnson who were employed by Swift Packing Company to play at the Swift's Bridge of Service Exhibit. Eddie Johnson recalls that the Melody Mixers played two shows a day seven days a week.

The Century of Progress was blatant with its Jim Crow employment policies. In September 1933, State Representatives Charles J. Jenkins, Harris B. Gaines and State Senator Adelbert Roberts joined forces in reaction to the condition at the 1933 Fair by fighting against the passage of legislation to pro-

State Representative Charles A. Jenkins.

Lloyd Wheeler, president of Supreme Life Insurance Company.

State Representative Harris B. Gaines.

Left: Sally Rand, the famous fan dancer was a major attraction at both the 1933 and 1934 World's Fair. Right: The Melody Mixers. (Left to right), Jimmy Jones, Leroy Wimbush and Eddie Johnson, a sensational teenage act.

mote another Chicago World's Fair in 1934. They reasoned that if the ills of racism that were visited upon blacks during the 1933 Fair were not cured, that there was not a single reason to have another Century of Progress for "Whites Only" on the shores of Abe Lincoln's city by the lake.

On Wednesday March 2, 1934 House bill No. 114 was passed by the Illinois House by a vote of 98 to 2. The bill essentially stated that all persons entering the Fair grounds in the summer of 1934 would be accorded equal rights in employment and enjoyment of the total facilities and the various pavilions and concessions.

The racism at the World's Fair simply mirrored a large cancer that was consuming the bowels of race relations in Chicago and the state of Illinois. Black Illinois legislators were fighting for Negro rights in Chicago that they could not enjoy in the capital. The colored law makers could not eat in any Springfield restaurant nor spend the night in a hotel.

Ten years later, hotel and eating accommodations for blacks in Springfield had not improved. In January 1943 State Senator-elect C. C. Wimbush and Representative-elect Corneal Davis, caught the 4:00 P.M. Abraham Lincoln train enroute to Springfield to be present for their swearing in ceremonies the next morning. Senator C. C. Wimbush had made reservations at the Abraham Lincoln Hotel in his name for both him and Davis. After they arrived, they got a cab to the Abraham Lincoln. Upon arriving at the hotel, they noted a long line of legislators waiting to be checked in by the registration clerk.

Left: State Senator Christopher C. Wimbush. Center: State Representative Corneal Davis. Right: Members of Representative Corneal Davis' family in Springfield. (Left to right): His cousin, Oneida Cockrell; Pearl Davis Darden, his mother; Elma Howell Davis, wife; and Pearl Penn, sister.

Wimbush and Davis got in line to wait their turn; however, when they reached the front desk, the clerk that had been handling the guest registration book looked up and said: "You boys don't live here."

Wimbush retorted: "Do I look like a boy?"

The clerk repeated: "I know you don't live here. You know you can't stay in any hotel in Springfield."

Wimbush shouted: "Don't you see that I've got reservations."

The clerk grimaced when he snapped: "I don't give a damn what you got. You don't stay here." The clerk then came out from behind the counter with his fist balled up and spewed: "Before I'd let any niggers stay in the Abraham Lincoln Hotel, I would tear it up or burn it down."

Corneal Davis then grabbed C. C. Wimbush by the arm and started pulling him toward the door. Davis said to Wimbush: "Listen to me. Don't worry about this. Just don't worry. Let's get sworn in first. Hell, this man is trying to get us in trouble. I know if you hit him, he will call the police and file a charge against you."

Wimbush said: "Shit! I'll kill him."

Davis pleaded: "Don't pull no gun out here. Let's get sworn in first."

Wimbush and Davis left the Abraham Lincoln and went down the street to the Leland Hotel where they were also refused a room. They then proceeded to go to every hotel in Springfield that night in an attempt to find some over night accommodations. The two newly-elected black legislators ended up spending the night sleeping on a bench in the Gulf, Mobile and Ohio Railroad Station. Ralph Stewart, a black Masonic brother who heard about the plight of Davis and Wimbush, came down to the railroad station the next morning and took them to his home to wash up and make themselves presentable to meet their families who came down in a sleeping car on a midnight train from Chicago.

When the two men arrived at the train station, Davis took command because Senator Wimbush was still steaming from the Abraham Lincoln Hotel experience. Davis invited everybody to have breakfast on him. He was taking them to the Thompson Restaurant on Fourth Street because he knew that that establishment had a good race relation policy in Chicago. The group entered the restaurant, picked up the serving trays and stood in line at the counter. The waitress ignored them and continued to serve and direct white customers around the spot where they were standing.

Davis said to the waitress after ten minutes had passed: "Wait a minute! Just a minute! We want to be served!"

The waitress stopped her serving activites and said: "Are all of these people in your party?"

"Yes!" Davis replied.

"We don't serve colored people here," she retorted.

At this point State Representative-elect Corneal Davis broke loose and shouted: "Where in the hell do you serve people with dark skin in this town?"

With a polite smile, the waitress rejoined: "I can't help you and I can't think of any place where colored people eat in Springfield except in their homes."

At this point Davis who is an octoroon (12.5% black) turned blood red and yelled: "I see what the problem is you don't serve colored people." He then jumped over the food counter and started loading up the trays with coffee, rolls, milk and fruit juice for all of the ladies in his party.

At the same time, his mother was pleading that he was going to get them all into trouble. Davis looked at his mother and in a gentle tone said: "Ma! We are not in Mississippi. This is Illinois, and they have a Civil Rights Law that they don't obey!"

The Davis party sat down and finished their breakfast without any additional incidents. They all peaceably left the Thompson Restaurant and went to the state house to witness Davis and Wimbush being sworn in and pledging to uphold the laws of the state of Illinois.

Springfield in 1943 was a reflection of the black experience in Abraham Lincoln's city by the lake in 1934. John Marcus, manager of the Annee Restaurant at 91 West Randolph Street in Chicago, Illinois, was arrested on Monday, February 26, 1934 on a warrant sworn out by Rev. R. H. McGavock, a mortician, Arthur J. Wilson, C.P.A. and Miss Johnnie Lou James because Marcus had refused to serve them meals in his establishment. The NAACP Legal Redress Committee represented by Attorneys Irvin C. Mollison and William H. Temple won a verdict against the Annee Restaurant. The two NAACP lawyers had tried another case a week earlier on Monday February 19 against the Log Cabin Restaurant located at 863 East 63rd Street because a waiter had refused to serve Miss Theresa Pratt and her escort, Herbert Williams. The damages awarded for that suit were only $35.00 and costs. The case represented the fifth successful victory by the NAACP Legal Redress Committee against restaurants in Chicago within a year.

Mayor Edward J. Kelly was a political master at putting distance between himself and the Jim Crow acts being exercised on black people by his white constituents. In January 1934, Kelly came out whole-heartedly in support of Attorney Arthur W. Mitchell as the candidate to oppose Congressman Oscar DePriest, the folk hero. This act sent a positive signal to the black community because the Democratic Organization had never supported a black candidate for a congressional race. Supporting Mitchell was Kelly's first step up the political ladder in the Black Belt.

In the fall of 1934, Kelly's popularity soared even higher in the colored community when he balked at the racist practices white parents were attempting

Attorney William H. Temple, member of the NAACP Legal Redress Committee.

Arthur J. Wilson, C.P.A. and Civic Leader.

Attorney Irvin C. Mollison, chairman of the NAACP Legal Redress Committee; first black lifetime federal judge, appointed by President Truman to the U.S. Customs Court.

Dr. Arthur G. Falls, M.D., a representative of the Chicago Interracial Council.

to implement at Morgan Park High. A delegation of white parents visited Superintendent William J. Bogan and Mayor Kelly with the threat that their children would not return to class at Morgan Park High School until thirty-three Negro freshmen had been withdrawn from the school premises and sent back to a newly-formed branch of Morgan Park High that had been set up in the all black Shoop Elementary School. Mayor Kelly made it clear to the 200 white persons who had stormed into his anteroom on Thursday October 11,

1934 that he was not intimidated by their presence. He further stated: "I am not going to interfere with the board of education in its policy of giving every citizen of Morgan Park the rights and privileges he or she is entitled to under the laws of the land. Moreover, I am definitely opposed to any movement that will deny the right of any citizen of Chicago the privilege of attendance at any public institution of learning regardless of race, color or creed."

A tall blond man in the center of the crowd responded in an angry tone: "If the coons can stampede the board of education into taking niggers into Morgan Park High School, we can play that game, too."

A middle age white woman shouted from the back of the room: "We moved out in Morgan Park to get away from these niggers. And now we have got to contend with them again. We ought not stand for it."

Another member of the delegation yelled across the room: "The mayor of Chicago violated the school law by interfering with an edict of the board of education when he rescinded the transfer of the black freshmen students who had been sent back to the John D. Shoop Elementary School and demanded that they be readmitted to Morgan Park High." The mayor made this switch in events after he had been visited by a delegation of black parents who were accompanied by State Representative Charles Jenkins and officials from both the NAACP and Urban League.

Arthur W. Mitchell saw the Morgan Park High racial flare as another occasion to stroke Mayor Edward J. Kelly. Hence, he wrote the following note to the mayor on October 18, 1934, seven days after Kelly had the anteroom confrontation with the white racist delegation:

> The stand taken by you was not only manly and right, but required the highest type of courage. In this matter you have made thousands of friends among Negroes not only for yourself, but for the Democratic party. Heretofore, the argument has been that Democrats are not sympathetic toward Negroes in matters of this kind. The work you did here stands out. There is nothing in the career of "Big Bill" Thompson, or any other Republican, which is so heartening to Negroes.

Mayor Edward J. Kelly articulated his dream for integrated public schools the night he dedicated the all black New Wendell Phillips High School in January, 1935. (The name New Wendell Phillips was subsequently changed to Jean Baptiste Point DuSable in April, 1936.) During the dedication ceremony, the mayor made the following observation:

> I have been thrilled at the sight of the two colored boys in the Hyde Park School Glee Club which sang here tonight. I was further thrilled at the sight of the colored boys in the Tilden Tech School Band here before me. It made

me think that time is not far away when we shall forget the color of a man's skin and see him only in the light of the intelligence of his mind and soul. . .

Mayor Edward J. Kelly articulated the kind of talk that black folk wanted to hear. In this sense, he was akin to William "Big Bill" Thompson. The only difference between "Big Red" Kelly and "Big Bill" Thompson was their names and political parties. Black people believed that both men could walk over water. Kelly's good record in the black community was built on his efforts to implement the dream he talked about the night he dedicated the New Wendell Phillips High School.

During the big Union Stockyards fire on May 19, 1934, Kelly went out of his way to praise the heroic manner in which the members of black-staffed Engine Company #19 stationed at Thirty-fourth and Rhodes and Truck 11 at Thirty-sixth Place and State Street fought the blaze. The fire swept twelve blocks and was the worst in Chicago since 1871.

In June 1934, Kelly appointed Major A. E. Patterson, a leading black Democrat and an exceptionally good lawyer, to the position of assistant corporation counsel. In the same month, he appointed Attorney Nathan K. McGill—general counsel for the *Chicago Defender,* a Republican-oriented newspaper—to the Library Board.

A racist ghost from Mayor Kelly's past attempted to climb out of the grave and haunt him in July, 1934. Present at the resurrection were A. L. Foster of the Chicago Urban League and Dr. Arthur G. Falls, representing the Chicago Interracial Council. The grave side meeting was called so that Mayor Edward J. Kelly's South Park Board could explain the Jim Crow wire fence on the south boundary of the Negro section on Jackson Park Beach and why eleven white persons from the University of Chicago were arrested because they chose to peacefully play games and bathe in what was commonly known as the "For Colored Only" section of Lake Michigan. Superintendent George Donoghue attempted to explain the mystery of the Jackson Park Beach fence. Mr. Donoghue said: "There is not now, nor has there been any segregation on Jackson Park Beach."

Mr. Donoghue then turned to Mr. V. K. Brown, recreation director of the South Park Board, to give a broader explanation. Mr. Brown continued: "The reason the fence and the enclosure were erected was to set aside a section of the beach from which the park could derive summer revenue. There was no fee charged for using the section outside of the fenced in section. We can not force colored people to use the enclosure unless they want to, but we have done nothing to stop them."

The physical enclosure was subsequently removed; however, Jim Crow was still being practiced on South Side beaches as late as Sunday August 28,

A picture of the Union Stockyard fire taken from the el platform on May 19, 1934.

The Robert S. Abbott mansion at 4742 S. Parkway (King Drive).

1960, when the Youth Council of NAACP waded in at Rainbow Beach, located on East 75th Street at the lake. The black NAACP youngsters were stoned off the lake front by white hoodlums while ninety-six white policemen watched.

Kelly may have been haunted, but never daunted by these racist ghosts from the past. He simply charged through the colored community with his brotherhood theme. On Sunday, September 16, 1934, Mayor Kelly presided over a pageant at Soldier Field entitled "Drama of Chicago on Parade." Blacks were particularly pleased to see Elmer Williams, a popular ex-*Chicago Defender* employee, in the pageant parade posing as Jean Baptiste DuSable, Chicago's black founder. Knowing the part that DuSable played in Chicago's history, Kelly saw to it that the DuSable float was given a very conspicuous part in the pageant. A thunderous cheer went up from the audience of 120,000 people who had jammed Soldier Field to see the event when the DuSable float initially appeared from beneath the stadium tunnel. Kelly added still another touch that night that pulled the heart strings of the black community. He sent his personal limousine and a special motorcycle detail to pick up the number one black Republicans—Mr. and Mrs. Robert S. Abbott, publishers of the *Chicago Defender,* at their home which was located at 4742 South Grand Boulevard (King Drive) and escorted them to the stadium where they were guests in the mayor's official box.

Kelly's political maneuvers to attract black people to the Democratic party were carried out with the skill of a brain surgeon. On October 15, 1934, he appeared at a rally sponsored by the Colored Women's Division of the Illinois Democratic Organization. Thirty-five hundred South Siders packed the Bacon's Casino Ballroom, located on the northeast corner of Forty-ninth and

Wabash, tighter than a package of frozen spinach to hear Mayor Kelly, Arthur Mitchell, Bryant Hammond, Edward Sneed, and the Third Ward Democratic Committee. Kelly gave a brief speech but was interrupted a half dozen times when he talked about his dream of a better and more equitable New Deal for colored Chicagoans. Equally as important to those present was the fact that Mayor Kelly remained more than a half hour, listening to other candidates talk about the New Deal and its worth. Kelly's patience and willingness to listen to what black folk were saying and thinking put more votes on the Democratic side of the ledger than his speech that night. The next week, people had possibly forgotten what the mayor said; however, they were still talking about the fact that the mayor did not give them the "hello and goodbye" treatment.

Twenty-one days after the Democratic rally held in the Bacon Casino, Arthur W. Mitchell defeated Oscar DePriest in the general election on November 6, 1934. Roosevelt's Democrats were in the saddle and riding higher than they ever had in the past 132 years. It was not a common consensus, but it was widely believed that no single individual in the Democratic party's management contributed more to the election of Arthur W. Mitchell as congressman from the First Congressional District than Edward J. Kelly. It was from Kelly's mouth that the word went out: "We want Mitchell for Congress." A letter cited earlier in this chapter indicates that Mitchell was seeking Kelly's support for more than a month before it was generally known that Kelly was going to be the next mayor.

At 5:40 P.M. on Wednesday, November 7, 1934, Oscar DePriest sent the following telegram to Arthur W. Mitchell.

Left: Third Ward Committeeman Edward Sneed. Right: Professor Alain Locke, eminent philosophy scholar at Howard University and major contributor to Arthur Mitchell's congressional campaign.

CU 153 7-CHICAGO ILL 7 540P
HON ARTHUR W MITCHELL
    CONGRESSMAN ELECT 417 EAST 47 ST-
CONGRATULATE YOU AS FIRST NEGRO DEMOCRATIC CONGRESS-
MAN-
     OSCAR DE PRIEST.

Sixteen days after Mitchell was elected, he sent a letter to Mayor Kelly which read as follows:

November 22, 1934.

Mayor Edward J. Kelly,
City Hall,
Chicago, Illinois

Dear Mayor:

Just now a great deal is being said as to who will be appointed Colonel of our Eighth Regiment. I am enclosing herewith a copy of a letter I am writing the governor touching this point. I hope my ideas meet your approval and that you can see the strategic importance of having a Democrat in charge of this stronghold in the Second and Third Wards where we are working night and day to strengthen Democratic lines. It is my honest conviction that no Republican should have this post at this time because of what it will mean to our party in the colored wards. I know with your good judgement , you will weigh over the fact carefully and will use your influence to the very best interest of our party.

I want to again thank you for that unparalleled interest which you have shown in me personally and in my political career.

I am

Sincerely and gratefully yours,

ARTHUR W. MITCHELL

AWM:LB
Enc.

Note the last sentence in the letter from Mitchell to Kelly dated November 22, 1934 makes it clear that Mitchell recognized his political indebtedness to Mayor Edward J. Kelly.

Mitchell defeated DePriest by a plurality of 3,130 votes out of a total of

52,810. Mitchell polled 27,970 to Oscar DePriest's 24,840. With the Kelly-Nash machine's support, Mitchell whipped the first black congressman from the North decisively in both the predominantly white Fourth and Eleventh "Back of Yards" Wards. While DePriest outdistanced Mitchell on the flat land in the Black Belt, he could not put enough miles between them on the high land to make up for the snow capped mountain of white votes.

DePriest recognized after the fact that his voting record against Roosevelt's alphabet program defeated him. He was hurt most by his stand against national welfare for the hungry. In addition, the intra-party fight between William E. King and William L. Dawson weakened DePriest's political base. However, the bottom line on the political balance sheet for the fiscal year of 1934 reveals that the big depression killed Abraham Lincoln, and DePriest collapsed on his grave.

Only in a severe economic depression could a candidate achieve so much with so little. Arthur W. Mitchell collected a total of $1,325.00 in political contributions between October 8, and November 2, 1934. Two of the largest white contributors were Jacob M. Arvey and Benjamin Lindheimer. They both were from the Jewish political bloc, and each gave $100.00. Louis B. Anderson, a prominent black Republican also gave $100.00. James Knight, wealthy gambler and owner of the Palm Tavern at 446 East 47th Street, gave $50.00. Professor Alain Locke, eminent philosophy scholar at Howard University, donated $50.00. Peter M. Kelly, cook county board commissioner, gave $2.00. Mitchell's total list of seventeen contributors during the twenty-five day period between October 8, and November 2, indeed, consisted of a group of strange political bedfellows.

After being elected and supported by such a strange alliance of political folk, Mitchell, unlike Oscar DePriest forgot that he was black. Having to choose between the poltical slave or political slavemaster, he chose the slavemaster and turned his back on the 12,000,000 Negroes who looked to the lone black congressman from Illinois to represent them. Mitchell literally spat in the face of the national black community when he said: "I do not represent Negro people in anyway, but the First Congressional District of Illinois."

His congressional district included the Chicago Loop and was known as the richest square mile on earth. Mitchell's statement meant he represented the downtown financial interests although their names were not listed among his contributors. Mitchell refused to associate himself with what was considerd a purely Negro matter. He contended that it was time to look at life through new economic spectacles. As a result, the resentment on the part of black people gave rise to an aborted movement to oust him from Congress.

Attorney C. Francis Stradford, a life long Republican, was sympathetic to Mitchell's plight as evidenced in the following letter:

Drexel 4171   Residence Drexel 7955

Law Offices of
C. FRANCIS STRADFORD
Suite 205 Citizens Bldg.
(n.W. Corner 55th & State Sts.)
CHICAGO

February 5, 1935

Congressman Arthur W. Mitchell
House of Representatives
Washington, D.C.

My dear Mr. Mitchell:

I wish to thank you for your favor of January 24th and to say that I am receiving regularly the Congressional Record.

Had a brief talk, today, with Mr. Tittinger, and he showed me a copy of the bill which you have introduced. Of course, you know that I wish you much success.

I am quite concerned about the unfavorable publicity which I have noted in the colored papers concerning your activities. No doubt, your friends at the *Chicago Defender* are largely responsible for it. The articles published by Melvin Chism and the *Crisis* were particularly vicious. I suppose the only consolation to be had is that your record will overcome all of this envious and unfriendly opposition. That is one of the penalties, however, that every public official has to face and endure with courage and faith in the ultimate triumph of right.

In connection with the memorandum that I gave you as you were about to leave, I am enclosing an article which appeared in the *Nation* which may be of some service in stressing the wisdom of making such an appointment. I understand that another similar article appeared in this week's issue of the *Nation,* but I have not read it. Mr. Tittinger told me today that you were expected in Chicago soon, so perhaps we may be able to confer about the matter.

Please give my regards to Mrs. Mitchell. I see your son occasionally and in that way keep somewhat in touch with your problems. In the event that I can do anything to assist on this end, please do not hesitate to call upon me.

With very best wishes, I am

Sincerely,

C. Francis Stradford

CFS:P

Congressman Arthur Mitchell making his famous "I Don't Represent Negro People Anyway" speech.

Mitchell's rising unpopularity in the Black Belt caused Mayor Edward J. Kelly to raise both eyebrows and put some distance between himself and the congressman. Kelly's replacement for Mitchell was waiting in the wings at City Hall. He was William Levi Dawson, a Republican alderman and an elephant, who had been voting in the city council like a donkey.

Franklin Delano Roosevelt.

Chapter *XII*

The Franklin D. Roosevelt Years: A Time for Change

The conversion of blacks from Republicans to Democrats was as much spiritual as it was political because the basic transformation took place within the walls of the black church, and the black preacher was a drum major for change. The message for a new political direction came from the mountain tops and was reiterated to the multitude from the pulpits of the Lord's House. The spiritual manifestation of a typical religious sermon interlaced with a political message that was unfolded in bold relief at a Wednesday Night Prayer Service held at Quinn Chapel, an African Methodist Episcopal Church, located at 2401 South Wabash Avenue. The presiding church official at the meeting was Deacon Corneal A. Davis, an active precinct captain in the Second Ward Republican Organization.

Davis recalls that the service took place in October 1936, several weeks before President Roosevelt was re-elected to his second term. Davis' ministerial text that Wednesday evening was about the fact that God had sent President Franklin Delano Roosevelt to feed the poor colored people, had given them jobs on the WPA (Works Progress Administration) and placed their restless young men on jobs in the CCC (Civilian Conservation Corps) where they could earn thirty dollars per month, twenty-two dollars of which was mailed directly to the enlisted youths' families to buy food and keep a roof over their heads. In the middle of Davis' sermon, a senior citizen affectionately known in the church as "Mother" Spencer, jumped out of her seat and started running up and down the aisles of the chapel shouting: "Thank God! for President Roosevelt! Thank God for President Roosevelt! He took my feet out of the miry clay and put them right down on the WPA."

Later that week, when a Democratic precinct captain delivered a basket of

Quinn Chapel, African Methodist Episcopal Church located at 2401 So. Wabash Ave., Chicago, Illinois.

Frederick Douglass, the most distinguished black American of the 19th Century.

food to "Mother" Spencer's apartment, she thanked the captain and said: "The devil (Democrats) brought it, but the Lord (Republicans) sent it. Praise the Lord! Let Jesus lead you and Roosevelt feed you." Psychologically, "Mother" Spencer reflected the mixed emotions that burdened many blacks when they made the political changeover from Republican to Democrat.

After the 1932 presidential campaign, Roosevelt's Democrats dealt effectively with the Negroes' basic problems of hunger and jobs but failed to remove the psychic mystique that blacks had for Republicanism. However, during the 1936 political crusade, the Democrats with the aid of the black minister unveiled the sainted Abraham Lincoln and the Republican philosophic myth about being the black man's savior. The Republicans' true posture was anchored in a plank of the 1860 platform. The plank referred to slavery, and it read:

> That the maintenance inviolate of the rights of the states, and especially the right of each state to order and control its own domestic institutions according to its own judgment exclusively is essential to that balance of powers on which the perfection and endurance of our political fabric depends; and we denounce the lawless invasion by armed force of the soil of any state or territory, no matter under what pretext, as among the gravest of crimes.

Lincoln was elected on this platform which essentially preserved slavery. In his *First Inaugural Address,* he explained: "I have no purpose directly or indirectly to interfere with the institution of slavery in the states where it exists. I believe I have no lawful right to do so, and I have no inclination to do so."

In 1863, the Union government faced the following problems: the necessity of increasing the size of the army, the necessity of placating Abolitionist-Democratic feelings of the North, and the necessity of cutting off England's indirect support of the South. England consistently purchased large amounts of cotton from the southern slave plantations.

Therefore, Lincoln, as a war measure, issued the Emancipation Proclamation which applied only to slaves held by the Confederate states. Within a year, Lincoln stated that over 100,000 Negroes were fighting in the northern armies for the preservation of the Union. In a letter to Horace Greeley, Lincoln gave his real reason for the Emancipation:

> My paramount purpose in this struggle is to save the Union and is not to save or destroy slavery. If I could save the Union without freeing any slave, I would do it; and if I could save it by freeing all slaves I would do it; and if I could save it by freeing some and leaving others alone, I would also do that.

In 1865, the Thirteenth Amendment to the Constitution was adopted. This amendment constitutionally freed the slaves. At the time of its adoption, all but three southern states had themselves by legislative action freed their slaves. When slavery was abolished, congressional representation with reference to the Negro was increased to two-fifths whereas previously a slave was counted as three-fifths of a free man in determining representation. Immediately, the Republican party, seeing in this a threat to its control of the government, pretended to befriend the Negro by giving him the vote. This political expedient became the Fourteenth and Fifteenth Amendments.

The real effect of all this Republican recognition of the Negro, in the words of Frederick Douglass, the most distinguished black American of the nineteenth century, was:

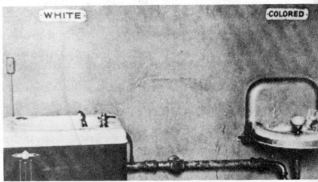

Left: President Herbert Hoover's 1932 integrated "soup and bread" lines. Above: Segregated drinking fountains.

> The government left the freed man in a bad condition. It made him free, and henceforth he must make his own way in the world. Yet, he had none of the conditions of self-preservation or self-protection. He was freed from the individual masters, but the slave of society. He had neither money, property nor friends. He was freed from the old plantation, but he had nothing but the dusty road under his feet. He was freed from the old quarter that once gave him shelter, but a slave to the rains of summer and to the frosts of winter. He was turned loose, naked, hungry and destitute to the open sky.

The Republicans' gifts to blacks were the Thirteenth, Fourteenth, and Fifteenth Amendments of the American Constitution. Very little time elapsed before the three amendments were rendered ineffective and obsolete within earshot of the Grand Old Party's perennial election battle call to blacks reminding them that "Lincoln freed them". Piece by piece and stitch by stitch, patches of America's constitutional and civil rights clothes were snatched from the political bodies of black folk until they were totally disrobed.

The political stripping of black folk began in a dimly lit smoke-filled room in 1877 when the Republicans secretly agreed to abandon the new black freedmen to secure the election of Rutherford B. Hayes. However, it was not until 1908 that President William H. Taft declared in an article that appeared in *The Outlook* that he proposed to carry out publicly what the Republican party had started clandestinely in 1877.

Taft's anti-Negro public policy was in step with the legal opinions of the highest court in the land. In the 1883 Civil Rights case 109 US 3 (1883), the U.S. Supreme Court opined that Congress did not have plenary power and that the refusal to serve black people was a question of states' rights, and therefore, must be redressed in the state court. The court also declared the Civil Rights Acts of 1875 and 1876 that were passed by the virtue of the 1868 Fourteenth Amendment were unconstitutional, hence, extending the precedent set in the 1873 Louisiana Slaughter House case 16 US 36 (1873) when the court held that federal citizenship did not include the protection of ordinary civil rights from infringement by state governments. Moreover, the court declared that the federal government could not regulate the behavior of private individuals in matters of race relations.

The court system has repeatedly been used to advance racism in America and to prevent blacks from obtaining the implicit rights guaranteed under the Constitution and its various amendments. A classic example can be found in Plessy vs. Ferguson 163 US 537 (1896). In that case, the Supreme Court held that a Louisiana statute requiring railroads to "provide equal but separate accommodations for the white and colored races" did not constitute a denial of the Fourteenth Amendment, which granted "equal protection of the laws" to all citizens. Therefore, the court said that if blacks wanted protection under the law, they must seek it from the states, which under the Tenth Amendment retained all powers not specifically assigned to Congress. In effect, the U.S. Supreme Court had the fox protecting the chicken house.

The U.S. Supreme Court chartered an anti-black course for the state courts and legislators to follow. In 1890, Mississippi led the way by requiring all voters to prove that they could read and interpret the Constitution. White registration officials applied totally different standards for blacks and whites. A black college graduate would be flunked as an illiterate and ineligible for a ballot whereas a white illiterate would be declared a constitutional scholar and eligible to vote. A Birmingham, Alabama ordinance mandated that blacks and whites be distinctly separated by well-defined physical barriers. Water fountains were labeled "For Whites Only" while sections of ball parks were separated by chicken wire. Blacks used "For Colored" side doors to theaters and were always confined to seats in the balcony or in the roped-off sections in the rear of the movie house. Mobile, Alabama passed a curfew law requiring blacks to be off the streets by 10:00 P.M. Atlanta, Georgia required separate Bibles, commonly known as "Nigger Bibles" for black witnesses. Blacks were, and still are to a lesser degree, buried in "Jim Crow" graveyards throughout the North and South and blessed into separate heavens. A New Orleans' law confined black and white prostitutes to separate red light districts even though the black district of joy was never legally off-limits to white males.

The long dark shadow of the Republican U.S. Supreme Court was not lifted until 1938 when an enlightened court ruled in the Ex rel. Gaines vs. Canada 305 US 337 (1938) that a black man who had sought admission to the state law school in Missouri could not be denied admission although the state had offered to pay his tuition in a northern law school. Chief Justice Charles Evans Hughes reasoned that it was the duty of the state to provide education for all of its citizens and that the provision must be made within the state and to fail to do so for Negroes "is denial of the equality of legal rights to the enjoyment of the privileges of the state, and the provision for the payment of tuition fees in another state does not remove the discrimination." The decision may have caused some states to turn over in bed in the middle of the night, but they were not fully awakened because in 1944, some six years after the Gaines vs. Canada decision, the majority of southern states were still appropriating out-of-state tuition for black professionals to be trained in the North.

In 1944, Cecil A Partee, Chicago's current city treasurer, was a recipient of the out-of-state tuition program when he came North with a scholarship to attend Northwestern University Law School. The fellowship was awarded to Partee, former president of the Illinois State Senate, by the University of Arkansas because its all white admission requirements obviated the attendance of colored people. The registrar at the University of Arkansas Law

Attorney Cecil A. Partee, former president of the Illinois State Senate and currently Chicago City Treasurer.

School told Partee: "If you don't hassle us by trying to get into our law school, we will pay your tuition at any northern law school that will admit you."

Looking back, Partee reflects on the fact that if he had been admitted to the University of Arkansas Law School, he could not have attended because he did not have tuition money. The University of Arkansas paid Partee's tuition directly to Northwestern University Law School in Chicago. Partee graduated in 1946 in an accelerated two-year program and went to work for Attorney Joseph Clayton, the dean of black criminal lawyers, whose offices were on the second floor at 3518 South State Street in the same building where Congressman William L. Dawson maintained his First Congressional Democratic headquarters on the street level.

Nine years earlier, a meeting to endorse Alderman William L. Dawson for re-election was called by former alderman and Republican stalwart, Louis B. Anderson, on Wednesday January 23, 1935 at 3140 South Indiana, the headquarters of the original Second Ward Republican Organization. Anderson addressed some seventy-odd men and women who were once considered the political pillars of the Second Ward Republican Organization. He opened his remarks with the following statement:

> I have been informed by Mayor Edward J. Kelly himself that he is sufficiently impressed with the services rendered by Alderman William L. Dawson, who is a candidate for re-election, and is, therefore, desirous of seeing him returned to the city council. The mayor is so impressed with Dawson that he has caused the information to be imparted through me to my friends in the ward in hope they would give Dawson whatever aid possible in consummating his re-election.

Ex-Alderman Anderson continued:

This statement from the mayor I deemed wise should be transmitted to you
people, knowing as I do that your interest can be best served and your wants
and ambitions best complied with by you re-electing Alderman William L.
Dawson, who will help the mayor inaugurate his program. I am not asking
you to change your politics and turn Democratic, but I am endeavoring to
bring you to the realization that Edward J. Kelly will also be re-elected
mayor, and I want you to so conduct yourself as to be able to call upon him
for whatever you may want and justify that call by making your presence
felt by a voting strength that will help him carry out his program. I feel
perfectly justified in saying to you that in so far as your interest is concerned
in Edward J. Kelly as mayor, you have another "Big Bill" Thompson, the only difference being the name.

On February 26, 1935 Alderman William L. Dawson was re-elected to the
city council by an overwhelming vote. In his victory statement Dawson said:

Many churches, civic organizations, neighborhood improvement clubs and
businessmen contributed to my election. I am sincerely grateful to all of
them. It is my hope to be able to coordinate the interest of all the people of
the ward, regardless of political affiliation, and to work to the end that the
civic and industrial interests of the people may be better served. I have
many friends to reward but no enemies to punish. I am willing to do my part
to bring about a harmonious working agreement to the end that my constituents will receive what they are entitled to as a political sub-division of the
city. My slogan in the campaign was the Second Ward for Second Warders.
That was not only a campaign slogan but I propose, as far as humanly possible, to put it into effect in deed and action. I am in complete harmony with
the program of civic improvement enunciated by Mayor Edward J. Kelly,
and gratefully acknowledge his wonderful contribution to the success of my
election.

The tenor of the speeches given by Alderman William L. Dawson, former
Alderman Louis B. Anderson, and former State Senator Adelbert H. Roberts,
on March 8, 1935 in the Congressional Hall at 3140 Indiana Avenue, suggested
that Mayor Edward J. Kelly had taken over the Republican party, "boot, bag,
and underwear". Each speaker addressing the meeting urged the 1,200 people
present to carry the word to their friends and acquaintances that the Second
Ward intended to give Mayor Kelly 20,000 votes in the April election. Oscar
DePriest was the only major black Republican who did not get on the Kelly
bandwagon. Twelve years earlier, DePriest had lead the black Republicans of
the Second and Third Wards into a political battle supporting the Democratic

mayoral nominee, William E. Devers, who won the race for the seat on the fifth floor in 1923.

The Congressional Hall was packed to the rafters with Republicans on Friday, March 28, 1935, four days before the mayoral election. It was at this meeting that Louis B. Anderson delivered his strongest indictment against the Republican party. In his final instruction to the Grand Old Party faithfuls, he said:

> Lincoln is dead. You don't need no ghost from the grave to tell you what to do when you go to the polls Tuesday. When Lincoln died most of the principles for which he fought also died. What is true of Lincoln and his principles is also true of Jefferson Davis. Neither of those men nor their principles play any part in Tuesday's election. Your vote on Tuesday April 2 must be measured in economics, social, and political terms of 1935 and not of 1863.

Former State's Attorney Robert E. Crowe wrapped up the meeting that Friday night with the following words: "The Republican party is in the hands of hoodlums, hustlers, grafters and political confidence men. The only way to get rid of those hounds is to completely destroy the meat house."

The push for Kelly's election was twofold. In addition to getting him re-elected, the black community wanted the mayor to select a black Second Warder to replace Joseph Tittinger, the white ward committeeman. Edward M. Sneed, committeeman of the Third Ward, was the black model that was constantly brought to Mayor Kelly's attention as a reminder of what a black man could do as the representative of his people. The Second Warders further argued that if they had to do the voting, why should they have to defer to someone else to count their votes and claim the credit? Moreover, it was reasoned that if blacks were in the minority in the Second Ward, they would not expect to lead, but conversely because they were in the overwhelming majority, they should begin to flex their political muscle and to leverage their voting strength.

The morning after election day on April 2, 1935, Mayor Edward J. Kelly was declared winner by an awesome majority. His margin of victory exceeded the most optimistic pre-election polls. He carried the black precincts in the Second, Third, and Fourth Wards by 80.5 percent of the votes cast. The Second Ward was one of seven that exceeded 20,000 votes. The three major black wards voted as follows:

WARD	KELLY	WETTEN	JENKINS
2	20,137	5,058	373
3	13,158	3,428	289
4	20,669	3,769	772

Joe "The Brown Bomber" Louis was appointed mayor of Chicago for ten minutes by Edward J. Kelly, October 2, 1935.

Mayor Edward J. Kelly, Pat Nash and George F. Ross, secretary of the Democratic Central Committee kept a close tally on the votes coming in from the black wards throughout election night, April 1, 1935.

The Joe Louis Brain Trust. Left to Right: assistant manager, Chicago policy king and real estate man Julian Black; trainer Jack Blackburn; Joe Louis; manager, Detroit policy king and life insurance executive John W. Roxborough with traveling companion Russell Cowans.

Kelly began his first full four year term riding on an extremely high popularity wave in the black community, and the mayor intended to keep it there.

On Tuesday afternoon October 1, 1935, Mayor Edward J. Kelly, a past master of public relations, made Joe "The Brown Bomber" Louis the mayor of Chicago for ten minutes. The "Brown Bomber" became Mayor Joe Louis as he sat in Kelly's chair posing for a battery of newspaper photographers and shaking hands with high city and county officials. It was at this time that Joe Louis told the group that he was now a resident of Chicago and would live in the Third Ward with his wife, the former Marva Trotter, in the Rosenwald Garden Apartments which occupied four square city blocks bound on the north and south between Forty-sixth and Forty-seventh Streets and on the east and west by Michigan and Wabash Avenues.

Following Joe Louis' ten minute reign as Mayor, he was escorted into the council chambers by ex-Alderman Louis B. Anderson where America's "Black Hope" was praised by the city fathers. Third Ward Alderman R. R. Jackson formally introduced Joe Louis as the man who many say will be the world's next heavyweight champion of the world. A bit bashful, Joe stood up and said: "I am glad to be here and meet you gentlemen. I am no speech maker, but I will fight anybody in the house." The chamber went into an uproar. Joe Louis glanced around the chamber in his poker face manner to make certain there were no challengers who wished to take him on. In a chamber that was now gripped with silence, the "Brown Bomber" gently and meekly took a seat next to former Alderman Anderson. There was a brief discussion among the aldermen about the possibility of organizing a celebration for Louis. The fighter responded to the suggestion: "It's mighty nice of you folk to want to honor me, but let's wait until I am the world's champion. Then we can all celebrate."

Congressman Arthur W. Mitchell did not have anything to celebrate because the word flashing through the tendrils of the Black Belt's political grapevine was that "Mitchell must be beaten." The Republican opposition lead by former Congressman Oscar DePriest was saying that Mitchell was a "public enemy to the progress of the American Negro." In addition, the ostentatious Mr. Mitchell appeared to be about as popular among his colored constituency as three cockroaches in a cup of soup. The silver lining behind the thunderous black political clouds hanging over Congressman Mitchell's head was the heavy support that he knew he would receive from the white section of the First Congressional District because he was their "boy." Moreover, his chief opponents, former Alderman Louis B. Anderson, ex-Congressman DePriest, Alderman R. R. Jackson, and Alderman William L. Dawson were in an intra-party dog fight. To make matters worse, the leader of the conservative right wing of the black Republicans, Mr. Robert S. Abbott, publisher of the *Chicago Defender,* took a laissez-faire posture during the black congressional fight and threw his editorial support behind Colonel Robert R. McCormick, publisher of the *Chicago Tribune* and candidate for the United States Senate. McCormick contended that the fabric out of which President Franklin Delano Roosevelt's New Deal proposals were being manufactured could not endure without a change in the constitution. At the same time, McCormick was quietly and wisely advising Mayor Edward J. Kelly on how to spend the millions of public works dollars that Roosevelt was pouring into Chicago. Kelly and McCormick carried on a sort of Chinese campaign in that they publicly grimaced and made thunderous sounds at each other; however, behind the scenes, they cooed like two Coca-Cola buddies.

McCormick was Mayor Kelly's guiding light in the use of federal dollars for major improvements along the lakefront such as the new Outer Drive. He also advocated the creation of landfill in the general area of the Chicago Tribune Tower, land that has been subsequently used to undergird skyscrapers that overshadowed the Chicago Tribune Building, McCormick's gothic cathedral, on North Michigan Avenue. Government monies were also being spent on the South Side. Improvements at Midway Airport alone digested $6,426,942. In addition, millions of dollars were employed to create thousands of jobs for men who worked on hundreds of miles of new streets, new sewers, sidewalks and new public buildings, none of which required bonds or special assessment against taxpayers or homeowners.

Roosevelt money was also being used to acquire land in the Ellis Park area in the heart of the Black Belt for a project which would house hundreds of families between Thirty-seventh and Thirty-ninth Streets on Cottage Grove and South Parkway. Seventy-four new parcels of land were acquired in the fall of 1936 bringing the total number in the area owned by the federal government to 267. The seventy-four parcels cost the government approximately $400,000. George F. Harding, the realtor and Republican national committeeman, owned twenty-eight of the seventy-four parcels, and therefore, received approximately $150,000. The demolition of these properties compounded the housing crisis for blacks because they were fenced into the area by restrictive covenants. Mr. and Mrs. Carl A. Hansberry, parents of Lorraine Hansberry, author of *Raisin in the Sun,* in an effort to climb over the "Jim Crow" barricade that surrounded the black community, moved into an apartment at 549 East 60th Street that they had sublet from a white woman whose name was Mrs. Rose Huffman. R. M. O'Brien, prominent realtor, served the Hansberry's on Friday, August 28, 1936 with an eviction notice because they were black folk and occupied the premises in violation of a restrictive covenant which prohibited members of the Negro race from residing in the building as a tenant or in any other capacity other than that of servant or employee until January

1948. Mrs. Huffman, the owner of the building, was also served with an order demanding that she vacate her apartment because she had violated the agreement by renting to people of African ancestry. The eviction notices were served despite the fact that the agreement between property owners restricting Negroes from living in certain areas was in direct violation of the constitutional rights of colored people. Illinois courts elected not to enforce the civil rights laws on behalf of blacks. Judges in the District of Columbia and Kansas, on the days they felt the spirit, refused to uphold similar covenants when such cases were brought before their courts. Illinois courts continued to rule in favor of racial housing covenants until 1948 when the U.S. Supreme Court ruled in the Shelly vs. Kraemer case that restrictive covenants were judicially unenforceable.

The following letter to the Hills Brothers Realty Co. is reflective of the prevailing attitude of many white citizens of that period and the judicial temperament of the Illinois courts.

Central Shore Voters League
Chicago, Illinois

September 23, 1936

Hills Brothers Realty Co.
366 East 47th Street
Chicago, Illinois

Gentlemen:

This will advise that the property located at 3844 South Ellis Avenue which you are offering to colored people is situated in a restricted territory, the title to said property carrying a 20-year clause limited sale or rental to persons of white race only. Will you, therefore, kindly advise your client that if she rents to colored people, she must be prepared to take the matter into court? In all cases where such matters have been brought into court, the property owners restrictive clause has always been upheld. Since its inception in this community eight years ago, this restriction has never been violated, and we do not intend to allow it to be so violated now.

Very truly yours,

Central Shore Voters League
Mrs. Hugh T. Martin
President

Restrictive covenants and tenants' rights were at the top of Alderman William L. Dawson's legal agenda. Dawson and Joseph Jefferson organized the Consolidated Tenants Association which had offices in the Supreme Life Insurance Building at 3507 South Parkway. The objective of the organization was to halt the rent hogs who were the beneficiaries of the racist covenants. Dawson made his feelings known when he held the city council spellbound on Wednesday April 7, 1937 with the following statement:

> Fellow members of the council, one hundred and ninety thousand colored people live on the near South Side. It is terribly congested. Often one family lives in each room of an apartment originally meant to house only one family. East of Cottage Grove and south of Sixty-third, there are covenants against these people which aggravate the situation. When people cannot find a place to live, they become anti-social. When landlords have long waiting lists, they exploit tenants with high rents. The renting and housing conditions have become unbearable.

Alderman Dawson had not taken his seat before Mayor Edward J. Kelly took the floor and stated he was well-acquainted with the problem on the South Side and favored passage of the Egan Resolution which earlier had been sidetracked. The resolution called for the appointment of a committee to investigate the present housing crisis on the Negro reservation. Dawson and seven other councilmen were appointed to serve on the committee for the purpose of doing some additional research on the living conditions of colored people in Chicago. The councilmen appointed to the committee were John Egan, William Rowan, James Bowler, Walter J. Orlikoski, Roger J. Kelly, and John J. Grealis.

Joe Jefferson, civil rights' activist and executive secretary to Dawson's tenant organization, was not impressed with the fact that the mayor had appointed these public leaders to research black folk. It was Jefferson's opinion that Negroes had been researched and studied more than any other ethnic group in America, and they were still on the bottom rung of the economic ladder.

Frazier T. Lane, director of the Department of Social and Civic Improvement of the Chicago Urban League, supported Joe Jefferson's position in a letter written to John Somsteby, chief justice of the municipal court. Lane's letter included the following remarks:

> The landlords, for the most part, live outside the district and have been parties to restricting Negroes to certain areas. This legal restriction on the south, north, east and west plus demolition of buildings creates a scarcity which makes it possible to increase rents even when there has not been an

The Rosenwald Garden Apartments were developed by the Julius Rosenwald Foundation. Mr. Rosenwald was one of the three founders of Sears Roebuck & Company.

Construction work being completed on the Ida B. Wells Housing Development located on East 37th Street near South Park Boulevard (Martin Luther King).

increase in the tenants' income and the landlord is offering minimum to zero building services. The establishment of a government housing project in the area of 37th and South Parkway which might give some relief is bitterly fought by those forces which have built up the restriction against Negro migration across borders outside the Black Belt. The borders and barricades have arbitrarily been set up by white absentee real estate interests.

Copies of the Chicago Urban League letter reached the desk of President Franklin D. Roosevelt via Governor Henry Horner and Mayor Edward J. Kelly.

Blacks were on the horns of a dilemma over President Roosevelt's housing plans for the near South Side. They all seemed to be elated about the fact that the district was being rejuvenated with modern homes and buildings, but worried sick about what was going to happen to them during the period that the old houses were being demolished and the new houses built.

Alfred M. Landon's overwhelming defeat by Franklin D. Roosevelt was one of a mountain of signals on how colored folk felt about President Roosevelt's housing programs. Along with a sundry of other benefits such as the W.P.A. paychecks and his new style dinner pail, Roosevelt's New Deal formula had wrapped its arms around the colored brothers and sisters so tightly that a graveside political meeting to evoke the spirit of Abraham Lincoln failed for the first time. The Grand Old Party called repeatedly upon the spirit of Lincoln to perform magic on behalf of Alfred Landon, the G.O.P. candidate, but the spirit of Roosevelt's materialism was too strong to be invaded from the grave.

3

THE DECADE THAT BLACKS LEFT THE PARTY OF LINCOLN

William "Bill" Dawson, the people's man.

Chapter *XIII*

Bill Dawson: The People's Man

The aura of Dawson's 1937 aldermanic re-election victory was still in his nostrils when he shifted his sights in 1938 to a higher political horizon, the congressional seat of Arthur W. Mitchell. The spring primary field was crowded with black Republicans seeking an opportunity to challenge Congressman Mitchell in the fall general election for the sole black occupied seat in the United States House of Representatives. Dawson was one of five candidates who threw his hat into the political ring to run in the Republican primary. The 1938 race was not a virginal congressional campaign for William L. Dawson. His first effort occurred in 1928 when he ran against Congressman Martin B. Madden, the white political leader of the First Congressional District, and garnered a respectable twenty-nine percent of the Republican votes.

In the 1938 congressional race, Alderman Dawson competed against black political giants such as former Congressman Oscar DePriest; the former Second Ward Alderman Louis B. Anderson; the great national orator, Roscoe Conkling Simmons; and Attorney Benjamin W. Clayton. Dawson was the victor in the primary. He won the five-sided Republican primary race by a plurality of 355 votes, polling a total of 4,295 against 3,957 for his closest opponent, Louis B. Anderson. Oscar DePriest came in third with 3,695. Clayton and Simmons were snowed under in an avalanche of white paper ballots in favor of the three other candidates.

Although Dawson was the occupant of the aldermanic chair in the Second Ward, he did not have access to any political patronage. The patronage and political power rested with Senator William E. King, the Second Ward Republican committeeman and Dawson's political enemy. King thwarted Dawson's political ambitions at every turn because he felt that "Bill" Dawson had the capability to take control of the ward. Dawson's victory was achieved through the efforts of his own independent Republican organization, aid from the Democratic county chairman Pat Nash through Nash's man, Daniel Serritella, the First Ward Republican committeeman, and more importantly, from his own personal popularity with the little man on the street who saw Dawson as a champion for common causes. Dawson spent seventy-five percent of his time daily giving free legal service in the municipal courts defending downtrodden tenants who were about to be evicted from their apartments. Attorney John T. Jones recalls that in 1937 (Jones) represented Dr. James A. DeRamus, owner of a large apartment building at 4336 South Vincennes Avenue, in an eviction suit. Dawson came into court without the pretense of a defense, representing twenty-three tenants including the two that Attorney Jones was evicting. Dawson told Jones privately after the cases were heard that (Dawson) knew that he only had "one legal leg to stand on"; however, Dawson felt he could get his people a few extra days. The judge would usually give Dawson's impoverished clients an additional eight to ten days to vacate the apartments simply because of the alderman's stature and popularity in the black community. Dawson was speaking figuratively when he said he had "only one legal leg," but in essence he was telling the truth because nine years earlier, he had lost one of his legs when he slipped on the steps of an Illinois Central train that pulled out from the Forty-third Street Railroad Station. Dawson's destination on the day he lost his limb was to have been Detroit, Michigan where he was to fulfill a speaking engagement for, the nationally popular and newly-elected, Congressman Oscar DePriest.

Dawson's ability to talk political sense to the common man put him within a razor's edge of defeating DePriest's successor, Congressman Arthur W. Mitchell, in the November 1938 general election. In that uphill battle, Dawson polled 26,396 votes against Mitchell's 30,207. Dawson lost the election by less than 4,000 votes because the powerful Senator William E. King and his Republican cohorts elected to sit on their hands during the campaign in face of the fact that King had announced publicly that he was supporting Dawson one hundred percent. King hated Dawson with a passion both personally and politically because he felt that Alderman Dawson had betrayed the party by supporting Edward J. Kelly in the 1936 mayoral election.

Congressman Arthur W. Mitchell's re-election victory over Dawson did not elevate him to a status that would warrant his being treated any differently than any other black man or woman who attempted to ride first class on a pullman coach in some parts of "up-South" Illinois and south of the Mason and Dixon line. While traveling from Chicago to Hot Springs, Arkansas, Congressman Mitchell was insulted and humiliated by a railroad conductor who refused to give him a pullman berth. He was cursed, called a nigger, and forced to ride in a "Jim Crow" coach which was covered with coal dust. The colored coach was next to the coal car and the train engine. The congressman

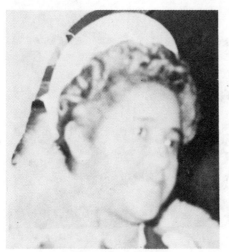

Mrs. Marjorie Stewart Joyner

Attorney John T. Jones, real estate lawyer par excellence.

Madame C. J. Walker, president of the National Beauty Culturist.

Metropolitan Community Church, 4100 S. Parkway (King Drive), the scene and platform for many political events during the 1930s and 1940s.

was doubly chagrined because he had paid first class fare for the ticket he purchased at the Illinois Central Railroad's Twelfth Street Station in Chicago. Earlier in the year, Mrs. Marjorie Stewart Joyner, a Chicago civic leader, president of the National Beauty Culturist, national supervisor of the Madame C. J. Walker Colleges, and current president of the Chicago Daily Defender Charities, was seated comfortably in a day coach on the Burlington

Congressman Arthur W. Mitchell being congratulated upon his re-election victory by two of his congressional colleagues.

and Rock Island Railroad while traveling through Texas after attending a Zeta Boule in Houston. Mrs. Joyner was told by a red neck conductor picking up the tickets that she had to move up front to the car next to the train engine. The train did not have a "Jim Crow" coach; therefore, she was forced to ride in the baggage car alone with a corpse. She later said to a *Chicago Defender* reporter: "It would not have been so bad had it been in the day time . . . but it was at night."

Joseph E. Tittinger, Second Ward Democratic committeeman, operated a Chicago style "Jim Crow" coach at Thirty-fifth and Michigan Avenue. Tittinger demanded that colored women and men seeking his aid wait in a small anteroom until he had interviewed every white person who wished to see him that evening. Once the office was totally cleared of whites, he declared a "colored folks hour" which he used to talk to his black constituents. The committeeman's philosophy on housing was similar to the one that he employed in operating his Second Ward Democratic headquarters. Tittinger felt that the South Parkway Garden Apartments (Ida B. Wells) should be built west of State Street on the old Black Belt site next to the railroad tracks where the Stateway Gardens and Robert Taylor projects are currently located.

In June, 1938 "Boss" Tittinger decided that every person who received a job through the Regular Second Ward Democratic Organization must pay three percent of his salary to him to help maintain the small two room second floor headquarters at Thirty-fifth and Michigan Avenue. The black precinct captains howled about the unfairness of the dues and proceeded to draw up a petition that was to be presented to Mayor Edward J. Kelly and Patrick Nash requesting that Tittinger be replaced in the next election in favor of a black who would show some sensitivity and interest in the colored community. The grievances in the petition were many, including the fact that the white committeeman ran his headquarters like a Mississippi plantation. They further pointed out that whites such as Tony Razzo, Kelly Lapin, Johnnie Ward, Myron Frazen, and a son-in-law of Morris Lapin were not precinct captains and lived outside the ward. However, they all held lucrative positions on the city payroll on the strength of the Second Ward Regular Democratic Organization's support which was ninety-five percent Negro. The colored precinct captains further pointed out in their petition that Jim Keho, a white precinct captain, repeatedly lost his territory but retained a high paying white collar job with the city whereas blacks with higher academic qualifications who consistently carried their precincts in all elections were working in the ward yards on low status blue collar jobs for pittance. The yard workers with editorial support from the *Chicago Defender* planted the seeds for change in the Second Ward Democratic Organization.

Nineteen thirty-nine was a year of dramatic change in the political structure of the Second Ward. On January 24, 1939, the following men filed to run in the February 28th aldermanic campaign: William E. King, the ex-state Senator, 4140 South Parkway; Earl B. Dickerson, 3842 South Parkway; Corneal A. Davis, 3221 South Calumet; Augustus L. Williams, 3646 South Michigan Avenue; James P. Durden, 532 East Fortieth Street; James Allen Grant, 3133 South Prairie Avenue; and the present incumbent William L. Dawson, 532 East Forty-second Street.

The *Chicago Defender* endorsed Alderman William L. Dawson as a man who should be re-elected because he had been loyal to his trust and the voters of the Second Ward. Conversely, the *Defender* stressed that former-Senator William E. King was a miserable failure as the Republican committeeman of the Second Ward, a master at creating dissension, and an unemployed politician in search of a job. In contrast, Earl B. Dickerson had several jobs. He was assistant attorney general for the State of Illinois and a director of Supreme Liberty Life Insurance Company. Neither position gave Dickerson the platform or the power he needed to fuel his political ambitions.

When the smoke from the political rhetoric had cleared the air on February 28, 1939, Mayor Edward J. Kelly's man, Alderman William L. Dawson had finished third behind Democrat Earl B. Dickerson and Republican William E. King. King received 9,217 votes to 8,513 for Dawson, Dickerson won the Democratic nomination with 9,241 votes against 1,597 for Corneal Davis, who had been sponsored by Dawson in an effort to siphon votes from Dickerson. Kelly had won the Democratic primary by a margin of 300,000 over State's Attorney Thomas J. Courtney. Mayor Kelly had asked Earl Dickerson not to run in the February election because he felt it would impede the incumbent alderman's chances of being re-elected and enable King to fulfill his deathwish of burying William L. Dawson politically. Dickerson with his eyes wide open aided King in spading the dirt on Dawson's Second Ward grave site.

In boardroom of the Supreme Liberty Life Insurance Company at 3501 South Parkway (King Drive). Left to right: General Counsel Attorney Earl B. Dickerson; Harry H. Pace, president; A. P. Bently, director; Dr. Midian Othello Bousfield, medical director; W. Ellis Stewart, secretary; T. K. Gibson, Sr., chairman and treasurer.

Dawson's political grave was not spaded deeply enough or packed tightly enough because on Sunday, March 19, 1939, the politically-buried Alderman's ghost walked into the Congressional Hall at 3140 South Indiana Avenue locked arm and arm with Dickerson, the Democratic Aldermanic nominee on his right and Tittinger the Second Ward Democratic committeeman on his left. They all walked proudly and erectly as they strolled toward the speaker's platform. Trailing Dawson in the line of march were eighty of his Republican precinct captains. Dawson made a stirring address to an enthusiastic audience that afternoon. He ended his partisan campaign speech with the following remarks: "I want Kelly to be re-elected in the general election because he has always been fair to my people. I want Dickerson elected because he represents the best thoughts of the people of the Second Ward and is capable by training and experience of making the most outstanding alderman in the city council. He will be a credit to his people, his community and his country."

William E. King did not believe that retribution from the grave was possible until he heard Dawson's voice from the beyond bellow: "I shall haunt him. The knife King stuck in me makes rest impossible." Dawson did not rest until April 5, 1939, the day after the final vote was counted, and Earl B. Dickerson had been declared the winner with a total of 19,287 votes against 16,917 for William E. King.

Alderman Earl B. Dickerson was the first black Democrat to represent the Second Ward in the city council. A similar honor went to Mike Sneed's man, Deputy Coroner Benjamin A. Grant, who defeated Alderman Robert R.

Jackson in a three corner Third Ward race which included former Congressman Oscar DePriest. The Democratic sweep in both the Second and Third Wards was made possible by petty jealousies and constant bickering among black leaders of the Republican party. William E. King, a master of duplicity, had literally locked "Bill" Dawson out of the Republican party because Dawson had been a cheerleader for Kelly in the city council chambers. The mayor wanted to reward the dethroned alderman for past loyalties. The only obstacles that stood between the two men were the Republican dog tags that Dawson wore around his neck.

In the mid-summer of 1939, Dawson met with Kelly and informed him of his decision to switch parties. Kelly was elated but Pat Nash had some deep reservation about a person who changed parties for personal benefit. The benefit for Dawson was obvious. Tittinger's precinct captains had revolted in June of 1939, and the Second Ward Democratic Organization was in search of a black leader. The three front runners for the position of Second Ward committeemanship were Christopher Wimbush, Bryant Hammond, and William L. Dawson. The former alderman's popularity and political effectiveness gave him the inside track. Mayor Edward J. Kelly made an astute political decision in November 1939 when he selected Dawson to replace Tittinger after first getting Alderman Dickerson's blessing. Later that month, he revealed his choice for Second Ward committeeman at a City Hall news conference.

Mayor Kelly needed a strong and cohesive Democratic organization in the Second Ward for the upcoming 1940 presidential campaign. Tittinger was not the man to lead the black political troops into a major political battle because in the last judicial campaign the Second Ward Democrats turned out a very low vote. One of the reasons given by the captains was that hungry, unfed warriors could not win fights. They cited the fact that there were eight truck driving jobs available in the predominantly populated black ward, and blacks had only one of the eight driving slots.

Kelly immediately granted Dawson, his new committeeman, access to state and local patronage to put a quick fix on the deep wounds that Tittinger had inflicted on the Second Ward's black foot soldiers. Although Dawson was the functioning committeeman, he was not politically-sainted by Pat Nash and the boys in the smoke-filled room at the Morrison Hotel until late December. Now with the full blessings of the Democratic Central Committee and new deal patronage jobs bulging out of all four of Dawson's pockets, he was able to attract a large number of stalwart Republicans into his re-organized Second Ward organization. To appease Christopher C. Wimbush, the runner-up for the Second Ward committeemanship, Dawson appointed him president of the ward organization. Dawson also threw some bread on the water for the white minority in the Second Ward by slating Joseph F. Tittinger for state representative. Dickerson and Dawson were now sleeping on the same soft, chicken-feathered, political mattress. Although the mattress was soft, they were both restless and uncomfortable as "king size" bedfellows.

Before the December snow of 1939 could lose its white glisten to the soot of Chicago's smoke stacks, Alderman Dickerson and Committeeman Dawson were at each other's throats. Kelly had appointed Dickerson and Dawson co-chairmen of a South Side fund raiser for his annual Christmas charity. Dawson's Second Ward Organization raised five thousand dollars to buy toys, food and clothes to be distributed several days before Christmas. Dickerson claimed credit for Dawson's organization fund raiser. Dawson was angry because he felt that Dickerson was trying to curry favors with the mayor by riding on Dawson's back. The stuffing in the mattress of the Dickerson-Dawson king size bed was beginning to turn from feathers to rocks.

The blood vessels in Dickerson's temples were protruding by March of 1940 because he felt that Dawson had double-crossed him by supporting the incumbent Arthur W. Mitchell for Congress for a fourth term. Dickerson claims that he made a deal with Dawson to support Dickerson for Congress in exchange for his backing Dawson for ward committeeman over Tittinger. Corneal Davis, Dawson's man, claims that such a deal, in his opinion, was doubtful because Dickerson could not have been elected alderman over William E. King without Dawson's total support. In this adversarial environment, Dawson found it necessary to quarantine Dickerson from the sensitive nerve center of the Second Ward Organization. Dawson's action infuriated Alderman Earl B. Dickerson to the point that Dickerson became a rebel with a cause but without a political army.

Dickerson did not make matters better for himself by refusing to campaign for Congressman Mitchell. Neither did the alderman's calcified position endear him to the Kelly-Nash machine because the machine demanded blind support for the ticket by all elected Democratic officials. Moreover, Dickerson became the mayor's antagonist in the council along with such independents as Paul Douglas from the Fifth Ward. Dawson and Dickerson found themselves playing the good cop and bad cop routine without the benefit of a partnership agreement. Dickerson and Dawson could have become partners without peers. They served together in 1918-1919 as officers in Company A of the 360th Infantry of the 92nd Division in the First World War. Dickerson credited Dawson early in their army careers as being a brilliant man. The writer has been in the presence of Dawson when he lauded Dickerson's talents. In spite of the separate roads they took politically, they covertly had a mutual admiration society. Dawson was on target politically, and Dickerson hit the bull's-eye philosophically which is supported by the following statement which crystallizes Dickerson's personal allegiance to the Democratic party. Dickerson said:

I could not accept the widely promoted notion that the Republican party was the party of Lincoln; therefore, the blacks should a priori (by preference), support its cause. I would not accept the "Trickled-Down" Laissez-Faire economic policies of the Republican party in the midst of economic catastrophe. Black politics, as it existed, had lost its foundation in the black cultural and institutional life. The black politicians' primary obligation was not to the community, but to the "organization" and to the white sponsors who supported their personal ambitions, appointed them to minor offices and provided financial assistance to their campaigns.

Dickerson's rhetoric was in the right pew, but his political judgment showed serious flaws when he failed to support Mitchell and Dawson in the April, 1940 election. Arthur W. Mitchell, the most unpopular congressman to ever serve in the First Congressional District, swamped Willard S. Townsend, international president of the United Transport Service Employees, who opposed him. Mitchell beat Townsend by 13,510 votes. The congressman polled a total of 16,667 votes against 3,157 for his opponent whereas Dawson polled 8,807 votes for re-election to the Second Ward committeemanship against no visible opposition.

The political gap between Mayor Edward J. Kelly and Alderman Earl B. Dickerson grew wider and unfathomably deeper between 1940 and 1942 because Dickerson became the strident and militant voice for such organizations as the Midwest Committee for Protection of the Foreign Born, National Lawyers Guild, Free Earl Browder Conference, Abraham Lincoln School, International Labor Defense Organization and the Progressive Party. These organizations were the advance guards for the civil rights struggle of the 1950s and 60s. To white folk generally, and Mayor Kelly specifically, too much civil rights and race talk spelled trouble. To Kelly, Dickerson was trouble.

In early January, 1942 when Mitchell decided not to run again, it was too late for Dickerson to get organizational support because Kelly had branded him a political untouchable. Dickerson belatedly realized that he did not have a ghost of a chance of receiving the Kelly-Nash endorsement because the die had already been cast. Dickerson subsequently heard through Alderman George Kells, a ward committeeman who sat on the six man congressional nominating committee, that William L. Dawson had appointed himself to the committee in order to position himself to replace Arthur W. Mitchell in the United States House of Representatives.

Alderman Dickerson reacted to Dawson's political maneuver by calling a meeting at the Quincy Club on Saturday, January 24, 1942. Represented at the meeting were church, labor and civil organizations. The meeting was chaired by Reverend A. Wayman Ward who asked Alderman Earl B. Dickerson if he would run for Congress. Dickerson readily accepted the draft. He then said:

> I fully appreciate the responsibility that would fall upon me as congressman from the First District of Illinois, but I am willing to make the fight for the office because I do not believe that Kelly and Nash and the downtown Democrats should tell the wards what to do and when to do it, who their candidates shall be even though the downtown selections are against the will of the people.

He further said that he was committed to the fight to bring home rule to the voters no matter how hard the fight might be. Dickerson later told the writer that he was a fool to undertake the congressional campaign because he was in the city council making a few thousand a year in addition to the money made from his private law practice. Dickerson recalls that he did not have much money but that he was doing reasonably well. That is, well enough to borrow $3,000 from the First National Bank of Chicago to launch his race for the United States House of Representatives. A group of ministers who supported Dickerson's campaign philosophy held a mass meeting at the Metropolitan Community Church located at 4100 South Parkway (King Drive) on Sunday, April 11, 1942 and raised between two and three thousand dollars in an effort to stem the tide in little David's battle against the Second Ward Goliath.

Dawson's campaign meetings in the week preceding the election took on the flavor of both a religious revival and a political convention. The assembly at Wendell Phillips High School was packed to the rafters with precinct captains, WPA workers and "big gun" Democrats from downtown, who pledged their support for Dawson in the congressional primary. The words that were continually echoed from the stage of the school auditorium indicated that Dawson was the man for the job. The stone wall that Dawson put in Dickerson's political path meant little to the alderman in his fight to tumble the giant Second Ward Organization. Alderman Dickerson, the standard bearer for the "silk stocking" crowd, leaped into the center of the congressional battle with a paper sack full of publicity and sound political arguments in contrast to Dawson's big duffle bag jammed with downtown pull, patronage and power.

The morning after the battle between the two young lions, the Dickerson forces recognized that they never had a chance. The election results were:

Dawson	13,787
Dickerson	4,187
King	9,032
Cyrus	1,157

With the exception of Dawson, Mayor Kelly was the happiest man in Chicago on Wednesday morning, April 15, 1942. He believed that all of his political dreams had come true because he came out of the primary war with a victory in every pocket.

The battle was now narrowed down to a Dawson vs. King "free for all" until the November congressional election. It also meant the renewal of a feud that went back to 1933 when Dawson was initially elected to the city council. A decade had not eroded the hostility between the two men. Dawson and King harbored a streak of meanness toward each other that was almost as deadly as a controversy with guns and tanks.

William E. King's continued duplicity within the Second Ward Republican Organization resulted in State Representative Harris B. Gaines losing his seat in the spring primary. Gaines responded by instructing his entire independent Republican organization to support William L. Dawson for Congress in the November election. However, Gaines made it clear that he had not jettisoned the Republican party because of his support for Dawson, whom he considered the logical choice for Congress.

Richard J. Lyons, a King supporter, pounded on the rostrum in the Olivet Baptist Church at 3100 South Parkway (King Drive) before an audience of 2,000 people and stated: "No man or woman with Negro blood who votes the Democratic ticket has any business in Illinois."

The crowd responded with cheers, applause, laughter and the ringing of cow bells.

Edgar G. Brown, director of the National Negro Council in Washington, D.C., returned to Chicago to introduce Senator Wayland Brooks to a gathering of 2,500 people at the DuSable High School auditorium on Forty-ninth and State Street. Brown's introduction included the following remarks:

> I am a registered Democrat in Chicago, but I returned here this Sunday before election, prepared to cast my ballot for Senator Wayland Brooks and the straight Republican ticket. Senator Brooks made every Negro in America his debtor by his successful championing on August 24th and 25th on the floor of the United States Senate, the anti-Poll Tax amendment to the Soldier Vote Law. This act gave ballots to 400,000 Negro troops for the first time in the nation's history.

These rallies had pollsters predicting that the First Ward might go Republican for the first time in about fifty years. Nevertheless, William E. King, Second Ward committeeman and Republican nominee in the First District, declared: "All the money the Democrats spend can never do more than delay the long overdue return to the Grand Old Party by my people."

Harold Smith, a *Chicago Tribune* reporter, made the following observation in a story that appeared under his by-line on November 1, 1942.

> Democratic leaders pooh-poohed their opponents' prognostications . . .The evidence is behind the G.O.P. claims. Sign ups under the new permanent

Congressman William L. Dawson standing on the steps of the U.S. House of Representatives, Monday, January 4, 1943.

Above: Wendell Phillips High School, Thirty-ninth and Prairie, the site of Second Ward committeeman William "Bill" Dawson's giant rally during his congressional primary campaign in the fall of 1942.

Right: Olivet Baptist Church, 3100 S. Parkway (King Drive).

registration law downstate were generally heaviest in the farm areas where Democratic disaffection is most evident. G.O.P. workers everywhere are fired with optimism whereas the Democrats, sensing defeat, are apathetic.

In the preponderantly colored First District, solidly Republican from 1904 to 1934, former State Senator William E. King, G.O.P. nominee, now as in 1940, is favored over former Alderman William L. Dawson, the Republican nominee four years ago, for the seat from which A. W. Mitchell is retiring.

The Democrats in the First Congressional District made the Republicans the new believers in a second Easter because William L. Dawson defeated his arch foe, William E. King, by a margin of 2,965 votes. Dawson received a total of 26,593 votes to King's 23,628.

On Wednesday morning November 4, 1942, Dawson was red-eyed and tired from sitting up all night in his headquarters at 330 East 35th Street watching the votes slowly trickle in from all of the wards. Dawson's fatigue did not camouflage his glee over the victory. Neither did his tiredness dilute his ability to generate that second burst of energy that one needs in the homestretch. Dawson's boundless energy that morning was reflected in the brisk tone of voice in which he explained his plans for Congress. He stated:

> We must stand united because the one congressman that the Negro people have in our national forum in Congress should not only represent his constituents in Chicago but the interests of all colored Americans.
>
> There can be no question that the aims, interests and aspirations of all Negro citizens in America are identical with those of the 275,000 on Chicago's South Side. All must stand together united as one in striving to attain full integration into American life.
>
> The right to work is the right to live. And I shall labor with every God-given talent to the end that the rights of all who work are protected and that no person shall be discriminated against in his right to work by reason of race, color or religion.

As to his victory over Republican William E. King, Dawson proclaimed: "Despite all the clamor and claims by some extra loud dopesters that the Negro is anti-administration, I believe this election shows that the South Side is still loyal and devoted to the best friend it has in the nation — President Roosevelt."

Dawson was sworn in as a member of the House of Representatives on Monday, January 4, 1943. His initial salary was $10,000 per annum. He received an additional $8,500 per year for three aides. The moment Congressman William L. Dawson took the oath of office is significant because it marked the hour that the model for the first black political "submachine" rolled off the American political assembly line.

Dr. Mary McLeod Bethune, president of Bethune-Cookman College and president of the National Council of Negro Women.

Chapter *XIV*

Congressman Dawson:
The Organization Man

Alderman Earl B. Dickerson was in Washington D.C. in mid-January 1943 attending to law business when he decided to pay a brief visit to the offices of the newly-elected Congressman Dawson. During his conversation with the congressman, Dickerson states that he extracted a promise from Dawson to support him for re-election in the February aldermanic race. According to Dickerson, Dawson agreed to make their mutual understanding known to the Second Ward Organization when Dawson returned to Chicago. Dickerson thought that Dawson's commitment was an exchange of favors because after the April 1942 congressional primary race in which Dawson defeated Dickerson, Dawson had accepted Dickerson's support silently. However, had Dickerson thrown his political force to the Republican Second Ward Committeeman, William E. King, Dawson would have been defeated. Hence, Dickerson felt he had earned Dawson's support; he returned to Chicago from the Washington meeting with a smile on his face. He felt confident that he had Dawson's blessing to be nominated for re-election as alderman of the Second Ward.

On Monday, January 18, 1943, two days before the Second Ward Regular Democratic Organization meeting was to be held, Dickerson learned through a Dawson precinct captain, Leroy King, that Dawson had returned to Chicago early and had taken William H. Harvey, a city fireman and a loyal member of the Second Ward Organization, down to Mayor Kelly's office to get the mayor to support Harvey for alderman of the Second Ward. On Wednesday night, January 20, Dickerson attended the Second Ward Organization's endorsement meeting at Dawson's headquarters which was located at 330 East 35th Street. The hall was packed with people, but very few knew what was going to happen. Dickerson felt that many people attending the meeting expected him

Left to Right: Mayor Fiorello LaGuardia of New York; A. Phillip Randolph, president of The Brotherhood of Sleeping Car Porters; Mrs. Eleanor Roosevelt; Dr. Mary McLeod Bethune, president and founder of Bethune-Cookman College.

to get Dawson's sanction. The hour of truth came when Dawson got up and made a spirited speech endorsing William H. Harvey, a city fireman, as the aldermanic nominee over Dickerson, the incumbent. Dawson's endorsement oration was followed by a string of glowing speeches given by C. C. Wimbush, Bryant Hammond and Corneal Davis who extolled Harvey's preparedness for the job and his loyalty and dedication to the Second Ward Democratic Organization. Although Dickerson was steaming as he sat in the chair of honor on the platform next to Congressman Dawson, he was not permitted to speak until the final endorsement speech for Harvey had been made. Dickerson then rose from his chair and gave a fire and brimstone speech attacking the way he had been mistreated and betrayed. Alderman Dickerson further promised that this would be the last Second Ward Organization meeting that he would ever attend.

Dawson's actions were justified said Corneal Davis who believed that:

Dickerson would not play politics in an organizational manner. He was a prima donna who regarded himself as more important than the party, and there was no other alternative for Dawson to take except to crush him. However, Dawson later offered Dickerson a big federal appointment which the alderman rejected. Hence, Dawson acted on the premise that to the victor belongs the spoils.

In a moment of reflection forty-two years after Alderman Dickerson's dramatic exit from the Second Ward Democratic Organization's meeting, Dickerson, the ninety-four year old former alderman, explained:

> That fellow Dawson was a very bright man. There is no question about that; however, he was a fellow who would do anything for power, and he sought power so that he could control the political and patronage appointments of blacks. He never would appoint anybody he thought might challenge his authority. Dawson never challenged the system publicly.
>
> Mayor Edward J. Kelly was also a bright man, but he had a plan to segregate black people just like Martin H. Kennelly and his successor, Richard J. Daley. The Robert Taylor Homes are monuments to remind us of what these men have done to black Chicagoans.

Dickerson's observations about Dawson and his general thirst for power were in focus; however, Dickerson had the lens cap on his camera when he stated that Dawson would not challenge the system publicly.

On Monday, February 8, 1943, the Georgia-born-freshman congressman from the First Congressional District in Illinois flew to Washington to defend Dr. William Pickens who was to be removed from the federal payroll because he had been accused of being a communist by Representative Martin Dies, Democrat of Texas and chairman of the Special House Committee to Investigate Un-American Activities. A dramatic episode developed when Congressman Dawson rose to get the floor. After Dawson had been recognized by the chair and as Representative Dies gathered his paper and prepared to leave the lectern, Dawson met Dies halfway up the aisle and stopped to converse with him for a few seconds. Dies apparently expecting a personality at-

Left to Right: State Senator Christopher C. Wimbush; Senator Fred Smith; Alderman William H. Harvey; and State Representative Corneal Davis. They were all dues paying members of Dawson's Regular Democratic Second Ward Organization.

Dr. William (Dean) Pickens, a staff member of the U.S. Treasury Department.

tack from Dawson addressed the entire Pickens' matter without expressing his racial feelings. Representative Dies had misjudged Dawson in thinking that he was a confrontational spokesman. Dawson was known in Chicago as a very low keyed persuader.

A tombstone-quiet enveloped the House Chambers when Dawson opened his mouth to make his maiden address before the congressional assembly. Congressman William Levi Dawson said:

> Mr. Chairman, it is with the greatest measure of hesitation that I, a new member, rise to address this august body at this time. I am sustained only by the knowledge that I can bring to this committee an understanding of the background of this subject matter better than any other person in this assembly.
>
> I have known William Pickens for more than forty years. I know his activities among my people and when I say "my people," I am not one who is sensitive to color. I am not one who is ashamed of what God made me. I stand before you further sustained by the knowledge that no man can question the loyalty of William L. Dawson to the United States of America. During the last war, although I was above draft age and did not have to go, yet, believing it was the duty of every citizen to rally to the colors in time of danger, I volunteered, was commissioned a First Lieutenant of Infantry and led black Americans into battle. I saw them fight, and I saw them die for this flag and country of ours. And if the years had not shattered this old frame of mine and if an accident had not maimed me, instead of standing in Congress of the United States, I would today, if I had my way, be back once again defending the flag, the only flag we know.

William Pickens has been charged with being a Communist. The gentleman who recited the great organizations that he belongs to, and so forth referred to 1927. I wish I could command words well enough to convey to you something of the psychology of an underprivileged people, something of the psychology of a people who are told they have every right in fact, but who know they do not have those rights in actuality. I wish you could envision in your own minds how we struggle wherever we can to make the Constitution and our democracy a living reality. I know something about communism; I know how the Communists have tried to infiltrate among our people, playing upon the ills we have suffered and so forth. And I know how often they did not come to us under the name of Communist but came with loud-sounding names, talking of freedom, talking of democracy, and talking of inalienable rights, things that are dear to the heart of every American, be he white or be he black. At some time or other, the names of many of us have been found connected with some of these organizations before we knew their true complexion because the more prominent the individuals were, the more insidious was their approach. I am telling you things you know.

You refer to 1927. That is a long time ago. Many names might be found on the rolls of some organization that has since been deemed a subversive organization. I say to you, William Pickens is not a Communist and has never been a Communist. William Pickens has not knowingly affiliated himself with a Communist organization, knowing it was Communist.

Certainly, he might have spoken at communistic meetings. I have done the same thing; in fact, I do not fear Communists. I do not fear them. I fight them, and I know that is the only way we can hold to our ideals. We have not yielded to them in their effort to infiltrate our group; and certainly, I know the voice of William Pickens has always been heard in defense of the high ideals of this country.

I say to you, Mr. Chairman, that his name has been used, but I know of my own knowledge that when he found it out, he sent in his resignation. This has been done by many loyal Americans, white and black, who went into the thing for an ideal only to find that the thing had been organized for another purpose.

Mr. Chairman, this thing is far-reaching in its effects. I know this Congress will not condemn any man because of his race, and I am not standing here pleading for that reason, because I have been the American sense of fair play demonstrated on many an occasion. The only hope black America has is the fundamental ideal of fair play that we know rests deep down in the bosom of the majority of the American public.

So, I am not saying that this thing is done on account of color, but I am saying to you that those who make the charge are not in a position to know of their own knowledge whereof they speak.

I do not know who their agents are. I know William Pickens was never called before the committee and given an opportunity to answer any charge against him.

I do not know who their agents are, but let me tell you their agents do not know William Pickens like we know him. They only know what might be seen in a list of a certain number of organizations.

But we know William Pickens in the flesh. We know that William Pickens has been the means of going up and down the length and breadth of this country teaching Americanism.

I tell you of my own knowledge, and from my knowledge of doing work among my own group, that he was deserted by a certain crowd that was insistent on certain demands, and William Pickens demanded that the government be placed first.

He was for the preservation of America above all domestic problems, and for that reason he was deserted by many of those who at one time had been associated with him.

He has been the means of millions of dollars of our money going into war bonds. One insurance company alone has bought over a million dollars worth of bonds. Others have bought up to the limit and will buy more. The rank and file of us are going down in our pockets to buy.

We do not care what the organizations may be I may say to the gentleman from Texas, but this we do know that William Pickens has never been a Communist.

William Pickens is a true American, and I state that with all the integrity of a man who would fight and die for America today.

When Dawson finished his maiden speech, the members of the House lifted the roof with thunderous applause and cheers. The first person to shake Dawson's hand and congratulate him after he had completed his address was Representative Hatton W. Sumners of Texas, chairman of the House Judiciary Committee.

Tuesday afternoon, February 9, the day following Dawson's speech, the house voted 267 to 136 to rescind its actions against Dr. William Pickens, ruling that he should be given a hearing along with 38 others who had been accused of communist affiliations including the eminent Dr. Mary McLeod Bethune of the National Youth Administration. Dr. Bethune, a decade earlier, had caused tears to stream down the cheeks of President Franklin Delano Roosevelt:

Mr. President, in many parts of the South, the fifteen and twenty dollar monthly checks the young people are receiving have meant real salvation. We are bringing life and spirit to these many thousands who for so long have been in darkness. I speak, Mr. President, not as Mrs. Bethune, but as the voice of 14,000,000 Americans who seek to achieve full citizenship. We must continue to open doors for these millions.

It was the spirit and character of the Dr. Bethune and Dr. Pickens of America that Representative Martin Dies' Committee on Un-American Activities was attempting to dye red.

Preceding the 267 to 136 vote in the House, the following comments were made by various members of that body. Representative George H. Bendar, Republican from Ohio said, "I have too much respect for Abraham Lincoln and that which he represented to vote for this amendment" whereas Representative James F. O'Connor, Democrat of Montana, bellowed, "I brand this proposal a conviction without trial in accordance with the American tradition of fair play and trial by jury of your peers."

Two reasons were given by Representative Louis Ludlow, a Democrat from the great state of Indiana:

> Mr. Pickens should not be forced off the treasury payroll. The Treasury Department denies categorically everything that has been said about Mr. Pickens, and I don't believe that the House can be taking action when we are the judge and the jury and the executioner without any evidence whatsoever to support such action.

Representative Frank B. Keefe, Republican of Wisconsin uttered:

> We are fighting to preserve the constitutional government and democracy and democratic processes and not to emulate Hitler; therefore, I still will not destroy my faith in the democratic process by denying an individual who is inferentially accused of a crime, an opportunity to be heard in a court of law.

Representative Malcolm C. Tarver, Democrat of Georgia in a slow southern drawl remarked, "I do not want to participate in any legislative lynching of men who have simply been charged with communistic affiliations without the submission of adequate proof to sustain the charges." Representative Francis Case, Republican of South Carolina, moaned in a deep voice, "I cannot believe that Abraham Lincoln would vote for the proposition now before us."

Representative Harold Knutson of Minnesota shouted:

> I brand the attack upon Dr. Pickens as lynch law. In my section of the country, this is what we call "shotgun" justice. I do not care what technicality the sponsor of this amendment hid behind. This is a race issue, pure and simple. The fact that in this body there are 435, of which 434 are white, and we vote to separate this lone, colored man from his job is all the proof the nation needs. I am opposed to what this Congress is attempting to do.

Congressman Dawson was consistent in his fights for equal rights. On June 12, 1943, he launched a vigorous attack against the southern poll tax. Dawson raised the following question on the floor of the House before his congressional colleagues. He queried:

> Who believes that the framers of the constitution intended to put it into the hands of any state to impose such qualifications as would take from the majority of the people of the state the right to express themselves at the polls in the election of federal officers?

In the fall of 1943, Dawson in his continuous fight against the poll tax, appeared before the Senate Judiciary Committee with facts and figures to prove that school expenditures in the poll tax states were less than the national average and that homicide rates were three times as high. Dawson further argued that the passage of a poll tax bill would not restore the right of participation in government to those who needed to raise their standard of living.

Dawson's constitutional viewpoint fell on impaired ears because it took a rumbling chorus of voices from the mid-nineteen fifties to the early nineteen sixties along with Dr. Martin Luther King's civil rights movement and the tramp, tramp, tramping of a million pairs of feet to get an amendment to the Constitution outlawing the poll tax. The amendment was passed in 1962, one year short of two decades after Dawson made his initial constitutional query before the House of Representatives.

During the interim twenty years, Dawson travelled up and down the dusty roads of his native South encouraging blacks to register, vote and organize. "Walk Together Children and Don't Get Weary" was a phrase that Dawson frequently used in his speeches during his organizational efforts.

Organizing the political troops to get William H. Harvey elected over Mack Akins in the April 6, 1943 election was a major task that Dawson undertook to make the Second Ward Democratic Organization a major cylinder in the Kelly-Nash political machine. Harvey beat Atkins in the aldermanic race by a close count of 14,058 to 13,349.

Mayor Edward J. Kelly received 61.1 percent of the black vote in that April 1943 election moving his up from 59.5 in 1939, which was a gain of only 1.5 percentage points in a four year period. In the same spring election, "Mike" Sneed's Third Ward Democratic Organization failed to re-elect Alderman Benjamin Grant after the two men patched up their differences because the Republican party had enticed the old warrior, Oscar DePriest, to come out of retirement and suit up for a political war. Although DePriest, the Republicans' black warrior, was in frail health, he trounced the Democratic incumbent. The Third Ward debacle weakened Committeeman "Mike" Sneed's voice within the Kelly-Nash inter-council and strengthened "Bill" Dawson's arm grip around a pork barrel full of patronage rewards.

The recipients of Dawson's Second Ward Democratic Organization's patronage had to display loyalty and total commitment to the committeeman. Dawson was strictly an organization man and also an excellent organizer and administrator. His life was politics. To play the game, he gave up his law practice and a stable home life for a place in Chicago's political sun. Dawson's earthly, creature comforts were few. He had a great fondness for poetry and was known to recite from memory poems written by the masters for as long as a half an hour at a time without stopping. He found reading detective and western novels relaxing. Occasionally, he played poker with his local political colleagues in the backroom of his headquarters, and sometimes these games lasted all night. He was also a great jazz buff; he collected Ellington, Basie, Armstrong, Calloway, and Jelly Roll Morton records by the hundreds. As a matter of fact, he was known to have one of the largest private collections of records on the South Side. Dawson owned a farm in Michigan where he, on rare occasions, took his family for a quiet weekend.

The congressman could be both earthy or suave depending on the audience. Dawson could switch from a dramatic spiritualist to a humorist spellbinder like Bill Cosby, leaving his listeners rolling in laughter. "Bill" Dawson, the man, was complex, but his political philosophy was simple. A decision was never based on black or white without weighing the political benefits that would accrue to the Second Ward Democratic Organization. Thus, Dawson never considered supporting a black man against a white man if the black man was not a card carrying member of the Democratic Organization. Dawson frequently said: "You would not expect Willie Mays to drop the ball just because Jackie Robinson hit it."

William Levi Dawson had no patience with anyone who wanted to be independent, buck the machine, or refuse to vote a straight Democratic ticket. Judge Sidney A. Jones, who was a member of Dawson's Second Ward Organization, stressed that because the "Old man" became a Democrat convert late in his political career, Dawson found it necessary to prove that he was a one hundred and fifty percent loyal Democrat all the way. And he was. Moreover, Judge Jones pointed out that Dawson was not interested in helping people who were on par with him intellectually. Jones recalled discussing with Congressman Dawson one afternoon the need to have a black man as an assistant attorney general of the United States and also the need for some black judges.

Dawson responded to Attorney Sidney A. Jones' observation with the following remark: "I don't think we have any black men qualified to hold the assistant attorney general's job. Jones retorted with several names of super

Attorney Sidney A. Jones, a member of the Second Ward Regular Democratic Organization.

Attorney Wendell E. Green, a member of the Civil Service Commission.

qualified blacks who had graduated from Harvard, Yale, Northwestern and the University of Chicago Law Schools. The Congressman rebutted with this remark:

> Do you think I am going to build up some guy so big that I will have to use all my energy to bring him down to my size? Furthermore, I prefer spreading the political gospel in the Second Ward Organization through ten small patronage jobs as opposed to one big one.

The Second Ward's patronage armies arms were too short to build Dawson's political empire to the sky; therefore, he reached out for help from the only cash intensive business in the black community. It was called policy; today, it is known as the Lottery. The policy Kings were the bankers of the black community. The following statement about the policy kings was noted in *An Autobiography of Black Chicago:* "The Jones brothers policy wheels in the 1930's and 40's operated like clockwork, as efficient and as well run as any marble-lined bank or brokerage house on LaSalle Street and many times more profitable."

Three decades later, the House of Representatives Policy-Numbers Game Study Committee chaired in 1973 by State Representative Lewis A. H. Caldwell, author of *The Policy King,* and State Representative Harold Washington, the committee's secretary, proposed a bill to legalize policy the same as bingo had been legitimatized. On June 27, 1975, Caldwell, Washington, Gaines and others introduced House Bill 3123 for the purpose of authorizing the organization of businesses to operate policy numbers, providing for their regulation and imposing a tax of 10% from the gross receipts of the operations. The bill would have also amended the criminal code to exempt games conducted under this act from penalties for gambling and syndicated gambling. Although Lewis A. H. Caldwell's policy bill died, it has subsequently been resurrected, relabeled and gentrified by white folk and is currently generating millions of dollars annually for the state of Illinois.

Policy, which is a gambling game, was a financial undergird in Dawson's political, civic and church work. According to Reverend Corneal Davis, Dawson did not have a personal financial interest in policy; however, he had more than a nodding acquaintance with the game because he accepted contributions from the policy kings to support the financial needs of the Second Ward Organization. Davis, who was also president of the Dawson Second Ward Organization for many years, said that Dawson's personal financial interest was in the Jitney Cabs that ran up and down South Park and Indiana Avenues on the South Side of Chicago. Dawson's partner in the cab venture was Nathan Kellogg McGill, a black lawyer, the former general council for the *Chicago Defender* and brother-in-law of Robert S. Abbott, the publisher. Although Dawson's business interests were elsewhere, he took the position that as long as it was legitimate to place bets at the race track in the Cook County or play Bingo in the Catholic churches, he would not brook any interference with the policy operations in his district from the police department or outside white gangsters.

Left: State Representative Lewis A. H. Caldwell, author of a book entitled Policy King, *and State Representative Harold Washington were co-sponsors of a bill to legalize policy to the status of Bingo, or Lottery.*

Frank "the enforcer" Nitti, treasurer of the Al Capone organization.

Illy B. Kelly, policy king and son-in-law of former Alderman Louis B. Anderson.

The policy business was so lucrative that Frank "The Enforcer" Nitti of the Al Capone mob bribed police captains to enforce the law against black policy operators in an effort to pry open the golden gates for white mobsters to muscle into the business. In each instance that this tactic was brought to Dawson's attention by the black policy kings, he went to Mayor Edward J. Kelly and had the police captain involved transferred out of the district.

Prior to the mob's attempt to use bribery to get into policy business, it used deadly force. On Sunday, January 8, 1939, the face of Walter J. Kelly, a policy king was blown off with four shotgun blasts fired from a moving vehicle while he was seated in his expensive new sedan which was parked in front of 3033 South Michigan Avenue, just a few blocks north of Dawson's Second Ward headquarters on Thirty-fifth Street. Kelly whose nickname was "Hoppy" reportedly was kidnapped ten years earlier by white mobsters and held for a $35,000 ransom. Walter Kelly's partner in the policy business was his very popular and younger brother, Illy B. Kelly, son-in-law of the powerful ex-alderman and Mayor Thompson's floor leader, Louis B. Anderson. As a matter of fact, when Corneal Davis chauffered for Anderson, Alderman Anderson instructed Davis to pick up Davis' weekly pay check at the Kelly Brothers' policy wheel which was located at 5051 South Michigan Avenue.

The political power of the policy kings is best exemplified by a statement made by John H. Sengstacke, publisher of the *Chicago Defender* newspaper chain and nephew of the late Robert S. Abbott, founder of the paper:

My Uncle Abbott told me to go down and tell Mayor Edward J. Kelly that he would like for him to appoint Attorney Wendell E. Green to the Civil Service Commission. Kelly told me that he did not have a problem in making such an appointment because of his close relationship with Mr. Abbott. However, Kelly advised me that I would have to go to Edward Jones to get final approval. I went back to my uncle and told him that they were in a hell of a situation. Here he was the publisher of the largest black owned newspaper in America, and he had to go to a policy king and get his approval before Mayor Kelly would put Wendell Green on a commission. "To hell with that," I said to my uncle: "I am not about to go and ask Ed Jones for anything."

The *Chicago Defender,* however, continued to campaign through its columns for Green's appointment, and Kelly subsequently placed Green on the Civil Service Commission.

The Reverend Philip Yarbrough, chairman of the Chicago Church Federation, called a meeting of civic and church organizations to protest the unparallel, demoralizing conditions caused by policy games, bookie joints and illegal liquor selling in Chicago. Yarbrough argued in his opening statement that:

John H. Sengstacke, publisher of the Chicago Defender.

He had been in Chicago for 31 years, through the days of the saloons before World War I and through the various periods when the city was notorious as a wide-open town, and yet, he had not seen or known any condition to be as vicious as the current crime and wave of corruption that was enveloping Chicago.

Hence, Reverend Yarbrough laid the responsibility for the widespread gambling squarely on the shoulders of Mayor Edward J. Kelly.

Dr. Arthur J. Todd of Northwestern University followed Rev. Yarbrough to the lectern and added:

The immense buying power absorbed by the rackets run by the gambling syndicate and the liquor business accounts for the paralysis in law enforcement that has laid Chicago low.

You can't pour a quarter of a billion dollars a year which is the estimate put on gambling and vice without robbing the legitimate business of needed trade to keep it prosperous and keep employment up.

It took federal aid to break the Capone gang. Now, it seems necessary to crush the gambling syndicate.

George Willington Lambert, a black civic leader and president of the Property Owners Improvement Association, told the group of civic leaders that gathered at the downtown YMCA for the Federation Conference that "the policy racket is devastating the Negro section of the South Side." He assailed ward committeemen as leading factors in the protection of gambling because they controlled the police through the electon of aldermen, the sheriff, the mayor and judges.

The power of the policy racket in the political and civic life of black Chicago from the 1920's through the 40's is illustrated by the fact that 15,000 people made a living off policy annually. There were 4,200 policy stations on the South Side alone. It has been estimated that nearly 100,000 persons played policy each day, and according to the files in the offices of former Attorney General Homer S. Cummings, one policy operator alone had an annual take of $2,016,000.00 of which thirty percent was profit for the wheel.

Some of the better known policy kings and the policy books (drawings) that they controlled were: the Jones brothers, who controlled the Bronx and the Rio Grande wheels from 4724 South Michigan Avenue; the Kelly brothers and their survivor, Illy B. Kelly, who controlled the Lucky Strike, Greyhound and the Lake Michigan wheels at 104 to 108 East 51st Street; Julius Benvenuti, one of the original policy wheel owners on the South Side, who controlled the Red Devil and Gold Mine drawings from his headquarters at 2900 South LaSalle; and Charlie Farrell and Henry Young, owners of the north and south and east/west book, who operated their wheel from 35th and State Street. Other policy kings were Earl White and Pop Lewis, owners of the Monte Carlo books, who operated their wheel from a building near Pop Lewis' Vincennes Hotel which was located at 36th and Vincennes Avenue and Jim Knight who operated the Royal Palm, the Iowa and The Wisconsin books from his Palm Tavern at 446 East 47th Street although his drawing wheel was located on Michigan Avenue near 51st Street.

The policy kings were very intertwined with the political, social, civic and religious life on the south and west sides of Chicago; hence, it was difficult to tell the direct source of the money that supported the legitimate businesses, charitable institutions, and churches. Moreover, policy money was the foundation for a number of legally established businesses. For example, Henry Young owned several large drugstores whereas Jim Knight owned a shoe store on 47th street. The Jones brothers, during the 1930's and 40's, owned numerous hotels and apartment buildings on the South Side in addition to a Ben Franklin department store on East 47th Street and also a milk dairy. The Jones brothers also owned villas in both Mexico and France. Moreover, the Jones brothers employed precinct captains as runners for their policy wheels; hence, they expanded the political patronage system.

Terms and Definitions Used by Policy Players, Runners, and Owners

A.M. Drawing	The lottery drawing usually held at 2:30 p.m.
P.M. Drawing	The second of the daily drawings usually held at 10:30 p.m.
Class	A numerical designation which identifies the particular series of numbers [called legs] on which a bet is wagered. There are three classes in each drawing— a series of 24 numbers are pulled first [the double leg] then a series of 12 [a single leg] and then a series of 3, 4, 5 or 6 numbers [referred to as the "short" or "junior" leg].
Hit	A winning bet.
Keg	A cylindrical drum containing numbers 1 thru 78 from which the numbers are drawn.
Over Looks	Late claims made by winners.
Parent Organization	The organization which conducts the lottery. Also known as the wheel or wheel headquarters.
Policy Station	A fixed location where a bettor goes to wager.

Policy Slip	A printed sheet showing the results of the drawing. One side shows the result of the 24-number drawing and the reverse side carries the result of the "single" leg and "short" leg drawing.
Runner	The person who picks up the money and betting records from the "writers" and the "policy stations."
Walking Writer	A person who walks the streets looking for bettors.
Wheel Operators	The people who operate the lottery.
Top Sheet	A sheet of scrap paper stapled to the betting records containing the identity of the writer or station, the gross amount bet, and the amount due to the wheel.
Fancy	Certain numbers or combinations which by custom have grown popular.
Gig	A bet on any three numbers appearing in any order.
Saddle	A separate bet that any two numbers of the "gig" will be drawn. A gig bet is a prerequisite to a saddle bet.
Flat	Two numbers played.
Horse	Four numbers played.
Jack	Five numbers played.

In 1973, three years after Congressman William L. Dawson's death, State's Attorney Bernard Carey created a furor by charging that Mayor Richard J. Daley would never let the police stamp out policy because many black Democratic precinct captains were employed in the racket. Policy was an underbelly in the political structure in that policy money was used to grease a succession of political machines.

William R. (Billy) Skidmore, the millionaire Chicago junk dealer and gambler, was the conduit for many years through which South Side policy money was sent downtown. Edward Jones was Skidmore's bagman because he collected weekly dues of $250.00 per week from each policy wheel that operated in the Black Belt and delivered it to Skidmore at his junk yard at 2840 South Kedzie Avenue. The federal government subsequently managed to put both Skidmore and Edward Jones in the federal penitentiary at Terra Haute, Indiana on income tax violations. William L. Dawson's hands were clean; his coat tail was never touched by anything stronger than a rumor.

Congressman William L. Dawson never bit the hands that fed the Second Ward Democratic Organization. He was known to be friendly and cordial with all the policy men. As a matter of fact, Dawson came back from Washington in February, 1944 to deliver the principal speech at the inaugural of Leon Motts, popular realtor and former policy man, when Mott's was installed as president of the Appomattox Club. Dawson's popularity was so high in 1944 that he could have touched a skunk with both hands, and each hand would have smelled as though it has been dipped in Chanel No. 5 perfume.

Dawson was so certain of winning the pending election in 1944 that he spent very little time in Chicago campaigning against William E. King, his perennial opponent. He left that matter in the hands of the Second Ward Organization and Mayor Edward J. Kelly. As a matter of fact, Dawson spent a great deal of time in New York State directing the presidential campaign for Franklin Delano Roosevelt.

The following speech was delivered by Congressman William L. Dawson on behalf of President Roosevelt over the mutual network on Sunday, October 1, 1944 from the Golden Gate Ballroom which was located in the Harlem section of New York City.

My fellow Americans, the outcome of this election may well determine whether the Negro citizens shall continue his upward march towards the realization of unrestrained citizenship or whether as a weak minority, he shall be pushed aside as an object of charity and again descend into the depths of poverty, hunger and despair.

The battle lines are drawn, the issues are clear, and the sponsoring forces of each candidate are known. Party lines have been forgotten. Behind the candidate's running on the Republican ticket, you find all the old gang reactionaries and isolationists who before Pearl Harbor fought every effort of our president to fortify, arm and prepare our nation for a war which was inevitable.

This country can never reach its highest influence as long as it permits a system of segregation and discrimination to be practiced against one-tenth of this population because of race and color. Deep seated prejudices and animosities cannot by legislation alone be removed from the minds and hearts of men, but the attitude of the nation's head can do much to determine the attitude of the nation. Under President Roosevelt, the Negro has forged ahead in the fight for full participation in American life because of a devout understanding and splendid courage of the president. He did not create the problem; he inherited it from those who preceded him. He has not equivocated. The world knows where Roosevelt stands. He has not done all he would like to have done; he has not done all that everybody wanted him to do, but by the living God, I defy any person to deny that he has not done more to promote a square deal for the Negroes than all the presidents since Lincoln combined.

The Negro hating, Negro baiting traditions of the South existed before

Attorney Oscar Brown, Sr., manager of the Ida B. Wells project; U.S. Vice President Henry A. Wallace; and Captain Harry B. Deas.

President Franklin D. Roosevelt in the door of his special car parked on a sidetrack in Chicago.

Roosevelt was born; the discriminatory and prejudicial customs and traditions of the American military establishment existed before Roosevelt was born, but Roosevelt since becoming president has done more to destroy these restrictions than any person now on the political stage. For twelve years, President Roosevelt kept faith with us. On November 7th, Negroes will keep the faith with him.

Dawson had every reason to keep the faith with Franklin Delano Roosevelt because the week prior to the National Democratic Convention in July 1944, President Roosevelt summoned Congressman William L. Dawson to the White House to discuss Negro issues that might come before the delegates. The president was concerned about the black vote, but at the same time, he was attempting to head off what he felt was a southern rebellion against his New Deal policies. The Texas Democratic party had split down the middle with New Dealers and anti-New Deal regulars coming to the Chicago convention with each group seeking to be recognized as the Texas official delegation. To make bad matters worse, the South Carolina Progressive Democratic party strategized for a floor fight against the Carolina Conservatives at the convention. Therefore, it was necessary for the president to make a major political move to solidify his New Deal supporters which, of course, included the majority of the black registered voters. The president had already decided that Vice President Henry A. Wallace could not help the ticket in the South. Therefore, he sent Wallace to China two months prior to the convention in an effort to accommodate the southern whites and, at the same time, distance himself from Wallace's progressive New Dealism.

Although President Roosevelt's nomination was never in question, it was unclear who he would select as a vice presidential running mate. Vice President Henry A. Wallace was the candidate favored by labor, liberals, and blacks whereas James S. Byrnes, a southerner, was the choice of conservatives and racists. In an effort to carry water on both shoulders, the president reached out for Supreme Court Justice James S. Byrnes as his selection for a running mate in an effort to pacify the South. The big bosses, Ed Flynn of New York, Ed Kelly of Chicago, and "Boss" Crump of Memphis, did not favor either Wallace or Byrnes because they felt that both men were losers and could not help the ticket against Governor Thomas E. Dewey of New York.

Robert Hannegan, the chairman of The National Democratic Committee, called Mayor Edward J. Kelly to ascertain his position and to determine whether Kelly could deliver Illinois. Kelly answered in the affirmative with the following proviso. He maintained that:

> If he could deliver the black vote, he could control the state. However, if he couldn't deliver the black vote, he would lose the state. Therefore, it would be necessary for him to confer with Congressman William L. Dawson to see if Dawson could in fact deliver the Chicago black vote.

Dawson had indicated to Kelly earlier that Byrnes was not acceptable to the black voters. Hence, a compromise candidate would have to be found. Kelly's Irish philosophy would not let him believe that a southern Irishman would not be acceptable to the black voters. Therefore, he asked Dawson to compile a list of reasons explaining why Justice James S. Byrnes was not acceptable to blacks. Dawson and his staff went to work in his office at 3520 South State Street on Monday afternoon, July 17, 1944, and worked throughout the night compiling and documenting reasons why blacks could not support Byrnes, a known southern racist. As a matter of fact, Dawson pointed out to Mayor Kelly that he was afraid that blacks would probably vote Republican in the 1944 presidential election if Byrnes were crammed down their throats.

Mayor Edward J. Kelly, being the tough Irishman that he was, did not give up the fight in his efforts to satisfy President Roosevelt's quest to get the blacks in Illinois to go along with Byrnes' candidacy. Therefore, Kelly asked Dawson if Dawson would meet face to face with Justice James S. Byrnes at the Blackstone Hotel and discuss in detail the grievances of black folk. Inasmuch as Dawson owed his success in the Democratic party to Mayor Kelly, he cordially agreed to such a meeting. The meeting between the two men took place at the Democratic headquarters, which was in the Blackstone Hotel, located on the northwest corner of Michigan and Balboa in Chicago, which was di-

The Democratic National Convention, 1944.

rectly across from the Stevens Hotel (Hilton). The two men met for three straight hours. Mayor Kelly waited in the foyer of the suite hoping that some kind of reconciliation might be made. After 185 minutes of conversation, Congressman Dawson rose from chair and said to Byrnes, "Mr. Justice, you cannot by my candidate."

He then turned and walked slowly with a limp, caused by his left wooden leg, into the foyer where Kelly was waiting. When Dawson reached the spot where Kelly was sitting, he stopped, placed his hand on Kelly's left shoulder, and said "I am sorry, Mr. Mayor, but Mr. Byrnes cannot be my candidate."

July 18, 1944 was a crucial day for President Franklin Delano Roosevelt and the Democratic party in Illinois. The southern Illinois Democrats were notorious with their conservatism and anti-New Deal sentiment. Illinois Republican leaders were buoyant because they felt that blacks were going to return to the Abe Lincoln fold. Therefore, it was imcumbent upon President Roosevelt to select a man who would be acceptable to the black voters, that is, if the Democratic party wanted to control Illinois, which had been a pivotal state in all major national elections.

Word about the outcome of the meeting between Dawson and Byrnes was dispatched to President Roosevelt, who waited in his special railroad car parked on a side track in Chicago. The president sent the following letter by messenger to Robert Hannegan, the chairman of the Democratic National Committee:

July 19, 1944

Dear Bob:

You have told me about Harry Truman and Bill Douglas. I should, of course, be very glad to run with either of them and believe that either one of them will bring real strength to the ticket.

Always sincerely.

Franklin Roosevelt

There are several versions of the July 19, 1944 letter written by President Franklin Roosevelt. One version has the president writing the letter from the White House on July 11 before he left for the West Coast via Chicago. That version does not seem feasible because a determination on whether Byrnes would be acceptable as a vice presidential candidate was not actually ascertained until Tuesday, July 18, 1944, seven days after that letter was to have been written. Grace Kelly, Roosevelt's secretary, maintains in her memoirs that President Roosevelt had put Bill Douglas' name first, that is before Truman's, and that Bob Hannegan had her retype that letter reversing the order. There is no evidence in the Roosevelt library file supporting this version. Bob Hannegan denied it in a conversation with Judge Samuel I. Rosenman only a few weeks before Hannegan's death in 1949. In addition, Margaret Truman made the following statement about her father in her book, *Harry S. Truman:*

> Whether the president wrote the letter in Chicago or Washington, it is very clear that he was reaffirming his decision to back my father for the vice presidential slot. The addition of William O. Douglas' name was designed to make it appear that Roosevelt was not dictating anything to convention. At this point, Mr. Douglas had no organized support whatsoever, and the nomination was totally beyond his grasp.

Although Dawson is not mentioned in either Margaret Truman's book or in Truman's memoirs, it is a fact that Dawson's behind-the-scene-preconvention activities opened the door for Truman's selection as vice president of the United States. Dawson's political movements before Truman's nomination are documented by Doris E. Saunders in an *Ebony* Magazine article entitled "The Day Dawson Saved America From A Racist President."

Senator Harry S. Truman comments in his memoirs about the events leading up to his election as vice president:

On Tuesday evening, July 18, 1944, The National Chairman, Bob Hannegan, came to see me and told me unequivocally that President Roosevelt wanted me to run with him on the ticket. This astonished me greatly, but I was still not convinced. Even when Hannegan showed me a long hand note written on a scratch pad from the president's desk which said, "Bob, it's Truman. F.D.R.," I still could not be sure that this was Roosevelt's intent, although I later learned that the handwriting in the note was the president's own.

Truman further states:

On Thursday afternoon, July 20, the day before the vice president was to be nominated, Hannegan called me from his room in the Blackstone Hotel and asked me to come to a meeting of the Democratic leaders. When I arrived there, they all began to put pressure on me to allow my name to be presented to the convention, but I continued to resist.

Hannegan had put in a long distance telephone call to the president, who was in San Diego at the time. When the connection was made, I sat on one of the twin beds, and Hannegan with the phone sat on the other. When Roosevelt used the phone, he always talked in such a strong voice that it was necessary for the listener to hold the receiver away from his ear to avoid being deafened, so I found it possible to hear both ends of the conversation.

"Bob," Roosevelt said, "Have you got that fellow lined up yet?"

"No," Bob replied, "He is the contrariest Missouri mule I've ever dealt with."

"Well, you tell him if he wants to break up the Democratic party in the middle of a war, that's his responsibility."

Truman states that the president banged down the phone and left Hannegan holding a voiceless receiver. The president's remarks put Truman on the horns of a dilemma.

Truman jumped to his feet and began walking around the room in search of a solution to Roosevelt's displeasure. He then suddenly blurted out to Hannegan: "Well, if that is the situation, I would have to say yes, but why the hell didn't he tell me in the first place?"

On Friday, July 21, 1944, the convention chose Harry S. Truman as its nominee for the vice president of the United States.

The president sent the following telegram:

From the White House

Washington
July 21, 1944

Telegram

Honorable Harry S. Truman
United States Senator
Stevens Hotel
Chicago, Illinois

I send you my heartiest congratulations on your victory. I am, of course, very happy to have you run with me. Let me know your plans. I should see you soon.

Franklin D. Roosevelt

Dawson, in an intransigent position against Byrnes' vice presidential bid, was the circuitous route on which Harry S. Truman ascended to the presidency of the United States.

Harry S. Truman served as vice president of the United States for only 89 days because of Roosevelt's untimely death on April 12, 1945. Although Truman later forgot to put the role that Dawson played in helping Truman become president in history books, he remembered his good friend William L. Dawson immediately after he took up residency at 1600 Pennsylvania Avenue. On Sunday afternoon, President Truman frequently placed calls directly from the Oval Office in the White House to Dawson's Second Ward headquarters at 3520 South State Street in Chicago.

Corneal Davis, who was the president of Dawson's Second Ward Democratic Organization, recalls one such occasion:

> I always came down to our headquarters at 3520 South State Street on Sunday afternoon, after I left church. It was a good time for me to talk with Congressman Dawson. I usually sat at the switchboard which was just outside his door. He always left the door open so that we could talk back and forth. On this particular Sunday, I was sitting by the phone when it rang. I picked it up and said, "Hello."
>
> A voice said, "is Bill there?"
>
> I said, "Who the hell is this, and who do you want to speak to?"
>
> The voice on the other end of the phone replied. "This is Harry S. Truman."
>
> While holding the open phone in my hand, I shouted back to Congressman Dawson and said "Chief. What do you think? I got some damn fool on the phone talking about he's Harry Truman, and he wants to speak to you."
>
> Dawson said: "Wait a minute," and he picked up the phone.
>
> I was still holding the receiver when the person said "Hello, Bill."

> And Dawson said, "Hello, Chief. How are you Mr. President?"
>
> I felt like running and jumping in the lake. I had called the president of the United States "a damn fool."
>
> The president asked Dawson who was that that answered the phone, and the congressman said: "Oh! He's my boy. He's been with me for many years."

Truman was fond of Dawson because of Dawson's ability to organize and get out the vote, and Dawson had ample opportunity to display that talent during the fall of the 1944 presidential campaign. When President Roosevelt came to Chicago for a giant campaign rally on Saturday, November 3, 1944 at Soldier Field, Congressman William L. Dawson was very prominent on the dais along with Vice President Henry Wallace.

Wallace stayed overnight in Chicago for a Sunday rally which was held on the South Side at the Savoy Ballroom on 47th and South Parkway (King Drive). When the vice president arrived at the ballroom where some 5,000 people had jammed every crevice of the hall, he was greeted by John H. Sengstacke, president of the *Chicago Defender* and co-chairman of the event along with Representative William L. Dawson.

The Sunday, November 4th rally at the Savoy was probably one of the most significant events to take place on the South Side of Chicago for a Democratic president in the history of the city. The doors of the Savoy Ballroom were opened at 12:30 P.M. to accommodate the tremendous crowd that was anticipated. Churches dismissed their services promptly that day in order that their members might hear the "champion of the common man." Another highlight of the program that afternoon was the parade of Negro clubs marching into the ballroom carrying banners extolling the virtues of the Roosevelt administration. Wallace, the speaker of the day, struck a theme that the black audience wanted to hear when he said: "Nobody can guarantee full employment or good wages. But by their fruits, you shall know them. Franklin D. Roosevelt believes in the people, and the people give him strength. The president spoke truly when he said the whole problem of reconversion can be summed up in one word—jobs."

Congressman William L. Dawson bought thunder to the event when he remarked: "If you can bring Abraham Lincoln back, I will vote for him. That failing, I will vote for Franklin Delano Roosevelt."

The crowd jumped to its feet and screamed in a frenzy in response to Dawson's statement.

Also present that afternoon on the dais was Dr. Mary McLeod Bethune who lauded Wallace's early remarks: "I think the vice president has raised a solid platform of hope on which the common many may stand. All thinking Americans should support Roosevelt's re-election because they know that Dewey's election would be a catastrophe." The master of ceremonies for that gala event was David "Bud Billiken" Kellum, the *Chicago Defender*'s city editor.

The enthusiasm and spirit from the rally at Soldier Field and the Savoy Ballroom spilled over into the election booths on Tuesday, November 7th because Dawson beat Second Ward Republican Committeeman William E. King decisively. Dawson who had been expected by some pundits to have an uphill battle against King showed surprising strength in the early returns on election day. In the 1942 election, Dawson went into office with a bare majority of 3,000 votes. This time, he beat King by over 14,000 votes. The voting tabulation showed the following: Dawson 42,473, King 26,196. In the Second and Third Wards, Roosevelt got 52,355 votes representing 64.1 percent against Dewey's 29,262 votes or 35.9 percent. However, Chicago was not as heavily Democratic as New York City because the black Harlem precincts gave Roosevelt 116,044 votes which represented 79 percent compared to 30,668 votes for Dewey which was 21 percent. Roosevelt carried New York's Harlem over Dewey by a 4 to 1 ratio even though Dewey and Roosevelt were both New Yorkers.

Wednesday, January 3, 1945, was a day of historical significance in America. For the first time in the twentieth century, two black men took their seats in the hall of Congress. The historic Seventy-ninth Congress of the United States convened before a gallery packed with several hundred people, although fewer than thirty blacks witnessed this swearing in ceremony. In the gallery was Hazel Scott, the movie and nightclub star, whose name had been romantically linked with that of Adam Clayton Powell and also very visible

Left: U.S. Representative Adam Clayton Powell of New York. Right: Dr. W. E. B. DuBois, director of the Department of Special Research of the National Association for the Advancement of Colored People (NAACP).

were Mrs. Mary McLeod Bethune, president of the National Council of Negro Women and Mrs. Bernice Spraggs, correspondent for the *Chicago Defender*. It was a day in the sun for both Congressman William L. Dawson (D) of Illinois and Adam Clayton Powell, Jr. (D) of New York as they took their oaths along with the entire body of congressmen.

Powell, the new member of Congress and the first Negro from the state of New York, was escorted into the legislative chambers by Dawson. Their offices were next to each other in the old House Office Building. The two Negro congressmen sat together during the preliminary organization of the House during which time Representative Sam Rayburn (Democratic of Texas) was re-elected Speaker.

It had been rumored that Powell would be seated next to Representative John Rankin (D), the Mississippi "Nigger" hater. The clash between the Union and the Confederate failed to materialize because during the first session Rankin occupied five different seats. No one was assigned to any particular seat, and Powell by choice was seated on the Democratic side of the House although he was elected on a coalition ticket composed of Democrats, Republicans and the American Labor Party.

The bright sun that glistened on the heads of Congressman William L. Dawson and Congressman Adam Clayton Powell Jr. was clouded by the stark reality that American blacks were still denied at home that brand of democracy that they had bought with their lives and blood on the battle fields of Africa, Europe and the Pacific. The facts of racism in America were echoed and re-echoed in all quarters from federal offices to the streets, and from civilians to servicemen of every station. Blacks seriously questioned whether things would be better.

April 12, 1945 is a day that I shall never forget. I was standing in the post exchange at Aberdeen Proving Ground, Maryland when President Roosevelt's death was announced over the radio. All the soldiers standing in the PX at that time reacted to what they had just heard the same as if someone in their immediate family had just passed. Roosevelt had indeed been considered by most to be the savior of black folk. The death of President Franklin Delano Roosevelt was indeed an irreparable loss to the Negro race. On street corners, in the barber shops, in markets—in all places that working men frequented—the effect was the same. Everyone felt that "The greatest man is dead."

War workers recalled the federal aid Roosevelt had extended them in the days of peace. They remembered the WPA, NYA, PWA and many other government programs that had helped take away the bitter taste and stain that was left by the nation's worst depression. The servicemen had their own thoughts. Todd Barrett, private first class declared, "I regret his death very much. I only hope the man who takes his place will follow the same policies."

Staff Sargent Leo Parker lamented, "He was America's greatest President.

Sgt. Dempsey J. Travis, Post Exchange Manager, third from left, in 1945 Army picture taken at Aberdeen Proving Grounds, Maryland.

Roosevelt died serving his people as surely as any soldier on the battlefield."

Private Mason E. Howard uttered, "I'm too hurt to talk about it; the news has gotten to me."

And these comments were made by others. Private Edward Mosely, "We lost a friend and leader; he's done so much for us."

Master Sargent Robert Hammon: "He did more good than any man that ever lived—surely he's the greatest president in the history of the United States."

Private Marion Bridges: "We lost a real friend, and I am seriously concerned about Harry Truman's ability to succeed Franklin Delano Roosevelt in the White House."

Two days after Roosevelt's death, I travelled to Washington from Aberdeen, Maryland to visit some relatives. The Washington D.C. Union Train Station was jammed with dignitaries of all types awaiting the 10:30 A.M. arrival of the Roosevelt Funeral Train. Black and white folk stood integrated in the "Jim Crow" District of Columbia—on both sides of the streets, sidewalk deep, from the Union Train Station to the Capitol at 1600 Pennsylvania Avenue. Many of the spectators wept openly. The hot and humid Potomac weather made waiting for the funeral procession onerous. It was heart breaking to stand there among a throng of blacks and whites who had become unified in tears over a fallen leader. The vibrations of my heartbeat seemed louder than the clop, clop from the hoofs of the six white horses pulling the caisson carrying President Roosevelt's flag covered coffin. The mourns from the crowd as the coffin passed were subdued by the drone of planes overhead and the humming from the motors of the slow-moving black limousines.

The war moved swiftly after Roosevelt's death. Within twenty-five days, the German government surrendered unconditionally at General Eisenhower's headquarters on May 7, 1945. That day was declared VE Day (Victory in Europe).

W. E. B. Dubois, director of the Department of Special Research of the National Association For the Advancement of Colored People, reacted to VE Day:

> Germans for 12 years have followed their ideas of race superiority, the right of might and a use of lives. We have conquered Germany but not their ideas. We still believe in white supremacy, keeping Negroes in their places and lying about democracy when we mean imperial control of 750 human colonies.

Congressman William L. Dawson reflected on VE Day:

> Victory in Europe has been won with the lives and blood of all races, creeds and colors of men. And in unifying effort, they have given their utmost in an endeavor to rid the world of the cancerous doctrine of racial superiority espoused by Hitler, and the cause has been great, and for their sacrifices, we are indebted. It seems to mean, here in America, that ours will be a hollow victory, indeed, that is unworthy of their sacrifices unless we are willing to begin now to show all of our citizens, Negroes and whites, that justice, that freedom, and that economic and political equality we have sought to secure for the world. And that we join other peace-loving nations in building a world order based not only on the sovereign equality of all nations, but on the equality of all races in which all men can live in security.

The words of the leaders were reflective of what was going on in the cities around the nation and specifically in Chicago during the final weeks of World War II. The Morgan Park 111th Street branch of the Young Men's Christian Association in Chicago, Illinois discontinued in 1945 the recreational swimming classes for infantile paralysis students because one of the new students happened to be black. At Hines Veteran Hospital in Hines, Illinois, Charles G. Beck, administrator of the institution, revealed that the army hospital would continue to adhere to a segregation policy for returning soldiers. On the South Side of Chicago, Oscar C. Brown, president of the Chicago branch of NAACP made valiant efforts trying to get W. H. Johnson, superintendent of schools to open the Washburn Trade School to black returning veterans. The only

Left: (Left to right) Attorney Sylvester White; State Representative Paul "Shoebox" Powell, whispering into the ear of President Harry S. Truman; and State Representative Corneal Davis. Right: Congressman William L. Dawson and President Harry S. Truman.

response to Brown's demand was the echo of his own voice. At the same time, the National Postal Alliance in Chicago attempted to get Postmaster Ernest J. Kruetgen to discontinue the ever-present discrimination policy of not promoting black employees. The United States Army prepared to place 22 black medical doctors on an inactive status because the army refused to integrate the hospital staffs to handle the thousands of casualties that were returning from the fronts of Europe and the far east.

Less than 120 days after Roosevelt's death, President Harry S. Truman issued an ultimatum to the Japanese to surrender or face prompt and utter destruction. Truman waited a week, and on August 6, 1945, his promise of destruction fell out of the sky over the city of Hiroshima in the epoch-making form of an atomic bomb. The city was obliterated; 75 to 100,000 people were killed while thousands more were permanently injured.

On August 14th, Japan agreed to surrender as GIs from all over the world came marching home.

President Roosevelt was indeed a great man, but he left black America with a heavy racist cross to bear. Congressman William L. Dawson had a prescription for carrying the cross of racism. He always said: "Don't get mad, get smart, organize and win your right to walk in the political sun through the ballot box."

Above: Roosevelt College, 1945. Right: In November, 1945, founding President Edward J. Sparling assisted Mrs. Eleanor Roosevelt as she dedicated the college in the name of her late husband, Franklin Delano Roosevelt.

190

Chapter *XV*

A Post-World War II Political Trial

Five days after President Franklin Delano Roosevelt's death on April 17, 1945, Roosevelt College was founded and emerged in Chicago as an instant beacon for democracy in higher education. The college permitted blacks and other minorities to receive a college education without butting their heads against a WASP created student quota system. Roosevelt College, with a bundle of economic opportunities wrapped in a package called the Servicemen's Readjustment Act or the G.I. Bill of Rights, was a godsend for black war veterans returning home from the four corners of the world. In the absence of a Roosevelt College, ninety-nine percent of the black servicemen returning to Chicago would not have had an opportunity to study for university degrees. Although their servicemen's benefits paid for their education in a heterogeneous student body, the prevailing admission policies of most colleges and universities set quotas for blacks that limited their presence to less than one half of one percent of the total academic population. The Servicemen's Bill was an opportunity of a lifetime for black vets because it provided living allowances, tuition fees, and money for books and supplies. Hence, Roosevelt College's open door approach to higher education was indeed good news to returning black veterans.

The Roosevelt College story was so unique in America that Nancy Washington, a student at the new institution and the wife of First Sergeant Harold Washington (current mayor of Chicago), was inspired to write Harold who was stationed on the Island of Guam in the South Pacific about the good news. She told him about all the glorious educational opportunities at this citadel for higher learning, which was located in downtown Chicago at 231 South Wells Street.

On January 20, 1946, First Sergeant Harold Washington was discharged from the United States Army Air Force and returned to Chicago. His first observations, after returning home after years in the South Pacific were:

> After staying in the tropical climate of the South Pacific for a very long period, I forgot how cold and mean the hawk (wind) could be in Chicago in January. To my surprise, when I arrived home, I couldn't find any clothes. I walked around for several months wearing both G.I. and civilian garments

Above: Staff Sergeant Harold Washington shortly before being promoted to first sergeant. *Below:* Harold Laskey, of the London School of Economics and visiting professor at Roosevelt University during the spring of 1948, with a group of student leaders (from left): Louis Roundtree, Torch reporter; Harold Washington, chairman of the Student Fund Drive; Irving Horwitz, editor of the Torch; Ray Clevenger, president of the Student Council.

Above: Roosevelt University Student Council meeting. Seated left to right: Frank London Brown; Ray Clevenger; unknown; Harold Washington.

Above: Harold Washington addressing a student *"Thank You"* assembly at Roosevelt University. Seated (left to right): Wayne R. Lyes, dean of The School of Arts and Sciences; President Edward J. Sparling; Marshall Field, a member of the university's Advisory Board; Harold L. Ickes, chairman of the Board of Trustees.

because I couldn't find a suit, that is, one within my price range. After an extensive search, I was able to find some trousers and later a sports coat, never two things in the same store. For reasons that I could not understand, I didn't have any trouble finding an overcoat in my size at the Rothchilds' Clothing Store on South State Street.

Had I known that I was going to have such a difficult time finding clothes, I would have brought a duffel bag full of G.I. garments home with me and used them until I could make an adjustment from army life to civilian life. The army actually allowed a soldier 30 days after discharge to get out of uniform. However, I hated the army with such a passion that I left everything that it ever gave me except the clothes I had on my back and toilet articles such as tooth paste, a brush and a comb.

I had no problems at all getting my old job back in the Bond Department at the U.S. Treasury which was located in Joseph Patrick Kennedy's Merchandise Mart Building. The Treasury Department was only a short hike from 231 South Wells Street where Roosevelt College was located. I decided that I would see what it was like. After I got there and looked around, I said, "Hell, this place is as good as any." Although the structural facilities were a far cry from those at Northwestern University, the democratic climate and spirit of the school's faculty and student body were unlike any other college or university within the confines of the forty eight states.

Marian Despres, wife of former Alderman Leon Despres, remembers Harold Washington when he enrolled in February, 1946 as a freshman student in her introductory psychology class at Roosevelt College. Mrs. Despres describes Harold Washington's early years as a college student:

> I remember Harold, and yet I don't remember very many students, but he had a presence. As a teacher, you notice somebody who would talk up in class; but at the same time, he never talked too much. Yet, he always made a great deal of sense to me.

Harold Washington remembers Marian Despres' psychology class primarily because it was overcrowded with at least fifty students enrolled, most of them mature veterans with a "no-nonsense" attitude. One afternoon after class, Harold recalls Mrs. Marian Despres approached him and declared:

> The Student Council is looking for members, and I would like for you to represent our class. I feel that you would make an excellent spokesman in that you would be able to articulate the sentiments of the other members of the class.

Washington's initial reaction to Mrs. Despres' suggestion was negative because he was holding down a full-time job at the Treasury Department and carrying a sixteen-hour class load. Mrs. Despres' suggestion prevailed. Harold was elected to the Student Council. Harold recalls his initial contact with college activities:

> The bottom line was that with Mrs. Despres' support, I was elected to the Student Council with almost one hundred percent of my classmates' votes, and that marked my initial involvement in student government. From the council, one thing lead to another which involved me in more student activities. There was no resistance to it. It was the kind of stuff that I was concerned about. In the army, I was always running lectures on the government. I was the education officer, in effect, if not in name, because the commissioned education officer was a southern white gentleman who could hardly read. Therefore, he turned the classes over to me, and I did a lot of teaching. I wrote the battalion's newspaper. I drafted the battalion's history. I was just involved in a lot of that kind of stuff. So the Student Council was sort of an extension. I don't recall any metamorphosis or awakening as a result of sitting on that student body.
>
> However, I must confess that the Student Council was my first sustained on-going relationship with a large segment of white folk. Like most black kids on the South Side, my relationship with whites was spasmodic involving contact with the grocery man, the butcher, the streetcar conductor, the bus driver and on the job. And then, of course, after being inducted into a segregated army, my relationship with whites was limited to white officers, non-commissioned officers and an occasional contact at the Army Post Exchange or in the Post Theatre.
>
> As a young kid, my only contact with whites was either to play ball with them or fight them in what we used to call gang fights. I had a cosmopolitan attitude although I went through the same kind of "Jim Crow" nonsense that most black people experienced in Chicago. I lived in an incubator. The South Side was my world. I would get my bicycle and ride all over the entire South Side and not come in personal contact with a single white person. Therefore, I really never had any meaningful relationship with whites until I attended Roosevelt University.

Mayor Edward J. Kelly was not unmindful of the absence of a meaningful relationship between blacks and whites. Segregation in the post World War II years hovered over the Chicago Public Schools and the housing market like a vulture circling over a dying animal. Following school walkouts by white students in protest over integration at Englewood, Morgan Park, and Calumet High schools, Mayor Kelly issued a statement condemning their actions and guaranteeing blacks access to all public schools. He ordered the Chicago Police Department to break up demonstrations, arrest white strikers, and to escort black students to school.

Mayor Kelly's pro-integration activities in public school matters fell like a red Chicago brick on the heads of some white folk, and they resented them. They were also mad about the stand he took on a proposed integrated housing complex in Morgan Park when he maintained that: "as long as I'm mayor, any person will be allowed to live where he wants to and can afford to live."

White resentment against Mayor Edward J. Kelly's pro-black attitude and his civil rights posture was reflected in the results of the November 5, 1946 election returns when the Democrats took a severe beating and lost many of their Cook County offices. Republican leaders like Governor Dwight Green and Robert R. McCormick, editor and publisher of the *Chicago Tribune,* interpreted the November election returns to mean that the Democratic machine had been cracked and was now ready to be smashed. They felt so certain about the possibilities of winning the next mayoral election that before the official vote count had been acclaimed, they announced that an obscure politician, Russell W. Root, was their next mayoral candidate for the 1947 election.

Jacob M. Arvey, chairman of the Cook County Democratic Committee, reacted to the Republican strategy by taking steps to replace Kelly as the Democratic mayoral candidate. In fact, Arvey met with Kelly and told him:

> Ed, if you run, you might win, but it would only be by a slight margin. The stand you took on open housing in Morgan Park hurt you. The Irish, Poles, and Bohemians resent the position you took when you said, "As long as I'm mayor, any person will be allowed to live where he wants to and can afford to live." Therefore, Ed, I am concluding that you have been hurt by something that you believe in, and something I believe you are right in. However, our straw poll indicates that your chances of winning are slim. Ed, for the good of the party, we are suggesting that you step down.

Mayor Kelly did not believe that his popularity had plummeted so deeply as a result of his pro-civil rights activities. However, when it was shown that the poll was taken by Spike Hennessey, his very closest friend and speech writer, Kelly had a change of heart and agreed not to run for re-election.

On the morning of December 19, 1946, the Democratic Central Committee met in its headquarters at the Morrison Hotel for a slate making session of the mayoral and aldermanic candidates for the 1947 election. Jacob M. Arvey, chairman of the Cook County Democratic Central Committee, told the assembled group of committeemen that his selection to replace retired Edward J. Kelly was Martin H. Kennelly, a multi-millionaire and president of Allied Vans and Warner Brothers-Kennelly Company, a warehouse organization.

The selection of Kennelly, a civic-minded do-gooder, confounded most political pundits along with the press because Kennelly had been director of

Governor Dwight Green.

Left to right: Martin H. Kennelly, a multimillionaire and president of Allied Van Lines and Warner-Brothers Kennelly Company; President Harry S. Truman; unknown; Jacob M. Avery, chairman of the Cook County Democratic Central Committee.

Attorney Roy Lee Washington, father of Mayor Harold Washington.

Rev. Archibald Carey, Jr.

Al Benson, a popular disc jockey, collecting a political contribution for the Roy Lee Washington aldermanic campaign from Dinah Washington, a national pop and blues singer.

the Chicago Crime Commission and a long time active enemy of the Kelly administration, which Kennelly considered totally corrupt. Therefore, it appears that Arvey, on his own, selected Kennelly because Arvey saw Kennelly as a winner because of his unquestionable triple "A" credentials; Kennelly was an independent who was politically clean and free of scandal.

On the South Side, in the Third Ward, there were eight candidates: Roy L. Washington (father of Harold Washington), Rev. Archibald J. Carey, Jr., Oscar DePriest, Edgar G. Brown, C. Udell Turpin, Rev. B. H. January, Clinton A. Brown and Homer Lewis, vying for the aldermanic position. Roy L. Washington had asked Third Ward Committeeman Mike Sneed to support him for the aldermanic slot. Sneed, a hard-headed, tough and rough South Sider with political savvy who deeply resented educated blacks, was intimidated. Roy Washington was well-educated and the only lawyer in the Third Ward Organization. He had paid his political dues through loyalty to the party and hard work as a precinct captain. Therefore, he felt he should have an opportunity to run for alderman.

Attorney Roy L. Washington's first choice was to be a municipal judge. Sneed supported Wendell Green over Washington for the post, which made Washington furious. In a final effort to get some recognition, Washington jockeyed around, and after a great deal of persuading and arm twisting, got 65 of the 90 precinct captains in the Third Ward to support him as candidate for alderman in the Third Ward.

In the February primary, Roy L. Washington polled 4,813 votes while Republican Rev. Archibald J. Carey, Jr. was close on his heels with 4,427. The incumbent, Oscar DePriest, who failed to gain regular G.O.P. backing, polled 3,609 while a protest vote of 2,331 went to Edgar G. Brown. Also C. Udell Turpin polled 1,066; Rev. B. H. January polled 513; Clinton A. Brown received 238 and Homer Lewis 113. Inasmuch as Roy Washington did not have the majority of votes, he was forced into a run-off election between himself and Archibald Carey Jr., the runner-up.

Harold Washington, the Roosevelt College political science student and his older brother, Roy Lee Washington, threw their efforts into the political campaign to help their father beat Rev. Archibald Carey, Jr., Al Benson, the popular radio disc jockey, joined them in their efforts and became Roy Washington's campaign manager. Harold and Roy Lee divided twelve precincts between them, knowing that the other precincts in the ward were Democratic strongholds. On April 1, 1947, Archibald Carey, Jr. beat Roy Washington in the general election. Carey received 13,960 votes while Washington got 11,978. An analysis of precincts' votes revealed that Roy Washington had been sold out by Sneed. Committeeman Sneed got some policy men to bankroll Archibald Carey, Jr.'s campaign, and they literally bought the election. Roy Washington knew he had been double-crossed, and he was fuming. Harold Washington describes his father's post-election day behavior:

> Although my old man was a minister, he started carrying a gun on his hip, and for a period of about three weeks, he looked for Sneed. I had never seen him that mad in my life. I remember asking my father, "Why are you walking around with that gun?" He knew he was not going to use it. Anyway, Sneed was out of town; I reminded my father that although he had spent $8,000.00 on the campaign that if he shot Sneed, it would take more than that to get him out of jail. My father replied, "I'm going to shoot him, Harold. I'm going to shoot him, Harold."
>
> Whenever my father called me "Harold," he was mad. When he wasn't mad, he called me "son." He repeated, "I'm going to shoot him, Harold." While Mike Sneed was still out of town, my old man cooled down. He went downtown and talked with old man Arvey and Mayor Kelly and told them that Mike Sneed had ripped him off. When Sneed came back to town, several things happened. Jacob Arvey took the Third Ward committeemanship away from Sneed. However, Arvey let Sneed keep his seat as a Cook County commissioner. They made Sneed give my father the $8,000.00 back that he spent on the campaign, and they fired about 15 precinct captains, temporarily. They then put C. C. Wimbush in as the Third Ward committeeman in early 1948. There was no election necessary; they simply shifted the patronage from Sneed to Wimbush. Sneed was through as a power broker in the Third Ward.

Christopher C. Wimbush became Third Ward committeeman with the stamp of approval and blessings of Congressman William L. Dawson. Wimbush was a Dawson protégé and former president of Dawson's Second Ward Organization. With Wimbush as the Third Ward committeeman, Dawson was able to invade and control the patronage activities of the Third Ward Organization. Dawson's political troops invaded the adjacent Twentieth Ward, and in the same year made Colonel Kenneth E. Campbell the committeeman.

In 1952, when Committeeman C. C. Wimbush got out of line, he was replaced by Ralph Metcalfe. Again, as had been the pattern in the Third Ward, the downtown bosses simply shifted the patronage to Metcalfe. In 1956, the Dawson machine rolled into the Fourth Ward and placed Claude W. B. Holman in the committeeman's chair, and in 1965, the Dawson troops marched into the Sixth Ward and made Robert H. Miller, a prominent mortician, committeeman in the Grand Crossing section.

Congressman William L. Dawson's organizational genius was recognized and respected by members of the old guard such as Mayor Edward J. Kelly

Left: Congressman William L. Dawson welcoming Ralph H. Metcalfe into the fold to replace C. C. Wimbush as committeeman of the Third Ward. Right: Third Ward Committeeman Christopher C. Wimbush.

and Jacob M. Arvey. However, Martin H. Kennelly chose to treat Dawson as if he were the corrupt boss of a political submachine. Dawson did not take kindly to Kennelly's behavior. Dawson was also displeased with Kennelly's lack of sensitivity on the black housing issue. While Mayor Kelly had shown a modicum of concern about the Negro housing difficulties, Kennelly showed total indifference. Kennelly was silent on the riot against black war veterans who moved into the airport homes, a public housing project on south Cicero Avenue. When the Trumbull Park riot occurred in the Fernwood area, Kennelly made no public statement. Mayor Kennelly was exasperated with his housing authority for what he called "its intransigent and unreasonable stand for integrated housing." As a matter of fact, Kennelly told Ms. Elizabeth Woods, executive secretary of the Chicago Housing Authority that, "he could see no sense in calling out a thousand policemen at a fantastic cost per day, just to protect eight Negro families." He further asked her, "If these people couldn't be taken care of in some other fashion?" Kennelly's housing sympathies were unquestionably on the side of the signatories of the housing restricted covenants.

In Dawson's opinion, the covenant's signers were directly responsible for the burning deaths of ten Negroes in a human furnace at 942 West Ohio Street. Negroes were forced to live in firetraps because they were hemmed in by written and unwritten laws that took the form of restricted covenants.

Kennelly stepped on Dawson's corns with both feet shortly after Kennelly was elected in 1947 because he sent white policemen from downtown into Dawson's districts. The white cops brutalized policy runners and arrested policy operators. The policy runners and operators, who were being arrested

Whites overturn a car belonging to a black resident of the airport homes.

Mr. & Mrs. Donald L. Howard, the first black family to move into the Trumbull Park Housing Project.

in the Second and Third Wards, were precinct captains of Dawson's organization. Hence, Kennelly's action disrupted Dawson's cash flow and also his political organization because the policy operators were large financial contributors to the Dawson submachine.

After several months of continuous harassment by Kennelly's downtown "goon" squad, Dawson had State Representative Corneal Davis drive him downtown to City Hall to discuss the problem with Mayor Martin H. Kennelly. Congressman Dawson attempted to explain to Kennelly that policy was a nickel and dime game played by black folk and that it was a form of recreation to blacks the same as bingo was to Catholics. Dawson further pointed out that since blacks could not afford to take trips to Washington Park or to the Hawthorne Race Track, they resorted to policy as a diversion. According to Corneal Davis, Kennelly treated Dawson with a great deal of contempt. Moreover, Kennelly refused to call off the police raids. Representative Corneal Davis became very angry when Kennelly told Dawson, "I'd rather you'd not come to my office."

Dawson replied, "Alright, I won't be back Mr. Mayor, but you can mind my word when I come back you will not be the mayor."

From late 1947 until December 1950, Dawson did not speak with Kennelly again. He had internalized his antagonism against the mayor, that is, until Joe Gill, the chairman of the Democratic Committee called a meeting at the Mor-

Martin H. Kennelly being sworn into office by Mayor Edward J. Kelly.

Clerk of Cook County Richard J. Daley and John Mortimer present Certificate of Election to Martin H. Kennelly.

Richard J. Daley and James Mean present Martin H. Kennelly with a birthday cake.

rison Hotel and announced that Kennelly was available again and wanted to be elected. State Representative Corneal Davis drove Fred Walls, Dawson's right hand man, down to the Morrison Hotel and waited for him outside the caucus room as Joe Gill went through a political ritual of expousing the virtues of Kennelly and the desirability of having him to run as a candidate again. As is the custom when Gill called for a vote, he started with the First Ward.

And the First Ward voted yea in support of Kennelly's candidacy. When Gill called on the representative of the Second Ward, Fred Wall, secretary of the Dawson organization, lifted his two hundred and sixty pound body from his chair and in a slow and deliberate fashion said, "Mr. Chairman, the candidate is not acceptable to Congressman Dawson."

The fifteen man slating committee reacted to Wall's statement in total disbelief. The atmosphere in the smoke-filled room was in such a state of bedlam that Joe Gill had to adjourn the meeting. Joe Gill, upon gaining his composure rushed to the phone to call Dawson at his office in Washington, D. C. where Dawson confirmed that he did not want Kennelly. Gill and Arvey interchangeably pleaded with Dawson to return to Chicago and attempt to iron out his differences with Kennelly.

Dawson, out of respect for both Arvey and Gill, consented to meet with Kennelly. The meeting took place in a private conference room in the Morrison Hotel. When Dawson entered the meeting, he found Kennelly sitting at a long highly polished conference table, flanked on both sides by party leaders. Neither Dawson nor Kennelly exchanged greetings. Dawson was offered a seat by Joe Gill, but he stated that he preferred to stand. The congressman then began to pace the carpeted floor with a limp caused by his wooden leg. He walked up and down the room heaping verbal blisters at Kennelly as Kennelly sat there white haired, silent, stone-faced and crimson. At one point, Dawson stopped walking long enough to point his finger directly at Kennelly's beet red nose and bellowed:

> Who do you think you are? My people had the votes to put you in office, and you tell me that I am not welcome in the mayor's office to discuss my people's problems. Black votes put you in office, and yet you treat us as if we were lepers. We don't need you. You need us.

After Dawson had completely humiliated Kennelly, Albert J. Horan, former municipal court bailiff, grabbed Dawson by the arm and took him to the side murmuring: "Okay you kicked his ass good. But we don't have another candidate." Dawson knew there was no other candidate on the horizon. Hence, he reluctantly agreed to support Kennelly for only one more term. Kennelly did not have the slightest notion that that meeting with Dawson was his political last supper.

Kennelly's days in office were numbered, and Dawson counted each day with the intensity of a prisoner serving time. Dawson considered Kennelly a Gold Coast Republican sitting in a Democratic chair. There was some evidence to support Dawson's contentions. When Kennelly was elected in 1947, he received fifty-seven percent of the votes. However, when he was re-elected in 1951, he only received fifty-four percent of the vote. Kennelly's margin of victory came from the black wards headed by Congressman Dawson, the Irish wards headed by Al Horan and the Jewish west side block led by Jacob M. Arvey.

Dawson felt that Mayor Martin H. Kennelly had turned back the civil rights clock for Negro people through his silence on the subject. The acts accomplished through his silence, paralleled those of any southern white supremacist. Two weeks after Kennelly was re-elected, Congressman Dawson was back in Washington fighting a southern inspired Winstead Amendment which would have allowed white selective service inductees to request assignments in racially segregated units. The Winstead Amendment was an attempt to negate President Truman's Equality of Treatment and Opportunity Report in the armed services which had been adopted by the army in 1949.

House Democrats with the aid of a group of Republicans made a strong bid to retain the pro-segregation provision of the Winstead Amendment. The segregationist were defeated by a vote of 226 to 178. It was Dawson's forceful speech on the House floor against the Winstead Bill that turned the tide. Dawson captured the ears and minds of the House of Representatives when he asked: "How long, how long my conferees and gentlemen from the South, will you divide us Americans on account of color?"

Again the Georgia born Congressman from Chicago inquired:

Why will this body go on record to brand this section of citizens' second class?

God didn't curse me when he made me black any more than he cursed you when he made you white. Give the test that would apply to make anyone a full-fledged American by the living God. If it means death itself, I will pay it, but give it to me.

Dawson looked up from the well of the chamber and pleaded to his fellow congressmen:

You see this mark on my forehead. It is the result of German mustard gas. I served in a segregated outfit as a citizen trying to save this country. I would give up this life of mine to preserve this country and every American in it, white or black.

Deny to me if you will all that American citizenship stands for, and I will still fight for you, hoping that under the Constitution of the United States all of these restrictions will be removed, and that we will move forward as one people, American people, joined in a democracy toward all the world.

I say to you, who claim to love America in this hour of its stress, that the greatest argument that the Soviet Union is using among the Black people of the world to turn them against us is your treatment of me, an American citizen.

I believe that the South is big enough for all of us to live in peace and happiness.

Peace is what Congressman William L. Dawson did not find in Martin H. Kennelly. Thus, Dawson undertook a one man crusade to find a politician to replace Kennelly. State Representative Corneal Davis explains:

That from time to time Dawson would ask him and State Senator C. C. Wimbush about various men serving in the legislature in Springfield. He once asked about this man, Richard J. Daley. He would say, "You guys should know him. You're down there with him."

I told him that Daley was a good man and a person that was nice to work with.

Dawson seemed to have chosen Clarence P. Wagner, alderman of the Fourteenth Ward. Dawson had known Wagner from the days when they both served in the city council. However, Wagner was killed in an automobile accident on July 10, 1953 near International Falls, Minnesota. His death possibly changed the course of political history in the city of Chicago because on July 21, 1953 Clerk of Cook County, Richard J. Daley, was elected chairman of the Cook County Democratic Committee in a very routine ceremony. Had Wagner lived Daley's ascent to chairman might have been blocked by the John Duffy, Judge James McDermott and Dawson's forces. Clarence P. Wagner had prevented Daley's nomination on July 8, 1953, two days before Wagner was killed. The John Duffy plan was to elect Judge McDermott as chairman of the Cook County Democratic Committee. Since McDermott could not be both a judge and a chairman, Clarence Wagner had agreed to step down from this post as committeeman of the Fourteenth Ward, and McDermott was to replace him. Thus, McDermott could have become chairman of the Cook County Democratic Committee while Alderman Wagner would have been in a position to become the 1955 Democratic mayoral nominee. Death intervened in Daley's favor, the same as it had in the past. The winds were blowing at Richard J. Daley's back because he was always standing with the proper wingspread and a prepared script ready to alight on center stage.

Historically, a fatality always seemed to have overtaken those who got in

Left to right: President Harry S. Truman; John H. Sengstacke, editor and publisher of the Chicago Defender; *and Clerk of Cook County Richard J. Daley wave to the crowd during the Bud Billiken Parade. Truman was the first U.S. President to ride in the Bud Billiken Parade.*

Senator Richard J. Daley. Congressman William L. Dawson frequently asked State Representative Corneal Davis and Senator Christopher Wimbush about Daley's record on the color question when Daley was serving in the Senate.

Daley's way. In 1936, David Shanahan, a Republican member of the Illinois House of Representatives died. Later, Daley ran as a write-in candidate for his seat and won with eighty-five hundred write-in votes. In 1938, Senator Patrick J. Carroll died, and again Daley filled the breach as Mayor Ed Kelly's man in Springfield. He stepped up from the state house to the state senate. In 1950, Michael J. Flynn, clerk of Cook County died. Once more the luck of the Irish kissed Daley because the wind under his wings permitted him to land in the shoes of Michael J. Flynn. The only time in Daley's political history when the wind was not at his back was in 1946. He ran for sheriff and lost to Elmer Michael Walsh, a Republican.

As clerk of Cook County, Richard J. Daley became an important person in the political machine. In addition to prestige, he gained control of a substantial amount of patronage and a top salary. Daley had started building prestige among black politicians in Springfield during the early 1940's when he was minority leader in the state senate. Daley assisted both Senator Christopher C. Wimbush and State Representative Corneal Davis with the preparation of their bills when they first came down to Springfield in 1942. As a matter of fact, Corneal Davis states that Daley expressed sympathy with them because of their inability to get decent housing in Springfield. Daley also voted for pro-civil rights legislations in the senate. However, none of the bills ever passed because the Democrats in the senate were in the minority. The mere gesture of appearing to be in favor of civil rights legislation was enough to endear Daley in the minds of both Wimbush and Davis. As a matter of fact, it was Senator Wimbush who was always singing Daley's high praises to Congressman William L. Dawson. After Daley became clerk of Cook County, he frequently stopped by Dawson's office at Thirty-fifth and Calumet while enroute to his home in Bridgeport and visited for periods of as long as an hour. Former State Representative Lewis A. H. Caldwell was present on a number of occasions when Daley paid visits to the congressman. Although hatreds of blacks was indigenous to Daley's Bridgeport community, Daley found it politically expedient to fraternize with such blacks as Congressman William Levi Dawson and Senator C. C. Wimbush.

Black faces were not a strange sight to Richard J. Daley. He had attended school at DeLaSalle where he studied bookkeeping. The Catholic high school was located on the northeast corner of Thirty-fifth and Wabash in the heart of the Black Belt. Daley saw thousands of black faces enroute to and from school on a daily basis between 1916 and 1919. During that period, Thirty-fifth Street was considered the Mecca of black capitalism and social life. In late July, 1919, one month after Daley had been graduated from DeLaSalle, the worst race riot in the history of the city broke out. Young Daley was the president of the Hamburg Club which had some members who were believed to have been in the front lines of violence during the riot. Daley was only seventeen at the time. There is no evidence to show that he was personally involved in the violence of that red hot summer. Since Daley was a member and the president of the Hamburg Club, it is believed that he certainly must have been on the fringes of the crowd. Daley's 1919 race riot sentiments could have very well been reflected in his shoot to kill order during the 1968 Martin Luther King, Jr. riot. However, private sentiments never got in the way of his political astuteness. Daley was an excellent bookkeeper who knew how to count black votes.

While Kennelly was politicizing and burying blacks beside the Rock Island Railroad tracks at the Robert Taylor Homes in the early 1950's, Daley was stroking Congressman Dawson for his support. Daley knew that Dawson would make the difference in the 1955 mayoral election. He remembered vividly the role Dawson played in delivering the Negro vote for Truman, the vote that enabled President Harry S. Truman to carry Illinois in his race against Thomas E. Dewey in 1948.

Mayor Kennelly was oblivious to Richard J. Daley's game plan. Therefore, he blindly pursued a third term as mayor of Chicago, Kennelly in his naivete' attempted to pacify Dawson's followers by having a publicity photo taken with trumpet star, Louis Armstrong. The following week, Kennelly was scheduled to have a photo taken with the all-American football great, Jim Thorpe, the American Indian's red hope. Shortly before Thorpe arrived, Kennelly turned to his press secretary and queried: "He's not another one of those colored fellows, is he?"

Kennelly was so desperate in his effort to salvage a third term that he directed the Chicago Housing Authority to hire John M. Daley, Richard J. Daley's second cousin. The housing authority's commissioners acquiesced to Kennelly's wishes. Kennelly's order to hire Daley was in direct conflict with his own civil service policies which had reduced the amount of patronage jobs available to the ward bosses by 12,000. Elizabeth Woods, executive secretary of CHA, publicly protested the political nature of the proposed appointment and noted that the candidate had but five years of legal experience (CHA regulations demanded at least eight), and that he ranked 183rd in a class of 191 at his law school. John M. Daley withdrew his name from consideration, but the political stench of Kennelly's act lingered on.

Kennelly's move to satisfy the ward bosses was too little and too late. The die had already been cast because he had irritated the ward bosses by abolishing some 1,000 "no collar" city jobs, soft jobs and fat money the kind that precinct captains hunger for. He later added insult to injury by insisting that civil service promotions be based on merit and not clout. Moreover, he eliminated patronage from city purchases.

Congressman William L. Dawson, the boss of bosses had given Kennelly the political kiss of death when Dawson had not consented to support him in the 1951 mayoral election. The heir apparent that the bosses had agreed on for the 1955 election was none other than Richard J. Daley, clerk of Cook County, a man who understood patronage and who was cut from the Edward J. Kelly mold.

In December, 1955, when Kennelly appeared before the slate making committee at the Morrison Hotel, he said that he had "always put public service ahead of politics, and that he intended to continue to do so." When Kennelly concluded his statement before the committee, there was utter silence in the room for perhaps sixty seconds or more until Kennelly broke the still and continued: "I presume gentlemen it's unanimous?"

Congressman Dawson recoiled: "It's unanimous."

Dawson didn't have to elaborate to Kennelly because Kennelly knew exactly what he meant. The word was out: Dawson wouldn't stand for Kennelly. Kennelly wore a very sad smile when he came out of the committee room and went back to his fifth floor office in City Hall. Kennelly should not have been surprised by the cold shoulder he received at the slating session because nobody had asked him to run.

Less than an hour had passed, and the fragrance of Kennelly's cologne had not cleared the room on that cold December 15, 1954 afternoon when Richard J. Daley appeared in front of the same committee that had just crushed Kennelly. When Daley came out of the committee room, the reporters ran up to him and asked: "Are you candidate for mayor?"

Daley replied innocently: "That's up to the committee."

December, 1954 was a month full of politics and games because on the sixteenth, Alderman Robert E. Merriam, a registered Democrat, opened his headquarters to seek the Republican nomination as a mayoral candidate. The Republican committeemen were delighted to embrace Merriam, the Hyde Park intellectual, because he was the best and brightest candidate on the scene. Republican county chairman, Ed Moore, was solidly behind Merriam while Governor William G. Stratton had given his tacit approval. Two days later on the eighteenth, Kennelly announced that Frank Keenan, cook county assessor, would manage the "Great Chicago Committee for the Re-election of Mayor Kennelly." Kennelly had decided to run with or without the regular organization's blessings. However, on December 20th, "Santa Clause" O'Hare kissed Richard J. Daley, a soft spoken ruddy-faced Irishman of 52, the father of seven children, a veteran of 30 years of Chicago's political wars, and the clerk of Cook County. Forty-nine of the fifty ward committeemen had agreed that Daley would be their candidate for mayor of Chicago. Kennelly received only one vote, and that was from Keenan, his campaign manager.

Kennelly entered the 1955 primary campaign blasting "The Morrison Hotel Gang" generally and Congressman Dawson specifically. In a speech delivered on Sunday, January 30, 1955, Kennelly attacked Dawson:

> The congressman is a political boss. I am not a boss. I refuse to be subservient to bossism.
>
> I can understand why Dawson passed the word that he couldn't stand for Kennelly. I haven't been interested in building up his power. Without power to dispense privilege, protection and patronage to preferred people, bossism has no stock in trade.
>
> During the last eight years while I have been mayor, the inventory in those commodities has been very greatly reduced in Chicago.

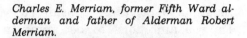

Charles E. Merriam, former Fifth Ward alderman and father of Alderman Robert Merriam.

Governor William G. Stratton 1953–1957.

On Monday, January 31, Adlai Stevenson, former Governor of Illinois, endorsed Richard J. Daley with the following statement:

> Aside from my personal respect and friendship for him, I think that Dick Daley's contribution as a political leader and public official commends him highly to the confidence of the voters of Chicago.
>
> I think the people of Chicago are fortunate to be able to choose from three men such as Mayor Kennelly, Benjamin Adamowski, and Richard J. Daley. All are good men competing for the Democratic nomination.
>
> Richard J. Daley was my director of revenue part of the time I was governor, and he has served the people faithfully and well in public office.

Governor Adlai Stevenson's enthusiastic endorsement of Richard J. Daley was important because the political waters in Chicago were muddled. Alderman Bob Merriam, the GOP candidate, was a Stevenson Democrat and former speech writer for the governor. Also, Merriam's father, Charles E. Merriam, who had been elected to the city council shortly after the turn of the century and served several terms, was also a professor of political science at the University of Chicago. The elder Merriam enjoyed a national reputation for political integrity. He also was an advisor to President Roosevelt. Stevenson must have privately considered Merriam a more formidable obstacle to Daley's ambitions to becoming mayor than he thought Kennelly to be. However, Kennelly's chief supporter was the *Chicago Tribune*, the spear carrier for the Republican party in Chicago. The thirty-six year old energetic Bob Merriam, without the support of the world's greatest newspaper, had a very good chance of becoming the first GOP mayor of Chicago since the defeat of William Hale Thompson in 1931. The leaders of both parties believed that if only 1.2 million Chicagoans voted, Daley would win. But they predicted that if Robert Merriam could bring out the independent and "protest" vote in the general election, he could beat Daley.

The political wires in the Black Belt were as crossed as they were in the white community. Governor William Stratton and Senator Everett Dirksen, both Republicans were playing a very small part openly in the primary campaign in predominantly Democratic Chicago. They didn't want to make Robert Merriam seem too Republican. On the other hand, influential Democratic leaders like Representative William L. Dawson stayed in the background because they didn't want to identify Daley too closely with the Democratic machine. The wires were indeed crossed.

Arthur B. Knight, a prominent South Side insurance broker, was joined by five black pro-Kennelly aldermanic candidates in a blast against Congressman Dawson. Knight charged Dawson with "deceiving Negroes and with inciting the political bosses to dump Kennelly."

Knight continued his charges:

> We will fight Dawson and his political machine to the finish. We predict that decent people of the South Side will join the good citizens of all parts of Chicago to secure an overwhelming victory for Mayor Kennelly and his running mates.

Joining Knight in the statement against Congressman William L. Dawson were these aldermanic hopefuls: Marshall Knox, Second Ward; Gordon W. Lawson, Third Ward; Julius Pryor, Fourth Ward; Chauncy Eskridge, Sixth Ward; and William S. Bridgeforth, Twentieth Ward.

Dawson was a black political power broker in Kennelly's opinion and had to be dethroned. The Kennelly forces were determined to accomplish that objective. Kennelly thought that he had found Dawson's achilles' heel in the policy racket.

A full investigation of a congressman accused of collecting policy racket graft was promised by the U.S. attorney, Robert Tieken. Tieken indicated on Friday, January 21, 1955 that Congressman Dawson's name had been mentioned to a January federal grand jury by Claude Murphy, a convicted and confessed graft collector, who told of gambling payoffs in an interview with news reporters after testifying before the grand jury for more than thirteen hours. Tieken said that "investigators were seeking solid evidence that the congressman named by Murphy got the money."

Government prosecutors were concentrating on an inquiry into whether income taxes were paid on policy graft. Murphy said that "the congressman received from ten to twelve thousand dollars a month." Murphy further asserted that the money bought protection in the Wabash Avenue, Prairie Avenue, Chicago Avenue and Hudson Avenue police districts. Although Murphy did not name names, he declared that "police captains rated ten thousand dollars a month; lieutenants split between forty-two hundred to five thousand dollars monthly; and sergeants split four thousand dollars monthly." He also maintained that "there were about forty policy wheels on the South Side that the mayor wouldn't let run the way they wanted them to and that all the policy workers were out trying to beat the mayor." Claude Murphy further stated that "the decision 'to get' the mayor was made in 1951 because Kennelly had successfully cut policy operations about fifty-five percent during his four year administration."

Irvin N. Cohen, chief council for the Chicago City Council Emergency "Big Nine" Crime Committee had many cell block interviews with Claude Murphy at Statesville Penitentiary. Alderman Benjamin M. Becker (40th) the "Big Nine" committee chairman claimed that the group had not been asleep on the policy investigation. If seventy-five percent of what Claude Murphy said was true, "It would blow the lid right off of this town."

When Murphy was questioned by Alderman Becker about the payoff system, Murphy repeated once more that a different amount was paid for each rank and that politicians got the largest amount as this excerpt shows:

Becker: "Who sets the price on it?"
Murphy: "I don't want to go into that now."

Becker: "Did the biggest amount go to the politicians?"
Murphy: "I think that would be right. That's where the power comes from. Doesn't it?"

Kennelly was still smarting because an alleged graft taking politician had had him dumped. The mayor's anger heightened when Richard Daley's wing of the Democratic organization circulated a pamphlet stating that Kennelly had not been reslated because of a civic protest. Kennelly responded to the allegation at the Fifth Ward meeting held on Thursday, January 20, 1955 by saying: "I wonder if the gamblers came before the committee too. And I wonder if some people came in who wanted to get their friends on the city payroll."

Kennelly further continued:

> I am not so sure the boys are telling the whole story. Maybe there are still some other reasons why it was done. And maybe the other reasons the boys in the Morrison Hotel understand and would not want to make public.

Six days earlier on January 14, 1955 the *Chicago Sun Times* headlines screamed:

GAMBLING RAIDERS HIT DAWSON'S BALIWICK AGAIN

> Eight are charged as patrons and four as operators of a policy game after a raid and arrest Thursday night at 4621 South Champlain Avenue. The raid was led by Detective Timothy Allman. Allman and his men reportedly took orders directly from Mayor Kennelly by the way of Police Commissioner O'Connor. Earlier in January, Allman and his men had raided three other gambling establishments in Dawson's district. Allman denies that the raids have any political implications.

"POLICY AND POLITICS"—was the title of this editorial that appeared in Saturday's, February 5, 1955 edition of the *Chicago Defender*.

> The tactics being used by Mayor Martin H. Kennelly to win the Democratic nomination for mayor are both dirty and dangerous. Moreover, the Kennelly forces and the daily newspapers have found Congressman Dawson "guilty" of many crimes without benefit of any court of law.

The editor also stated that Congressman Dawson had never been indicted nor convicted for any crime by a judicial body and added that:

> Kennelly's strategy is clearly designed to arouse the indignation of whites against a powerful Negro leader and influence them to vote their prejudices rather than their well-founded convictions.
>
> After eight years as mayor with the entire police force at his command, Kennelly has suddenly discovered the policy racket. His own police department would tell him that this racket is owned and operated by the same syndicate gangsters who have been assassinating citizens on Chicago's streets ever since the rise of Al Capone.

Congressman Dawson does not now nor ever has had the power to prevent Mayor Kennelly from wiping out policy. The basic issue is not policy. It is politics. The majority of Negro voters are the same as voters in other wards: hard working, law-abiding citizens who want a clean, decent city and who want, above all, to avoid racial bitterness.

A Hitler rose to power in Germany by accusing high-placed jews of treason and whipping up anti-Semitism. Race baiting in our country has won victories in such states as Georgia and Mississippi. By building up a powerful Negro congressman as a symbol of hatred, the Kennelly forces can exploit racial prejudices for all it is worth, while at the same time pretending to be crusading against corruption. This is a greater crime than any attributed to Dawson.

It is the responsibility of all decent citizens of both races to make certain that race baiting will produce no victories in Chicago.

Kennelly's response to the *Chicago Defender's* editorial was:

We're going to win. The ticket of Kennelly for mayor, Marian W. Isbell for city clerk and Morris B. Sachs for city treasurer will be swept to victory. We will win because the people of Chicago will not abdicate their rights of self-government to a click of cynical self-serving political machine bosses. The political bosses who gave the order to 'dump Kennelly' have underestimated the people. They think that the people won't care to vote. That's where they're wrong. The people will vote on February 22nd, come rain, snow or high water. They will ask for a Democrat ballot and mark them in the interest of the whole people. That's why we will win.

Kennelly had every reason to believe he was going to win the primary campaign against Richard J. Daley because every major Chicago newspaper was laced daily with stories exalting Kennelly's administration and the fact that it had been scandal free. Unfortunately for Kennelly, newspapers do not elect mayors. Electing mayors is an organizational function. Kennelly lost the election to Daley by 100,064 votes. The vote count showed: Daley, 364,839; Kennelly, 264,775; Adamowski, 112,072.

The saddest sight on election night was Morris B. Sachs, a man of small statue and a prominent State Street clothing merchant, and tall, patrician, white-haired Kennelly embracing each other as they wept over the election returns. They looked sadder than professional mourners at an Irish funeral.

As Kennelly and Sachs wept over the returns, the saloon keeper, Paddy Bauler, gloated: "Chicago ain't ready for reform yet!" Bauler who was a Democratic boss of the Forty-third Ward and a member of the Cook County Democratic Committee spoke for the whole organization:

The sad night that Martin H. Kennelly and Morris B. Sachs wept unashamedly because they had lost the election to Richard J. Daley.

The organization is working now like it did when Ed Kelly and Pat Nash ran it. The proof of the pudding is in the voting. This guy Kennelly took a lot of jobs away from us. Kennelly never learned one of the first rules of politics: you've got to help people before they'll help you. When you live with people, you have got to take care of them. I get the streets paved and new street lights and new ash cans, and I make sure everybody in my ward knows where these things come from. They may not like Paddy, but they like the service they get.

That's what comes from living with people. But Kennelly ain't lived with people. He picks a fancy apartment, an elevator to take him up away from the people, and when the elevator brings him down, his car is waiting.

But Richard Daley lives in a bungalow, walks to church, sees his neighbors, and understands people. Those seven kids of his don't hurt. I was the one that told him to get their pictures in his ads: I was one of thirteen kids, and I know they like a family man.

This election has revived the whole damn party. It's fired up the precinct captains like they ain't been in thirty years. My guys are going all out for Daley in the general election. They like a guy who takes care of them.

The *Chicago Defender* shared Paddy Bauler's opinion. It endorsed Richard J. Daley for mayor, Morris B. Sachs for city treasurer, and John C. Marcin for city clerk. On April 2, 1955, a *Defender* editorial entitled "ELECT MAYOR DALEY" stated:

Whether the Democrat party will continue to administer the affairs of Chicago for the next four years or whether the power of government will pass into the Republican hands will be decided Tuesday, April 5th when the next mayor, city clerk and city treasurer are elected.

It is the duty of every man and woman who aspires to first class citizenship to go to the polls and participate in that election. In our considered opinion, citizens who approach the ballot box guided by the undisputable facts of the record and with the best interest of Chicago at heart will vote for Richard J. Daley for mayor. Mr. Daley has been a good honest, able public servant. He has served without blemish for twenty years as state representative, state senator, state director of revenue, as deputy controller of Cook County, and as clerk of Cook County.

During all that time, there has been no hint of dishonesty or corruption regarding Mr. Daley. Even his opponents, no matter how they talk of dishonesty and corruption, have not committed the ultimate folly of a personal attack upon a man with Mr. Daley's record.

Mr. Daley is not a talker—a trait which has great value in campaigns. It is of dubious worth in the mayor's chair—he is doer.

Leaders from all walks of Chicago's life, including men and women who

On a happier day in March, 1955, the following men join hands in unity: (Left to right), Morris B. Sachs; Richard J. Daley; Adlai Stevenson; and Dr. Carl Meyers.

backed Martin J. Kennelly came out in full support of Richard J. Daley's campaign for mayor. The list was headed by Adlai E. Stevenson, the former governor of Illinois and 1952 candidate for president, Senator Paul Douglas and Congressman William L. Dawson, leader of one of the most powerful sections of the Democratic party of Chicago. Stevenson said of Daley "effectiveness and integrity are not big Daley's boast. They are his record. Daley has proven himself a friend of good government, a friend of Chicago, and a sincere and tender friend of Chicago's millions."

However, Robert E. Merriam, Daley's Republican opponent, charged that "if Daley is elected, it will be an open invitation for the hoodlums and gangsters to come running back from Florida and New Orleans. The choice for the Chicago voters is a choice between corruption and reform."

On Tuesday, April 5, 1955, the voters spoke. Daley defeated Merriam 708,222 to 581,255, a plurality of 126,967. Nine predominantly Negro wards accounted for 77% of Mayor-elect Richard J. Daley's 127,199 margin of victory. Five central South Side wards: the Second, Third, Fourth, Sixth and Twentieth accounted for a 49,363 edge. The Sixteenth Ward, Englewood, gave Daley a 5,840 margin. And three west side wards: the Twenty-fourth, Twenty-seventh and Twenty-eighth accounted for 42,473 of the bulge. The Negro section of the Forty-Second Ward on the near north side gave him, 5,644, which brought Daley's total to 103,320 in areas where there was a heavy black vote. If the black voters had voted for the ghost of Abraham Lincoln, as they had in the past, Robert E. Merriam would have been elected mayor of the city of Chicago.

4

THE
DALEY
YEARS

The warning.

Chapter *XVI*

Richard J. Daley: The Mayor

On Thursday November 12, 1970 at 11:00 A.M., Congressman William L. Dawson's body lay in state in a lustrous wooden casket before more than 2,000 mourners who had come to pay their last respect to a great statesman. The culturally diverse crowd filled every seat in Reverend Retha Brown's Progressive Baptist Church located at 3658 South Wentworth Avenue in Chicago, Illinois. Dawson's coffin was nestled between several hundred floral arrangements that were blanketed across the front of the pulpit in the huge tabernacle and stacked like soldiers along both the north and south walls of the auditorium. Political figures at the service included Lieutenant Governor Paul Simon, United States Senator-elect Adlai E. Stevenson III, United States Representative Daniel Rostenkowski (D, IL.), Representative-elect Ralph H. Metcalfe (D, IL.), Representative Charles Diggs (D, Mich.), John H. Sengstacke, publisher of the *Chicago Defender*, State Representative Corneal Davis, State's Attorney Edward V. Hanrahan, County Board President George W. Dunne, and Mayor Richard J. Daley. They all had come to say a special good-bye to a man who had played a substantial role in Daley's rise to the pinnacle of Chicago's politics. In a very moving and emotional eulogy for his friend, Daley said the following:

> Dawson was a great man. His greatness was embraced in people. He loved people.
>
> Look around here today. There are people from all walks of life and from all communities. He lived a productive life with programs for his people.
>
> He was a great man not as an artist or an architect is great, but as a man who leads his people.
>
> Congressman Dawson was a great man who fought long and hard for black people everywhere.

He was a strong leader and vital force for progress in this city where he labored so effectively for so many years to advance the cause for racial justice and the general welfare.

Daley's voice quivered. His misty sky blue eyes could barely hold back the tears as he continued: "We need his faith today. He had faith in people and in the future that was unshakable. We have lost a great and valiant soldier, and I have lost a personal friend."

After Daley finished speaking, he looked down from the pulpit at Congressman Dawson's body in the open casket, extended his right hand in a farewell salute and said: "Bill. You were a great guy."

The funeral service on that cold, grey and windy November day was a majestic political event. Persons ranging in rank from mayors, U.S. senators and congressmen to the newest precinct captain in Dawson's Second Ward Organization were present to pay homage. There were one-hundred, twenty-five honorary pallbearers. Among them were the names of former presidents, Lyndon Baines Johnson and Harry S. Truman. Eighteen persons spoke during the two hour ceremony reminding those in attendance that Dawson was elected to congress at a time when Negroes were being denied hotel rooms in every major city in America, specifically in Washington D.C., Springfield, Illinois and Chicago, Illinois.

Mayor Richard J. Daley and family on the day of his inauguration in April, 1955. (Left to right): Michael, Bill, John, Mary Carol, Richard, the mayor, Mrs. Daley, Michael Daley, his father and Eleanor. Patricia was away studying to be a nun when picture was taken.

Mayor Richard J. Daley in a moment of con-templation in November, 1970.

Mahalia Jackson, the great gospel singer, sang "You've Got To Walk This Lonesome Road."

Mahalia Jackson, the great gospel singer, sang "You've Got to Walk This Lonesome Road." She also told how she used to come down and sing for the precinct captains at Dawson's ward meetings.

A very special eulogy was delivered by Dawson's "political boy", State Representative Corneal Davis (D, Chicago), a minister known as the "Happy Warrior" of the Second Ward Organization. Rev. Davis said that "Dawson was in the forefront of registering Negro voters in this country and that it all began with Dawson saying, 'We've got to get them on the books Davis."

As this writer stood by the church door watching the mourners file out, he could hear some of them singing, "Walk together children and don't get weary. There is a great camp meeting in the promised land." Those were the words that Congressman Dawson always voiced at the end of his Second Ward Organization's meetings.

Mayor Richard J. Daley had not been sworn into office sixteen days when Brigadier General Julian Dawson, M.D., brother of Congressman Dawson, died on May 5, 1955. Attorney Ira Dawson, son of the general and nephew of the congressman, remembers Mayor Daley coming to their home at 5226 S. Michigan Avenue an hour and a half before the funeral services to visit and offer his condolences to the family. The mayor stayed and mingled and talked with members of the Dawson clan for approximately an hour.

Daley and his security men then proceeded from the Dawson homestead to the Episcopal Church of St. Edmonds at 6105 South Michigan Avenue where the funeral service was held. There Daley rejoined the family and other city and state officials, along with Dr. T. M. Smith and a large number of the Provident Hospital medical staff with whom General Julian Dawson had served as senior surgeon for twenty years.

Ira Dawson, in a moment of reflection, states:

> My father and uncle were two brilliant and stubborn men. Neither wanted to bend his different perspective on the routes blacks in Chicago should take, particularly, those blacks who were in a position of leadership. My dad felt that principle took precedent, at all times, over compromise whereas Uncle Bill felt that the only way to get the best for blacks was through the art of compromise even if sometimes that compromise diminished principle.

Dawson and Daley were both graduates of a political school in which compromises and principles sometimes balanced the scale. Dawson brought balance to Daley's 1955 campaign when he delivered 103,320 black votes in a mayoral race in which the winner's plurality was only 126,967 votes. Dawson's ballot strength made him a creator and not a creature of Richard J. Daley; however, the congressman never fully exercised the political leverage that came with the power of a large black voting block.

Between 1955 and 1959, Daley slowly gained power and control in Dawson's black wards by dividing the blacks so that each committeeman reported to him. He, in turn, gave the committeemen greater patronage benefits than they had had previously. This patronage detour slowly sapped the energy of Congressmen Dawson, the political Sampson of black Chicago.

As chairman of the Cook County Democratic Organization, Daley controlled patronage. A committeeman without patronage was like a bird without wings. The committeemen controlled the aldermen, and Daley as mayor of the

Mayor Richard J. Daley seized power early through giving recognition to black centers of influence outside the political establishment. Daley declared February 2, 1956 Negro History Week. (Left to right): James A. Furgeson; Theodore R. Hawes; Benny D. Brown; Vernon B. Williams, Jr.; and Mayor Richard J. Daley.

city and chairman of the Democratic patronage machine controlled both the aldermen and those committeemen who opted for wings.

Attorney Harold Washington wore wings Wednesday evening, May 25, 1955 when he shared the dais with such heavyweights as Mayor Richard J. Daley, Mrs. Eleanor Roosevelt, and Supreme Court Chief Justice Earl Warren. Both Justice Warren and Mrs. Roosevelt received honorary degrees from Roosevelt University that night. Warren was presented with the honorary Doctorate of Law degree for his "vital contribution to the achievement in American society of equality of opportunity, academic freedom and Democratic self-government." Mrs. Roosevelt was presented with a Doctorate of Humanities as a "eminent American citizen, who in times of uncertainty and crisis, spoke clearly for the principles of social justice and welfare." The occasion was Roosevelt University's tenth anniversary Founders and Friends' Dinner held in the International Amphitheater at 4220 S. Halsted Street. More than three thousand persons attended the event.

Harold Washington recalls that delightful evening and the events that followed with a smile and these observations:

> I felt good for a lot of reasons that night other than the fact that I was sharing the dais with Mrs. Eleanor Roosevelt and Chief Justice Warren. Also Richard J. Daley was my seat mate. Daley had only been in office about six weeks, and I was working in the Corporation Counsel's Office. Actually, I worked for Daley. He didn't know me. I didn't know him. I had worked for him in the campaign. So, here we were sitting next to each other. We were making small talk when I was introduced to make my speech. I spoke on behalf of the Roosevelt alumni that night.
>
> After I finished my speech and sat down Daley said: "Are you in the Corporation Counsel office?"
>
> I said, "Yes." We chatted in greater depth and got more intimate.

Dr. Jonas Salk, U.S. Supreme Court Chief Justice Earl Warren, and Eleanor Roosevelt receive the first honorary degrees awarded by Roosevelt University. Left to right: Donald Steward, Kendall Taft, President James Sparling, Dr. Edward Chandler, Mrs. Eleanor Roosevelt, Arthur Hillman, Board Chairman Leo Lerner, and Chief Justice Earl Warren. Right: Eleanor Roosevelt, shown exchanging pleasantries with Trustee Dr. Percy Julian during Roosevelt University's Tenth Anniversary.

Harold Washington displayed his best oratorical skills that night. If applause is a barometer, then everybody in the audience was pleased with his presentation. There were more than one thousand blacks present that evening, and they all seemed to be bursting with pride. Their boy and Roosevelt University's first black class president showed that he was endowed with speaking talents that could be matched with the best that America had to offer.

Young Washington did not have the slightest notion of the great impact his speech had had on Mayor Richard J. Daley until the following week. He recalls what occurred on his first day back at City Hall after the Roosevelt event:

When I went into work that Monday, John Melaniphy, the Corporation Counsel, called me into his office and said, "Daley is interested in you. He really wants to put you out there." I said: "What's wrong?" He lowered his voice to a confidential tone and uttered: "I'll tell you confidentially. The city's chief prosecutor is going to be replaced. I think he wants to groom you to be the city prosecutor."

I was already in the prosecuting division. So, sure as hell for the next six months, I was transferred from one prosecuting section of the city to another, from narcotics to family court, gambling court, all around. They were grooming me for the big job.

I never quarreled with anybody, but my new position created a lot of animosity in the office. The white folk were trying to get me out because they thought I was Daley's "boy." I hadn't said a word to them other than, "How are you feeling?" I hadn't even talked to Daley.

The subtle harassment continued. They gave me a hard time. It was really rough in there. It was so bad I threatened Judge Samuel Leibowitz. He came into my office one day talking a lot of B.S. I asked him: "What are you talking about?" And we got into a real argument. I threatened to throw him out of a closed window. He started yelling and screaming and folk came running into the office.

Daley heard about the riff and sent Attorney Edith Sampson to talk to me. Edith came down and said: "Daley wants you to know he really likes you. However, you have got to get along with these dudes."

I yapped: "I couldn't get along with the racist mothers." I ran all the stuff down to her. Even as my confidant, I shouldn't have told her all of that mess, but I did anyway. And the harassment continued. Finally I just left. I was young and unsophisticated.

I didn't know how to handle those white folk. Instead of getting rough, I should have jumped cool and by-passed them. Maybe everything happened for the best, so I left. Daley was concerned. He called me at home one day and asked, "What happened?"

I thanked him for his concern and replied: "I couldn't handle that thing. It's just not for me." He wished me well and all of that.

The new role that Mayor Daley gave Washington in the city's Law Department was not on the traditional Negro job track at City Hall. His sharp intellect and no-nonsense mannerism umbrelled behind an infectious smile made him a professional threat to the white lawyers who wanted to move up in the city's law office.

Attorney Roy Washington, Harold's father, had worked in the Corporation Counsel's Office earlier. However, the elder Washington had always had the typical colored assignment such as prosecuting attorney at the 48th and Wabash Avenue Police Station where he held a strong position for a number of years.

Washington had only been practicing law less than two years when his father died in 1954. His father had been a precinct captain in the old Third Ward Organization and worked under a succession of committeemen: Sneed, Wimbush, and Ralph Metcalfe. Although Harold Washington had never formally joined the Third Ward Organization, he assisted his father during the elections by working in the precincts. Several months before his death, Attorney Roy Washington told Harold: "You ought to get to know Ralph Metcalfe better. As a matter of fact, you should work for Ralph. He's a young man, and he's going up the ladder."

In deference to his father, young Washington replied:

> Okay! I will try it. I had no particular interest, and I didn't really think it out. My father had only been dead a week or two when Ralph called me to come down to his office which was located at 366 E. 47th St. The moment that I walked into Metcalfe's private office, he looked up from his desk and said, "Are you going to take your father's precinct and also take the job in the Corporation Counsel's office?"

Washington replied in the affirmative and accepted both the corporation counsel's job and also the precinct captain's position which was really not a challenge because he had lived in the Third Ward all of his life and had done practically all of the precinct work for his father for at least two or three years prior to his death. The corporation counsel's job paid $4,800 annually which was a little better than a pedestrian's salary. In 1985 dollars, that would be equivalent to between $18,000 and $20,000 per annum. Thus, in addition to holding the city job, young Harold practiced law on the side.

Washington had only been working with the Third Ward Organization about three months when Alderman Ralph Metcalfe approached him again with a new assignment. The alderman asked him if he would take over the

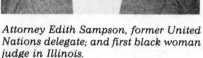

Attorney Edith Sampson, former United Nations delegate; and first black woman judge in Illinois.

Sam Patch, presently administrative assistant to Mayor Harold Washington and also the contract compliance and affirmative officer for the city.

Third Ward Young Democrat Organization. Congressman Dawson had told Metcalfe that he wanted to rejuvenate that political sector and pull all of the young people together from the Second, Third, Fourth, and Twentieth Wards.

In eight months, Washington developed the Third Ward Young Democrats into the largest minority political organization in the city with a membership of five thousand. At its annual affairs, the Young Democrats had a bigger turn-out than the Third Ward parent organization. The Third Ward Young Democrats turned over between seven and eight thousand dollars per year above expenses to the parent organization. In addition, Washington always got a large number of blacks in his precinct to vote. He was never further down than fifth on the list of precinct captains in his ward in getting blacks out to vote. Washington was usually second and occasionally first when he outdistanced J. D. Jones, the fireball of the Third Ward precinct captains.

In 1959, Metcalfe made Harold Washington the supervisor of the precinct captains and ultimately Washington ended up working ten of the precincts himself. In addition, Washington taught political science and government operation classes to the Young Democrats and older members of the parent organization. The youth organization's growth actually became a threat in Metcalfe's eyes. The Third Ward Young Democrats took on some independent forays. They challenged the Cook County Young Democrats which was predominantly white and defeated them on more than one occasion. The blacks were dominating the county organization to the point where the chairman, David Bradshaw, son-in-law of W. Clement Stone, went down to Mayor Richard J. Daley and screamed for assistance.

Sam Patch recalls that he met Harold Washington in April, 1963 at a convention being held by the Young Cook County Democrats Organization. Patch had gone to see Alderman Ralph Metcalfe about getting into politics, and Metcalfe had suggested that he go down to the Morrison Hotel and talk with Harold Washington. Harold Washington was the campaign manager for William Harris, current commissioner of Building and Zoning for Cook County, and in 1963 was a candidate for chairman of the Young Cook County Democrats. Patch recollects his activities that evening:

> I went down to the Morrison Hotel at 9:30 P.M. that Friday night, and I knocked on the door of room number 506. Harold opened the door, and I told him that Ralph Metcalfe had sent me down to see him. He responded: "Fine. Who are you?"
>
> And I said: "I'm Sam Patch." We exchanged some pleasantries during what was known as a social hour among the young group, and then, Harold told me to pick up some literature, go out in the lobby of the hotel and buttonhole everybody I saw.
>
> I said: "What do you mean by buttonhole?"
>
> Harold recoiled: "Just stop everybody you see and tell him how great Bill Harris is and that you would like for him to vote for Harris."
>
> I followed his instructions and worked to approximately three o'clock in the morning. I then went back to Harold's room because I was tired. I said to Harold: "I guess I'll go home."
>
> Washington looked up from a stack of papers and said: "Wait just a minute. The politicking has just started."
>
> And I said: "But it's three o'clock."
>
> He replied: "That's when it starts. Now, if you want to be a politician, I'm going to teach you how to be a politician. Now we are going to politic. We're not going to sleep! I stayed with Washington talking to people and buttonholing people until six A.M. It appeared to me at that early hour we had everything buttoned down. I told Harold that I was going home and that I'd see him early that afternoon.
>
> He said: "Oh! No! I want to see you back here between eight thirty, and nine o'clock this morning." This was a Saturday. He reminded me that the election was going to be held that evening.

Patch explains that the following thoughts continued to pop up into his mind as he travelled home on the Englewood Express El Train: "I don't want to be bothered with this. This guy is crazy. What is wrong with this man. Here I am just a Young Democrat. This ain't even the big stuff, and he's already got me working around the clock."

It had been traditional although not constitutional among the Young Cook County Democrats that if a person served an interim period as first vice president, he automatically ascended to the chairmanship. However, when it became William Harris' time to step up to the chairmanship, the young white Democrats didn't want him because he had the wrong paint job which was black.

At the election that evening, Harold Washington made the nominating speech for Bill Harris. Sam Patch recalls that it was the first time in his life that he had ever seen a black man stand up in a public meeting and point his finger at prominent white folk and call them racist. Washington screamed: "You don't play the game by the rules. When we get in the game, you change the rules."

Harold was pointing his finger at men who are now some of the biggest political names in this town. Patch recalls he was very nervous. He had never seen or witnessed anything like that. Here was a black man in a white hotel pointing his finger and shaking his fist at white folk during a period when they were calling blacks "colored" to their faces and "niggers" behind their backs. In the finale of Harold Washington's nominating speech for Bill Harris, he told the group:

> I will never appear before the Cook County Young Democrats again. This is my last time. I've been in this organization for a long time. I've worked hard. We have paid our dues. We have come up through the ranks. We've done everything you've told us to do. Our ward, the Third Ward, is the number one ward, the top ward in the state. We have won national recognition. Now when it comes our turn, this man, Bill Harris, who has served so diligently, is not acceptable.

Patch recalls that Harold's speech was not only passionate but very emotional:

> You will not change the rules when it's our turn. You will accept us for our worth. Now if you don't vote for Bill Harris this time, don't look for me to come back anymore.

Prior to his farewell speech to the Cook County Young Democrats, Harold Washington had almost succeeded in pulling off a political coup that afternoon. Washington had set up a deal with the Young Democrats from the Second, Third, Fourth, and Twentieth Wards to support a white state president if they in turn would change the constitution so that the first vice president of the Cook County Young Democrats would automatically succeed to the chairmanship, which, of course, would have meant that Bill Harris would have succeeded Richard J. Elrod as chairman. William Harris remembers Harold Washington's plan with a broad smile on his face:

> Harold had pulled together a package that was going to put the first black in the seat of the chair. We had counted heads and knew exactly who was going to support our resolution. We had the numbers. I will never forget when we read the resolution. Eddie Roswell who was taking the minutes almost

fell off of his chair because he knew passage of that resolution would block his opportunity of becoming the next chairman. Elrod, the chairman, immediately called for a recess. The chair prevailed, and so the recess was in order. From that point on they used every technique known to man to try to get us to kill our resolution. They even called their committeemen, who in turn called us in an effort to get us not to vote on that resolution. The credentials of our delegates were challenged. When they discovered that they could not turn us around, they adjourned the meeting. Although we had the majority in that room by head-count, the chairman had the prerogative to adjourn the meeting because he simply called for a voice vote as opposed to a roll call. The 'I's' had it, and the meeting was adjourned. Elrod supported Eddie Roswell because Roswell had supported him when he became chairman.

Although Harold Washington never attended another Cook County Young Democrat's meeting, he continued to monitor and teach the Third Ward Young Democrats. He told the young black Democrats that staying active in the Young Democratic organization was important. He explained that the Cook County Young Democrats' Organization was the training ground for white folk who were preparing to ascend the organizational ladder. Before Washington came on the scene, blacks had treated the Young Democratic organization as a social club. Harold Washington turned that social club around and made the Young Democratic organization a place for political education.

Harold Washington states that in 1960, he went to Congressman William L. Dawson and told him that discrimination was destroying the Young Democrats. Dawson told Washington that he would take care of it, but nothing happened. Subsequently, Bradshaw went to Daley and told him that the Negroes were flexing their muscles. Daley told him to straighten up or resign. Bradshaw got his act together and completed his term as chairman. Richard J. Elrod, current Sheriff of Cook County, succeeded Bradshaw.

Bill Harris followed Washington's advice and stayed in the Cook County Young Democrats because he was determined to become the chairman of the group. Harris voiced the following:

> I went to Eddie Roswell, the current treasurer of Cook County and told him if he would support me for chairman in the 1964 election that I would in turn support him. Eddie agreed. We spent 1963 pulling everybody in line. If I had not been elected chairman in 1964, it would have been an embarrassment, not only to me but to the total party if the members had selected somebody else. There was no way they could by-pass me without embarrassing themselves totally. And they knew I would walk, and that I wasn't controlled by the party because I didn't have a political job.

Above: Attorney Harold Washington making a passionate nominating speech on behalf of Bill Harris before the Cook County Young Democrats. Below: A group of young Democrats in a lighter moment. (Left to right) Attorney Harold Washington, Richard J. Elrod, chairman of The Cook County Young Democrats, Clifford Kelly, Bill Harris, and John Stroger.

The Morrison Hotel, headquarters for Cook County Democrats.

Left: (First row extreme left), David Bradshaw; (third from left), Richard J. Elrod, Mary Ella Smith; (extreme right), Bill Harris; (third row left) Alvin Robinson; (third from left), Attorney Harold Washington. Right: John F. Kennedy campaigns in Lake Meadows Shopping Center at 35th and South Parkway (Martin Luther King Drive). (Left to right) Corneal A. Davis (at microphone) touting Senator John F. Kennedy for President during the 1960 campaign; Alderman William H. Harvey (Second Ward); John H. Sengstacke, publisher of the Chicago Defender; Congressman William L. Dawson; State Representative James Y. Carter; Alderman Kenneth E. Campbell (Twentieth Ward); State Representative Skyles; John F. Kennedy; and Richard J. Daley.

There was no way they could come to me and make a switch by saying that they would give me something better if I waited a couple more years. I was in a position where they pretty much had to accept me. I have to give Harold Washington credit for engineering this election because he was the one that was giving us the cues and guidelines. We all spent many many hours in his law office after we left the Cook County Young Democrat's meetings figuring out strategy for putting together a package that would make it possible for a black to become chairman of the Cook County Young Democrats. I served two terms and was succeeded by Alex Seith.

Although the Young Cook County Democrats were publicly independent of the regular organization, John Stroger, currently a Cook County commissioner, remembers that when he was the secretary of the Cook County Young Democrats and David Bradshaw was chairman, Mayor Richard J. Daley called them into a meeting at his office in the Morrison Hotel for the purpose of organizing a voters' drive for John F. Kennedy in the suburbs. Stroger states that Daley furnished a number of taxi cabs every evening for thirty plus days to enable young black Democrats to travel into the suburbs of Markham, Harvey, Robbins, and other black populated areas in Thornton Township to distribute literature for the presidential campaign of the handsome Harvard educated Boston Irishman.

John Stroger and Charlie Ford, president of the Third Ward Young Democrats, both worked diligently in the Kennedy crusade, and both later became co-campaign managers for Harold Washington when he ran for the House of Representatives in an at-large election in 1964. Out of a field of several hundred candidates running statewide, Washington came in among the top forty winners who were elected to the House in Springfield, Illinois.

It was during Washington's tenancy in Springfield as both a member of the House of Representatives and state Senator that he commenced having problems with Mayor Richard J. Daley. Washington states: "In Springfield, I was totally independent, and in Chicago, I was part of a machine. I never got the two things confused."

Washington said that all hell broke loose when he and Renault Robinson got together on a bill for a Police Review Board. Washington went from sugar to salt in the Daley camp. Daley called Ralph Metcalfe into his office chambers and told him to dump me. Ralph Metcalfe in turn went to Harold Washington and said: "The mayor wants me to dump you."

Washington asked: "Why?"

Metcalfe retorted: "You know why. You are messing around with the police department."

Washington recoiled: "What do you mean? I'm cleaning the mother up."

Washington asked Metcalfe: "What did you tell him?"

Ralph replied: "I told him that if he wanted to dump you, he would have to do it himself. I wasn't going to do it."

Washington bristled: "You're inviting him to my behind man. You should have told Daley to get lost and that I was your man."

Ralph retorted: "I did the best I could."

"Hell, you left me out there." Washington rebounded.

After a brief pause in the conversation, Washington turned to Metcalfe and bellowed: "I'll call Daley!"

Ralph rose from his chair and said: "You can't call Daley; he won't talk to you."

With a quizzical look on his face, Washington asked: "How do you know?"

Ralph responded: "I know he won't. You should understand the psychology, Washington. The boss won't talk to anybody other than another boss."

Washington fired back: "You got your white man, and I got mine."

After the conversation with Metcalfe, Washington called Jack Touhy, Speaker of the House, and said: "Jack, Daley has asked Ralph Metcalfe to dump me".

Touhy responded: "Hell, I told you to leave that got damn police stuff alone. You just won't learn. I'll take care of it."

A single call to Touhy ended the first in a series of dump Harold Washington episodes. Since Ralph Metcalfe never understood why Daley's thunder and lightning subsided. Ralph Metcalfe later asked Washington: "What happened?"

Harold replied: "I don't know." Harold Washington knew that he owed Jack Touhy one, and he recalls when the payoff came. One afternoon Touhy called Washington and said: "Daley wants you to go on the Chicago Crime Commission."

Washington replied: "I am no damn sleuth. I don't want to go on the Crime Commission. That's not my ball game. I am not made for that kind of stuff. I wasn't even a good prosecutor. I'd prosecute a guy, get a conviction and then I'd want to let him off."

Touhy became annoyed listening to Washington's excuses and in a thundering voice interrupted the conversation and said: "Daley wants you on the Crime Commission!"

Harold recognizing he was in a no win situation replied: "Okay, if you insist." Touhy made it clear that I owed him, that he had saved my behind and now it was time to pay up, Washington recalls.

Washington still did not fully understand why Daley wanted him on the Crime Commission until one day he read an editorial in the *Chicago Daily News* entitled "SIRAGUSA, STAFFED UP AGAIN," which explained the

Right: Patrolman Renault Robinson, the man who beat "clout city."
Below: An investigative hearing was held in the State of Illinois
Building on discrimination against the Afro-American Patrolman's
League and other minorities. (Right to left) State Representative Otis
Collins, Senator Harold Washington, Senator Richard Newhouse,
and Attorney Howard Savage.

Crime Commission was doing a good job and that it had gotten bills to clean up crime in Chicago passed against overwhelming odds to clean up crime in Chicago. The kicker in the editorial stated that "Representative Harold Washington looks like a stand up guy who is not a tool and may well bring a refreshing change to the Commission."

Reflecting on the *Chicago Daily News'* editorial, Washington mused and then uttered: "Daley knew well what he was doing. I was his dump-off cat. This was the way he chose to use me as his showcase nigger."

Mayor Richard J. Daley's assignment for Harold Washington on the Chicago Crime Commission was a spear carrying role in a major operatic tragedy when compared to the parts that were played by Aldermen Ben Lewis and Claude W. B. Holman in dismantling the power of Congressman William L. Dawson.

In 1958, Mayor Richard J. Daley was instrumental in getting the absentee white leaders of the rapidly racially changing Twenty-fourth Ward to name Ben Lewis as alderman to fill the unexpired term of Sidney Deutsch. In 1961 after Deutsch's death, Daley named Lewis the ward committeeman of the Twenty-fourth Ward, which had been labeled the best in the country by Franklin Delano Roosevelt during the presidential campaigns of 1932 and 1936.

Third from left: Alderman Ben Lewis of the Twenty-fourth Ward on December 4, 1962, files petition for re-election. Ninety days later he was murdered in his office at 3604-06 W. Roosevelt Rd.

Lewis became Daley's "house boy" and took great pride in attacking Dawson publicly on signal. He constantly bragged about the fact that none of his precinct captains were "Dawson men" and that his telephone line ran directly to the fifth floor in City Hall and not to Dawson's headquarters at 34th and Indiana Avenue. During the period that the bulldozers were attacking Dawson's constituents in the Second Ward, Ben Lewis had been heard gloating that "Everytime that an iron ball bats down one of those slum buildings on the South Side, twenty families move west."

Black displacement caused by the iron ball of urban renewal prompted Alderman Leon Despres in 1958 to introduce an open housing ordinance in the city council. Alderman Claude W. B. Holman, initially an independent Democrat, co-sponsored the housing ordinance to Despres' amazement. Alderman Despres was delighted with Holman's support because without a black alderman's endorsement, the measure had a slim to no chance of passage.

Congressman William L. Dawson passed the word that Chicago wasn't ready for open occupancy. While Daley was opposed to an effective open occupancy law, he gave the measure lukewarm support because he wanted to cultivate Holman, who was using the issue to liberate the Fourth Ward from Dawson's umbilical cord. Daley and Holman toyed with Despres' occupancy ordinance for five years before it was finally passed in a watered down version in 1963

Alderman Holman and Congressman Dawson quarreled openly about

Holman's position on open occupancy and patronage. Dawson wanted to nominate Edith Sampson for a judgeship while Holman was opposed to it. Although she lived in his ward, Holman wanted to appoint someone else that he felt was more deserving among his troops. Edith Sampson was not known as a Holman disciple. Daley stepped into the fray shortly after he had been re-elected to a second term in 1959. His second victory enabled him to secure control of forty-seven aldermen out of fifty. He also froze all of the patronage in Holman's Fourth Ward. On the surface, this appeared to be an impartial move. However, it was a covert move on Daley's part to convert Holman from a "field boy" to a "house boy" within Daley's black kitchen cabinet. Hence, 1959 was the year when Dawson was effectively cut down from his role as "the black political leader" to a simple Second Ward committeeman and the Negro congressman from the First Congressional District.

Daley established direct lines from the fifth floor in City Hall to the various ward committeemen's offices. Holman (Fourth Ward) became Daley's man. Miller (Sixth Ward) was his man. Dawson (Second Ward) was his man. Campbell (Twentieth Ward) was his man. Lewis (Twenty-fourth Ward) was his man. Harvey (Second Ward) was his man, and finally Metcalfe (Third Ward) was his main man. Six black aldermen and one black congressman had been transformed within four years from black power brokers to political overseers on Daley's plantation.

Dawson's political stranglehold up to 1959 gave him the power to fire any patronage worker in any of the black controlled wards. Daley's new political realignment negated that power. The six black aldermen became known as the "Silent Six". They did not open their mouths unless they got a signal from either Tom Keane, Daley's floor leader, or Daley himself.

Alderman Claude W. B. Holman became Daley's defender on all subjects raised by the opposition. Holman was a short, five foot-six, freckle-faced mulatto with white hair. His booming thunderous voice was Daley's biggest piece of rhetorical artillery. Holman was frequently seen on the five o'clock news standing in the front row of the city council wearing a loud checkered jacket and a bow tie that bobbed fiercely as he spoke. There were many occasions when he could be heard saying: "I always speak on administration matters. All I have to know is what we are going to talk about, and I'll back the mayor. I'd be drawn by wild horses before I fail him."

On another occasion, Holman attacked a bill that was supported by Governor Richard Ogilvie. From the floor of the city council, Holman screamed:

> That the deceit and unadulterated hypocrisy of the Republican legislation is now exposed for all the world to see. By their tricky maneuvering, the Republicans have raped, murdered, and killed the people of Chicago. They have sold the old, the sick and infirmed down the river. This act of

Republican legislation is the greatest frame-up since the crucifixion of
Christ.

Mayor Richard J. Daley made Alderman Leon Despres Holman's special
assignment. Despres recalls:

> Whenever I would raise a point about discrimination, segregation, oppres-
> sion, civil rights, or an ordinance on those matters, which I increasingly did,
> Daley would always sick one of the "Silent Six" to answer me. It usually was
> Holman. At the beginning Alderman Harvey would get up and be very
> courteous and say, "I like and appreciate what Alderman Despres is doing,
> but it's the wrong way." Then Holman would get up and talk on the same
> matter. But of course, Holman was noted as a man who exhaled fire.
> Anything I suggested, Holman would find a way of twisting it and showing
> that it really wasn't for freedom, or if it was a good measure, he'd get up and
> say that my motives were bad. Holman had no inhibitions. He would flatter
> Mayor Daley and tell the mayor publicly in the city council that he was the
> greatest mayor in the glare of the cameras and radio microphones. I
> remember once he said, "You are the greatest mayor in history, greatest
> mayor in the world and in outer space too."

Leon Despres found Holman to be both a mean and vindictive person
whereas Despres opined that Ralph Metcalfe didn't have a streak of meanness in his entire body. Part of Holman's meanness surfaced because of his opposition and resentment toward Despres, a white man, representing the Fifth
Ward which was fifty percent black. When Attorney Aaron H. Payne supported Despres for re-election in 1963, Holman put Payne on ice. Payne made
the following remarks about Holman's action:

> I guess I raised too much hell over there at the Sanitary District Civil Service
> Board. Holman had recommended me for the five thousand dollar a year
> post in 1960. Holman was definitely opposed to my renomination, and it
> stemmed from my support of Despres, a political independent in the Fifth
> Ward and a frequent critic of Mayor Richard J. Daley.

When asked by the *Chicago Daily News* about the Payne appointment,
Holman stated: "It is completely out of my hands."

At the time Payne also noted that, "the price of independence comes high."
He said: "Since I spoke out for Despres, Holman hasn't even spoken to me. If
you're going to succeed in this business, I guess you have to conform, I can't do
it."

A classic Holman versus Despres streak of meanness came out in a debate that took place in the city council chambers on January 31, 1963. Involved were zoning changes from business to residential classifications on nine small parcels of land in the Hyde Park-Kenwood urban renewal area which embraced both wards.

Then Alderman Emil V. Pacini (Tenth) called the amendment up for passage. Despres urged the passage with the remark that all had been agreed on at a series of meetings in both wards. Holman leaped to his feet, rushed to the one microphone set up for the meeting, and shouted that he would handle matters in his ward. Despres shouted back that he had the floor and had not yielded it. Pacini quieted them down and said the matters would be handled separately. Despite Pacini's effort to quiet them, the quarreling continued.

After Despres charged that Alderman Holman did not attend the community meetings, Holman shouted: "I was busy attending meetings with other city officials. I am not like a certain alderman on 55th street who puts his feet on the desk and smokes cigars."

"I resent the slurs on Alderman Campbell", Despres countered. (Alderman Kenneth E. Campbell (Twentieth Ward), a political ally of Holman, also had an office on 55th Street).

"I am referrng to Despres." Holman quickly responded.

Before Holman could finish his allegation, Despres recoiled: "Let the records show I don't smoke."

Pacini suggested that the two men shake hands. When Despres held his hand out, Holman turned his back and stormed from the room remarking: "I am particular with whom I shake hands with."

Alderman Timothy Evans, of the Fourth Ward, Holman's successor, analyzes the fights between Holman and Despres:

> Holman's vicious attacks against Despres enabled Holman to get the largest slice of Daley's patronage pie within the black wards. There was not necessarily any substance to what Holman was articulating in a thunderous voice against Despres on the city council floor. What you saw was his style. The substance is what was going to take place the next day after the speech had been delivered. It was then that Holman would frequently go to Daley and say, "I stood up for you, Daley. Now I want the next series of judicial appointments for my people; I want some specific jobs in city hall, etc." Holman, in fact, got more judicial appointments and high administrative jobs for the Fourth Ward than any single black alderman in the city of Chicago. Holman was perceived by most middle-class blacks as an extreme Uncle Tom who did Daley's bidding at every beck and call. It appears that Holman was prepared to take the Uncle Tom lumps publicly as long as he could produce for his people privately.

Left: Aaron Payne, in happier days, was toastmaster at many civic events and frequently introduced Mayor Richard J. Daley. (Standing left), Aaron Payne and Mayor Daley.

Left: Mayor Richard J. Daley, Alderman Claude W. B. Holman (Fourth Ward), and Alderman Kenneth E. Campbell (Twentieth Ward).

Left: Mrs. Wendell Green being sworn in by Mayor Richard J. Daley as a member of the board for the Chicago Public School system. Right: Former Municipal Judge Sidney Jones is currently commissioner of Liquor Control.

Alderman Timothy Evans was also a young lawyer in Claude W. B. Holman's law firm. Evans also thought highly of Holman.

> Holman was a very low-keyed, very modest, unassuming and truthful to the fault to your face. I mean whatever it was he thought was a fact he told you. In addition, he was a brilliant man in that he was able to finish law school at night while attending two schools and holding down a full-time job during the day as a court reporter. Earlier in his career, he had been a secretary to the first black Democratic congressman, Arthur Mitchell.

Timothy D. Black, Jr., a civil rights activist, saw Alderman Holman as a Daley turncoat because Holman had been elected as a Kenwood-Hyde Park independent with the overwhelming support of the Independent Voters of Illinois. As a matter of fact, Tim Black and his constituents were so livid about Holman's behavior that they decided to run a candidate against him in 1963. Black, who was the chairman of the Fourth Ward branch of the Independent voters of Illinois, was successful in getting Gus Savage, who lived in the Fourth Ward, to consider running against Holman. Tim Black states:

> I will never forget because it was just before Christmas in 1962, prior to the primary. We had agreed that we were going to give Augustus Savage our wholehearted support, and we were busy pulling all the pieces together. We called a meeting at John Nesbitt's home in Madison Park where we were going to make the press announcement. We were really exuberant because we had an independent in Despres in the Fifth Ward, and now we were going to have an independent in the Fourth Ward.
> We certainly felt that we could win with Gus because Gus Savage was well-known through his articles and editorials in the *Hyde Park Herald.* The evening wore on, and there was no Gus. Finally people at the party kept asking me, since Gus was late, if I was sure Gus was going to be our candidate. And I told them that I was very confident. Somebody at the party who knew Gus a little better than I did said: "If he doesn't run Tim, will you run?"
> I said, "Oh, no, I won't run. I'm sure Gus is going to run." It was near midnight when Gus arrived. Everybody was feeling good and very enthusiastic until Gus abruptly announced that he was not going to run.

Congressman Gus Savage states that he decided not to run in 1963 for the following reasons:

> I was editing three newspapers for the South Town Economy Chain: the *Hyde Park Herald,* the *Bulletin* and the *Booster.* In addition, they had me scouting the west side in search of some additional papers to add to the chain. I thought that somebody should challenge Holman, so I encouraged

them not to give up the challenge simply because I didn't want to be the candidate, and I suggested Tim Black. Tim finally decided to run, and I agreed to be his campaign manager. Let me point out another factor. I never felt that a journalist should be a candidate or involved directly in electoral activities. Therefore, I never directly ran for an office. I was always involved in campaigns to help other independents. Never would I have run and would not be in congress today had it not been for a peculiar set of circumstances in 1967 that compelled me to do what I said I would never do which was to run for office. Unfortunately, Tim Black lost the 1963 election to Claude W. B. Holman.

Tim Black contributes his loss to the fact that the Independent Voters of Illinois and the labor people did not support him after it appeared that Alderman Leon Despres was going to be in trouble in the Fifth Ward.

Mayor Richard J. Daley did not oppose Despres; however, Alderman Thomas E. Keane (Thirty-first Ward) and Congressman William L. Dawson did. Daley backed off Despres because he did not want to rock the boat in the liberal Kenwood-Hyde Park district in any way that would affect his own April re-election bid. Alderman Kenneth Campbell, an ex-Fifth Warder, was undergirded by Keane and Dawson when he invaded the Fifth Ward with his troops from the Twentieth Ward in support of Chauncey Eskridge, an attorney and close friend of Dr. Martin Luther King, Jr.

The political trio put its strength behind Eskridge and against Despres for the February 26, 1963 election. Despres saw Eskridge, Campbell, Keane and Dawson as threats and called Walter Reuther, president of the United Auto Workers Union in Detroit Michigan, and asked for help. Reuther's response to Alderman Leon Despres was positive. In addition to being a labor lawyer, Reuther shared with Despres a common sensitivity about people and liberal causes.

In response to Reuther's decision to move the labor troops from the Fourth to the Fifth Ward, Tim Black states with a tinge of bitterness in his voice: "I was left high and dry to build an organization from scratch, to run against Holman who was now a full-fledged machine candidate."

Alderman Kenneth Campbell (Twentieth Ward) felt that Despres was vulnerable because the Fifth Ward had been redistricted and fifteen thousand blacks from Woodlawn had been added to the voting roles in the Fifth Ward. Campbell did not know if these blacks would vote for Despres. Despres contends that Daley did not support Kenneth Campbell when Campbell invaded the Fifth Ward.

Campbell's political troops were isolated, and his campaign really was a fiasco in that Chauncey Eskridge ended up carrying only one precinct in the entire Fifth Ward. Moreover, Marshall Korshak went to Daley and asked Daley for his permission to support me because I had beaten Marshall the last time out. Marshall, obviously had adopted the philosophy, "if you can't beat them, join them."

Despres' voice reflected a great deal of satisfaction as he continues to describe his campaign for re-election:

My forces were strong in that Walter Reuther sent Willoughby Abner, regional vice president of the United Auto Workers Union, to campaign in my behalf. And, of course, he brought the union troops. We had the Independent Voters of Illinois troops and, of course, the Korshak troops. Chauncey Eskridge, my opponent, in desperation attempted to enlist Dr. Martin Luther King, Jr. into sponsoring a registration drive in the Fifth Ward and, of course, oppose me in the campaign. It was really a disguise on the part of Eskridge to bring King into the politics of the community. I was very pleased that Dr. King decided not to participate.

Those supporting Despres, in addition to Walter Reuther and sanitary district trustee, Marshall Korshak, were Benjamin S. Adamowski, Republican candidate for mayor, and Senator Paul H. Douglas (D, IL.). Douglas supported Despres because Despres was an honest and an extremely bright man. However, Marshall Korshak who was somewhat more practical noted that although Despres was a remarkable man, he and his ward precinct captains supported Despres because the residents of the Fifth Ward would never permit outsiders (Campbell, Keane and Dawson) to invade it and dictate policy. Alderman Despres smashed Chauncey Eskridge in the Fifth, and Holman vanquished Tim Black in the Fourth. Holman won by a plurality of 7,000 out of a total of 10,000 votes cast.

Timuel D. Black, Jr. subsequently told Claude Holman that: "I have found it embarrassing to have to depend on Alderman Leon Despres, a white man, to carry the message for black folk, particularly when there are six black aldermen sitting in the city council who see nothing, say nothing and hear nothing. It's unfortunate that the only black voice in the city council is a white one."

Sidney Jones, former municipal judge and alderman of the Sixth Ward (1955–59), saw Despres' actions in the city council on the behalf of blacks as positive. Jones, who is currently Commissioner of Liquor Control, verbalizes Despres' role in the cause of civil rights:

I don't see any reason why a man just because he is black is the best representative for black people. We could very well have a black guy like that Clarence Pendleton, chairman of the U. S. Commission on Civil Rights, who is currently doing more damage to the black liberation struggle than the late Senator Bilbo of Mississippi. I would rather see a good white man like Father Theodore M. Hesburgh of Notre Dame University, or a good liberal like Leon Despres, rather than a guy like Pendleton. There are more Pendletons in the world than you would want to believe.

Leon Despres was not part of the Daley machine; therefore, he could afford to just speak out. He is a very fine man who is cultured and intellectually and humanly sensitive. The black aldermen during that period could not speak out because they were part of the machine. There was good justification for designating Despres as the finest black alderman who happened to be white in the city council.

Daley would send his program and budget down to the city council, and no one dared to raise a question, white or black, except Despres and perhaps the single Republican alderman that was in the council at that time. Bill Harvey of the Second Ward had no occupation or profession. He wouldn't do anything to disturb Daley; Campbell (Twentieth Ward) had no occupation or profession but was a smooth and suave politician who would tell me: "Man, I ain't no lawyer. I don't have no profession. Politics is my business and I'm not going to do nothing to get myself in bad with the man who has the power."

In the Third Ward there was Ralph Metcalfe who had no profession, and his claim to fame was the fact that he was a world renown athlete. Holman in the Fourth and Bob Miller in the Sixth fell in a different economic category. Holman was a lawyer bent on proving to Daley that he was the most loyal person in the world to the mayor. He wanted the world to know that he was the mayor's man. Bob Miller (Sixth Ward) was a successful mortician. However, he was a 'died in the wool' Dawson-Daley man and wouldn't do anything to rock the boat.

In April, 1963, Alderman Leon Despres ceased being the only independent voice espousing the Negro cause in the Chicago City Council. Despres was joined by Charlie Chew, who defeated the white Seventeenth Ward incumbent Arthur Slight by 7,069 to 5,654. Blacks from the Second and Third Wards had migrated southwest into the Seventeenth giving blacks a numerical advantage in a ward that was shifting swiftly from all white to all black. The ward was fifty-fifty in 1959; however, when Chew was elected in 1963, it was ninety percent black.

Agitation for the election of a Negro alderman in the Seventh Ward had not come from Chew's forces alone. William L. Dawson (D, IL.) wanted a Negro in that ward and also was insistent that a Negro be elected to run in the Twenty-first Ward. His candidate for the Twenty-first was Melvin McNary, vice president of Chicago Metropolitan Mutual Assurance Company, who ran third against two white candidates: James J. Driscoll and Samuel Yaksic.

Alderman William Cousins, Jr. (Eighth Ward).

Senator Richard H. Newhouse, Jr., Democrat of the Twenty-fourth District.

Attorney Chauncey Eskridge, candidate for alderman of the Fifth Ward.

Alderman Charles Chew, Jr. (Seventeenth Ward).

Alderman Leon Despres (Fifth Ward).

Charles Chew, Jr., a very articulate man with a deep ebony complexion and a clean, bald head, commented immediately after his election to the aldermanic seat that "the majority of the Negro clergymen worked against me. One pastor would not even let me stand on the sidewalk in the front of his church and hand out literature."

The former Fifth Ward alderman, Leon Despres analyzes Chew's election somewhat differently, noting that "It was easy for Charlie as a black candidate with energy to defeat Arthur Slight. Chew's key to success at that time was the fact that he was black and the machine was white."

In Chew's first three years as an elected official, he attempted to fulfill his promise to pound and chisel away at Daley's machine in the city council. His actions made good ingredients for press releases, but were exercises in political futility because Daley controlled forty-seven of the fifty aldermen. Despres, John Hoellen, a Republican, and Charlie Chew were really the only reasons that the city council had to meet because Daley had a figurative political power of attorney from the other forty-seven.

Charlie Chew in his colorful style lashed out at Daley on the issues of school superintendent, Ben Willis (who was doing his best to keep Chicago schools segregated), and police brutality. He also chided the other six black aldermen whom he called the "Silent Six". In retrospect, Chew states that he knew the "Silent Six" were aware of the needs of their people. They couldn't help themselves because their heads were bowed while they ate from Daley's trough.

Chew recalls a conference that he and a few other aldermen had with Daley about the public schools in Chicago. Chew describes the events that took place at that meeting:

> The meeting heated up when I made some pointed remarks to Daley. Daley was called away for a phone call, Claude Holman, one of the "Silent Six" wheeled around in his chair and waved his finger in my face and said: 'You don't come in here and talk to the mayor like that. As long as you serve in the city council, you will never get anything out of it. I am one of the mayor's lieutenants, and I am going to see that you get nothing out of this council or go anywhere within the Democratic party because you are too damn mouthy.'

According to Chew, Holman really meant what he said and that he was puzzled by how his people would find Daley's actions acceptable. Holman's threats and his substantial power of persuasion was used to hold Chew in line along with the two white liberal independents. Holman frequently stressed that, "blacks have benefited from the regime of Mayor Richard J. Daley more than any other mayor in history." Therefore, Holman's love and loyalty for the mayor caused him to literally stand in the door of the council chamber and block the other six black aldermen from organizing an effective "Black Caucus."

In 1966, the ground in Chicago had been hollowed by the foot steps of Dr. Martin Luther King, Jr. and his followers. Anti-machine sentiment was high. A remap had created a senate district with no incumbent, and Alderman Charlie Chew saw this as his opportunity to escape from the confines of City Hall and the bellowing voice of Claude Holman.

Russell DeBow, the administrative aide to Mayor Richard J. Daley and also former aide to Congressman William L. Dawson, was selected to run for the newly created Twenty-ninth District State Senate seat. DeBow was Daley's hand-picked candidate slated to run against Alderman Charlie Chew, the independent, who had already rivved up his campaign wagon and was crusading through the black community with his pate shining brighter than an August midday sun and shouting from the top of his lungs that his campaign was a "People's Movement."

Charles Chew, Jr. was a very effective speaker and campaigner. He could spellbind an audience to the point that it would believe that a giraffe was an ant. Chew would frequently refer to his opponent, Attorney Russell DeBow, the regular organization's candidate, as the flunky who worked downtown in Daley's office. However, when he really wanted to put his cleat hills down on his opponent's head, Chew would refer to DeBow as "The Boy" employed on the fifth floor at City Hall. His audience would react to Chew's anti-establishment rhetoric with both laughter and thunderous applause because Chew was an independent champion with enough raw audacity to place his right foot in the political establishment's behind.

In contrast, Russell DeBow was a low-keyed gentleman's gentleman with degrees from Southern Illinois University and the University of Chicago Law School. He was a very talented, sensitive and decent man who did not have the stomach to fight in the arena of jugular vein politics where blood frequently splattered on the shoes of the contestants.

On June 14, 1966, Chew defeated DeBow 16,773 to 11,638. His victory rendered a devastating blow to Daley's machine and lifted the spirits of the independent political movement on the South Side of Chicago. Chew stated on election night that "this is a direct rebuff of the Daley organization and its attempt to dictate policy for my people. I'd like to serve notice on them, that my people are tired of do-nothing representation.

Despres went out to Chew's headquarters election night to congratulate him upon his victory as a newly elected Illinois senator. Despres remarked that "Chew's senate victory is more sigificant than the victory he got when he became alderman. This time the important issues are his record, his policy and his freedom from the machine."

Sammy Rayner of 318 East 71st Street, a Chew supporter and campaigner, noted the metamorphosis that took place in the personality of Charlie Chew after his victory. He recalls:

> Before his primary, I heard Chew make a speech where he damned Mayor Daley so badly, I thought nobody could feel that badly about anyone. He actually won his seat in the senate on the strength of his dislike and disdain for Daley. His actual hate and dislike for Daley could not have been very deep because it wasn't long after his victory that he began to love the mayor. You've heard of the fine line between love and hate?

At this point Rayner broke into loud laughter saying that "it didn't take Charlie Chew long to jump over that fine line."

The ballots had not had time to dry from the sweat on the palms on the ballot counters' hands before Chew made a deal with the Daley organization. According to Congressman Gus Savage, the following scenario occurred on the morning after the election:

> Les Bland and I got the word at 11:00 P.M. on election night that Chew had cut a deal with Mayor Daley. We didn't want to believe it because this was the first time in the history of the state that an independent had won an office larger than a ward.
>
> The next morning Les Bland and I went over to Chew's house at 37 W. 78th Street to confront him. We rang the first floor bell for about a half an hour, and nobody answered. Then, we went around the back and rang the back door bell. There was no answer. We knew that Charlie was in the house because his car was parked in the driveway. Les and I decided that we would cover both doors. Les agreed to watch the back door, and I said I would watch the front door in order to see what was happening at the Chew household. We were prepared to stay there all day and all night, if necessary. Low and behold, an hour hadn't passed before Russell DeBow, the guy that we had just beaten, came out of the front door. I then knew for certain that a deal had been made.
>
> I said to DeBow, "Man, what the hell are you doing here?" DeBow just smiled and continued to walk towards his car. At this point Chew's son, Lorenzo, who was a young police officer, opened the door and said, "Fellows come on up. Dad wants to talk with you." So Les and I proceeded upstairs.
>
> Chew greeted us with his usual pepsodent smile, extended his hands and said: "I'm certainly glad to see you fellows."
>
> The first question I asked Chew was, "What the hell was DeBow doing there?"

Chew said, "Man, let me tell you. I have cut a permanent deal with Daley and I had planned to tell you guys about it but I didn't want to blow it before it was set."

Charlie then invited us to go down to City Hall the next day when he was to see Daley and cement his proposition.

I told Charlie, "I will not be with you tomorrow when you go down to City Hall because I'm going to print in my paper what you have done. I'm going to tell on your ass."

His son, Lorenzo said, "Daddy, Gus is right. The people have too much confidence in you for you to betray their trust."

Charlie disagreed with his son, and his son broke down in tears right there in front of us while sitting on the sofa.

At this point, Les and I left the room with me turning to Chew saying, "I'm going to expose you, man. I'm going to expose you."

I don't think Chew believed that I would do it. But I did. Frankly, I don't think the community believed the stories I was writing in the *Citizen*. It actually took several months before it was obvious to the general public that Chew had really deserted the independent movement.

Above: The late Melvin McNary, vice president of Chicago Metropolitan Mutual Assurance Company and candidate for alderman of the Twenty-first Ward.

U.S. Congressman Gus Savage (Second District).

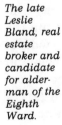

The late Leslie Bland, real estate broker and candidate for alderman of the Eighth Ward.

Chew's election to the state senate was a historical development in the black independent movement. It proved that a solid black vote could break the machine. It was also a validated fact that middle-class blacks could function effectively without the benefit of any small political favors from Daley's "Silent Six". The black community won the senatorial election but lost the candidate. The operation was a success, but the patient died.

The members of the South End Voters Conference were enraged because of Chew's betrayal. Chew had been the lightning rod for the movement. Gus Savage, the chairman of the group, was livid because he had been instrumental in getting the conference to accept Chew as a candidate at a meeting held in the offices of the late Leslie Bland's realty company which was located at 409 East 79th Street, near Dr. Martin Luther King Drive. Others present at that conference meeting were A. A. (Sammy) Rayner, Jr., Attorney William Cousins, Attorney Roland Burris, Milton Lamb, Bennett Johnson, and representatives from the Chatham-Avalon Community Council, the West Chesterfield Council and the Park Manor Neighbors.

Savage's argument in favor of Alderman Charlie Chew as their candidate for state senator was so persuasive that evening that he got the South End Voters Conference to endorse Chew, although Charlie Chew was not present at that meeting. The jettisoning of the independent political movement by Chew hurt Savage deeper than most because of Savage's early endorsement and support of Chew.

Gus Savage editorialized Chew's defection in his Citizen's newspapers for several months before deciding that the South End Voters Conference would expand its political wings to challenge the incumbent candidates in the Sixth, Eight and Twenty-first Wards. The conference decided to run William Cousins in the Eighth against Leslie Bland who had become a recent convert to the Dawson and Chew team. A. A. Sammy Rayner, Jr. was slated to run against the incumbent Robert H. Miller, a Daley Democrat and a member of the "Silent Six". However, before the South End Voters Conference could decide on a candidate for the Twenty-first Ward, Senator Charlie Chew selected Attorney James Montgomery as his aldermanic candidate for the Twenty-first Ward. Montgomery had served as Chew's campaign manager in the state senate race.

In addition to Montgomery being a ten year resident of the Twenty-first Ward, he enjoyed an excellent reputation as a trial lawyer. In 1961, he put the fear of God in former school superintendent Benjamin C. Willis in the federal courts when he challenged de-facto segregation in the Chicago schools and sought an injunction to end it. Montgomery ultimately negotiated the school case and got some relief. The law suit represented an adventure in the "art of the possible" because Superintendent Willis never regained his balance of power and finally resigned. In the "hot summer" of 1965, Montgomery acted without fee in coordinating the efforts of forty lawyers defending more than one thousand civil rights demonstrators who had been arrested while marching from Grant Park to the Loop in connection with their campaign against Willis.

Gus Savage, chairman of the South End Voters Conference, made the following observations about Chew's endorsing James D. Montgomery:

> The selection of Jim Montgomery by Charlie Chew created a problem for the South End Voters Conference. Jim had been associated with us but had agreed to run under Chew's flag in the 1967 aldermanic race. His candidacy created the illusion that he was our candidate whereas his obligations flowed to Charlie Chew, his sponsor. Thus, Montgomery would have been an extension of the Regular Democratic Organization and a potent political arm for Daley in the Twenty-first Ward which is a stable middle class black community.

The Twenty-first Ward included Chatham and Chatham Village, Avalon Park District, Chesterfield, West Chesterfield, Roseland Heights, Princeton Park, and the new areas of Euclid Park and Oakdale and an old section of Morgan Park.

James D. Montgomery of 9714 South Union, a former assistant U.S. attorney told a *Chicago Daily News* reporter on Sunday, November 13, 1966 that "although he supported the Chicago freedom movement, he didn't consider himself an 'anti-organization' candidate." Montgomery further stated that he planned to seek the votes of whites, who made up about twenty-five percent of the ward, as well as those of the Negroes.

Gus Savage chronicles his own moves and actions and those of Attorney James Montgomery:

> Jim Montgomery was an attractive candidate, and we couldn't find another person in the Twenty-first who we felt was strong enough to beat Jim. Although I didn't live in the Twenty-first Ward, the South End Conference group decided that I was the only person with enough name recognition to possibly beat Jim in the February 28, 1967 race. Initially, I was reluctant, but I felt so serious about the necessity of stopping Charlie Chew that I agreed to move to 9907 South Morgan which was located in the ward in order to run against Jim Montgomery. The chairman of my campaign was school board member, Warren H. Bacon. Co-chairmen were Rev. Maceo D. Pembroke of the St. Mark Methodist Church and Charles Hayes, district director of the United Packinghouse Workers.
>
> At the start of the aldermanic campaign, I shut down the Citizen newspaper because my backers and I were in disagreement over support or non-support of the Daley-Dawson ticket.

Montgomery became disillusioned when he found out that he had been cranked into a political quagmire. It turned out that while Jim was playing footsie with Senator Charlie Chew, Charlie in turn was playing tootsie with Joseph Robichaux, the ward committeeman of the Twenty-first Ward, who had his own candidate picked. His selection was Attorney Wilson Frost of 8458 S. Michigan Avenue, who had been endorsed by the Regular Democratic Organization and secretly by Charlie Chew. Frost had the support of the machine's precinct workers.

Jim Montgomery had been deserted by both Charlies: Mr. Charlie (downtown political bosses) and Charlie Chew. I beat Montgomery, but I lost to Frost by approximately five hundred votes, and Frost, in turn, unseated Alderman Samuel Yaksic of 10204 South Wentworth, a white Republican.

Charlie Chew sold out the independent voters on the South Side. He played the role of a Trojan horse and became a Democratic party man. U.S. Representative William Dawson (D, IL) and Charlie Chew were now a part of the same machine.

The Chew-Montgomery episode was the genesis of the peculiar circumstances that caused me to run for my first elective office. I often referred to Wilson Frost during the campaign as the "pick" and Jim Montgomery as the "trick."

In retrospect, Attorney James Montgomery, former corporation counsel for the city of Chicago, believes that Chew shadowboxed with his efforts to become alderman in the Twenty-first Ward in order to kill Gus Savage's chances of defeating Wilson Frost. Doris Saunders, an *Ebony* magazine editor and Montgomery supporter saw Congressman William L. Dawson's hand on the wall of the Twenty-first Ward and attempted to get Montgomery to drop out of the race. Montgomery states that his pride would not let him quit. Both Montgomery and Savage were attractive to the same independent voting constituency in the Twenty-first Ward. Hence, they effectively cancelled each other out.

Although Wilson Frost appeared to outsiders to be the man who had come in out of the snow to challenge Savage and Montgomery in the aldermanic campaign, he had been an inside bonafide member of the Twenty-first Ward Organization for several years. As a matter of fact in 1964, prior to Daley taking the patronage away from Committeeman James J. Driscoll and giving it to Joseph J. Robichaux, Judge Duke Slater and others in the ward had been agitating for Frost to become the first black ward committeeman in the Twenty-first. Robichaux, an Illinois athletic commissioner and a former basketball coach at St. Elizabeth High School, was a Roman Catholic, and had the support in November, 1963 of Alderman Ralph Metcalfe (Third), who was Daley's number one black Roman Catholic. Joe also had the blessings from on high of Congressman William L. Dawson. In order to avoid a faction fight, Congressman Dawson had Frost come down to his office at Thirty-fourth and Indiana and asked him to support Joe Robichaux. The youthful Frost acquiesced. Frost said: "Both Charlie Chew and Doris Saunders switched from Montgomery the moment Congressman Dawson officially endorsed me as the Twenty-first Ward Organization's aldermanic candidate. However, Mayor Daley did not throw his resources into our campaign until after the February, 1967 race."

A. A. (Sammy) Rayner, Jr., a South End Voters Conference member, was also deserted by Chew but had better luck than either Savage or Montgomery because he defeated the Sixth Ward Regular Democratic Organization candidate, Alderman Robert H. Miller, who appeared to have the backing of Dawson and Daley. The victory was decisive with Rayner receiving 6,677 votes to Miller's 4,286 votes.

Right: An ad hoc committee for William Cousins. (Left to right), Attorney William Cousins; Dr. Robert L. Kimbrough; Dempsey J. Travis; Attorney Nelson Brown; Charles S. Smith; Graham White. (Standing left to right), Toy Jordon and the late Jimmy Lynch, owner of The Urban-Nite on East 75th Street.

Left: Thirty-four year old James D. Montgomery, aldermanic candidate in the Twenty-first Ward, explaining his platform to some devotees in the ward. Montgomery advocated strong and effective independent political leadership for the Twenty-first Ward.

Right: James D. Montgomery and friends predict victory: (Front row left to right), Fredrick D. Sengstacke; Mrs. Howard Savage; Attorney Howard Savage; Fred Cole; Senator-elect Charles Chew, Jr.; Attorney James D. Montgomery, candidate; Elson Hutchinson, campaign manager; Fred Hubbard, independent candidate for alderman in the Second Ward; Attorney Leo Holt, former law partner of James Montgomery and candidate for alderman in the Sixth Ward. Rear (left to right), Clifford O'Neil, Philmore Jones, and Thomas Howery, president of Maple park Homeowner's Association.

Despres, who was unopposed in his bid for re-election in the Fifth Ward, aided Rayner throughout his campaign and was present at Rayner's headquarters Tuesday night, February 28, 1967 for the victory celebration. Rayner, Savage, Hubbard and Cousins had been supported by a group called the Committee for an Effective City Council which offered money, platform help, and political advice. The co-chairmen of the thirty-seven man committee were former State Representative Abner Mikva, Warren H. Bacon, Timuel D. Black, Jr. and Dr. Marvin A. Rosner. According to Warren H. Bacon, "the council had been a band of sluggish followers, not leaders." He strongly believed that Rayner and the others would become a dynamic and independent new force in the city council.

Abner Mikva also viewed Rayner as part of this new dynamic movement:

> I think Sammy's impact on the council is going to be very great indeed. He's bright and articulate and can speak in a strong voice without being offensive. Even when he is making a strong statement, he has a smile on his face. He should be an important voice for the whole community and particularly for the Negro community.

Sammy Rayner, Jr., father of six and a mortician, understood better than most the events that surround the beginning and the ending of life. Rayner explains the events that caused his election:

> I really won by default, Richard J. Daley was angry with Alderman Robert H. Miller. Miller had voted, in the committee, against Mrs. Wendell Green who was Daley's selection for the Chicago Public School Board. Although Miller changed his committee vote on the council floor in favor of Mrs. Green, Daley wouldn't forgive him for going against his wishes.

Left: Abner Mikva, former U.S. Congressman.

Right: Warren Bacon, businessman, civil rights leader and political activist.

When election time rolled around, Mayor Daley simply pulled all of the workers out from under Miller and barred them from giving any assistance at all. It was a negative election. They voted against Bob Miller and for me because there was nobody to protect Bob at the polls.

Attorney William Cousins, Jr., an independent and like Rayner a member of the Independent Political Organization (IPO) and the South End Voters Conference, managed to win the run-off spot against the organizational candidate, Leslie N. Bland, Dawson's man in the Eighth Ward. Cousins subsequently defeated Bland in the April 4th election.

In that same season, Fred D. Hubbard ran only 1,500 votes behind Alderman William Harvey in the Second Ward where Harvey had the blessing of William L. Dawson. Hubbard had a strong showing in both the public housing projects which lined South State Street and in his home district around the middle-class Prairie Shores and Lake Meadows developments. The Daley-Dawson machine was beginning to show critical leaks in the Second, Sixth, Eighth and Twenty-first Wards. Daley had declared the traditional liberal Fifth Ward off-limits during the aldermanic campaign.

The trees that Dr. Martin Luther King, Jr. planted in Daley's Chicago in 1966 indeed bore a strange political fruit, fruit alien to the soil on Daley's plantation. Richard Newhouse was elected to the state senate from the Twenty-fourth District, which includes the Fifth Ward, at the same time that Charlie Chew was elected in the Twenty-ninth District. When Newhouse heard that Charlie Chew had crossed over to the regulars, Dick Newhouse anticipated a call from City Hall. The call finally came via Marshall Korshak, the Fifth Ward committeeman.

A meeting was called by Korshak in the Democratic headquarters at the Sherman House which was located on the northwest corner of Clark and Randolph. Present at that meeting were Alderman Ralph Metcalfe (3rd Ward), William Shannon (17th Ward), Claude Holman (4th Ward), Kenneth Campbell (20th Ward) and George Collins (24th Ward). Senator Richard Newhouse describes the dialogue that took place during that conference:

It's important that I bring to your attention the fact that all of the chairs at the small conference table were filled except one, and it was to my left. Initially, we started talking about the problems that were occurring in the streets because of Dr. Martin Luther King, Jr. and his civil rights' staff's presence in Chicago. That discussion didn't last too long before Marshall Korshak said: "We would like for you to come into the organization. It's just like a marriage. I will vote you in."

Newhouse responded: "Isn't there a courtship before the marriage?"

Dead silence fell over the room. I changed the conversation back to the kids out in the streets and reminded Korshak that the future of the Democratic party could very well be in those kids. I further pointed out the fact that their constituency should certainly be cornered, trained and cultivated. Right in the middle of the development of that discussion, the door opened and guess who walked in? Richard J. Daley.

It didn't occur to me until after I had left the room that Daley was giving signals to the group from that chair on my left. The meeting was cordial. Nothing really developed. They weren't crazy enough to make me any offers. They knew it was a "principle thing". The question that they had to find out was where my line of principle was drawn. The fact that Chew was on their side effectively cancelled out my voting power in the Senate.

On the other hand, I have to give Charlie Chew credit for stimulating a lot of people, which of course, made his betrayal even worse. Charlie was the King of the Hill. Charlie could do no wrong. He was standing out there damn near by himself. He was flamboyant. He came in the Senate with assets and behavior that boarded on the outrageous. He had the hallmark of a seasoned public relation's grabber. So I just have to say that Charlie did a lot to change the political atmosphere, which made a sell out on his part that much more damaging.

Chew's defection could have been devastating if he had been the genesis of the independent political movement. Thank God! He was simply the messenger because the roots of the movement were imbedded in such people oriented organizations as the Park Manor Neighbors, the Chatham-Avalon Council, the West Chesterfield Council and numerous other small home owner groups located in the areas south of Marquette Road and north of the city limits.

Gus Savage surfaced consistently as the political science teacher for the independent movement. He was in constant contact with the federation of block clubs and councils as the editor and publisher of the Chatham Citizen newspaper chain. His newspapers were used as a political science textbook. Through his columns and editorials, he preached and taught the need for breaking the chains of plantation politics in the black community.

Moreover, Savage publicized the block clubs' and councils' activities and teas which, in turn, gave him a public relations' credit card with an unlimited ceiling among the membership of the various clubs. On a one-on-one basis, he got an opportunity to know, by first name, most of the leaders of the block clubs and councils throughout the south central, southeast and southwest side communities. Frequently, he would pull one hundred or more block captains together and tell them that they were stronger than any political precinct captain. As a matter of fact, Savage would tell them that they were even better than the precinct captains because they could expedite community services for the block club via direct contact with the alderman or committeeman. He also told them that they did not realize their political strength. If they pulled their forces together, they would be able to elect the public officials who represented their wards, districts and ultimately the city. He would constantly remind them that they were middle-class and that they did not need a precinct captain to bring them a turkey for Thanksgiving, a chicken for Christmas or a ham for Easter in exchange for their votes. That moonbeam talk put heart in the people of the Sixth, Seventh, Eighth and Seventeenth Wards. That fact was reflected at the polls because these were the first wards to pull out front and show a total independence from the Daley machine.

The political independence that Augustus A. Savage taught and preached through the columns of his *Citizen* newspaper and from various political forums throughout the South Side was born out of the pain he had suffered from a lifetime struggle against plantation politics. Savage cut his baby teeth in 1948 B.D. (before Daley) working in the 1948 presidential campaign of Henry A. Wallace.

In 1950, he was campaign manager for Sam Parks in Parks' United States House of Representatives' race against Congressman William L. Dawson. The Dawson-Daley machine kicked their behinds. In 1952, he adopted a G.O.P. strategy with Oscar Brown, Jr. who entered the congressional race against Dawson on the Republican ticket. Both were crushed by the Dawson-Daley machine.

In 1948, Savage cofounded the Chicago League of Negro Voters. Other founding members were Attorney Lemuel E. Bentley, Frank London Brown, Newell Brown, Oscar Brown, Jr., Margaret Goss Burroughs, Gloria Carter, Herman Gilbert, Luster Jackson, Albert Janney, Mr. & Mrs. Bennett Johnson, Carter Jones, Attorney William Moore, Robert Wimbush, and the Reverend Morris Tynes. In 1959, the Chicago League of Negro Voters sponsored the candidacy of Attorney Lemuel E. Bentley for city clerk. Bentley was the first Negro to run in a major primary for one of Chicago's top three executive posts. Gus Savage managed the Bentley campaign, which secured over fifty-eight thousand votes citywide with a budget of only three thousand dollars.

After the defeat of Lemuel Bentley, Gus Savage, the new guru of independent politics recognized that the Chicago League of Negro Voters had to broaden its structure to include the civil rights movement. Hence, he told civil rights' groups such as the NAACP that in order to be more effective, they should increase their arsenal by including political registration in their civil rights' package. Registration was the first step in political education. Moreover, it was non-partisan in that a person could register and vote for whomever he wanted. If the Chicago League of Negro Voters had advocated electoral politics, it would have meant partisan politics. Hence, the charters of most of the civil rights organizations would have been violated.

Savage did not really learn how the Democratic machine operated until 1958 when he moved into the Twenty-fourth Ward on the west side and started publishing the *Lawndale Booster* newspaper and the *American Magazine*. It was through these vehicles that he had attempted to organize blacks in both the Twenty-fourth and Twenty-ninth Wards. The white hoodlums in the Regular Democratic Twenty-fourth Ward Organization decided that they would teach Gus Savage a lesson about politics. First, they harassed and intimidated the advertiser of the *Booster* newspaper which ultimately caused it to fail. Secondly, they started to intimidate Savage and his family. Late one night, the hoods came to Savage's home, jerked his baby son, Tommy, out of bed and threatened to throw him out of the window. Savage still had not gotten the message, so they took him for a ride from which he miraculously escaped. Savage was lucky because the last Negro who tried to buck the west side machine was a lawyer by the name of Octavius Granady. Attorney Granady was shot down in the streets by the white political hoodlums on election night April 10, 1928. His driver, Attorney Euclid Taylor, was wounded but managed to escape.

Bennett Johnson and Randolph Savage, Savage's brother, packed his furniture and his family up in the middle of the night and moved them and Gus Savage to a farm in Michigan where he stayed for over a year to rid himself of the traumatic experience that he had gone through in his efforts to politically organize blacks on the west side. It was during his stay in Michigan that he decided to come back to Chicago and set up shop on the South Side and start a new organization which became known as the South End Voters Conference.

When Dr. Martin Luther King, Jr. was preparing to come to Chicago and set up shop in 1965, he sent his advance men, Andy Young and Jim Bevel, to Chicago to find out exactly where they should let down their bucket. Before starting up the movement in Chicago, Chicago leaders were invited to a five day conference in Lake Geneva, Wisconsin to discuss Chicago and its politics. Gus Savage was among those that the Southern Christian Leadership Conference invited. Gus took Les Bland, the realtor, along to represent the business community. Savage recalls that when he addressed the audience, Dr. Martin Luther King, Jr. was present. Savage argued that the South Side, which consisted of stable home-owner communities would be the proper place for King to start his campaign in Chicago, but Jim Bevel and Andy Young argued that since housing was the main issue in Chicago, the S.C.L.C. should go to the west side because the housing situation there was deemed to be critical. Savage countered their argument with the fact that he had lived on the west side during 1959 when his life had been threatened and that he didn't feel that the Lawndale community was stable enough to support a movement such as King anticipated bringing to Chicago. He further argued that the people on the west side did not have a stake in preserving the community and that everybody there was getting ready to move some place else. As a matter of fact, he exaggerated the point that the west side was so transient that families were renting apartments on a week-to-week basis. Gus Savage continued to reiterate that the people living on the South Side in the areas like Park Manor, West Chesterfield and Chatham were not transient, that they had a stake in the welfare of the community and that they wanted more than a bottle of wine or a turkey at Christmas time. Savage closed his argument by saying that Chicago was a political town and that the housing problem could not be solved without attacking the political problem because the housing problem, was a mere reflection of the political disease that infected the city. He reminded Dr. Martin Luther King, Jr. that Mayor Richard J. Daley had the key to the closet where the political antibodies were stored. Therefore, Savage took the position that if Dr. Martin Luther King, Jr.'s mission was to get the key to that closet, he should start his Southern Christian Leadership Conference movement for an open city on the South Side of Chicago.

Dr. King listened quietly and politely to Savage's arguments but followed the advice of his S.C.L.C. disciples, Reverend James Bevel and Reverend Andrew Young, now mayor of Atlanta, Georgia. Both Bevel and Young had debated in favor of the west side. Bevel agitated for Lawndale because it was dominated by street gangs. He wanted Dr. King to introduce them to nonviolence and also be accessible to the gang leaders. Dr. King started his Chicago Freedom Movement on January 26, 1966 from a $90.00 per month third floor apartment that was selected by Bevel in a dingy three story walk-up located in the North Lawndale community at 1550 South Hamlin Avenue. The site is presently a littered vacant lot, not a shrine to King's efforts in Chicago.

Pickets marching around City Hall in protest of the Jim Crow policies of Chicago Board of Education Superintendent Benjamin C. Willis and the gerrymandering of school districts by him and Mayor Richard J. Daley.

Chapter *XVII*

Daley vs. the Civil Rights Movement

On Sunday, August 28, 1955, Emmett Louis Till, a fourteen year old Chicago boy, was kidnapped at pistol point by Roy Bryant and his half brother, J. W. Milam, from Till's uncle's home in Money Mississippi and then murdered. Till's water swollen body, with one side of his face beaten to a pulp, a bullet hole in his head and a cotton gin fan lashed to his feet, was fished out of the Tallahatchie River near Greenwood, Mississippi three days later and shipped back to his home in Chicago where it was viewed in horror by thousands who passed his open casket in a church on South State Street. Ninety-five days later on December 1, 1955 in Montgomery, Alabama, Mrs. Rosa Parks refused

Left: Emmett Louis Till, a 14-year-old Chicago boy, whose vacation ended on the bottom of the Tallahatchie River near Greenburg, Mississippi because he allegedly whistled at a white woman. Right: Mrs. Rosa Parks, a seamstress whose refusal to sit in the back of a Montgomery, Alabama bus, changed the course of civil rights history in America.

Attorney Lemuel E. Bentley ran for the office of Chicago city clerk in 1959 and thus became the first black to run for a citywide post.

to move to the back of the bus in defiance of an Alabama state law and a direct order from a white bus driver. Although both the Till and Parks events took place more than seven hundred fifty-three miles from Mayor Richard J. Daley's Chicago, they were destined to play a role in the fermentation of the black independent political movement which first surfaced in 1959 with the candidacy of Attorney Lemuel L. Bentley for city clerk of Chicago.

Congressman William L. Dawson refused to speak out in the halls of Congress or in the Negro community on issues such as the Till murder in Mississippi or Dr. Martin Luther King's Montgomery, Alabama Bus Boycott. Dawson did not believe in raising a stink about a civil rights issue unless he could be reasonably certain of victory. Willoughby Abner, a local official of the United Auto Workers Union and president of the Chicago Branch of the NAACP in 1956 and 1957, attacked Dawson in absentia on public forums and in open letters to the press about his silence on equal rights for black folk. Abner became further incensed with Congressman Dawson because Dawson had refused to confront Mayor Daley with the NAACP's documented evidence that revealed unquestionably that de facto racial segregation existed in the Chicago school system. The survey placed the school districts in Chicago in three groups: those that were predominantly white students, those that were predominantly Negro, and those which included a significant number of students of both races. The president of the Chicago Board of Education was R. Sargent Shriver, Jr., brother-in-law to Senator John F. Kennedy.

The National Association for the Advancement of Colored People's survey revealed that in 1956, one hundred ninety-two dollars was appropriated per child for institutions in the districts with predominantly white students and one hundred seventy dollars per child for instructions in districts that had predominantly Negro students, a difference of twenty-two dollars between the predominantly white and predominantly Negro districts. In summarizing the report, NAACP President Willoughby Abner said:

> It would certainly be a conservative estimate to say that the city of Chicago spends at least fifteen percent more on instructions per white child than per Negro child and the percentage of inexperienced general studies teachers (under three years of experience) in a predominantly Negro district is shockingly disproportionately higher than in predominantly white districts. Less than ten percent of the teachers in the predominantly white districts are inexperienced. But an average of thirty-four percent of the teachers in the Negro districts are inexperienced. Racial integration should be a prime factor in districting and redistricting the Chicago school system.

The straw with which Abner broke the camel's back was the picket line that he threw around Daley's City Hall in spite of strong opposition from both the black political and civil rights establishments. The conservative political leaders did not want to get rid of Abner as president of the Chicago Branch of the NAACP because he had served them well. In June, 1957, he had organized and staged the largest civil rights rally in the history of the Chicago branch. More than seven thousand persons attended the meeting which was held at the Coliseum on 14th and Wabash Avenue. Roy Wilkins, NAACP executive secretary and Reverend Ralph D. Abernathy of Montgomery Alabama headed up a list of important speakers. More ministers cooperated in that mass meeting than any previous activity in the association's history. Abner also quarterbacked the most successful Freedom Fund Dinner to be held by the Chicago branch. The more than twenty-five thousand dollars raised at the banquet enabled the branch to expand its staff to include an executive secretary. Jackie Robinson, the baseball hero, was the principal speaker for the event which was held in the Terrace Casino in the Morrison Hotel on July 14, 1957.

The conservative black leaders could tolerate the talents of a quasi-militant like Willoughby Abner because he was kicking on the doors of racism that other leaders dared not touch. They wanted a rebel rouser but one they could control. They would let a militant drive them down the street. However, they wanted the power to tell him when to shut his mouth and turn the corner. Abner violated the conservatives' rules when he put his foot on the gas pedal and drove full speed north to the loop and formed a picket line around Chicago's City Hall. The conservative civil rights leaders thought that Abner was selling wolf tickets to white folk when he threatened to picket, but when he actually pulled it off, he became a real threat to both the black and white political establishments.

United States Representative William L. Dawson was not willing to play dead and let Abner use a civil rights platform to attack him politically and continue to embarrass him and his good friend, Mayor Richard J. Daley. Hence, the congressman adopted a business strategy employed by monied corporate outsiders when they positioned themselves to take control of a publicly owned stock company. Dawson converted six hundred plus precinct captains and their assistants into instant civil rights workers by personally buying each of them a share of stock (membership cards) in the Chicago Branch of the NAACP. On the surface, it looked like a benevolent act for civil rights. In reality, it was a very shrewd way to stack the officership and board of the largest NAACP branch in the country with individuals who owed or needed favors from the Dawson-Daley Democratic organization.

Dawson's timing for the purchase of the NAACP membership cards was a master stroke. He waited until the very last business hour on the last day that members could qualify to vote in the NAACP annual election before he plunked down the money and closed the transaction. The purchase of the large block of membership cards by Dawson was not known to Abner because it was handled by some of the congressman's inside NAACP folk. Since a person must be a card carrying member of the NAACP thirty days prior to election to be qualified to vote, it was too late for Willoughby Abner to enlist forces from the United Auto Workers Union to launch a counter membership campaign.

On Friday, December 13, 1957, Dawson's brand new civil rights stockholders invaded the annual NAACP election meeting which was held in the DuSable High School auditorium located on the northwest corner of the block long building at 49th and South State Street. The orders from the Dawson-Daley machine were to unseat Willoughby Abner and his entire board with the exception of those Dawson insiders who were concealed in the Democratic organization's "Trojan horse." The bottom line was to get rid of Abner or not report to patronage jobs the next morning. Abner had to be punished for having the audacity to pin the tail of segregation on Mayor Richard J. Daley's donkey. Congressman Gus Savage made the following observations about the dumping of Willoughby Abner:

> The annual election meeting had been under way for about an hour when I
> decided to go out into the outer lobby of the auditorium and have a smoke.
> To my surprise, the lobby was jammed with people whom I had never seen at
> a NAACP meeting. I looked through the crowd and spotted an old friend
> from Wilson Junior College, who today is a very prominent political figure. I

walked over to him and said: "Man! What in the hell are you doing here? You are not a member of the NAACP. My friend replied: "Yes I am a member. I have been a member for thirty days along with all these other precinct captains and workers. We are waiting out here until we get the signal to come in and vote. We are going to kick Willoughby Abner's ass tonight."

Willoughby Abner, the tall handsome and articulate labor leader with a baby face and infectious smile, was soundly defeated at the polls that night after a number of high profile blacks including the Reverend Archibald Carey denounced him from the stage of the DuSable High School auditorium as a front man for a left wing organization. All the denouncers to a person had political ties to the Daley-Dawson machine that were not as obvious as those of the precinct captains, but they were not less vital in oiling the wheels of the mayor's black political submachine.

After the heated election followed by a long count on that cold December night, Theodore A. Jones, an executive of the Supreme Liberty Life Insurance Company emerged as the president of the Chicago Branch of the NAACP on

Left: Willoughby Abner, a militant civil rights leader and a local official of the United Auto Workers' union. He was president of the Chicago branch of the NAACP in 1956 and 1957. Right: Theodore A. Jones, vice-president and controller of the Supreme Liberty Life Insurance Company and president of the Chicago branch of the NAACP during the years of 1958 and 1959.

the morning of December 14, 1957. Others elected with Jones were Cora M. Patton, first vice president; M. T. Blanton, second vice president; Willis A. Thomas, third vice president; Mrs. Effie P. Norman, secretary; and Mrs. Ethel C. Dostal, assistant secretary. Those elected to the executive committee on the Jones slate were Reverend Clarence Cobbs; Reverend Theodore Richardson; Albert L. Brooks of the Postal Alliance; Dr. David Johnson; Joseph T. Johnson; Louis Martin, vice president of the *Chicago Defender;* Charles Thompson; John Lewis; Attorney J. Harold Mosley; Edward Todd; Seymour Margolis; Lewis J. Alexander; Reverend Gus Courts; Yolanda Johnson Cheatum; Attorney Odas Nicholson and Etta Moten Barnett, movie and stage star. The election supervisory committee which had been elected at the November NAACP membership meeting conducted the meeting. The members of the committee were Mrs. Amy Victor, Joseph McKinney and James H. Kemp, president of Local 189 Building Service Employees Union Workers.

Congressman Charles Hayes, a trade unionist and former international vice president of the United Food and Commercial Workers International Union, was a member of the defeated Willoughby Abner NAACP team. Hayes recalls:

> James H. Kemp, president of Local 189 Building Service Employees Union Workers, played an important role in Abner's defeat. Kemp was a member of the Executive Committee of the Chicago Federation of Labor headed by Daley's very good friend, William A. Lee. Kemp was a stalwart with the Democratic machine. He did not want to see anything happen that would reflect adversely on Richard J. Daley or William L. Dawson. Jim was opposed to opening the eyes of the sleeping black political giants on the south and the west side of the city of Chicago. He joined Daley and Dawson in wanting to make sure that the black vote was kept under control. Some of us tried to push reforms and make it easier for people to register. The resistance that was there from the machine was omnipotent. I remember going and trying to appeal to the Board of Election Commissioners to permit on-site registration for the people employed in the union stockyards. My request was denied, and it became obvious to me that they did not want an increase in black voting strength. The invaders of the NAACP were elected to make certain that no one in the newly elected NAACP hierarchy or their successors would ever rock Daley's political boat, and they didn't.

Ted Jones, in a victory statement that appeared in the *Chicago Defender* on December 14, 1957, said:

> We will take an inventory of the programs and projects in which the branch is committed. The new board will examine this in relationship to its program.

The new administration intends to make full use of the help, time and experience of the previous administration. We will offer them every opportunity to participate in the program.

Jones, like Abner, emphasized in his platform the need for action against segregation in housing and the public schools. He also said: "I will give special attention to the promotional procedures of the civil service system as they apply to policemen and firemen."

An interesting side fact about the NAACP election is that a colored woman who had served as executive secretary of the NAACP branch before and during the invasion by the Democratic machine turned up subsequently at a trespassing trial of the NAACP's "Truth Squad Mothers" as prosecuting attorney and a beneficiary of a Daley-Dawson patronage appointment. The same colored lady, as a staff employee of the NAACP, had helped document the case against race discrimination in the Chicago school system which provoked the actions of those she was about to prosecute.

The NAACP's "Truth Squad Mothers" felt that the former executive secretary of the NAACP had sold them down the river, a suspicion that is frequently validated by individuals that value greed over *principle*. This premise

Left: James H. Kemp, president of Local 189 Building Service Employees Union Workers and a member of the board of directors of the Chicago branch of the NAACP. At the time of his death, he was national president of the NAACP. Right: Charles Hayes (presently congressman for the First Congressional District) a trade unionist and former international vice-president of the United Food and Commercial Workers International Union, and a civil rights activist.

is supported by a survey made by James Q. Wilson, Ph.D., a Harvard University professor, in his 1960 classic book entitled, *Negro Politics: The Search for Leadership*. Wilson said:

> Suspicion of Negro leaders and the thought that they will sell out to white people is the single most common thought among the rank and file. As the most oppressed group, Negroes feel their leader ought to be a Moses leading them to the promised land. There is a constant clamor for a local Martin Luther King, Jr.

Wilson pointed out that his study on Negro politics was discouraged by intellectuals in the black community. They led him to believe that he was out to study something that did not exist. Contrary to their complaints, Wilson found that there were Negro leaders in abundance and in positions that required leadership ability. He cataloged them into three divisions: organizers, token leaders and prestige leaders. Examples of organizer-leaders were those who tried to mobilize the Negro public behind certain causes. He named Gerald Bullock, former president of the state conference of NAACP branches and Dempsey J. Travis, newly elected president of the Chicago Branch of the NAACP as representatives of this group. Wilson pointed out that in addition to Bullock's leadership in Abner's NAACP faction, Bullock was vice president of the Chicago Teachers Union and the Independent Voters of Illinois. Bullock had led a Chicago contingent of young people on a march in Washington, D.C. in behalf of civil rights whereas Travis, a real estate man, had been an outspoken critic of the racist practices of the white real estate and insurance interests in Chicago, which Travis described as both bigoted and unfair to Negroes.

Wilson noted in his 1960 study that token representative Negro leaders were most often criticized by members of their race, but rarely was this criticism made public. These leaders were the Negro appointees of public bodies such as the Board of Education and the Civil Service Commission.

Wilson described prestige leaders of that period as those whose names were on the letterhead of any group or cause to insure success. The epitome of the Negro prestige leader was Truman K. Gibson, Sr., chairman of the board of Supreme Liberty Life Insurance Company. Other examples of prestige leaders were John H. Johnson, publisher of *Ebony* and *Jet* magazines, John Sengstacke, publisher of the *Chicago Defender* and T. K. Lawless, prominent dermatologist.

Dempsey J. Travis, the man that Dr. James Q. Wilson labeled the organizer-leader type, rose to the top of the civil rights ladder in Chicago as Wilson had predicted prior to the publication of *Negro Politics*. However, Travis did not fit the silk stocking candidate mold that State Representative William Robinson pinned on him the night he was elected NAACP president on December 11, 1959 over Gerald Bullock who was Robinson's candidate. The election was held in the auditorium of the Dunbar Vocational High School, 3000 South Parkway (King Drive). Although Travis succeeded Theodore A. Jones to the presidency and was also a Dawson supported candidate, his leadership style was more in the vein of Willoughby Abner than that of Theodore A. Jones. As a matter of fact, it was his militant style as the president of the Dearborn Real Estate Board during the years of 1958 and 1959 that brought him to the attention of the NAACP. In 1959, Travis was also first vice president under George S. Harris of the National Association of Real Estate Brokers and the housing chairman for the Chicago Branch of the NAACP. Charles A. Davis, a DuSable High School classmate and a public relations consultant for the NAACP, cited Travis' record as head of the real estate board as the reason that the NAACP recruited him to run for president. Travis rejected the honor to serve on both the first and second times he was asked during the summer of 1959 and did not give it any more consideration until late November of that year, just a couple of weeks before the annual NAACP election was to be held.

Others elected on the Travis-Jones slate were Willis A. Thomas, secretary-treasurer of Local 356 Waiters, Bartenders, Waitresses and Cooks Union, first vice president; Reverend S. S. Morris, Pastor of Coppin A.M.E. Church, second

Left: State Representative William Robinson, a civil rights activist and a very prominent and articulate member of the Republican party. Right: George S. Harris, president of the Chicago Metropolitan Mutual Assurance Company and president of the National Association of Real Estate Brokers.

vice president; Albert Brooks, an official of the National Alliance of Postal Employees, third vice president; Reverend A. P. Jackson, pastor of Liberty Baptist Church, fourth vice president; Ethel C. Dostal, secretary; Charles A. Davis, president of Charles A. Davis and Associates, assistant secretary; and James H. Kemp, treasurer. Persons elected to the executive committee were Theodore A. Jones, CPA; Joseph Austin; Reverend Clarence H. Cobbs; State Representative J. Horace Gardner; George S. Harris, president of the Chicago Metropolitan Mutual Assurance Company; Charles Hayes; Dr. David Johnson; Joseph Johnson; Lucious Love; Mrs. Mattie Kelly Moore; Atheviant Moore; Phillip Oliver; Reverend Theodore Richardson, pastor of the Metropolitan Community Church; Mrs. Rachel Ridley; Edward Todd; E. Winston Williams, an official of Local 356 Waiters, Bartenders, Waitresses and Cooks Union; and Arthur J. Wilson, Sr., CPA.

The newly elected members of the NAACP board had their jobs cut out for them. The U.S. Civil Rights Commission had declared "Chicago the most residential segregated city in America." Fighting segregated housing in Daley's Chicago was like rowing a boat in the middle of Lake Michigan with a left thumb. Mayor Daley rationalized the "Jim Crow" community problems by saying that "human relations is not a one man job. You can't let a contract through the Purchasing Department for so many dollars worth of brotherhood signed, sealed and delivered by the next election, just like a sewer or highway express. It takes time, patience, energy and planning to erase prejudice, hate and sharp practices that have been built into American society and history for generations."

Edward Holmgren, staff director of the Chicago Urban League, made the following observations about Daley and the Chicago housing problem:

> In a straight comparison of administrations, achievements are slight, if any. They are not perceptible. Examine the party structure. There are a large number of Negro voters under Congressman William L. Dawson. But he is not pushing. Daley is not doing anything because nobody is pushing him. We, the Urban League, are of the 'do-good' type of organization. We can't compete with a machine.

The officers and board of directors of the NAACP were also confronted with the fact that "Jim Crow" was not just limited to the residential housing area in that Negro lawyers were filing civil rights complaints indicating that their firms ran into racist confrontation in a search of new office space downtown. Attorney Earl E. Strayhorn, of the law firm of Rogers, Rogers, Strayhorn, and Harth, a member of the Chicago Civil Rights Commission and a former assistant state's attorney, charged that there was as much racism in the Loop as there was in Deerfield. (Deerfield is a suburb northwest of Chicago

(Left to right): Attorney R. Eugene Pincham (currently an Illinois Appellate Court judge), Dempsey J. Travis, former president of the Chicago branch of the NAACP and Attorney Earl Strayhorn, currently a presiding judge in the Circuit Court of Illinois, examine a lease document that was voided by a Loop office building manager when he discovered that the tenants were black lawyers.

that opted to convert a residential site into a public park rather than to permit a black physician, Dr. Arthur Falls in cooperation with the Modern Community Developers to develop integrated housing in the area.) On December 15, 1959, Dr. Martin Luther King, Jr. commented on the proposed fifty-one home housing development in Deerfield during a press conference held at the Sherman Hotel in Chicago:

> I have no doubt it would work. Dr. Arthur Falls and the Modern Community Developers (the project backers) are just working in line with our democratic creed where a minority of homes in a project are sold to Negroes. It's alright, as an attempt to set an example in a community to prove that integration can work. This is not the ultimate aim. By setting it (integration) forth before people, they will be able to see it work.

Dr. King further stated that if the United States did not solve its integration problem within ten years, "it will be too late."

During the very same period, there were forty-two Negro physicians in Chicago who were nationally certified as specialists in their fields, but only fifteen of Chicago's two hundred and twenty-six black physicians had been appointed to the staffs of Chicago's sixty-three predominantly white hospitals. These problems were only the tip of the iceberg on the 1959–60 agenda of the Chicago Branch of the National Association for the Advancement of Colored People.

In February, 1960, Dempsey J. Travis accompanied by Reverend Carl Fuqua, the executive secretary of the Chicago Branch of the NAACP, travelled to Washington to meet with Clarence Mitchell, the National Lobbyist for the NAACP to buttonhole some Illinois congressmen to support a bill that was coming before the House of Representatives in which the national NAACP had an interest. During that trip, Travis visited with Congressman William L. Dawson in his Capitol Hill office suite. Dawson said:

> I'm not interested in controlling the NAACP or its policy making body. However, I do want to see the "right man" as the president. I don't think that a civil rights organization should be used as a political platform. I feel that a volunteer association that is agitating for certain civil rights goals is, in effect, tampering with politics.

Congressman Dawson made it clear to Travis during his visit that he had no intentions of interfering with the way Travis administered the affairs of the NAACP. However, Travis recognized that Dawson could take that position because Dawson had in place enough voting power on the board of the Chicago Branch of the National Association for the Advancement of Colored People after the election of Theodore A. Jones in 1957 to make certain that no one within the NAACP's structure strayed beyond the outer gate of Dawson's political back yard in his life time.

Looking back on his conversation with U.S. Representative William L. Dawson in the District of Columbia, Travis viewed Dawson a master politician because Dawson tailored his operation to the specification of a black pragmatist in a white political arena. Dawson may have irritated the young turks and civil rights activists such as Travis and others, but in Dawson's opinion, his method was the last and best hope for succeeding in what he considered the highly competitive game of politics.

William L. Dawson underestimated the strength of the black vote. He felt that a black leader could not negotiate on the basis of black power because Dawson apparently did not recognize the latent potential of these votes. He believed that wit was the black man's best weapon for striking bargains with the white political establishment. Illinois' only black congressman was not audacious and flamboyant in the styles of Congressman Adam Clayton Powell or Willoughby Abner, and unlike either, he never experienced the humiliation of defeat.

Dawson can only be understood in the context of the time in which his various political strategies were employed. The political climate was such in 1960 that ten southern television stations turned down the Chicago produced *Playboy Penthouse Party* because Negroes and whites mingled socially on the show. Negro performances were acceptable, but any hint of social acceptance was considered taboo. Victor Lownes II, promotion manager of *Playboy* magazine and associate producer of the television show said:

> We get a lot of complaints. In most cases the station manager would tell us that they would like the show but then they would say the people out there wouldn't accept its racial aspects.
> One manager said he liked our show but asked if we wanted his transmitter turned into a fiery cross.

It is interesting to note that the people out there are always the bigots and not the station managers. Hugh Hefner, *Playboy* magazine publisher and host of the show said: "We aren't going to back down on this issue. Television can be a great force in ending this discrimination nonsense, and we're going to be rational about it."

Dawson made his highest marks when dealing with senators and congressmen who represented the palace guards of racial discrimination. Exhibit A of that ability can best be noted in his close relationship with former President Harry S. Truman, an admitted former member of the Klu Klux Klan. A classic example of Representative Dawson's magnetic ability to crossover can be found in the following text of his seconding address on behalf of the nomination of Senator Lyndon Baines Johnson of Texas for the vice presidency:

> Mr. Chairman, fellow Democrats, ladies and gentlemen of the convention:
> America, these United States that we love must prepare to keep its rendezvous with destiny. What we do here tonight may prepare us for that rendezvous which may well determine whether we as a nation, as the leader, will survive or perish. We must prepare now to show a united front to all the enemies of freedom. We must lay aside all local, sectional and religious differences and unite into one force to oppose the evil forces of communism which now threaten the entire civilized world. We, as Democrats, we as a party of people must as the party of the people give to the people of the

United States that leadership which will resolve these differences, wipe out the lines of sectionalism, transcend any differences of religious belief and weld us into one mighty, indivisible force for freedom. We have selected for our president John F. Kennedy of Massachusetts, a man who has demonstrated that he has the quality to lead such a fight. We must decide upon a running mate for him; someone who will aid and assist him in completing his job; someone whose life has risen above all local, sectional and religious differences in the carrying out of his responsibility of high office.

I rise to second nomination of a man who has demonstrated that he possesses these qualities. I have been in Congress for some eighteen years now, and years ago, as a newcomer to Congress, I came to know Lyndon B. Johnson. My delegation from Illinois named me to be their representative on a Democratic congressional committee of the Congress. My name was put in nomination for the office of executive secretary of that committee.

The name of Lyndon B. Johnson, then a young congressman, was also presented and Lyndon Johnson in his speech declining the nomination, seconded the denomination of Dawson, a fellow member. And I hold that office today.

He wasn't thinking of the vice presidency. He wasn't thinking of any advantage that would come to him then, but what he did was an indication of the character of the man. The question of race, locality of religion did not enter his mind then and will not enter his mind now in dealing with the many vexing questions that trouble this beloved country of ours now.

I watched him through the years. I've seen him go up higher and higher in places of public trust where he spoke for and represented all the people of America. Never during any time of Lyndon B. Johnson's public life have I ever known him to do or say one thing that could be construed as based upon some question of differences of race, religion or sectionalism.

We need now to join hands with John F. Kennedy of Massachusetts to bring to America that unity which binds us together as one people, a mighty force to fight for freedom.

I am honored to second the nomination of honorable Senator Lyndon B. Johnson for vice president.

Clarence Mitchell, NAACP's national lobbyist's initial reaction to Lyndon Baines Johnson being nominated to run for vice president was negative. He made the following statement in Chicago on July 19, 1960. He said: "The Democrats gave the Republicans a Christmas gift when they put Lyndon B. Johnson on the ticket after endorsing a strong civil rights plank."

"If you want to shoot Santa Claus," he said to the Republicans, "come out with a plank full of innocuous and general statements." Mitchell did not share with William L. Dawson and Lyndon Baines Johnson the opinion that civil rights could be achieved by persuasion. Moreover, Clarence Mitchell felt that

Johnson was a hypocrite, and Mitchell attempted to justify his position when he stated that "if Lyndon Johnson believes in the Democratic pledge to eliminate poll taxes as a requisite for voting, why doesn't he start in his native Texas."

The week of July 11, 1960 when Senator Lyndon Baines Johnson was selected as Kennedy's vice presidential candidate, seven thousand blacks and whites marched and rallied outside of the Democratic convention in Los Angeles for a strong civil rights plank and an elimination of the southern poll tax. Dr. Martin Luther King flew in from South America to join the marchers. The NAACP's Clarence Mitchell observed that while they were waiting for Congressman Powell to join the march, the U.S. representative drove up in a white cadillac. "If he had to join us that way," Mitchell declared, "he could have used an integrated car."

Students held a round-the-clock "Freedom Vigil" to dramatize the sit-in movement. Dr. Martin Luther King Jr., Congressman Adam Clayton Powell, Roy Wilkins and A. Phillip Randolph who had been active participants and leaders of the Los Angeles march, demanded that the Democratic party write ironclad civil rights guarantees into its platform and expel segregationists from party ranks. From A. Phillip Randolph, to Dr. Martin Luther King, Jr., to Roy Wilkins and Adam Clayton Powell, the civil rights issues were being painted in iridescent colors, sketched in bold strokes which left no particle of a doubt as to their intent and purpose. Their demands were aired before the 108 member Democratic platform committee. The delegates to the convention approved the suggested civil rights plank almost intact after a last minute effort by some southern delegates to scuttle it. A minority report against the civil rights plank had been presented on behalf of the states of Georgia, North Carolina, Arkansas, South Caroline, Florida, Mississippi, Virginia, Tennessee and Alabama. An Alabama delegate who was asked by a reporter for his reaction to the electrifying civil rights plank that had just been passed replied with thunder in his voice: "No comment, suh! Go to hell! No comment!"

The civil rights plank that was adopted went far beyond the expectations of the Negro leaders. The fifty-four page document constituted a ringing triumph for the cause of human rights and called for: 1.) support for whatever action is necessary to eliminate literacy tests and payment of poll taxes as a requirement for voting. 2) a permanent civil rights commission and revision of congressional procedures to simplify the passage of anti-discrimination laws. 3.) action by the president and the federal agencies to prevent discrimination in federal or federally aided programs. 4.) formal approval of the U.S. Supreme Court's 1954 decision outlawing public school segregation.

The Southerners' minority report struck its hardest blow at voting rights for Negroes and the implied endorsement of "sit down" demonstrations.

Senator Ervin of North Carolina said, "The program seeks to make special favorites of colored people and to excuse them from the judgment under the same laws as other persons." Senator James O. Eastland of Mississippi added that "the government is not going to coerce the people of Mississippi into living with neighbors not of their own choice. This civil rights plank has no place in the platform if the Democratic party wants support next November from fifty million persons who live in the South." However, former Solicitor General Philip B. Perlman of Maryland supported the plank, describing it as a "blueprint for the future" saying that "it appeals to the mind and consciousness of all men of good will."

On June 1, 1960, a month prior to the Los Angeles march, America's two foremost civil rights leaders sent the following telegram to Chicago:

> S NNY049 NNZ48 LONG BOOK NYZ48 NL PO UUX NEW YORK NY 10
> DEMPSEY J. TRAVIS   1960 June 11 AM 12 2S
> 414 E. 47th St CHCO, IL.
>
> WE ARE REQUESTING YOUR COOPERATION IN AN IMPORTANT UNDERTAKING. WE BELIEVE A MIGHTY VOICE MUST BE HEARD AT THE FORTHCOMING POLITICAL CONVENTION DEMANDING ELEMENTARY JUSTICE FOR THE NEGRO. WE PLAN TO COME TO CONVENTION AND NEED YOUR HELP. EACH PARTY MUST REPUDIATE SEGREGATIONISTS WITHIN ITS RANKS. CHICAGO HAS HISTORICAL OPPORTUNITY TO MAKE A UNIQUE CONTRIBUTION TO CIVIL RIGHTS. COURAGEOUS SOUTHERN STUDENTS AND MILLIONS OF DISFRANCHISED NEGROES LOOK TO PEOPLE OF YOUR CITY TO REPRESENT THEM BEFORE THE CONVENTION. WE URGE YOU AND OTHER COMMUNITY LEADERS TO COOPERATE WITH US IN ORGANIZING A NONVIOLENT "MARCH ON THE CONVENTIONS MOVEMENT FOR FREEDOM NOW." LOS ANGELES LEADERS ARE BEING CALLED UPON FOR SIMILAR ACTION. JOAN SAULT, HUNTER O'DELL, AND NORMAN HILL IN CHICAGO ARE OUR REPRESENTATIVE TO ASSIST YOU IN CONVENING A COMMUNITY COMMITTEE TO IMPLEMENT OUR SHARED OBJECTIVES. PLEASE WIRE READINESS TO SERVE ON THE COMMITTEE TO COOPERATE WITH US AND REPRESENTATIVES IN ACHIEVING OBJECTIVES OF THIS PROJECT.
>
> A PHILLIP RANDOLPH AND MARTIN LUTHER KING, JR., 312 W. 125th ST., NEW YORK 27 NY.

The initial meeting of the Chicago March on the Convention Committee assembled in the Blue Room of the Parkway Ballroom at 45th and South Parkway (Martin Luther King, Jr. Drive) and was called to order on June 21, 1960, at 3:55 p.m. by Bayard Rustin, executive assistant to A. Phillip Randolph.

Some forty Chicago leaders attended. Rustin expressed his appreciation for their presence on the part of those community leaders in the hall and introduced A. Phillip Randolph. In his remarks, Randolph, often called the "Father of the Modern Civil Rights March," discussed both the purpose and the program of the "March on the Convention Movement for Freedom Now." He stressed the importance of the march in Chicago and in Los Angeles as a demonstration on the part of black people and their supporters in the labor and liberal movements for a strong civil rights platform for each of the two conventions. Randolph said: "This demonstration shall be a protest against the conspiracy of silence on civil rights and the piecemealness which characterized both the Republican and Democratic parties."

Randolph, who had been called the most dangerous man in America by President Woodrow Wilson, continued:

> The 'March on Convention Movement' would emphasize the need for a presidential executive order to implement court decisions ending segregation in housing and guaranteeing the right to vote. He wanted the march in Chicago to be a huge mass demonstration that would leave no doubt that black people stood firmly behind their leaders in the demands for an end to equivocation on the civil rights question.

Bayard Rustin, Randolph's heir apparent and the man who subsequently became architect of the two hundred thousand plus People's March on Washington in August, 1963, explained the importance of a large demonstration in Chicago at the Republican Convention which would follow the demonstration in Los Angeles at the Democratic Convention in six days. He

(Sitting left to right): A. Phillip Randolph, the father of the civil rights marches and Bayard Rustin, his ingenious protege.

Rev. A. Patterson Jackson, pastor of Liberty Baptist Church at 4849 South Martin Luther King Drive. Liberty was the site of many of Dr. King's early civil rights rallies.

said the Los Angeles committee was planning a demonstration with between five to ten thousand people, and he urged Chicagoans to set a similar goal. Bayard emphasized the fact that Chicagoans should not let the implication be left that the black leadership was concentrating on the Democratic party and endorsing the Republican party. "The March on the Convention Movement is a demonstration against the do-nothingness of both parties," Rustin bellowed.

During the question and answer period following Rustin's remarks, Randolph in his quiet, dignified style made clear that the march movement welcomed and solicited the cooperation of black Republicans in Chicago, especially those who would be delegates to the Republican National Convention. "As to the future plans by the march movement," Randolph said, "we will cross that bridge when we get to it." For the entire period leading up to the convention, the emphasis was to be on mobilizing the maximum number of people to take part in the demonstrations.

Randolph in his deep Harvard accented baritone voice, cultivated during his many years of orating on the street corners of Harlem, urged the selection of a coordinator to centralize the responsibility for the overall march. It was the consensus of the meeting that at the co-chairmen's meeting which was to be held the following week, a coordinator would be elected and that presently an interim convener of the co-chairmen should be selected. After being nominated by Reverend Owen D. Pelt, Dempsey J. Travis was unanimously appointed as interim convener and was subsequently unanimously elected as the general march coordinator at a later meeting. Nominations for additional co-chairmen for the Chicago Organizing Committee were made from the floor. Twenty-four nominees were accepted, representing a cross section of groups and organizations in Chicago. The body decided that ten additional co-chairmen would be nominated at the meeting of co-chairmen scheduled for the following week.

Immediately following the "Freedom Movement Now" meeting of the co-chairmen on Wednesday, July 6, 1960, thousands of pledge cards were ordered and circulated within seventy-two hours. The job performed during the next seventeen days by a small staff of five, which included Timuel D. Black, Norman Hill, Bennett Johnson, Joan Suall, and Carl Fuqua, executive secretary of the Chicago Branch of the NAACP, was to bring together support groups for the preconvention rally and the March which was monumental.

The organizational trees planted by the "Freedom Movement Now" staff and the co-chairmen bore fruit on Sunday, July 24, 1960, the day before the Republican National Convention was to open at the International Amphi-theater. More than fifty-five hundred persons filled the streets in front of the ultra modern quonset-shaped Liberty Baptist Church pastored by Reverend A. Patterson Jackson at 4849 South Parkway. Young people passed out literature and sold buttons that were emblazed "Freedom Now." The blue and white "Freedom Now" buttons had two shoe prints symbolizing marching feet on the move for civil rights. Twenty-five hundred people jammed the interior of the church. The mass meeting was covered by both the ABC and CBS televi-sion networks. It was the preconvention "March for Freedom Now" rally.

The speakers that afternoon at the Liberty Baptist Church were Governor Nelson A. Rockefeller of New York; Roy Wilkins, NAACP executive secretary;

Dempsey Travis, right, introduces Dr. King at a Freedom Now rally held Sunday, July 25, at the Stone Temple Baptist Church located at 3622 West Douglas Boulevard. In the background on the extreme left is Roy Wilkins, executive secretary of the national NAACP and on the extreme right is Gus Savage, a civil rights activist. (Currently congressman for the Second Congressional District in Illinois.)

A. Phillip Randolph, Negro labor leader; Hugh Scott, Pennsylvania senator; and Jacob Javits, New York senator. The Reverend Dr. Martin Luther King, Jr. was scheduled to speak; however, he arrived in Chicago too late to make that meeting. Governor Rockefeller, the lead speaker, began: "I will wage a convention floor fight if necessary for a Republican civil rights plank pledging military federal action to erase racial discrimination." The governor's remarks were interrupted twenty-eight times by applause and strong cheering ovations from the more than seventy-five hundred persons that formed an attentive crowd that spilled out into the center of South Parkway.

Roy Wilkins stated that "We want civil rights. We will take them from the Republican party, from the Democratic party, or from both of them rolled together."

Following the highly successful afternoon rally at Liberty Baptist Church, Dr. King and Roy Wilkins appeared at a second rally that evening at 7:00 P.M. for some four thousand "Freedom Movement Now" supporters at Stone Temple Baptist Church located at 3622 West Douglas Blvd. When King finished his highly charged oratorical task that evening, the crowd was prepared to walk water with its leaders.

Monday, July 25, 1960 at 4:00 P.M., the March on the Convention Movement for Freedom Now demonstrators assembled in front of Reverend Louis Rawls' Tabernacle Baptist Church at 4130 South Indiana Avenue. At 5:10 P.M. sharp, more than ten thousand black, white, and brown marchers, by police count, stepped off proudly en route to the International Amphitheater located at Root and Halsted Streets and the site of the Republican Convention. In the front line of the march was A. Phillip Randolph, 70, international president of the Brotherhood of Sleeping Car Porters, white-haired and walking with dig-

Left: Diane Nash Bevel, a Chicago student civil rights activist and a Fisk University student. She was also a leader in the Nashville, Tennessee student lunch counter sit-in demonstrations in 1960. Right: Mayor Marion Barry, student civil rights sit-in demonstrator and currently the mayor of Washington, D.C.

*A civil rights poster announcing a
Freedom Now rally to be held at the
Liberty Baptist Church.*

nity. To his left was Roy Wilkins, 58, executive secretary of the National
Association for the Advancement of Colored People. Wilkins' eyes burned
with what appeared to be a smoldering anger. On Randolph's right was
Reverend Dr. Martin Luther King, Jr., 31, of Montgomery, Alabama, president
of the Southern Christian Leadership Conference and a granite rock of a man.
To King's right was Reverend Ralph Abernathy, 34, vice president of the
Southern Christian Leadership Conference and Dempsey J. Travis, 40, march
coordinator and president of the Chicago Branch of the NAACP. Directly
behind the front line of marchers were student sit-in leaders: Diane Nash, Bernard Lee, and Marion Barry, current mayor of Washington, D.C. The Chicago
march on the Republican Convention was the largest civil rights march of its

Left: Looking south from the 40th and Indiana Avenue El platform at the tail end of the largest civil rights march, led by Dr. Martin Luther King, Jr., up to 1960. Right: Bennett Johnson pinning a Freedom Now badge on Dr. Martin Luther King just prior to the march of July 26, 1960.

kind ever held in America up to that point in history. The marchers proceeded north from 40th and Indiana to 39th Street and west on 39th Street to Halsted singing a civil rights lyric to the tune of "I've Been Working on the Railroad:"

> "We've been marching on the vigil
> All the live long day
> And we'll be marching on the vigil
> Till Americans change their ways.
> Can't you hear our plea for freedom?
> Rise up so early in the morn.
> Can't you hear our plea for freedom?
> Put Civil Rights in your platform!

Upon arriving at the International Amphitheater, Randolph, Wilkins and King stepped out of the line of march and waited on the west side of Halsted Street for a representative of the Republican National Committee to greet them. They waited, and waited, and waited. Wilkins, showing annoyance with having to wait, compared the Democratic Convention held earlier in July at Los Angeles with the current Republican Convention and said: "Paul Butler (Democratic National Chairman) was there waiting for us in Los Angeles when we arrived at the Democratic Convention site, and he made a hell of a speech." The Republicans had forgotten to trot out their symbolic Abe Lincoln to greet the sons and grandsons of America's former slaves.

The march leaders had been cooling their heels for about thirty minutes when an administrative assistant to Senator Kenneth B. Keating (NY) came out of the convention hall to tell the delegation that the senator had been designated by the National Committee to confer with the marchers. Soon thereafter, Senator Keating appeared before the group and said: "I have been appointed as a spokesman for the Republican National Committee. You know my views on civil rights. I asked and received permission to state those views explicitly to you."

Randolph then asked Keating: "Have the Republicans on the platform committee settled on a civil rights plank?"

"I can't tell you that," Keating said, "I don't know. I am not happy with the present civil rights plank." Keating continued, "But I think my selection to meet with you is significant."

"Do you think this is an indication that a strong civil rights plank will be adopted?" Wilkins asked.

"I don't know," Keating replied. "But it would indicate to me that the Republican National Committee, at least, favored adoption of a strong civil rights plank."

The Reverend Dr. King then said: "We feel the civil rights plank should include an endorsement of student sit-ins. Can you say whether the platform will consider that endorsement?"

"I can't tell you what the platform will contain," Keating replied.

Randolph, Wilkins, and King did not appear to be satisfied with their verbal interchange with Keating. They were also displeased because they had not been permitted to appear before the platform committee or the convention delegates. The group had been practically ignored by the total GOP leadership with the exception of Governor Nelson D. Rockefeller, who had been seeking black support for a presidential campaign that he aborted shortly after the convention opened. Vice President Richard Nixon, heir apparent to the Republican throne, unlike Rockefeller, rejected as "unsatisfactory" the "Freedom Now" committee's proposed measures on the civil rights issue.

Moments after Senator Keating left, A. Phillip Randolph turned to the freedom fighters standing in front of the International Amphitheater and said: "The right to life, liberty and the pursuit of happiness is a God given right."

"This is a turmoil issue," Reverend Dr. King told the assembled "Freedom Now" marchers. "You must show new determination in struggle and sacrifice. Walk together children. Don't get weary." Upon hearing those closing remarks, the orderly crowd dispersed.

Gus Savage, (presently Congressman of the 2nd District) a co-chairman of the "Freedom Movement Now" committee, was incensed and displeased with the disrespectful behavior that the Republicans had heaped upon the black marchers and their leaders. Hence, Savage decided to organize a group of men, women and children to picket the Republican Convention on Wednesday, July 27, 1960. Savage describes that picket experience:

When we arrived at the convention site and parked our cars, we were met by a Captain George Barnes, who was the head of the Chicago Police Department's labor detail. Barnes pointed to a group of tough looking Bridgeport whites standing near the entrance of the Amphitheater and said: "Look, I've got to protect you from those guys, and the only way I can protect you is that you stay on the east side of Halsted across from the entrance because if you picket directly in the entrance, there will be too many people around, and I can't protect you. You can understand that if you are in the middle of a crowd and people decide to do harm to you in any way, I cannot distinguish it. Therefore, I've arranged for your picket line to work on the east side of the street so that we can protect you from the hostility, and there is a lot of it down here."

Savage continues:

I agreed to Barnes' suggestion without too much thought after taking a good hard look at those tough looking white hoodlums. We had a number of women and children among the picketers, and I wanted to protect them. I passed out the picket signs and started walking the picket circle as the assigned policemen stood by to protect us against those white hoodlums who were hollering and calling us niggers, baboons, jungle monkeys, and threatening to bat our brains out if we crossed the street. For all practical purposes, the picket line was peaceful except for those guys screaming and hollering. Barnes told me he would escort the picketers out of the area at 9:00 P.M. because he anticipated that the longer we picketed the more hostile the mob would become. He also indicated that the group would get larger and meaner as the evening grew darker. Captain Barnes further indicated there would be no way we could get out of there without getting hurt without an escort.

When time came for the son of a gun to escort us out of the Bridgeport area, he was nowhere to be found. The picketers began to get nervous. After a half an hour had passed, I realized we were in trouble. These white folk were going to tear us apart. It was time for us to leave, and there was not a police escort in sight.

There was a white sergeant standing about twenty feet from the picket line. I walked over to him and said, "We are ready to go to our cars."

He replied, "I'm sorry Mr. Savage. I can't leave this spot. I was assigned to stand here by Captain Barnes. I can't leave until I get further orders."

Savage recoiled, "I'm ready to leave."

The sergeant bristled and said: "Well there's nothing I can do. You will just have to stay here."

The only black cop on the entire labor detail was standing within ten feet of where the sergeant and I were talking. I walked over to him and said, "Listen. You are black like me; you see what these people are trying to do to us. They are going to let these goons beat these women and children up. They know we have got to go back to our cars, and they're going to beat the hell out of all of us. They will kill us. How can you be a policeman and black and let us go out into that darkness with all those barracuda swarming around us? Don't you have no feelings?"

The son of a gun acted like he didn't want to answer. I kept on talking to him and finally he broke. He said, "What do you want?"

I said, "Just take me across the street to the Amphitheatre to see if Captain Barnes is still there."

He said, "You know I'm going against orders."

I said, "I know. The white sergeant don't want you to go."

That black policeman was so touched by my appeal that he left without orders and escorted me across the street to the Convention Hall to find Captain Barnes. I couldn't have made it across the street without that black officer. When we got there, we were told that Barnes had left. Here I am the leader of the picket line, I'm responsible for all these men, women and children. God damn! I didn't know what to do.

There was a second black cop inside of the Amphitheatre who recognized me. He said, "I'll tell you Savage what you can do. Call the local police station and tell them that there's a riot going on out here. That's the only way you are going to get any protection. These guys stationed out here are not going to assist you period!"

I asked, "Where can I find a phone?"

He said, "The nearest phone is down there at the El station."

The El stop was about a block north of the Amphitheatre at 40th Street. I turned to my black cop escort and said, "I got to make a telephone call down at the El station."

He said, "That's a block away. I can't go down there because I've already walked off from my assignment. I've got to go back to my post."

I talked about that mother like a dog. I said, "You are going to let me walk down there and let those tigers kill me before I get to a telephone? You sure are a big, bad, black policeman." I said, "I'm only half your size, but I am going to walk down there anyway. Whatever happens, I hope you m.f. remember me." So I started walking down the street, and the white hoodlums started following me.

I said to myself as I walked, "I don't know what I am going to do." There was nothing I could do. I looked back and low and behold, there was my black police escort. I will never forget. He had caught up with me and was walking about ten paces behind me. He smiled, held his arms down with the palms of his hands towards the ground in sort of a shifty like way, which means everything is all right. That black cop will never know how good he made me feel. I never felt better in my life because I knew that palm down signal meant he was not going to let anything happen to me.

The overt hostile attitudes of the white Bridgeport hoodlums against Gus Savage and his picketers were the covert sentiments of many of the white officers on duty at the Republican Convention. The public display of hatred for blacks exhibited by the Bridgeport mob mirrored the private policy of the Chicago Police Department towards black citizens generally. Thus, the white policemen were symbols of urban occupation troops, white power, white racism, and white repression. The fact that the police department would permit a group of thugs to assemble and openly threaten to do violence to peaceful pickets reinforces a strongly held opinion about the double standard of justice and protection in urban America. Hence, it's factual to conclude that two standards do indeed exist: one black and one white.

Another example of unequal protection raised its ugly head before the International Amphitheater's janitorial staff could clean up the confetti from the Amphitheater convention floor after the Richard M. Nixon victory. On Friday, July 29, teenage violence flared at the Bessemer Park swimming pool on the southeast side of Chicago because some Negro and Mexican youths attempted to use the pool. The ethnic minorities were confronted by armed whites who shouted, "Go home niggers." Captain Philip Briatzke, commander of the South Chicago District Police, was in charge of the area in which the disturbance took place. Just a few years earlier in the same general area, Frank London Brown and his family had been greeted with the yell "Coon, Coon, you've come too soon. You and your kind should go to the moon." This was the Brown family's greeting when they moved into the Trumbull Park development, in addition to receiving a welcoming brick thrown through their window and gunfire. The siege of Trumbull Park was the longest and most costly racial incident in Chicago's history up to that date. In the late summer and fall of 1953, as many as twelve hundred policemen patrolled the area around the four hundred and twenty-seven unit Trumbull Park project on some days. This kind of man power was needed to protect fewer than ten black families who resided within that complex.

Black families didn't have a ghost of a chance in the hands of a white policeman because white cops did not respect black police officers in or out of uniform. Renault Robinson, former executive director of the Afro-American Patrolman's League, cites the following case histories:

> The Afro-American Patrolman's League started in 1967 as a way of stopping the Chicago Police Department from being so inhumane and brutal to blacks. The police were beating the hell out of everybody but not providing any service. You were as afraid of the police as you were of burglars and robbers because if you ran into a white police officer, he would rather kick your teeth in than help you. At the station where I was working on 22nd and Damen, they would bring a white woman in for a traffic violation, let her use the commander's washroom, let her sit down and call her counsel in an outer office. They did everything they possibly could to make white women comfortable. If they brought a black woman in on the same charge, they would make her sit on the floor in a filthy cell until she urinated on herself, which was inhumane treatment.
>
> Let me just cite a few incidents where black police officers had confrontations with white police officers. A black police officer went out to the Dan Ryan Woods at 87th and Western with his family on a picnic. A bunch of white guys jumped on him and his children, and a big fight started. Somebody called the police, and they came. Although the black officer was wearing his gun all throughout the melee, he never took his pistol out of its

holster. As a matter of fact, he never did anything except try to defend himself. When the white cops arrived, they beat the hell out of him and his family, although they saw his gun and badge. They broke his wife's arm and beat up his eldest son although he kept yelling, "I'm a policeman, I'm a policeman." They said, "You are a nigger out here molesting these white kids."

In another incident, a black officer went to the police station to inquire about his sons who had been beaten up by a couple of white police officers. He was looking for the policemen involved so that he could get some details on exactly what happened. The cops in the police station surrounded him, jumped on him (some fifteen of them), beat him up, and he subsequently got fired.

White cops very frequently issued traffic tickets to black policemen although the black policemen showed their badges. They would reply: "Nigger you know that badge on you don't mean nothing to me." And they would write the ticket anyway. He could be a sergeant, lieutenant. It didn't matter. He was a nigger.

In another episode, a black officer was married to a white woman. He worked in a police district that was predominantly white. He was leaving a restaurant where he had celebrated his wife's birthday. He was pulled over by a squad car, and one officer said, "Hey! Nigger. What are you doing with that white woman in your car?"

The second officer said, "You know she must be a whore. Otherwise she wouldn't be in there with a nigger." They told the black officer to get out. They started talking very nasty to both him and his wife. The black officer kept telling them that he was a policeman. They said they didn't care anything about that and that a nigger shouldn't be a policeman anyway because they marry white women. They ended up beating him up. The Afro-Patrolman's League went to his aid, and he decided in the end that since he was married to a white woman he would let the white police association help him instead of us. We said fine, if that's what you think is the best thing to do. The police association let him get strung out and got him fired.

There was a classic case involving a black officer who had been made a commander. His mother was abused by some white cops. The commander refused to do anything about it because he was afraid that if he did or said something that might offend his white bosses, they would snatch his commander's badge away from him. So he continued to take their abuse.

The sores of police abuse and brutality festered in the ghetto midnight sun with little or no attention from Mayor Richard J. Daley or Superintendent James B. Conlisk until Dr. Herbert Odom, a South Side dentist and founder of the Mal-Mart Medical Center at 6333 South Green St. was stopped in his white 1969 Cadillac on March 13, 1972, because the light over his red license plate was out. Dr. Odom identified himself, but the two white Brighton Park area

Left: Dr. Herbert Odom, president of both the Mal-Mart Medical Group and also the Wentworth Nursing Center, Inc. Right: Dr. Daniel Claiborne, a prominent dentist and popular social leader.

Task Force Police Officers were not impressed with his status or station in life. To them he was just another nigger. The cops told Dr. Odom that the violation merited a ticket. An argument ensued, and the good doctor was body searched and thrown across the hood of his pretty white Cadillac, his arms were twisted behind his back, and handcuffs were placed tightly around his wrists. He was subsequently hauled off to the Englewood District Police Station at 6120 South Racine on charges of disorderly conduct, resisting arrest and simple battery, and locked up like a common criminal for three and a half hours. He was not freed until a friend posted a one thousand dollar bond.

Although the Odom arrest received substantial print media attention, the Chicago Police Department ignored it and arrested another doctor a month later. Dr. Daniel Claiborne, a prominent dentist and popular socialite, was imprisoned after a minor automobile accident. He was thrown into a jail cell at the Forty-eighth Street Police Station and held for six hours. Dr. Claiborne had been declared hopelessly drunk by the arresting officer and dragged unconscious from his 1972 black Fleetwood motorcar. His crime was allowing his vehicle to strike an empty jalopy in the Fifty-seven hundred block on South State Street. A few weeks after the accident, Dr. Claiborne died. The medical prognosis revealed that Dr. Claiborne was not drunk, but had suffered a severe stroke. His detention in jail and the delay it caused in getting medical attention contributed to his early demise.

The odds for Dr. Herbert Odom, Dr. Daniel Claiborne or any other black man getting care, protection, and justice while in the custody of some white police officers were about even with that of a snowball's chance in hell. These everyday facts of black life seemed to have escaped the attention of the

Congressman Ralph Metcalfe, a crusader against police brutality in the black community.

celebrated Olympic track star, Congressman Ralph Metcalfe, until Dr. Herbert Odom, his chief fund raiser and confidante became a victim of police brutality. When Dr. Odom told Congressman Metcalfe his police brutality story, the congressman's mental anguish figuratively propelled him through the roof of his office with the speed of a jet fueled by a mixture of indignation and emotional shock.

The Dr. Odom experience prompted Congressman Ralph Metcalfe in lightning fashion to pick up the phone in a state of rage and anger and call Superintendent James B. Conlisk, Jr., who immediately arranged a hasty meeting for Metcalfe and members of Metcalfe's Third Ward Crime Prevention Committee. Metcalfe told the Superintendent that he and his constituents were sick and tired of the brutal and insensitive treatment that was being crushed upon the heads of black folk by the Chicago Police Department. "Mr. Superintendent, you will be hard pressed to go into any home in the black ghetto and not find at least one member of that household who either feels that he has been abused verbally or physically by some member of the police force, or has first hand information from such an incident," Metcalfe said.

It should be noted that between 1968 and 1972, the Chicago Police Department's own Internal Affairs Division, which alone had the official mandate to probe citizen's complaints received 5,251 charges of police abuse. Only 144 (2.6%) were sustained. The questions that the Afro-American Patrolmen's League continued to raise were just how exhaustive and how impartial were the investigations by the Internal Affairs Division.

On April 17, 1972, two days after Dr. Daniel Claiborne had been incarcerated, Congressman Metcalfe, Dr. Odom and eight members of the Third Ward Crime Prevention Committee stormed into Superintendent Conlisk's

Eleventh and State Street office without an appointment and plunked down on his desk a hastily drawn list of six demands. They included:

1. The termination of all activities by the police task force.
2. The establishment of a citizen's board at each police district.
3. The promotion of at least one black to a policy making position in the department.
4. The recruitment of more black officers.
5. An investigation of police advancement procedures.
6. A promise to fulfill all these demands by May 31, which, of course, was just three weeks away.

According to George Sims, a former commander of the Chicago Police Department and a member of the Catholic church, a major prerequisite required to fulfill Ralph Metcalfe's third and fifth demands was to join the Catholic church. John T. Scott, the first black police captain, was promoted to that rank after serving thirty-three years in the department. He was a converted Catholic. Harry B. Deas, the second black police officer to make captain, had served in the department for thirty-one years before he was promoted in 1946. He was also a Catholic convert. Kinzie Bluitt, the third black to become a police captain, was also an active member of the Catholic church. Harold L. Miles, Robert Harness and William Griffin were members of the Catholic order before they were promoted to the rank of captain. Fred Rice, the present superintendent of the Chicago Police Department is a Catholic. Approximately nine percent of blacks in the general population of Chicago are Catholics as compared to more than fifty per cent of the blacks in the upper ranks of the Chicago Police Department.

In March of 1960, there were ten thousand five hundred seventy-five police including 65 captains, 170 lieutenants, 697 sergeants, 1,373 detectives, 8,140

From left to right: The first black to be appointed captain was John T. Scott, who joined the department in 1903, and was appointed by Mayor Edward J. Kelly in 1940. Second was Harry B. Deas, who joined the department in 1915, appointed to captain 3/31/46. Third was Kinzie Bluitt, who joined the department 1/24/29, appointed to captain 7/16/54. Fourth was Harold L. Miles, who joined the department 8/27/45, appointed to captain 12/21/62. Fifth was Robert Harness, who joined the department 3/33, appointed to captain 1/15/62.

patrolmen, 72 policewomen, 41 matrons, one chief surgeon and thirteen assistant surgeons. Included in that number there were 1,500 Negro police, only four black sergeants, no black lieutenants and one black captain. Between the years of 1956 and 1960, not a single Negro was upgraded in the department, while at the same time, more than three hundred whites were promoted in various departments of the police department.

In 1870, Martin B. French, a black man, became the first gentleman of color to be appointed to the Chicago Police Department. During the next one-hundred year span between 1870 and 1970, progress for blacks as law enforcement officers has been deliberately slow. Although in 1970 the black population in metropolitan Chicago was 1,230,719, there were only 2,100 Negro police officers in the department including two deputy superintendents, one assistant deputy superintendent, five captains, seventeen lieutenants and thirty sergeants.

Former Commander George Sims, a Catholic convert, made the following observation:

A helpful way in the days of yore to get ahead in the department was to avoid congregating with other black police officers. Daley did not want three blacks to get together and discuss anything without his permission. He actually tried to enforce the old law against mob action, which decreed that any three blacks who got together were in a conspiracy to commit violence or overthrow the government. I can recall on one occasion during the Christmas holidays that Superintendent Fred Rice, who was a captain at that time, invited a bunch of us guys over to his house to celebrate the occasion. You wouldn't believe it, but the next day, I got a call from Jim Rockford who told me about a specific commander who attended the gathering and reported to him exactly what was said and by whom at that holiday party. It appeared that there were more than a fair number of guys around bucking to be promoted to a position high enough to kiss Mayor Daley's mistletoe.

The primary method for keeping blacks out of the top ranks can be found in the three part testing system employed to control the number of blacks in the hierarchy of the police department. The efficiency rating system is very subjective and can cause the brightest man to flunk. Here is an example of a case that came before me when I was sitting on the board. A black fellow by the name of Erskine Moore was given a seventy. He was a commander and a graduate of Northwestern University; he had both a Bachelor's and a Master's degree. There was no doubt about his integrity and ability, but they gave him a seventy on the efficiency test. Right behind him came an Irish Catholic by the name of Clark, who had been a lieutenant for only three months, but those bastards gave him a 100 efficiency rating. I said, "No way!" I had to fight like a dog to get Moore's rating increased to 93 and the other fellow's reduced. However, when the deal went down, the Irishman was made a captain. Apparently, the board's decision didn't mean anything because those fellows would go behind closed doors in an upper room and cut their own promotional deals for their family and friends.

When Father George Clements of Holy Angels Church on 607 East Oakwood Boulevard and some other white priests decided to support the Afro-American Patrolman's League and attempt to get a square deal for black patrolmen, they were called to attend a meeting at Mayor Richard J. Daley's office. Father Clements said: "The moment we were seated in Daley's inter-office, Daley started telling us that we should realize we were getting into an extremely sensitive area in the city and that we were playing with dynamite. The best thing for us to do was to reconsider our entire approach."

One of the Irish priests interrupted Daley and said, "Mayor Daley, all we are trying to do is to redress some of the evils that have been taking place in our city by the police for a very long time."

Daley looked at the priest and asked, "What kind of book do you have in your hand? Isn't that a breviary (a book of prayers)?"

The priest answered, "Yes."

Daley said, "Aren't you priests supposed to be reading that book every day?"

The priest responded, "Yes."

Left: Father George Clements, pastor of the Holy Angels Church. Right: George Sims, former police commander of the Filmore District.

"If you read that book more, you wouldn't have time to be getting into my book," Daley recoiled. "You see, the city of Chicago is my book. Therefore, I'm suggesting that you stay out of my book and stay in your book." Daley's tone was definitely vehement.

After the Daley meeting, Father George Clements was called to a meeting by Cardinal John Cody. The Cardinal was pacing the floor when Father Clements was escorted into the study at the Cardinal's home on 1555 North State Parkway. Before Father Clements could take a seat, the Cardinal started reprimanding the black priest. The Cardinal shouted, "Of all the things that I have had against you up until this point, the Afro-American Patrolman's League is the crowning point. This time you are really flirting with being suspended from the priesthood."

Cardinal John Cody.

Father George Clements replied, "Your Eminence, what you don't seem to understand is that there are a lot of ethnic groups within the police department, and all of them have their various organizations. We have the Polish Patrolman's Association, the Italian Police Federation, the Irish Police Association, and I am against all of these groups because they are building walls around people where we should be building bridges. Your Eminence, if you recall, not too long ago, you gave the invocation at the Irish Policeman's Association banquet."

The Cardinal retorted: "And there are other things I don't like about you."

Father Clements noted that the Cardinal's response was the typical response of most white folk. They didn't see anything wrong with something being white. But the moment black people got together in an association like the Afro-American Patrolman's League, it suddenly denoted a conspiracy of some kind, which means that the Illinois Black Laws of the nineteenth century were still "alive and well" and living in Chicago.

The slave and master mentality of the last century was alive and well and living in Chicago. The fact was exemplified by another scene between Cardinal John Cody and Father George Clements.

Father Clements explained:

I had a black unity mass at Holy Angels Church, and priests from all over the country came to bear witness. There was a huge crowd, and a lot of media play. I had tiger skins on the altar to symbolize our blackness. Cardinal Cody was furious when he saw the event on the five o'clock news. He called and told me to meet him at his home promptly, within forty-five minutes. I knew I had been a bad boy because the Cardinal only invited priests to his home, located at 1555 North Parkway, when he was going to chew them out. If the Cardinal simply wanted to transact some business, he would have had me come to his chancery office at 155 E. Superior. On the other hand, if he was going to tell me something positive like giving me a promotion or a new church, he would show up unannounced at my parish.

The Cardinal made no pretense in doing anything positive because he started screaming and yelling the moment I stepped into his study because he felt that I had been insubordinate in putting the tigers' skins on the altar. The Cardinal got up from his desk, shook his fingers in my face, and said, "Listen, don't you know you belong to me. You belong to me! Don't you understand that!" He was yelling at the top of his voice.

I looked up at him and said, "Yes suh boss!"

The Cardinal responded, "Yes! That's right!"

He then sat down calmly as if nothing had happened and asked, "How is your dear mother?"

Father Clements continued:

> The irony of what had happened in our dialogue had been totally lost on the
> Cardinal because in his mind, he said this boy now realizes his place and
> therefore, we can now go on and take care of something else. It really wasn't
> so much a racial thing as it was a thing of authority. Privately, we priests
> used to refer to Cardinal Cody as Mayor Cody and Mayor Richard J. Daley
> as Cardinal Daley because neither of them would make any important move
> without consulting the other.

Membership in the Roman Catholic Church was helpful to ambitious black
fire fighters, but not as much as in climbing the promotional ladder within the
Chicago Fire Department as it was in the police department. There have been
only sixteen black fire chiefs appointed within the one hundred and thirteen
years that blacks have been working for the Chicago Fire Department. It was
not until September, 1958, eighty-six years after the first Negro was appointed
to the department, that a black gentleman, who was a Catholic convert was
permitted to rise to the rank of fire chief. His name was Grant Chaney. Edwin
Williams, Mike Ellis, and Woodie McCune, the second, third, and fourth black
fire chiefs were not members of the Catholic church. Crawford Smith, the fifth
black fire chief was Catholic. Fred P. Morgan, the sixth, Jessie Stewart, the
seventh, and Oswald Lewis, the eighth fire chief were all Protestants. As a
matter of fact, only two of the first eight black fire chiefs were Catholics.
However, some of the black firemen, like the policemen, joined the Roman
Catholic church for a very practical reason. They felt that the Catholic priests
could help them and many of the firemen who gave large donations to the
church were helped. Some priests had open lines of communication to either
Tom Donnovan, Daley's patronage chief, or directly to Mayor Richard J.
Daley, which was not a handicap for a parishoner seeking job opportunities
through a clout-laden priest.

There were blacks who worked in the "Jim Crow" firehouses as acting
engineers (fire truck drivers) until 1954; however, they had never been appointed as such officially. In 1954, twelve whites were officially appointed
engineers, and they replaced the acting blacks. The only whites in the black
firehouses were the engineers, the lieutenants, and the captains. Mayor
Richard J. Daley did not use the power of his office to integrate the Chicago
Fire Department until the west side riot of 1965. Until that time, the firehouses
were either all black or all white with the exception of the omnipotent
presence of white officers.

Les Outerbridge, president of the Afro-American Fireman's League states
that "As of February, 1980, there were 500 black fireman on the force and 300

Top row, left to right: Grant R. Chaney, entered department 12/19/29, promoted to chief 9/1/58, retired as deputy marshal 6/1/63; Edwin Williams, entered department 9/16/43, promoted to chief 1/1/62, retired as first deputy marshal 4/30/78; Mike Ellis, entered department 12/16/29, promoted to chief 7/12/64, retired 7/13/65. Bottom row, left to right: Woodie McCune, entered department 2/8/54, promoted to chief 6/1/65, retired deputy marshal 6/5/81; Crawford Smith, entered department 8/23/43, promoted to chief 1/1/67, retired as division marshal 7/16/76; Fred T. Morgan, entered department 2/8/44, promoted to chief 4/1/72, retired as deputy marshal 4/29/82.

of them had less than five year's service. The 300 were hired in 1977 as a result of a suit brought against the Chicago Fire Department by the Justice Department that commenced in 1973."

The Chicago Fire Department's cotton curtain engulfed Russ Ewing in its "Jim Crowism" when he joined Engine Fire Company #48 in 1956. The fire station was located on 40th and Dearborn Street, the current site of the Robert Taylor Homes.

Russ Ewing, Channel 7's (ABC) Emmy Award Winning investigative reporter and former fire fighter, explains:

> I resented every day that I had to work under the racist conditions that existed in the Chicago Fire Department. However, I needed a job, and that was

the best job available for a guy who was married and working his way through college. I found a fun way to relieve my frustrations and survive working under adverse conditions. At night, when my fellow fire fighters were upstairs in the bunk room playing cards, I would spray paint and stencil over the large Chicago Fire Department letters on the side of our fire trucks and substitute it with "Colored Fire Department." The next day, when we rolled down the streets in our fire trucks, the Negroes would look and see Colored Fire Department and fall out laughing. Of course, when the white chiefs would see the sign, they would nearly have a heart attack.

The white chiefs tried from time to time to find out who was doing it, and they never could. And yet, all the black fellows knew it was me. The lieutenant would make us wipe it off as soon as he discovered it, but the next night I would put it right back on again. I saw it as a way of giving vent to my resentment of having to work under "Jim Crow" circumstances.

Russ Ewing's no-nonsense attitude was resented by the white officers in his fire station. They finally got even with him when he took the engineer's examination. Russ Ewing recalls:

When I took the engineer's and lieutenant's examination, I received the highest mark any black person had gotten up until that time. But I got the lowest mark in efficiency. At that time, they gave you an efficiency mark based on what they thought of you. My efficiency grade was so low that it indicated I couldn't even walk. However, there was another guy in our company by the name of _____ _____ who couldn't add up a grocery bill, but he was an ace Uncle Tom. He got a low mark on the written exam because he couldn't figure out water pressure and other mathematical formulas, which didn't matter, because he had the blessings of the Great White Fathers. They made him engineer because they loved him. In fairness to _____, he was basically a good fireman. He just couldn't count.

Later, I started writing an anonymous column for the Chicago Defender about racism in the Chicago Fire Department. They really jumped down on my behind about that action.

Commissioner Robert Quinn called Ewing down to his office one day and said:
"Russ, are you going to shut up?"
Ewing retorted, "Shut up about what?"
Quinn shouted, "We know what you are doing. We know you are the one causing all the trouble. I'm talking about that integration stuff. What I want to know is are you going to shut up?"
Ewing recoiled, "I don't know how to shut up."
Russ Ewing's behavior created a dilemma for Quinn. The commissioner

Seated to the left is Russ Ewing, former firefighter and current Emmy award-winning newscaster for the ABC Television Network, interviewing the Honorable Elijah Muhammad, spiritual leader of the Nation of Islam.

did not want to fire Ewing, but he had to discipline him. To do otherwise would lower the morale of the white officers at Engine Company #48 and also encourage other black firemen to follow Russ Ewing's anti-establishment behavior. Hence, Commissioner Quinn took the road least travelled. After reflecting for a moment, and with a broad smile on his face, Ewing described Quinn's actions:

> Quinn decided to take me out of fire station #48 because I was a troublemaker. He put me to work in his office down at 840 N. Orleans where they could watch me like a hawk eight hours a day. When I was working in the fire station, I worked twenty-four hours straight, and then was off for the next forty-eight hours. When he placed me in that north side office for punishment, it meant I had to show up for work every solitary day.
>
> Since I did not have to go to any fires, I just sat there and studied my college courses everyday for two years. Sometimes when Ruth (my wife) and I reminisced about the old days when I was a fireman and the pranks I used to pull, we frequently cracked up with laughter that bordered on hysteria.

In 1960 the pickets marching around the Chicago Board of Education were not laughing as they protested against the double shifts in some of Chicago's public schools. The pickets represented three organizations: Mothers on the March, Lawndale Citizens Committee, and the Chicago Committee of Racial Equality. The groups contended that there was no shortage of classrooms in the city and that if the school districts were revised and the buses used to transport people, the double shift could end immediately. Dr. Faith Rich, chairman of the Chicago Committee of Racial Equality (CORE), said, "Our committee found potential classroom seating capacity for 50,000 people unused in one hundred and seventeen schools, many of them near the double shift areas." However, Sergeant Shriver, Jr., president of the Chicago Board and brother-in-law of Senator John F. Kennedy, the Democrat's nominee for president, denied there were enough classroom seats available to end the double shift.

Meanwhile, as CORE picketed against the Chicago School Board's gerrymandered boundaries, Dr. Martin Luther King, Jr. and thirty-five student demonstrators remained in jail in Atlanta, Georgia. They chose jail rather than post bond for the pending trial on charges that Dr. King and the student demonstrators violated Georgia's new state law aimed at stopping sit-in demonstrations against segregation. Dr. King and the thirty-five student demonstrators had been bound over to criminal court on the five hundred dollar bond on charges that they violated the anti-trespass law to make it a misdemeanor to refuse to leave a legal business establishment at the request of the owner. King said after his arraignment: "I cannot in all good conscience accept bail. I will stay in jail a year if necessary. It is our sincere hope that the acceptance of sufferance on our part will serve to awaken the dozing consciousness of our community."

Dr. King's incarceration was a result of his sit-in demonstrations at Rich, Woolworth's and several other stores in the Atlanta area. There were no Rich stores located in the Chicago area; therefore, the Chicago Branch of the NAACP picketed the Woolworth's stores locally in support of Dr. Martin Luther King, Jr.'s crusade against injustice.

On October 21st and 22nd, conferences were held in Atlanta at the request of Mayor William Hartsfield with members of the Southern Christian Leadership Conference. Mayor Hartsfield agreed to use his influence with the merchants to have charges against the students and Dr. King dropped and their release effective immediately. The student sit-in demonstrators agreed to a thirty day truce while the mayor worked to end discrimination in Atlanta's downtown lunch counters.

The charges against Dr. King and the students were subsequently dropped, but officials in DeKalb County intervened to prevent the release of Dr. King. Judge Oscar Mitchell of the DeKalb County court issued an order directing Dr. King to explain why the results of his participation in the sit-ins should not void his suspended sentence imposed for a minor traffic violation of failing to obtain a driver's license. Dr. King had previously pleaded guilty to the traffic charge and was fined twenty-five dollars and placed on probation for one year. On Tuesday, October 25, Judge Mitchell revoked the suspended sentence, refused bail, and ordered the Montgomery-bus-boycott leader to serve four months in prison.

Lyndon Baines Johnson, vice presidential candidate.

Present in the courtroom at the time King was ordered to go to prison were NAACP Executive Secretary Roy Wilkins and a host of other Negro leaders from Atlanta schools and colleges. Tension in the courtroom was so high that Dr. Samuel W. Williams, president of the Atlanta NAACP branch, was arrested for simply standing too close to a white spectator.

While Dr. King sat in the jail cell in Reidsville State Prison, located two hundred miles south of Atlanta, Richard J. Daley, mayor of Chicago, located exactly 702 miles north of Atlanta, was busy preparing to stage a whooping, hollering, floor stomping rally at the Morrison Hotel for vice presidential candidate Lyndon Baines Johnson. Daley was also directing his Democratic precinct troops to deliver a quota of three thousand persons per ward to march for Senator John F. Kennedy, the Democratic candidate for president, in what was billed to be the largest torch light parade in the history of Chicago. More than seventy-five drum and bugle corps, some from as far away as two hundred miles, signed up for the two mile parade from Grant Park to the Chicago Stadium at 1800 West Madison Street. One hundred and ten floats representing every ward and township in Cook County had signed on to participate in electing the first Catholic to the presidency of the United States.

Dr. King's incarceration did not receive any comments from Richard Milhouse Nixon who was the Republican presidential candidate. But Robert Kennedy, Senator John F. Kennedy's brother, called Judge Mitchell, and Senator Kennedy called Mrs. King. This act of humanity delivered more Negro votes than any Texas style get-together or torch-light parade ever could. When presidential candidate John F. Kennedy phoned the Rev. Martin

Luther King Jr.'s pregnant wife, Coretta, he said: "This must be very hard on you and Dr. King. I want you both to know I'm thinking of you, and I will do what I can to help." Dr. King walked from behind the white walls of Reidsville Prison shortly after the Kennedys intervened.

Judge Mitchell denied that he had been influenced by the Kennedy call. The Judge said that "pressure favoring King's release had come from those close to a candidate for president of the United States." The actions of the Kennedys were in such a contrast to Nixon, that many Abe Lincoln politically oriented Negroes publicly admitted that this deed helped make up their minds in favor of the Democratic candidate. Ministers such as Dr. King's father openly stated that although they had been adverse in voting for a Catholic,

President John F. Kennedy and Mayor Richard J. Daley of Chicago.

the humane Kennedy action now warranted their support. Dr. Martin Luther King, Jr., after being released from jail said: "I feel it's my duty to remain free to criticize both parties, but for fear of being considered an ingrate, I want to make it clear that I am grateful to Senator John F. Kennedy."

John F. Kennedy's election gave Mayor Richard J. Daley an opportunity to offer Congressman William L. Dawson a bite out of an apple from the Garden of Eden. Daley and Dawson were in a heated disagreement over Edith Sampson's ambition to become a judge. Daley supported Edith, but Dawson was opposed because he felt that her behavior around white folk was not creditable. Hence, Mayor Daley encouraged President-elect Kennedy to offer Dawson a job as postmaster general (and the honor of being the first Negro cabinet member), but the seventy-four year old man did not bite the apple. Had Dawson accepted the cabinet position, it would have given Mayor Daley unobstructed power over Chicago's black political submachine.

In December, 1960, when Dawson was queried about the postmaster general's appointment by some members of the Second Ward Organization, he retorted, "If I had taken that job Kennedy offered, he would be my boss, and I don't want no damn boss." Dawson then leaned back in his chair and looked out of the second floor window of his office at people passing on the west side of the street on Thirty-fourth and South Indiana Avenue. He pointed his finger at the people and uttered, "How many votes does the postmaster general have?"

Edith Sampson was appointed a municipal judge in 1962 by Mayor Richard J. Daley without Dawson's blessing. The seventy-six year old congressman was visibly upset about Daley usurping his committeeman power and appointing Sampson, who was a member of Dawson's Second Ward Regular Democratic Organization. Daley had moved in on Dawson's political domain in the same fashion that the congressman had castrated the Chicago Branch of the NAACP. There has been little to no opposition for the once coveted office of the presidency of the Chicago Branch of the NAACP since December, 1959. Dempsey J. Travis refused to stand for re-election for a second term in that office in December, 1960.

Members of CORE and other civil rights groups picket the White City Roller Rink at 63rd and South Parkway (Martin Luther King Dr.) in 1946 in protest of its policy of excluding Negroes.

Chapter *XVIII*

Fracturing the Chains of Racism and Plantation Politics

In January of 1960, Chicago, the city that Edwin C. Berry, the executive director of the Chicago Urban League had characterized as the most segregated city in the United States was without an effective mainstream civil rights organization. The Chicago Branch of the NAACP, the largest branch in the nation, had been co-opted by the Daley Democratic machine and, therefore, ceased to articulate the black experience except in toothless rhetoric that was designed not to offend Mayor Richard J. Daley or the Chicago business establishment.

The void of civil rights leadership left both black and white youth floundering and searching for a vehicle with which to counterattack political and economic oppression in Chicago. CORE, the Congress of Racial Equality, came to the rescue and re-entered the Chicago civil rights market in full force in February 1960. CORE began its campaign by wrapping a picket line around a Woolworth store in the Loop in support of the students' lunch counter sit-in movement in the South against the Kresge and Woolworth stores. The Chicago Branch of the NAACP in an effort to catch up with the young tigers joined CORE in March 1960 by picketing the Woolworth store in the Lake Meadows Shopping Center on the South Side.

It was most appropriate for CORE to step up to the civil rights batter's box with a picket sign because CORE was founded in Chicago on the University of Chicago campus in March of 1942 by James Farmer, George Houser, Bernice Fisher, Homer Jack, Joe Guinn, and James R. Robinson. Farmer and Guinn were black; the other four men were white. CORE was both the father and the mother of sit-down demonstrations which CORE initially employed in Chicago in 1942 and 1943 against Stoner's Restaurant in the loop at 23 North Dearborn Street and at Jack Spratt's Restaurant at Forty-seventh and Kimbark Avenue. The management of both Stoner's and Spratt's had been persistent in their refusal to serve blacks while CORE was equally as persistent in seeking change. During the same period, the University of Chicago CORE members picketed six eating establishments near the campus that had refused to serve Negro students. The Hyde Park area eateries demonstrated against were Todd's Restaurant, Steak and Shake, Hagen's Steak House, Skelton's Drugs, Bidwell's Candy Shop and the Steak and Shake Drive-in.

Merle Todd, of Todd's Restaurant said that if there was a suit brought against him, he would fight it through all the courts if it took 15 years.

Attorney Jewel Stradford Lafontant, former member of CORE, a deputy U.S. solicitor general during the Nixon and Ford administrations, and currently a very successful legal practitioner.

Top left: Edwin C. Berry, the executive director of the Chicago Urban League. Berry characterized Chicago as "the most segregated city in America." Bottom left: James Farmer, civil rights leader and cofounder of the Congress of Racial Equality (CORE).

Jewel LaFontant, a law student at the University of Chicago in 1943, recalls:

> Interracial groups testing the various restaurants received a hostile reception. Sometimes we were served at Jack Spratt's but in an uncivil manner. In one instance, the dishes we blacks used were actually smashed in our presence by the manager. Stoner's downtown would seat the CORE test groups after a long wait and would serve them meat with eggshells scattered on it, a plate of food salted so heavily that it could not be eaten, or a sandwich composed of lettuce and tomato cores picked out of the garbage can. I remember there was a crippled white fellow with us, who was kicked. We were really abused. We would then turn around and file a lawsuit. I was on the Legal Redress Committee of the NAACP. We filed lawsuits against the various restaurants, and we ran Stoner's out of business.

Attorney Patrick B. Prescott, counsel for the Woodlawn AME Church, at 6456 South Evans Avenue, planned to file a $100,000 suit against Northwestern University for refusing to honor housing reservations for Ms. Robbie Shield of 6449 Eberhart in Willard Hall which was located on the campus of the university. Ms. Shield was sent away from the Evanston campus at midnight to a colored rooming house in the Black Belt section of that northern suburb because Northwestern University refused to house Negroes in any house or dormitory on its grounds. Reverend Archibald J. Carey Jr., pastor of Woodlawn AME Church, stated that he had received numerous telephone calls offering financial assistance for instituting legal proceedings and that the official board of the church had unanimously voted to back the suit. The Woodlawn AME Church was the site of CORE's first national convention, hosted by Reverend Carey, that took place the weekend of June 5, 1943.

In August, 1943, CORE widened its attack to include "Jim Crow" blood banks. The Chicago chapter of the American Red Cross and area hospitals had a policy of segregating the blood plasma of Negro and Caucasion donors. More than one hundred CORE protestants stormed the offices of the Chicago chapter of the American Red Cross Society at 5 North Wabash Avenue with leaflets outlining the bigotrous practice of blood segregation and referred to it as contrary to medical science democracy and the best national morale. The leaflets, in addition to the protest, quoted the *Journal of American Medical Association* in an article of July 4, 1942 which stated:

> There is no evidence that the blood of Negroes differs in any significant respect from that of white persons. The successful transfusion of whole blood from white persons to Negroes or vice versa can be accomplished quite as readily as between members of the same race . . . the segregation

of the blood of white persons from the blood of Negroes in blood banks is, therefore, not only unscientific but is a grievous affront to the largest minority in our country . . .

On February 8, 1947, the University of Chicago CORE group had a demonstration of approximately 1,000 students in a quarter-mile picket line around the university campus. This was a culmination of many years of work on the part of university CORE representatives and the University of Chicago students to end discrimination in the hospitals, clinics and the medical school of the university. As early as 1943, the Chicago CORE issued an action pamphlet documenting its case against the university's hospitals, clinics, and the medical school. In spite of the CORE investigation, nothing was done between 1943 and 1947 by the university officials to change the picture; therefore, direct action was mandatory. The campus newspaper, *The Daily Maroon* supported the two hour walk-out by the students.

Bessie Davis, a University of Chicago graduate and retired public school teacher currently living in Chatham, who was a student at the University of Chicago in 1941 recalls:

> I became ill while in class, and I was given some medicine at the student clinic which caused my condition to worsen because of an allergy. I subsequently developed jaundice and Billings Hospital refused to admit me although I was enrolled in the university's student health plan. My mother was directed by the Billings admittance office to take me to Provident, the colored hospital. When I returned to school the following year, I refused to pay the student health fee.

The earlier CORE research on the practice of racism in clinics and hospitals was one of the linchpins in a suit filed by a group of Negro physicians in February, 1961 alleging anti-trust violations against 56 Chicago hospitals for discriminating against Negro patients and physicians. The suit charged that restrictions and limitations had been placed on the appointment of Negro doctors to hospital staffs and the admittance of Negro patients. It further contended that the defendants were guilty of a boycott in violation of the Clayton and Sherman Anti-Trust Acts; and therefore, CORE was seeking a court order to stop the alleged practice.

The groups named in the suit by the Negro doctors include the Hospital Service Corp which adminstered the Blue Cross Plan and the Illinois Medical Service. Also named were the Chicago Medical Society, Chicago Hospital Council and the Illinois Hospital Association. The suit further contended that the boycott against blacks had been carried out since 1938 and that it had applied to all hospital services including administering drugs and medicines.

The physicians who filed the suit were Dr. N. O. Callaway, president of the Medical Associates of Chicago and a recent past president of the Chicago Urban League, John W. Coleman, Robert G. Morris, Arthur G. Falls, Audley R. Mamby, C. L. Martin, George Shropshear, John Standfield, Charles L. Williams and Charles W. Wren. The list of 56 hospitals named included all the major hospitals from the American Hospital to the Woodlawn Hospital.

The history of CORE and its ongoing student action committees made it attractive to both black and white activists in the 1960's when their kind were literally locked out of the Chicago Branch of the NAACP's decision making activities by black Daleyites on the board. It was not uncommon to have a black Daley supporter whisper in another member's ear that Joe Blow was a communist simply because Joe Blow wanted to challenge the political plantation system in Chicago. Therefore, in 1960 when Robert Lucas, the current executive director of the Kenwood-Oakwood Community Organization (KOCO) and past chairman of the Chicago Branch of the Congress of Racial Equality, looked for something to do other than work in the Post Office, he joined CORE. Bob Lucas observed:

> CORE was the only organization with an agenda in place to actively fight "Jim Crow" in the schools, "Jim Crow" in the hospital, and "Jim Crow" in housing. I joined the University of Chicago unit of CORE because it was the strongest in the city. Most of the officers in the unit were white. This was also true at the national level. Although CORE had moved its headquarters from Chicago to New York in the mid nineteen forties in search of a more favorable climate for its cause, the local chapter of CORE got a tremendous amount of support from the liberal Jewish community.
>
> We got involved in school boycotts in 1961 because we felt Ben Willis, who was then the superintendent of Chicago schools, was containing blacks in so-called "Willis wagons". If a school was on the border between the white and black community, Superintendent Willis would contain blacks in "Willis wagons" or mobile units stuffed into school playgrounds.

Chicago CORE played a crucial role in the early school boycott demonstrations; however, it was outgeneraled in the struggle by a twenty-eight-year-old black militant, Lawrence Landry, who was the chairman of Chicago Area Friends of the Student Non-violent Coordinating Committee (SNCC). CORE was literally buried in the school battle in a broad base coalition of neighborhood groups called the Chicago Committee of Community Organizations that had come together under one umbrella specifically to fight both "Big Ben Willis" and Chicago's "Jim Crow" school system.

On September 4, 1963, Chicago's "Jim Crow" school system swung open its doors to 553,000 pupils and 21,000 teachers. Mobile school rooms or "Willis wagons" had been the target of demonstrations during the hot summer of 1963. The summer had included a mass demonstration led by Dr. L. H. Holman, president of the Illinois state branches of the NAACP. The ranks of the Holman march against "Jim Crow" schools were enlarged by the fact that the national NAACP held its fifty-fourth annual convention in Chicago during the first week in July, and eight hundred delegates from that body joined Dr. Holman in the protest march against "Willis wagons". Conspicuously absent from that march was Reverend W. N. Daniels, president of the Chicago chapter of the NAACP. The national NAACP delegates marched in front of the Board of Education Building at 228 North LaSalle Street chanting, "We Shall Overcome" for a period of one hour, and then they circled the blocks from LaSalle Street west to Wells, north on Wells to Wacker and back to LaSalle a half a dozen times carrying signs which read, "Jim Crow Must Go" . . . "Mr. Willis . . . Away with Segregated Wagons". When the delegates completed their sixth circle, they returned to the NAACP convention headquarters which was at the Morrison Hotel.

June Shagaloff, the NAACP special assistant for education, said:

> The march has a two-fold purpose, first to protest the refusal of the Chicago Board of Education and superintendent of schools, Benjamin Willis, to end defacto segregation in the public schools of Chicago and to highlight the NAACP's nationwide desegration drive in the north and west which now extends into seventy communities in eighteen states. The Chicago school board and Mr. Willis, who is known as the "darling" of the Ford Foundation, maintains one of the most rigid and extremely segregated school systems outside of the South.

Left: Parents and friends picketing the use of "Willis wagons" because they were employed by Mayor Richard J. Daley and Superintendent Benjamin C. Willis as instruments to maintain "Jim Crow" schools in Chicago. Right: Superintendent of the Chicago Board of Education, Benjamin C. Willis.

Reverend Joseph H. Jackson, president of the National Baptist Convention, USA, Inc.

On June 30th, three days before the NAACP demonstration at the Chicago Board of Education Building, Dr. Lucien H. Holman launched a verbal attack upon Mayor Richard J. Daley and Governor Otto Kerner as they sat smiling sheepishly on the platform of the Progressive Baptist Church at the opening mass meeting of the Fifty-Fourth NAACP Convention. Holman accused both Mayor Daley and Governor Kerner of not doing enough to advance the cause of Negro people. He also attacked Negro aldermen, commonly known as the "Silent Six," although the number had been reduced to five because Benjamin F. Lewis had been assassinated.

Holman criticized the aldermen:

> The Negro people in Chicago are tired of the slow pace and are impatient. They resent the pace set by their elected leaders. Alderman Leon Depres (who is white) acts more like a Negro than you Negro aldermen. Negro leaders should be more militant, and in this day and time, Negro leadership is going to have to be more vocal. Negroes will not be pacified by one federal judge (James B. Parsons) or Bill Dawson (William L. Dawson), congressional leader from the First District. These two men have been presented to black folk as idols. If either one of them died or retired, there would be only a single Negro leader left.

Dr. Holman did not stand alone in his criticism of Negro leaders, white and black advocates for equal rights who picketed Mrs. Wendell E. Green, a Daley-appointed colored member of the board of education twice during the month of June because the leaders felt she had betrayed them. They also picketed Dr. Joseph H. Jackson, president of the National Baptist Convention, USA, Inc., on the eve of the NAACP convention because he advocated a moratorium on civil rights demonstrations.

Leaders of the National Association for the Advancement of Colored People lead a civil rights parade down State Street during their 1963 Chicago Convention. In the front line center are Bishop Stephen G. Spottswood, chairman of the Board of Directors of the NAACP; Mayor Richard J. Daley, carrying a flag and Roy Wilkins.

Dick Gregory, the popular comedian, joined a demonstration protesting the erection of "Willis wagons" at Seventy-First and Lowe Street and was arrested. In the meanwhile, a group of parents continued to demonstrate at the Guggenheim Elementary School, 7146 South Sangamon Avenue, in protest of mobile units that had been moved there during the summer. Five demonstrating picketers were arrested. They included Marcia Lee, 19; Vickie Harris, 20; Robert Brown, and Kitt Pleune, all members of CORE. Pleune, Lee and Brown were released after they were charged with disorderly conduct and fingerprinted at the police station whereas the other two persons were charged with interfering with police after they chained themselves to a squad car.

As a result of the turmoil involving Dick Gregory, the board of education in an unusual move overruled Superintendent Benjamin Willis and announced that mobile classrooms would be removed from the Seventy-First and Lowe Street site. Superintendent Willis steamed but did not boil over the Seventy-First and Lowe decision by the board. However, when he was compelled by an order handed down by the Superior Court on October 3, 1963 to transfer twenty-four students, mainly blacks to schools that they had chosen pursuant to a board of education directive, the superintendent blew up and resigned the following day. The Coordinating Council of Community Organizations was ecstatic. The daily press, with the exception of the *Chicago Tribune*, was in accord with Superintendent Benjamin C. Willis' decision to resign while the *Chicago Defender*, unlike the other daily papers attacked Willis.

The editorials from the various newspapers read:

"Dr. Willis (. . . is not irreplaceable . . . we do not think that the board should return from its own concept of progress by the petulance of its administration." (Editorial, *Chicago Daily News*, October 9, 1963)

"The resignation of Dr. Benjamin C. Willis has been inevitable for some months . . . whatever the reason may have been, Dr. Willis lost contact with both his board and his public . . . it is the obligation of the superintendent to carry out the policy of the board, once decreed, or, if he disagrees, as Mr. Willis did, to resign." (Editorial, *Chicago Sun-Times*, October 6, 1963)

"We wish the superintendent well: there are many positions, we are sure, that will benefit from a hard driving executive who wants his word to be law. But in this tense and touchy year of 1963, the directorship of the Chicago school system is not one of them." (Editorial, *Chicago American*, October 7, 1963)

"(Dr. Willis) still not without his power. He's the Madam Nhu of racial progress in Chicago—the Charles DeGaulle of American education—the Governor Wallace of Chicago standing in the doorways of an equal education for all

Negro kids in this city—A one man educational John Birch Society, incarnate, inviolate." (Editorial, *Chicago Defender,* October 12, 1963)

On October 7th, black Chicagoans were treated to the sickening spectacle of the school board crawling on its collective knees seeking an absentee employee, the superintendent of public schools. The board went into special session to vote to reconsider Willis' resignation. Six voted to reconsider while two voted against it.

The Student's Non-Violent Coordinating Committee (SNCC) posted a thinly-veiled threat of a massive school boycott against the board of education for refusing to accept Willis' resignation. Lawrence Landry, Co-chairman of the Chicago Area Friends of SNCC said: "If the board is waiting for the reaction of civil rights groups, it will not be disappointed. We predict a massive unified form of direct action, probably a school boycott soon." The Coordinating Council of Community Organizations (CCCO) scheduled a special meeting to take up the Willis matter. However, the Reverend Wilbur N. Daniels, president of the Chicago branch of NAACP said, "the NAACP had not planned any action as of yet."

On Wednesday, October 16th, the board of education hearing room was packed with a predominantly segregationist group representing the Southwest side communities. When Superintendent Benjamin C. Willis strolled proudly and arrogantly into the boardroom, the white community

Coordinating Council of Community Organizations (CCCO) officials hold a press conference the day before the October 21, 1963 school boycott. It was Chicago's first major school boycott. (Left to right): Reverend Arthur Brazier, former chairman of the CCCO; James Forman, leader of SNCC; Lawrence Landry, chairman of the Coordinating Council of Community Organizatins; Rose Simpson, civil rights activist and Carl Fuqua, executive secretary of the Chicago branch of the NAACP.

representatives stood and gave him a thunderous round of applause. Claire Roddewig, president of the board of education, immediately asked the board members to retire to an inner office for a private session. After the members had deliberated for ninety minutes, they returned to a hearing room that was quieter than a cemetery tombstone. Thomas Murray, chairman of the committee, read the long awaited report which in substance said the superintendent had the support of the board. The anti-integrationist group broke into a loud round of cheers and applause.

Warren Bacon, opposed the acceptance of the report without detailed clarification on the relationship between the board and the superintendent. Bacon was voted down by the seven other members of the board including the other colored member, Mrs. Wendell E. Green. Hence, Benjamin C. Willis was back in the driver's seat.

A strange thing happened on Tuesday, October 15, 1963. Mayor Richard J. Daley, Benjamin Willis' creator, gave permission to the "Silent Six" black aldermen to open their mouths, speak up and attack the "Frankenstein" of the Chicago educational system. He further instructed them to run as fast as hell and catch up with the majority of their constituents who were apparently hell-bent on following the dicates of Lawrence Landry and the CCCO in boycotting the Chicago school system on October 22nd, a day which had been declared "Freedom Day" by the Coordinating Council of Community Organizations.

The temporary liberated aldermen made the following statements. Alderman Ralph Metcalfe, Third Ward:

> I'm in complete agreement with the philosophy behind the October 22nd boycott. If the city is not aware of the depth of feeling of Negroes regarding the inferior education Negro children are receiving, the one day boycott should be dramatic proof that Negroes are nearing the breaking point. Willis has become a symbol of segregated education in Chicago. He is asked to be relieved of his duties. I think the board of education is bowing to unreasonable pressure by trying to retain Dr. Willis. The board of education is obligated to set policy which will benefit all the people in the system. It must not advocate this responsibility which is a mandate from the public.

Alderman Claude W. B. Holman, Fourth Ward:

> I am definitely opposed to the board of education retaining Superintendent Willis. I think the one day boycott is a good thing, something to rivet in the minds of Chicago that there are thousands and thousands of people in the city who do not want the school board to ask him to return. We have a school's problem committee in the Fourth Ward that is ready to carry the message to the school board by participation in the October 22nd boycott.

Alderman Robert Miller, Sixth Ward:

I have been opposed to Superintendent Willis and his policies since the beginning. I had a heated quarrel with him when he proposed the building of the John Foster Dulles Elementary School at 63rd Street and Calumet, which is opposite the elevator noise, taverns and heavy traffic. I pointed out to the superintendent how these things would harm the children in their attempts to study and the threat to their safety in travel to and from home. Willis told me in no uncertain terms that I could forget it. He was going to build the school anyhow, and he did. I am against his dictatorial attitude towards the board of education and his procedures in the business that affect our children. I also blame the board for weakening its position with him. They have allowed things to happen by default because of its weakness. As for the boycott, I endorse it because it will not hurt the students.

Alderman Charles Chew Jr., Seventeenth Ward:

I feel that Superintendent Willis has served his usefulness to Chicago as the head of the school system. The board should accept his resignation without equivocation. If his resignation is not accepted, all of the liberal, forthright citizens of this town should march on the board of education members in an attempt to have them reconsider.

I would say that it is about time that my fellow aldermen started turning their positive actions to work on the council floor.

All the things that are needed to aid us should be done by changing the law. I think they should stop establishing new organizations and start acting like representatives of the people.

Alderman Kenneth E. Campbell, Twentieth Ward:

I endorse the one day boycott, but I am definitely against a sit-in because I do not approve of any action which would interfere with the normal, legal function of government. I feel the boycott is a demonstration for an American principle. I do not think keeping the students away from the school for one day is as harmful as the segregation which can harm them for the rest of their lives.

Alderman William Harvey of the Second Ward was out of the city, but Lawrence Woods, Congressman William Dawson's administrative assistant said: "The Second Ward is backing the boycott one hundred percent. We will take whatever steps that are necessary to make it effective. We will go out, bar none. That means furnishing ward workers, precinct captains, everything."

The endorsement of an independent civil rights protest by Chicago's black

Alderman Charles Chew Jr. of the Seventeenth Ward and the only black member of the city council who supported the school boycott.

ward political machines marked a 100% turn in Chicago politics. The all-out endorsement by the black aldermen indicated that Richard J. Daley had given their actions his blessings and that he did not object to a strong anti-Willis protest inasmuch as Superintendent Willis was already back in the saddle at the board and riding herd over his minions. Daley obviously felt that a full-blown Willis protest would give the Negro community an opportunity to get a small taste of victory and blow off some steam.

8:30 A.M. Tuesday, October 22nd, was one of the finest hours for Chicago Negroes and liberal-minded white folk. Streets that were usually jammed with little Negro children enroute to segregated schools were empty. Twenty thousand boycott supporters had encircled City Hall. Later that morning, the human wave floated down LaSalle Street to the Chicago Board of Education Building chanting, "Willis Must Go, Willis Must Go." Several hundred Chicago policemen formed a human barricade at the board headquarters to prevent the huge spirited crowd that had gathered to hear Dick Gregory and others from spilling onto Wacker Drive. James Farmer, executive director of CORE said: "You came here today to see that Willis goes. He must go. And we will help you keep that promise."

Lawrence Landry, boycott leader, stated:

> The retention of Superintendent Benjamin Willis by the school board was conceived in ignorance and dedicated to the proposition that cynical politics shall reign forever. The school board has issued an overt and public insult to those of us who seek high quality integrated education in Chicago.

James Foreman, national chairman of the student Non-Violent Coordinating Committee, asked the crowd if it would be prepared to "do this again next month", and the crowd roared its willingness.

Seventy-five days had not lapsed before the need arose to call a second school boycott. Lawrence Landry declared on January 2, 1964: "The city council stabbed Chicago Negroes in the back . . ." The council's school committee had voted to approve the appointment of Cyrus Adams and Mrs. Lydon Wild to the board of education. SNCC and several other civil rights organizations had opposed the appointments in the belief that at least one black should have been submitted to Mayor Daley for consideration. Adding insult to injury, the council committee's lone Negro member, Sixth Ward Alderman, Robert H. Miller, voted with the majority in the thirteen to one vote to confirm both Adams and Wild. Fifth Ward Alderman, Leon Depres voted against the confirmation.

To counter the second school boycott, eight Negro committeemen formed a new civil rights organization which they called "The Assembly to End Prejudice—Injustice—Poverty". Their first action was to immediately launch an attack on other civil rights groups such as the Coordinating Council of Community Organizations. They also denounced the proposed boycott of public schools which the CCCO had set for February 25, 1964.

Alderman Kenneth E. Campbell of the Twentieth Ward was elected president of the group which included among its members Alderman Metcalfe, Third Ward; Claude W. B. Holman, Fourth Ward; Robert H. Miller, Sixth Ward; George Collins, Twenty-Fourth Ward; Joseph Robichaux, Twenty-First Ward; William H. Shannon, Seventeenth Ward; and Congressman William L. Dawson. According to Campbell, Congressman William L. Dawson was one of the first signers of the new organization's declaration of purpose. On the other hand, Alderman Charles Chew Jr., who was elected without the Democratic party's support was not invited to join, and neither was State Representative Willim N. Robinson, one of the leading Negro Republicans and a civil rights activist.

Rose Simpson, chairman of the Parent's Council for Integrated Schools said: "Captain Richard J. Daley has cracked the whip, and his plantation overseers jumped in line to form their own short-line freedom train."

If there was any doubt about the purpose of the new organization, Alderman Kenneth E. Campbell made it clear at a press conference on February 4, 1964 when he said:

> We hope the school boycott fails, and we're working hard toward that end. I have conducted a poll in my ward to test the will of the people. I've sent out ten thousand leaflets asking parents to send their children to school and explaining the boycott procedures would not reach the civil rights objectives. I also attached a pledge card to comply with my plea. The ten thousand leaflets that I sent out were far too few. There was demand for five thousand additional.

Timuel Black, a civil rights activist, Independent Voters of Illinois leader and college professor.

When Campbell was asked if Mayor Daley had instructed him to form the organization, he replied emphatically, "No." Earlier in the day, Mayor Daley denied he had anything to do with the formation of the organization and said, "They sent me a copy of their program and objectives. That's all I know about it."

Frank L. Mingo, candidate for Seventh Ward Democratic committeeman, said: "Apparently the civil rights groups such as CCCO and Protest at the Polls have the machine worried, so suddenly it is trying to jump on the civil rights bandwagon. Where were these double dealers last week, when only Chew and Despres voted against confirming segregationists on the school board?"

The success of the first school boycott revealed that the Negro community was marching to a different political drum beat and that its black elected officials were out of step. The six black aldermen were late in joining the freedom march, and when they did, they found that young Negroes like Lawrence Landry, Timuel Black and Albert Raby had emerged from the ranks to fill the void. The Negro councilmen had abdicated their leadership on the most dominant issue of their time because of their blind allegiance to Mayor Richard J. Daley.

Mayor Richard J. Daley and his black political machine called in all of the outstanding IOU's in an effort to stop this second school boycott. The NAACP with the support of the Chicago Urban League engineered a proposal that was supported by the majority of the members of the Coordinating Council of Community Organizations. The proposal approved by the group stated that the second school boycott should be held in abeyance until negotiations with the board president, Carl Roddewig, or Mayor Richard J. Daley could be held. Those members of the CCCO who did not support the motion for abeyance believed that the motion was a clever effort on the part of the black and white political establishment to ground this second boycott effort into the dust.

Nine of the major objections to a second school boycott in Chicago were: 1) It was illegal; 2) It was immoral; 3) It should be postponed until after the survey of Chicago schools alleged defacto segregation by five educators is completed March 31st; 4) It might fail; 5) It was unfair to use children to fight the civil rights battles of adults; 6) It would accomplish nothing; 7) The conference table was the place to solve such issues; 8) Leaders of the boycott were only interested in personal aggrandizement; and 9) The more experienced leaders, for example, the Negro politicians led by Alderman Campbell should direct the civil rights movement in Chicago since their record of accomplishments spoke for itself.

The Democratic machine rolled out its legal artillery in an effort to intimidate the boycotters. State's Attorney Daniel P. Ward and Police Superintendent Orlando W. Wilson pledged to arrest and prosecute any persons attempting to stop children from going to school. This warning was, undoubtedly, directed at members of the Coordinating Council of Community Organizations. Wilson said that he had instructed his men to arrest anyone who threatened or physically blocked children wishing to enter the school building. However, he stated that this did not apply to parents. They had a right to keep their children out of school if they wished to *so*.

State's Attorney Ward said:

> Prosecution will be instituted under a provision of the Illinois School Code which states in part. Any person who induces or attempts to induce a child to be absent from school unlawfully is guilty of a misdemeanor upon conviction of that, therefore, shall be punished by a fine of no more than $550.00 or imprisonment in the county jail for not more than twenty-five days or both. The boycott is an expression of lawlessness. It does not serve any useful purpose or aims.

Comedian and civil rights leader Dick Gregory, fresh from a stay in a Pine Bluff, Arkansas jail, reacted to State's Attorney Daniel P. Ward's threat at a CCCO rally in Stone Temple Baptist Church, at 3622 West Douglas Boulevard by saying:

> A good legitimate Negro wanting to go into politics in Chicago not only has to run against a handkerchief head Negro but also against a machine getting kickbacks from dope and prostitution. The law enforcement agencies in this town can enforce the laws against civil rights people but not against gangsters.
>
> You have to respect Daley. He has a big job being mayor, governor, prosecutor and president of the Chicago Branch of the NAACP.

The second school boycott was being conducted against the concerted efforts of the six black aldermen, Congressmen William L. Dawson, Mayor Richard J. Daley and without any support from the Chicago Urban League or the National Association for the Advancement of Colored People. NAACP board member, Charles A. Davis, resigned as convener of the Coordinating Council of Community Organizations in November of 1963, shortly after the first school boycott. Davis was replaced by Albert Raby, a Chicago school teacher and civil rights activist. The NAACP's reason for not a participating in the second boycott was a bland one in that the organization maintained that it was running a voter registration campaign and that a school boycott would be counter productive to that effort.

On February 23rd, two days before the boycott, Alderman Kenneth Campbell, Alderman Claude W. Holman and Mrs. Daisy Bates, a civil rights leader from Little Rock, Arkansas, spoke at the rally at the Greater Bathesda Church located at 5301 South Michigan. Mrs. Bates appeared as a representative of the registration education platform for the Democratic National Committee. Outside the church, fifteen pickets from the Afro-American Heritage Association in favor of the boycott chanted and sang, "Go Ben Willis Go," referring to their demand for Willis to resign. A few blocks north of the Greater Bathesda Baptist Church, at the United Packing House Workers' Community Center on 49th & Wabash, more than a thousand people attended a rally in support of the school boycott. Reverend Fred J. Shuttlesworth, executive board member of the Southern Christian Leadership Conference said, "Chicago has got things boiling throughout the country, and it is spearheading the movement (civil rights) in the North. I urge you to continue non-violent direct action and a generation of uneducation, miseducation and noneducation shall begin to come to an end on Tuesday, February 25th."

Despite the strong and organized opposition to the second school boycott, it was a success because 172,350 students did not report to their classrooms on February 25, 1964. There were no demonstrations on that Tuesday to prevent the children from attending school. The weather was sunny and mild in spite of the weatherman's predictions that it would be cloudy and cold with possibly a few snow flurries. The second boycott was more indicative of the mood of the Negro people than the first because it succeeded in the face of determined opposition by Mayor Richard J. Daley and all of the Negro aldermen except Charles Chew who supported the effort by conducting a black studies class for fifty boycotting students in a local church in the Seventeenth Ward.

At the Jenner Elementary School at 1009 North Cleveland, only 250 out of an enrollment of 2,518 students showed up for class. There were only 300 students present out of an enrollment of 947 at the Byrd Elementary School at

363 West Hill. Willard A. Johnston, principal of the Beale Elementary School at 6006 South Peoria, noted that only 500 pupils showed up for classes out of a student body of more than 1,800. Johnston considered the 500 student population a victory as compared to the 136 students who showed up during the October 22nd boycott. Just a block away at Beale Upper Grade Center at 6043 South Sangamon, Melvin M. Lubershane, the principal, reported that one-fourth of the 945 students were present.

Alderman Kenneth Campbell charged that the student absenteeism was due to some teachers' indirection and encouraging their students to stay home. He quoted one teacher as saying, "We will see you Wednesday", which implied that school would be closed on Tuesday. In Alderman Kenneth Campbell's ward, which included parts of school districts thirteen and sixteen, the absenteeism ranged from 62.4 percent to 85.5 percent of the elementary and high school students—whereas in Alderman Holman's ward which included school districts thirteen and fourteen, the absenteeism ranged from 42.5 percent to 85.5 percent. A. A. Sammy Rayner Jr., front running contender for Dawson and Mayor Daley huffed and puffed, but it could not blow out the flame of freedom."
Dawson and Mayor Daley huffed and puffed but it could not blow out the flame of freedom."

Superintendent Benjamin C. Willis reacted to the successful boycotts by blaming the parents of the boycotting students for increased student assaults against teachers. At a board meeting Willis pointed to a map indicating where teachers were most frequently assaulted, stating:

> If you would relate the locations of the instances of assault to absence on the boycott days, you will see that there appears to be an extreme degree of correlation. There is no excuse for students to exhibit disrespect for teachers (and others) in schools through words, gestures, actions or any manner whatsoever. Certainly there is no justification for people ever striking a teacher. Are we to hold students solely responsible for the alarming increase in undesirable attitudes and actions? I think not. Good discipline originates in the home. Parents must teach and require of the child respect for law, for authority, for the rights of others and for private and public property.

Warren Bacon called Willis' statement a hysterical attempt to blame the boycott for violence against teachers and increased pupil misbehavior. Raymond Pasnick, another board member, told the superintendent he had no right to accuse parents of defiance of authority in participating in the boycott since he "ran down the back stairs" of the board of education building to avoid a subpoena issued in October during the controversy over the permissive transfer plan. Willis' actions, Pasnick said, were definitely in defiance of the law.

The second boycott differed from the first not only in size but in political ramifications. During demonstrations, the second boycotters showed greater anger at Mayor Richard J. Daley and the Democratic party as opposed to Superintendent Willis who was the original target. They also heaped attacks upon State's Attorney Daniel P. Ward, U. S. Representative William L. Dawson, Alderman Kenneth E. Campbell and Alderman Claude W. Holman. On the other hand, Alderman Leon Depres and his wife were seen marching with the one thousand demonstrators on February 25th around City Hall where one picketer was carrying a sign that read, "If Daley won't give up Ben Willis, we won't give him LBJ in the upcoming November presidential election."

Alderman Leon Depres remarked following the City Hall demonstration:

> I've supported the school boycott because I felt it was legal. I made a careful study of the statues and cannot find where a one day boycott is illegal. Boycotting is a legitimate expression of the people and their presentation of rightful grievances. The illegal and proper conduct of the school officials in regard to segregation in the school should eliminate any qualms about illegality. When I speak of boycotting, you must understand that I mean the effort of sincere parents and citizens involved, who believe in orderly demonstrations to emphasize their needs. All right thinking citizens should support the boycott to show they are tired of school officials shortchanging the entire city in education.

Alderman Chew, who also joined the demonstration and picket line around City Hall, noted that "the Democratic machine is no longer oiled, and the Negro politicians hand-picked by Daley are no longer effective in their wards. We don't need them to misrepresent us."

Lawrence Landry, who set the political pace for the boycott, observed that: "I think that for the first time in the history of Chicago, black people were given a chance to choose between Daleyism and freedom, and they chose freedom."

Daley said that he did not regard the second boycott as a success. "How can anyone figure this is a success? I don't think keeping children out of school is a success, and furthermore, I don't believe that the boycott has any political implications, none whatsoever. Anyone who tries to make a political issue out of civil rights will find himself flirting on soft grounds in pretty thin ice." Reverend Wilbur N. Daniel was not afraid to walk on thin ice because he resigned from the presidency of the Chicago Branch of the NAACP and an-

Reverend Wilbur N. Daniel, popular church leader, former president of the Chicago branch of the NAACP and a candidate for Congress on the Republican ticket to replace William L. Dawson.

nounced that he planned to devote full time to campaign for the Republican nomination as a candidate to replace Dawson in the First District. Albert Brooks, the first vice president of the NAACP, replaced Daniel in that chair.

Lawrence Landry and the other civil rights organizations, including the NAACP and the Urban League, were unanimous after the Freedom Day II victory in their demands that Mayor Richard J. Daley not appoint Mrs. Wendell L. Green to the school board. Alderman Robert Miller (Sixth Ward) broke ranks and declared: "I can't see the school nomination committee coming up with Mrs. Green's name, and I can't see the mayor naming her. I can't see myself voting for her. It would be a mistake. The image she has left is just like that of Ben Willis. I can't see Mrs. Green serving on the school board for another term.

Edwin C. Berry, executive director of the Chicago Urban League, declared: "Reappointment of Mrs. Green would be a monumental tragedy of the greatest magnitude. I urge the mayor to consider the league's slate of board candidates: Mrs. Carey B. Preston, Mrs. Eugene Cotton, Professor Allison Davis and Dr. Seymour Banks."

Alderman Chew (Seventeenth Ward) stated: "I think Mrs. Green has outserved her usefulness as a member of the school board; she should retire with honor rather than seek reappointment and risk embarrassment."

The Chicago civil rights leaders extended an olive branch to Mayor Daley when they asked him not to reappoint Mrs. Green. Daley, in turn, ignored their request and gave them a cactus bush. He reappointed Mrs. Wendell L. Green to the board in May, 1964.

Mayor Richard J. Daley defied the wishes of the black community and reappointed Mrs. Wendell L. Green for a second term on the board of education in May, 1964.

State's Attorney Daniel Ward had met earlier with the board of education president, Claire Roddewig, to discuss action to be taken against the boycott leaders. Attorney Raymond Harth said that in his opinion any legal action brought as a result of the February 25th boycott probably would not stand up in court. Harth further stated, "I don't think that the board of education or the state's attorney can make the charges stick. The stature of law is such that there would be a good defense for parents, CCCO leader's Lawrence Landry and Al Raby to charges brought against them."

Hence, State's Attorney Daniel Ward's legal threats festered "like a raisin in the sun" while Landry and Raby continued to organize and demonstrate.

A march on Chicago's City Hall against unequal education for blacks. In the first row behind the parade marshals are (Left to Right): Sydney Finley, acting executive director of the Chicago chapter of the National Association for the Advancement of Colored People; Reverend Walter Fauntroy, member of the Southern Christian Leadership Conference (and currently the congressman for the District of Columbia); Albert Raby, chairman of the Coordinating Committee of Community Organizations; Dr. Martin Luther King, president of the Southern Christian Leadership Conference; Rev. Ralph Abernathy, Vice President of the Southern Christian Leadership Conference. Inset: Bill Berry, executive director of the Chicago Urban League and Rev. C. T. Vivian, of the Southern Christian Leadership Conference.

Chapter XIX

Marching and Rallying Against Pharaoh

Superintendent Benjamin C. Willis' re-election by the board to head the Chicago school system for a fourth term was tantamount to lighting a match to a short wicked bomb. The civil rights organizations exploded and fragments of the freedom struggle flew in every direction. The NAACP instantly proposed a two day school boycott to protest Willis' re-election whereas CORE wanted a five day boycott and felt that anything less would not be effective. An accord could not be reached between NAACP and CORE; hence, both the Congress of Racial Equality and the Student's Non-Violent Coordinating Committee pulled out of the NAACP boycott plan. Their withdrawal from the boycott was based upon both tactics and objectives. The two militant organizations within the federation of Chicago civil rights groups saw Daley as their objective as opposed to Ben Willis. They felt that Daley was the key to Ben Willis' removal despite Daley's Buddha-like posture of noninvolvement in public school matters.

There were others opposed to the boycott for different reasons. Circuit Court Judge George N. Leighton made some cogent comments about the boycott that was scheduled by the Chicago Branch of the NAACP for both Thursday and Friday, June 10th and 11th. Judge Leighton said:

> The most important objective we must keep in mind is a continued education of the children as we continue efforts to solve the many problems that now exist in our school system. As a member of the Friends of the Schools Committee, I know of the concern for good education for all of the children in Chicago. We have had, in Chicago, two school boycotts. It is not an exaggeration to say that very little was accomplished by this form of public demonstration. I sincerely urge that parents do not withdraw their children from the schools while efforts are being made to improve the quality of education in Chicago.

Left: Attorney George N. Leighton, United States district judge for the Northern District of Illinois and former appellate court judge in the First District of Illinois. Right: Edward Gardner, a past president of the West Chesterfield Community Association, former assistant principal in a public elementary school and the co-founder with his wife Bettiann of Soft Sheen Products.

Edward Gardner, president of the West Chesterfield Community Association, a businessman and an assistant school principal, said:

> I am not speaking for the association, but I feel, personally, that the boycott is simply an attempt at an easy solution of a major problem. To rely on a boycott to solve the education crisis is feeding ourselves with false reality. We must wake up to the real world. This does nothing to solve the major problems that the Negro has including education. I suggest that we work on positive projects. Continuous use of the boycott, which has been very effective in the South, should not be applied here in Chicago. The boycott certainly appeals to the emotions. Until we begin to structure realistic programs and face ourselves as we are, we will be simply going around in circles.

On June 8th, the day that Judge Leighton and Edward Gardner aired their concerns, Judge Cornelius J. Harrington issued an injunction banning the school boycott. On the morning of June 10th, NAACP attorneys Raymond E. Harth and Garland W. Watt appeared before Judge Julius Hoffman in the Federal District Court to get the injunction set aside. Judge Hoffman declined to accept jurisdiction and told both Attorneys Watt and Harth that they had not exhausted their remedies in the state court. The injunction had been issued by Judge Harrington on a petition by the board of education. The court document named the Chicago branches of the NAACP, Congress of Racial

Equality, the Student Non-Violent Coordinating Committee, the Coordinating Council of Community Organizations, A.C.T. and seventeen officers of that group.

The Coordinating Council of Community Organizations had several battle plans because within fifteen minutes after Judge Hoffman had refused to lift the ban, Al Raby, the convener of the civil rights groups declared:

> We are under an injunction which prevents us from abdicating or inducing children to participate in a boycott. We will abide by the injunction. Our lawyers have advised us against inducing anyone to boycott; however, we will proceed with a scheduled march on City Hall this afternoon from the south parking lot at Soldier Field. Roy Wilkins, national director of the National Association for the Advancement of Colored People will participate. I have also sent a telegram to Reverend Martin Luther King inviting him to attend.

Both Al Raby and Dick Gregory had been arrested three days earlier on Monday evening, June 7th, after initiating an around the clock, twenty-four hour vigil, at the board of education building, 228 North LaSalle, against the retention of Superintendent Benjamin C. Willis. Others arrested that Monday were Mrs. Evelyn Geter, Elinor Miller M.D., Ronald Woodward, Frank Ditto and John Hanna. Gregory and Hanna refused to put up bond and were placed in the central district lockup.

The Federation of Civil Rights Organizations, led by Al Raby, was determined that twelve non-negotiable demands be fulfilled before they would call off the vigil and march. The major demands were: 1) Daley would make a statement saying that Willis should begin a paid leave of absence immediately; 2) the school board should fire Willis and hire a panel of nationally known

Attorney Garland W. Watt, former judge in the Circuit Court of Cook County, Illinois and chairman of the Legal Redress Committee for the Chicago branch of the NAACP.

educators to find a successor who favors integration; 3) integration of all summer schools; 4) abandonment of new school districts in the South Shore and Forrestville areas; 5) withdrawing of all school boundaries to conform with the American law, which forbids drawing boundaries that perpetuate de facto segregation.

Inasmuch as none of the demands were met, two hundred marchers assembled in the parking lot at the south end of Soldier Field shortly before noon on Thursday, June 10th. At approximately 12:30 P.M., they commenced to march north of Lake Shore Drive, where they were joined by other marchers who had been waiting on the sidewalks. The marchers turned west on Balboa Drive, north on State Street, west on Madison and north on LaSalle. Civil rights officials estimated that the number of marchers increased from two hundred to seven hundred by the time they reached City Hall. The police advanced guards stayed approximately a block ahead of the marchers, diverting traffic onto side streets and permitting the demonstrators to occupy all lanes of traffic on all of the streets they used. The police barricaded LaSalle Street between Washington and Randolph after the marchers arrived in front of City Hall because the demonstrators and onlookers jammed the entire block from curb to curb.

A delegation of the marchers, which included Albert Raby and Dick Gregory, went to the fifth floor of City Hall in an attempt to see Mayor Daley. They were met at the outer door of the mayor's office by Colonel Jack Reilly, Daley's director of special events. He told the delegation that Daley was not in the building and would not be back for the rest of the day, but Daley would be happy to meet the committee at 9:30 A.M. on Monday. Raby informed Colonel Jack Reilly that another march would be held the following day which was Friday, June 11th. The march would start at the same time and the same place, in the south lot at Soldier Field and its destination would be City Hall; moreover, the delegation would return to the mayor's office again on the chance that he might be available. Raby also let it be known to Reilly that the around the clock picketing of City Hall, which had started on Tuesday, would continue on a twenty-four hour basis. An hour before Raby and the demonstrators moved from City Hall to the board of education building where the board was holding a meeting, the board ratified the emergency action of its president, Frank Whiston, in seeking the court order against the school boycott that was planned for Thursday, June 10th, and Friday, June 11th.

Daley was angered by the fact that the marchers had blocked traffic enroute to City Hall on Thursday; thus, he met with a group of reporters on Friday morning and told them that he had directed Police Superintendent O. W. Wilson to enforce the law. The mayor said, "Nothing like yesterday will happen today," meaning that he didn't intend to let the demonstrators obstruct traffic and not be arrested for violating the law.

The second march to City Hall on Friday, June 11th, started at 1:10 P.M., forty minutes later than the march the day before. The delay was caused by the fact that the number of demonstrators who had assembled in the south end parking lot at Soldier Field had increased from two hundred on Thursday to approximately one thousand on Friday. The rules for the march had changed. Mayor Richard J. Daley had directed his police department, through Superintendent O. W. Wilson to prohibit the marchers from blocking traffic and to restrict the march to a single traffic lane as opposed to occupying all the traffic lanes as they had done the day before.

The first half mile of the second day march went peacefully with the marchers occupying the two western lanes in the northbound portion of Lake Shore Drive. Police on three-wheel motorcycles patrolled the lines of march to make sure that the marchers did not crowd into the other two northbound lanes and cause a traffic block. As the marchers neared Columbus Drive, eighty policemen, who had been waiting in parked police vans joined another forty or so policemen on the scene and formed a line to fondle the marchers into a single traffic lane on the north side of Balboa Drive. At this point, the march came to a halt. There was a conference among John T. Kelly, deputy chief of the patrol; Captain Robert Lynskey, task force commander; Captain James Riordan of the first district; and Al Raby, convener of the Coordinating Council of Community Organizations. Raby protested that the single lane restriction was a violation of an agreement that they had made before the march started which permitted the demonstrators to use two traffic lanes. Captain Lynskey disputed Al Raby's version of the earlier discussion and said they would have to use one lane from Balboa to City Hall, but had been permitted to use two lanes on Lake Shore Drive because there were four northbound lanes and four southbound lanes.

Al Raby then went into a huddle and had a conference with James Farmer, national director of the Congress on Racial Equality, Rev. William Hogan of the Catholic Interracial Council, Edgar Riddick of the Student Non-Violent Coordinating Committee, and Dick Gregory. After the brief conference, Raby turned and told the police officers if they could not use two lanes, they would sit down. Lynskey responded, "If you do, you will be arrested." Al Raby and the group leaders then began shouting, "Sit down, sit down," to the marchers. About one-fourth of the marchers sat down while the others moved to the sideline.

It was at this point that two hundred and twenty-eight of the demonstrators sat down and were promptly arrested. Included in the first wave of ar-

Reverend George E. Riddick, former member of the students' non-violent coordinating committee and currently the vice president of Operation PUSH. And also pastor of Blackwell Memorial AME Zion Church.

rests were Dick Gregory, James Farmer, Albert Raby, Syd Finley, acting executive director of the Chicago chapter of the National Association for the Advancement of Colored People, John McDermott, executive director of the Catholic Interracial Council, Rev. William Hogan of the Catholic Interracial Council and Edgar Riddick of the Student Non-Violent Coordinating Committee. Many of the demonstrators went limp. Others, white and Negro, men and women, squirmed, kicked, and fought when they were shoved into the six large blue and white prison vans.

Twenty-eight of the demonstrators were arrested that same afternoon a mile from Balboa Drive when they knelt and sat down on the sidewalk outside of City Hall. One of the demonstrators, Mrs. Betty Johnson of 4919 Woodlawn Avenue, the wife of Professor Walter Johnson of the University of Chicago, lost a tooth in a scuffle. She refused to let a police surgeon examine her when she was taken to the women's lockup. The City Hall pickets were arrested when they changed from a single line of march to walk four abreast, blocking the sidewalk, and sat down when the police ordered them to return to a single file. Some of the City Hall pickets taken to the first district lockup at 1121 South State Street refused to give police their names. Instead they told the police their names were Ben Willis, Mayor Daley, Mrs. Daley, and so on.

After the mass arrest, Mayor Richard J. Daley said: "As long as I am mayor, there will be law and order. I hope these people involved realize we are trying to cooperate with them, and I repeat, they have the right to protest and the right to demonstrate. They haven't the right to take the law in their own hands."

Daley's law and order talk after the mass arrest on black Friday, June 22nd, fell on deaf ears. The defiant Chicago Public School freedom fighters moved their staging area on Saturday, June 12th, from the south parking lot at Soldier Field to Buckingham Fountain in Grant Park on Lake Michigan, just east of the business district and in the shadow of Roosevelt University. The third march on City Hall started without fanfare. At 2:30 P.M., at the height of the shopping period, on a bright and sunny Saturday afternoon, several hundred tranquil marchers trudged two abreast along the sidewalks, westward bound to Daley's City Hall. The character of the march changed abruptly as the demonstrators turned west off State Street onto Madison Street. At that moment, the demonstrators rushed wildly to the center of State and Madison Streets and staged a sit-down in the heart of what was reputed to be the world's busiest corner. Their actions tied up traffic for almost an hour. Commander Robert Lynskey raised his baton to signal for the police vans to move forward and arrest the demonstrators. The demonstrators then backed up into the middle of the intersection in a circular wagon type formation.

When the police vans moved in, the crowds, by this time, included several hundred spectators who had surged into the street. Police then locked arms at all four corners of the intersection of State and Madison to hold back the spectators and permit the clearing of the streets. Most of the demonstrators went limp and let police carry them to the vans. The six nuns in the front line of the march from Marillac House of the Daughters of Charity located at 2822 W. Jackson Boulevard stood up and walked. Some of the demonstrators struggled and scuffled with police. Before the vans could move away from the intersection several youthful civil righters threw themselves under the vehicles to prevent them from moving. Police, who had encountered this tactic before, appeared in coveralls to drag the demonstrators free. The driver of one of the police prison vans stepped on the gas which sent out a cloud of exhaust fumes that forced the freedom fighters from under the van.

A preliminary count showed that one hundred and ninety-six persons were arrested. Most of them were taken to the Central District Police Station which counted as its prisoners thirty-five juvenile girls, nine juvenile boys, sixty-two women and seventy-seven men. Eleven men and two juvenile boys were taken to the Prairie Avenue Police Station.

Six additional prisoner vans and a number of other police vehicles were needed to remove the balance of the Ben Willis and Mayor Daley protestors. The strongest resistance was offered by a group of young white and Negro demonstrators who sat in the middle of the street in a circle singing and chanting, "Ben Willis must go! Ben Willis must go!" Four of the young demonstrators tried to block the paddy wagons by throwing their bodies under the wheels and stoically lying there until the police dragged them away.

Among the demonstrators who were arrested were Reverend John Porter, a Negro minister who was the leader of the Chicago affiliate of Rev. Martin Luther King Jr.'s Southern Christian Leadership Conference, Bob Lucas, chairman of the Chicago branch of the Congress on Racial Equality and Mrs. Lillian Gregory, wife of comedian Dick Gregory. The total number of demonstrators arrested in the two day period exceeded four-hundred.

After the police restored the flow of traffic, about one-hundred of the demonstrators, who had stayed behind the police lines, fell into a marching formation and started walking west toward City Hall singing freedom songs. When the demonstrators reached the County Building, they found the City Hall side of the building on LaSalle Street locked and the building surrounded by a wall of policemen, standing six feet apart, with an equal number of officers standing along the curb monitoring and watching the movement of the freedom fighters. The marchers and pickets were restricted to marching back and forth in an area between the City Hall door and Randolph Street. The other three sides of the building were ruled off-limits. As they marched up and down the sidewalk carrying signs assailing both Superintendent Benjamin Willis and Mayor Richard J. Daley, they sang freedom songs such as "We Shall Overcome" and "We Shall Not Be Moved."

Mayor Daley, in an effort to forestall any demonstrations and disruptions of motorists and shoppers in the Loop on Saturday afternoon, sent Al Raby a telegram before the march began. He offered to meet with Raby and a committee of leaders in his office at 2:30 P.M. Although the City Hall door was locked against pickets and marchers, Daley remained in his fifth floor office until late afternoon and would have received the civil rights leaders even if they had arrived late.

After the mass arrest, Raby announced he had sent the following telegram to Mayor Daley: "We regret that the police department has again prevented our peaceful march from reaching City Hall. We shall try again tomorrow."

In addition to announcing plans for a demonstration on Monday, Raby said: "This is an all summer operation. Sunday we will hold rallies in Washington Park at 3:00 P.M., in Mozart Baptist Church, 1900 W. Adams at 5:00 P.M., and in the First Congregational Church, 1613 W. Washington Blvd. at 7:30 P.M." Raby also asked that Mayor Daley release all those arrested and make a public statement in support of a policy of integration in Chicago Public Schools.

Al Raby had avoided any possible arrests by remaining out of the line of marchers and out of the demonstration. He had explained to the civil righters, prior to the commencement of the march at 2:30 P.M. on Saturday afternoon, that he could not further their cause by getting arrested again within two days. Dick Gregory, who was also absent from the Saturday march and

Albert Brooks, former president of the Chicago branch of the NAACP and also past treasurer of Local 701 of the National Alliance of Postal and Federal Employees Union.

demonstration, was not released from custody until early Saturday morning on a one-thousand dollar bail bond on charges of battery against two policemen, resisting arrest, obstructing traffic and disorderly conduct. Dick Gregory was scheduled to appear in court on June 23rd. One of the arresting officers said that Dick Gregory had kicked him while another officer said Gregory had bit him on the left thumb. Dick Gregory, in turn, charged them with police brutality because they had caused him injuries that resulted in treatment at Provident Hospital where he had complained of pain in his back, injuries to his thumb, ankle and head.

"We are not marching tomorrow," Albert Brooks, president of the Chicago Branch of the NAACP, said shortly before Dick Gregory and other protest groups met to consider several proposals that would be severely destructive during the parade through the Loop to City Hall for the astronauts, James A. McDivitt and Edward H. White. Brooks further stated: "There's too much opposition to a seriously disruptive action; therefore, we are considering suggestions such as standing along the line of march with signs, merging into the parade, or stepping from the curb to attract attention." In addition, Brooks said that the NAACP delegation intended to keep its scheduled appointment with Mayor Daley on Monday to discuss the situation and that the NAACP group would continue other forms of protest which it felt were necessary and effective, and planned to carry on the court fight against the boycott injunctions."

A member of the Coordinating Council of Community Organizations said: "I am frankly surprised that the NAACP took part in the sit-down protest last week. I understand that the group's board of directors met on Friday and decided they could not participate further in the protest demonstrations because it was costing their organization too much money to provide bail bond for persons arrested in the anti-Willis activities."

Al Raby, convener of the CCCO, said that the Monday's demonstration would "tarnish" Chicago's national image but would not indicate a "lack of respect" for the astronauts; however, "we plan to demonstrate tomorrow in a manner which will bring Chicago to the attention of the whole country, but at the same time, not embarrass the civil rights movement." Raby also announced that the protestors would meet at 11:00 A.M. on Monday in front of Buckingham Fountain in Grant Park.

"We have something planned for Monday that will upset this whole country," Dick Gregory, the comedian and protest leader told six hundred and fifty persons at a Washington Park Rally, which was one of three held Sunday to drum up support for Monday's demonstration. "If any of us gets a scratch, Mayor Daley had better leave town because we will close down the city," Gregory shouted at the top of his voice. The federal government stepped into the controversy over school Superintendent Benjamin Willis after demonstrations against Willis had been called off that afternoon out of courtesy to the visiting astronauts. George Culberson, associate director for Mediation of the Federal Community Relations Service, met into the early hours Tuesday morning with Al Raby at the First Congregational Baptist Church, 1613 W. Washington Blvd. Al Raby and five other leaders aired the grievances against Superintendent Willis and also the demands they intended to make upon Mayor Daley. They requested that Culberson use his office to mediate. George Culberson said after the meeting: "Today I will meet with the city officials and hear their side of the story." In the meantime, while Culberson and Raby had been meeting, other civil rights leaders in another room in the same church were planning another march on City Hall from Buckingham Fountain at 11:00 A.M. on Tuesday, June 13th, 1965.

When the demonstrators met early on Monday morning at Buckingham Fountain, Dick Gregory told the group of more than three hundred that the planned march had been called off. A member of the CCCO said the decision not to protest the march was made at a meeting Sunday night at the First Congregational Church. A majority of the protest group voted against a march while the astronauts were in town. Jets flying over Grant Park to herald the arrival of the astronauts frequently drowned out some of Dick Gregory's comments. Several ministers and three Catholic priests were in the group listening to Dick Gregory. The protest group's forces were weakened because one-hundred and seventy of the demonstrators were in the Criminal Courts Building waiting to appear on charges against them after the sit-down strike on State and Madison Streets on the previous Saturday.

Al Raby was absent because he was on the payroll of the Chicago Board of Education as a teacher at Hess Upper Grade Center at 3500 W. Douglas Boulevard. Raby had exhausted his leave time and was back teaching. Leo J. Wernick, principal at the Hess Center, where Raby was a seventh grade English teacher said: "We have a definite understanding. He tells me in advance when he will be out for personal business. He has agreed not to mix his outside business with his classroom work." Wernick also stated that Raby was an excellent teacher and that Raby was out of school Thursday, present Friday morning and out Friday afternoon. He added, "Leaves by teachers for personal business are restricted to three days in succession."

George W. Conley, superintendent of district nineteen, in which the Hess School is situated declared: "Any action against Raby for outside activities would have to be up to John F. Erzinger, assistant superintendent of schools in charge of personnel." Conley described Raby as a "meticulous hard working teacher." Erzinger said, "Any action against Raby would have to be started by Wernick, his principal, and Superintendent Conley. Erzinger said he had not heard from either of them.

Meanwhile, the marches in the Loop continued. Eighty-five persons were arrested in midafternoon on Wednesday during a sit-down in the middle of State and Madison Streets. For three hours, Monsignor Daniel Cantwell, chaplain for the Catholic Council of Working Life; Dr. Edward H. Chandler, head of the Church Federation of Greater Chicago; the Reverend William Johnson, Pastor of the Greater St. John Church, 48th and Michigan Avenue; and Rabbi Ernest Lorge of Temple Beth Israel, conferred alternately with Daley and the protest leaders in hopes of bringing both sides together. Al Raby, convener of the Coordinating Council of Community Organizations and head of the protest marchers, handed the clergymen three conditions for talks with Daley: 1) that charges against all persons arrested in the demonstrations yesterday and last week be dismissed; 2) that a mutually agreeable date be set for a meeting; and, 3) that on that date, a march from Buckingham Fountain to City Hall be permitted in two lanes of any street the police department selects.

Daley replied through the clergymen that he would meet with the protest leaders at any time and any place. He also said that they could apply for a parade permit. However, the mayor asserted in reference to the first condition that it was beyond his authority to dismiss the charges.

George Culberson, associate director for Mediation of the Federal Community Relations Service in Washington, D.C., also attempted to arrange a meeting yesterday. He conferred with Al Raby and Dick Gregory, the Negro comedian and comarch leader, and then went to see Daley. Culberson's mediation fell on the protestors' deaf ears because Daley would not meet the condition of dismissing the previous days' charges against the marchers.

Three hundred marchers set out from Buckingham Fountain at 2:25 P.M. to arrive at City Hall by 3:30 P.M.. Al Raby carried a copy of the *Havighurst Report on School Integration* to give to the mayor. When the marchers reached the intersection at State and Madison Streets, a group of them suddenly sat down. Police moved in and cleared the streets in fifteen minutes, arresting forty-five men, thirty-two women, five girls and three boys. Charges of disorderly conduct against one of the women who had a five-year old girl and a three-week-old infant with her, Miss Eursell Johns, 30, of 1135 East 79th Street, a Cook County Hospital Technicians, were dismissed for lack of evidence.

On Thursday, June 16th, Reverend John Porter, a local leader of the Southern Christian Leadership Conference, led a delegation of one hundred anti-Willis demonstrators to City Hall. The marchers were escorted gingerly by members of the Chicago Police Department. Many of the marchers were middle-aged and dressed in suits and ties in contrast to the younger marchers of the previous days who wore slacks and shorts. Upon arriving at City Hall, a delegation of five demonstrators including Reverend Porter were escorted into Mayor Daley's inner office. Reverend Porter handed the mayor a copy of the *Havighurst Report* which Raby had attempted to deliver to Daley a few days earlier.

Reverend Porter asked Mayor Daley to read the report on school integration. Mayor Daley replied, "I have already read it twice."

Reverend Porter retorted, "I hope you will read it again and implement it."

Neither Al Raby nor Dick Gregory were present at the meeting with Mayor Daley. Raby had returned to Hess Upper Grade Center where he taught school while Dick Gregory took a lie test to disprove charges that he bit and resisted police who arrested him in the prior week's demonstrations.

On the night of June 16th, Mayor Daley gave an emotional speech at the South Shore Commission's 12th Annual Meeting held in St. Philips Neri Auditorium located at 2110 E. 72nd Street. He appealed to the community organization to cooperate with public officials in matters concerning civic improvements. With tears in his eyes, Daley asked members of the South Shore Commission to support his program which was designed to create a City Department of Development and Planning and to serve as a liaison between governmental agencies and community improvement organizations in the areas of urban renewal, schools, traffic control, business, housing, and transportation. He concluded his speech in a choked voice, but at no point did he make a direct reference to the demonstrators who had blocked Loop traffic repeatedly in protest of a new contract which was awarded by the school board to School Superintendent Benjamin C. Willis.

In concluding his speech, Daley said, "I come from a people who had no say in their government, so they came to this country. When they elected an official there, they had respect for him. I recall that during the funeral parade for Governor Dunne, my father turned to me and said as the governor's body went by: 'There is the governor of Illinois, son. Take off your hat.' But people today have forgotten this. Unless we have free men and women who uphold order and the law and have respect for public officials they elect, then we have anarchy and conflict."

On Monday, June 28th, six-hundred civil rights demonstrators, led by Al Raby and Robert Lucas, staged a "lie down" on LaSalle Street outside of City Hall at the height of the evening rush hour. The "lie down" demonstration did not begin until Raby and a delegation came out of a two hour meeting with Mayor Daley.. After the session, Raby remarked: "The meeting with the mayor was totally unacceptable, and we plan to get arrested."

Raby and Robert Lucas were the first to lie down. Following their lead, the demonstrators began sprawling on the asphalt pavement in the middle of LaSalle Street. About fifty persons were arrested in a matter of minutes by police who waded into the reclining protestors when they refused orders to get up off the ground. Police Commander James Riordan demanded that the demonstrators leave the thoroughfare. Police vans moved into position like battle tanks as scores of patrolmen, who were stationed around City Hall, poured into the streets to end the traffic blockage. A free-for-all developed in one police van between cops and battling demonstrators. A clergyman affiliated with Dr. King was struck several times. As one van pulled away from the demonstration scene, a water bomb fell from an upper window of the State of Illinois Building on some spectators who watched the demonstration.

On Tuesday, July 6th, 1965, following Dr. Martin Luther King's appearance as the principal speaker at the United Church In Christ's National Convention held at the Palmer House, Al Raby and Dr. King held a press conference. Raby announced to the news media representatives that Dr. King had agreed to accept an invitation to spend some time in Chicago beginning July 24th to assist the fight for quality integration and education for Chicago children. Dr. King indicated that Negro leaders in Chicago had extended several invitations to him in recent weeks to join the Chicago struggle. He said that the Southern Christian Leadership Conference had maintained constant communications with the Chicago civil rights leadership and that he would be joined by members of his staff. King said their purpose would be:

> 1) To acquaint ourselves with the leadership of the civil rights movement and the forces of good will in the community. 2) Get a first hand picture and understanding of some of the problems faced in the northern cities by visiting local leaders. 3) To assist local leadership in interpreting the issues of the movement to a broader base of the community through a tour of

Negro and selected white communities. 4) To hold frequent rallies on street corners and in churches in an effort to rally the support of a coalition of forces of good will around common goals.

Dr. King was queried by a *Chicago Defender* reporter as to whether there was a distinction between civil rights disobedience in the South and civil rights disobedience in the North. Dr. King retorted:

> There is a distinction; while in the final analysis, it is the same. In both situations, there are differences. In one situation, you break laws that are unjust which are usually local laws in conflict with federal laws. In the North, laws appear just on their face but are unconstitutionally applied; also in the North legal segregation doesn't exist in the same overt and separate sense as it does in the South. Civil disobedience is used in the North to call attention to the overall aliveness of unjust situations. It is a weapon whereby we dramatize the evils of segregation and discrimination both in the North and in the South.

Dr. Martin Luther King came to Chicago as promised on July 24th and spent the day touring Chicago in an intensive effort to enlist recruits for the anti-Willis march which was to be held on Monday, July 26th. Dr. King made eight stops that included El Bethel Baptist Church at 5657 Lafayette Avenue. King spoke to three hundred clergymen at El Bethel, and from there went to Altgeld Gardens, the Robert Taylor Homes, the Kenwood District, Stateway Gardens, Oak and Orleans Streets on the near north side, 15th & Loomis on the southwest side, 1940 W. Madison Street and concluded his day in a vacant lot adjacent to the Friendship Baptist Church at 3409 Douglas Boulevard. Dr. King told all of his audiences, "If we walked from Selma to Montgomery, Alabama, with the Klan all around us, you can march in Chicago. Bull Conners in Alabama found out what the power of numbers means and when the white power structure sees us on Monday, they too will know we mean business."

Dr. King also hammered home the idea that Negroes should be willing to take a day off work if necessary to take part in the march:

> People in the South have taken weeks off; therefore, you certainly can take one day off to show Daley that you want your freedom. I want you all to be there Monday because right now the world thinks the Negro is satisfied with his lot in Chicago. When you start marching down that street, the world is going to know you don't like it and are not going to put up with it anymore.

Dr. King repeatedly advised his listeners about the power that resides in numbers. He emphasized that numbers turned the tide during the Montgomery demonstration against bus segregation. "There were thirty-four hundred Negroes already in jail," Dr. King explained, "but we lined up five thousand more who were ready to march. That's when the police realized we had won. There were no more jail cells in which to throw us."

There were two significant omissions in all of Dr. King's speeches throughout the day on July 24th. Even though Dr. King was in Chicago to lead the march and aid the Coordination Council of Community Organizations in its fight to oust Benjamin C. Willis as Superintendent of Schools, Dr. King never mentioned Willis by name. In fact, during all of his speeches, he placed as much emphasis on inadequate housing and lack of job opportunities as he did on segregation in the schools. Secondly, King declined to spell out how many marchers he expected to lead through the Loop on Monday, July 26th, at 3:00 P.M. The closest Dr. King came to making an estimate of the crowd was when he said to his listeners: "When we march tomorrow, I want us to have so many people they won't be able to count us." However, earlier in the day, Dr. King's closest aide, Reverend Ralph Abernathy, predicted during a talk at Altgeld Gardens that there would be ten thousand persons taking part in the march. In Dr. King's continued crusade to gain support for the march on Sunday, July 25th, he delivered two sermons, one at Quinn A.M.E. Church at 2401 S. Wabash at 11:00 A.M. and another at Progressive Baptist Church, 3658 S. Wentworth. He also gave five street corner speeches and ended his day at 8:00 P.M. speaking to ten thousand people, mostly white, on the Village Green of Winnetka. It was before the Winnetka group that Dr. King said the march must draw ten thousand people to be considered a success. King concluded his Winnetka, On-The-Green speech, with the following quotation: "We must learn to live together as brothers, or we will perish together as fools."

Dr. King's crusade for supporters to demonstrate against City Hall paid off in large dividends on Monday, July 26th. Thirty thousand people followed the Nobel Prize winner to City Hall in the greatest civil rights demonstration ever held in the history of the city. The chanting and shouting followers of Dr. King clogged the downtown streets at the height of the evening rush hour. The demonstrators marched fourteen abreast, shoulder to shoulder and from curb to curb. At one point, the line of march stretched back eight city blocks. The two and one half mile trek from Buckingham Fountain to LaSalle Street required less than an hour because there were no incidents, and five hundred and fifty police were on hand to make certain that the spectators did not interfere with the demonstrators. Peace and nonviolence characterized every foot of the march. Mayor Richard J. Daley, City Hall's principal occupant, was absent from the city the day of the big march because he was attending the 42nd Annual National League of Cities Convention in Detroit, Michigan.

Mayor Daley's absence from the city was not enough to permit him to escape the wrath of the Chicago demonstrators. Four carloads, filled with

Thirty thousand supporters stood with King on North LaSalle Street as he ended his historic march in front of City Hall on Monday, July 26, 1965. Mayor Daley was out of town attending the 42nd Annual National League of Cities convention in Detroit, Michigan.

members of the Chicago chapter of the Congress of Racial Equality journeyed to Michigan where they were joined by Detroit members of the SCLC, thirty Detroit CORE members and representatives of the Northern Student Movement in picketing at Cobo Hall in protest against Mayor Daley's refusal to meet with Dr. Martin Luther King in Chicago. Detroit's Mayor Jerome Cavanagh frowned at the pickets saying, "We had plenty of pickets before, and I'm sure we'll have plenty in the future. I obviously don't agree with their picketing Richard Daley who is an outstanding mayor and man." Henry Herman, 26, a social studies teacher at Chicago's Crane High School declared that "we want to demonstrate the kind of educational system Daley stands for to the rest of the nation." Dick Gregory stated that he was going to Detroit on Tuesday to join the demonstrators who felt that Daley should have remained in Chicago to discuss alleged de facto school segregation with Dr. Martin Luther King.

When the front line of marchers reached LaSalle Street, an observer looking south up the LaSalle Street canyon from the vantage point of City Hall saw a wave of men, women and children, both black and white, twisting north off West Madison Street and pouring down LaSalle Street like water rolling over a mountain waterfall. Upon reaching the front of City Hall, the Reverend Shelvin J. Hall, chairman of the Westside Federation, announced that members and supporters of the demonstration would proceed to march against Charles Swibel, chairman of the Chicago Housing Authority at Marina Towers where he resided. The Reverend Clay Evans, pastor of Friendship Baptist Church stated that "we have to let Mayor Daley know that it won't do any good to have a good educational system and still have to live in rat-infested slums."

Dr. King bellowed from over a loudspeaker in front of Pharaoh's Palace, "We asked for ten thousand, but if my eyes serve me correctly, we have ended up with more than thirty thousand."

After the crowd roared its approval, Dr. King declared:

> Chicago is the North's most segregated city. Negroes have continued to flee from behind the cotton curtain, but now they find that after years of indifference and exploitation, Chicago has not turned out to be the new Jerusalem. We are now protecting the educational and cultural shackles that are as binding as those of a Georgia chain gang. The chains have now been replaced by emotional stratagem. We march here today because we believe that Chicago, her citizens, and her social structure are in dire need of redemption and reform.

King's big march was slow getting underway; he was more than an hour late. Dr. King had been treated for exhaustion at Williams Clinic, 406 East

Marquette Road during the morning, and for a while it was doubtful if he would march. He was exhausted from his three day campaign through the city to enlist recruits for the march. After speaking before the huge rally on LaSalle Street, King was rushed back to his 16th floor suite in the Conrad Hilton Hotel where he again was examined and treated by his physicians for exhaustion and an attack of bronchitis, in addition to a slight fever that caused him to stay in Chicago overnight. Dr. King and his entourage left Chicago Tuesday morning, July 17th, in an auto caravan that was preceded and followed by two police cars that escorted them to O'Hare International Airport.

At the same hour that Dr. King was leaving Chicago, Congressman Adam Clayton Powell (D., N.Y.), chairman of the House Education and Labor Commission held a hearing in Washington, D.C., where both Superintendent Benjamin C. Willis and Professor Philip M. Hauser of the University of Chicago were testifying. Professor Hauser, a sociologist, maintained that "Willis had become the symbol of segregated schools." He accused Willis of sabotaging sound educational policies and called him "an example par excellence of trained incapacity."

Representative Roman C. Pucinski (D., IL), a member of the committee, told Professor Hauser that Hauser's testimony would be more persuasive if there were less personal bitterness on his part. Superintendent Benjamin C. Willis told the committee: "Our goal is to provide for the best possible education—intellectual, social and emotional for every child, white or black so that each, as an individual, may become all that he is capable of becoming for his own benefit and that of his family and nation." Superintendent Willis further pointed out the shifting of population groups within the city, the influx of families from Mississippi and other states in the deep South, and the fact that half the elementary pupils who live in poverty areas were among his difficulties. Between 1950 and 1960, Willis said that "the number of white children under the age of five living in the city of Chicago decreased by 22,643, or 8%. In the same period, he said the number of non-white children under the age of five increased by 76,139 or 141%. Willis also said that "if these trends continue, it will become increasingly impossible to provide any meaningful integration."

Dr. Hauser, who was chairman of the Advisory Panel on the Integration of Chicago Public Schools and the author of what is known as the *Hauser Report,* summarized the 18 month old report before the committee. Hauser made three points: 1) The Chicago schools are "very much segregated" having 84% of the Negro pupils in Negro elementary or high schools, or in schools with fewer than 10% whites. 2) The Negro teachers "are very much segregated." 3) The education available to Negroes is "by a number of measures inferior" to that available to whites. Hauser charged that Willis was "unalterably opposed" to putting most of the report's recommendations into effect, and that it was virtually impossible to get a copy of the report from the Chicago Board of Education.

Hauser further asserted:

> Much is being made these days out of civil disobedience of demonstrators in Chicago. White and Negroes have taken their grievances to the streets. But there is civil disobedience to be found also in the Illinois State Legislator which has refused for decades to heed Chicago's needs including her educational needs. There is also civil disobedience among members of the board of education, who are failing to follow national policy and Illinois law to integrate the schools. There is civil disobedience in the general superintendent's office in also refusing to follow national policy and Illinois law.

About seventy-five anti-Willis marchers, led by James Farmer, national director of the Congress of Racial Equality, marched from Grant Park to City Hall as Dr. Philip M. Hauser, along with Timuel Black, Charles Smith and Sydney Finley, presented their grievances before the House Education and Labor Commission in the District of Columbia. During the march, a heavy down pour of rain started as the marchers reached State and Madison Streets, but none of the demonstrators sought cover. When the group reached the door of the LaSalle Street entrance to City Hall, they sang three verses of "We Shall Overcome." Farmer told the group that he would not make a speech, because "you have said it all by your walk in the rain."

Dr. King left Chicago enroute to Cleveland three hours before the anti-Willis march led by James Farmer; however, prior to leaving, he stated: "The response to the march yesterday was beyond our greatest expectations, and I really think it was magnificent. I will certainly return if the Chicago leadership asks me to. If something isn't done about the school situation, we will have to have another massive march and school boycott." (Superintendent Benjamin C. Willis and Mayor Daley had been the targets of forty-three marches from Buckingham Fountain to City Hall.)

Dr. King's statement was prophetic because in a relatively short period of time, the marches from Buckingham Fountain to City Hall dwindled to Raby plus nine marchers and a mongrel. Raby knew he would never see the end of the tunnel in the equal education struggle without the support of a magnetic leader like Dr. King. Hence, Raby journeyed to Birmingham to remind the nonviolent crusader of his promise to return to Chicago if circumstances warranted. Dr. Martin Luther King Jr. was searching for a city north of the Mason and Dixon line that would serve as a testing ground for his nonviolent direct-action campaign. Therefore, he agreed to give Al Raby's request for him to return to Chicago careful consideration.

In the meantime, the Watts ghetto of Los Angeles exploded on every television set in the country while Americans witnessed the worst race riot in American history on their living room television sets. Blacks burned and looted stores for six consecutive days before the local police force and the California militia could put down the disturbance. Thirty-four people were killed, nine hundred injured, some three thousand five hundred arrested, and forty-six million dollars worth of property was destroyed.

The underbelly of the Watts riot was a cast of people who were being systematically dehumanized. One-sixth of the Los Angles half million blacks were packed into Watts' dilapidated housing stock like caged animals. The Watts area was four hundred percent more congested than the rest of Los Angeles. "Jim Crow" and unwritten restrictive covenants prevented blacks who could afford to live elsewhere from moving. The employment picture was dismal. More than thirty percent of the potential wage earners in Watts were unemployed at the time of the riot. Thousands of Watts' skilled and unskilled blacks had no hope of employment. The stores in the Los Angeles' Black Belt preferred white employees over blacks and the employees, like the white owners, lived outside of Watts' ghettos. All of the elements for human exposure were present in Watts in August, 1965. The missing ingredient to ignite the bomb presented itself when 21 year old Marquette Fry was arrested for drunken driving, and a white policeman chose to draw a gun in the process of making the arrest. The black witnesses became angry and began to fight the white police officer, and the holocaust in Watts began.

Dr. King's nonviolent movement was on trial in the Watts' section of Los Angeles. In defense of the movement, Dr. King, who flew to Los Angeles with Bayard Rustin and Bernard Lee, walked the streets of Watts pleading with residents to understand that violence and rioting were not the answers to their problems. Many of the people that he spoke to on the streets of Watts were both skeptical and angry; some even heckled the bearer of the cross for nonviolence. Dr. King was literally shocked to learn firsthand that some young people in Watts thought they had won.

Dr. King queried, "How can you say you won when thirty-four Negroes are dead, your community is destroyed, and white people are using the riot as an excuse to accelerate a white backlash?"

"We won because the whole world is now paying us attention," retored an unemployed young man with a wife and two babies.

To hear such a remark from an intelligent young black man was an excruciating experience for Dr. King. King labeled the young man's statement: "The language of the unheard; a desperate and suicidal cry; one who is fed up with the powerlessness of his existence and who asserts that he would rather be dead than ignored." Dr. King and Bayard Rustin noted that the rioters moved in an almost direct path toward Mayor Sam Yorty's City Hall and the Los Angeles establishment.

Blacks in Los Angeles invited him to stay, but King knew where he had to go. Upon his return to Atlanta, he informed his staff that the Southern Christian Leadership Conference was heading for Chicago where it would mount its northern direct-action campaign to spotlight the myriad slum conditions, substandard housing, unequal job opportunities, racist real estate practices, police brutality and de facto segregation. Chicago had the strongest Negro leadership in place and functioning more effectively than any other city that the Southern Christian Leadership Conference had considered. Moreover, Dr. King had great faith in Al Raby and in CCCO and felt that an effective campaign could be built around them. On the other hand, he considered Chicago the northern city that was the closest equivalent to Birmingham, Alabama in that it was the most considered "ghettoized" city in America, the symbol of segregation in the North. King felt that if he and the Southern Christian Leadership Conference could solve the Negro problem in Chicago, they could expunge the racial problems in cities all over America.

Reverend James Bevel, a veteran SCLC fire-eater who wears a shaven head, a skull cap and a string of battle scars from the sit-in campaigns of the early 1960's, states that he supported Dr. Martin Luther King's move to Chicago for the following reason:

> I picked Chicago because if you're going to have a nonviolent movement, the first thing you have to do is have a place where somebody is in charge. As it relates to Birmingham, Bull Conner was definitely in charge; if you went to Selma, Jim Clark was definitely in charge. Come to Chicago, Mayor Daley was definitely in charge. That is, you must have someone who can make a decisive decision on a constitutional issue, and it will be carried out.

Earl Bush, Mayor Richard J. Daley's press secretary, believed that Dr. Martin Luther King had another reason for selecting Chicago. Bush said:

> King considered Daley to be in complete control of Chicago, which in a way he was. King thought that if Daley would go before a microphone and say, "Let there be no more discrimination," there wouldn't be. King overestimated Mayor Daley's power. Daley did not have the power to make all men brothers, nor was brotherhood necessarily a priority for Daley, who was also concerned about white flight to the suburbs. He saw whites running, and the real issue to him was how to keep them from running. Daley had no answers, but he wasn't anti-black. He felt that he had to preserve the foundation of the city.

Dr. King had some answers and solutions for Daley's Chicago. He felt that Chicago deserved an alternative to the Los Angeles riot and that Chicago could be saved with a large dose of redemptive healing, administered through a direct-action, nonviolent campaign. Hosea Williams, one of Dr. King's disciples, was not in accord with King's thinking in trying to save Chicago. Williams urged King to stay at home in the cotton and tobacco belt and register Negroes under the new voting law. He felt that Chicago was not their turf. Bayard Rustin, a New Yorker, agreed with Hosea Williams. Rustin saw Dr. King's battle in the North unlike anything King had experienced in the South. Rustin recognized the North as a complex, interlocking chain of real estate interests, political machines, banks, and other "Fortune 500" interests that were unlike anything King had encountered in Albany, Selma, or Birmingham. Rustin also knew from firsthand experience in organizing the 1960 Chicago March on the Republican Convention that Mayor Daley had "super highways" into the black community through black elected officials such as Congressman William L. Dawson, Alderman Ralph H. Metcalfe (Third Ward), Alderman Kenneth Campbell (Twentieth Ward), and Alderman Claude W. B. Holman (Fourth Ward).

The black political submachine controlled the NAACP, Chicago's largest civil rights organization, and members of the "Fortune 500" companies reached into the Chicago Urban League's decision-making process with their financial contributions. Bayard Rustin questioned whether King was prepared to fight Daley and whether he was equipped to do battle with Daley's Chicago brand of Negroes. Rustin told King: "You will come away from Chicago with nothing meaningful for all your efforts." Bayard was prophesying because when King acted on inspiration as opposed to preparation, as he had in Albany, Georgia, he was usually wrong.

Alderman Dorothy Tillman, who was a teenage Southern Christian Leadership Conference staff member and one of the advanced guards that came to Chicago with Reverend James Bevel in the fall of 1965, made the following observations about the brand of Negroes she found in Chicago:

> Chicago was the first city that we ever went to as members of the SCLC staff where the black ministers and black politicians told us to go back where we came from. I was so stunned and stabbed that I told Reverend Bevel I didn't want to stay here if they didn't want me to. He said no, that Dr. King said we have to stay here to liberate these Negroes.
>
> Although there were Uncle Tom's in every city that we went to across the country, nobody ever had nerve enough in any other town to stand up and tell Dr. King and his staff members to leave. Blacks in Chicago actually

Dorothy Tillman, a teen age member of Dr. Martin Luther King's Southern Christian Leadership Conference advanced guard, which came to Chicago in 1965. She is currently alderman of the Third Ward.

allowed other blacks to go on television and say that we were not wanted in Chicago. I called my mother in Alabama and told her there were some s-t-r-a-n-g-e Negroes in Chicago. As a matter of fact, we could not find a church pastored by a black minister on the west side that would give the SCLC office space. Therefore, we ended up with a white minister by the name of William Briggs who pastored the Warren Avenue Congregational Church. It became SCLC's headquarters in Chicago. After Dr. King got settled on Hamlin Avenue, he occasionally would joke with us during staff meetings about the weird Negroes in Chicago. Dr. King delivered a sermon one night at 1550 S. Hamlin at a meeting that was restricted to the staff. The sermon was entitled, "The Strange Negroes In Chicago". Dr. King would frequently say to me, 'You ain't never seen no Negroes like this, have you Dorothy?' I would reply, "No, Reverend." He said, 'Boy, if we could crack these Chicago Negroes we can crack anything.'

Hosea Williams echoed Dorothy Tillman's sentiments when he said: "I have never seen such hopelessness. The Negroes of Chicago have a greater feeling of powerlessness than I've ever seen. They don't participate in the governmental process because they are beaten down psychologically. We are used to working with people who want to be free."

Mr. Hankerson, another SCLC staff member said: "A lot of folks here in Chicago won't even talk to us. I would still rather be working in Mississippi. People here are not interested in first class citizenship."

The observations of Tillman, Williams and Hankerson are borne out by the fact that on the west side of Chicago, in April, 1964, the Daley machine was able to elect a dead white man Thomas J. O'Brien to congress over a qualified young black woman by the name of Mrs. Brenetta Howell. Chicago Negroes were so apathetic and intimidated by the Daley machine that they would vote for Frankenstein and make him a winner if Mayor Daley put him on the ballot.

Dr. King witnessed the kinds of experiences sighted by Tillman and others. Since he could not compete with Daley in the patronage, ham, chicken, and wine department, he realized that Chicago would be tough. As a matter of fact, he knew it would be the toughest challenge he had ever faced in his whole civil rights nonviolent struggle. However, he was unwilling to stay away from the windy city because the odds were against him. King respected Rustin's opinion but was unwilling to surrender to "the paralysis of analysis." King felt that he had "divine guidance." He also felt that God was calling him to work in the valleys of Chicago. The poor people needed him there; he had to go. God wanted him to go to Chicago.

The socio-political analysis of Chicago that Bayard Rustin unveiled before King and the Southern Christian Leadership staff left many of the staffers in a hypnotic state. However, Andrew Young answered the analytical dilemma Bayard had placed before the staff when he said: "Martin has been called by God to Chicago; therefore, he should go." With planning and effort, Andy Young thought that SCLC could raise a nonviolent army of one hundred thousand or more people in Chicago because the black population in the windy city numbered almost a million people and exceeded the population in some states. Young felt that an army of one hundred thousand nonviolent crusaders could accomplish the impossible dream in Daley's Chicago.

On Wednesday, January 5, 1966, Dr. Martin Luther King flew into Chicago from Atlanta, Georgia, with a staff that included the Reverend Ralph D. Abernathy, vice president at-large and treasurer; Reverend Andrew Young, executive director; Reverend Bernard Lee, King's personal assistant; and Junius Griffin. The group was met at the airport by Reverend Walter Fauntroy of the Southern Christian Leadership Conference's Washington Bureau and several Chicago leaders. King and his four disciples were whisked away in a caravan of cars to the Sahara Inn, 3939 Mannheim Road, in Schiller Park, where they immediately went into a two day closed door session. The Chicago leaders who were present at the secret meeting with King were Al Raby, convener of the Coordinating Council of Community Organizations; Edwin (Bill) C. Berry, executive director of the Chicago Urban League; William Robinson, of the Church Federation of Greater Chicago; Eugene Turnour, regional director of CORE; Bob Lucas, Chicago CORE director; Robert Mueller, of the Westside Christian Parish; and Dr. Alvin Pitcher, from the University of Chicago and a member of the CCCO. Also present from the Chicago SCLC staff were the Reverend James Bevel, Reverend C. T. Vivian, and Reverend C. K. Steele.

Although King had been secreted into Chicago, the Chicago media became aware of his presence in the area within less than three hours after his arrival. The print and television media's interest in Dr. King was both intense and skeptical. When Dr. King finally emerged from the closed door two day shirt sleeve conference, he made the following announcement to a clamoring press corp that had been camping at the Sahara Inn for twenty-four hours. King said: "The CCCO and the SCLC have now combined their efforts into what will be known as the Chicago Freedom Movement. Our objective will be to bring about the unconditional surrender of forces dedicated to the creation and maintenance of slums. The Chicago Freedom Movement will press the political power structure to find imaginative programs to overcome the problem."

Dr. Martin Luther King outlined a proposed civil rights drive for Chicago that fundamentally followed the strategy he had used in the South. The plan called for mobilization of the city's nearly one million Negroes in training workshops, possible school and economic boycotts and mass demonstrations. King described his battle plan as having three major phases. The first phase was that of organization and education, which had already begun to take shape several months earlier under the direction of Reverend James Bevel and twenty SCLC staff members, who had been directing workshops on the west and near north side of Chicago. The second phase, which was timed to commence around March 1, called for demonstrations against specific targets. Phase three would launch what he called "massive action", which was set to begin on May 1.

Al Raby was at King's side during the January 7, 1966 press conference when Dr. King said:

> This is the first significant northern freedom movement ever attempted by major civil rights forces. It will be directed against public and private institutions that have created infamous slum conditions directly responsible for the involuntary enslavement of millions of black men, women and children. I will demonstrate my support for this cause by spending two or three days of each week in Chicago. I plan to live in a west side apartment that will symbolize the 'Slum Lordism' that I hope to smash.

On Wednesday afternoon, January 26, Dr. King and his wife, Coretta, moved into a three story walk-up, located at 1550 S. Hamlin Avenue, on the west side of Chicago in the Lawndale district. More than three hundred people greeted Dr. King and his wife when they arrived at the building. Children and adults from the community jostled one another for a spot where they could be

Dr. Martin Luther King and his wife Coretta held their first joint Chicago press conference on Wednesday afternoon, January 26, 1966, in their third floor apartment at 1550 South Hamlin Avenue, which is located in the Lawndale district on the near West Side.

Above: Dr. Martin Luther King and Al Raby, leader of the CCCO, carry trash from Dr. King's westside apartment building at 1550 South Hamlin Avenue. Left: Dr. King cleans up a gangway next to his apartment building in the Lawndale area on the west side.

Dr. King addresses some of his Lawndale neighbors from the back porch of his apartment building at 1550 South Hamlin Avenue.

near the minister and hopefully get an opportunity to touch his hand or garment. While standing in the entrance, Dr. King turned to the crowd and said, "I have to be right here with the people. I can learn more about the situation by being here with those who live and suffer. I will live in the apartment about three days a week, and I hope that my being here will dramatize the slum conditions in this city." Beautiful Coretta King in a Persian Lamb coat with a mink-trimmed collar was standing by his side as he addressed the crowd.

Dr. and Mrs. King turned to enter the building; then he stopped dead in his tracks. He had had an afterthought. King did a complete about face and said: "We have a big job to do. Not just in this building, but in the whole slum operation. We will be organizing tenant unions to end slums . . . and we will engage in rent strikes if necessary."

Dr. and Mrs. King and the herd of news reporters ascended three flights of stairs that had been drenched with urine so frequently that the strongest disinfectant could not remove the strong stench. When they reached the third floor and opened the door to their new apartment, Coretta and Dr. King saw a living room which had been painted white by amateur decorators. There were a fake fireplace, one sofa, a single chair, and a small table in the front room. The master bedroom was painted a jailhouse gray. There were a new Hollywood type bed and no chairs in the large bedroom. In an adjourning bedroom which was also painted gray, there was a queen-sized bed in in addition to a folding bed, which could be stored in a closet. The kitchen had been painted a jaundice yellow. The cook room had a sink on legs, a used stove and a reconditioned refrigerator. The unwashed windows in the kitchen looked out over a row of rooftops that were cluttered with whiskey and wine bottles and an assortment of beer cans and rocks. Next to the kitchen was a bathroom. The cracked tile on the bathroom floor was symbolic of the run-down condition of the apartment. Next to the washbowl, was a bathtub on legs that was both dirty and stained from age. Mrs. Coretta King spent Wednesday night in the apartment and left for Birmingham, Alabama the following day. Before leaving town, she made the following comment about the apartment: "In all my life I had never seen anything like it. There were no lights in the hall, and only one dim light at the head of the stairs. There was not even a lock on the door."

Dr. King's staff managed to keep his calendar filled because on the evening of the 26th his staff arranged for him to attend the hearing at a local church where some five hundred Lawndale residents were present and prepared to recite chapter and verse on the horrors of living in slum property. One woman got up and testified:

> I get down on my knees and scrub all day. I'm tired of giving away my hard-earned money to slum lords. I am filled to the brim: tired of being walked

over, tired of being mistreated. Thank God you are here, Dr. King, because I
don't intend to pay rent no more where there are rats, and I know you won't
let nobody throw me out.

After listening to individuals testify late into the night, Dr. King responded:

Many things you said tonight, I heard in the same kind of sessions out in
Watts right after the riots. I say to the power structure in Chicago that the
same problems that existed and still exist in Watts, exist in Chicago today,
and if something isn't done in a hurry, we can see a darkened night of social
disruption. We are going to organize to make Chicago a model city.
Remember, living in the slum is robbery. It's a robbery of dignity and the
right to participate creatively in the political process. It's wrong to live
with rats.

Mayor Richard J. Daley returned to Chicago on Monday, January 31 after
an eight day vacation in both the Florida Keys and Puerto Rico. Daley announced shortly after his arrival that he would go to Washington on Friday to
participate in a discussion with President Lyndon Baines Johnson on a 2.3
billion dollar program for clearing slums in American cities. Daley said that
"the elimination of slums is the number one program of this administration,
and we feel we have done more in this field than any other city. All of us, like
Dr. King, are trying to eliminate slums."

While Mayor Daley was in Washington, D.C., conferring with President
Lyndon Baines Johnson, Dr. King was in conference with Archbishop John P.
Cody, head of the Chicago Roman Catholic Archdiocese at the prelate's
residence. Dr. King and Cardinal Cody talked for approximately one hour and
fifteen minutes about racial injustice in Chicago. After the meeting, King told
the press: "We agreed to keep each other informed about activities in areas of
mutual interest, but there was no other agreement. It was the kind of discussion that could lead to an agreement." At the time that King and Cody were
closeted together, Dr. King was not aware that Cody had been briefed about
him by the FBI and that Cody was reported to have said to some Catholic insiders that he was not impressed with King and thought that he had a glib
tongue. Cody also had made it known to Mayor Daley that he intended to be
most circumspect in his dealings with the Negro leader.

Dr. King was not satisfied with simply wooing influential white religious
leaders like Archbishop John P. Cody; he was also intent on bringing into the
fold as many black religious clergy as possible. However, many of the black
clergymen treated King as if he had leprosy because they did not want
anything or anyone to disturb their relationship with the Daley machine.

Reverend Clay Evans, pastor of the Friendship Baptist Church, seated second from the left, plans fund-raising event to build church after his first mortgage was rejected by several major life insurance companies because of his affiliation with Dr. Martin Luther King. Seated left to right: Sid Ordower, civil rights activist and director and producer of the Jubilee Showcase; Reverend Clay Evans; Dr. Martin Luther King, president of the Southern Leadership Conference; Lucille Loman, administrative assistant to the Reverend Jesse Jackson, Operation Breadbasket. Standing left to right: Robert Weaver; Roebuck Staple, of the famous gospel Staple Singers; Reverend Jesse Jackson, recently appointed to head Operation Breadbasket by Dr. Martin Luther King; Bell "Dock" Lee and Jesse Forley.

Reverend Clay Evans, pastor of Fellowship Missionary Baptist Church and president of the Chicago branch of the Baptist Ministers Conference, was an exception because he opened church doors for Dr. King that had been closed until Evans interceded for King in behalf of the Chicago Freedom Movement. The Reverend Jesse Louis Jackson, a young Southern Christian Leadership Conference staff member, was very instrumental in getting Reverend Evans involved in the Chicago Freedom Movement. When Reverend Evans embraced Dr. King and the movement, there was thunder in the House of the Lord. Reverend Evans said: "Many ministers who were with us had to back off because they didn't want their buildings to be condemned or given citations for electrical work, faulty plumbing, or fire code violations." The building department was a plain clothes arm of the police department and was frequently used to keep black ministers and real estate owners in line politically.

Reverend Clay Evans paid a big price for joining the Chicago Freedom Movement. Evans recalls:

I was trying to build an edifice at 45th Place and Princeton Avenue. The basement foundation had been laid, the steel structure was up, insurance companies and banks had agreed to come together to make the loan, and the contractor was prepared to move forward. It was at this time that I decided that Dr. King, Jesse Jackson, and I would go down and talk with the mortgage broker about the construction payout.

I introduced Dr. King to the mortgage broker, and he looked across the table at King and Jesse and me and said, "Reverend Evans, I have cautioned you about getting involved. Dr. King, you might mean well but if Dr. Evans stays involved in the movement, people have said to me they are not going to let him have the money. I know you must be well aware that Mayor Daley can stop any structure in Chicago that he wants to."

Reverend Clay Evans' water filled basement and naked steel beams remained a monument to the Chicago Freedom Movement for seven years. The church edifice was finally completed in 1973, with a loan from the Amalgamated Bank and Trust Company. The Reverend Jesse Louis Jackson, as president of Operation PUSH (People United to Save Humanity), and Reverend Donald Benedict of the Community Renewal Society who put together an ecumenical group that guaranteed the bank loan coordinated the transaction with the bank for Reverend Clay Evans.

Reverend Evans' prominence among some black ministers enabled King to reach into Chicago's black churches and address the real grass roots people. On Saturday, February 5, 1966, King urged residents of the East Garfield Park area to be "dissatisfied" until improvements were made in housing, employment, and educational facilities as he spoke before the East Garfield Park People's Conference Meeting in the Mozart Baptist Church, 2900 W. Madison Street. King also said that "we must organize to solve these problems, and there is power in numbers. Forty-six percent of the Negroes in Chicago live in dilapidated conditions. We don't have wall-to-wall carpeting to worry about, but we do have wall-to-wall rats and roaches."

On February 10, Mayor Daley announced a massive city and county assault on slums and rats in a counter attack that he hoped would dilute the effectiveness of King's war against slumlords. Landlords of 331 welfare families were ordered by Daley's Department of Building to repair their apartments or face rent withholding and lawsuits. Daley set the end of 1967 as a target for clearing every slum in the city. Raymond M. Hillard, Cook County Public Aid Director, with Daley at his side in a City Hall press conference said, "I believe we now have in sight the complete wiping out of slums in Chicago. Slums have been winning the battle up to now, but this changes the tide."

On February 11, 1966, Dr. Martin Luther King threw another tactic into the arena in an effort to stay abreast of Mayor Daley. He threatened to lead economic boycotts against local industries which refused to hire Negroes for "bigger and better jobs". He said his SCLC Chicago subsidiary, Operation Breadbasket, was programmed to bring more than fifty million dollars in income to Chicago Negroes. "If you respect one's dollars, one must respect the person. The Negro has buying power, and his right to maintain that buying has to be upheld." The man named to head Operation Breadbasket by a reluctant Dr. King was a young 24 year old CCCO and SCLC organizer named Reverend Jesse L. Jackson. Jesse was selected because Ralph Abernathy saw him as a winner, and secondly, he was not a threat to other ministers who pastored large churches. Thirdly, he was based in Chicago and was not opposed to holding the Operation Breadbasket meeting on Saturday morning, which was a time that was not a threat to regular Sunday church services and collections. King, in his efforts to get support for Breadbasket's economic boycotts, told a group of fifty labor leaders which included William L. Lee, president of the Chicago Federation of Labor, that the civil rights movement in Chicago would emulate labor techniques and would also seek financial support from that body. King emphasized: "We have mutual interests and concerns. If there are any two movements that have an identity of purposes and objectives, they are the labor movement and the civil rights movement."

Chicago's white labor leaders and some blacks in labor were not in tune with King's Chicago Freedom Movement because its practices were contrary to the gospel as practiced by Daley. Moreover, the American Federation of Labor trade unions, in the light of their support for Mayor Daley, were able to negotiate highly favorable contracts for their members who worked exclusively for the city of Chicago; these union workers received the regular private industry higher pay scale with all the additional municipal fringe benefits plus the advantages that accrue to city payrollers who were not in union monopoly categories such as all state and national holidays, gold brick work assignments with casual to no supervision. Unlimited gold bricking was the city payrollers most cherished perk. Blacks, with very few exceptions, were excluded from the craft trade unions and the municipal goodies; therefore, anything that King said to union leaders about Mayor Richard J. Daley was blasphemous. To make bad matters worse for King, William A. Lee, president of the Chicago Federation of Labor and head of the Bakery Drivers Union (AFL), William McFetridge, international vice president of the Flat Janitors Union (AFL), Stephen Bailey, president of the AFL Plumbers Union, and Joseph Germano of the CIO Steel Workers, were all part of Daley's inner circle. One of Daley's best friends, Thomas J. Murray, vice president of the board of education, was also president of Local 134 of the Electrical Workers Union (AFL) and president of the Building Trades Council of Chicago.

The *Hauser Report* pulled the white sheet off the interlocking relationship between City Hall, the trade unions, and the board of education. It had been claimed for years by white politicians that the reason blacks were not employed in the trades around City Hall was that they were lazy and simply did not want to work whereas the real reason that blacks were not working in the trades was that Superintendent Benjamin C. Willis was part and parcel in a conspiracy with a league of American Federation of Labor unions in denying training for black youth. The *Hauser Report* showed that black students were denied admission to the apprenticeship training programs at the Washburne Trade School because the anti-black trade unions of Chicago ran the institution as opposed to the board of education. The trade unions decided which student applicants would be able to matriculate at the Washburne Trade School and the trade school was run by Tom Murray, Mayor Richard J. Daley's very close friend. Therefore, it was impossible for Daley not to have known of the unions' exclusionary policies as they applied to blacks and other minorities. Moreover, the trade union's "Jim Crow" policies could not have been implemented without the tacit approval of Superintendent Benjamin J. Willis and Mayor Richard J. Daley.

The vice president of the board of education, Thomas J. Murray, snarled when questioned by reporters about the racist politics at Washburne: "If the board of education interferes in union membership practices, the trade unions will pull out of Washburne and start their own school." It's true that Daley did not directly hire Superintendent Willis, but Daley appointed Murray and the six additional board members who hired him; therefore, no one could say with a straight face that Daley did not have influence on any action that took place in the board of education generally and at Washburne Trade School specifically.

The trade unions that supported Dr. Martin Luther King were few, and they all surfaced with financial support for a massive Freedom Festival, which was held on March 12, 1966, at the International Amphitheater at 41st and Halsted Street. The five trade unions that made substantial cash contributions were Teamsters Local 743, Warehouse, Mail Order Employees, the United Auto Workers, International Ladies Garment Workers Union, the United Steelworkers of America and the United Packinghouse Workers of America. The five trade unions all had a long and consistent history in supporting civil rights causes. The Freedom Festival was attended by some thirteen thousand eight hundred King supporters. The event grossed one hundred thousand dollars for the Chicago Freedom Movement. The celebrities that appeared on the program that Saturday evening were Sidney Poitier, Harry Belafonte, Dick Gregory and Mahalia Jackson. In a major address that night, Dr. King observed:

> Never before in the history of the civil rights movement has an action campaign been launched in such splendor. Never had a community responded more splendidly to the call for support than you have in Chicago. The

> Chicago Freedom Movement will continue to encourage sit-ins, stand-ins, rent strikes, boycotts, picket lines, marches, civil disobedience and any forms of protests and demonstrations that are nonviolently conceived and executed.

The huge crowd responded to Dr. King's remarks with thunderous applause and a long standing ovation.

Between the Freedom Festival on March 12, and Freedom Sunday on July 10, Superintendent Benjamin C. Willis handed in his resignation to the board of education to become effective August 31, 1966. Benjamin Willis broke the news of quitting his school post at a hastily assembled five minute press conference on Monday afternoon, May 24, 1966, in the board of education office. Superintendent Willis said, "I picked the early resignation date in order give the incoming superintendent, James F. Redmond, an opportunity to familiarize himself with the Chicago system. My resignation should dissolve a current dilemma of the board of education, which, if permitted to continue, could only be detrimental to those whom I am deeply interested."

Although Superintendent Willis had an ironclad contract which would have continued him in his job for an additional two and a half years. In response to pressure for his removal, he had promised that he would resign on December 23, 1966, his 65th birthday. The decision to toss in the towel approximately three and a half months earlier than the agreed date was apparently in response to the unrelenting agitation for his ouster from a large segment of the Negro community. Dr. Martin Luther King and other black leaders held both Willis and Daley responsible for the continuance of de facto segregation in the Chicago school system.

The reactions to Superintendent Benjamin C. Willis' resignation were extreme in that some members of the board of education were stunned and sad whereas the troops in the civil rights movement were collectively jubilant. "Black day for Chicago," was the reaction of Thomas J. Murray, vice president of the Chicago Board of Education." He continued I feel that Dr. Willis' resignation is one of the worst things that could have happened. I might have been doing some wishful thinking when I thought there might be a way to prevent him from resigning. I would like to see him reconsider. He's been a great superintendent. He has much to offer the city of Chicago."

Al Raby, convener of the Coordinating Council of Community Organizations and a long time foe of Willis said, "I am overjoyed by Willis' decision. I think he made a wise decision to get out fast. He represented a major stumbling block in quality integrated education in Chicago."

"Hurrah!" was the immediate reaction of Urban League Executive Director Edwin Berry to the news of Superintendent Willis' resignation. Berry characterized the school superintendent's actions as follows: "A segregationist who was so taken with the idea of keeping the schools segregated, yet trying to call it something else. He was totally ineffective as an administrator. He was so anxious to maintain segregation that he tried to put a school on every corner in the ghetto in order to enforce it."

Inasmuch as in the late spring of 1966, Dr. Benjamin C. Willis' reign as superintendent of the Chicago Public School system was rapidly becoming a historical footnote, the season dictated that Dr. Martin Luther King Jr. shift the Chicago Freedom Movement's gears into its second phase which was mass demonstrations and then into the third phase which was direct action.

In addition to seeking black and white support for the mammoth rally, which was to be held at Soldier Field on July 10, 1966, Dr. King extended an invitation to the Chicago Latin American leadership to join the human rights movement. Reverend Daniel Alvarez, president of the Spanish American Ministerial Association, appeared to favor Kings' invitation. Rev. Alvarez, who had participated in numerous civil rights protests and marches said that he agreed with the content of King's invitation and message. King's full invitation read as follows:

> The incident of social disruption which occurred on June 12, 1966, in Chicago' predominantly Puerto Rican neighborhood is indicative of the flagrant gross callousness exhibited by law enforcement officials who reportedly are assigned to protect a city's citizenry.
>
> Those who praise the efficient work of the riot-control trained policemen and dogs should also be vocal in their denouncements of those city agencies which ignore dangerous social conditions caused by deprivation in housing, job opportunities, welfare and education. It is also ironic that the power structure will not listen to minority communities' grievances until an atmosphere of violence threatens to blight the whole community.
>
> This same power structure is then joined by so-called responsible elements of the community in heaping verbal abuse upon that particular ethnic group or race which traditionally is always victimized by forces representing the status quo.
>
> It is time for Chicago's entire community representing the forces of good will to join the city's oppressed minorities in seeking nonviolent methods to eliminate the hideous conditions which plague this city. I am issuring a special appeal to Latin American residents of Chicago to join me and my Southern Christian Leadership Conference, along with organizations represented by the Coordinating Council Community Organizations, in a mammoth freedom rally and march on Sunday, July 10, to demand of the city fathers an open city for all men regardless of their race, religion, or national origin.

Right: A burned-out squad car is hauled away from the disturbance scene. A crowd tipped it over on the corner of Damen and Division.

Above left: A priest appeals to the crowd to disperse and go home. Above right: Cruz Arcelis, 20, 1665 North Wolcott, prisoner being removed from St. Mary of Nazareth Hospital to the Bridwell Hospital after being treated for a leg wound inflicted by Police Officer Munyon who was attempting to apprehend the revolver-toting street fighter. This incident set off a full-scale riot in the Puerto Rican community on June 12, 1966. Right: Policemen, with their dogs, face crowd during disturbance near Damen and Division. The canine corps was used in several instances to hold the crowd at bay.

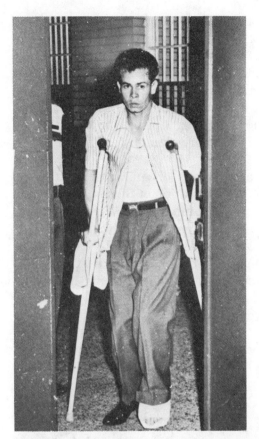

Left: The shooting of Arceilis Cruz, 21, shown leaving the county jail after making bond, by a Chicago policeman was the prelude to the Puerto Rican riot which started on Division Street near midnight on June 12, 1966. Above: A Puerto Rican community representative is seen (mouth agape) in the background yelling for quiet so that police officials and Puerto Rican leaders inside of a nearby record shop on Division at California can proceed with peace negotiations.

Members of the Chicago Police Department assemble at Division and Washtenaw before making a nightstick swinging drive North on Washtenaw to clear the area of rioters.

Freedom Sunday rode into Chicago the afternoon of July 10th on a heat wave that reached 98 degrees by 4:00 P.M. A half million people inundated the Chicago parks and beaches in search of relief from the scorching sun. Only forty thousand of an earlier estimated one hundred thousand showed up that afternoon at Soldier Field for the Freedom Sunday Rally. Several hundred persons quickly claimed the few shady spots in the Soldier Field stand when gates were opened for the rally at 12:15 P.M. Those arriving later had to sit in the hot sweltering sun-drenched seats. Many of the more thoughtful ones brought umbrellas.

Scattered throughout the stands were various organizations sitting in groups. Among them were the American Confederation of State, County, and Municipal employees, AFL-CIO, Local 6 of the United Auto Workers Union, the Woodlawn Organization, the West Side Organization, the Englewood Organization, the Lawndale Organization, the East Garfield Park Organization, and many other groups representing segments of Chicago's seventy-five communities. Vendors of cold drinks, ice cream, and straw hats had more business than they could handle.

Before the speeches began, two hundred youths, most of them claiming to be members of the Blackstone Rangers, a South Side youth group, demonstrated in the stadium's infield with a banner inscribed, "Black Power," and placards bearing the legend, "We Shall Overcome," and "Freedom Now," with

National and international entertainers appeared at the Chicago Freedom Fest. (Left to right): Sidney Poitier; Dr. Martin Luther King, Jr.; Harry Belafonte (partially hidden); Mahalia Jackson; unidentified woman and Al Raby.

a drawing of a submachine gun. Following this unscheduled demonstration, the excited and restless crowd was entertained by many performers including Dick Gregory, the international comedian who had announced earlier his independent candidacy for mayor of Chicago, Mahalia Jackson, the great gospel singer, WVON disc jockey Herb Kent, who acted as master of ceremonies, Oscar Brown Jr., the Andrew McPherson sextet, Peter Yarrow of the Peter, Paul, and Mary folk singing act and the very young and talented Stevie Wonder. Rev. Arthur Brazier, sitting on the speaker's platform listening to the entertainers and waiting for Dr. King's arrival, said the following thought streamed to his mind:

> I felt a real sense of belonging to something that was happening positively for black people in the city of Chicago and in the nation. Chicago was a part of a national movement. Black people were coming out of a state of economic and social oppression. We were now saying and doing things that were almost unheard of five years earlier.

The spirit of the afternoon was lit by King's wife, Coretta, who sang the National Anthem. She was followed on the program by a series of speakers who had struck a pledge of basic unity in the human rights fight. Religious, labor, and civil rights leaders made pleas, demands, warnings and commands under the blazing sun from the shadowless speaker's platform. Thunderous applause boomed through the humid atmosphere in response to the words of Dr. Edgar H. S. Chandler, executive director of the Church Federation of Greater Chicago; Reverend Ralph Abernathy, vice president of the Southern Christian Leadership Conference; Al Raby, convener of the Coordinating Council of Community Organizations; Ralph Helstein, president of the United Packinghouse Workers of America; Sergio Herrero, president of the Spanish-American Federation; Floyd McKissick of CORE; and James Meredith. Irv Kupcinet, the Sun-Times columnist added a bit of humor and wit that put the crowd in stitches that afternoon when he introduced Rev. Brazier and said, "Ladies and gentlemen, let me introduce you to a man who holds the ladies' up, The Rev. Arthur 'Brassiere'."

The most deafening ovation and response was reserved for Dr. Martin Luther King, president of the Southern Christian Leadership Conference. Cheers and applause shook the heavens like a sonic boom when Dr. King rolled through the gates onto Soldier Field in a white convertible Cadillac. As Dr. King stood waving at the crowd from the car as it circled the stadium, an announcement came over the public address system indicating that dozens of buses were backed up for miles along the Outer Drive. The news that additional people were enroute to the rally brought cheers from those in the throng

When Dr. King's motorcade rolled into Soldier Field, he received a standing, thunderous ovation.

who were disappointed because the crowd was under the original estimate of one hundred thousand.

Archbishop John P. Cody, who was to introduce King at the rally, was out of town on an official visit to mission parishes in Panama had the introduction read in his name by Bishop Aloysius Wycislo, auxiliary Bishop of Chicago and pastor of Immaculate Heart of Mary Parish. The introduction by the archbishop read:

> You've come this afternoon to hear a man who has become a symbol of all this (civil rights, racial, human freedom) to America and to the world. The man has awakened the conscious of a nation. This man has taught us that wherever there is segregation, no man can be truly free. This man has achieved mightily for all Americans and never, even under the most severe tests, betrayed the idea of nonviolence and love.

When King arose to speak, the crowd jumped spontaneously to its feet and gave him a roaring ovation that must have lasted at least six minutes. Efforts to stop the adulation were fruitless because the crowd was determined to show King how much they loved him and his nonviolent philosophy. In response to the crowds reactions, King said:

> We are here today because we are tired.
> We are tired of being seated in the flames of withering injustice. We are tired of paying more for less.

We are tired of living in rat-infested slums and in the Chicago Housing Authority's cement reservations. We are tired of having to pay a median rent of $97.00 a month in Lawndale for four rooms while whites in South Deering pay $73.00 a month for five rooms.

We are tired of inferior, segregated, and overcrowded schools which are incapable of preparing our young people for leadership and security in this technological age. We are tired of discrimination in employment which makes us the last hired and the first to be fired.

We are tired of a welfare system which dehumanizes us and dispenses payments under procedures that are often ugly and paternalistic. Yes, we are tired of being lynched physically in Mississippi, and we are tired of being lynched spiritually and economically in the north.

We have also come here today to remind Chicago of the fierce urgency of now. This is no time to engage in the luxury of cooling off or to take the tranquilizing drug of gradualism.

We have also come here today to affirm that we will no longer sit idly by in agonizing deprivation and wait on others to provide our freedom. We will be sadly mistaken if we think freedom is some lavish dish that the federal government and the white man will pass out on a silver platter while the Negro merely furnishes the appetite. Freedom is never voluntarily granted by the oppressor. It must be demanded by the oppressed.

We must not wait for President Johnson to free us. We must not wait for the Supreme Court and Congress to free us. We must not wait for Mayor Daley to free us. These forces will only respond when they realize that we have a powerful inner determination to be free. The battle is in our hands. So, we must go out with grim and bold determination to free ourselves. We must desegregate our minds. We must believe and know that we are somebody. We must not allow anybody to make us feel that we are inferior.

We must appreciate our great heritage. We must be proud of our race. We must not be ashamed of being black. We must believe with all of our hearts that black is as beautiful as any other color.

This day, we must declare our own Emancipation Proclamation. This day, we must commit ourselves to make any sacrifice necessary to change Chicago. This day, we must decide to fill up the jails of Chicago, if necessary, in order to end slums.

This day, we must decide to register every Negro in Chicago of voting age before the municipal election. This day, we must decide that our votes will determine who will be the mayor of Chicago next year.

This day, henceforth and forever more, we must make it clear that we will purge Chicago of every politician, whether he be Negro or white, who feels that he owns the Negro vote rather than earns the Negro vote.

This day, we must continue our already successful efforts to organize in every area of Chicago, unions to end slums. Together we must withhold rent from landlords that force us to live in subhuman conditions.

This day, we must make it clear that we will withdraw our money 'en masse' from any bank that does not have a non-discriminatory lending policy.

We must affirm that we will withdraw economic support from any company that will not provide on-the-job training, and employ an adequate number of Negroes, Puerto Ricans, and all other minorities in the higher paying jobs.

This day, we must decide to give greater support to Negro-owned businesses which will aid in building our economic strength.

I understand our legitimate discontent. But I must reaffirm that I do not see the answer to our problems in violence.

Our movement's adherence to nonviolence has been a major factor in the creation of a moral climate that has made progress possible. This climate may well be dissipated not only by acts of violence but by the threats of it verbalized by those who equate it with militancy. Our power does not reside in Molotov cocktails, rifles, knives and bricks.

The ultimate weakness of a riot is that it can be halted by superior force. We have neither the techniques, the numbers nor the weapons to win a violent campaign.

Many of our opponents would be happy for us to turn to acts of violence in order to have an excuse to slaughter hundreds of innocent people. Beyond this, violence never appeals to the conscience. It intensifies the fears of the white majority while relieving their guilt.

Nonviolence does not mean doing nothing. It does not mean passively accepting evil. It means standing up so strongly with your body and soul that you can not stoop to the low places of violence and hatred.

As we think of our methods we must avoid the error of building a distrust for all white people. In seeking the profound changes full integration will involve, Negroes will need the continued support of the white majority.

We must face the realistic fact that we are only ten percent of America's population and no romanticized call for black separatism can be validated in reason, or in morality.

Beyond this, we must see that within the white community, there exists a substantial group of white Americans who cherish democratic principles above privilege, and who have demonstrated their will to fight with the Negro against injustice. Indeed, some have died for our freedom on the highways and in the byways of the South.

The Negro needs the white man to free him from his fears. The white man needs the Negro to free him from his guilt.

Any approach that overlooks this need for a coalition of conscience is unwise and misguided. A doctrine of black supremacy is as evil as a doctrine of white supremacy.

Finally, we assemble here today to march to City Hall to demand redress of our legitimate grievances. I am still convinced that there is nothing more

Left: Dr. Martin Luther King addresses a crowd of more than 50,000 at Chicago's Soldier Field for the campaign to end slums in Chicago on Sunday, July 10, 1966. Below: At the conclusion of Dr. King's speech, he joined hands with others on the platform and they sang several choruses of "We Shall Overcome." (Left to right): Reverend Stroy Freeman, pastor of New Friendship Missionary Baptist Church; unidentified Catholic priest; Dr. Martin Luther King; Reverend Theodore M. Hesburgh, C.S.C., president of Notre Dame University; Dr. Edgar H. S. Chandler, executive director of the Chicago Federation of Greater Churches.

powerful to dramatize and expose a social evil than the tramp, tramp, tramp of marching feet.

As we march, some silent onlooker, some detached spectator will probably ask where are these people coming from. The answer will come in the words of John the Relevator, "These are they that are coming up out of great trials and tribulations."

These are they coming up out of many years of neglect and exploitation. These are they, whose children have been so scarred by the system of oppression that they often have clouds of inferiority floating in their mental skies.

These are they who with tear-drenched eyes have had to stand over the coffins of four little beautiful innocent, unoffending Negro girls in Birmingham, and Emmet C. Till, and Medgar Evers in Mississippi.

After Dr. King concluded his historical speech, he led 38,000 of his followers on a march from Soldier Field to City Hall where he posted demands of the NonViolent Freedom Fighters on Mayor Richard J. Daley's front door in the fashion of his namesake Martin Luther, the German theologian, who nailed ninety-five theses (statements for debate) on the door of Castle Church in Whittenberg, Germany, on October 31, 1517.

Six hundred police officers were assigned to the King march. Dr. Martin Luther King led the march on that hot, humid afternoon in an air-conditioned automobile. An ambulance accompanied the marchers to give first aid to those who were fallen by the heat. The marchers sang civil rights songs and chanted, "Mayor Daley Must Go," as they proceeded west on Balboa to State Street, north on State to Madison Street, west on Madison to LaSalle Street, and north on LaSalle to the City Hall. As the front of the column of marchers neared City Hall, the rear was marching west on Balboa Drive and over the Illinois Central Railroad tracks. The marchers filled the streets from curb to curb.

Banners and placards attacking the city administration of Mayor Daley and his Democratic political organization cast the theme of the march. "End Modern Slavery—Destroy the Daley Machine," one plaque read. Another plaque that was destroyed by fellow marchers along the route read, "Don't Hate the White; Don't Be Anti-White or Poor White Trash; Be Pro-American; Vote for George C. Wallace in 1968". Wallace, an ardent segregationist, was governor of Alabama. As Dr. Martin Luther King and Al Raby posted their demands on the City Hall door, the crowd roared its approval. After Dr. Martin Luther King completed the posting, he turned to the cheering multitude. The radiant gleam on his face reflected the fact that he hoped that July 10, 1966 would mark the symbolic beginning of the American reformation. A condensed version of King's demands follows:

REAL ESTATE BOARDS AND BROKERS

1. Public statements that all listings will be available on a nondiscriminatory basis.

BANKS AND SAVINGS INSTITUTIONS

1. Public statements of a nondiscriminatory mortgage policy so that loans will be available to any qualified borrower without regard to the racial composition of the area.

THE MAYOR AND CITY COUNCIL

1. Publication of headcounts of whites, Negroes and Latin Americans for all city departments and for all firms from which city purchases are made.
2. Revocation of contracts with firms that do not have a full scale fair employment practice.
3. Creation of a citizens review board for grievances against police brutality and false arrests or stops and seizures.
4. Ordinance giving ready access to the names of owners and investors for all slum properties.
5. A saturation program of increased garbage collection street cleaning and building inspection services in the slum properties.

POLITICAL PARTIES

1. The requirement that precinct captains be residents of their precincts.

CHICAGO HOUSING AUTHORITY AND THE CHICAGO DWELLING ASSOCIATION

1. Program to rehabilitate present public housing including such items as locked lobbies, restrooms in recreation areas, increased police protection and child care centers on every third floor.
2. Program to increase vastly the supply of low-cost housing on a scattered basis for both low and middle income families.

BUSINESS

1. Basic headcounts, including white, Negro and Latin American, by job classification and income level, made public.
2. Racial steps to upgrade and to integrate all departments, all levels of employment.

UNIONS

1. Headcounts in unions for apprentices, journeymen and union staff and officials by job classification. A crash program to remedy any inequities discovered by the head-count.

2. Indenture of at least 400 Negro and Latin-American apprentices in the craft unions.

GOVERNOR

1. Prepare legislative proposals for a $2.00 state minimum wage law and for credit reform, including the abolition of garnishment and wage assignment.

ILLINOIS PUBLIC AID COMMISSION AND
THE COOK COUNTY DEPARTMENT OF PUBLIC AID

1. Encouragement of grievance procedures for the welfare recipients so that recipients know that they can be members of and represented by a welfare union or a community organization.
2. Institution of a declaration of income system to replace the degrading investigation and means test for welfare eligibility.

FEDERAL GOVERNMENT

1. Executive enforcement of Title I of the 1984 Civil Rights Act regarding the complaint against the Chicago Board of Education.
2. An executive order for Federal supervision of the nondiscriminatory granting of loans by banks and savings institutions that are members of the Federal Deposit Insurance Corporation or by the Federal Deposit Insurance Corporation.
3. Passage of the 1966 Civil Rights Act without any deletions or crippling amendments.
4. Direct funding of Chicago community organizations by the Office of Economic Opportunity.

PEOPLE

1. Financial support of the freedom movement.
2. Selective buying campaigns against businesses that boycott the products of Negro-owned companies.
3. Participation in the Freedom Movement target campaigns for this summer, including volunteer services and membership in one of the Freedom Movement Organizations.

Out of the twenty-four demands that Dr. Martin Luther King posted on the door of Chicago City Hall, the boycott provisions under the people category held out the most immediate promise for concrete results because of the earlier successes of both the SCLC and CCCO in that arena. Hence, Operation Breadbasket, an arm of the Southern Christian Leadership Conference, yielded the earliest and most solid accomplishments for the Chicago Freedom Movement under the leadership of the charismatic and youthful Reverend

Jesse Louis Jackson, a rhetorician who fully understood the use of the boycott leverage.

Between April and September in 1966, Reverend Jackson persuaded five major milk companies and two major soft drink firms to upgrade 295 qualified blacks from manual labor to skilled jobs. A few landed in sales positions, thus collectively increasing the income in the black community by $2,225,000 annually. Operation Breadbasket's job lift program was simply the first step of a strategy that ultimately would loosen the plantation chains on the lips of Daley's black "Silent Six" aldermen. On an even higher rung on the economic ladder, the Breadbasket strategy would redefine and help implement marketing reciprocity between black entrepreneurs and major white firms.

Dick Gregory, popular international comedian, was arrested protesting the erection of "Willis wagons" at 71st and Lowe Avenue.

Chapter *XX*

Tramping for Democracy in Chicago

Dr. Martin Luther King's demands had not been posted for more than forty-eight hours on the front door of Mayor Daley's City Hall when a police riot erupted on Tuesday, July 12, 1966 in the heart of Chicago's west side ghetto where three hundred thousand blacks had been crowbarred into the worst slums in North America. The west side peoples' eruption was the second within a thirty day period in Chicago. On Sunday, June 12, 1966, there was a brown peoples' explosion on the northwest side of Chicago when patrolman Thomas Munyon shot a twenty-one year old Puerto Rican, Arceilis Cruz of 1265 North Winchester Avenue, in the leg after the victim pulled a revolver.

A screaming, jeering crowd of more than one thousand Puerto Ricans formed rapidly after the shooting. Many were women. During the height of the melee, one hundred patrolmen in wedge formation charged the enraged throng but were repeatedly met by a hail of bricks, bottles, and debris. The enraged mob tore fire hoses from the hands of firemen attempting to extinguish the blazing police squad cars. Before daybreak on Monday, June 13, 1966, bands of young Puerto Ricans and others broke into and looted business establishments along Division Street, which was the main street in the barrio.

Ironically, the black explosion came exactly thirty days after the Puerto Rican riot and two days after the leading advocate of nonviolence, Dr. Martin Luther King, had addressed an audience of thirty thousand people in Chicago at Soldier Field. The black rebellion was more intense and covered a wider geographic area than the Puerto Rican Division Street riot. The black explosion was not ignited by a shooting. In contrast, it was inflamed by a one hundred degree temperature which caused black west side youths to seek relief from the scorching sun under a neighborhood fire hydrant because the nearest Lake Michigan beaches were closed as a result of water pollution. Patrolmen Melvin Clark and Arthur Scor shut the fire hydrant off in front of 1233 South Throop in compliance with a municipal ordinance. In a superman posture, Donald Henry, 26, of 1246 Taylor Street, stepped up and reopened the hydrant. Clark and Scor grabbed Henry and told him he was under arrest. Henry shouted to the gathering crowd, "You are not going to let these policemen arrest me. Why don't you do something about it?"

After making a quick survey of the gathering crowd, Patrolman Scor ran to his squad car and put in a call for assistance. Fifteen squad cars responded. The crowd instantly converted into a mob and began hurling rocks at the squad cars and other passing vehicles. Donald Henry and six other adults, in addition to two juveniles, were arrested. After the prisoners were removed from the scene, the mob reacted by roving from 12th and South Throop to 14th Street and Racine Avenue and then east to 14th and Blue Island Avenue, north back to Roosevelt and Halsted and west to Roosevelt and Ashland, smashing windows and looting shops as they moved along the street. Most of the damage was inflicted in the Liberty Shopping Center in the thirteen hundred block of Racine Avenue, where almost all the windows in eight of the nine shops in the center were smashed in a forty-five minute barrage. Gerald Waszkowski, 24, of 2033 Rice Street, an employee of the drug store in the shopping center, described the attack:

> There were two to three hundred persons, mostly teenagers in the crowd that approached the center from a park across the street. Twenty youths stepped out in front of the rest and began hurling beer bottles, cans, and rocks at the windows in the shop. They were soon joined by others in the crowd. Our drug store and a supermarket were open at the time. We had twenty customers in the store. An elderly blind man and a Puerto Rican man who had been struck in the head and was bleeding profusely sought refuge in the store as we closed our iron gates to prevent entry by the crowd. We then took refuge in the rear as the window smashing continued. In addition to the drug store and supermarket, a laundromat, furniture store, cleaning shop, medical center and jewelry store were damaged. A restaurant owned by a black man in the center was not touched.

Later in the evening, a homemade bomb known as a Molotov Cocktail, was hurled at a police squad car on Roosevelt Road east of Ashland Avenue, but it did not ignite. Fifteen persons were arrested at the scene while five other homemade bombs were confiscated. Irving Frank, owner of the Continental Laundry at 1417 Roosevelt Road, asked Monroe Street police for more protection. He said windows in his plant were broken and that he feared for the safety of employees working inside.

Chester Robinson, director of the West Side Organization at 1527 W. Roosevelt Road, was at the scene when Donald Henry was arrested. Robinson said:

> I told the police officers the seriousness of the problem and explained that the area's lack of recreational facilities including the need for a swimming pool was undercutting our ability to control the activities of the youngsters. As a matter of fact, we sent forty of our West Side Organization's people out into the streets to try to get the kids to march away from the scene singing freedom songs. But more police were flushed into the troubled area, and the crowd grew angry and began pelting the law officers with bricks and bottles. Other teenagers were jostling one another, some swearing. Even in play, there was defiance on the faces of some of the youngsters and curses on the lips of others; Negro officers seemed to be torn between duty and something else.

Neither the temperature nor the tempers had abated on Wednesday morning, July 13, because the community people continued to display their collective unrest and wrath over the fire hydrant incident and the need for recreational facilities on the west side. The seething anger over the fire hydrants on the near west side was a mental throwback for older blacks who remembered vividly their inability to eat hamburgers in white restaurants in Chicago and throughout the confederate states; hence, both the fire hydrant and the greasy hamburgers were superficial elements of a problem that had its roots in the bowels of a greater discontent that manifested itself in a violent rebellion led by their children.

On Wednesday evening, apartment building bricks and the asphalt street pavements in the west side ghetto were regurgitating the heat of the midday sun. The smoldering anger of the mob erupted into a second night of violence and destruction in the Fillmore district when a mob of several hundred blacks came to the rescue of an ex-convict, William Young, who screamed for help and claimed that two white detectives were trying to kill him. Detectives Biadgio Panepinto and James Rizzi described their encounter with William Young which poured gasoline on tempers that were already at an incendiary intensity that hot smothering summer night. The detectives said:

> We were driving along in plain clothes and spotted William Young standing in front of a liquor store at 137 South Pulaski Road and recognized him from the bulletin "WANTED" picture. Young tried to shield his face with an umbrella when we approached him. When we asked him for identification, he stuck a piece of paper in his mouth and swallowed it. At this point, he began to scream and call for help. He was yelling to bystanders that we were trying to kill him. He broke away and began to run, and we caught him. His

screams attracted a crowd of about two hundred people. He again broke away from us, and we chased him into an alley and drew our revolvers. He stopped, but as we approached him and attempted to place him in handcuffs, he began to struggle, knocking both of us to the ground. While we were wrestling with him, he yelled that he would rather be dead than sent back to jail, and he again asked the crowd to assist him in making his escape from us. The crowd had completely encircled us and began to make threats and warn us that if we did not release the prisoner we would be in big trouble. At this point, we were rescued by other policemen arriving on the scene. But the crowd that had formed because of the incident did not break up. Instead, it moved to Pulaski Road and Gladys Avenue where a hardware store was looted and then east on Madison Street looting and smashing windows in the nonblack owned shops and offices along the way. (A high rise office building located at 2400 West Madison, owned by a black man named Henry E. Fort, was not touched by the looters and arsonists.)

What Mayor Richard J. Daley described as some acts of juvenile delinquency on Tuesday afternoon, July 12, 1966, developed into a mini riot Wednesday morning because of the callousness of the police officers in handling the fire hydrant episode. Policemen coming off the Wednesday, 4 P.M. to midnight shift in the Monroe Street, Fillmore, Marquette, Wood Street, Deering, Wabash, Englewood, Central, East Chicago, and Shakespeare districts were held over for what obviously was becoming a full scale riot. Nine hundred police officers were deployed to the battle zone on the west side. The cry of "police brutality" became a litany. Innocent persons were herded from the streets like cattle and civil rights workers representing SCLC and CCCO, attempting to restore order in the neighborhood, were accorded the same treatment as rioters by police.

Essentially, the west side had become a confrontation between blacks and whites. The black community was under siege by a predominantly white police occupational force. Dr. King and his lieutenants pleaded with the young people in the streets to adhere to the principles of nonviolence by getting off the streets and returning to the safety of their homes. King's pleas fell on the ears of the dead. However, Dr. King continued in his efforts to resurrect the minds of the young rioters throughout the night, speeding from one battle zone to another in a desperate effort to stop the violence and destruction. By dawn, Thursday morning, July 14, two people had been killed, fifty-six injured and two hundred and eighty-two arrested. One of the dead was a girl fourteen years old and pregnant.

A one hundred and forty square block area of Chicago's strife-ridden west side was cordoned off Thursday night by fifteen hundred national guardsmen. Residents taunted the heavily armed soldiers with jeers, curses, and mock applause. The fifteen hundred soldiers were part of a more than thirty-nine hundred man force mobilized earlier on Thursday and fanned out from six Chicago armories. They had rolled into the west side area riding in over one hundred trucks and jeeps, some with thirty caliber machine guns mounted on the back. Major General Francis P. Kane, commander of the Illinois National Guard's 33rd Infantry Division, said as he deployed the troops: "My men have orders to shoot back and shoot back to kill, if they are fired upon."

More than two hundred guardsmen were assigned to patrol 16th Street between Kedzie Avenue and Pulaski Road where police had encountered heavy looting during the daylight hours on Thursday. Sixteenth Street was closed to vehicular traffic at 11:30 A.M. and was filled with soldiers carrying carbines and walking in groups of four and five. A dozen jeeps with guardsmen manning machine guns rode up and down 16th Street and surrounding arteries.

Sporadic incidents plagued the police and guardsmen. A firebomb was thrown at the rear of the home of a white family at 4340 W. 21st Street, but it went out without causing damage. A volley of firebombs was hurled at a passing freight train at Morgan and Kinzie Streets while the flame caused a small brush fire. A second fire broke out in Big Ben's Shoe Store at 1435 South Pulaski Road and caused some damage. A band of youths looted the store but eluded capture by the guardsmen or police.

The total geographic area being patrolled by the national guard was bounded by Kedzie Avenue on the east, Kilbourn Avenue on the west, Harrison Street on the north, and 16th Street on the south. A large section of this area had been the scene of violence and widespread looting since the riot broke out on Tuesday night. By late Thursday evening, an additional forty-four persons had been arrested on charges ranging from disorderly conduct to resisting arrest and burglary. Thirty-three were juveniles, three were women, and eight were adult men. Taverns throughout the area were closed by orders of the police department; the sale of liquor by anyone was forbidden.

Standard weapons carried by the national guardsmen included 45 caliber automatic pistols, carbines, rifles, machine guns, tear gas, and bayonets. The 33rd Division had moved into the west side area on orders issued by Governor Otto Kerner in Springfield, acting upon the urging of Mayor Richard J. Daley who requested the mobilization on the recommendation of Police Superintendent Orlando W. Wilson. Daley requested the guardsmen in the wake of the third night of violence, when more than thirty persons were injured including six policemen who were shot.

Mayor Richard J. Daley and Police Superintendent O. W. Wilson accused "teenage criminals, outsiders, and hoodlums" with responsibility for the outbreaks. Daley and Wilson hinted that King had been the blame for part of the trouble, pointing out that members of King's SCLC staff had been working with black teens on the west side and had encouraged violence by showing

Police Superintendent O. W. Wilson (left) and Mayor Richard J. Daley attempted to lay the blame on Dr. Martin Luther King, Jr. for the west side riot.

films of the Watts riot in Los Angeles. Reverend James Bevel denied the charges. He said the films had been shown in combination with films on King's nonviolent movement in order that teens could compare the results of both violence and nonviolence.

Prior to an unscheduled meeting with Mayor Richard J. Daley on Friday afternoon, July 15, 1966, Dr. Martin Luther King recoiled to a *Chicago Tribune* reporter at City Hall in the hallway on the fifth floor in front of Daley's outer office in response to earlier comments made by Daley and Wilson: "This is absolutely untrue. It is very unfortunate that a mayor of the city would perpetuate such an impression. My staff has preached nonviolence. We have never veered away from that at any point. The films showing the Watts riot were to demonstrate the negative effect of riots."

After the ninety minute meeting with Daley, Dr. Martin Luther King expressed satisfaction and said, "We had a very fine meeting. I plan to go back among the people and urge respect for law and order."

A Daley aide made it known to a *Chicago Tribune* reporter that none of the demands that King had taped on the City Hall door that previous Sunday had been covered in the meeting. Archbishop John P. Cody, Rabbi Robert J. Marx, the Reverend Donald E. Zimmerman, and the Reverend Dr. H. S. Chandler issued the following joint statement after attending the King-Daley meeting:

> Unfortunately, there are some who have connected these disturbances with legitimate efforts by men of good will to correct the injustices which some members of minority groups are still forced to endure in our society. While we call for an immediate return to law and order, we pledge ourselves to pursue every avenue which would lead to a society in which all citizens, regardless of race or creed or religion, may enjoy equal opportunity.

Dr. Martin Luther King, Jr. and Mayor Richard J. Daley shake hands after a ninety-minute private session in Daley's fifth floor City Hall offices.

The clergymen further said that they were confident that the Negro community did not support acts of violence.

Daley announced in his pressroom in the presence of King and other members of the clergy that he and those attending the meeting had agreed on five steps to be taken in an effort to pacify residents of the riot area. The steps included:

1. Sprayer attachments will be put on fire hydrants, which will be maintained by firemen on corners near fire stations.
2. Park district and police officials will take steps to see that all persons have equal access to swimming pools and parks.
3. Political precinct workers in the riot area, which is predominantly Democratic, will urge residents to stay in their homes and obey the law.
4. Daley's pledge that more swimming pools and playgrounds will be constructed in the area.
5. Daley would appoint a citizen's committee to advise him and make recommendations to the police department, with special emphasis on relations between police and the community.

King appeared elated at Daley's latest declaration and retorted:

> We think this is a good step for the moment. It is a move in the right direction. We will be going back to the people saying some positive things are being done, that changes are being made. Although the citizen committee Daley said he would appoint fell short of the police review board that we requested, I feel that the appointment of a committee to review police-community relations was an important concession.

After the Daley press conference in City Hall, Dr. King rushed back to his apartment at 1550 South Hamlin and put out a call for the fifteen top gang leaders of the Cobras, Vice Lords and Roman Saints to meet with him in his home. The three gangs had been in the forefront of destruction and disorder in the west side rebellion. By 8:30 that evening, all of the gang members had assembled in Dr. King's third floor flat. For six hours the various youth chiefs poured out their grievances against the police, the Daley machine, and its Negro "pawns". After the gang leaders had placed all of their problems on the table, Dr. King responded to the litany of injustices item by item. At the same time, he kept asking the gang leaders to renew their vows and commitment to nonviolence. He reminded them of what he had said to them during their first meeting shortly after he arrived in Chicago in January 1966. King then reiterated: "Demonstrations are far more effective than aimless destructive rioting."

King also told the gang leaders that hot July night that he was about to launch his attack on segregated housing in Chicago and to employ civil disobedience techniques. He told the gang leaders that he wanted them and their followers to serve as marshals in his open housing campaign. After more dialogue and deliberation, Richard "Peanut" Tidwell, the leader of the Roman Saints, pledged himself to King and the nonviolent movement and then proceeded to walk around King's living room twisting arms and persuading other leaders to do the same. At the conclusion of the meeting, there was accord. They all joined hands as Dr. King said a prayer for the group. The gang chiefs left Dr. King's apartment committed to prevent their followers from causing any more trouble. Within thirty-six hours, peace had returned to Chicago's west side. The peace that blanketed Chicago's west side can be attributed to that all night meeting in Dr. King's apartment and his influence over the gang bangers as opposed to the show of military force exhibited by the Illinois National Guard.

On Saturday, July 30, Dr. Martin Luther King publicly announced the launching of his open housing campaign at the New Friendship Missionary Baptist Church located at 848 W. 71st Street. King told his followers that the time had come to employ "creative tension" in Chicago. The plan, King said,

New Friendship Missionary Baptist Church, 848 West 71st Street.

would be to march against a bastion of segregated housing which typified the white noose that ringed the neck of the black ghetto on the southwest side of Chicago. Gage and Marquette Parks had been selected as the targets. King felt that a crusade in these two communities would dramatize the racist practices of the white realtors and expose Chicago's fair housing ordinance to the nation as a pack of unfilled promises. King also felt that a march into these white communities would put the fear of God in City Hall, the state and the national capitals, and therefore, coerce them into guaranteeing open housing to blacks throughout the nation; thus, blacks would be removed from the end of America's housing assembly line for hand-me-down and dilapidated housing stock.

Dr. Martin Luther King was out of the city on a speaking engagement in Atlanta when his followers assembled on Sunday, July 31 at 3:00 P.M. in the New Friendship Missionary Church to get their last minute instructions before their initial march into Marquette Park. Al Raby and Rev. Andrew Young instructed the marchers to adhere to "Doc's" (Dr. King's) nonviolent philosophy whereas Robert Lucas, local director of the Congress of Racial Equality, told the marchers, "We can't continue the passive reaction to all hatred."

At the conclusion of the briefing session, five hundred and fifty Negro and white demonstrators were loaded into a caravan of ninety cars and driven to Marquette Park. Seven hundred angry whites waited at Marquette Park for the demonstrators to arrive and begin to march. When the demonstrators drove up to the parking lot of 71st and California Street at 4:10 P.M. in their caravan of cars, they were immediately jeered. Firecrackers were exploded. Riot helmeted police were pressed to keep the angry crowd from the demonstrators amidst cries of "Nigger-loving cops", "Go back to Africa," and "We don't want you here".

The marchers began their walk west on 71st Street and then north along Kedzie Avenue which bisects the southwest side park. Seven white youths attempted to block the march but were hauled away by policemen. Officers confiscated three brickbats from whites in the crowd. As the march moved north on Kedzie, bottles, rocks and other debris showered the marchers, who stayed on the sidewalk throughout. As the march turned into a residential area, cars that were locked and empty were rolled into the pathway of the marchers. Policemen smashed one car window to release the emergency brake and push the car away. Police wielding night sticks scuffled several times with angry crimson faced young whites, and some middle aged women, in their efforts to clear a path for the march.

The original destination for the marchers was a planned "prayer vigil" in front of a white church in the predominantly Irish, Lithuanian, Polish and German working class community. The prayer vigil for open occupancy never came off because the jeering, screaming whites prevented the marchers from getting near the church.

At West 66th Street and South Kedzie, the first marcher was struck by a bottle. A Negro woman demonstrator collapsed into the arms of a fellow marcher after being hit. Captain Paul McLaughlin ordered his men to use night sticks to protect the marchers. The crowd of neighborhood residents had swelled to an estimated four thousand in size although less than that number was involved in the actual attacks on the two block long line of marchers.

Cries of "White power, "Go home Niggers" and "Wallace for President" mingled in the air with the pop of exploding firecrackers and the sound of bottles, bricks, and rocks bouncing off the heads and bodies of the marchers. One nun, Sister Mary Angelica said, "I have never seen so much hate. I can't believe it."

"I see sheer rage and unadulterated hatred in the faces of these folks," retorted Haki Madhubuti (Don L. Lee).

Another Catholic sister was struck on the head by a brick. Several stitches were required to close her wound. More than fifty-four persons were injured, including two policemen, and at least fourteen persons were arrested. Reverend Jesse Jackson was hit with a rock. Al Raby was struck four times by thrown objects as he trudged through a hail of stones, bottles and curses. More of the marchers would have been injured had it not been for members of the Cobras, Vice Lords and Roman Saints street gangs. The three tough youth gangs marched and worked as marshals and monitors for the demonstrators, batting down with their bare hands hundreds of bricks and bottles that were thrown at the marchers. The street gangs were perfect models of nonviolence during the Marquette march.

As the marchers returned to the park where demonstrators were to disperse, a semicircle of about one thousand whites, five and six deep were waiting. A police captain, ordering his men to use their night sticks, yelled, "Alright, alright. Let's go." About fifty officers charged as the whites quickly dispersed. A number of the demonstrators' parked cars were set afire, thirty-seven were overturned and damaged, and two were pushed into the Marquette Park lagoon. When the marchers attempted to return to their cars, they were diverted by the police and escorted east on 71st Street away from their automobiles.

Bottles and rocks showered the demonstrators until they crossed South Ashland Avenue into the Black Belt. By the time the last demonstrators had left Marquette Park on Sunday night, twenty-two persons, including five policemen, had been treated at Holy Cross Hospital for injuries. At least, seventeen persons were arrested on charges ranging from disorderly conduct to possession of fireworks before the disturbance subsided about 9:00 P.M. Sunday night. Fourteen of the demonstrators were given first aid treatment after they returned to the march headquarters in the New Friendship Missionary Baptist Church at 848 West 71st Street. Raby told the group that he planned to talk with Dr. Martin Luther King on Monday and discuss the lack of police protection given the demonstrators. (On Sunday July 6, 1986, twenty years after the King march, the home of the Aleem Waheed family, a black family living in Gage Park, was fired bombed).

On Monday, August 1, 1966, the Reverend Dr. Martin Luther King Jr. and Albert Raby, convener of the Coordinating Council of Community Organizations, in a joint statement said:

> It is clear that the police were either unwilling or unable to disperse the riotous mob that so brutally attacked Negroes and whites. This failure is especially appalling in view of the huge mass of police and national guardsmen that were mobilized to put down the violence of a few hundred Negroes on the west side. It is clear that the Marquette, bigoted mob destroyed more property on the southwest side than did the west side rioters. We will continue to demonstrate in all white communities in Chicago in our nonviolent effort to open housing for all. In this process, we demand the full and active protection of the local police.

"We got to go back," said the Reverend Jesse Jackson, a worker in the Southern Christian Leadership Conference.

"These people (Chicago Lawn residents) will have to realize that they are going to have to stop cheating progress," Al Raby said.

Police Superintendent O. W. Wilson blamed "a lack of communication between civil rights leaders and police for the near riot Sunday in Marquette Park". He stated that notification of Sunday's parade to Gage Park reached the police department at 3:00 P.M. and the march was scheduled to get underway forty-five minutes later. At 3:45 P.M., Assistant Deputy Superintendent James P. Hackett asked Raby to delay the march for fifteen minutes. Raby complied. Hackett immediately put thirty men to work in Gage Park clearing space in the parking lot for the cars of thirty of the demonstrators. Ninety vehicles showed up. The other cars had to be parked outside of the legal parking area. By 4:00 P.M., according to Superintendent O. W. Wilson, there were two hundred thirty-seven men on hand in the park. They were joined shortly thereafter by seventy-six others. The superintendent observed that three hundred and thirteen men is quite a body of policemen.

In response to Superintendent O. W. Wilson, the Reverend Jesse Jackson said, "The police had promised to protect the cars while the marchers covered the eight mile route. On that promise, the marchers abandoned plans to have their cars driven away from the park during the march."

On Wednesday, August 3, 1966, Dr. King stated that, "There will be more demonstrations against housing discrimination in Chicago's troubled Gage Park section, and I will lead the march myself. We will go back to Gage Park this weekend." Dr. King, his aides: the Reverend James Bevel and Albert Raby, whipped up enthusiasm for the Friday march at a rally that was held Thursday night in the New Friendship Baptist Church. Between fifteen and eighteen hundred individuals jammed into the church while about two hundred and fifty stood outside. About one-fourth of the crowd was white and mostly young. Among the whites in the crowd was the Reverend Richard Morrisroe, 27, a Chicago Roman Catholic priest who had been seriously wounded in a civil rights demonstration the prior year in Alabama. The young priest received a standing ovation from the audience.

The Reverend James Bevel told the crowd: "You haven't seen anything yet." Bevel threatened to organize a group to camp out in the neighborhood of any real estate firm that did not agree to sell or rent houses in the area to Negroes. He also said that other marchers would be organized in the all white areas of the Bogan High School, Bridgeport, and in the west suburb of Cicero.

Raby in brief remarks just before the close of the rally at the New Friendship Missionary Baptist Church reminded all of those intending to march on

Friday that they must remain nonviolent. He said that anyone in the line of march who became violent endangered his own life and that of the marchers.

The five hundred demonstrators who had volunteered at the Thursday night rally to march with King on Friday appeared early Friday afternoon at the New Friendship Missionary Baptist Church. As each one entered the church, he or she was handed a printed fact sheet advising him or her about how to avoid injury, if attacked, how to act, if arrested, and how to exercise his rights, in case of arrest. Each demonstrator filled out an information fact sheet prepared by the Human Rights Legal Committee for the purpose of arranging bail in case of arrest. A first aid station was set up in the basement in the New Friendship Missionary Baptist Church, the South Side action center, for the Southern Christian Leadership Conference. The fearless Reverend Stroy Freeman was the pastor of the church.

The Reverend Dr. Martin Luther King told the marchers that the protest would be directed against four real estate offices that allegedly discriminated against Negroes who wanted to buy or rent housing in the Gage-Marquette Park area. The proposed plan for the demonstration called for the demonstrators to march in three groups east on Marquette Road to California and then north to 63rd Street to picket the various real estate offices.

Meanwhile back in Gage Park, Alderman David W. Healy (13th) whose ward included the Chicago Lawndale areas said the Gage-Marquette Park community leaders had gone through the area urging residents to refrain from gathering on the streets during the demonstration. "Our main effort is to get parents to talk to their children. Most of the trouble last Sunday night involved teenagers," Alderman Healy said.

White teenagers in open convertibles began gathering in Marquette Park about 2:00 P.M., some two hours before the first civil rights demonstrators were expected to arrive. Police struggled to keep traffic moving on Marquette Road north of the park as roaming gangs of youths stoned the passing cars of Negroes on their way home from work.

"Go home, you apes," was a frequent cry.

When the first carload of demonstrators drove into the west end of the park about 4:00 P.M., crowds of young whites smashed their windows before police could form a protective cordon. Dr. King entered Marquette Park at the opposite end from his followers. Reverend Andrew J. Young said they had been separated in traffic from the rest of the motorcade.

By the time Dr. Martin Luther King Jr. and the last wave of marchers arrived at the staging area in the park, it was 5:00 P.M. Members of the Marquette mob had already begun to throw eggs and cherry bombs which are highly explosive firecrackers. More than twenty-five policemen escorted Dr.

King from his car to the staging area as a volley of stones, pop, beer, and whiskey bottles flew over their heads. It was at this point that a stone struck Dr. King on the right side of his head; he stumbled to his knees. As Dr. King rose to his feet with assistance from fellow demonstrators, he ripped off his tie and opened his shirt collar and said: "I've never seen anything like it in my life. I think the people from Mississippi ought to come to Chicago to learn how to hate." The stone had left a visible mark above Dr. King's right ear. A man walking directly in front of Dr. King was dazed and bleeding from a stone that struck him just above the nose. Moments after Dr. King was struck by the

Left: Dr. Martin Luther King, Jr. is hit on the side of the head by a rock before the Marquette-Gage Park march against Jim Crow housing was five minutes old. Below left: Dr. King falls to one knee after being struck with a missile. Frank Mingo (partially visible at right) and other aides rushed to protect him from further attacks by shielding his head with their hands. Right: Dr. Martin Luther King, Jr. regains his composure and is seen rubbing the right side of his head where the rock impacted just above the ear. His aides continue to shield him with their hands.

stone, a phalanx of seventy-five husky bodyguards surrounded him and maintained a tight shield around the crusader for nonviolence for the balance of the one hour march.

The marchers stepped off from the staging area one hour and a quarter late to an amplification in the volume of jeering from the white hecklers, who lined the sidewalks along the demonstrators' line of march. The five hundred marchers included whites and Negroes, about one hundred and seventy-five women, and approximately fifty-five clerics. Teenage gang members acted as parade marshals. Intermittent barrages of bottles and rocks continued to pelt the demonstrators as they moved north on California Avenue. Kale Williams, of the American Friends Service Committee was the "white" target for one of the rocks. He was marching alongside "Ma" Houston of Operation Breadbasket carrying her Bible when he was struck in the head with a brick. He instinctively threw up the hand in which he was carrying "Ma" Houston's Bible to shield his bloodied cranium from any additional damage. "Ma" told Kale that the Lord saved his life that day when he told her to hand him the Bible. Demonstrators with first aid kits patched up Kale and other marchers bloodied by the missiles. Nine hundred and sixty police officers bore the brunt of the pressure from the milling mob.

"It was bloody California Avenue for us," said Lieutenant Thomas P. Hayes, who had recently been named head of the Police Community Relations Unit. Negro and white policemen either stood or walked shoulder-to-shoulder, night sticks ready to protect the five hundred civil rights demonstrators from the throngs of screaming hostile whites. It was the Negro policeman, however, who took the greatest abuse from the crowds. "You got to take it easy. Remember. You got to take it easy," one of the big Negro sergeants shouted to fellow Negro officers as they moved through Marquette Park. The mob seemed to take delight in taunting the Negro officers with shouts of "lousy Nigger cops" and other epithets. Five Negro detectives were booed and jeered. Their cars were hit with a barrage of rocks near Marquette Road and California Avenue.

Two white youths, hanging in a tree at 65th and California, were pulled down by the police after the youths hurled rotten eggs at the marchers. At the intersection of 64th Street and California, about one hundred whites sat down in the middle of the street to block the marchers. Police, led by Task Force Commander John Mulchrone, waded into the crowd with night sticks held waist high. Most of the youths arose and ran. When the marchers turned west on 63rd Street and headed toward Halborsen Real Estate Office, they saw fifty white youths who had halted a CTA bus near 3000 West 63rd Street. The young hoodlums were attempting to assault Negro passengers on the bus through the open windows. The police drove them away.

When the five hundred marchers knelt in front of Halborsen Real Estate Office for a prayer vigil, shrieks from whites drowned out their prayers. "Go back to Africa," was one of the cries.

To the Roman Catholic priests, white youths screamed, "You won't have anything in the collection box Sunday."

The vigil at the real estate office lasted about three minutes. The hostile climate on West 63rd Street dictated that the marchers return to the staging area immediately to retrieve their cars and buses. The police department had chartered buses to expedite the marchers' exit from the 63rd Street shopping area. Back in Marquette Park, approximately twenty-five hundred whites had gathered on a knoll overlooking the parking area where the demonstrators had parked their cars.

Bottle after bottle was hurled at the demonstrators from the crowd on the knoll. When the buses and cars began leaving the parking lot, the crowd chased them, smashing windows and battling policemen when the officers attempted to disperse them. One group of about one hundred whites mobbed a half dozen policemen and then were beaten back by a wave of police reinforcements, who came running, firing pistols in the air, and pummeling and clubbing whites with their night sticks.

"You Nigger lovers! S.O.B.'s!" said an aged man in a green Ivy League style suit. "I will never vote for Mayor Daley again."

"God! I hate Niggers and Nigger-lovers," screamed a gray-haired woman who appeared to be in her sixties.

The last of the civil rights demonstrators' vehicles left the Marquette Park area at 8:00 P.M., but the rioting continued. At 9:30 P.M., bands of whites still rushed through the streets, waving confederate flags and heckling the policemen who remained in the area. Policemen beat crowds back again and again only to have the whites regroup and continue their rock-throwing forays through the area. Whites occasionally stoned police cars when they were unable to find cars with Negro passengers.

In a post Gage-Marquette Park rally at the New Friendship Missionary Baptist Church, Dr. King told his followers:

> I was happy that somewhere, sometime my parents taught me not to hate. Stones are not going to stop us. Our numbers will grow larger. We are going back. We are in the right. We will accelerate our open housing campaign by marching in both the Bogan area and the suburb of Cicero. If they want us to stop marching, make justice a reality. I don't mind saying in Chicago or anyplace else, I'm tired of marching, I'm tired of marching for something that should have been mine at birth. If you want a moratorium on demonstrations, put a moratorium on injustice. If you want us to end our

moves into communities, open those communities. I don't mind saying to you, I'm tired of living every day under the threat of death. I have no martyr complex. I want to live as long as anybody in this building. And sometimes, I begin to doubt whether I'm going to make it through. So I will tell anybody, I'm willing to stop marching. I don't march because I like it. I march because I must, because I'm a man, because I'm a child of God.

The spirit of the post Gage-Marquette Park rally was captured in the Chicago Freedom Movement song:

Ain't going to let no King Richard turn me around,
Turn me around, turn me around.
Ain't going to let no King Richard turn me around.
Gonna keep on a-walking, gonna keep on a-talking,
Gonna keep on marching to the Freedom Land.

Dr. Martin Luther King's July 31st march into Marquette Park caused Mayor Richard J. Daley a great deal of concern because it was affecting his southwest side political base. Therefore, he attempted to derail King's second march into Marquette Park by giving the black political submachine led by Alderman Ralph Metcalfe permission to meet with King at the YMCA on Thursday morning, August 4, the day prior to the second march into Daley's southwest territory. Alderman Leon Despres was the only white elected official present at that meeting. He observed:

King told the group of elected black officials present at the meeting that he needed a victory. What he was really saying was that "I am ready to give up, but I need a victory to save my face."
Ralph Metcalfe took the lead and said, "Dr. King, let us put our arms around you." And Metcalfe physically put his arms around Dr. King's shoulders. This sight made me very, very sad, to see King willing to give up his fight in Chicago. Metcalfe could hardly conceal his pleasure with the thought that King was ready to leave town.
Despres reports that Metcalfe said: "If you want us to arrange some face-saving device so you can get out of town, we certainly will take care of you."

He didn't use those exact words, but that was the impression he conveyed, Despres recalls. The forty-five minute meeting ended at the YMCA with Metcalfe agreeing to take King downtown to work something out in a way that King would get a victory and leave town in dignity and hold his head high.

Civil rights leaders in a surprise move Wednesday, August 10, 1966, called off a scheduled open housing march into the Bogan area until at least Friday and a march into Cicero indefinitely. The decisions were made at a four hour secret strategy meeting held at the Chicago Theological Seminary, 5757 South University and attended by about thirty persons. Among the top civil rights leaders taking part in the secret strategy meeting were Al Raby, the number two man in the march organization; the Reverend James Bevel, number three man; and Reverend Jesse Jackson, the number four man.

Sarah Wallace, a spokesman for the Coordinating Council of Community Organizations, explained the postponement of the Bogan march in these words: "The element of surprise was gone. The psychological shock wouldn't be there. The Bogan plans had been too widely publicized."

Ms. Wallace further maintained that, "the march into Cicero was delayed for the same reason." She further added: "The Reverend Jesse Jackson, number four man in the Martin Luther King civil rights movement here, had not been authorized to announce that a march into Cicero will be held late this week." The Reverend Jackson had made the announcement at a rally Monday night, August 8, in the Warren Congregational Church located at 3101 West Warren Boulevard. Ms. Wallace also said, "Such marches must be approved by the sixteen member action committee of the Local Coordinating Council of Community Organizations and by Dr. King's Southern Christian Leadership Conference."

Left to right: Reverend James Bevel, Reverend Ralph Abernathy and Reverend Jesse Jackson discuss a strategy for future marches as they prepare to participate in a demonstration that is in progress in front of the Chicago Real Estate Board building at 105 West Madison Street.

Dr. King, reached by phone in Jackson, Mississippi, said, "The delay of the marches into Bogan and Cicero doesn't change a thing except the timing. We certainly plan to march into both places shortly. Cicero is a symbol of a community that has refused to move forward for several years. Nothing has changed. We are going to continue to march."

On August 19, 1966, Mayor Richard J. Daley asked for and got a temporary injunction drastically limiting civil rights marches and demonstrations in Chicago. The injunction was issued by Judge Cornelius J. Harrington in chancery court. The document prohibited eight individuals and their associates and three organizations from staging more than one march or demonstration a day within the city limits and limited the maximum number of participants to five hundred.

The temporary injunction also restricted the civil rights marches and demonstrations to daylight hours and banned them during the rush hour, from 7:30 to 9:00 A.M. and from 4:30 to 6:00 P.M. It also required twenty-four hours of advance notice in writing to Police Superintendent O. W. Wilson of any march and demonstration plan and mandated that the communication give the time and the route.

In an effort to clarify the intent of the injunction, the mayor appealed to citizens of Chicago over television stations WBKB, WFLD, and WGN. He spoke for ten minutes during prime time, from 10:00 P.M. to 10:10 P.M. and said:

> My fellow citizens, I'd like to visit with you in your homes tonight and discuss a matter which directly affects the safety and well-being of every family and every person in our city.
>
> After conferences with Superintendent of Police O. W. Wilson and the corporation counsel of the city of Chicago at my direction filed suit in the Circuit Court of Cook County seeking a temporary injunction to reasonably regulate street demonstrations in the city of Chicago. Judge Harrington granted the injunction.
>
> As mayor of Chicago, I feel it is my responsibility to report to you directly tonight because of the great moral and legal questions involved in this suit.
>
> There is no desire on anyone's part to interfere with these orderly civil rights demonstrations. The only purpose of this suit is to end the kinds of street demonstrations which have adversely affected the rights of all people by making it impossible for the police department to adequately protect the lives and property of all citizens. In the past two years, there have been more than two hundred civil rights demonstrations, and only in two instances have police been given in writing the information essential for the protection of lives and property.
>
> Under normal circumstances, the police have approximately one thousand men on patrol in neighborhoods. This is not possible with the marchers.

392 / An Autobiography of Black Politics

Dr. Martin Luther King responded to the court injunction obtained by Mayor Daley to limit his demonstrations with indignation and said:

> The marches will go on. I might ignore the court order. The city's move is unjust, illegal, and unconstitutional. It is the Chicago real estate dealers who should be enjoined and not the demonstrators. I deem it a very bad act of faith on the part of the city in view of the fact that we are negotiating. This just stands in the way of everything we are trying to do.

The Reverend James Bevel, one of Dr. King's top aides, said, "The mayor is more interested in false peace than in justice. The injunction is probably unconstitutional and if two thousand persons want to see a real estate dealer, they can legally do so in spite of the injunction."

Leo Holt, an attorney, who represented the Coordinating Council of Community Organizations said: "He might go to a higher court to seek an order to halt enforcement of the city's injunctions which was obtained in the circuit court. If the police department can't protect the marchers, the national guard could be called out. And if that is not enough, they should call on the United States Army."

Police Superintendent O. W. Wilson in explaining the reason for the injunction stated:

> The police for two years have done its best to provide protection for marchers. It has become increasingly difficult, particularly in the areas where there are counter demonstrators. This problem is aggravated when the marches take place at night and when we'd like information on the number of persons marching, the route, the time of starting, and other essential details.

Two Republican aldermen, John Hoellen (47th) and Edward T. Scholl (41st) criticized Daley's injunction request saying he was shifting his responsibility to enforce the law to the circuit court. They maintained that the city ordinance governing marches and street demonstrations was the law of Chicago and questioned why the mayor didn't have the courage necessary to enforce it.

In response to a resolution introduced in the city council and supported by forty-five aldermen to praise the mayor's injunction and the mayor's actions in "dealing with the great legal and moral question involved," Alderman Leon M. Despres made the following remarks against that resolution on the floor of the city council on August 25, 1966. Alderman Despres said:

The city administration's resolution to praise the mayor for the injunction against peaceful demonstrations is ill-advised. It was divisive. It placed the full punitive force of the city behind one group of Chicagoans against another.

In the history of our city and nation, the injunction has been a traditional repressive instrument against the oppressed in their efforts for social progress. Starting with the railroad strikes of the 1870's and going on for sixty years, the injunction was a device to stop, injure, harass, punish, and undermine railroad workers, building tradesmen, eight-hour day advocates, coal miners, mill hands, printers, clothing workers, automobile workers, and others in their quest for recognition and a better life. Chicago was one of the chief centers for the issuance of injunctions and used to be one of the injunction capitals of America, but since the Republic Steel Injunction and massacre of 1937, for nearly 30 years Chicago has been free of massive injunctions. The action we are asked to approve today returns Chicago to the pre-1937 policy and establishes Chicago as the injunction capital of America.

The injunction is one-sided. It is directed only against persons seeking to end Chicago's housing discrimination. It contains no balancing provisions to protect demonstrators and restrain others from interfering with their lawful rights.

In the resolution, we are asked to condemn persons because they live outside Chicago. However, the city administration's most intimate advisor lives outside Chicago and in eleven years has not found Chicago inviting enough to live or vote in. Just this morning we honored an outsider, a man who came from Poland to head a demonstration here—Bishop Rubin, the representative of the Polish Cardinal. Recently, the city council honored the Prince Consort of Great Britain, the mayor of Lourdes, and many others. We delight in honoring outsiders, unless we disapprove their aims. All of us disapprove the Nazis and Fascists, but the "outsider" part of the resolution we are asked to pass today is directed principally against America's most distinguished Nobel Prize winner—Dr. Martin Luther King Jr. So far, we have not even asked him to come to the city council although we ask other outsiders regularly and although a resolution to invite him has been languishing for months.

We know what we ought to do in Chicago. We ought to end the two city structure. We ought to open each neighborhood. We ought to change housing policy from support of housing segregation to support of housing integration. Our support of housing integration ought to be by personal example in every neighborhood in Chicago, not merely in Hyde Park-Kenwood and a few others. We ought to pass the city council ordinances and resolutions which have been ordered to lie in committee but should have been passed long ago—the pending resolution supporting the right of all Chicagoans to find housing regardless of race or religion and disapproving the bombing of the James Brown home at 10624 Lafayette; the pending resolution disapproving the interference with Chicagoans' rights to find housing and expressing regret over the city's failure to protect two Negro tenants at 3309 South Lowe Avenue; the proposed ordinance directly forbidding racial or religious discrimination in the sale, lease, rental, allocation, assignment, or offer of housing; the resolution expressly petitioning Congress to enact federal legislation against discrimination in the rental or sale of housing; and the resolution to request Chicago Housing Authority to end its ghetto policy on the location of public housing. There are the measures we ought to pass at once and not a resolution to approve a punitive injunction and a policy of segregation.

There is constant talk in the council of resort to the "conference" as a substitute for progress. Conference is vitally important, but when used in the context of injunction and segregation, the call to "conference" can cover resistance to progress. A "conference" by stubborn men who support injunction orders and segregation becomes a Berlin-type wall supporting the two city division of Chicago and resisting the effort to make Chicago one city.

We ought not to pass the proposed resolution. I propose the following substitute and move its adoption:

RESOLVED that the city council of Chicago affirms the following statement as basic policy for Chicago:

"Let us break the chains that bind the ghettos by banishing discrimination from the sale and rental of housing."

(The substitute was lost, and the main resolution was passed 45-1).

On Friday, August 26, 1966, Dr. Martin Luther King announced after a "Summit Meeting" held in the Palmer House with the Chicago political, business, and religious estalishments that an agreement had been reached and that he was, therefore, declaring a halt to street demonstrations against housing bias in the Chicago area. Dr. King made the announcement after his team of civil rights workers had reached a unanimous agreement with civic officials and real estate interests on a ten point program designed to end discrimination in residential renting and sales. Dr. King hailed the accord as the most significant program ever conceived to make open housing a reality in the metropolitan area. Dr. King further said, "As a sign of the Chicago Freedom Movement's good faith that the agreement would be carried out, it would defer its plans to send three thousand marchers into the all white suburb of Cicero on Sunday."

The "Summit Meeting" was sponsored by the Chicago Conference On Race and Religion. Seventy-nine persons were present at the two and one half hour meeting and not a single vote was cast against the proposed accord which had been worked out the day before the summit meeting by a twenty member subcommittee.

Harvey Clark, Jr., his wife and two children are escorted into an apartment building at 6139 19th Court in Cicero, Illinois under heavy police security.

Above: The Clark family's furniture and personal belongings were thrown out of the third floor window of the 6139 19 Court apartment building by a Negro-hating mob of Ciceroites. The city fathers of Cicero flooded the front yard of the building after the first riot-filled night in order to keep the mob from assembling directly in front of the building on a second night of disorder.

Following the destruction of the Clark's personal property, the Clark family received a check from the national office of the National Association for the Advancement of Colored People. Shown making the presentation to the Clark family is Willard Townsend, national vice president of the NAACP, standing at the extreme right; Nelson M. Willis, left, and Attorney John W. Rogers, (currently a circuit court judge in the county of Cook) second from the right, look on. Little Michelle Clark, the daughter of the Harvey Clarks, second from the left, later became the first black woman correspondent for CBS Television. Michelle was working in that capacity when she was killed in an airplane crash at Chicago's Midway Airport on December 8, 1972. The plane crashed near 63rd and Cicero.

Chester Robinson, executive director of the Westside Organization, said the accord was a toothless tiger and that his group and six others which he did not identify were going ahead with plans to send at least three hundred demonstrators into Cicero. "We will march into Cicero come hell or high water. We feel that the poor Negro has been sold out by this agreement."

The last time a Negro family ventured to move into Cicero, the most vehemently defended bastion of white racism in the western suburbs, was in 1951. On June 8, 1951, Harvey Clark Jr., his wife and two children were permitted to move their furniture into an apartment building at 6139-19th Court in Cicero under the watchful eyes of a group of white racists.

The Clark family was never allowed to physically occupy the apartment. Under the cover of night, teenage hoodlums broke into the building and threw the Clark's furniture, clothing, and other property out of their third floor apartment windows. Each time a window was broken or an object was hurled out, the mob would roar in delight. The roars amplified to a frenzy when the Cicero rioters began to lynch the Clark family in absentia by setting fire to the Clark's furniture and clothing that had been thrown to the ground.

On the second night, a Cicero mob of five thousand gathered below the window of the apartment that had been rented by the Negro family and created an atmosphere of a Ku Klux Klan carnival without mask. The sheetless mob was in search of a collective orgasm through racial hatred. It took five hundred bayonet wielding guardsmen to end the incident. The Clark family never occupied the Cicero apartment. (Dempsey Travis, An Autobiography of Black Chicago, Urban Research Institute, 1981, Page 129)

Chester Robinson of the Westside Organization and Robert Lucas of CORE considered the "summit agreement" and the deferment of the Cicero march a civil rights "cop out". According to its terms, the toothless Chicago Commission on Human Rights would require real estate brokers to post a summary of the city's open housing policy, and the city itself would redouble efforts to enforce it and to encourage state housing legislation; the real estate board, which had been lobbying against such a bill would no longer do so (though it refused to drop a legal battle it was waging against Chicago's own fair housing ordinance); Chicago Savings and Loan Association would agree to lend money to qualified families regardless of race, thus meeting one of King's cardinal demands; and finally the Chicago Chamber of Commerce and an impressive array of other business, labor, and municipal organizations, all pledged themselves to work on behalf of fair housing.

Robert Lucas, chairman of the Chicago chapter of CORE was present at the Palmer House meeting and noted:

Blacks were not really asking for anything. Usually when blacks have whites on the run, their demands are very weak. Here are all these establishment white men from various institutions in the city sitting in this room, and they believe that at any moment this rebellion was going to spill over into the Loop and destroy all the stuff downtown, and they were rightly afraid. Yet you had blacks in the room from the Urban League and from the CCCO and even Dr. King and nobody knew what to ask for, nobody really made any demands of any significance. I remember I got up and said that one of the reasons for the rebellion was because of social conditions, and I ran down the whole list; and I was ignored at the time. I was known as a renegade anyway, and I was ignored. It was at this point that the white leadership members felt that they could trust me. But it was at the same point that the black leadership felt that King could not be trusted. He shouldn't have been involved in that kind of meeting. I remember that out of that meeting at the Palmer House all that blacks could think to ask for, and Bill Berry asked for it, were some portable swimming pools. They said the reasons blacks were rioting was because these little kids wanted to get cooled under these fire hydrants. Bill got up there, and in a sense, he was begging these white folk for some portable swimming pools. And they respected Bill. As a result of that we got the portable swimming pools.

The Southern Christian Leadership Conference had made all these threats about marching in Cicero, and we were getting feedback. Blacks were working in Cicero; none lived there. Blacks were being beaten up by whites because of SCLC threats. West side blacks didn't believe anything was going to happen, and they were complaining because Dr. King was making these threats and not carrying through with them. If you remember, a young junior high school kid named Jerome Huey had gotten killed in Cicero that year looking for a job, and we were angry about that.

The summit agreement was really an agreement to do nothing. They had really agreed to nothing. They had an agreement, but the agreement wasn't worth the paper it was written on. The agreement did say in a kind of vague offhanded way that blacks would be able to live throughout the city, but there weren't any teeth to the agreement. There was no way to enforce it, and I believe that Dr. King wanted out. I mean it was a face-saving kind of thing. Dr. King and the Freedom Movement really wanted out!

Yeah! And Mayor Daley. There was a lot of pressure on Daley. Whites were beginning to say, "Hey, you may not be re-elected." So Daley got what he wanted. Daley was the only one that really won. The whites won also, but the blacks got nothing. Dr. King had a face-saving thing, but I believe until this day that King was ill-advised; he just had the wrong cats around him.

On Wednesday, August 31, 1966, four days before Robert Lucas and Chester Robinson were to march into Cicero, Dr. Martin Luther King Jr. was interrupted by cries of "Black Power" as he spoke to an audience of one thousand who had filled the auditorium of the Liberty Baptist Church at 4849 South Parkway. Dr. King called out to the dissidents seated in the back of the

Above: Liberty Baptist Church, at 4849 South Parkway. Below: Dr. Martin Luther King, Jr. is heavily surrounded by security from the Chicago Police Department as he leaves through the side entrance of Liberty Baptist Church in an attempt to avoid the huge crowd. Liberty is pastored by Reverend A. Patterson Jackson.

church: "I hear somebody back there calling for Black Power. Let that man come to the platform and address the meeting. This is a democratic meeting."

Monroe Sharpe, Chicago area director for the Student Nonviolent Coordinating Committee (SNCC), strolled down the aisle from the back of the auditorium to the platform and said: "We say you don't deal with Mayor Daley because his power lies in economic strength, and you can't beat that. What you have to do is get rid of the man," Sharpe began. "Oh it's all right to have the tramp, tramp, tramp of feet going through white areas. We want tramp, tramp, tramp through the black man's neighborhood too." As Sharpe spoke he received scattered applause from his disciples at the back of the auditorium. Neither Dr. King nor any of his followers attempted to challenge Mr. Sharpe. Sharpe continued: "Black Power" means you tell the man to get out, not he must hire some more Negroes or sell better merchandise because before we get to Gage Park we want to stand on our own corner and call it our own." Sharpe's statement received warm applause from a handful of his followers.

At this point Dr. King returned to the podium and began a seventeen minute oration which may have been the most important and impassioned speech of any he had delivered since coming to Chicago. Dr. King thanked Mr. Sharpe for his views but said he never would debate with him anywhere and explained why with a Biblical allusion. "Whenever Pharaoh wanted to keep the slave in slavery, he kept them fighting among themselves. The cry for 'Black Power' is made because the white power structure didn't make important concessions in recent years." As Dr. King reviewed the history of Negro suffering and the harm done by hate, his audience exceeded itself repeatedly in its ecstatic exclamations of approval. Dr. King bellowed:

> We are one tenth of the population of this nation. How can we expect to gain power unless we share power? It's absurd to think we can go it alone the way some people are saying we should. The only power I believe in is human power. The Negro in America has taken Jeremiah's question mark about suffering and turned it into an exclamation point. Everyone gets discouraged about the slowness of the civil rights movement including myself. However, I am not worried about Chicago. I am not worried about the Freedom Movement. My eyes have seen the glory of the Lord.

King took his seat, and the audience jumped to its collective feet and gave him a roaring ovation.

Momentarily, Dr. Martin Luther King Jr. looked like a man stunned, and then he was suddenly jostled from his chair by the congratulatory pummeling of the pastors on the dais and the members of the audience who could reach him. He was also engulfed by SCLC colleagues which included the Reverend Andrew Young, executive director of SCLC; the Reverend Jesse Jackson, head of Operation Breadbasket; and the Reverend James Bevel, head of the Chicago project. The SCLC ministers pulled Dr. King to the front of the platform. Dr. King threw his arms high in the air acknowledging the thunderous applause.

Before the applause abated, Dr. King joined hands with the ministers on the platform and started singing his customary closing song of "We Shall Overcome." It was sung as if it would never be sung again. There they stood, Dr. King, Reverend Jesse Jackson, Reverend James Bevel, Reverend Andrew Young and others on the platform singing their lungs out, bobbing, weaving, and rocking to the melody of the Southern Christian Leadership Conference's theme song. The major message of the meeting was the fact that the Freedom Movement was going after economic goals and that round one on the housing front had been won.

On Sunday, September 4, 1966, Robert Lucas, chairman of the Chicago chapter of the Congress of Racial Equality (CORE), picked up the torch that he felt that Dr. King had dropped in the "summit meeting" on August 26th and marched into Cicero, Illinois, the Selma, Alabama of the North, on behalf of open occupancy.

Two hundred marchers assembled in the street at 15th and Kolin on the far west side of Chicago. Clusters of blacks who lived in the area watched with some amazement at this group that was bold enough to march into racist Cicero, the western suburb that had a reputation for beating and killing blacks. Nearby on the corner of 16th and Kostner stood thirty state troopers wearing yellow helmets and carrying long billy clubs. Some of the troopers had shotguns, and all carried revolvers in their holsters. There was also a jeep full of national guards at the assembly point, a reminder that twenty-five hundred Illinois guardsmen were on the alert in various armories in Chicago in case a full scale riot broke out.

In accordance with the orders from Cicero officials, the march started more promptly than most previous civil rights demonstrations. The marchers stepped off at exactly 2:10 P.M., only ten minutes behind schedule. The demonstrators walked on the sidewalk while in Chicago. They proceeded south along Kolin and then west on 16th Street. Some one hundred and twenty-five Chicago policemen guarded the marchers until they went through the Belt Railway underpass and entered Cicero. Ten Chicago policemen were posted on top of the underpass. Just inside the Cicero town limits, the marchers formed ranks of ten abreast in the street. Several truckloads of guardsmen rode ahead of them and more guardsmen in trucks rode behind

Robert Lucas, chairman of the Chicago chapter of the Congress of Racial Equality (CORE), marched into Cicero, Illinois (the Selma, Alabama of the North) on September 4, 1966 with two hundred of his followers.

them. Seventy-two Cicero policemen and one-hundred county sheriff policemen marched on both sides of the demonstrators.

Bayonet-wielding Illinois national guardsmen, club-wielding Illinois state troopers, and helmeted Cicero and Chicago policemen kept an angry mob of onlookers at bay as the marchers entered the town of Cicero. Thus, the march was relatively peaceful going into Cicero with the exception of spectators shouting, "Go back to Africa! White Power!" and, "Two, Four, Six, Eight! We don't want to integrate!"

The marchers in turn, yelled back, "Black Power! Black Power!"

When the demonstrators reached a closed service station at 25th Place near Laramie, they paused to hold a prayer vigil where a black boy, Jerome Huey, was beaten to death by four white youths several months earlier. Huey was in Cicero searching for employment when he was killed. Huey's parents, Isaac and Ruth, were among the marchers. Mrs. Huey broke into tears as Norman Williamson, a theology student at the Maywood campus of the Lutheran Theological Seminary, said a vigil prayer on behalf of her son. Seven hundred young white Ciceroites, some wearing swastika bands taunted the demonstrators during the prayer.

The most violent flare-ups in Cicero occurred as the marchers were returning to Chicago and going through the Belt Railroad underpass on 16th Street which roughly marks the Chicago-Cicero border. The Chicago police were there to prevent hecklers from following the demonstrators across the boundary. Young white spectators began throwing rocks and bottles at the demonstrators. The marchers started throwing the objects back at the crowd. The youthful goons reacted to the demonstrators throwing objects back at them by attempting to physically move in on the demonstrators and engage them in hand-to-hand combat. The police and guardsmen prevented that from happening. In the process, one white youthful heckler was grabbed by the policemen and was beaten into submission with clubs as he was dragged into a prisoner van.

Cook County Sheriff Richard B. Ogilvie said that "the demonstrators were much more unruly than Dr. Martin Luther King's group. They retaliated against the onlookers with profanity and by throwing missiles back." Although Bob Lucas correctly portrayed himself as being a nonviolent person, he also pledged his marchers to nonviolence before the Cicero march. Apparently, some of the marchers forgot the pledge when they felt the pain of bricks and bottles bouncing off of their bodies.

Major General Francis P. Kane estimated that the shouting, taunting, and brick-throwing crowd consisted of approximately three thousand people. To

Cook County Sheriff Richard B. Ogilvie observed that Lucas' Cicero demonstrators were much more unruly than the Dr. Martin Luther King marchers. They retaliated.

maintain peace among that crowd, it was necessary for the national guard to bayonet six individuals and for the policemen to arrest forty-two white Ciceroites during the demonstration.

Robert Briscoe, executive director of the League of Labor and Education, supported Lucas and SNCC in their march into Cicero. Chester Robinson and the Westside Organization did not participate in the march for reasons that were never explained. Briscoe said:

> We marched in Cicero with the Congress of Racial Equality and SNCC last Sunday not because we want to live in Cicero, but because we believe beyond a doubt in open occupancy. We believe we have a right to march anywhere if we decide to do so. If Dr. King started to march, he should have gone ahead and done so. We are tired of Dr. King starting local warfare then running and leaving it to the local people as he did in Alabama and other parts of the country.

Police Superintendent O. W. Wilson accused the Congress of Racial Equality and its Chicago Chairman, Robert Lucas, of twitching the tail of a race riot during the Sunday march in Cicero. "Core's action was reprehensible, but apparently legal," Wilson said.

The September 7, 1966 edition of the *Chicago Sun-Times* editorial labeled the Cicero march as irresponsible and said:

> The CORE march on Cicero was an irresponsible and pointless act that hurt the cause of racial understanding and good will. The hoodlums who tried to break it up are irresponsible lawbreakers who deserve the rough treatment from the police and national guardsmen. But there should have been no march in the first place. The best criticism of it has come from a top figure in the Chicago Freedom Group which staged the housing marches in Chicago in August.
>
> The Chicago marchers made a point. They called attention to the violation of Chicago's Fair Housing Ordinance by real estate dealers. Their marches resulted in a summit agreement to utilize the services of public and private agencies to try to ease the Negro housing problem.
>
> What was the objective of the march on Cicero, staged by the dissident group, the Congress of Racial Equality, headed by Robert L. Lucas, a post office employee who advocates civil disobedience as a protest weapon?
>
> "The march was successful," Lucas said, "because Negroes felt good."
>
> "That's no reason for demonstrating," said Reverend James Bevel, a top aide of Dr. Martin Luther King Jr. "A demonstration has to educate and make clear its objectives. Lucas has not given any clear reason why he is demonstrating."

Dr. Martin Luther King, Jr. returned to Chicago on the occasion of the Chicago Freedom Movement's unveiling of a $4,500,000 Housing and Urban Development mortgage commitment for the rehabilitation of apartment buildings on the loan starved west side. Seated left to right at the December 20, 1966 unveiling in the lower auditorium of the Liberty Baptist Church are: Dempsey J. Travis, real estate broker and author; Al Raby, convener of the Coordinating Council of Community Organizations; Dr. Martin Luther King, president of the Southern Christian Leadership Conference; Ernest Stevens, director of the local insurance office, of the Federal Housing Administration; Frank B. Palmer, board chairman of the Community Renewal Foundation and Jess Gill, project director.

The Reverend Bevel criticized Lucas for demonstrating without work, study, investigation or discussion. Lucas who did not join the earlier King marches and who says the summit meeting was meaningless, now threatens to duplicate the King marches in all white Chicago neighborhoods. The Reverend Bevel suggests, "Lucas is trying to get personal enhancement."

Both James Bevel and Robert Lucas were marching in the same direction but to the beat of a different drummer. Bevel and Lucas have looked back at the days of the Chicago Freedom Movements, marches and demonstrations and agreed that Dr. Martin Luther King, Jr. left monuments and civil rights blueprints in Chicago that are still being used to build towers of racial equity and fairness. The current movement for fairness and equity in politics is a legacy of the Chicago Freedom Movement. Operation PUSH, formerly known as Operation Breadbasket, is a national monument to Dr. King's efforts in Chicago. The Leadership Council For Metropolitan Open Communities was given birth in a summit meeting held at the Palmer House in Chicago on August 26, 1966, and is a by-product of a marriage between the Chicago Freedom Movement and the Chicago Establishment. Today, the Leadership Council is still laboring in the vineyards daily to make Dr. King's dream of open-occupancy in the Chicago metropolitan area a reality. King lives.

Chapter *XXI*

White Politics and Black Justice

Prevent the coalition of black nationalists groups. In unity there is strength, a truism that is no less valid for all of its triteness. An effective coalition . . . might be the first step towards a real "Mau Mau" in America, the beginning of a true black revolution.

Prevent the rise of a "messiah" who could unify and electrify the militant black nationalist movement. Malcolm X might have been such a "messiah"; he is a martyr of the movement today . . . Elijah Muhammad is less of a threat because of his age. King could be a very real contender for this position should he abandon his supposed "obedience" to "white liberal doctrines" (nonviolence) and embrace black nationalism. Stokely Carmichael has the necessary charisma to be a real threat in this way.

> J. Edgar Hoover, Director
> Federal Bureau of Investigation
> March 4, 1968

Dr. Martin Luther King, Jr. was assassinated on April 4, 1968, exactly one month after J. Edgar Hoover issued the aforementioned directive. Following the death of Dr. Martin Luther King, Jr., Hoover called the Black Panthers "the single most dangerous threat to the internal security of the United States." Out of two hundred and ninety five actions taken to disrupt black nationalist militant groups, two hundred and thirty three were aimed at the Panthers. One of the objectives of the FBI's COINTELPRO (Counter-Intelligence Program) was to provoke warfare between the Panthers and other black organizations, such as the Black Stone Rangers. These actions according to the Staff Report of U.S. Senator Frank Church's committee on intelligence activities, "involved risk of serious bodily harm or death to the target." All the

Left: J. Edgar Hoover, director of the Federal Bureau of Investigations. Below: The Honorable Elijah Muhammad, spiritual leader of the Nation of Islam, (left) and Dr. Martin Luther King, Jr., president of the Southern Leadership Conference.

Left: Malcolm X, a fearless black national leader and one of America's most electrifying speakers. Center: Stokely Carmichael, chief advocate of black power. Right: Fred Hampton was considered a threat to the establishment before he reached his seventeenth birthday.

Dr. Martin Luther King, Jr. was assassinated on April 4, 1968, exactly twenty-four hours after the above picture was taken on the balcony of the Lorraine Motel in Memphis, Tennessee. (Left to right): Reverend Hosea Williams, staff member of SCLC: Reverend Jesse L. Jackson, staff member of SCLC; Dr. Martin Luther King, Jr., president of the Southern Leadership Conference and Reverend Ralph Abernathy, vice president of the Southern Leadership Conference.

weapons in the COINTELPRO's arsenal were used in Chicago against the rising black "messiah", Chairman Fred Hampton of the Illinois Black Panther Party, according to documents released in a suit in which FBI Agent Roy Mitchell was a defendant. Mitchell was an expert handler of FBI informants and a script writer for their activities.

A confrontation that was not in Roy Mitchell's script book took place on December 18, 1968 between the Black Panthers and the Black Stone Rangers. A Black Panther was shot by a Ranger for selling papers in the Woodlawn area on the South Side of Chicago. Twelve members of the Black Panther Party and five members of the Black Stone Rangers were arrested as a result of that shooting incident. On the evening of December 18 around 10:30 P.M., thirty Black Panthers went to the Black Stone Rangers' headquarters which was in the First Presbyterian Church, located at 6400 South Kimbark in Woodlawn. Upon arrival, Jeff Fort invited Fred Hampton, Bobby Rush and other Black Panther Party members to come upstairs and meet with him and the Ranger leadership. A FBI informant gave the following description of what transpired that evening at the meeting:

> Everyone went upstairs in a room which appeared to be a gymnasium,
> where Fort told Hampton and Rush that he had heard about the Panthers
> being in Ranger territory during the day attempting to show their "power",

First Presbyterian Church, 6400 South Kimbark Avenue was the headquarters for the Blacstone Rangers street gang.

and he wanted the Panthers to recognize the Rangers' "power." At that point, Jeff Fort gave orders, via walkie-talkie, whereupon two men marched through the doors carrying pump shotguns. Another order and two men appeared carrying sawed-off carbines, then eight more, each carrying a .45 caliber machine gun, clip type, operated from the shoulders or hip. Then other rangers came into the room with over and under type weapons.

The FBI informant stated that after this procession, Fort had all Rangers present, approximately one hundred, display their sidearms and about one half had .45 caliber revolvers. All the weapons appeared to be new.

The FBI spy stated that they left the gym, went downstairs to another room where Rush and Hampton of the Panthers, and Fort and two members of the "main twenty-one" sat at a table and discussed the possibilities of joining the two groups. Prior to sitting down, Jeff Fort took off his jacket and revealed the .45 caliber revolver that he was wearing on a shoulder holster and a small caliber gun he was carrying in his belt.

The FBI informant said that nothing was decided at the meeting about the two groups actually joining forces. However, a decision was made to meet again on Christmas Day. Fort did indicate during the meeting that the Rangers were behind the Panthers but were not to be considered members. Fort wanted the Panthers to join the Rangers while Hampton wanted the opposite, stating that if the Rangers joined the Panthers, then together they would be able to absorb all other Chicago gangs. Hampton also stated that they couldn't let the man keep the two groups apart.

The FBI informant further related that Fort gave Hampton and Rush one of the .45 caliber machine guns to "try out." Based upon the conversation during the meeting, Fort did not appear very anxious to join forces with the Panthers. Neither did it appear that he wanted to terminate the meeting for this reason.

, On December 26, 1968, Fort and Hampton met again to discuss the possibility of the Panthers and Rangers working together. This meeting was held in a bar in the Woodlawn area and broke up after several Panthers and Rangers got into an argument. On December 27, Hampton received a phone call at the Black Panther Party's headquarters on West Madison from Fort telling him that the Black Panthers had until December 28, 1968 to join the Black Stone Rangers. Hampton told Fort that Fort had until the same time for the Rangers to join the Black Panther Party, and they hung up.

In light of the fact that the Black Stone Rangers and the Black Panther Party could not amalgamate their operations, the Black Panther Party decided not to conduct any additional activity or do any recruiting in the Rangers' territory, thereby, bringing peace. However, a peaceful solution was not in the Federal Bureau of Investigation's plot. Therefore, it decided to pour gas on a smoldering fire and send the following letter to Jeff Fort:

> Dear Jeff:
>
> I spent some time with some Panther friends on the west side lately. And I know what's been going on. The brothers that run the Panthers blame you for blocking their thing, and there's supposed to be a hit out for you. I am not a Panther, or a Ranger, just black. From what I see these Panthers are out for themselves, not black people. I think you ought to know what they're up to. I know what I'd do if I was you. You might hear from me again.
>
> (Sqd) A black brother you don't know

The FBI's Chicago office believed that the letter to Jeff Fort would intensify the degree of animosity between the two groups and occasion Fort to take retaliatory action which would disrupt the Black Panther Party or lead to reprisals against its leadership.

To further its efforts of disruption and dissension between the Stones and the Panthers, the Chicago FBI field office, in March, 1969, approved the following anonymous letter:

> Dear Hampton:
>
> Just a word of warning. A Stone friend tells me [(name deleted)] wants the Panthers and is looking for somebody to get you out of the way. Brother Jeff is supposed to be interested. I am just a black man looking for blacks working together and not more of this gang-banging.

A page that had not found its way into the Federal Bureau of Investigation's Counter-Intelligence scenario was that of a possible affiliation of the Mau Mau, a self-defense organization, with the Black Panther Party. The Mau Mau joined the Panther party in mass and was subsequently having trouble following the Illinois Black Panther Party's orders. Therefore, the FBI saw this as another opportunity to cause dissension. Hence, it sent the following letter:

> Brother Kenyatta,
>
> I am from the South Side and have some Panther friends that know you and tell me what's going on. I've known these two _____ that run the Panthers for a long time and those mothers been with every outfit going where it looked like there was something in it for themselves. I heard, too, they are sweethearts and that _____ has worked for the man, that's why he's not in Vietnam. Maybe that's why they're not playing like real Panthers. I hear a lot of the brothers are with you and want those mothers out but don't know how. The Panthers need real black men for leaders, not freaks. Don't give up brothers.
>
> A black friend

Federal Bureau of Investigation documents also indicate that during this letter-writing period, a FBI informant within the Black Panther Party was involved in maintaining a division between the Panthers and the Black Stone Rangers.

On April 2, 1969, a ploy that bordered on genocide was used by William O'Neal, a member of the Black Panther's inner circle and a person who in 1973 was uncovered under cross examination in the Stanley Robinson and William H. Tolliver trial by Attorney R. Eugene Pincham as one of seven FBI spies who had been planted inside the Panther party, called the Panther headquarters at 2350 West Madison Street and said "Some Black P Stone Rangers are firing on Panthers in Robbins, Illinois, and the brothers need some help."

Fred Hampton, Bobby Rush and a dozen other Panthers jumped into three cars after loading themselves to their teeth with weapons of all kinds, including shotguns with flashlights on them, plastic machine guns and other automatic weapons. When they arrived in Robbins, they indeed found people lurking in the shadows of the moonlight with guns and started shooting at them. There was a heavy exchange of fire. However, there were no Black P Stone Rangers in Robbins. In the interim, a FBI informant called the police. The local police responded, saw that they were outarmed and outgunned, and left. In the meantime, the Black Panthers heard the sound of some familiar

Police Superintendent James Conlisk and former police sergeant Stanley Robinson, who is presently serving time for murder, in happier times.

shouts from the other side and realized that they were shooting at each other. Before the Panthers had an opportunity to make a clean getaway from Robbins, the local police returned with reinforcements from Blue Island and other neighboring communities.

One of the Panthers' cars had its tires shot out, so the occupants took off on foot. Fred Hampton and Bobby Rush had been the occupants of the disabled car. Fred had to be in court the next morning on a Good Humor Ice Cream truck robbery case. At 1:00 in the morning, Hampton started running toward Chicago in a very fast and deliberate speed, whereas Bobby Rush ran through fields, woods and dells and came out where there was an old farmhouse. There, he saw a man who looked as if he was about to leave for work. Bobby asked, "Would you let me use your phone?"

The man replied, "No way, I don't have a phone."

Bobby continued, "Well, will you take me where I can find one?"

The man dropped Bobby Rush off at the Village of Robbins Police Station. Bobby walked into the building, reached up and grabbed the public phone which was near the doorway. While Rush was talking, his jacket fell open and a police officer sitting at the desk spotted a big forty-five hanging from Bobby's waist.

The cop shouted: "Oh my God, there is a gun. Oh my God, that's Bobby Rush." Of course, Bobby Rush was arrested right there on the spot in the police station.

Attorney James Montgomery, brilliant trial lawyer and the former Corporation Counsel for the City of Chicago.

Attorney James Montgomery, one of the lawyers for the seven surviving Black Panthers, recalls that both Fred Hampton and Bobby Rush came into his office late one evening several days after the Robbins, Illinois shoot out and related to him in a very animated fashion, the details of the Robbins episode. Montgomery explains:

> Hampton was extremely articulate and descriptive. He was full of life, and he was enjoying telling what had gone down. Hampton was a very talented and free-spirited man, in spite of the problems that had been heaped upon him. One of the things that I noticed about him, in the times that I was around him, was that he always carried a paperback book of some kind, either in his back pocket or in his hand. He had read the philosophy of Mao Tse-Tung extensively. He was also well versed on Malcolm X's work and the small body of published material by other black writers. Fred could command your attention just talking about the rights of the people or any other subject. He certainly held me spellbound that evening talking about the contrived Panther vs. Panthers gun battle in Robbins, Illinois.

Fred Hampton was born in Chicago on August 30, 1948. The middle class family of five which included his father, Francis; his mother, Iberia; his brother and sister, William and Deloris, lived in Blue Island until they finally settled in

Maywood, Illinois, a small western suburb adjacent to Chicago. At age 17, young Hampton was a black candidate earmarked to succeed in the white establishment. He graduated from Proviso East High School in Maywood, Illinois with academic honors, three varsity letters, and a junior achievement award and then enrolled in Triton Junior College.

While in high school, he became president of the youth council of the Maywood Branch of the National Association for the Advancement of Colored People. Under Fred's leadership, the NAACP Youth Council's membership grew in a relatively short period of time from forty members to over five hundred. Hence, he made the Maywood junior branch one of the largest NAACP youth councils in the state of Illinois.

On June 16, 1967, tranquil suburban Maywood, Illinois was rocked by racial unrest. Young black men were demonstrating to have a swimming pool built in the ghetto section of Maywood inasmuch as they were not allowed to use the one in the "For Whites Only" area. Hampton, along with some adult members of Maywood's Negro community, converted what could have become a violent racial confrontation into a peaceful march on City Hall. They convinced the young and the restless suburban blacks that the solution to their discontent could not be resolved by violence. However, the Maywood Police's reaction to the Negroes' audacity to march was such that they arrested everybody who appeared to be in a leadership position in the march. Hampton saw his actions in the march as right. He could not accept the contradictions of a system which lauded him as an athlete and praised him as a scholar but wouldn't let him use the swimming pool facilities because of his skin color. He didn't feel that the white establishment had given him a choice. The police charged Hampton and the several other march leaders with mob action.

When the mob action case went to trial, Attorney James Montgomery represented one of the older gentlemen who had participated in the march on the Maywood City Hall. Fred Hampton was represented by Dennis Cunningham, a lawyer who was from the People's Law Office in Chicago and was basically the Panther's representative throughout the time that they were active in Chicago. Attorney James Montgomery recalls:

> We asked for a jury trial and learned they did not have jury trial facilities in Maywood. Therefore, we tried the case in the old county building in Chicago before an all white jury. It was during this trial that I became very knowledgable about Fred Hampton and the Panthers. I had been schooled very well during my legal career in the art of persuading judges and juries in a racist society. My feeling was that the best approach for me to take with

respect to my client was to disassociate him from Hampton and the young radicals and cast him as a reasonable man concerned about issues in his community. I showed my client as stable with a good job and so forth, and I did so without protest or rancor.

What amazed me about Fred Hampton and his approach to the trial was that he was the target. He was the focal point of the trial. Everybody was after him. And Fred got up on the stand as if he were on a podium speaking to a crowd of people that were partisans or enemies. He didn't seem to care which it was. He got up and answered his questions in the language that he might use in answering questions out on the street. When his lawyer said, "Did you do it because so and so?", Fred would reply, "Right on!" with the same enthusiasm and vigor that he might employ in a street corner conversation.

An amazing thing happened during that trial as I sat there and cringed and panicked in the thought that this radical approach in dealing with a white jury was going to rub off on my client. However, it turned out that the jury for some miraculous reason turned everybody loose including Fred. Everybody was acquitted in the case.

On July 10, 1968, a Good Humor Ice Cream man was beaten and robbed by a gang of black youths. Fred Hampton was arrested. He was identified, in what some believe to have been a political frame-up, to be the ring leader of a criminal gang that had robbed the Good Humor Ice Cream truck and distributed the ice cream in "Robin Hood" fashion. Hampton was convicted on April 7, 1969 in connection with the robbery of the Good Humor truck and given a two to five year prison sentence. Hampton's conviction came despite his testimony that he was not on the Maywood school playground when the ice cream was stolen. In an out-of-court statement, Hampton told reporters: "I may be a pretty big mother, but I can't eat no seven hundred and ten ice cream bars." The ice cream bars had a retail value of seventy one dollars.

The sentencing of Fred Hampton in the Good Humor robbery case is recalled by Circuit Court Judge Sidney Jones, the presiding jurist in that case:

Fred Hampton appeared to be a very conscientious young man. He was represented by Attorney Jean Williams, a relative of the late Claude Holman, the alderman of the Fourth Ward. She was a spunky little lawyer. However, she started her jury selection process by asking the prospective jurors the following question: 'You wouldn't be prejudiced against this man because he is the leader of the Black Panthers movement in Chicago, would you?' I took a recess and called her and the state's attorney into my chambers and said, Don't ask the jurors that question. You should not attempt to get anything into evidence about him being a Black Panther because it's going to prejudice them (the jurors). He would be prejudiced and hurt in the eyes of the jury.

Attorney Williams retorted, 'I want to bring it all out about his Black Panther connections.'

I replied, 'Alright, but that's going to be harmful to him.' At any rate, during the trial, the Black Panthers were involved in a disturbance that got a great deal of newspaper coverage. So again, she wanted to raise a question of whether or not the jurors had read anything about it in the newspaper, which again in my opinion was a mistake.

Judge Sidney Jones made the following observations about the Hampton trial:

I had never heard of Fred Hampton until his case came before me. Although he was a clean cut young fellow, he led a gang of black youths who attacked a young white boy who was working his way through college as a vendor for the Good Humor Ice Cream Company. Hampton and his group broke into the ice cream truck and told the young man that he did not have any business in that neighborhood. They pushed him around, knocked him down and then proceeded to have a picnic with the ice cream.

The Hampton people really treated their juvenile criminal action like it was a joke. However, the victim was able to drive his truck away from the scene and to get a police squad car and return. The victim picked Fred Hampton out of a group as the person who came into his truck and knocked him down. The jury found Hampton guilty. However, I let him stay out on bond, pending the ruling on a motion for a new trial. Once a fellow's found guilty, we have a probation officer make a pre-sentence investigation. I told Hampton I was going to let him stay out on bond until I ruled what punishment he would receive. But I asked him to refrain from demonstration activities of any sort. But the very same night, he went out and led another demonstration somewhere. I was severely criticized by the state's attorney's office for letting him out on bond after he had been found guilty.

The investigating social worker's report on Fred Hampton was not bad. He had a small criminal record from Champaign, Illinois where he had been in a motel and had not paid the bill. He had had a meeting, a conference down there and had been found guilty and convicted for not paying the obligation. However, I would have considered that petty theft.

When the time came for me to sentence him, the state's attorney was asking for a long jail sentence because he had been convicted of robbery and aggravated battery. The state's attorney asked Hampton did he believe in Karl Marx. Hampton said, 'Yes. I believe in Karl Marx, W. E. B. Du Bois, Mao, Dr. Martin Luther King, or anybody else that I think can help my people.'

The state's attorney then asked Hampton if he believed in violent revolution by force or anything of that sort. And Hampton answered that question, 'Yes, I do, by whatever means we can get our freedom, etc.'

So based on his conduct between the time he was found guilty and the arguments on what we call mitigation and aggravation and the receipt of reports from the probation officer, I decided that I was not going to put him on probation. But I sentenced him as I recall, from two to five. That was the minimum. He subsequently got out on bond through an appeal in the appellate court. However, later, the conviction was confirmed. He was supposed to have been picked up and taken to jail on the day before he was killed.

Lucy and Kenneth Montgomery gave a fund raising party for Fred Hampton while he was out on bond for the Good Humor Ice Cream robbery. Attorney and Mrs. James Montgomery (not related to the hosts) were guests. They recalled how impressed they both were with Hampton's presence and his ability to expound on the theories and philosophies of the great thinkers of the past and the present. They felt that he commanded the attention of both the elitists and the young kids who had no jobs. Mrs. James Montgomery recalls very vividly some of the highlights of a speech Hampton made at Lucy's home. She said:

> While Hampton stood there talking and searching the crowd with his bright intelligent eyes he said, 'As I put my ear to the cold concrete floor in my cell at Menard Prison, I heard the beat (he started patting his feet), and it was the beat of the heart of the people.' He then smiled and said, 'I love my people more than I love women, and the Lord knows I love women.' His tone was tremendously powerful as he built up his beat of the people theme into such a crescendo that everybody in the entire room was both spellbound and captivated by this young man, who had just celebrated his twentieth birthday in the Menard Prison at Joliet, Illinois.

Hampton frequently expounded on why he was weary but how the beat of the people motivated him to move on. He understood the needs of the people, and he explained explicitly how he intended to satisfy those needs. By any measurement, Hampton was a tremendous force. He was a real threat to the establishment. He was fearless. "Fred was fired energy, very passionate, very eloquent in his pronouncements. His eloquence was a young cross between Malcolm X and Dr. Martin Luther King, Jr., leaning more toward Malcolm," Haki Madhubuti, the renowned poet observed.

Overnight, the squeaky clean black kid with the excellent mind, silver tongue and junior achievement award from Maywood, Illinois was branded a criminal while in the pursuit of justice for his people. Ironically, Fred Hampton's talents were at the root of his problems because he was using them to help the underclass. That kind of activity marked him as a future leader. Hence, it warranted his name being place in the FBI file as someone to watch and possibly waste.

William Hampton, who was three years older than Fred, made the following observations about the metamorphosis of his kid brother:

> My brother was always an active, outspoken person, even when he was twelve or thirteen years old. He was just one of those natural leaders. Fred always wanted to help people out, but he had no real political ideas back in early high school. He was a typical student, was active in junior achievement and athletics and had top grades. I'd say it was in 1966 when he was seventeen years old that Fred developed a true black identity. That was also when he began to notice all of the oppression and bigotry around him. Fred with his natural outspokeness began to get involved. He began to rankle his teachers and school administrators. They said he was inciting things. Their idea of a good black student was the guy who plays football and keeps his mouth shut. Fred wanted to be a lawyer. But events were beginning to gather him up and transform him. The militancy was forced upon him by the news media, by the racist policemen in Maywood, by the school administration, by the entire white power structure that fingered him as the enemy. This made him angry, and the angrier he got, the more militant he got. He was very young.
>
> By 1967, my brother was beginning his career as a police-blotter radical. That summer, he was arrested and charged with mob action in leading a demonstration in Maywood to have a swimming pool built in the suburb's black neighborhood. He felt white kids had pools to swim in. Why not us? Now that pool is finally built.

The transformation of Fred Hampton can be seen in the following note written by him in October, 1968, when he was the president of the Youth Council of the Maywood NAACP. It read:

> We in the youth council believe that anyone who sees for themselves the evils that the black race has been subjected to, and listens to the atrocities that still exist today, must admit that the only way to think is with the thought of total and immediate liberation of oppressed people by any means necessary.
>
> Understand us. We can and will work with anyone at anytime by any means to eliminate all the social, economic and political evils that confront the oppressed peoples of the United States today.

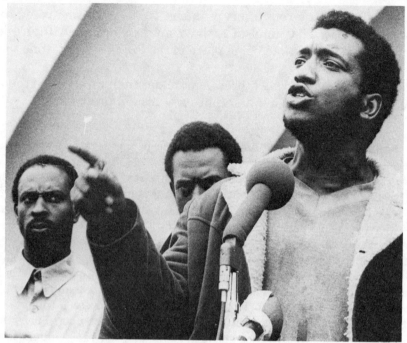

Chairman Fred Hampton delivers a fiery address on the campus of the University of Illinois in Chicago. (Left to right): Chaka, Calvin and Fred.

In June 1968, two months after Dr. King's assassination, Fred Hampton, Bobby Rush, Jewell Cook and Billy Brook founded the Illinois branch of the Black Panthers; however, it was not officially recognized by the national office in Oakland, California until October 1968. Fred was now ready to transcend the marches, demonstrations, sit-ins, kneel-ins and pray-ins. His message was "Get out of my way _____," and "Off the pigs." The radicalization of Fred Hampton was now complete.

Fred Hampton's public utterances were generally fiery calls for revolution and bitter attacks on the "racist pig" American system. But when the weatherman faction of the Students For A Democratic Society came to Chicago on October 8 and tore a swath through the near north and the Loop, Hampton and his Black Panther Party disavowed the group, noting that the climate was not right yet for a revolution in this country.

The Illinois branch of the Black Panther Party adopted the October 1966, National Black Panthers Ten Point Platform and Program which follows:

1. We want freedom. We want power to determine the destiny of our black community.

We believe that black people will not be free until we are able to determine our destiny.

2. We want full employment for our people.

We believe that the federal government is responsible and obligated to give every man employment or a guaranteed income. We believe that if the white American businessmen will not give full employment, then the means of production should be taken from the businessmen and placed in the community so that the people of the community can organize and employ all of its people and give a high standard of living.

3. We want an end to the robbery by the CAPITALIST of our black community.

We believe that this racist government has robbed us, and now we are demanding the overdue debt of forty acres and two mules. Forty acres and two mules was promised 100 years ago as restitution for slave labor and mass murder of black people. We will accept the payment in currency which will be distributed to our many communities. The Germans are now aiding

When the Students for a Democratic Society came to Chicago on October 8, 1969, Chairman Fred Hampton disavowed any affiliation with that group. The radical rhetoric of the SDS and the Panthers may have been the same, but their timetables for action were different.

Jews in Israel for the genocide of the Jewish people. They murdered six million Jews. The American racist has taken part in the murder of fifty million black people; therefore, we feel that this is the greatest demand that we make.

4. We want decent housing, fit for shelter of human beings.

We believe that if the white landlords will not give decent housing to our black community, then the housing and the land should be made into cooperatives so that our community, with government aid, can build and make decent housing for its people.

5. We want education for our people that exposes the true nature of this decadent American society. We want education that teaches us our true history and our role in the present-day society.

We believe in an educational system that will give to our people a knowledge of self. If a man does not have knowledge of himself and his position in society and the world, then he has little chance to anything else.

6. We want all black men to be exempt from military service.

We believe that black people should not be forced to fight in the military service to defend a racist government that does not protect us. We will not fight and kill other people of color in the world who, like black people, are being victimized by the white racist government of America. We will protect ourselves from the force and violence of the racist police and the racist military by whatever means necessary.

7. We want an immediate end to POLICE BRUTALITY and MURDER of black people.

We believe we can end police brutality in our black community by organizing black self-defense groups that are dedicated to defending our black community from racist police oppression and brutality. The Second Amendment to the Constitution of the United States gives a right to bear arms. We, therefore, believe that all black people should arm themselves for self-defense.

8. We want freedom for all black men held in federal, state, county, and city prisons and jails.

We believe that all black people should be released from the many jails and prisons because they have not received a fair and impartial trial.

9. We want all black people when brought to trial to be tried in court by a jury of their peer group or people from their black communities, as defined by the Constitution of the United States.

We believe that the courts should follow the United States Constitution so that black people will receive fair trials. The 14th Amendment of the U.S. Constitution gives a man a right to be tried by his peer group. A peer is a person from a similar economic, social, religious, geographical, environmental, historical and racial background. To do this, the court will be forced to select a jury from the black community from which the black defendant came. We have been and are being tried by all-white juries that have no understanding of the "average reasoning man" of the black community.

10. We want land, bread, housing, education, clothing, justice and peace. And as our major political objective, a United Nations' supervised plebiscite to be held throughout the black colony in which only black colonial subjects will be allowed to participate for the purpose of determining the will of black people as to their national destiny.

When, in the cause of human events, it becomes necessary for one people to dissolve the political bands which have connected them with another, and to assume, among the powers of the earth, the separate and equal station to which the laws of nature and nature's God entitle them, a decent respect to the opinions of mankind requires that they should declare the causes which impel them to the separation.

We hold these truths to be self-evident, that all men are created equal; that they are endowed by their Creator with certain inalienable rights; that among these are life, liberty, and the pursuit of happiness. That to secure these rights, governments are instituted among men, deriving their just powers from the consent of the governed; that, whenever any form of government becomes destructive to these ends, it is the right of the people to alter or to abolish it, and to institute a new government, laying its foundation on such principles, and organizing its power in such forms, as to them shall seem most likely to affect their safety and happiness. Prudence, indeed, will dictate that governments long established should not be changed for light and transient causes; and, accordingly, all experience hath shown that mankind are more disposed to suffer, while evils are sufferable, than to right themselves by abolishing the forms to which they are accustomed. But, when a long train of abuses and usurpations, pursing invariably the same object, evinces a design to reduce them under absolute despotism, it is their right, it is their duty, to throw off such government, and to provide new guards for their future security.

The Black Panther Party of Illinois followed the same table of organization and philosophy as the founding body in Oakland, California. There was an executive committee of six who were known as ministers of defense, information, education, culture, finance, and a chairman who was the spokesperson for the group.

Chairman Fred Hampton propelled the growth of the Illinois Black Panthers from a small cadre of thirty-three in April 1968 to over one thousand within a year. In the spring of 1969, young men and women flocked to Chicago from all parts of the Midwest to become part of the Panther movement and to follow Fred Hampton, the compelling speaker and very popular folk figure among young blacks.

The Black Panther's political program was not as much Maoist as it was an adaptation of an old wives' tale which said, "The way to a man's heart is through his stomach." The free breakfast program for children was certainly an adaptation of that wives' tale philosophy and also the centerpiece for the Chicago Black Panther movement. People in the community responded positively to their free breakfast program and the Peoples' Medical Center at 3850 West 16th Street. The medical center was staffed by twenty doctors, and affiliated with Mount Sinai Hospital. Ronald Satchell, of 6846 South Clyde Avenue, a brilliant 19-year-old Black Panther, was the director of the center.

The Black Panthers' breakfast program reached the minds of people of the community folk through feeding the stomachs of their hungry children.

The first free breakfast program was served by the Panthers early in April 1969, at the Better Boys Foundation located in the fifteen hundred block on South Pulaski Avenue. By the end of May 1969, the Chicago Panthers had expanded their free breakfast program across the city. Members served children at the Marcy-Newberry Association on 16th and Homan, the Peoples' Church at 201 South Ashland, the Precious Blood Church on Congress and Western, and at St. Dominic's in Cabrini-Green. The white Catholic priests responded positively to the idea of the Black Panthers feeding kids on their premises whereas the black Protestant churches closed their doors to the idea for fear of retaliation from the Chicago Democratic machine.

The political establishments, both national and local, became paranoid about the breakfast program because it exposed to the community a need and a service that was not being fulfilled by their duly elected officials. The Chicago political establishment retaliated against the Black Panthers because of the popular community support they were getting for their free breakfast program among the machine's voting constituents. In an effort to intimidate the promoters and supporters of the breakfast program, members of the Chicago Police Department, acting as an occupational military force, visited the breakfast sites and took pictures of the youngsters while they ate breakfast. In addition, the police would snatch community volunteers working in the breakfast program off the streets for questioning as if they were suspected of committing some criminal act. After interrogating the volunteers, they would ride them around in the squad car and then put them out of the police vehicle miles away from their intended destination. The police also followed a general pattern of harassment and arrests which drained the modest treasure chest of the Panthers who were attempting to make bail for those arrested and also pay for legal counsel. The Federal Bureau of Investigation even got into the act and attempted to get Robert Lucas, head of The Kenwood-Oakwood Community Organization, (KOCO), and former head of the Chicago branch of the Congress of Racial Equality, (CORE), to criticize the Panthers' breakfast program. Lucas reacted by calling a press conference and commending the Black Panthers for feeding some four thousand kids daily without a cent of government money or government control.

The Federal Bureau of Investigation's efforts to disrupt the Black Panthers covertly by pitting the Black Stone Rangers against them or by converting grassroots groups such as the Kenwood-Oakwood Community Organization into federal mouthpieces failed. Therefore, Marlin Johnson, special agent of the Chicago FBI office decided to make a frontal attack against the Black Panther Party.

On Wednesday, June 4, 1969 at 5:35 A.M., Merlin Nygren, assistant deputy superintendent of the Chicago Police Department, received a telephone call from the local FBI office informing him that the local bureau would be directing a raid on the Black Panther headquarters at 2350 West Madison Street within minutes. Therefore, the FBI wanted all Chicago police cars to stay out of the vicinity. Before Assistant Superintendent Nygren could hang up the phone and alert the squad cars in the district, a blockade of the area between 2300 and 2400 on West Madison Street had been affected. FBI agents wearing light olive green bullet-proof vests and white arm bands with red letters that read "U.S. Department of Justice" rerouted traffic away from Western Avenue and Madison Street as the red revolving mars lights on top of their vehicles gave the detoured motorists the eerie and frightening feeling that envelopes those who are making an effort to escape from a combat war zone.

Marlin Johnson, the FBI special agent in charge of the raid, arrived at the combat zone dressed to kill in a cocoa brown suit, white-on-white shirt, and a wide brimmed Borsalino hat similar to the kind Al Capone was noted for wearing. Johnson's FBI raiders came equipped for combat with submachine guns, shotguns, rifles with telescopes, tear gas, bullhorns and a helicopter. Several agents had positioned themselves on the top of the Panthers' headquarters building and were postured to hit any moving target. On the ground level, federal agents took cover behind automobiles and fixed their cold and unemotional eyes on the building's entrance at 2350 West Madison which lead to the second and third floor offices occupied by the Black Panther organization.

FBI Agent Johnson used his bullhorn to demand that the Panthers come out of the building with their arms raised high. When the Panthers did not respond, two agents were directed to tear down the fort-like door with a sledge hammer. The agents then rushed up the stairs with their weapons in firing position and took into custody eight Panthers, including two women. The Panthers did not offer any resistance in the face of the FBI's overwhelming weapon power.

After the raid was over and the Panthers' offices were secured, the federal agents went on a rampage, tearing revolutionary posters off the wall, throwing food for the children's free breakfast on the floor and trampling it, and then methodically wrecking the entire office. In addition, they confiscated a list of several thousand names of Panther supporters and lawyers. They also took between $1700 and $2500 in cash, office equipment and six legally purchased weapons. The bureau's excuse for making a raid was that the agents were searching for a Black Panther by the name of George Sams, who was a fugitive wanted for a crime he had committed in New Haven, Connecticut. George Sams was not only an active member of the Panther party, but also an undercover agent for the FBI. At the time of the raid, the FBI agents knew, according to their own intelligence reports, that Sams was not in Chicago.

When Fred Hampton received notice of the FBI raid, he rushed over to the headquarters building and, in an exhausted voice that was beyond bitterness, said to a reporter: "I told you yesterday this was coming."

For Hampton, police and FBI harassment became a way of life that he no longer took personally, and he stated that "the federal pigs' war on the Panthers was in fact war on the people." The Panthers were now the buffer for what black people had been taking all along. Therefore, Hampton felt firm in his belief that the Black Panther Party was in the vanguard of playing its proper role as a defender of black folk. Later Hampton wrote:

> The trend as we have predicted before is towards total fascism. Anyone whose political aspirations differ from those in authority are in danger and could at any time become the victims of indiscriminate arrest and innumerable forms of harassment. It is perfectly clear that the so-called law enforcement officials will stop at nothing including genocide to keep the legitimate political grievances of oppressed people from being expressed. Some people will contend that our actions are of an extreme nature, but I know of no other intelligent way to act in extreme situations other than extreme.

Members of the Chicago Police Department, working under the umbrella of Cook County State's Attorney Edward V. Hanrahan, and he in turn was being advised by the FBI, meted out the most extreme penalty when they took the life of Fred Hampton and Mark Clark before daybreak on Thursday morning, December 4, 1969. At about 4:40 A.M. on that cold December morning, Police Sergeant Daniel Groth was driving west in an unmarked squad car and leading a motorcade of three additional vehicles when he made a call over his radio to the nearby Thirteenth District Police Station and announced that he was enroute to make a raid on the Black Panthers in a building at 2337 West Monroe and that he needed two patrol cars to assist in covering the street and alley sides of the dwelling. A few minutes later, Sergeant Groth and the fourteen officers who had been assigned by the Chicago Police Department to the office of Cook County State's Attorney Edward V. Hanrahan alighted from their three cars and a truck, which they parked approximately two hundred feet east of the building and proceeded towards the target site on foot.

FBI Agent Roy Mitchell had furnished Cook County's State's Attorney Edward Hanrahan's police with a detailed map which showed the layout of Fred Hampton's apartment. The map also indicated the exact arrangement of the furniture in the various rooms, interior doors, closets, windows and the exact location of the bed where Hampton slept. In addition to the map, William O'Neal, the Black Panther and FBI undercover spy, furnished the raiders with a list of the legally purchased weapons that were stored in the apartment.

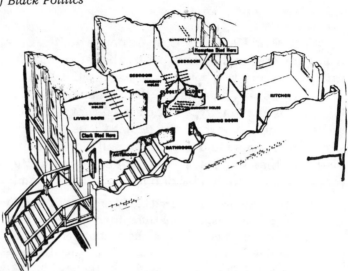

The FBI furnished the Hanrahan raiders with detailed floor plans of Hampton's apartment at 2337 West Monroe Street.

Sergeant Groth, noting that all of the lights were out in the building, climbed quietly up the front stoop accompanied by Officers Jones, Hughes, Garmon and Davis. Officers Carmody, Ciszewiski, Broderick, Kelly, Joseph and Corbett tiptoed around to the back door of the apartment. Officers Marusich, Harris and Howard remained outside to cover the front and rear of the building. The building was also being covered by police with riot guns and rifles who had been stationed on the roof of 2337 West Monroe and other nearby roof tops. Police from the Woods Street Station cordoned off the entire 2300 block.

At 4:46 A.M., four of the Cook County state's attorney's police officers were standing in the foyer of the 2337 West Monroe dwelling with deadly weapons that were loaded and unlocked: Sergeant Groth had a .38 caliber revolver in his right hand. Jones carried a .38 caliber revolver and his own 12 gauge, double-barreled shotgun. Garmon had a .357 caliber revolver in his holster and cradled a .45 Thompson submachine gun. Davis had both a .38 caliber revolver and his own .30 caliber carbine rifle.

At this point, Groth knocked on the door to the first floor apartment. A woman who lived in the second floor apartment above Hampton at 2337 West Monroe confirmed that she heard somebody knock on the first floor door. According to Hampton's second floor neighbor, the sound of the knock was instantly followed by a bellowing male voice that said, "Open up! Police!" There was a moment of deadly silence, and then World War II broke out in the Hampton apartment. The loud cannon blast at the front door literally shook the building and that nerve-shattering impact was followed by rapid machine gun fire followed by the intermittent loud barking sound of small firearms. Simultaneously, shots were heard coming from the rear of the apartment.

It was the sound of the gunfire that awakened Verlina Brewer, a sixteen-year-old kid from Ann Arbor, Michigan, who had run away from home to join the Black Panther Party. Verlina was sleeping in the front bedroom which was located adjacent to the living room with two other Panthers. She told her lawyer, R. Eugene Pincham, when she heard the shooting that she and the two others in the bed simply rolled out of the bed onto the floor and then rolled under the bed to get out of the line of the gun fire. When the shooting stopped, officers rushed into the bedroom with flashlights and herded them out from under the bed. When Verlina attempted to stand, it was then that she realized for the first time she had been shot. She fell to the floor. The state's attorney's police picked her up and carried her out into the hallway. Her two roommates stood in the hall with their hands high above their heads, while she sat on the floor. While sitting there, Verlina heard one officer say, "There's a son-of-a-bitch back here, and he's pretty bad."

She then heard two shots and a voice say, "If he wasn't dead, he's dead now." The voice had come from the second bedroom which was the room where Chairman Fred Hampton had been sleeping.

Verlina Brewer, shown with her left leg in a cast and crutches as a result of the gun shot wounds she received in both her leg and buttocks during the police raid on the Hampton apartment.

Debra Johnson, mother of Fred Hampton's son, told Attorney James Montgomery, her lawyer at the time of the raid and throughout the eighteen month trial which involved all of the surviving seven Black Panthers, about the events that took place at 2337 West Monroe between 12:15 A.M. and 6:00 A.M. on Thursday, December 4, 1969:

> I arrived at the apartment at 2337 West Monroe shortly after midnight. Fred and Louis Truelock were talking about something in the living room. We spoke. Then I went into the back bedroom and returned to the living room. I exchanged some thoughts with Fred, went back to the bedroom, and went to bed. Fred got into the bed about 1:00. We phoned his mother and sister and talked about thirty or forty minutes. In the course of the phone call, Fred fell asleep in mid-conversation. After I got off the phone, I tried to wake him, but I couldn't. I then went to sleep. The next thing I remember was Louis Truelock, the eldest of the nine Panthers in the apartment, shaking Hampton on the bed, trying to wake him up.
>
> 'Chairman, chairman, wake up. The pigs are vamping,' Truelock yelled.
>
> By then, the darkened apartment was lit with gunfire. Hampton still had not stirred. I heard what sounded like gunshots. It was so many I couldn't count them. I looked up and saw what appeared to be shooting coming from the front of the apartment to my right and also from the back, the kitchen area. Truelock was partly on the bed next to the still-dormant Hampton. I crouched over Hampton. I started to move Hampton towards the edge of the bed furthest from the door, where the police were now firing into the room with such rapid fire that the mattress was vibrating real fast from the bullets being shot into it. In the meantime, Fred raised his head and looked towards

Debra Johnson, the mother of Fred Hampton's son, was forcibly removed from Hampton's bedroom moments before two bullets were fired into his brain by a Chicago policeman.

the door. He didn't make a sound. That was the only movement he made. I laid my head down beside his because I thought I was dead.

Truelock had moved away from the bed and was crouching by the wall. He kept yelling, 'Stop shooting, stop shooting. We have a pregnant sister in here,' Truelock shouted.

The shouting continued. Truelock kept shouting, 'Stop shooting, stop shooting.' Then they stopped shooting. Truelock called, 'We're coming out.' I put my house shoes on. I had my hands up. Truelock was coming behind me. Then I heard two single shots. I couldn't see where they came from. I jumped, kept my hands high in the air.

Outside of the bedroom, I saw two lines of policemen in the hall. One of the policemen grabbed my robe and threw it down and said, 'What do you know, we have a broad here.' Another grabbed me by the head and shoved me into the kitchen.

While standing in the kitchen, I heard a voice that appeared to come from my bedroom saying, 'He's barely alive. He will barely make it.'

Then I heard two shots and a sister scream from the front. Then the shooting stopped. I heard someone say, 'He's as good as dead now.'

Within thirty minutes after the Chicago police had removed the dead, the wounded and the three ambulatory Panther survivors from the building at 2337 West Monroe, the telephone rang at Malcolm X College, where Fred Hampton had once been a student. The college is located ten blocks from the site of the Monroe Street slaughterhouse. The voice on the phone said, "Renault, you better get over here quick. The cops have murdered Fred Hampton and Mark Clark. It's a mess, man, a mess." The stunned Renault Robinson, president and co-founder of the Afro-American Patrolman's League, who was on leave from the Chicago Police Department and working as a security guard at Malcolm X College, hung up the phone, jumped into his car and headed for the Hampton apartment. When Robinson arrived at the two-story brownstone building, about 20 ashen-faced young men and women were milling around outside in the cold morning air. Recognizing Robinson, the contingent assembled around him and filled him in on the details.

Responding to the information, Robinson said, "It must have been a shootout."

A Panther retorted, "Shootout hell, it was a slaughter. Come and see." And Robinson followed the young Panthers into the apartment and what he saw was a mess. The doors and walls were ripped by what appeared to be hundreds of bullet holes. It was immediately clear to Robinson that someone wielding a machine gun and standing in the hall had systematically riddled the entire length of the wall. The Panthers pointed out to Robinson Hampton's blood-soaked mattress and bits of flesh and tissue that were strewn around the room. Robinson, who admittedly is no evidence technician, observed that the bullets with one exception all seemed to have been fired from the outside in. Hence, he concluded that if it had been a shootout, it was one-sided.

In the late afternoon after the shootout, as the rigid cold bodies of Fred Hampton and Mark Clark lay in the county morgue with identification tags on their big toes, State's Attorney Edward V. Hanrahan declared that the shootout involving the fourteen policemen that raided the Panther apartment as nothing short of heroic. He boasted that "the fourteen men who went on the raid were from among the one hundred four Chicago Police Department members who are permanently assigned to my office." At the press conference, Hanrahan displayed nine shotguns, seven pistols, two carbines and several hundred rounds of ammunition confiscated from the Panther apartment and said, "We wholeheartedly commend the police officers for their bravery, their remarkable restraint and their discipline in the face of this vicious Black Panther attack. We expect every decent citizen of our community to do likewise."

Sergeant Daniel Groth, Hanrahan's man, later gave the following version of the Panther raid to a group of reporters:

> I knocked on the door, and there was a response. "Who's there?"
>
> I identified myself as a police officer and stated I had a search warrant to search the premises. There was no response. I repeatedly demanded entry. Several minutes passed before I finally put my shoulder to the door and forced it open. Once inside the apartment's darkened hallway, I spotted a woman with a shotgun at about a forty-five degree angle from my position. Next to me was Patrolman James Davis.
>
> The woman fired the shotgun, and Officer Davis fell to the floor while I returned the fire. The flash of the shotgun lighted the darkness of the hallway enough for Davis to spot a man behind a nearby door with a shotgun leveled at me. Davis exchanged shots and subdued the man.

At this point, Groth said:

> I feared that my men entering from the rear might begin firing at the policemen entering from the front. So I called a halt to the firing. I then ordered the Panthers to come out with their hands up. This demand was answered by a man's saying, 'Shoot it out.'
>
> I then resumed the shooting, and I heard the voice of Patrolman John Ciszewski shouting he had been shot. I again called for a halt to the shooting. And this time I relayed a call for police reinforcements.
>
> Again the voice from a backroom said, 'Shoot it out.' The man may have said, 'Shoot it out with the pigs.' I just don't recall the exact words. Shortly thereafter, the fire ceased, and we secured the apartment. The police began rounding up the wounded and the arsenal of weapons in the apartment.

The Reverend Jesse Jackson held a memorial service for Fred Hampton at his Operation Bread-basket meeting, which was held in the Capital Theatre at 7941 South Halsted on Saturday, December 6, 1966. More than five thousand people attended. On the stage at the Capital Theatre (from left to right) were William Hampton, brother of the slain Illinois Black Panther Party Chairman Fred Hampton; Reverend Jesse Jackson; Bobby Rush, Black Panther Party official and Renault Robinson, president of the Afro-American Patrolman's League. Wanted by police for questioning, Rush surrendered to Renault Robinson and several other officers while still on stage in front of some five thousand persons in the theatre audience.

Taken to the Cook County Hospital were Alondo Harris, 18 of 1848 South Hamlin, with a gun wound in the hand and right leg; Verlina Brewer, 16 of 128 West 107th Street, wounded in the buttocks and left knee; Blair Anderson, 18 of 6943 South Justine, wounded in the stomach and right leg; Ronald Satchell, 19 of 6846 South Clyde Avenue, wounded in the right leg, right thigh and right hand. The three uninjured Black Panthers who were taken into custody and placed in cells at the Woods Street Police Station were Debra Johnson, 19, of 2337 West Monroe; Louis Truelock, 39, of 1900 West Jackson and Harold Bell, 23, of Rockford, Illinois.

Black Panther leaders vehemently denied the police version of the shooting death of party Chairman Fred Hampton. They called the raid "a planned murder." Bobby Rush, deputy minister of defense of the Illinois Black Panthers, said:

> Evidence gathered since the predawn Thursday raid proved that state's attorney's police entered the first floor apartment where Hampton lived with the intention of killing everyone there. A look at the holes in the wall would show anyone that all the shots were made by persons who entered the apartment and then went from room to room firing in an attempt to kill everyone there.

Jewel Cook, Illinois Panther field secretary, said, "The pool of blood on Hampton's bed clearly indicates that he was shot while still in the bed and had no chance to return the fire as police said in their story."

Reverend Jesse Jackson said, "I am personally grieved over the death of Fred Hampton because he was a personal friend of mine."

Alderman William Cousins, Jr. (8th) called for an investigation of the shooting. And Alderman A. A. (Sammy) Rayner (6th) called Hampton's death "an assassination" and further said, "The shooting was another example of the systematic extermination of the Black Panther's leadership."

Alderman Leon Despres (5th) said:

> It appeared the raid was a clear violation of civil liberties—an abuse of the search warrant. No one can condone violence, and I hate possession of guns. But from all the evidence gathered, Hampton was killed in bed. A commission such as was suggested by former Supreme Court Justice Arthur Goldberg to investigate the alleged Pinkville massacre in Vietnam should look into the Hampton-Clark slayings.

"This is a tragic story for Chicago," was the view of Clayton Kirkpatrick, editor of the *Chicago Tribune* and a staunch supporter of law and order.

At first, the Chicago news media, with the exception of the *Chicago Daily Defender,* misjudged the public mood. An editorial in the *Daily Defender* which totally captured the mood of the black community read:

> In the babble of angry and excited voices rising from every quarter, it may not be easy to arrive at the truth in the slaying of the Black Panther leaders in their west side apartment by the state's attorney's special police force.
>
> Carefully concealed political partisanship, racial bias and plain constitutional myopia may so fog the facts as to impede the search for truth and end, instead, in confusion and mutual suspicion.
>
> Yet the clouds that hang over the deaths of the Black Panther leaders must be dissipated if anguish, bitterness, and racial strife are to be allayed. The black community is in an ugly, dark, ominous mood. The people seem ready for a showdown with the police or any other symbol of white power. Polarization of the races is sharper now than it has ever been in this city.
>
> Unguarded public utterances by city officials do not calm the troubled waters. Though a search for truth is urged, no vindication of the state's attorney's precipitous action will soothe the frayed nerves of the black communities across the nation. This is not to say that the Black Panther movement has reached general acceptance. It simply means that the belief in a wide-spread conspiracy to destroy the movement is indelible. Moreover, it will be difficult to sweep away the assumptions that the attempt to do away with the Black Panthers stems primarily from the fact of their racial identity.

There is no great, sustained public outcry and no governmental effort to stamp out the knights of the invisible empire despite its unsavory record of cross-burning, of flogging and killing. Membership in hooded orders includes some men in Congress, some federal judges and some policemen.

American society has been built on violence, but a violence that becomes national concern only when it is perpetuated by black citizens. It is then that the litany of law and order is recited daily as a scriptural commandment.

The downtown media reports flatly accepted the police definition of the incident of a shootout. *Chicago Today* headlines blared "Panther Bosses Killed In Cop Shootout." It was a familiar case of journalistic double talk since doubt was present even in the cityroom where those first stories were written. One *Sun-Times* reporter quit when editors buried his story which was the first news story that revealed that the location of bullets in the Panther apartment did not square with the police version of the raid. Another editor told a group of reporters who wanted to dig deeper that nobody would be interested in it. Yet a week later, local news men rushed to catch up with the story, seeking rumored witnesses and charting investigations.

The hundred and eighty degree turn by the Chicago print media was caused by a unanimous outcry of the black and liberal white community to know the truth. Alderman A. A. (Sammy) Rayner, a prominent mortician and the co-signer of the lease for the Black Panther headquarters at 2350 West

Alderman A. A. (Sammy) Rayner, a prominent mortician, World War II fighter pilot in the all black 99th Pursuit Squadron, civil rights activist and the signer of the lease for the Black Panthers' headquarters' offices at 2350 West Madison.

Madison, was in the forefront of those seeking to know the truth. Rayner said to a *New York Times* reporter, "I think what happened to Fred Hampton shook up every black man in the city. It made middle class people think black for the first time."

Thousands of white folk and middle class Negroes began to really think black after visiting the site of Fred Hampton's and Mark Clark's murder at 2337 West Monroe Street. Inadvertently, mass visitations were made possible by the state's attorney's police who failed to have the Cook County Coroner's Office seal the apartment after the bodies of the two Panthers had been removed. During the thirteen day period that the dwelling was not sealed, members of the Black Panther Party conducted open house tours through the Monroe Street facility for thousands, among whom were bereaved mourners, concerned citizens and just plain nosey people. The Panther building was open from mid-morning December 4th until early afternoon on the 17th, the day the apartment was finally sealed.

Everyone who visited the Monroe Street slaughterhouse saw signs of death everywhere. There were powder burns on the outside of the entrance door where the state's attorney's police had fired a bullet that passed straight through it. Mark Clark was standing behind the entrance door when the state's attorney's police's bullet struck him in the upper part of his torso and killed him. The large circular blood stain just inside of the front door was evidence of where Clark made his final fall.

For thirteen days, there were literally thousands of mourners who waited in block-long lines for an opportunity to visit the shrine where Hampton died. In the center of the crowd in the forefront, with the light coat, is Reverend Ralph Abernathy, vice president of the Southern Christian Leadership Conference.

State's Attorney Edward V. Hanrahan, second from left, with arms folded, visited the scene of the Clark-Hampton assassination for the first time on July 10, 1972, which was more than two years after the event.

The five room apartment was bone-chilling cold from the winds sweeping through the broken windows in the kitchen and in Hampton's bedroom. Moreoover, the front door was always wide open because neighbors, young members of the Panther party, friends, foes and thousands of the curious kept coming, coming to see the genocidal scene that they read about but could not believe. To some older folk, the murder site was reminiscent of the 1929 St. Valentine's Day massacre. However, the 1969 version was different in that the murders were committed by members of the bonafide Chicago Police Department as opposed to members of a rival gang masquerading as law enforcement officers.

The Black Panthers who conducted tours through the apartment were courteous and very matter-of-fact as they pointed to the bullet holes that had penetrated the south wall from the north, where the police entered the building and thereby disproving the official position that State's Attorney Hanrahan was espousing about the police firing in response to a Panther attack. In the living room, the guide counted forty-two bullet holes in a straight line on the south wall. On the back side of the south wall in the living room was the front bedroom, where Verlina Brewer and two other Panthers were sleeping when they were awakened by the whiz, boom and bang sound of bullets. In addition to the wall in Verlina's bedroom being full of bullets, so was her door. On the exterior hallway just outside of Ms. Brewer's bedroom were two clusters of pellet holes that looked as if they had been made by a shotgun blast fired at a forty-five degree angle into the bedroom from the doorway.

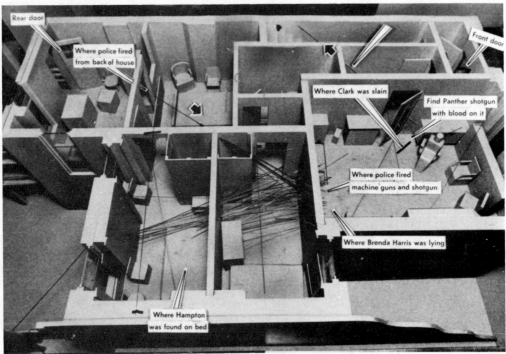

FBI model of the Monroe Street apartment in which the December raid by state's attorney's police took the lives of Fred Hampton and Mark Clark. The federal grand jury condemned the raiders, who entered through both the front and rear door, firing a total of eighty-two to ninety-nine shots. One shot was fired by the occupants of the apartment, the jury found. It went through the front door of the flat. The mass of wires shown in the model indicates the path of the bullets fired by the police. Labels have been added to this FBI model.

There were twenty-five bullet holes in the North wall of the back bedroom where Chairman Hampton slept. Twenty-five of the forty-two bullets fired into the living room penetrated the walls in both the front and rear bedrooms. Walking into Hampton's bedroom was impossible without stepping into a large pool of coagulated blood. The four-foot-long crimson pool was caused by the profuse bleeding from Hampton's fatal head wounds which were caused by a hand gun fired at close range. The bloody area in the doorway marked the spot where the state's attorney's police laid Hampton's body after removing it from the bed.

The sheets and pillows on Hampton's bed had been removed. But blood still seeped into the head of the mattress beside a tuft of stuffing where the bullets penetrated. There was also a great deal of blood at the foot of the bed which seems to have flowed down the mattress onto the floor where it splashed onto books such as *Lenin, Malcolm X Speaks* and Franz Fanon's *The Wretched of the Earth*. The double mattress on the bed had been thoroughly punctuated with bullet holes.

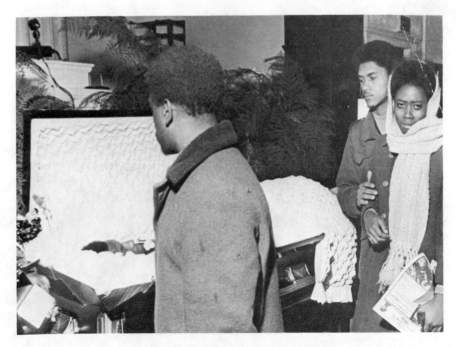

Top: Thousands of mourners waited in line for hours in sub-zero weather to pay their last respects to Chairman Fred Hampton. Bottom: Hampton's funeral was held on December 9, 1969 at the First Baptist Church in Melrose, Illinois. He was buried in a family grave site in Haynesville, Louisiana, which was his mother's hometown.

Left: Gun shot holes punctuated the walls of the bedroom and the blood soaked mattress upon which Fred Hampton was slain. Literature, which was once the property of a bright young man, laid scattered on the floor. Below: Senator Charles Chew (left) and Senator Richard Newhouse inspect bed (bullet hole) in which Black Panther Fred Hampton died.

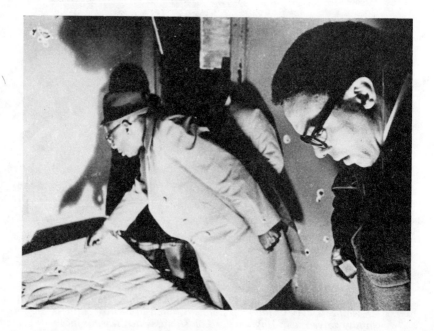

Congresswoman Shirley Chisholm, D—NY.

Congressman Charles Diggs, D—Mich.

Congressman John Conyers, D—Mich.

Left: Congressman William L. Clay, D—Mo. Right: Congressman Robert N. C. Nix, D—Penn.

Left: Congressman Louis Stokes, D—Ohio. Right: Congressman Augustus Hawkins, D—Calif.

The blood of Fred Hampton and Mark Clark could not just simply be washed away by a special coroner's jury inquiry because the black community's belief in the fairness of the judicial system had been punctured. Therefore, through the efforts of Senators Charles Chew and Richard Newhouse and State Representative Harold Washington, a special congressional hearing was convened at 10:00 A.M. on Saturday, December 20, 1969 at A. R. Leak's Colonial House, 914 E. 79th Street, in Chicago. Members of congress conducting the one-day public hearing were Congresswoman Shirley Chisholm, D—NY; Congressman Adam Clayton Powell, D—New York; Charles Diggs, D—Mich; John Conyers, D—Mich; William Clay, D—Mo; Robert Nix, D—Penn; Louis Stokes, D—Ohio and Augustus Hawkins, D—California; Illinois' lone black Congressman William L. Dawson, who was ailing, did not attend the hearing.

The United States government was motivated to start its own investigation as a result of the hearing by the black congressmen in Chicago. Representative Adam Clayton Powell of New York made the following comment about the Justice Department's proposed investigation. "We have no faith in the power of justice." Powell's statement was indicative of the mood of the black community, which increasingly viewed Chicago and America as a police state bent on genocide. Likewise Jay Miller, head of the Chicago branch of the American Civil Liberties Union said, "An investigation by the Justice Department is like asking the wolf to investigate the lamb."

David Hillard, national chief of staff of the Black Panther Party, who flew in from California to attend the hearings, said:

Congressman Adam Clayton Powerll, D—NY, said of the federal inquiry of the Hampton-Mark Clark case, "We have no faith in the power of justice."

Mayor Richard Hatcher of Gary, Indiana served on a blue ribbon commission investigating the slaying of Fred Hampton and Mark Clark. The commission was chaired by former U.S. Supreme Court Justice Arthur Goldberg.

> We see the vicious murder of Hampton and Clark as a checkered flag which signals a systematic plot of genocide against the Black Panther Party. We feel without a doubt that the vicious attack upon our leadership, particularly here in Chicago, shows a revanchist policy of the Chicago Police Department, and this has served as a convincing indictment against the U.S. government and all of its agencies that are unleashed against the Black Panther Party.

Another commission to investigate the Hampton-Mark Clark slaying was headed by former U.S. Supreme Court Justice Arthur Goldberg and Roy Wilkins, executive director of the National Association for the Advancement of Colored People. The only persons from the Chicago area that served on that commission were Reverend Jesse Jackson, national director of Operation Breadbasket and Mayor Richard Hatcher of Gary, Indiana.

Renault Robinson, president of the Afro-American Patrolman's League, said his group was, "collecting evidence to use to prove beyond a shadow of a doubt that there are conflicts in the state's attorney's report."

On December 11, 1969, two days after Renault Robinson announced his investigation, Superintendent of Police James Conlisk ordered the Internal Inspection Division to investigate the Hampton raid. The Conlisk investigation was abruptly stopped for political reasons and then resumed as a public relations' ploy at Hanrahan's request. With State's Attorney Edward V. Hanrahan's blessings, Superintendent Conlisk ordered Deputy Superintendent John F. Mulchrone to conduct "a complete, comprehensive investigation of the facts." Mulchrone passed the buck down to Captain Harry Ervanian who was the director of the Internal Investigation Division. Ervanian made a loud public announcement that "all information relating to the raid would be examined, including arrest records from the raid and all physical evidence, statements from the witnesses and photographs of the apartment."

On December 19, 1969, seven days after the IID investigation had been resurrected by Hanrahan, Captain Ervanian made the following statement:

> The Internal Investigation Division's report indicates that physical evidence has fairly established that the occupants of the premises at 2337 West Monroe fired upon the officers who were in the process of executing a search warrant. There is no apparent misconduct or impropriety by any of the officers. . . . The officers were in the process of lawful execution. . . . They were met with deadly force. . . . The officers were obligated and lawfully justified in countering this deadly force. . . . This investigation is classified as exonerated and recommended that no complaint registered number be issued.

Following in the tracks of the IID investigation was the report of the special Cook County Coroner's jury, which on January 7, 1970, twelve days after it had convened, entered a finding of justifiable homicide in the deaths of Hampton and Clark. The criminal justice system in Chicago was on a roll against black Americans because on January 30, 1970, a Cook County Grand Jury which had been summoned by State's Attorney Hanrahan indicted the seven surviving Panthers for "attempted murder," and other crimes such as "aggravated battery" and "armed violence." The said indictment read:

> The grand jury chosen, selected and sworn in for the county of Cook in the state of Illinois in the name and by the authority of the people of the state of Illinois, upon their oath is present that on December 4, 1969, at and within said county, Brenda Harris, Verlina Brewer, Blair Anderson, Ronald Satchell, Harold Bell, Debra Johnson and Louis Truelock, and also known as Louis Trueluck, committed the offense of attempted murder and that they with intent to commit the offense of murder, intentionally and knowingly attempted to kill Daniel Groth, James Davis, Joseph Gorman, George Jones, Edward Carmody, Phillip Joseph, Raymond Broderick, William Corbett, William Kelly and John Ciszewski, without lawful justification, in violation of Chapter 38, Section 8-4, of the Illinois revised statute, 1967, contrary to the statutes, and against the peace and dignity of the same people of the state of Illinois.

The indictments were based primarily on the testimony given by the fourteen state's attorney's policemen before the special coroner's inquest; also used was the police scientific evidence which had identified recovered shotgun shells from the Panther apartment, two of the shells according to the police report had been fired from a shotgun that was manned by Brenda Harris.

The two investigations and the Cook County Jury indictment raised more questions than they answered. Therefore, the impaneling of a federal grand jury under the direction of Jerris Leonard, assistant attorney general of the United States, was certainly in order. The problem with the federal grand jury investigation was that it was limited in its scope and action to federal offenses such as a violation of the federal civil rights act. It could not act upon such state offenses as murder, manslaughter, or obstruction of justice, which are crimes only against the state law. Therefore, it was absolutely necessary for a state grand jury proceeding to be held. Harry Kalven, of the University of Chicago Law School, and Jon R. Waltz, professor of law at Northwestern University, suggested the urgent need for such an inquiry at the county level. The Chicago Council of Lawyers, a new bar association, the American Civil Liberties Union, and a progressive civic group called Businessmen in the Public Interest issued demands for the convening of a special county grand jury and the appointment of a disinterested special prosecutor to assist it. Judson M. Minor, who was president of the council and is currently the corporation counsel for the city of Chicago, remembers "other civic groups laughed at first," probably believing that the Daley machine would block a potentially damaging review.

The federal grand jury's report, which was handed down on May 15, 1970, was indeed a damaging review to Daley's heir apparent, Cook County State's Attorney Edward V. Hanrahan. And it also poured rain on Mayor Richard J. Daley's sixty-eighth birthday party. The thunder of the report was found in the physical evidence presented by the FBI which proved conclusively that between eighty-three and ninety-nine shots were fired into the Hampton apartment by the raiders, and only one was possibly fired out by one of the Panthers. The grand jury report was also critical of the inconsistencies of the accounts given by the state's attorney's raiders. It spoke of the police investigative accounts given by the state's attorney's police as a cover up for the raiders. Hence, the federal grand jury's report actually labeled the police investigation as purposeful malfeasance.

On the heels of the federal grand jury report, demands for a county grand jury investigation were heightened. State's Attorney Hanrahan filed a petition in the circuit court opposing any such proposed grand jury. City Hall, by its inaction, supported Hanrahan. However, for reasons only known to God, someone at City Hall changed his mind and decided that a special investigation would be for the good of the city. By the time the city father reached this decision, more than seventy civic organizations, including the very ultra conservative Chicago Bar Association, had joined in a call for a special investigation.

Late in June, 1970, Mayor Richard J. Daley gave Judge Joseph Power instructions to appoint Barnabas F. Sears as special prosecutor to conduct a second grand jury investigation into the Panther affair. Chicago's black community had wanted the appointment of a black attorney. Bobby Rush, the new leader of the Illinois Black Panther Party, preferred Attorney Thomas N. Todd, a law professor at Northwestern University Law School; he knew Todd and felt that he could trust him. Instead the mayor, whose approval constituted a command, ordained the selection of a certified member of the city's white elite. Sears was a composite LaSalle Street establishment lawyer, portly, white-haired, well-tailored, a pipe smoker, who had also been president of the highly regarded American College of Trial Lawyers. Sears began his work as a special prosecutor very slowly. He screened a number of very capable lawyers as potential assistants.

One of the lawyers considered by Barnabas Sears as a potential assistant special prosecutor was Attorney R. Eugene Pincham, currently an Illinois appellate court judge. Judge Pincham recalls:

Attorney Thomas Nathaniel Todd, a practicing lawyer, civil rights activist, former professor of law at Northwestern University Law School and a nationally-renowned orator.

The Honorable R. Eugene Pincham, Illinois Appellate Court Judge for the First District.

Barnabas Sears called me one morning and asked if I would meet with him. I did not have the vaguest idea what he wanted. We met late one afternoon in a restaurant on LaSalle Street. First, he swore me to secrecy and then said he was going to have a free hand in investigating the Hampton-Clark case. Therefore, he would like for me to join him in that venture. He said we would have a free hand in the prosecution and that nothing would be revealed until he had gotten his staff in place. He assured me that nobody knew what he was asking me to do except him and me. He further said if I had any reluctance about the integrity of the investigation, I could resolve that reluctance by his assurance that it would be a full scale honest, candid and genuine investigation. He said the chips would fall where they may and anybody who did wrong would go to the penitentiary.

Sears made all of those assurances because I had expressed a reluctance in the integrity of the investigation because I had felt that it was a white wash up until that time. And I saw no reason why I should change my opinion. He assured me that the highest integrity would prevail, and I in turn agreed to join his team.

I went home that night, and went to bed. About 3:00 in the morning a drunk called me. I won't call his name because he's still living. He was feeling very good, and he said to me, 'I'm glad you've agreed to work with Sears. If the things come out alright, you will have given the investigation some credibility in the black community. You will be able to get anything you want from Daley.'

Keep in mind that this drunk who called me was far removed from the inner circle of what was going on. If he knew it, everybody knew it. The next morning, at 8:00, I called Barnabas Sears, went down and told him exactly what I have just told you about the call from the drunk. He said, 'Obviously somebody knew about it. And I am sure you are honest and sincere in telling me about it.'

I responded, 'The perception is that this thing is going to be a whitewash, and I don't want to be involved in it.' I told him I would not serve.

He said, 'I understand.'

Barney and I remained friends up until the day he died. That incident proves something to me that Claude Holman, alderman of the 4th Ward said many, many years ago, and that was, 'There are no secrets in a democracy.' That adage certainly proved true. I genuinely believe, and I think Sears believed that nobody knew about our meeting except him and me.

After interviewing a number of lawyers, Barnabas Sears finally selected Ellis Reid and Howard Savage; both were black. He then picked Wayland B. Cederquist and James W. Collins, two white lawyers from his own firm. The selection of a salt and pepper prosecuting team was reflective of Sears' independence and his commitment to both fairness and affirmative action. On the other hand, Judge Joseph Power was a neighbor and lifelong friend of Mayor Richard J. Daley. He was also a former law partner of the mayor and was indebted to him for his judicial post. Therefore, in Judge Power, Daley had a checkmate for any action by Sears that might prove politically embarrassing to him or his protégé, Edward V. Hanrahan.

Therefore, when Barnabas Sears said, "I have sworn to uphold my oath, and I will do it. Let the chips fall where they may," that declaration by Sears did not seem to visibly concern Daley or Hanrahan, because in Sears they had created a little Joseph with the knowledge that their Goliath wore a black robe and would sit in judgement on any move that Attorney Barnabas Sears made.

Sears did not impanel his twenty-three jurors until December 7, which was the twenty-eighth anniversary of the bombing of Pearl Harbor. Special State's Attorney Barnabas Sears had waited until December because he did not want to have his investigation embroiled in the November election. On December 14, Sears began calling his witnesses. Sears guarded the secrecy of his grand jury sessions like a mother hen covering the eggs of her unhatched chicks. He did not provide a running, daily commentary to the media. However, after the jury had heard fifty witnesses, received approximately one hundred and fifty exhibits and generated a record of more than five thousand pages, Sears felt ready to hand down some indictments.

On Thursday morning, April 22, to the surprise of a group of reporters in the Criminal Court Building press room, Barney Sears dropped in and told them that he thought he might have a story for them later that day. Shortly after lunch, Judge Power gagged Sears by conducting a closed session with the grand jury. Sears was livid, and he said:

> Judge Power has gone beyond his power in the law in trying to tell the grand jury what witnesses had to be called. The grand jury is independent of any judge or any elected official. The judge had no right to frustrate its proceedings.

The smoke from Sears' blast about Judge Power had not completely settled Thursday afternoon when Hanrahan rushed into the chamber of the Chicago City Council and caused Daley to step down from the rostrum to have a hasty conference with his protégé. When reporters later questioned Daley about the conference, Daley responded, "He just stopped by to say hello."

"Did you discuss the grand jury?" a reporter retorted.

Daley scowled and snapped, "What grand jury?" and walked away.

Rumors were flying thick and fast among reporters as they discussed the week's events at their favorite watering holes. Mike Royko, the *Chicago Daily News* columnist, who currently writes for the *Chicago Tribune,* spoke openly of "a fix." On Sunday, three suburban newspapers broke the story that the grand jury had voted to indict Hanrahan and several others for obstruction of justice, but that Judge Power in his secret meeting with the jurors had refused to sign the formal presentation.

The following scenario took place between the jurors, Judge Power and Barnabas Sears. Despite some misgivings, the jurors had decided to indict a number of persons including Hanrahan, and on April 22 had tried to present their "True bill" to Judge Power. The judge had refused to receive the indictments and had launched into a heated argument with Sears. Occasionally screaming at him, the judge ordered a puzzled-looking Sears to make a "complete investigation" by summoning not only Hanrahan, who had already flatly refused to testify but also an assortment of sixteen to twenty witnesses who had appeared before the federal grand jury but whose testimony, in Sears' opinion, was irrelevant to the quite different criminal charges being considered by the state panel. It was believed by some astute legal observers that Judge Power's demand for additional witnesses was merely an attempt to delay the return of the indictments or avoid them in some way.

Hanrahan, apparently alerted to the imminence of the indictment rushed to the courtroom for a possible last minute appearance before the grand jury. A few court watchers thought that if Hanrahan, who had a fiery temper like Mayor Richard J. Daley, could keep his temper in check and soften his abrasive personality, he might be able to talk his way out of the jam. (According to several of Hanrahan's Notre Dame University classmates, his apparent arrogance was a shield for his basic insecurity and shyness.)

When Barnabas Sears walked into Judge Joseph Power's courtroom on Monday morning, April 26, the judge's complexion turned beet red, and his face became distorted at the very sight of Sears. The judge immediately summoned Sears to the bench, which he pounded with his left fist while pointing his right index finger at Sears' nose and shouting, "I want a full and complete investigation." Power continued to insist that Sears take testimony from every witness who had appeared before the federal grand jury.

The unflappable Sears quietly responded, "Your honor, do you honestly believe you have the power you are seeking to exercise? You have absolutely no such power at all. It would impeach the integrity of the grand jury."

Power, in laying the foundation for a contempt citation against Special Prosecutor Sears said, "I now order you to subpoena all witnesses. I don't care who they are. I want them all to appear." He then fined the intransigent Sears one hundred dollars "for a contemptuous attitude," and a continuous fine of fifty dollars per hour.

The Assistant Special Prosecutor Howard Savage, who was standing with Barnabas Sears before Judge Power's bench, said:

> Judge Power, you mean you're going to charge Attorney Sears fifty dollars per hour during the working day from nine to five? You don't intend to charge him while he is sleep.
>
> However, Judge Power responded, 'Yes. I mean fifty dollars an hour at all times, even while he's sleeping.'
>
> When we left the courtroom, Barney said, 'Well Howard, at least you got me fined while I am sleeping.'

The undaunted Barnabas Sears and the grand jury refused to hear anyone except Edward V. Hanrahan himself. Hanrahan, on the following day, commenced what stretched out into twenty hours of belated testimony. After his first three-hour session, the state's attorney was observed smiling and joking with some of his associates, but as one Chicago reporter later remarked, "a smile and some Irish blarney was not enough to sway the jury." (It later developed that it may have been enough to sway four disgruntled jury members.)

While Edward V. Hanrahan appeared to be cool and laid back in the presence of the grand jury, twelve of his fourteen raiders and two assistant state's attorneys were seemingly getting hot and uncomfortable because on April 29, lawyers representing them asked that the grand jury be dissolved. In early May, Sears launched a counter-attack against the scheme to dissolve the grand jury and Judge Power's unwarranted interference with the jurors by going directly to the Illinois Supreme Court for relief. First, he asked that the contempt citation be set aside and that the court design rules "to guide the future conduct of the special grand jury, as it is investigating a matter of grave public concern." The court agreed to hold an expedited hearing. However, in the interim, Judge Power bestowed upon himself the authority to find out if the jury had been improperly influenced by Barnabas Sears. Hence, he directed Sears to give him a copy of the record of testimony to date. *(A judge is never present during a grand jury's day-to-day proceedings.)*

Judge Powers subsequently held a private meeting with two of the jurors. Sears again appealed to the Supreme Court, asking it to stop Powers from meeting privately with the jurors and to also deny his request for the jurors' transcript and to direct him to dismiss the petition filed by the three defense lawyers on the grounds that their clients, not yet known to have been indicted, had no standing to attack the jury.

On May 26, the Supreme Court, sitting in Springfield, heard oral arguments. Barnabas Sears presented himself to the justices of the Supreme Court on that day and gave them both a scholarly and brilliant outline of the history of grand juries. The Supreme Court justices were not moved or impressed with Sears' historical recitation. On the other hand, they were very impressed with the arguments of Don Reuben, one of Chicago's most brilliant and adept lawyers, who argued vigorously and poignantly before the court on behalf of Sears.

On June 25, two days after the release of the Supreme Court's opinion in favor of Sears, the sealed brown envelope made its first public appearance in Judge Power's courtroom. The grand jury's foreman, Richard Balla, an electrical engineer said, "Your honor—I would like to present to you in open court this indictment so that it shall be entered into the court's records."

Judge Power, looking as though a bottle of hornets was about to be uncapped under his nose, instructed the foreman to "hold it a moment." Powers then turned and began listening to the various pleas of the defense counsels as to why the envelope should be kept sealed.

Special State's Attorney Barnabas Sears stood before Judge Power's bench for what must have appeared to him to be an indeterminate amount of time waiting for the judge to accept the sealed brown envelope. Sears then broke the silence of the court when he said, "Your honor doesn't have any discretion except to accept these indictments." And then Sears added, "No bail is necessary." Judge Power seemed surprised because he apparently had feared the worse.

He said, "No bail? I thought this was a murder case." (Murder is not ordinarily a bondable offense.)

Sears quietly repeated, "No bail is necessary." Judge Power's face showed signs of relief.

Then he began talking as if he had not read the Supreme Court decision of June 23, saying, "I might consider getting from you the list of witnesses that testified before the federal grand jury and determine whether there are any witnesses that should have been called. Moreover, I want to determine whether the indictments had been procured in a proper manner. That is something that is still to be determined."

On June 30, the grand jurors again attempted to present the brown envelope to Mayor Daley's old friend, Judge Joseph A. Power, who angrily refused to accept more than its cover page. Sears with a straight face tore off the cover page and handed to him. Power then told the jurors that he had obtained a list of the federal grand jury witnesses *(Sears had supplied it to him earlier)*. Judge Power stared down at the cover page which he held in his lap and then slowly raised his head and revealing the painful look on his face as he said to Sears, "Tragically!, it comes too late. You have already had your deliberations!"

With the jurors still in the courtroom, he leaned further over the bench and stared directly into Sears' eyes and said, "The petitioners (that is potential defendants) feel that some action of yours may have prejudiced this grand jury; therefore, it should be dismissed."

Sears responded, "Well now, I take exception to the statement that this grand jury has been tainted."

Special Prosecutor Barnabas Sears filed an answer to the petition seeking the dismissal of the special grand jury on July 26. In the meantime, Judge Power set the matter down for a hearing on August 5. However, on August 5, Judge Power pulled another trick out of his sleeve when he disclosed that he was appointing Mitchell Ware, who had taken a leave of absence as director of the Illinois Bureau of Investigations, as an amicus currae (a friend of the court) to investigate whether the grand jury had been improperly influenced by Sears and his associates. He also said that he wanted Ware to investigate what had been done on those crucial days immediately preceding the vote to indict because there had been no verbatim transcript taken on April 20, 21 and 22. *(Sears and his associates had repeatedly pointed out that, pursuant to the practice long followed by the state's attorney's office, no court reporter was present because the jurors had devoted those three days to hearing the special state's attorney's evidence summary, prior to deliberating and voting.)* Judge Power ignored Sears' explanation and set August 17 as the next court date to hear matters that Sears felt were not relevant to the case.

A very weary Barnabas Sears found it necessary to make another shuttle trip back to Springfield to ask the court to do three things: prohibit the August

17 hearings, set aside Ware's appointment and, most important of all, order Power to open the envelope with the indictment without further delay. Chief Justice Robert C. Underwood ordered a stay of all proceedings until his court, then in recess, could be assembled. Despite the stay order, Hanrahan showed up in Judge Power's courtroom on August 17 and announced that he wanted to make a statement. Power promptly informed the spectators that the Underwood order "does not preclude my hearing other evidence. I can not deny anyone coming into court the right to make a statement." Since Sears was aware of Underwood's stay order, he did not appear in court on the 17th. Therefore, it was necessary for Power to set Friday, August 20, as the day to hear the Hanrahan statement. Hanrahan never delivered it. Instead, on Monday, August 25, he petitioned the Supreme Court to require Judge Power to conduct an investigation "personally" into the charges that Sears had coerced the grand jury into indicting. If Power found evidence of wrongdoing argued Hanrahan, the judge could order the indictment destroyed without making it public. The Supreme Court immediately took under advisement Hanrahan's petition and those previously filed by Sears.

Meanwhile, back in the city that works, the most diverse elements of Chicago opinion were growing restive. In an editorial entitled, "Open the envelope now, the *Chicago Tribune* said:

> The best way Judge Joseph Power could serve the interest of the public and of justice would be to stop his delaying tactics and open the sealed envelope—. Judge Power's excessive activity on Mr. Hanrahan's behalf serves no public purpose other than to remind everyone that both he and Mr. Hanrahan are close friends of Mayor Richard J. Daley and other leading figures in the Democratic machine.

A *Sun-Times* editorial spoke of Power's "outrageous zeal to protect certain public officials," of his assumption of "dictatorial powers" and called on the Supreme Court to rectify "this parody of justice."

Mike Royko, in the *Daily News* said that, "Because of this envelope, the whole ancient system of grand jury indictments is undergoing an instant overhaul by Judge Power."

Jack Mabley, conservative columnist for the *Chicago Today,* decried "the shameless exhibition of a double standard of justice." Mabley ended his August 15 column by saying, "No matter how this mess turns out, our judicial system has been irreparably besmirched, and we all suffer for this."

Mabley's newspaper ran an editorial headed, "Judicial Tyranny" and charged Judge Power with "making an insult on the integrity of the grand jury."

Television station WMAQ (NBC) lamented editorially "the legal maneuvering to discredit the work done by the grand jury and Barnabas Sears and his associates."

At 10:15 A.M. on Tuesday, August 24, the Supreme Court spoke for the second time on the almost hopelessly tangled Black Panther affair. Attorney Mitchell Ware's appointment to prosecute the prosecuted prosecutor was rescinded, and the brown envelope with the indictments was to be opened. At 2:05 that afternoon, the opening of the envelope became history as Hanrahan gritted his teeth and said that this was what he had always wanted.

Hanrahan and his thirteen co-defendants were arraigned before Judge Power on August 31. When asked how he pleaded to the charge against him, Hanrahan replied, "I make no plea. I do not recognize this as a valid indictment." Although normal practice in such a situation dictates that the arraigning judge enter a not guilty plea on behalf of the mute accused, Power refused Sears' request that he do so in Hanrahan's case. Power's second act in his three-act play entitled: "The Public Be Damned," was to reassign the case, not to a disinterested downstate judge or even to a Chicago Republican judge *(there were a few),* as requested by practically everyone, but instead he assigned it to Philip Romiti, a Democratic county judge who had been reslated for judgeship by the Daley machine. As his very final act, Judge Joseph A. Power discharged the grand jurors in an almost unprecedented move and gave the following advice to the defendants' counsel, "You are at liberty to talk to them and use them as witnesses (in support of your motions to bury the indictments) again." Power's political affinities overrode his judicial identity.

A petition asking that another judge be assigned to the Hanrahan case was filed by attorneys for the American Civil Liberties Union, Chicago Council of Lawyers and the Businessmen in the Public Interest. Alexander Polikoff, representing the ACLU, argued that the Supreme Court had the responsibility to ensure "the appearance as well as the reality" of justice for all of the parties concerned. In essence, Polikoff's petition argued that all persons involved in the case had the same political backgrounds and connections. All were Democrats. He pointed out not only was Hanrahan a Democrat but Criminal Court Chief Judge Joseph A. Power, who received the grand jury indictments, was a Democrat. Criminal Court Judge Romiti, to whom Power assigned the Panther case for trial, was a Democrat, and Police Superintendent James A Conlisk, an unindicted co-conspirator in the case, was a loyal member of the Democratic party.

Hanrahan, representing himself, said that to petition for a change of venue to intervene in a case was "based on nothing but innuendos. It clearly attacks the court itself and is a scurrilous pleading."

Polikoff responded, "The petition was simply and wholly to maintain impartiality in the case."

Illinois Supreme Court Justice Walter V. Schafer refused on Wednesday, September 1, to assign a circuit court judge from outside of Cook County to hear the case of State's Attorney Edward V. Hanrahan and the thirteen others indicted in the Black Panther hearing. Judge Schafer's ruling appeared to clear the way for Judge Philip Romiti to hear the defense motions on Friday in which Hanrahan and others were seeking permission to question members of the special grand jury that had returned the indictments. An emergency motion filed by Sears in an attempt to halt questioning of the grand jurors by defense lawyers was denied by Criminal Court Judge Philip A. Romiti.

Reverend Jesse Louis Jackson, who observed the Democrats' three ring circus from the sideline, demanded that Hanrahan be removed as state's attorney and replaced by any of the four following lawyers: R. Eugene Pincham, Thomas N. Todd, James Montgomery or Kermit Coleman. Jackson stated, "Most of us in the black community believe that the charge of conspiracy is much too anemic and should be changed to murder. The indictment does raise the question of Hanrahan's fitness to hold any office of public trust." Jackson also called on Mayor Daley and Governor Ogilvie to join in his demands for Hanrahan's replacement. *(Almost simultaneously, Daley was declaring that there was no reason for the state's attorney to step down from his office.)*

Jackson then queried:

> How do you fire eighty-one bullets in a darkened house at 4 A.M. and kill two innocent people and not call it murder? The same raiders have the authority and the weaponry to conduct that raid tonight on the headquarters of Operation Breadbasket. It can not be forgotten that the federal government conspired to cover up, hide and protect the actions of the state's attorney and his raiders with the federal grand jury report.

Daley treated Reverend Jackson as though he was the invisible man by totally ignoring his statement. In turn, the mayor blasted the Chicago Council of Lawyers, a legal reform group, and other organizations that commented on the Panther case as "wholier-than-thou" groups and suggested that they reread the Magna Carta, the Declaration of Independence and the United States and Illinois Constitutions.

Daley's loyalty to his protégé, Edward V. Hanrahan, was not wrapped in the American flag or in the Illinois Constitution. Daley's support was based on the fact that he was the boss of the Democratic organization and that Hanrahan had been a loyal member. Loyalty and ethnic pride were the glue that held the Democratic machine intact. To dump Hanrahan would mean breaking the Democratic oath of loyalty. In an effort to avoid jettisoning Hanrahan, Daley used every conceivable maneuver to sidetrack the indictments of Hanrahan and his helpers. He worked the political smog machine overtime to remove any signs of judicial battle scars from the face of the organization.

Many changes other than the weather took place between September and December. In this instance, it was Richard J. Daley's sentimental loyalty to Edward V. Hanrahan. When the Illinois Supreme Court voted in mid-December four to three against Hanrahan and the other Panther raid defendants, it became evident that their trial would fall in the midst of the 1972 political campaign. Therefore, on Monday, December 20, 1971, Daley called the party together, and it decided in its own self interest that the man who led the Democratic ticket in 1968 and who had just been re-slated to run again by the Democratic committeemen, in a meeting which was held on December 7, 1971, must now be ceremonially dumped. The party leaders went to Edward Hanrahan and asked him to step down, and he balked. They, in turn, slated Raymond K. Berg at that meeting on December 20, just six hours before the filing deadline. Petitions were whipped together in short order for Berg's candidacy and, of course, the petitions included thousands of alleged forgeries.

The Irish in Hanrahan told him to defy the slatemakers and run anyway. Alderman William Cousins (8th) immediately responded to Hanrahan in the following manner:

> As a candidate for state's attorney, Hanrahan is public enemy number one and the single most divisive force in the county.
>
> No one's support of Hanrahan should be conditioned on the trial verdict. Independently of the Black Panther episode, Hanrahan has shown that he is unfit for office. His temperament, the low value he puts on human life, his overtly racist approach and his constant resort to demagoguery indicate his true character. He talks tough, but his performance is consistently weak.
>
> Although I am a Democrat, I am compelled to endorse Bernard Carey, the Republican, for state's attorney. Mr. Hanrahan is public enemy number one not only for blacks but for whites as well.

In contrast to Alderman Cousins' position, Alderman Claude W. B. Holman (4th), Mayor Daley's black leader in the council, predicted that the Democrats would carry the black wards with Hanrahan on the ticket. Holman further noted that the "extremist who attacked Hanrahan would attack any candidate we might slate for that job."

State Senator Richard Newhouse, (D-26), disagreed totally with Alderman Claude W. B. Holman when he said that Edward V. Hanrahan was:

A certified public bigot who is determined to eventually take over as the leader of the state Democratic party.

I am going out after him. I am going to teach and recommend ticket splitting so the black voters can register their feelings.

Newhouse further pointed out that it would be dangerous for opponents of Hanrahan to continually harp on the Black Panther case because that case, in his opinion, was an argument in his favor with the backlash voters.

Newhouse continued:

The horror of the Panther raid must be underplayed if we're going to talk about the real issue, a terribly unstable man who wants the key position in the political system. There's much more involved here than the state's attorney's office. The leadership of the Democratic party in the state is the prize he's after. And the state's attorney's office is just a step along the way.

Hanrahan has designed and introduced some of the worst civil rights legislation imaginable, including a provision for the court trial of defendants even when they are not present. These proposals were so bad that some of the sponsors withdrew their names after I vigorously opposed the legislative package.

Hanrahan is a menace to minority people and effective government. I hope every minority political figure will join me in a campaign to make certain that he is not re-elected and thus prevent him from eventually becoming a leader of a major political party in this state. Such a development would be an unmitigated disaster for the people.

Edward Hanrahan defeated Traffic Court Judge Raymond Berg in the Spring primary, and on October 25, 1972, Hanrahan was welcomed back into the Democratic fold after being acquitted of the conspiracy charges. Daley and his co-horts were delighted that Hanrahan had indeed returned, but the black community was mad. The voices of Jesse Jackson, Senator Richard Newhouse and Alderman Cousins about the likes of Edward Vincent Hanrahan had not fallen on deaf ears.

Reverend Jesse Jackson transcended the rhetoric of vote splitting and started teaching classes with the assistance of Alice Tregay, head of the political education division of Operation PUSH, in the vote splitting techniques at the Operation PUSH headquarters.

Through his regular Saturday morning radio broadcasts, the Reverend Jackson was able to appeal to and attract over one thousand individuals from every stripe of life who were willing to volunteer and go out into the community. The Operation PUSH mission was to teach others how to ride the donkey and the elephant at the same time.

State's Attorney Edward Vincent Hanrahan, said: "I shall return" at his post election press conference following his defeat.

On November 8, 1972, the voices of both Fred Hampton and Mark Clark were heard from the grave by the voters in voting booths on the South and West sides. The black voters gave the Republican candidate, Bernard Carey, in their anti-Hanrahan campaign, sixty percent of their vote, thus, defeating Hanrahan by a county-wide margin of 129,000. Only Alderman Claude W. B. Holman's ward carried for Hanrahan, and it carried by only a couple of hundred votes.

On Thursday, November 11, 1972, State's Attorney Edward V. Hanrahan held a post-election press conference at the Civic Center. He said:

> There's nothing I hate more than defeat, but you don't roll over and cry. I shall survive. To paraphrase General Douglas MacArthur, 'I shall return.' I will be around in '74 (the next general election), and I will certainly be around in 1975 (Chicago's next mayoral election).

Reverend Jesse Jackson's response to Hanrahan's parroting of General Douglas McArthur's famous last lines "I shall return" was:

> Wherever you turn up, Ed, we will be there to defeat you. You will have a long time to consider why you lost the election. For the first time in decades, emergence of a city-wide independent black voting bloc will result in bargaining leverage for the black community, since both parties have to compete for the black vote. The attitudinal winds have shifted. It is no longer fashionable to say 'I'm a Democrat.' It is more prestigious to say 'I am an independent.' However, don't get too carried away. The new state's attorney is still a white man, and white people only respond to blacks from pressure. Since we elected Carey, it's now time to give him our assignment for jobs and investigations we want conducted.
>
> *(Hanrahan was also defeated when he entered a 1974 Congressional race, and in the mayoral race against Daley in 1975.)*

5

THE
WASHINGTON
YEARS

1943

1ST
SGT.
U.S. ARMY

SOUTH
PACIFIC

MAYOR
OF
CHICAGO

1983

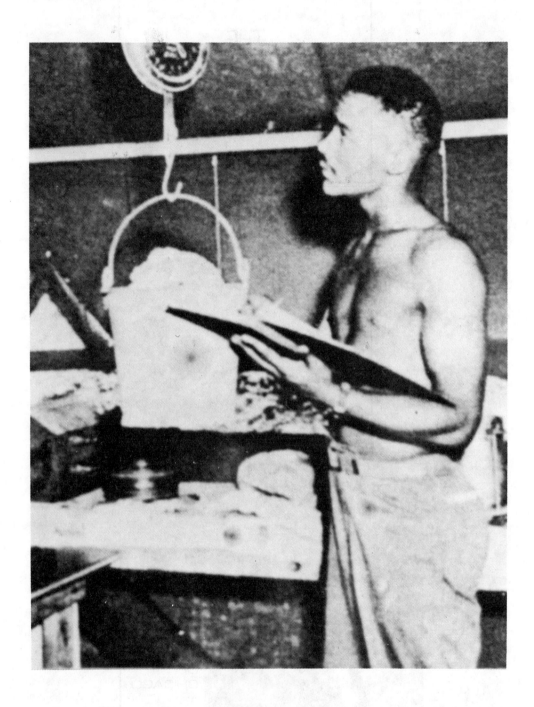

First Sergeant Harold Washington of the Headquarter and Supply Company in the 1887th Engineer Aviation Battalion, is shown performing one of his many functions as a soil technician on the island of Guam in the South Pacific in December 1944.

Chapter *XXII*

Harold: A Roaring Twenties Baby

On April 15, 1922, there was not a visible cloud on the Chicago skyline. The outdoor temperature was a mild fifty-six degrees. Bertha and Roy Lee Washington became the proud parents of a fourth child, a baby boy named Harold, who was born shortly before high noon in Chicago's Cook County Hospital, the common man's health institution located on the near west side at 1835 West Harrison. William "Big Bill" Thompson was mayor of Lincoln's city by the lake, and Edward "The Iron Master" Wright was serving his maiden term as the first black ward committeeman in the history of the windy city. Louis B. Anderson had replaced Oscar DePriest, Chicago's first black alderman, in the Second Ward.

The Chicago Kent College of Law conferred a hard earned law degree upon Roy Lee Washington, Sr. in June, 1922, who joined the other ninety-five black lawyers practicing in Chicago, many of whom held down full-time jobs as postal clerks in the main post office. Washington had attended law school at night while working full-time as a common laborer for Wilson and Company in the Chicago stockyards. Roy Lee Washington, Sr. continued working in the horrible smelling stockyards for two years after he received his law degree. Nineteen twenty-two was indeed an eventful year for Roy Lee and Bertha Washington in that they had been the recipients of another healthy baby boy. Moreover, Roy Lee Sr. had successfully passed the Illinois bar examination and proudly hung out a gold lettered shingle in front of his spanking brand new law office to indicate that he was ready to serve the public. The Washingtons were looking forward with great anticipation to their fortune ballooning like the Chicago black population which had grown from 30,150 in 1900 to 109,000 in 1922.

Left: Roy Washington, Sr., the father of Mayor Harold Washington, on the night of Roy Washington's graduation from Chicago Kent College of Law in June 1922, two months after Harold was born. Right: A 1947 photo of Bertha Washington Price, the mother of Mayor Washington, his three full siblings and his seven half brothers and sisters. She nursed an early secret ambition of one day becoming a star in the theatre.

Harold's parents, Roy Lee and Bertha Washington, bestowed upon their latest addition to the population the middle name of Lee, the same as they had given their other three children. They had even refused to let their only daughter, Elizabeth Lee Washington, escape without being stuck with the Lee moniker. Harold, the omega child of the union between Bertha and Roy Lee, rejected the surname of Robert E. Lee, the commander and chief of the Confederate Army, as soon as he could spell it. In 1924, two years after Harold was born, Adelbert H. Roberts, a three-term state representative, was nominated and elected the first black senator in the state of Illinois.

In the summer of 1926, before Harold Washington was old enough to enter kindergarten, Bertha and Roy Lee were divorced. William E. Dever was mayor at the time, and Albert B. George was elected the first black lawyer to ever sit on the bench and preside over a municipal courtroom in Cook County, Illinois. Roy Lee Washington Sr., a practicing lawyer and minister with a degree from Garrett Theological Seminary, was given custody by the court of all four children, which supports Harold Washington's contention that his dad was an unusual man. The divorce caused the Washington siblings to be separated. Roy Lee Jr., the eldest son, was sent to live with his maternal grandparents down in Carrier Mills, Illinois. Elizabeth Lee joined her paternal grandparents, Reverend Isaiah and Amanda Washington, in Springfield, Illinois, a city filled with layers of "Jim Crowism" that paralleled the racism practiced in any city located in the bowels of Mississippi or Alabama. Roy Lee, Sr. and his two youngest sons, Edward Lee and Harold Lee, moved into his elder sister's home on the near South Side in Chicago's Third Ward. They had been living in their aunt's home for only several months when Roy Lee Sr. decided, in the fall of 1926, to send his two small boys off to be educated at St. Benedict The Moor, a Catholic boarding school for colored children located in Milwaukee, Wisconsin. Harold was only four and a half years old, and Edward had just celebrated his sixth birthday.

Six days after Harold and Edward set their feet inside the interior of St. Benedict The Moor, the two free-spirited young brothers became disillusioned about being institutionalized in a boarding school ninety miles away from their father and thus showed their disenchantment with St. Benedict The Moor by running away from the school fourteen times within a thirty-four month period. The two young lads successfully hitchhiked back to Chicago on eight occasions. They bummed rides in T-Model Fords, Moons, Packards, Hudsons, Pierce Arrows, trucks, horses hitched to wagons and any other moving object that was headed south toward Chicago, Illinois. Each time, they managed to arrive safely and without incidence at the doorsteps of their aunt's home in Chicago where their father maintained a single room.

Although Roy Lee Washington, Sr. always greeted his two young sons warmly, he tenderly but firmly packed them up and delivered them back to the Catholic sisters at St. Benedict The Moor in Milwaukee. The sisters frequently told Roy Lee, Sr. that Harold and Edward were both high-spirited youngsters who did not like regimentation and described them as impetuous kids who could be nuisances, but never classified as bad or incorrigible.

3936 South Grand Boulevard, now Dr. Martin Luther King Drive.

In the winter of 1928, while Harold and Edward were being contained at St. Benedict The Moor Boarding School, William L. Dawson mustered up enough audacity to run for Congress in the First Congressional District against Representative Martin B. Madden, the great white father and a political savior in the minds of some colored folk. Dawson made an impressive showing by garnering twenty-nine percent of the black Republican votes in the primary of the First Congressional District. Considering the temper of the times, his success at the polls was unprecedented.

The following summer in 1929, Edward and Harold received permission from their father to leave the boarding school and return to Chicago. Roy Lee, Sr. moved with his two young sons into a white stone Victorian three-story mansion owned by his friend, Mrs. Davis. The building was located at 3936

Earl "Father" Hines, at the piano surrounded by a bevy of pretty Grand Terrace chorus girls. Inset: Al Capone.

South Grand Boulevard (now Dr. Martin Luther King Drive) directly across the street from the famous Grand Terrace Night Club, which was the musical headquarters of the world famous piano player, Earl "Father" Hines and his orchestra. Young Harold spent many of his early evenings looking out of his second floor bedroom window at white women draped in mink coats and jackets and at white men in tuxedos, tails, and top hats riding up to the door of the Grand Terrace Cabaret in their chauffeur driven cars to be entertained by Earl Hines and his all-star black orchestra and a jewel-studded colored floor show spiked with shapely mulatto chorus girls.

The plush Grand Terrace Night Club was controlled by the Al Capone syndicate, and although it was located in the heart of the Black Belt, it catered to a "white only" crowd. Occasionally, the owners made a colored movie celebrity like Hattie McDaniels or a policy king like Ed Jones an "honorary white," and in that status such persons were permitted entry to the night club. Harold learned early in life that his Chicago was one hundred percent black because the only white folk he saw on a daily basis were the community merchants and those rich looking folk whom came nightly to the Grand Terrace to enjoy black music and black entertainers.

In 1929, Oscar DePriest, a political celebrity, became Chicago's first black man to be elected to the United States' Congress in the twentieth century. In September of the same year, Edward and Harold were enrolled in Felsenthal Elementary School, located at 4101 S. Calumet Avenue. The boys attending Felsenthal were known for their rough and tough behavior, but Harold, being a slender child, was bait for several of the school's oversized roughnecks who would alternately pick Harold out of the crowd to be a punching bag almost every Friday afternoon right after the school bell rang at 3:15. If Harold managed to escape from school without getting whipped by the bullies, Edward, who was a year and a half older and much larger than he would frequently exercise his fist against Harold's head when he got home.

Harold Washington's head was obviously put on straight because he started reading before he was four years old and had developed a ferocious appetite for the printed words in newspapers, magazines and books by the time he was seven. One afternoon in the early winter of 1932, while reading a dime detective magazine, he discovered an advertisement by Charles Atlas, the strong man, which showed a picture of a handsome muscular guy kicking sand in the face of a skinny guy who was lying on the beach with his girlfriend. The display advertisement showed the beautiful girl abandoning the skinny fellow and walking away with the young man with the muscles. The lead line in the advertisement read, "How Joe's body brought him fame instead of shame." Harold mailed the ad coupon to Charles Atlas in New York City for a copy of the free book on muscle development. The desire to become a

The Atlas ad that pushed Harold Washington into turning the tide on the playground bullies and becoming an after school hero.

muscular person like Charles Atlas kindled young Harold Washington's entrepreneurial juices. Hence, he created his own employment in the heart of the big depression by soliciting window washing jobs from the home owners and tenants in the 3900 and 4000 blocks of Grand Boulevard (Dr. Martin Luther King Drive) every Saturday from sun up to sun down.

Harold, the pint-sized business person, was paid a nickel for every two windows he washed. He saved every penny until he had accumulated enough to send for an Atlas instruction course on muscle building. Roy Lee, Jr., his oldest brother, recalls how Harold always wanted someone to feel his muscles regularly after he started practicing the Atlas dynamite tension technique. Underdeveloped, Harold was very serious about building up his body and worked extremely hard at physique building for almost two years until he was both confident and satisfied with his physical development.

Roy Lee, Jr. recalls that the day of reckoning arrived one Saturday morning when Edward decided he was going to exercise his fist on Harold's body. Harold shouted at Edward, "No! No! You don't fight me anymore," as he successfully employed his Atlas muscle achievements on Edward's head and body. Harold's ability to defend himself at home was transferred to the schoolyard. After several decisive victories on the playground at Felsenthal Elementary School, his problems with the school roughnecks ceased.

In the spring of 1933, William L. Dawson was elected alderman of the Second Ward on the Republican ticket. In the early winter of that year, Reverend Roy Washington, Sr. and his two sons, Harold and Edward, moved from 3936 S. Parkway into a large apartment located in a six flat building at 4507 S. Vincennes Avenue with a distant cousin, Prentiss Wheeler, who owned the newspaper and candy concession at the 47th Street elevator train stop. The Vincennes building was a three-story brick walk-up located right next door and south of the Ebenezer Baptist Church, which was the home base for many of Chicago's famous gospel singers and composers such as Mahalia Jackson, Willie Webb, Robert Anderson, Sallie Martin and Thomas A. Dorsey, the author of Dr. Martin Luther King's favorite gospel song entitled *Precious Lord.* The Washingtons were still living at the Vincennes address in 1935 when Harold's father met and married Arlene Jackson, a very cultured lady, who had been both a school teacher and a music instructor in Kansas City, Kansas. The marriage enabled Reverend Washington to stabilize his family life by reuniting his three sons in a rented apartment at 4444 S. Indiana Avenue, an apartment large enough to give everybody laughing room, that is, everybody except his daughter Elizabeth Lee who continued to reside with her paternal grandparents until she was married.

A year later, the Washington family moved around the corner to an even larger apartment at 111 E. 44th St. There Harold met a beautiful girl, Nancy Dorothy Finch, who lived on the third floor. Harold instantly became infatuated with Dorothy whom he affectionately nicknamed Peaches because of the peach-like fuzz on her face. It was truly puppy love at first sight. He was bowled over by the appearance of the five-foot-five inch striking beige beauty with whom he attended Forrestville Elementary and DuSable High School. In

The Washingtons having an evening on the town with friends. (Left to right): John and Delores Cheefus, Harold and Dorothy Washington and Theolene and James Dixon.

addition to fondly remembering the pretty little girl who lived on the third floor at 111 E. 44th Street, Harold recalls:

I was always involved in the political process. When we transferred from the Felsenthal to the Forrestville Elementary School, located at 622 E. 45th Street, I was always getting elected to some position, running for some office or serving on some committee. I actually worked in the precinct with my old man before I was fourteen years old. I used to help him pass out literature.

Politics was a centerpiece around our house. Before I reached my teens, I was aware of presidents, mayors, governors, aldermen and people of that nature. My father discussed politics at the dinner table almost every night. The only subject that superseded politics in our home was religion. Political personalities such as William L. Dawson, Oscar DePriest, Mike Sneed, Arthur W. Mitchell and C.C. Wimbush were frequent visitors in our home. I was literally raised in a political atmosphere.

Although Harold considered his father, Roy, an ideal role model, there was a teacher at Forrestville Elementary School, Miss Charlotte Roland, who made a great impression on young Washington. He describes her:

Very matronly, but firm, detached, and warm. She was just a strange kind of woman. She had a common influence on everybody. For example, in her class, there was never any loud talking or sounds. The kids were always orderly, mannerly, and courteous. She ran a tight ship, but everybody loved her. She was a robust, husky woman: a typical black woman, an earth mother. I don't recall any other teacher in grammar school having any real serious influence on me. Teachers like Miss Roland are never forgotten.

Jean Baptist DuSable High School at 4934 S. Wabash Ave

Left: Chauncey Willard, the five-foot-tall principal of DuSable High School, had a voice of authority that clapped like thunder. He had the full respect of both the faculty and the student body. Right: Annabel C. Prescott, assistant principal and daughter of the late Bishop Archibald C. Carey, Sr. and the sister of the late Judge Archibald Carey, Jr.

After graduating from Forrestville Elementary, Harold Washington enrolled at DuSable High School at 4934 South Wabash Avenue. He remembers his high school days:

> I was a good student. I did not really have to work very hard to maintain good grades. My main interest was the track team. I don't think I took a book home five times during the entire period that I was there. I used to do all my homework during the study hour; that was enough. Miss Mary Herrick was my division and study hour teacher. She was a kind person. Miss Herrick did not play favorites with her attention; she was a universal den mother. I probably studied a little better than an hour a day. That was about it. If I took school work home, it was usually for a book report or some other English writing assignment.
>
> I had an English teacher named Jeannette Triplett, who didn't take any stuff. Students had to produce in her class. I remember she was a stickler for punctuation and preciseness. I recall that she gave us a choice for our final paper. We could write about anything we wanted, as long as it was concerning Chicago. Of all things, I wrote about policy. I wrote about it, I guess, because of the economic rationale for the existence of policy, that is, the number of people who were employed by the policy barons, how much money was moved around and the glamour that seemed to envelope the individuals who were involved in the policy game. I recall when I got to class on the day the papers were to be turned in, I had to confess that I had not written the paper but that I had an outline and was prepared to deliver my theme orally.

Left: Mrs. Jeannette Triplett, the English teacher who made young Washington toe the line. Right: Miss Mary Herrick, the beloved DuSable civics instructor and Harold Washington's home room and study hour teacher.

Left: Mrs. Anna Sublette, the history teacher who made historical figures come alive and walk right off the pages of the book for Harold Washington. Right: Dr. Mildred Bryant Jones, the highly-disciplined music teacher who anointed Harold, a non-singer, to the position of hummer in the Glee Club.

Mrs. Triplett countered by saying, 'You were supposed to write it.'

I said, 'But I can give it orally; as a matter of fact, I don't mind giving it orally.'

The class then took a vote, and I was allowed to give my presentation orally. When I gave my talk, Mrs. Triplett literally went into shock. My stepmother and Mrs. Triplett were very good friends. After class, Mrs. Triplett chastised me. She said that giving a paper on an illegal subject like gambling was a horrible thing. Mrs. Triplett even went so far as to tell my stepmother, who was a very high moraled person. My stepmother said she thought it was a hideous thing for me to be supporting because it was improper for a person to be an advocate for any activity that was against the law. My father thought it was funny because he pitched in all those worlds. Although Mrs. Triplett gave me a passing grade, I was not considered one of her favorite people.

Dr. Mildred Bryant Jones was another teacher at DuSable who made a great impression on me. She taught harmony and voice. Dr. Jones insisted that I join the glee club although I could not sing a lick. I was not able to carry a tune. Therefore, she settled on the notion that I could hum. I was the best hummer in the class because I was the only one. The good doctor was a little bit of a lady but a powerful teacher. Dr. Jones was a good friend of Dr. W.E.B. DuBois, the great black scholar who earned a Ph.D. at Harvard University before the turn of the century. She would often mention Dr. DuBois as an excellent role model for her students to follow. She told us about DuBois' scholarly achievements and demanded that we pursue excellence the same as he did.

Mrs. Anna Sublette was my history teacher and a woman that I was just fascinated with. She had the most infectious personality of any person I had met in my life. Mrs. Sublette made history come alive. When she explained a historical incident, we could literally see the characters walking right off the pages of the book. Women influenced me in school. I can't think of a single male teacher throughout my high school days who had any influence on my thinking or behavior.

There was another lady I was very fond of, Mrs. Charlemae Rollins, a librarian at the George Cleveland Hall Library, which is located at 4801 South Michigan Avenue, two blocks from DuSable High School and four blocks from my home. I read through whole sections of that library. Miss Vivian Harsh, the head librarian at the Cleveland Hall Branch, was instrumental in pulling together the most comprehensive collection of books on Afro-American history in Chicago. It was in that collection that I was first exposed to black authors such as Carter G. Woodson, Dr. W.E.B. DuBois, and Booker T. Washington.

Reading was an excursion that took me places an urban kid would never see. Reading whet my appetite. It really wasn't the library but the books. The main value was the joy of reading. I can't imagine life without it.

Left: Mrs. Charlamae Hill Rollins was Harold Washington's favorite librarian at the Cleveland Hall Branch. Right: Miss Vivina Harsh, head librarian at the George Cleveland Hall Branch, pulled together the most comprehensive collection of books on Afro-American history in Chicago. Washington was introduced to great black literary giants such as Dr. Carter G. Woodson, Dr. W.E.B. DuBois, Arna Bontemps, Sterling Brown, Claude Mc Kay and Countee Cullen at the Cleveland Hall Branch.

Above: Cecil Hellman, the DuSable track coach. Right: The DuSable Thinclads. Seated in the first row, second from left is Harold Washington; third is Robert Ray, the captain of the track team. (Note: both are holding trophies.) Standing in back row, to the extreme left is Albert Brown; third from the left is Thomas "Mad Man" Jones.

My main interest in high school was sports. As a matter of fact, Robert Ray, the captain of the DuSable Thinclads and I were the winners of the city championship in 1939. Ray won the hundred-yard dash and the two-hundred-yard dash. I won the hundred and twenty-yard high hurdle and got second place in the two-hundred-yard low hurdle. We got third place in the relay and won the city title. If you look at us now, you probably would say, how did those cats run? We were both built about the same. Ray was stockier and more muscular than I. Our mutual friend, Albert Brown, placed third in the eight hundred and eighty-yard dash.

Cecil Hellman was our coach and a very decent and pleasant person. He was a big raw-boned Scandinavian, a fatherly-type man who showed great concern about the welfare of the members of the track team. He frequently asked you questions, for example, 'Is there anything I can do for you? Are you doing good? Is there anything bothering you?' Although he was kind, he was not of very much value to me because he did not know anything about hurdling. He was more of a calisthenics man, and my primary interest was track. Therefore, I learned hurdling by reading pamphlets on the subject and through trial and error.

The Regal, at 47th and South Parkway, where Harold Washington spent many hours watching the Pathe News reels repeatedly for the purpose of picking up pointers on how to run the low and high hurdles sans an instructor.

I recall my brother Roy told me about a Pathe News reel that was showing at the Regal Theater that had a small segment on hurdling. I made a mad dash to the Regal the next day and sat through the movie three times just to see that section of the news reel which went 'zip!' I also hung around the University of Chicago field house every time there was a meet just to catch the hurdlers. The longest hurdle at the field house, I believe was sixty yards, that goes in six or seven seconds, and it's over zip! If you were seated at the wrong angle watching a hurdle meet, you wouldn't get much out of it. And I was always seated at the wrong angle. I was usually sitting where the hurdlers were coming at me whereas in order to get the greatest benefit, you had to see it from the side. My teaching aides were limited to watching news reels at the Regal and Metropolitan Theaters and at track meets at the University of Chicago. Nowadays, you can record Foster or Wilson from television on to a VHS or Betamax and play it back fifty times or more if necessary in slow motion. How can you miss?

Albert Brown remembers Harold Washington when he joined the track team in 1937. Brown describes Harold:

> He was a jolly, friendly fellow, who trained hard and had a lot of ability. Harold was big for his age, muscular with a large chest area and big legs. He was the same height at age sixteen as he is today. Although young Washington had an outgoing personality, he never discussed his family. None of us knew that Harold's father was an attorney and that his step-mother was a social worker. He selected, for some reason, to hang out with the rough and rugged fellows.
>
> Harold was the best boxer in our group. He was good enough to turn pro-fessional. However, Eddie Plique, the Savoy Ballroom boxing promoter, discouraged Harold from turning pro because he felt that he had too much brain power to waste on the canvas of a boxing ring.

Although Harold never carried textbooks home from school, he was a "cafeteria" reader outside of the classroom on subjects far beyond the DuSable textbooks. He read everything that he could get his fingers on. He always had a book in his hand or a magazine sticking out of his hip pocket. Sometimes, he carried both in both hip pockets. He was a member of the neighborhood softball team called the "Falcons," and his standard baseball equipment as the team's third baseman was a glove and a book. Some of Harold's teammates John Cheefus, Frank and Kenneth Titus, Aaron and Albert Hart, Melvin Wilkins, "Red" Christian, Henry Adams, Booker T. Washington, not related, and Edward Washington, Harold's brother, fre-quently accused him of eating a dictionary for lunch. Harold would read snatches of Edward Bellamy's *Looking Backward, The Education of Henry*

Kenneth Titus, a 1939 DuSable High grad and a teammate of Harold's on a neighborhood softball team known as the "Falcons."

Adams, Henry David Thoreau's *Walden* and magazines such as *Modern Mechanics,* or *The Shadow* while walking from third base to the player's bench between innings. Often he would complete several of Dostoevsky's or Nathaniel Hawthorne's short stories while waiting his turn at bat. Harold picked up the reading trait from his dad, who had a large library loaded with books on power and self-determination. Attorney Roy L. Washington was a very reflective man and an omnivorous reader, who also spent a lot of time talking to his boys, mostly to Harold because he was the youngest and, therefore, could not get away.

In 1934, while the Washington family resided at 4507 South Vincennes Avenue, Arthur W. Mitchell defeated Congressman Oscar DePriest, the Republican stalwart, in his bid for re-election. Hence, Mitchell became the first black Democrat to serve in Congress. Reverend Roy Lee Washington, Sr., an associate minister at Bethel A.M.E. Church for many years under the leadership of Bishop Ward, supported Mitchell in his bid for Congress. Although Reverend Washington conducted the Sunday services at Bethel about once a year, he was frequently called upon to give the Sunday morning sermons and make political speeches at various African Methodist Episcopal churches on the South and west sides of Chicago. Reverend Washington always took young Harold with him to different houses of worship every Sunday and to an occasional Democratic party rally where Judge Richard Harewood recalls seeing Harold in the company of his father. Although the ministry was Reverend Washington's first love, and he wanted Harold to become a minister, he never tried to influence him. In contrast, Reverend Isaiah Washington, Harold's paternal grandfather, definitely tried to persuade him to become a minister, but "Master" Harold resisted.

Harold recalls:

> I always knew what my father's Sunday sermon was going to be about because he would start practicing on me on Monday. Although I was not exactly an inanimate object, I did not do much responding. If you have ever been around preachers, you know they start practicing their sermon on whomever they can get their hands on. Since I was the youngest child, I was his captured audience. He would articulate his sermon to me because that is the way preachers prepare for the next Sunday. I would always listen very carefully just in case he might ask me a question, which he occasionally did. Therefore, I have to credit the extensive knowledge I have about the Bible today to those Bible sessions with my father.

Harold Washington had some strong notions about church as a child. He thought the Lord wanted little children to play, not pray all the time. Harold continues explaining his father's influence:

Although I knew I would never become a minister, I was certain that some-day I would finish law school and be a public figure, not necessarily a politician. It never occurred to me to run for office. I don't recall figuring that out. As a matter of fact, I had a tinge of distaste for politics. My old man had a tempering influence on me; he was a good role model. He got his message across to his boys by example.

In addition to Reverend Roy Lee Washington, Sr. being an African Methodist Episcopal minister, he was also a practicing lawyer in the days when black lawyers didn't fare too well. It was a tough, tough hustle. He was also a politician and an active member of the Third Ward Democratic Organization. When Roy, Sr. first joined the Democratic Organization, most blacks were Republicans; he never really discussed with young Harold exactly what made him move into the Democratic party in those early years. Harold's face lights up like a two-hundred watt bulb, and his infectious smile radiates intensive warmth when he describes his father:

My old man was as tough as steel and as soft as butter. He was a very affectionate man who tried to play the role of mother and father. He could be both protective and rough, depending on the circumstances. My old man could get me to do anything. All he had to do was raise his right eyebrow, and I would jump as if he had stuck a firecracker to my backside.

My dad was an overriding influence in my life. There's no question about it. In retrospect, he was even greater than I thought. The role model thing is a fact of life. The role model could be the man at the corner store, a brother, a teacher, but in my case, it was my old man. I always made a crack when I was young that I knew who Santa Claus was. It was my dad because he made the year-round comforts at our home possible. I would say that Christmas was a big thing in terms of the day itself, but trading presents was never a factor. I always made my own toys. I made a wagon, a scooter, and put together roller skates. Children's toys as such were never high on my agenda. Somewhere along the line I may have gotten a catcher's mitt for Christmas.

Harold recalls with an even brighter and broader smile:

My father was very solicitous in his concern about his children. All through the years, my father kept a wonderful relationship with my mother; they remained good friends. So much so, that all six of my half brothers and sisters were just a part of the family. We children visited back and forth between our home and theirs at 4736 South Michigan Avenue, only four blocks apart. My half brothers and sisters were the Prices, four girls: Ernestine Price Scott, who lives in Washington, D.C.; Gwendolyn Price, who works for a Loop law firm; Elaine Price Lake, a nurse who lives in Harvey, Illinois; Patricia Price McDouglas, a buyer who lives in Maryland and two boys: Ernest "Sonny" Price Jr., who was named after my stepfather, a businessman who lives in St. Louis, Missouri, and Ramon Price, the Chicago artist and curator for the Chicago Museum of African-American History.

The Washingtons and the Prices got along like one big family. Even my stepmother got into the act. She never went over to my mother's house or vice versa. However, we children moved back and forth between the two houses. The two families sort of intermeshed, and that was due to the nature of the parents. My father and mother were good friends, and they remained good friends until my father died. They were civilized people who never visited whatever took them apart upon their children.

Judge Arthur Hamilton remembers Attorney Roy L. Washington in the following manner:

I was general secretary for the Cook County Bar Association in 1952. Attorney Roy Washington Sr. was a very active member of that association. I was impressed with Attorney Washington's no-nonsense manner. When he died, he left five hundred dollars to the Cook County Bar Association. That was the first I ever heard of anybody doing such a thing. I will always remember him for that magnanimous act. Roy Washington thought enough of the black lawyers' organization to will it some money.

The Honorable Arthur Hamilton, judge of the circuit court of Cook County.

Albert Brown, a 1939 DuSable grad who joined the Civilian Conservation Corps with Harold Washington in June 1939.

Attorney John T. Jones also recalls Roy Washington's gift to the bar association and that five hundred dollars in 1952 was not a small amount of money, particularly in light of the fact that the average income for a black family was less than twenty-four hundred dollars per year.

Harold Washington reflects:

> My dad was tight with a buck all his life. Whenever he parted with his hard earned money, you could bet it was for an absolute necessity or a very good cause. My dad never made a large sum of money. However, he managed to maintain what was considered a middle-middle class status throughout the depression years of the 1930's. When my father passed in 1954, he was in fairly good shape. He didn't really start making money until 1941, just at the beginning of the war years. He made it in real estate, not in the practice of law. I guess you would have called him upper-middle class. His estate was worth about $350,000. I know because I probated the will. I was the lawyer. The legalities of the will were so complex that nobody got rich. However, he took good enough care of his four children and my stepmother.

On Harold's seventeenth birthday, he decided to drop out of high school and join the Civilian Conservation Corps, which was commonly known as the "CCC camp". Albert Brown, who was a member of the DuSable 1939 championship track team, along with Harold, was surprised to see Harold Washington enlisting in the CCC camp at the same time he did in June, 1939. Brown still believes, almost fifty years after the fact, that Harold went into the CCC camp without his parents' consent. That notion does not hold water in light of the following statement made by Harold Washington.

I don't really know how my father got me in the Civilian Conservation Corps, but I got in. They may have removed the income level requirements at the time because the CCC camp was very popular during the middle and late 1930's. I was sent up to the camp at Bitely, Michigan, which is close to Baldwin. In addition to a land reclamation program, we planted evergreen trees in that area. After three months, I was shipped out to Stockton, Illinois, which is near the northwest border of the state. I was there for several months. Our job was quarrying limestone which is heavy, hard and just plain dirty Georgia buggy work. The bad thing about Stockton was the atmosphere. It was a very prejudiced little town. The limestone was given to farmers free. The members of the Conservation Corps used it to stop soil erosion. It was a very useful type of work, but to me it was not the most captivating experience I ever had, but I did not find it unpleasant. My only real gripe with the Civilian Conservation Corps was the fact that it reminded me of my earlier regimentation experience at St. Benedict The Moor Boarding School. The CCC camp was quasi-military although we did not have to march and drill. The similarities between the army and the CCC camp centered around the fact that we had to wear uniforms and line up for the mandatory reveille before breakfast and retreat before dinner. On balance, it was a mind-opening experience for a seventeen-year-old boy. I completed my six month tour of duty and returned to DuSable High School.

While Harold was planting evergreen trees in Michigan and quarrying limestone in Illinois in the Civilian Conservation Corps, William L. Dawson and Mayor Edward J. Kelly were cutting a deal which led to Dawson walking out of the Republican party and joining the Democrats. In December, 1939, when Washington completed his six-month tour of duty in the Civilian Conservation Corps, Pat Nash and Mayor Edward J. Kelly anointed Bill Dawson with the committeemanship of the Second Ward and gave him a bundle of patronage positions for his precinct captains. Earl B. Dickerson, an independent Democrat, was serving his first and only term as alderman of the Second Ward.

The next magnetic force to pull Harold out of DuSable High School before graduation was Nancy Dorothy Finch, the young beauty who lived on the third floor at 111 E. 44th Street. Harold and Dorothy were married in May of 1941. Since he had just turned eighteen and she was seventeen, they both had to get permission from their parents in order to get the marriage license.

Reverend Roy Lee Washington, Sr. performed the wedding ceremony for Nancy Dorothy Finch and Harold Washington in his living room on the second floor at 111 E. 44th St. Harold recalls, "My mother-in-law, Mrs. Sally Finch, a very stylish stout woman with a beautiful face kept raising the following questions: 'Is this legal Roy? Are you sure this is legal Roy?'"

Reverend Washington retorted, "I marry people all the time."

Mrs. Finch snapped back, "That is not what I asked you Roy."

The two sweethearts discovered almost immediately after taking vows that their "non-shotgun" marriage was going to be a stormy one. Both Harold and Dorothy were strong-willed people with volatile tempers.

Fortunately, prior to his marriage, Harold had landed a good paying job by ghetto standards as a common laborer working the same job that his father had worked twenty years earlier at Wilson and Company located in the stockyards at 40th and Ashland Avenue. There he was employed in the freezer department where he wore rubber gloves, boots, and several layers of clothing. He manually tossed frozen hams and slabs of pork bellies into a train of metal carts. From the freezer, the rock frozen meat was carted into the sweet pickle department where it was thrown into a defrosting tank. The author, like his father, also worked in the cold and wet sweet pickle (defrosting department) in the early nineteen forties for approximately a year. Harold's job in the freezer was even worse because the workers had to go outdoors into freezing weather to warm up. (The Union Stockyards employed more Negroes from 1918 through 1950 than any other industry in Chicago. The steel mills ranked second in the employment of colored men during the same period.)

Prior to the stockyards, Washington worked as a hawker for the station concessionaire for approximately six months selling cokes, sandwiches, and candy aboard Greyhound buses that stopped to pick up passengers at the 79th and Stony Island Avenue bus station. Earlier, he worked as a pin boy in a bowling alley and also as a teeth polisher in a dental laboratory.

White collar jobs in the government or private industry in Chicago during the nineteen twenties, thirties and early nineteen forties were strictly reserved for white folk. The only "clean shirt" jobs for Negroes found in more than token numbers were in black-owned business establishments like insurance companies, banks, burial associations, cosmetic companies, weekly newspapers and in government agencies such as the post office, the Chicago Board of Education, the Department of Agriculture, the Works Progress Administration (WPA), the National Recovery Administration (NRA), the Treasury Department and the Chicago City Hall, where a large number of blacks worked at low level jobs in the water department. As a matter of fact, so many colored people were working at City Hall during the Thompson era that the water department was called "Uncle Tom's Cabin" in the 1920's and early 1930's.

Harold, who was among the fortunate few who passed the civil service examination for a clerkship in the treasury department, which was located in the Merchandise Mart Building, worked in the E. Bond Divison manning data processing machines from 1941 until he was drafted into the army in 1942. In that same year, November 1942, William L. Dawson was elected to Congress

Sergeant Wildforster, the military instructor for DuSable High School's Reserved Officer's Training Corps.

in the First Congressional District which included the First, Second and Third Wards.

Harold Washington was processed into the U. S. Army at Fort Custer, Michigan. He, along with one hundred and fifty-two other recruits, was greeted at the 1609th Service Unit by "old soldiers," that is, civilians who had only been in the army for three days who laughed and shouted, "Shorty's got your gal and gone", at them. Harold Washington officially became an "old soldier" within forty-eight hours after receiving a metal dog tag which bore the serial number 36395331, (It was mandatory to wear the dog tags at all times, even in the shower,) his G.I. (Government Issue) clothes and his immunization shots. Buck Private Washington had had some preparation for army life because the U. S. Army was just a larger version of the Civilian Conservation Corps (CCC) minus the drills and guns. In 1937, at DuSable High School, Harold had opted to join the Reserve Officers Training Corps (ROTC), under Sergeant Wildforster, as opposed to taking gym because he felt that he got enough gymnastics exercise in his daily track practice. In the ROTC at DuSable, he learned the army's close order drill and weaponry ranging from the M-1 rifle up to the one hundred and five millimeter howitzer.

After three days at Fort Custer, Michigan, Private Washington and approximately two hundred other recruits were shipped out on a troop train to Tonpeah, Nevada for basic training. After a couple of days in Tonpeah, it became obvious to Washington and the other buck privates that they had been misassigned and were going to be simply marking time until they were shipped to another camp for training. Buck Private Washington recollects:

> There was a soldier at Camp Tonpeah with the surname of Shields who was a former Davis Cup tennis player. He asked me to help him recruit a boxing team to participate in the regional Golden Gloves finals, which were to be held in Reno, Nevada which was about one hundred miles from Camp Tonpeah. We recruited a team of boxers in the upper six weights. Theodore 'Red' Davis, a former co-captain of the DuSable High School football team, was our heavyweight. I was the light heavyweight. Another guy whose name I can not recall was the middleweight. We trained hurriedly for about three

Theodore "Red" Davis, former co-captain of DuSable's football team and an army buddy who served on both the state side and in the South Pacific with Harold Washington.

weeks. It was tough because we were above sea level, and nobody was accustomed to it.

Dawn finally broke on the day we were to make the trip to Reno, Nevada, the gambling capital of America. We were told we would be staying at the Hotel Golden. I'll never forget when we arrived at the hotel, we went in through the back door. We didn't stay in a hotel room, but in a converted pantry or storage room where they had set up seven cots and had stacked the hotel supplies in the room into a corner. They had moved us into the hotel so fast we didn't know what was going on. This was a very humiliating experience. During the five days that we were there, we occasionally went out the front door, that is, the 'for white only entrance.'

One day, Theodore 'Red' Davis said, 'Let's go to Harrah's gambling casino.' I wasn't much of a gambler. I played a little poker, but I wasn't going to play that kind of stuff out there. Anyway, 'Red' gambled a little bit.

As I recall, a fellow walked up to us as we were standing there watching a roulette wheel. He said, 'No coloreds allowed.'

I said, 'What?' I really didn't understand him at first.

He repeated, 'No coloreds allowed.'

Then 'Red' said, 'What did you say?'

So we made a game out of it. And the cat finally, in disgust, walked away. After that encounter, to make a long story short, we walked around in the casino with a sort of a braggadocio attitude for about ten minutes and then split. It wasn't my first encounter with prejudice, obviously, but it was kind of shocking because it was my first encounter with prejudice as a soldier. I remember after we got back to the pantry in the hotel, I was pretty upset about it. I wanted to get the hell out of town. But Shields calmed us down. We went on and fought. 'Red' got beat pretty bad in his bouts. I lost one of my three bouts. Max Baer, the former heavyweight champion of the world, was the referee, and I believe I would have had a better chance if he had not been. But 'Red' obviously went along for the trip because he wasn't a boxer.

Two days after we returned to Tonpeah from Reno, we were shipped to Hammerfield, California, which was a training ground. I stayed there for approximately thirteen weeks, after which I went to Marchfield, California, where I stayed for about a year. While there, I went to every damn school I could think of. I attended the Administration School, which came in handy because I was made a first sergeant and the Chemical Warfare School. I enrolled in something else that you would never think or imagine, a Soil Technician School, which was a fascinating business. The other school I attended was a Camouflage School.

At the Soil Technician School, I learned how to test soil, clay and gravel to determine whether or not the ground would support an airfield. When I came out of Soil Technician School, I was a technical sergeant. I was then sent overseas to Guam where I was made first sergeant. I was the only soil technician in the entire area. They shuttled me from island to island

A picture of the Headquarters and Service Company Units of the 1887th Engineer Aviation Battalion taken in Guam in November 1944. Standing at the extreme left in the first row is acting First Sergeant Harold Washington.

periodically to test the soil. There was a high mortality rate among soil technicians because they were getting bumped off. But I really didn't think too much about it.

I did a great deal of structured reading while in the service. I must have taken at least thirty correspondence courses. Every ninety days I would report to the company warrant officer, who was a resident teacher for correspondence courses, to take a test on the material I had completed. I took almost every course listed in the catalogues: history, literature, chemistry, and a great number of English courses. I didn't take any physics courses because the Soil Technician School had been an accelerated truncated course in physics. I devoured all that material. Some people drink and chew gum; I read. All of my correspondence credits were mailed back to DuSable High School by the company warrant officer. Hence, when I returned to Chicago after being discharged from the army in January, 1946, I went directly to DuSable and picked up my diploma because I had covered enough academic material in the service to graduate from high school three times. My brother Edward, who was afflicted with leukemia at age fifteen, died at age twenty-six in 1946, shortly after I returned to Chicago.

Harold Washington used his Servicemen's Readjustment Act (G.I. Bill), to complete his undergraduate studies as a political science major at Roosevelt University and law at the Northwestern University Law School, where he was the only black admitted out of an incoming freshman class of 185 in the fall of 1949 under the traditional quota system. City Treasurer Cecil Partee, a graduate in the Northwestern Law School class of 1946, and Judge R. Eugene Pincham, a member of the Northwestern class of 1951, were also the only blacks in their classes. Washington supplemented his seventy-five dollar per month G.I. income in several ways. In his junior year at Roosevelt University, he was employed part-time in the excellent political science department where the chairman was Dr. Jerome Watson. In his senior year, he was a full-time assistant instructor to Dale Pontius, a brilliant political science professor.

As a class lecturer, Harold Washington's paycheck was thin; therefore, he and his brother Roy Lee, Jr. started a decorating and maintenance service. Harold launched his marketing program by advertising the Washington brothers' decorating capabilities on the bulletin board at Roosevelt University. Roy Lee Washington, Sr. owned several small apartment buildings on the South Side of Chicago for which Roy Lee, Jr. and Harold already did the plumbing, plastering, carpentry, and decorating. In a relatively short period of time, the brothers were inundated with so much work that it was necessary for them to hire additional help.

During a moment of reflection, Harold Washington said:

> We had a lot of decorating gigs. Wilberforce Jones and four or five other guys used to work with Roy and me on the weekends. We scheduled all our work for Saturdays and Sundays. We must have painted half of the homes on North Sheridan Road. In my second year of law school, we made good money.

Harold Washington graduated from Northwestern Law School in 1952 with a brand new doctorate of jurisprudence degree. Two years prior to receiving the degree, Nancy Dorothy and Harold were divorced. They were married for ten years and lived together for the total period, with the exception of the three and a half years he spent in the army and the brief intermittent periods when they separated because of incompatible temperaments. Although thirty-six years have passed since their divorce, Harold Washington still speaks of Dorothy with a great deal of warmth and fondness. His former wife has since remarried and is a practicing grade school teacher living in Tennessee.

AUTHOR'S NOTE

Although Mayor Harold Washington has frequently said that he never dreamed of being mayor of the city of Chicago, he has never said that he did not have that particular ambition. Hence, I felt it proper to end this chapter with an article he wrote for an army battalion newspaper called the *New World* (February, 1945) while serving on the island of Guam in the South Pacific. The article is entitled "Ambition."

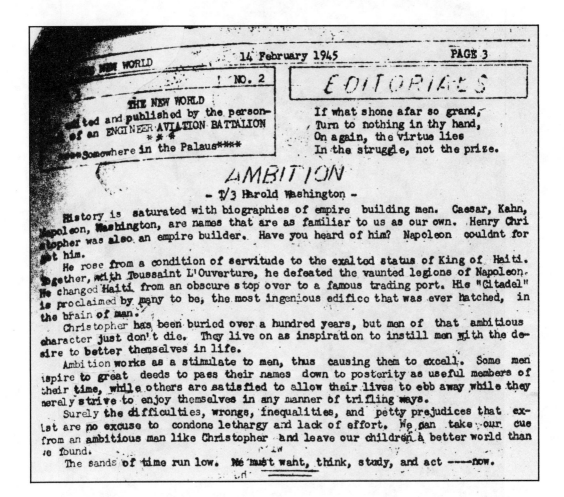

NEW WORLD   14 February 1945   PAGE 3

NO. 2   *EDITORIALS*

THE NEW WORLD
...ted and published by the person-
...of an ENGINEER AVIATION BATTALION
* * *
...Somewhere in the Palaus****

If what shone afar so grand,
Turn to nothing in thy hand,
On again, the virtue lies
In the struggle, not the prize.

AMBITION
— T/3 Harold Washington —

History is saturated with biographies of empire building men. Caesar, Kahn, Napoleon, Washington, are names that are as familiar to us as our own. Henry Christopher was also an empire builder. Have you heard of him? Napoleon couldnt forget him.

He rose from a condition of servitude to the exalted status of King of Haiti. Together, with Toussaint L'Ouverture, he defeated the vaunted legions of Napoleon. He changed Haiti from an obscure stop over to a famous trading port. His "Citadel" is proclaimed by many to be, the most ingenious edifice that was ever hatched, in the brain of man.

Christopher has been buried over a hundred years, but men of that ambitious character just don't die. They live on as inspiration to instill men with the desire to better themselves in life.

Ambition works as a stimulate to men, thus causing them to excell. Some men ispire to great deeds to pass their names down to posterity as useful members of their time, while others are satisfied to allow their lives to ebb away while they merely strive to enjoy themselves in any manner of trifling ways.

Surely the difficulties, wrongs, inequalities, and petty prejudices that exist are no excuse to condone lethargy and lack of effort. We can take our cue from an ambitious man like Christopher and leave our children a better world than we found.

The sands of time run low. We must want, think, study, and act ——now.

State Representative Harold Washington, a freshman member of the House, standing in front of the Illinois State Capital Building in the Spring of 1965. A statue of Abraham Lincoln looms in the background.

Chapter *XXIII*

The Rise of a Political Movement Within One Score

On January 6, 1965, Harold Washington was sworn in as a freshman in the Illinois House of Representatives in Springfield, Illinois. His seat mate in the Assembly was Adlai Stevenson, who was also a freshie in the class of "65." It was customary in those days for all of the Democratic members of the House and the Senate to receive a small piece of white paper on their desks each morning. The paper was called an "idiot sheet" by some of the independent members of those bodies because it listed the House and Senate bills that were coming up for a vote that day and also indicated how the public-elected officials should vote on each bill. If the member was not from a strong independent political base such as the Thirteenth or Twenty-fourth Legislative District and failed to follow the "idiot sheet" to the letter, he more than likely would not be reslated at the next election. There were some exceptions. For example, State Representative Harold Washington reflects:

> Adlai Stevenson was more independent than I or anybody else down in Springfield. He came in at the very top of a ticket with 236 candidates trailing him on the "orange ballot" of 1964 whereas I came in number forty, which was not bad considering it was the first time I had run for public office and the fact that it was an at-large statewide election.

Adlai Stevenson recalls:

> Well, Harold Washington was a maverick, but not totally, because he was also dependent on the Democratic organization for support. I frequently saw the agony and tension in his face as he wrestled with the notions of what he wanted to do and what the Chicago machine wanted him to do. Harold

Adlai E. Stevenson III, former State Represen-
tative, Illinois state treasurer, United States
Senator, and a candidate for governor in 1982 and
1986, and the son of an Illinois governor and
grandson of a vice president of the United States.

turned to me one day and said, 'I'm very envious of you because of your total independence.' His observations helped me to understand the difficulty others were facing. It also made me realize Harold Washington was somebody who was going to work for the people and do everything within whatever the limits were to represent his own conscience. Therefore, everything that Harold has done since those early days has not come as a surprise to me.

Harold Washington's subsequent moves in the Illinois House and Senate were not a surprise to Congressman Gus Savage, who has been a friend of Washington's since their college days. Congressman Savage states:

Washington was a freshman in the House when his committeeman and alderman, Ralph Metcalfe, along with Mayor Richard J. Daley conspired to get Dr. Martin Luther King to leave town. Harold's stomach must have churned at the sight of that kind of activity because he is a principle guy and a well-read intellectual. His heart certainly bled when his committeeman Ralph Metcalfe initially joined Daley in supporting Hanrahan after the Hampton-Clark murders. Harold was against that kind of skull-duggery because, in my opinion, in his heart he has always been with the people. Harold was independent by inclination, and he knew the kinds of things which the Democratic machine was doing were wrong. He had been personally wronged by the way the machine had treated his father. And he too had been held back because any white boy with Washington's qualifications for operating in the political arena would have been high on the political ladder by the time Washington put his foot in the state house for the first time. On the other hand, he was afraid to become an all out independent because he felt he could not win an election without the support of the Third Ward Organization.

In 1969, Harold Washington, Lewis Caldwell, Ray Ewell and Calvin Smith organized a black caucus in the House of Representatives. The Chicago Democratic machine was definitely opposed to black folk getting together for anything other than to dance. Lewis Caldwell said, "Two-thirds of the blacks in the House and the Senate failed to join the caucus because they feared losing their patronage jobs at City Hall." Harold Washington led the charge for a

Black Democrats in the 77th Illinois General Assembly. In front row: (left to right) Senator Fred E. Smith, State Representative Corneal Davis and Senators Richard Newhouse, Kenneth Hall and Cecil A. Partee. Second row: (left to right) State Representatives Richard A. Carter, Robert L. Thompson, James A. McLendon and Lewis A.H. Caldwell. Third row: (left to right) State Representatives Elwood Graham, Otis G. Collins and Genoa S. Washington. Fourth row: (left to right) State Representatives James Y. Carter, Harold Washington and James C. Taylor. Missing from the photo session were Senator Charles Chew, Jr. and State Representatives Raymond W. Ewell, Isaac R. Sims and Eugene M. Barnes.

black caucus in the House as a legislative maverick. He also succeeded in getting ten of the twenty black members of the Illinois legislature to join him on May 11, 1971 in a boycott against Vice President Spiro Agnew, when Agnew addressed the Illinois General Assembly.

Washington said that Agnew was, "anti-black, anti-student, anti-peace, and anti-poor. He's like the Klu Klux Klan; he's anti-everything."

On the other hand, when State Representative Harold Washington was in Chicago, he was an integral part of Richard J. Daley's machine. He ran his precinct in the Third Ward like a czar and was one of the brightest and the best in that organization. He survived with his mavericism in Springfield because many of his political peers liked his political style and integrity. In addition, he was an excellent legislator who served the party well in that capacity. On eleven occasions, his colleagues voted him one of the top ten state legislators. In addition, precinct captains like "Bill" Nolls in the Third Ward Organization loved him.

Washington was not a legislative mechanic. He was an innovative legislator and a very persuasive orator. In 1965, during his freshman year, he was in the forefront of a political fight to reform consumer credit and won. In 1969, he introduced a bill to make Dr. Martin Luther King, Jr.'s birthday a holiday. It passed in both the House and the Senate but was vetoed by Governor Richard Ogilvie. He submitted two additional bills over a period of four years to memorialize Dr. King's birthday. The second bill passed the House and Senate and was signed by the governor; however, the bill simply made King's birthday a commemorative day when the public schools in the state would give recognition to Dr. Martin Luther King, Jr.'s accomplishments. Representative Washington explained the importance of the bill after it was passed:

Governor Richard B. Ogilvie (R), 1969–1972.

Governor Daniel Walker, signing the Dr. Martin Luther King birthday bill on September 17, 1973, as State Representative Harold Washington, the sponsor of the bill, observes.

This legislation accomplishes two things: it honors a great American, and it attempts in a small way to fill a gap in our school curriculum which has given little recognition to black Americans. Recognition of Dr. King by the children of Illinois represents a great public honor and the continuation of his role as a symbol of morality, dignity, and integrity. For the black community, this new holiday provides a means of creating a sense of pride and dignity and honor in the black children that is so necessary for every child.

Representative Washington was also the chief sponsor of a third bill to have Dr. Martin Luther King, Jr.'s birthday declared a legal holiday in Illinois. The latter bill got full passage with the assistance of State Senator Cecil A. Partee and was signed into law on September 17, 1973 by Governor Daniel Walker. Illinois was the first of the fifty states to officially declare King's birthday a legal holiday.

The saga of the Dr. Martin Luther King birthday bill is best told by its sponsor, State Representative Harold Washington, who said:

The first year we filed a statewide King holiday bill, I was unable to get it passed because there was a tremendous resistance to that form of recognition to Dr. King at that time. I, therefore, amended the bill and provided for a commemorative holiday for Dr. King to be celebrated by all school children in the state through appropriate ceremonies on Dr. King's birthday. It was the only such commemorative holiday in the country.

With the help of such people as Harold Charles, a Farragut High School teacher and head of Operation Breadbasket's teacher division, and Sam Patch, we were instrumental in getting the state superintendent of public instructions and Dr. James Redmond to send out directives to every school in the state together with a proclamation setting up guidelines for the commemoration of Dr. King in all public schools. To that limited extent, the commemorative holiday law must be considered a successful innovation. It did not satisfy black folk's legitimate demands for recognition of Dr. King.

Nor were we satisfied with a commemorative holiday. And so, in 1971, I again filed bills for a statewide holiday in memory of Dr. King. At that time, I incurred no resistance in the House nor did Senator Partee in the Senate. Legislative attitudes had changed. Unfortunately, Governor Ogilvie, pursuant to some extremely bad advice, refused to sign the bill into law. He amended it to provide that Illinois would celebrate Dr. King's birthday only if it became a national holiday. I refused to accept Ogilvie's amendment because the southern-dominated Congress, as well as many northern bigots, are not about to make Dr. King's birthday a national holiday. Do you know that Abraham Lincoln's birthday is not yet a national holiday? And you know why!

At first, I could not understand why Ogilvie could commit such a blunder. Then the answer occurred to me. We had not taken time to alert the brothers to zero in on Ogilvie.

Nevertheless, I was incensed with Ogilvie's position and made no bones about it when he ran for re-election in 1972. Since he was defeated by only 75,000, I'd like to think that his refusal to sign the King holiday bill was instrumental in helping to bring about his defeat.

We then come to the present King holiday bill, which was maneuvered through the House and Senate, through the Washington-Partee effort, and sitting on Governor Dan Walker's desk. I did not think he would make the same mistake as Governor Ogilvie. However, I for one had decided to muster as much public sentiment for a King state holiday as possible and to involve all who wish to be involved.

Three weeks prior to the bill reaching the governor's desk, my staff circulated petitions throughout Chicago in hopes of acquiring 50,000 signatures on the petition urging Governor Dan to sign the King holiday bill into law. The response was terrific, and with the cooperation of such organizations as Operation PUSH, Kennedy-King College, approximately three hundred ministers and business establishments, the bill was signed by the governor on September 17, 1973.

In the final analysis, controversial legislation is not passed solely due to the efforts of even the most skilled legislators; it is passed and signed only when there is respect for and fear of those who stand behind the elected officials, mainly, the people.

In the year of the final King bill, Representative Harold Washington's legislative and leadership abilities had become so pronounced that State Representative Lewis A.H. Caldwell (D-24) announced that he was going to place the name of Representative Washington (D-26) in nomination for the office of speaker of the House of Representatives. Caldwell said that Washington, during his four terms in the House, had emerged as "an articulate, constructive spokesman for progressive legislation." Justifying his actions, Caldwell argued that:

> At this juncture in history, the Illinois House needs a leader of strength, dedication, knowledge and compassion. Washington has demonstrated a deep seated appreciation for the Democratic process and can direct those affairs without fear or favor.
>
> During his legislative career, Washington has been in the forefront to uplift the quality of life for all people by providing equal opportunity, protection for citizens who persecute criminals, voting rights for youth and equal opportunity for all sexes. This was characterized as his legislative input. He also has advocated decent housing and meaningful education, consumer protection and greater employment opportunities.

Caldwell continued:

> It is now time to elevate to the highest policy-making position in the Illinois House a person from the state's largest minority group. In my opinion, Washington possesses all the necessary qualifications to be speaker.

State Representative Harold Washington's legislative taste for reform ran the entire gamut from the Fair Employment Practices Act to providing protection for witnesses in criminal prosecution, from opportunities for small minority business contractors to reform of the Currency Exchange Act, from the passage of a state Human Rights Act to the enactment of a bill to save Provident Hospital, one of Chicago's oldest black institutions, with a $15 million grant.

Senator Cecil Partee handled most of State Representative Harold Washington's bills when they came to the Senate. "Many of Harold's bills had something to do with affirmative action. The Senate was deaf on those kinds of bills unless they were shepherded through by someone with political savvy and who could make the case," Senator Partee said. In most instances, Senator Cecil Partee was the man who made the case. Partee recalls:

> Harold was an excellent legislator, very dogged and determined all the time. Many of the things he wanted were considered controversial by the political establishment. For example, when Harold Washington and some others

organized a black caucus, I did not join because I did not think it would be kosher for me to do that being the leader of the entire Senate and segregating myself into a black caucus. But be that as it may, there was no doubt in my mind about Harold Washington's ability to lead in causes in which he believed.

State Representative Harold Washington with a chuckle and a broad smile explains Partee's involvement:

Having Senator Partee handle my bills was the best thing going. For one, we were both from the Twenty-sixth Legislative District. Secondly, he was the majority leader in the Senate and he subsequently became the president of that body. By the same token, I handled most of his bills in the House, not all of them because some had to be handled by the House leadership.

Senator Cecil A. Partee and Attorney Earl L. Neal, one of Chicago's most talented trial lawyers, were both members of Alderman Kenneth Campbell's Twentieth Ward Organization. Cecil Partee and Harold Washington were both graduates of Northwestern University Law School, while Washington and Neal took the Illinois Bar Examination at the same time in 1952. In addition to being lawyers, the three men had a common interest in organizational politics. Earl Neal organized the Young Democrats of the Twentieth Ward Organization. And Harold Washington had done likewise in the Third Ward. Neal remembers Harold Washington from those early years:

This amateur snapshot was taken by the author in the kitchen of his mother's home on December 23, 1952, one month after Harold Washington passed the Illinois Bar Examination. Left to right: Mayor Harold Washington, Congressman Gus Savage, the late Willie Wright, Attorney Lawrence Haliburton. Seated are: Mrs. Mittie Travis, the mother of Dempsey J. Travis, and Henry G. Forte, a former member of the Nat "King" Cole Orchestra.

Left: Attorney Earl L. Neal, the first black to be elected chairman of the board of trustees for the University of Illinois. He subsequently was elected chairman of First Federal Savings and Loan Association of Chicago, Chicago's second largest savings institution. Thus, Neal became the first black in the country to head a major savings institution. Right: The late Kenneth Wilson, a former justice of the Illinois Appellate Court in the First District and the man that Mayor Harold Washington succeeded in the Illinois House of Representatives as representative of the Twenty-sixth District.

A very forceful, articulate and bright man who was one of the pillars of the Third Ward Organization. When I think of the Third Ward, I think of Alderman Ralph Metcalfe, Kenneth Wilson and Harold Washington. All of them were excellent politicians. Harold replaced Kenneth Wilson in the House of Representatives when Wilson became a Cook County commissioner.

There was a strange turn of events that kept me from joining their ranks as an elected public official. In the first instance, Alderman Kenneth Campbell ran for a seat on the Sanitary District and lost. If he had won, I would probably have replaced him as alderman because that is the way he wanted it. Later, Campbell wanted me to take a seat on the Cook County Board when Mike Sneed died because Mike was a Twentieth Ward appointee. I believe someone from the Second Ward wanted the spot. Therefore, Daley appointed Josephine Sneed, Mike Sneed's widow, to avoid a Dawson-Campbell fight.

Although I did not get either appointment, I continued to work hard every night at the organization's headquarters. And I think it was one of the most invaluable services that I ever performed because it gave me an opportunity to develop a close relationship with the people and their problems. I'm pleased to say that in most instances I was able to find a solution to whatever the problem might happen to be. Alderman Kenneth Campbell taught me one lesson, 'If people are with you Earl, they will carry you to the mountain top. Don't ever betray the people that you are serving.' I guess it was during that period that I began to meet a lot of people and develop a lot of friends because I was constantly doing favors.

In a relatively short period of time after his arrival in Springfield, Illinois, Representative Harold Washington made many friends in both the House and the Senate because his reputation as a hard worker and a person with an unabrasive demeanor preceded him. He is remembered by members of the General Assembly in Springfield as the legislator who, in the heat of debate, maintained the aplomb of a seasoned diplomat. He never permitted himself to get into screaming and wrestling matches on the floor of the House or the Senate. On the other hand, he used kid gloves when he found it necessary to knock heads because he never wanted to leave his protagonist with a headache to remember him by. Like his father before him, he had the ability to be as hard as steel when the occasion demanded it.

There were many occasions when Washington found it necessary to be iron-fisted. In the fall of 1976, Senator Washington requested that the machine give the black caucus a right to select Kenneth Hall, a downstater from East St. Louis, as its Senate leader. Mayor Richard J. Daley said, "No! A thousand times no!" Washington countered Daley's refusal to honor the black caucus' request with a thumbs down attitude on supporting Thomas Hynes as majority leader in the Senate. The black caucus joined forces with Senator Dawn Clark Netsch and some other North Shore liberals, in addition to a group known as the "Crazy Eight" from downstate Illinois. In exchange, the black caucus supported the North Shore liberals and the "Crazy Eight" in their pursuit to get some Senate rules changed. The coalition of fifteen held out for rule changes, and the black caucus' right to select its own leader for six weeks. It took one hundred and ninety votes during that period for the Senate to realize

State Senator Dawn Clark Netsch, north side independent Democrat. She was the only female member and Harold Washington was the only black member in the Northwestern Law School graduating class of 1952.

Four members of the black caucus discuss strategy on the floor of the State Senate: Left to right, Senators Richard Newhouse, Harold Washington, Kenneth Hall and Earline Collins.

that the coalition meant business and before a compromise could be reached. Senator Philip J. Rock of Oak Park, Illinois successfully refereed the matter. Daley, for reasons of his own, would not let Tom Hynes negotiate the stalemate. Everybody was satisfied with the way the matter was settled except Richard J. Daley who resented Washington's leadership role in the Senate fight and never forgot it.

Although Harold always maintained a low profile, prior to being elected to the Illinois House of Representatives, his leadership and analytical abilities were both prized and sought, before and after he became an elected official, by many progressive political groups. In June 1974, the Committee for a Black Mayor chaired by Charlie Hayes, international vice president of the Amalgamated Meat Cutters' and Butchers' Union of North America, AFL-CIO, drafted a criteria for a black mayor to run in 1975 against Mayor Richard J. Daley. The following minimum qualifications were considered:

1) Absolute integrity which has been tested ad evaluated. He must have an unblemished record.

2) An affirmative and consistent record in the movement, and the ability to attract the type of high-level committee that will raise at least $1 million.

3) The candidate and/or the committee must provide the organizational understanding to get, keep and inspire the necessary foot soldiers to establish a meaningful precinct organization throughout the city.

4) The candidate hopefully will be both charismatic and scholarly with the multi-talents necessary to communicate with persons of all classes and races in the city. He should be exciting enough to cause non-registered black voters to become anxious to register and to vote.

5) The candidate and his top organization committee must have a complete understanding of the dog-eat-dog political processes operative in Chicago. He must understand these processes from the "nitty-gritty" to the most sophisticated forms.

6) The candidate must have the strength and ability to govern, if elected.

A subcommittee of the Committee for a Black Mayor chaired by Attorney James Montgomery, president of the Cook County Bar Association, interviewed persons who had been selected as potential candidates for mayor of Chicago. The interviews took place on Saturday, September 14, 1974 between 9:30 A.M. and 4 P.M. in the Marie Antoinette Room of the Shoreland Hotel. Among some of the candidates considered for interview were Joseph Bertrand, city treasurer; Roland Burris, the state comptroller; Alderman Wilson Frost; Attorney E. Duke McNeil; Senator Richard Newhouse; Senator Cecil Partee; Commander George Sims; Attorney Thomas N. Todd; Congressman Ralph Metcalfe and State Representative Harold Washington.

Senator Richard Newhouse indicated a strong willingness to run; the same was true of Attorney E. Duke McNeil. Congressman Ralph Metcalfe did not express an interest during the interview because he did not feel that the Committee for a Black Mayor had the ability to raise the funds necessary to run a credible campaign. Metcalfe said his initial prerequisite for running would be for the Committee for a Black Mayor to place a half million dollars in a campaign kitty at the Independence Bank. On the other hand, State Representative Harold Washington told the committee he was not the guy for the job. And he, in turn, pushed vigorously for Congressman Ralph Metcalfe to become the black candidate to run against Mayor Richard J. Daley in 1975.

To support his rationale for Metcalfe's candidacy, Representative Harold Washington read the following prepared statement to the Committee for a Black Mayor on Saturday morning, September 14, 1974.

I am greatly honored and highly appreciative of the opportunity to meet with you this morning. I consider your invitation to meet with you in order to consider me as a candidate for mayor of the city of Chicago, under the sponsorship of the black community, one of the crowning achievements of my career. There is no way in which I can adequately thank you individually and collectively. I am aware of the fact that I ran well in the name-recognition survey which you conducted, and I would like to believe that those votes were earned. I would like to think that those votes came as a result of my work and productivity in the General Assembly in Springfield, not from the electronic and print media. I would like to think that the support of the people came from their knowledge and belief that I have been a servant of the people.

In July of this year, I read a column entitled, "Daley Machine Black Target" in which syndicated columnist Victor Riesel wrote about the Committee for a Black Mayor. And although Riesel is not one of my favorite journalists, he did quote Mr. Hayes as saying '. . . we're rousing the black sleeping giant. After all, we are one of the two basic supports of the Illinois Democratic Party . . .' I agree with Mr. Hayes that the black voter in Chicago represents the potential political power to turn this city around, in fact, turn this state around. Again, I commend you all for your foresightedness in forming this group, taking the survey and interviewing those individuals who you believe have the basic qualifications for becoming the first black mayor of our city. You are to be congratulated.

I am known in many circles as an independent machine politician. Frankly, I take a great deal of pride in that title because it tries to explain how a black person can be within the party structure and yet and still be a man who represents the interests of black people. Some years ago, the Chicago League of Negro Voters in a pamphlet called *Freedom Now* described this phenomenon as 'intra-party independence.' Their postulate was that a black person within a political party could be in a better position to deliver than an 'independent' as long as the party politician concerned himself with the needs of his community. In spite of the regular party line, he could be more effective than someone outside of the organization. This has been the role I have attempted to play during my years of public service.

I would venture to say that the most effective candidate to oppose Mayor Daley in the upcoming race is a man who can attract support from those black voters who respond to the leadership of persons who are not primarily politicians. In other words, the candidate must appeal to the regular organization people as well as the independent voters, the black voter, the white, and the latino, the old and the young, and both sexes.

Another factor which I hope we can agree on is that name-recognition is an extremely important item. Many of the bush league, instant replay political analysts who were yesterday's front room revolutionaries have criticized this committee's progress to me. I have always asked them what have you done for the group. If you can't help them, leave them alone. Black folk don't need arm chair quarterbacks. Many of these people say it is too late to put together a campaign for a black mayor. Under ordinary circumstances, I might agree. But when the candidate has good name recognition among the entire community and when he can inspire confidence and

U.S. Representative Ralph H. Metcalfe, the 1936 Olympic gold medal winner who became a black folk hero when he broke with Mayor Richard J. Daley over police brutality.

trust because of a proven record which will bring financial support, I say it is not too late, if this committee is serious.

Let me quote Riesel again: 'Political realists predict Hayes' committee won't dent the Daley machine. But how much can the committee shake the 'entrenched labor-Daley establishment,' as Hayes puts it?'

I would like to beg your indulgence for a few more minutes because I am trying to make myself clear as possible, which is again the reason I wrote this statement, because if something was lost on you during this brief meeting, I hope you will pick this document up again and peruse it.

I am a person who fits most of your criteria, and I am one of the leaders in the survey, so I am going to take some liberties which I hope will be taken by you in good faith.

Until a few days ago, I was wrestling with the idea of seeking the high office of mayor of Chicago because I felt that I represented to a large degree the concepts mentioned above. In other words, I am able to draw votes from the regular voters as well as the independents. I have good name recognition, I meet most of the committee's criteria, and my record of public service is as good, and in some cases better, than any other person being considered.

After discussing the pros and the cons with some of my political advisors, we arrived at a decision that the man who fits the bill better than I do is Congressman Ralph H. Metcalfe. He has an illustrious record of public service. He can draw support from the regular voter and the independent voter. He can get support from the white, latino and black communities. He fits the criteria of this committee. It is my considered opinion that Congressman Ralph Metcalfe is your best candidate.

Let me again repeat that I consider myself a servant of this committee, and I would be hard pressed to say no to a legitimate draft. But we are all interested in promoting the empowerment of blacks in this city and throughout the nation. Based on that premise, I say let's go with our best. . . . Ralph Metcalfe.

In view of my support of Congressman Metcalfe, I do not think that any consideration of me as a prospective candidate for mayor of the city of Chicago is necessary, but I will wait upon the will of this group.

I will also strongly support any candidate selected by this group because I respect its judgment. If I may beg your indulgence, I would like to refer to the Riesel article a last time: 'This isn't militant black power, clenched-fist street horseplay . . . This is sophisticated power-block politics.' I buy it. If you have any questions, I would be glad to answer them.

In spite of the urging and cajoling by Charles Hayes, Howard Medley, Harold Washington and others to get Ralph Metcalfe to run for mayor, he held his decision until December 3, 1974. However, early in November in an interview with *Chicago Tribune* reporter Barbara Reynolds, he implied that he had not reached a decision but strongly hinted he was on the verge of running. He then said, "My initial requirements that the Committee for a Black Mayor guarantee a war chest of $500,000 before I consider the race may have been too stiff. And my other condition that the three other candidates (Richard Newhouse, E. Duke McNeil and west side developer Edward Allen) withdraw from the race in my favor may also have been unrealistic."

Having eliminated those two stiff preconditions, Metcalfe said, "I feel the pressure to move. The pressures on me are tremendous. And I would feel some pain about letting such a fine group of people down (the committee). I will feel more relaxed when I have made some kind of decision."

On Tuesday, December 3, 1974, U.S. Representative Ralph H. Metcalfe declared, "I will not be a candidate for mayor in 1975." Metcalfe, who had been urged to run by the Committee for a Black Mayor, further said, "The decision which had been expected had been difficult. But it became clear that time (to raise funds, gather support and otherwise put together a winning campaign) was not on the committee's side." The congressman's statement was made at a press conference held at the Sheraton-Chicago Hotel. Charles Hayes, Alderman Tyrone T. Kenner (3rd) and State Representative Harold Washington (D, Chgo) were on the podium with the congressman when he said, "The pressure on prominent blacks from Mayor Daley's Regular Democratic Organization was overwhelming and partly responsible for the committee's failure to come up with a minimum political war chest of $250,000. I was so moved by the collective hunger of my political respect and power that I spent many a prayerful hour trying to make up my mind."

Charles Hayes' face was flushed, and his voice reflected disappointment and anger when he stepped up to the microphone after Metcalfe finished his statement. Hayes said, "Without the support and sometimes actual resistance by members of the black affluent, the original goal of $500,000 was unrealistic. The total amount of money raised was $187,000, and every dollar will be returned to the donors."

Hayes concluded his remarks with a blistering attack against those affluent blacks who he charged with being controlled by Mayor Richard J. Daley. He then added in a softer tone, "We regret very deeply (Metcalfe's decision). We are convinced that a victory could have been the peoples, if he had decided to run."

In response to a question raised by Ellis Cose of the *Chicago Sun-Times* during a question and answer session at the end of the press conference, Ralph Metcalfe denied that he had been put up by Mayor Daley to draw support away from other black candidates. He also denied that anyone influenced or dealt with him in such a manner that forced him to make his final decision. However, there were political pundits who believed that Metcalfe had used the Committee for a Black Mayor as a leveraging tool to reingratiate himself with the Daley machine and to get his lost patronage back.

Two months had not passed before Metcalfe, who had declined to run under the banner of the Committee for a Black Mayor, endorsed Alderman William S. Singer as his choice to run in the February 25 Democratic mayoral primary. U.S. Representative Ralph Metcalfe said he had "broken with Daley and his regular Democrats because despite potential promises for the last twenty years, we remained the nation's most segregated urban area and suffered all the resulting plagues of systematic discrimination."

Metcalfe further said he was endorsing Forty-third Ward Alderman Singer, a white, over the only black candidate in the Democratic mayor's race, State Senator Richard Newhouse, because he did not support Newhouse's position on several issues. Metcalf added, "I can't conceive of a man running this city who doesn't support the ERA." Metcalfe said that he considered State Senator Richard Newhouse a friend but would not support him just because of the fact that he was black. On the other hand, he believed, "Singer can win this uphill battle against Daley with my help in the black community. His record is clear. He has always cast his votes in the city council for human rights and civil reform."

Metcalfe's endorsement of Singer came after Reverend Jesse Jackson, president of Operation PUSH, had hinted that he might back Singer. However, the following week, Reverend Jackson "in a clarification" of his earlier position said that he would not endorse Singer as long as Richard Newhouse was still in the running.

Left: Alderman William Singer, the man who wanted to be mayor and who successfully co-led with Reverend Jesse Jackson a delegation that unseated Mayor Richard J. Daley and his delegates at the 1972 Democratic convention held in Miami, Florida. Right: State Senator Richard H. Newhouse, Jr., an independent Democrat, was the odd man out in the state Senate because Mayor Richard J. Daley's regulars found that Newhouse's voting pattern did not necessarily follow the party line and, therefore, was unpredictable.

Newhouse stayed in the campaign despite Metcalfe's endorsement of Singer and said, "There is nothing devastating about this. It's a little sad. That's all."

Newhouse noted that:

> Metcalfe criticized the Daley regime as 'dictatorial, arrogant and over aged,' yet indicated that he would still support it in the April general election should Singer be defeated in the February primary.
>
> Like Congressman Metcalfe, I also am opposed to the record of Daley's administration. My opinion of it, however, will not change next month. The principal difference between my campaign and that of Metcalfe (Alderman Anna Langford and Singer combined) is simply this, they propose that someone new slice the present political pie, while I plan to bake an entirely new pie using black, white and brown ingredients from all of Chicago's communities.

In the February 25th primary, Senator Richard Newhouse came in third behind Richard J. Daley and Bill Singer. However, Newhouse beat former State's Attorney Edward V. Hanrahan, who had scraped the bottom of the political barrel in what he had hoped would be his last hurrah.

Congressman Ralph H. Metcalfe's endorsement of Alderman "Bill" Singer as a candidate to oppose Mayor Richard J. Daley in the mayoral primary election was the last straw in a bundle of straws needed to break the donkey's back. Daley was outraged and wounded by the congressman's actions and thus became determined to put the name of Ralph H. Metcalfe on the list of the unemployed.

Daley had given Metcalfe an early warning of things to come when he stripped him of his Third Ward patronage and switched it to Alderman Tyrone Kenner. When Edward Vrdolyak rebelled in 1974 against Daley and ran for Cook County Assessor opposite Tom Tully, the organization's man, Daley did not lift a finger. The same was true of Vito Marzullo when in 1972 he violated the machine tradition and threw his ward to Richard Nixon instead of the Democratic candidate. The Democratic Organization had an unwritten code which stated that independent Negroes need not apply. Metcalfe violated that rule when he vehemently protested against police brutality in the black community.

Daley's shadow was cast on the wall of the Third Ward when Kenner had a "high noon showdown" with Metcalfe over Metcalfe's endorsement of William Singer. Alderman Kenner displayed his defiance of the congressman with Daley's blessings when he moved out of the Regular Third Ward Organization headquarters at 45 E. 47th Street into his own Democratic quarters at 202 E. 51st Street. Most of the jobs and the precinct captains went with Kenner. Hence, Metcalfe did not have enough volunteer workers to carry Singer in his own Third Ward. The clout and the manpower were gone, and Metcalfe ceased to be even a silhouette of a ward "boss."

Inspite of his political impotence, Metcalfe maintained that he would run for ward committeeman in 1976 and fight to get his patronage back. Moreover, he indicated that he intended to run for Congress again regardless of whether the regular organization supported him. The congressman had good reason to believe that Daley would not support him in the 1976 campaign because in 1974 the organization put on an intensive search for someone to run against him. Several high profile names were mentioned and then buried because the polls showed anyone who ran against Ralph would be committing political suicide in the black community because the congressman was at the height of his political popularity as a result of his fight with Daley and James Conlisk over the police brutality issue.

Metcalfe did not lose the faith although he was carrying two visible crosses. On his left shoulder, he carried the burden of the loss of several hundred patronage workers and on his right shoulder, a federal indictment as a result of an Internal Revenue investigation growing out of alleged zoning bribes paid to him when he was the chairman of the zoning committee. The Internal Revenue investigation ran parallel with Metcalfe's public criticism of the police brutality that Mayor Daley's "boys in blue" were meting out in the black community. A city hall houseboy said that Mayor Richard J. Daley literally blew a fuse when federal prosecutor Sam Skinner dropped the indictment against Congressman Metcalfe on April 16, 1976 because of the statute of limitations.

In the fall of 1975, Mayor Richard J. Daley selected Erwin France as the organizational candidate to unseat Congressman Ralph Metcalfe. France had all of the prerequisites to succeed in his assignment. He was young, bright and very articulate, in addition to having an excellent stage presence. His only negative was the fact that he did not have good name recognition. On the other hand, Metcalfe, a world famous Olympic track star, was a symbol of black political independence. He was bigger than life, a Nat Turner leading a political revolt from the plantation of Mayor Richard J. Daley.

In response to Metcalfe leading a revolt from Daley's plantation, Erwin France is quoted in Vernon Jarrett's *Chicago Tribune* column, dated January 22, 1976, as saying:

> My opponent (Metcalfe) has confessed that he has spent most of his political life as an Uncle Tom. But now he poses as an independent militant. I say he has not changed. He's neither an independent nor a militant.
>
> If it is true, as Metcalfe says, that our party is a plantation, then all he is doing is trying to lead black folk from one plantation to another, a worse one, a plantation bossed by Governor Dan Walker and William Singer, his behind-the-scene sponsors and mentors.

Erwin France, the brilliant young Turk who was selected to run on a political fast track against Congressman Ralph Metcalfe, the old political war horse. The race was a repeat of the 1936 Olympics, Metcalfe won the gold.

When the question of name recognition came up in a political forum, Erwin France always pointed his finger at the nine ward committeemen who selected him on November 20, 1975 as opposed to Metcalfe to run on the regular Democratic ticket in the First Congressional District. Erwin France said, "It is the job of the nine ward committeemen in my district to make my name synonymous with my record. If Ralph wins, the message is that nine political leaders working together couldn't beat one man." The implication of France's remarks was that if Metcalfe won, there would be a post-election bloodletting and the onus would fall on the heads of the ward leaders and not on him.

"I am different from the nine ward committeemen. I don't control patronage; I have no precinct captains. My winning depends upon how well the volunteer ward leaders do their jobs," Congressman Metcalfe said.

As for Metcalfe symbolizing the free black spirit, Erwin France said that the political race had nothing to do with symbols and that "It's a simple matter of winning, so the winner can divide up the political pie, like in football, where friends play on opposite teams. Sometimes you work like hell to beat somebody you like." *(Metcalfe and France were fraternity brothers; both were members of Alpha Phi Alpha Fraternity, Inc.)*

France further stated that, "Symbolism confuses people. Too many people think this is a Metcalfe versus Mayor Daley race rather than a France versus Metcalfe race."

In his crusade for freedom and liberation, Metcalfe consistently stated his main opposition was Mayor Daley's machine and not Erwin France. He characterized France as a tool of the machine and Daley as his real opponent.

The day of reckoning came on Tuesday, March 16, 1976. Metcalfe beat France by a landslide victory. He received seventy-one percent of the vote against twenty-nine percent for Erwin France. It was the first time in history that anybody, black or white, had beaten the organization in a congressional primary or general election.

A wall-to-wall crowd awaited the arrival of the victor at the election night headquarters, which was located at 4859 S. Wabash Avenue. It was shortly after 10 P.M. when Metcalfe appeared amidst thunderous cheers and applause. As his bodyguards crowbarred a passageway to the stage for the conquering hero, the cheers swelled to elephant size and did not subside until Congressman Metcalfe commenced his softly spoken greetings, "My brothers and sisters, it is a great moment in history that you have written tonight."

His hands trembled, his eyes filled with tears and his voice yielded to an emotion that most men try to hide. Metcalfe paused a few minutes to gain his composure and then said, "This is a peoples' victory. It could not have happened without the grace of God almighty. It gave us the opportunity to say, we will be free."

There were chants of freedom and more applause as Metcalfe continued his speech. "Starting tonight, we will have a new day. This is our victory."

It was Reverend Jesse Louis Jackson who captured and outlined the issues of the campaign between Metcalfe and Mayor Daley with the chant that he led: "Down with Daley. Up with Metcalfe. Down with slavery. Up with freedom. I am somebody."

Attorney Thomas N. Todd, chairman of Metcalfe's campaign committee, called the victory "a reawakening of some of the spirit that had fueled the movement." Todd further noted, "Too often blacks have taken victory as an end in itself and are dissatisfied with a good feeling. If we're going to make any shift in power in 1979, we must begin tonight. We must stop rejoicing and get to work in building coalitions and organizations."

A week after the election, U.S. Representative Ralph Metcalfe observed, "It was not an empty victory. The people have spoken. They want to be free." Metcalfe continued, "People did not like the idea of Daley sending a puppet to destroy another man. And that sentiment was nationwide, going far beyond the boundaries of the First Congressional District." The people's victory gave Metcalfe a refueling to renew his feud with the mayor over police brutality. He accused Mayor Daley of practicing racism.

Within hours after the death of Mayor Richard J. Daley, on December 20, 1976, racism in its rawest form unmasked and displayed itself through the antebellum behavior of the white majority members in the Chicago City Council. Alderman Wilson Frost, president pro tem of the city council, thought that

Alderman Wilson Frost, the man that many feel should have been Chicago's first black mayor following Richard J. Daley's demise.

the conventional constitutional procedure would automatically elevate him to the position of acting mayor. Hence, the evening that Daley died, Frost publicly announced that he was the acting mayor of the city of Chicago. William R. Quinlan, the city's corporation counsel disputed Frost's contention and said that there was no specific statute outlining the order of succession and that the city council would have to elect an acting mayor from its membership.

Alderman Wilson Frost, in his rebuttal to Quinlan's argument said:

> I am the mayor of Chicago because of the way the law is structured in Illinois. All municipal bodies must have continuity. When Mayor Daley died, I was the only person who had the power to call a meeting and as the president pro tem, I am the only person who can preside over that meeting. Therefore, I am in fact the mayor until the city council holds its first meeting to elect one of its members as interim mayor. As a matter of fact, after Mayor Daley recovered from his stroke two years ago, he called me into his office and said, 'If I had died, you would be here now,' meaning that I would be sitting in the mayor's chair.

Daley's political old guards spit in mass in the collective faces of the black voters when they had members of the Chicago Police Department forcefully turned Frost away from the door of the mayoral fifth floor suite when he presented himself as the acting mayor. The old guards did not want a black man to even entertain the notion that he was the acting mayor of Abe Lincoln's city by the lake.

The black community was spitting fire over the way Frost was being treated by the city hall storm troopers. Gus Savage, congressman of the Second District in Illinois since 1981 and pioneer political and civil rights activist, felt the heat of the fire spitters and decided that the time was ripe for a black mayor. Savage went to Wilson Frost and said:

> You have the right credentials, and there's a momentum in the black community to support your candidacy. If you give me permission and your word that you will stand up to the end, I'll go out and mobilize the entire black community in your behalf. You won't have to lift a finger or spend a dime. Frost agreed.
>
> On Wednesday evening, December 22, we packed people into the Roberts Motel's 500 Room like sardines. The crowd was a mixture of both regulars and independents. People did not believe that Frost was going to come until I brought him through the back door. Frost did not want to come through the front door because there were a large number of reporters out there awaiting his arrival, and he didn't want to answer any questions.
>
> On Thursday morning, December 23, State Representative Harold Washington (D-26), State Senator Elect Earlean Collins (D-9), and I went to

Roberts Motel at 301 East 63rd Street was the site of a Frost for Mayor Rally. The motel facilities were used frequently by the Committee for a Black Mayor to hold meetings and interview potential candidates.

Alderman Edward Vrdolyak's office and attempted to persuade him to support Wilson Frost. The meeting erupted into a shouting match with Vrdolyak screaming, 'You are not going to come and threaten me in my office!'

On Monday, December 27, at 11 A.M., Harry Golden, of the *Chicago Sun-Times*, called me at home from the pressroom at City Hall and said, 'What's your rationale for Frost not running for mayor?

I replied, 'That's not what he said at a public mass meeting we held at Roberts Motel last Wednesday.'

Bob Lucas, who was at my house when Golden called, and I immediately organized a delegation that included Renault Robinson, of the Afro-American Patrolman's League; Tommy Briscoe, of the Coalition of Black Trade Unionists; and Ed Smith and Danny Davis, of the Westside Coalition for Unity. We went directly to Frost's office at City Hall where we confronted him.

I said, 'I heard that you have decided not to run for mayor. If that is the case, you're going to embarrass us because we have organized to have the City Hall chambers packed tomorrow.'

Frost replied, 'You got me wrong Gus.'

I retorted, 'Remember, all I asked you to do man is to stand up.'

Frost snapped back, 'That's right. And I intend to stick with my promise.'

Shortly after one o'clock on Monday, December 27, U.S. Representative Metcalfe met with Frost. Metcalfe, in turn, told reporters when he came out of the meeting with Frost that Frost had not agreed to a compromise. The white lawyers who were present when Metcalfe spoke to the reporters said that Frost had. Frost's lawyer, Jerome Torshen, said Frost had shaken hands on a deal. Reverend Jesse L. Jackson, head of Operation PUSH, visited Frost later that Monday afternoon with another delegation of blacks and later said to reporters, "There's no deal. Frost just told me he had never agreed to a deal."

In fact, an agreement had been reached on Sunday, December 26, in a seven and one half hour closed door marathon negotiating session involving members of the late mayor's palace guards. The meeting took place between two casts of characters in separate offices who bargained by telephone for the choice leadership position in the post Daley era. At City Hall, 129 N. LaSalle, were Corporation Counsel William R. Quinlan, patronage chief Thomas R. Donovan, Aldermen Fred B. Roti (1st) and Michael Bilandic (11th), who was then the finance committee chairman. In the law offices of Alderman Edward M. Burke (14th) at 39 S. LaSalle, were Burke, Aldermen Wilson Frost, Edward R. Vrdolyak (10th), Vito Marzullo (25th), Terry M. Gabinski (41st) and two of Frost's lawyers.

Below: Alderman Edward Burke, a young Turk in the shadow of Daley's old guard. Right: Alderman Edward Vrdolyak, the leader of the young turks' coffee rebellion in 1974.

After the political air cleared in mid evening on that smoky Sunday, everybody seemed set for a smooth transition at the upcoming Tuesday's council meeting: Bilandic would get the acting mayor's job with the understanding that he would not be a contender in the special mayoral race; Frost would take the chairmansip of finance; Vrdolyak would submerge, at least for the time being, his ambitions, for something higher and would become the president pro tem of the council, which was Frost's present post; and the sizeable Polish block would be mollified by being promised that their man would become vice mayor upon approval of the new post by the city council. It was also assumed that the new office of vice mayor would resolve the succession dilemma.

By 6 P.M. Monday, December 27, rumors of a Frost deal were thicker than a London fog. In response to a reporter's questions about the rumors, Reverend Jackson expressed the consensus of the black community.

> We are not concerned with a back room deal. For the black community, there are three options. One is to accept the humiliation of being dealt out. The second is for a group of people to have a back room meeting and give us something less than that which we deserve. Third is for us to line up our friends across racial lines in the council meeting tomorrow and to emerge victorious. It appears that the constituency of Alderman Wilson Frost and the Democratic party are on a collision course.

Contrary to what Wilson Frost had told Metcalfe, Jackson and Savage in his offices on the second floor of City Hall that Monday, there was physical evidence on the fifth floor that indicated that a deal had been made. The policemen who had been stationed at the double doors of the late Mayor Daley's suite on Christmas Eve had been removed, and the doors were unlocked and ajar. Folk working in the general area of the late mayor's office appeared to be very relaxed as opposed to being tense and agitated.

On Tuesday, the twenty-eighth, when the city council convened, Frost refused to stand up, and the deal that was negotiated with the palace guards on Sunday was put in place inspite of the threats by leaders of the black community to revolt from the Democratic party. Alderman Michael Bilandic was elected acting mayor by the city council by a lopsided vote of 45 to 2. Two policemen, one white and one black, were assigned to watch Gus Savage during the council meeting and to arrest him if he attempted to start a demonstration. The black officer confided to Savage that he was ashamed of his assignment.

Left: Alderman Michael Bilandic was elected acting mayor by the Chicago City Council eight days after Daley's death and was subsequently elected mayor of Chicago in a special election held in June 1977. Right: Vernon Jarrett, Chicago Sun-Times *columnist, television talk host on* Face to Face, *and a political commentator for ABC News (Chicago).*

After the council meeting, Frost said, "Why should I be the one to take the suicidal leap?" Vernon Jarrett, the political analyst, noted in his column in the *Chicago Tribune* on December 29, 1976, "What a sad reflection on the entire spectrum of black leadership that a black man would consider such a harmless move 'suicidal' in Chicago in 1976." Frost gave the following reasons for not committing political suicide on the floor of the city council:

> I could not muster more than nineteen votes out of forty-eight, and I needed twenty-five votes to be elected acting mayor. Therefore, I worked out an accord to accept the chairmanship of the finance committee which is the most powerful committee in the city council. On the other hand, I could have gone to the council floor fighting like a lot of people wanted me to do, but I would not have come out with any benefit other than knowing that I gave some people a good feeling.

Leaders of black community groups immediately reacted to Alderman Wilson Frost's accord with the Daley loyalists at a mass meeting held on Tuesday evening, at 7 P.M. in the Progressive Community Church, located at 56 E. 48th Street. Gus Savage, one of the organizers of the mass meeting, expressed his disappointment:

> I am deeply disappointed that Alderman Wilson Frost refused to stand for election this morning in the city council for the office of acting mayor of

Chicago. In his refusal to stand, he completely violated a solemn and specific pledge he made to a delegation of leaders who are present here tonight and who met with him Monday. We asked specifically, twice, would he stand Tuesday for election by the city council for the post of acting mayor, regardless of pressures of the office or lack of sufficient support to win. Twice, he replied, 'Yes!'

We were mobilized, particularly to oppose efforts to deny Frost the post because of his race. In general, we stand for the principle that political authority must be fairly shared by all minorities who make up Chicago's population, or these minorities will not be able to equally fulfill their responsibilities of citizenship.

Hence, the principle we support goes beyond the person we supported. Frost's failure to stand up this morning did not end our cause; rather it

The Progressive Community Church, located at 56 E. 48th Street, was the site of most of the mass meetings held by the Committee for a Black Mayor. The church is currently pastored by Reverend B. Herbert Martin, who is the president of the Chicago Branch of the NAACP. Mayor Harold Washington is a parishioner at The Progressive Church.

represented merely the end of our beginning. If the politicians would deny the most qualified person the post of acting mayor because he happened to be black, we propose that the people elect a qualified black as permanent mayor. This is the only effective way to reverse this racist decision. We ask Chicago to be fair.

Savage's emotional report to the people was interrupted by stomping feet and loud applause more than ten times. When the cheering and the applause subsided, Savage continued:

The first alderman to stand up for racism in the council this morning was one whose far southeast side constituencies is at least half black. 'Fast Eddie' Vrdolyak, of the Tenth Ward, placed in nomination Michael Bilandic, of the Eleventh Ward, which includes the late Mayor Daley's Bridgeport residence.

Two of the aldermen who spoke for Bilandic's nomination were black: Bennie Stewart, of the far South Side Twenty-first Ward and Eloise Barden, of the Sixteenth Ward, which includes Englewood.

White Alderman Ross Lathrop, of the Hyde Park Fifth Ward, and Dick Simpson, of the northside Forth-fourth Ward, sought to support Frost, but Roman Puchinski successfully objected on a point of order. Puchinski noted that Frost had not filed with the city clerk a written statement of consent to candidacy as required by the rules adopted by the council Tuesday to govern this election. Frost, presiding as president pro temporary, verified that he had not consented to standing for acting mayor.

Following that scenario, all aldermen (including Lathrop and the thirteen black ones), except white independents Simpson and Marty Oberman, of the near north side Forty-third Ward, voted for Bilandic. The black aldermen even held a press conference before the council meeting to indicate they would not support Frost.

It was wrong for Alderman Wilson Frost to permit prominent blacks and some whites to mobilize public sentiment for him as acting mayor. He appeared at a rally we organized for that purpose at Roberts Motel Wednesday evening of last week and inspired the audience with his apparent commitment to seeking the post.

Frost is not the main culprit. However, he should have stood, although he would not have won. The bitter and aging culprit is racism.

Racism brings to mind a question that was raised by a young white woman reporter earlier today. She asked me how I felt about Frost. I replied, 'Why don't you ask me how I feel about Vrdolyak, Stewart, Marzullo, Laskowski, Natarus and Cohen, who lead the fight against Frost running?' They, more than Frost, represent the main problem of racism.

I am distressed but not deterred. We can overcome by June at the special election expected to be announced by the council next Thursday. Let's let today's disappointment become a springboard for justice. Racism seriously aggravates the ills of our city. Hence, it harms us all, whites as well as blacks, and latinos. Be fair Chicago!

All of the people in that jam-packed auditorium jumped to their feet at the conclusion of Savage's statement and gave him a six minute standing ovation.

Following Gus Savage's report, State Representative Harold Washington introduced a resolution to elect Chicago's first black mayor in the 1977 special mayoral election. The motion to adopt the resolution was seconded by trade unionist Tommy Briscoe.

Specifically, the resolution called for the grassroot organization to: 1) select a search committee that would identify one or more qualified candidates; 2) present the candidates to the group on January 13, 1977, the date of the next public meeting; 3) organize a citizen's committee to raise funds and 4) mobilize to turn out the vote, particularly in the black wards, to elect a black mayor.

Representative Washington, who was one of many politicians, businessmen and civic leaders to attend the rally, said, "The resolution is a major move to set in motion a new direction for Chicago's minority population."

U.S. Representative Ralph Metcalfe (D-1st) urged for black unity, "a goal that has long passed us. We have paid our dues, and now it's collection time."

Reverend Jesse Jackson, national president of Operation PUSH, spoke of the resolution as, "a six month date with destiny. Nobody will save us from us for us but us. Therefore, the singular goal of the black community should be to elect a black mayor." Like many other black leaders, Reverend Jackson contended that Alderman Frost was denied his rightful position as acting mayor because of his race. "He should have challenged the council's racism," Jackson said. As a result of Frost's decision not to run for acting mayor, Reverend Jackson termed Frost's move, "a measure of embarrassment" for the entire black community. "We should have lost the vote without losing our respect," Jackson contended.

Following the mass meeting, State Representative Jesse Madison and Renault Robinson, along with a group of prominent business persons, were charged with finding one or more candidates for mayor and presenting them at a public conference to be held no later than January 13, 1977.

In less than a week, the Committee for a Black Mayor came up with three names: Cecil Partee, Richard Newhouse and Renault Robinson. Most surprising of the three was Robinson because he had never entered a political campaign. Yet Robinson had earned more respect at the grassroots level of the black community than perhaps any other leader in Chicago because of his nine year struggle against racial discrimination in the Chicago Police Department.

On Sunday night, January 2, a self-destruct explosion in the Committee for a Black Mayor was barely avoided when the group voted 12 to 13 to allow committee membership to several angry persons that showed up for the meeting, who had originally been excluded. Those voting against accepting the additional members cited problems of "manageability and possible troublemakers." Renault Robinson cast the deciding vote that granted membership to additional participants in the committee's deliberations.

Renault Robinson, the chairman of the committee, came under a lot of pressure from prominent black leaders because of the size of the selection committee. Robinson resigned rather than reduce the size of the body. The resignation of the chairman effectively put the broad based eighty member committee out of business.

A new nine member selection committee was formed. The new selection committee members were Charles Hayes (chairman), Reverend Jesse Jackson, Barnetta Howell Barrett, Gus Savage, Addie Wyatt, Dempsey J. Travis, Reverend Maceo D. Pembroke, Dr. James Buckner and Nancy Jefferson.

Among those who pressed for this smaller, "more manageable" group were businessmen John H. Johnson, George Johnson, Al Johnson, Alvin Boutte, U.S. Representative Ralph Metcalfe and Edwin (Bill) Berry. These leaders favored the smaller committee's structure because they felt a full public selection would lead to confusion, dissension and hurt feelings.

On January 12, 1977, the nine members of the selection committee received the following telegram:

On Saturday, January 15, from 3 to 8 P.M. at Roberts Motel, 301 E. 63rd Street, in Rooms 119 and 120, our committee will meet to interview possible candidates for mayor. Your presence is urgently needed because we must complete our report on that date. Notices have been sent to all remaining prospective candidates on our list. If you have any suggestions as to additions to the list, please notify them to be present between the hours of 3 and 8 P.M. on Saturday, January 15, 1977.

The suggested names to be called for mayoral interviews were Warren Bacon, Dempsey Travis, Alvin Boutte, Roland Burris, Thomas N. Todd, Renault Robinson, Harold Washington, Richard Newhouse, Cecil Partee, Wilson Frost, Addie Wyatt, Erwin France, Louise Quarles Lawson, George Sims, Jesse Jackson, James Montgomery, E. Duke McNeil, Jesse Madison, Leon Davis, Ralph Metcalfe and Robert Tucker.

Alvin Boutte, co-chairman of the Committee for a Black Mayor, and currently chairman of the board of the Independence Bank.

On January 12, 1977, the following letter was also received by the committee:

To: All members of the Committee for a Black Mayor

Dear Member:
Our group is reconvening at 4 P.M. on Monday, January 17, at Johnson Publishing Company, 820 S. Michigan Avenue to hear a report from the committee which was given the responsibility to seek the name of a suitable candidate that we could support for mayor of the city of Chicago. Please set aside two hours of your precious time to be in attendance at this meeting.
Sincerely yours,

Charles Hayes
Co-Chairperson

All of the persons who had been on the suggested list to be interviewed by the members of the Committee for a Black Mayor removed themselves from consideration with the exception of State Senators Harold Washington, Richard Newhouse and Attorney E. Duke McNeil. Harold Washington was the top choice of the low profile search committee of nine chaired by Charles Hayes. And he was also selected by a high profile west side committee headed by Tommy Briscoe and State Representative Jesse Madison. Inasmuch as the selection of Harold Washington as the mayoral candidate was unanimous. The following mailgram was received by each member of the Committee for a Black Mayor and other community leaders on January 20, 1977.

01/19/77   11:00 P.M. EST

Mr. Dempsey J. Travis
840 E. 87th St.
Chicago, IL 60619

We ask you to join us in standing with our candidate for mayor this Friday, January 21, at 7 P.M. in the Progressive Community Church, 56 E. 48th Street. Your participation in this historic occasion is essential to the progress of our community and the city. We look forward to locking arms on the platform with you Friday night.

Alvin J. Boutte and Charles Hayes

U.S. Representative Ralph H. Metcalfe dropped a bombshell on the crusade for a black mayor, five hours before the mass meeting was to take place on Friday, January 21, when he told the *Chicago Sun-Times,* "I have indicated to my associates on the committee that I can not support Harold Washington. We need a candidate who will advance the interest of black people and who will be a good mayor for all the city of Chicago." Metcalfe also said he had "a bill of particulars" against Washington, suggesting that Washington's confrontation with the Internal Revenue Service and a subsequent brief jail sentence made Washington unacceptable to him as a candidate.

At the meeting that evening when Gus Savage, co-chairman with Metcalfe of the Black Leaders Steering Committee, read Metcalfe's comments that appeared in the newspaper to the crowd, there were boos at the mention of Metcalfe's name. Many of the individuals in the audience had supported Metcalfe in his bouts with the Regular Democratic Organization and privately expressed the feeling of betrayal and confusion at Metcalfe's behavior.

Labor leader Charles Hayes attempted to pacify and assure the crowd that Metcalfe had not deserted them for the Regular Democratic Organization. "Ralph is recognized as the top black political leader," Hayes said.

State Representative Washington, the committee's top choice for mayor, in lieu of announcing he was willing and able to run for the office of mayor, pulled his name out of consideration that night before a very disappointed group of people who had come to celebrate the committee's selection.

Washington made the decision because his friend Metcalfe had publicly said he would not support him. Although Washington was obviously stunned by Metcalfe's opposition, Washington made no reference to the congressman in his speech. Instead, he said that the black business leaders had failed to come through with projected finances to fulfill the budget requirement that he thought was necessary to run a successful campaign.

Savage declined to make any further comments about Metcalfe's remarks and instead became very philosophical stating, "We are discouraged but no less determined." On the other hand, Tommy Briscoe, general chairman of the five thousand member Chicago local of the American Postal Workers Union, reacted angrily and said:

> Either Ralph has lost his mind or he's a god-damn fool. He's laying the ground work for the damn machine to make another overture to him. If Metcalfe does not back the black candidate this time, then he will not be elected again. We will defeat him.
>
> The same people who rallied to him and carried him past the Democratic party last year are now backing Washington. We tried to make a statesman out of Ralph. We tried to make him a symbol for black people, but we aren't creating a monster. We can drop him like a hot potato.

On the same day that Metcalfe dropped his bomb on Harold Washington, Edward Vrdolyak sent up a hot air balloon for the mayoral candidacy of Michael Bilandic. In an address to the city club, Alderman Vrdolyak said that the late Mayor Daley told him several times that he wanted Bilandic as his successor. "I have never said this in public before, but as I remember it, the last time he said something like, 'Mike would be a good man for the city of Chicago after I'm gone.' "

Alderman Vrdolyak was one of the Daley loyalists who engineered the negotiations that gave Bilandic the acting mayoral post on December 28, eight days after Daley's death. Mike Bilandic at that time said that he would not run, and he had not altered his position yet. Vrdolyak added, "However, I would hope he will change his mind." Vrdolyak further asserted that Bilandic was the best choice for mayor because, "his idea of a good time is doing research, and he knows the nuts and bolts of the business of running a government."

On Sunday, January 30, Attorney Robert Tucker threw his hat in the ring to run against Bilandic. He announced, "I am a candidate for the office of mayor of the city of Chicago. I promise to bring a new and enlightened leadership." Tucker as always was well-dressed, poised, urbane and articulate. *(Bob is the only man that the author knows who graduated from Tennessee State and Northwestern University Law School and sounds like he was breast fed at*

Attorney Robert Tucker, a man who threw his hat in the ring to become Chicago's first black mayor.

England's Oxford.) Tucker fielded questions from the reporters that Sunday after his mayoral announcement like Hank Aaron, the home run champion, facing a DuSable High School pitcher. In replying to a question about his experience to be mayor, Tucker replied, "As a teacher, lawyer and former assistant regional director of the Department of Housing and Urban Development, I handled a budget of over $400 million a year. The elements of government are by no means foreign to me." When queried about the source of funds for his campaign, Tucker replied, "If one hundred thousand (of the people of Chicago) respond to my call with a single contribution of $10, it will afford me the opportunity to present myself before my people."

Robert Tucker's mayoral campaign barely got off the ground because on Sunday, February 6, 1977, exactly one week after he announced, an article appeared in the *Chicago Tribune* stating that the federal government was seeking an accounting of a $300,000 loan to Tucker and some other businessmen. The money was to promote a plan conceived by Attorney Robert Tucker involving the purchase of real estate. Tucker claimed that the *Tribune* report was misleading. However, shortly after the story appeared, Tucker withdrew from the mayoral campaign.

Following Attorney Robert Tucker's withdrawal of his candidacy for mayor, the following letter was mailed to the Committee for a Black Mayor:

February 25, 1977

Dear Committee member:
You are herein notified that after our selection committee projected the name of Attorney Robert Tucker as our candidate for the office of mayor of the city of Chicago and he subsequently withdrew from the race. This ended the life of our committee.

This will make it unmistakably clear and avoid any possible misunderstanding. Anyone who was a part of our group is free to support whoever they desire for the office of mayor. My tenure as chairperson of the group obviously ended with the dissolution of the committee.

With sincere best wishes, I am very truly yours,

> Charles Hayes
> International Vice President
> Director of District #12
> Director of Organizing

Although Gus Savage had voted with the committee to support Robert Tucker's candidacy, Savage had had a premonition that Tucker was going to drop out of the race shortly before the deadline to file the mayoral petitions. Therefore, Savage, Renault Robinson, Tommy Briscoe, Sid Ordower and Slim Coleman had circulated petitions and had gotten 6,500 names for Harold Washington before Tucker dropped out of the race and without Harold Washington's permission or knowledge.

Senator Harold Washington recalls:

> Gus Savage and Sid Ordower came by my house and told me that they had gotten 6,500 names without my agreeing. I didn't agree. They didn't have any place to go.
>
> So Gus said, 'Look Harold. I will guarantee you that we will do all the work that has to be done. We will raise the necessary money. It won't cost you a dime. All you have to do is continue to breathe and agree to be our candidate.'
>
> I realized several things: 1) Somebody had to do it because the political apparatus in the black community was out of hand. 2) I didn't have anything to lose. 3) I was going to continue to have trouble with the machine because they didn't want me down in Springfield. However, they hadn't at that time made up their mind to take me on. I also realized that I was at a transition point in my life. Either go up or go down. What did I have to lose. Gus Savage and those fellows that I mentioned put the whole thing together. I didn't have to do anything. My first physical act in the 1977 campaign was to go down to a campaign office that Gus Savage had rented, at 6 E. Randolph, which was just above Walgreens drugstore on the northeast corner of State and Randolph. Gus had even had window signs printed with my name on them lying on the floor, and he had also installed a battery of telephones. Gus must have got a real good peek at my hold card. After spending a very brief time in the headquarters, I walked with Savage and a small delegation over to City Hall, had a press conference and filed my petitions.

Harold Washington took his mayoral campaign across the city and spent a great deal of time campaigning on the north side in the Uptown area.

Behind the mayoral campaign, I knew that in 1978 the machine was coming after me with everything including the kitchen sink, and I would have to fight them all. And at the same time, I had to stay in the Senate. So, the 1977 mayoral campaign offered me an opportunity to establish myself in the First District and build. For example, Bob Shaw, who lived in the Ninth, wanted to be alderman. He handled the Ninth Ward for my mayoral campaign. We took the Ninth. Niles Sherman wanted to be the alderman in Twenty-first Ward. We took the Twenty-first Ward. Monica Faith Stewart, who incidentally was running for an open aldermanic spot in the Eighth Ward, and we took that part of the Eighth which was black. Danny Davis over on the west side wanted to be an alderman. However, we didn't take the ward but we got 2,000 votes, which was unheard of. Alderman David Rhodes of the Twenty-fourth Ward was trying to save himself from the Bilandic administration because they were after him. We didn't take the twenty-fourth, but we got 2,500 votes. Gus Savage wanted to be congressman in the Second District, and I campaigned more in the Second District than I did in the rest of the city combined, putting that together. We got 11 percent of the vote and carried five wards. We carried the Fifth, Sixth, Eighth, Twenty-first and Ninth. We almost carried the Seventeenth. We ran well in all of the South Side black wards. And did well on the west side. But nobody really looked at it. It was revolutionary. It was really showing what could been done if you got out there and worked, even if you lost. In 1978, the Democratic machine came after me with everything but the atomic bomb. We won by 139 votes to go back to the Senate that year. They must have spent $150,000 in the Twenty-sixth district, an unheard of amount of dollars for a senatorial district campaign. I wouldn't have survived in the senatorial race had it not been for Cecil Partee and Shannon coming to my rescue. Ralph H. Metcalfe sat on his hands and didn't do one thing to help me. As a matter of fact, he hurt me. We were over the hump. The machine was literally dead on the South Side. There was no question in my mind about it in 1978. Ralph, as you know, had died. And Bennett Stewart was put in his place. The black community had been waiting to get Ralph.

U.S. Representative Ralph H. Metcalfe, the 1936 Olympic gold medal winner and former alderman of the Third Ward died suddenly, in his third floor apartment at 4530 S. Michigan Avenue, of an apparent heart attack on October 9, 1978. Before the funeral arrangements could be made, the local Democrats were pushing to meet the constitutional deadline of eight days to replace his name on the November 7 general election ballot. Bennett Stewart, Cecil Partee and Joseph Bertrand were the names that were frequently mentioned as possible replacements. However, Stewart had unofficially been designated as Metcalfe's successor in a secret meeting held by Mayor Bilandic's patronage chief, Thomas Donovan.

On Monday, October 16, 1978, more than two thousand residents packed the Liberty Baptist Church at 4849 S. King Dr. for the purpose of witnessing and participating in the ward committeemen's selection of Metcalfe's replacement. Samuel Ackerman, First District state central committeeman, chaired the meeting. Ackerman had hoped to allow nine individuals other than the committeemen to address the restless throng, but the regular Democrats quickly shut off participation after the first speaker, Augustus "Gus" Savage, representing black newspaper publishers, shouted, "Above all don't select Bennett Stewart."

Alderman Bennett M. Stewart, Sr. was selected as the candidate by seven committeemen from the First Congressional District to succeed the late Ralph Metcalfe.

When Bennett Stewart's name was put into nomination, more than half the crowd booed and shouted angrily. A large number of the people left the meeting shouting, "We won't vote. . . . vote socialist." Seven of the town ward committeemen voted for Bennett Stewart over County Commissioner John Stroger, Jr., and Loop City College Professor Timuel Black. John Stroger received two votes, his own and one from Joseph Bertrand whereas Timuel Black received one vote from Alan Dobry, independent committeeman from the Fifth Ward. Earlier in the meeting, Dobry had tried to put a motion before the ward committeemen to postpone the election for a replacement when Alderman Tyrone Kenner, who had just been elected earlier that day as a committeeman of the Third Ward by the Ward precinct captains, physically attempted to take the microphone out of Dobry's hands. The hostility between some of the committeemen and between some members of the audience and the committeemen was thick enough to cut with a knife. Senator Harold Washington, who was a Third Ward precinct captain, was seated in the audience that night at Liberty Baptist Church and later made the following observations:

> In 1980, it was very natural for me to run against Bennett Stewart for Congress. We had taken all kinds of polls. The polls showed in a solid five man race I would get 50 percent. In none of the polls did it go up or go down; it stayed at 50 percent. And that's the way it came out. I got 50 percent, and the other three candidates split the balance almost evenly.
>
> The Ronald Reagan thing, probably was as much responsible for me winning as Jane Byrne. There's no question about it. All during the congressional race, blacks kept saying, 'When are you going to run for mayor again?' That question came up all over the place. We took a series of about six polls, and they all showed 90 percent of the blacks in the city would vote for a black mayor unnamed. We started in the First District, were shocked

Commissioner John H. Stroger was one of several candidates who politicked to replace the late Metcalfe in the halls of Congress. Stroger was also the campaign chairman for Mayor Harold Washington when he ran successfully on the orange ballot in 1964 for a seat in the Illinois House of Representatives.

A happy and emotional constituent embraces Congressman-elect Harold Washington, in his campaign headquarters at 640 E. 79th St., upon learning that Washington was overwhelmingly victorious in the November 1980 congressional race against Congressman Stewart. Looking on (at far left) with childish admiration is Bennett Johnson III, son of civil rights activist and publisher Bennett Johnson. Also looking on in the background (wearing dark coat) is former representative Robert Mann; (right to left) unidentified voter; Lois Edwards (wearing headpiece), secretary to both the late Roy Washington, Sr. and Harold Washington; another unidentified voter and Paula Thomas.

with the figures, ran the poll again, and got the same results. We went to the Second District, again the same results. We went to the west side, and the figures were slightly lower. There was no question what was going on out there. The people were very, very angry at both Jane Byrne and Ronald Reagan. And they had not forgotten the treatment meted out to the black community through the way the Wilson Frost matter was handled.

The political frosting that was layered on the black community was one of several reasons why Senator Harold Washington ran for mayor in 1977 when he had no expectations of winning. In addition, there were layers of resentment against the Democratic machine that were beginning to manifest themselves as a movement in at least six South Side wards, and that resentment needed a political exit. In addition, Washington's running could prove that black folk could lose and still not end up on the debit side of the ballot box because out of the 1977 campaign came a group of bright young women and men who became the bedrocks for a large political cadre that subsequently functioned effectively during the 1979 aldermanic campaign, the 1980 congressional race when both Harold Washington and Gus Savage were victorious, and, finally, in 1983 when Harold Washington ascended to the seat that Wilson Frost had been denied because he was black.

Mayor Jane Byrne, 1979–83.

Chapter *XXIV*

The Fire That "Byrned" Down Black Political Apathy

When Chicago's black voters went to bed on New Year's Eve, Sunday, December 31, 1978, they had not been given the slightest warning from the weather forecasters that they would awaken to fifteen inches of snow on New Year's Day, snow that would be instrumental in changing the course of Chicago's political history. It was not until Saturday, January 13, 1979, when an additional twenty inches of snow fell on the city's streets, and people were snowbound and unable to attend church on that Sunday, that the eyes of Chicago's black political giant opened and began to blink and squint at the avalanche of white substance that had imprisoned cars and made the streets and expressways parking lots for thousands of stranded motorists.

Jane Byrne was not unhappy about the record snow fall.

Aileen Byrne, Jane's ex-sister-in-law, called her from Cleveland, Ohio and said, "Janie, I'm praying the snow will stop."

Jane replied, "Please don't do that. Pray that it keeps up."

Unlike Jane Byrne, Mayor Michael Bilandic asked his mother to pray for the snow to stop. To make bad matters worse for Bilandic, Jane Byrne went on the five o'clock news and called Mayor Michael Bilandic "the abominable snowman." She said that all the trash that had been allowed to accumulate in the alleys in the absence of garbage pick ups because of the snow should be piled in one huge stack and called "Mount Bilandic." Jane Byrne trudged through the snow drifts shaking hands with potential voters at taverns, super-markets, shopping centers and el stations where trains did not stop and at bus stops where people waited up to two hours for buses in the lake-chilled winds. She proclaimed to everyone within the sound of her voice that she had a cure for that "white stuff" that had fallen out of the sky and paralyzed the city that used to work.

The city's pharaohs laughed at the pronouncements of Jane "the snow killer," calling her "Crazy Jane." However, the people on the South and west sides of Chicago listened because el trains were passing their regular stops in the black community like bats out of hell loaded with white folk who were enroute to their jobs in Chicago's Loop. The Bilandic administration had displayed total disdain for the black community when it decided that the best way to appease the white Chicago Transit Authority (CTA) riders was to eliminate a number of stops between 95th Street and downtown on the Dan Ryan line and at stations heavily used by blacks on the Lake Street line. The hue and cry from the black community as a result of this racist action must not have been heard in the heavens because the Gods continued to cry snowflakes as the el trains continued passing blacks by.

Jane Byrne's prayers brought a total of eighty-seven inches of snow to Chicago that winter as compared to a norm of thirty-seven inches. Hence, when Jane Byrne, the snow queen, glided into the mayoral office on the tail of the snow storm, the eyes of Chicago's sleeping black political giant did not simply open, but widened with amazement because "Little Janie" had defeated Chicago's invincible political machine in the same way that "Little David" had defeated Goliath. She had accomplished this monumental achievement with very little money and a whole lot of guts and prayer. Her campaign debt was only $75,000 or fifty percent of the money that the machine had spent attempting to defeat Harold Washington in the Twenty-sixth District senatorial race in 1978. The Gods had also sent the black community a message through the blessings that they had bestowed upon Jane Byrne.

Three pages out of the chapter on the blessings of Jane Byrne were told by the Reverend Claude Wyatt and his wife Addie, a union executive and an internationally known women's leader. Addie Wyatt recalls:

> Jane Byrne visited with Charles Hayes and me in our offices in the headquarters of the Amalgamated Meatcutters and Butchers Workman of North America, AFL-CIO, at 2800 N. Sheridan Road. She said she was running for mayor, which is a position, she said, 'that you all (black people) should have, but you can't win it now, and I can. All I want is one term.' When Byrne made her closing statement in a fifteen minute political pitch, I rose from my chair and walked to the elevator with her and said, 'You can win. I will do whatever I can to help you win.'
>
> When Charlie and I talked to our people, some of them were unhappy about our position. However, we believed that supporting Jane Byrne was a step in the right direction towards obtaining our goal, and our goal was to

Addie Wyatt, director of the Civil Rights and Women's Affairs Departments of the United Food and Commercial Worker's International (UFCW) and Charles Hayes, former UFCW International vice president and currently United States Representative for the First Congressional District in Illinois.

ultimately get a black mayor elected in the city of Chicago. We firmly believed that if Jane Byrne would win, black people could win.

We saw a miracle at work during the Jane Byrne campaign. Reverend Claude Wyatt, my husband, and I sat in our living room and watched the snow pile up at our door so high we could not leave the house.

While looking out the window at the snow one day, Claude said, 'Addie, God works miracles all the time. I believe he's going to let the snow keep falling until it's time for election. God has to do something to anger the people enough to make them want to dislodge Mayor Bilandic from office. As a matter of fact, some of my parishioners have called me in the heat of anger to tell me that they can't get to church because they were not able to move their cars. I, in turn, called one of the city administrators and asked, where are the people supposed to put their cars, in their pockets?

When people become angry, they begin to look for something or someone upon whom to vent their feelings. Bilandic was the target. Lo and behold, just a few days before election, the sun began to shine, and the snow began to melt. The snow parted on the sidewalks and in the streets of

Reverend Claude Wyatt, Jr., pastor of Vernon Park Church of God located at 9011 S. Stony Island. Wyatt is a man of the cloth who has consistently been on the right side of the civil rights movement.

Chicago like the water of the Red Sea parted for the children of Israel, and He let my people march to the polls on Tuesday, February 27, 1979, and vote the pharaoh out.'

Jane Byrne defeated Michael Bilandic by only 16,775 votes. However, a statement made by Thomas Coulter, executive director of the Chicago Association of Commerce and Industry, in Bilandic's presence while Coulter addressed the annual luncheon of the association on March 2, 1979 hurt Bilandic as much as his defeat. Coulter said:

Two years ago, the mayor had a big pair of shoes to fill. He did a good job, and he got Chicago moving very well.

But late on New Year's Eve, he came home, took off his shoes, and it snowed. The next morning, those shoes were filled with ice and snow, and he couldn't get them on again.

There was some embarrassed laughter from the crowd of about 2,000 in the International Ballroom of the Conrad Hilton Hotel, but Bilandic did not smile, and his face flushed while Coulter talked.

Frank Considine, the outgoing president, attempted to soften "the below the belt blow" that Coulter had made about the mayor by departing from his prepared text and saying, "The city kept moving, kept operating. Chicago was inconvenienced, yes; slowed, yes; but stopped, no. However, the merchants lost an estimated one and a half billion in sales during those stormy days."

After the luncheon, a misty-eyed Michael Bilandic and his wife Heather, hurriedly left the hotel, brushed by reporters and refused to respond to questions.

Mayor Michael Bilandic was not the only loser in the February 27, 1979 Democratic mayoral primary. Blacks also lost because shortly after Mayor Jane Byrne was sworn into office, on April 16, 1979, she privately embraced Aldermen Edward Vrdolyak, Edward Burke and Charles Swibel, chairman of the Chicago Housing Authority. All were men she had earlier labeled as members of an "evil cabal." She totally ignored the independent aldermen who had supported her and who she had led to believe that they shared the same politics during the political crusade in the "good old snowy times." Moreover, Byrne purposely buried her head in the political sands of City Hall and permitted Aldermen Burke and Vrdolyak, her allegedly former political enemies, to reorganize the city council and gobble up all of the best committee chairmanships for themselves and their City Hall cronies.

The unpredictable behavior of Lady Jane caused many blacks to take a deep nose dive into the attitudinal sea of "you're damned if you do vote and you're damned if you don't vote". This negative mind set hung heavily over the black community as it watched Mayor Byrne dismantle its political dreams and aspirations one by one.

During one of her early political campaign marches across Chicago, Jane Byrne promised that she would demote Police Superintendent James O'Grady when she took office because O'Grady had politicized the police department by supporting Mayor Michael Bilandic. When Jane Byrne took office, the black community justifiably thought that Jane, the snow killer, would replace Superintendent O'Grady with someone from the black community. Byrne did a quarterback side-step and designated Samuel W. Nolan, as acting superintendent and then, subsequently, did a reverse step and replaced Nolan with a white career officer by the name of Richard Brzeczek, a move which was properly interpreted by the black community as racist.

Mayor Byrne was obviously insensitive to the needs and aspirations of the black community. How else could her actions be accounted for? In November, 1979, Joseph Hannon, superintendent of the board of education, resigned. The community leaders asked Mayor Byrne to promote Manford Byrd, Hannon's deputy superintendent. She haughtily turned her back to the entire black community and appointed Angeline Caruso, a white woman who was a subor-

Acting Superintendent of the Chicago Police Department Samuel W. Nolan, currently serving as Chief of the Cook County Sheriff's Police Department.

dinate of Deputy Superintendent Byrd. Dr. Manford Byrd had had the hands-on-experience of actually running the schools as the number two man under two successive superintendents, Superintendent James F. Redmond and Superintendent Joseph Hannon. In addition, he had impeccable educational credentials. And yet, he was denied the position by Mayor Byrne simply because he was black and reflected the heart-felt interest of the people who had given her sixty-three percent of their votes in the mayoral contest.

Byrne's dismantling of blacks' authority continued. In April, 1980, as part of Governor James Thompson's legislative package, Byrne was able to reorganize the board of education. She appointed five blacks and was desirous of having Thomas Ayers, former chief executive officer of Commonwealth Edison as the new president of the board. The black members wanted to select a member from among their own group. Byrne rebelled and called their actions immature. However, it came to the attention of Reverend Al Sampson, a former Martin Luther King disciple, that Thomas Ayers lived in the suburbs and maintained an apartment in the same Gold Coast building where Mayor Byrne lived at 111 East Delaware. With Sampson's non-residential information on Ayers under his arm, Lu Palmer grabbed the torch and led a successful boycott against Ayers' membership on the board. Ayers resigned, and Reverend Kenneth Smith was subsequently elected president. Dr. Ruth B. Love, of Oakland, California, was selected by Byrne over Manford Byrd despite the urgings of Reverend Jesse Jackson and other community leaders for Byrd to become superintendent of the Chicago Public Schools. Both Smith and Love were the first blacks to hold their respective positions of superintendent of schools and president of the board.

Lu Palmer made the following observations about Dr. Love's appointment:

> When they decided to allow a black to become superintendent, they brought
> in a white dude to handle all the money. The first black superintendent
> became the first superintendent who is not allowed to handle the budget.
> Byrne obviously feels that people who don't know how to count their voting
> strength might become confused when it comes to counting money.

In February, 1981, one month after Byrne had selected Ruth Love as
superintendent and Kenneth Smith as president, she announced that she was
replacing Leon Davis and Michael J. Scott, two black members of the board of
education with two white women who had been vocally opposed to desegrega-
tion in the Chicago school system. Her appointee from the northwest side was
Rosemary Janus, and from the southwest side, she appointed Betty Bonow.
These two racist appointments were so repugnant to the black community
that one elderly black woman, Ruby Blackburn said, "Mayor Byrne is a white
woman who does not believe that rice is white, and fat meat is greasy. If she
did, she would not continue to offend black folk the way that she has."

In support of Byrne's appointments, Alderman William Lipinski (23rd) said:

> The southwest side residents have been short changed for years in city ser-
> vices. The appointment of Mrs. Bonow will do little to improve the situation.
> City officials have neglected education, roads and public transportation in
> the area. Those people are entitled to representation because they make up
> thirty-five percent of the city's population and fourteen percent of the public
> school enrollment.

*Lu Palmer, journalist,
radio commentator, a
popular and highly
respected host on
WVON's* On Target *Talk
Show, and a political ac-
tivist extraordinaire.*

Leon Davis retorted, "But they already have representation on the board from the southwest and the northwest sides in Raul Villalobos and Martha Jantho." However, Lipinski felt that neither of those persons spoke for the views of the white ethnic.

On Friday, February 11, three black elected officials held a press conference at City Hall to protest the appointment of the two white women. U.S. Representative Harold Washington (D, Chgo) expressed concern that Dr. Ruth B. Love, who was expected in Chicago on March 25th to become the school superintendent, might reconsider and back off. "I hope Ms. Love doesn't get cold feet and think this is a political quagmire," he said. "This is a kick in the stomach to this wonderful black woman," he continued.

State Senator Richard Newhouse (D,Chgo) and State Representative Carol Moseley Braun (D, Chgo), who joined Washington at the press conference and were instrumental in passing the Chicago Public Schools' financial bail out legislation, said there was no intention to limit board members to one term as Mayor Byrne had contended when she announced that she was replacing Davis and Scott.

"Unconscionable," said James Compton, head of the Chicago Urban League. "Mayor Byrne has once again shown insensitivity to Chicago's blacks by replacing those who have served the board in good stead. To appoint a woman who is embroiled with the "Schochley mentality" and one who is a known leader of the segregated Bogan community is a slap in the face," reiterated Compton.

While Jane Byrne was politically castigating the black community, there were many blacks who were not just sitting around on their hands singing the "Jane Byrne blues." There were a number of community organizers making plans to do battle with the administration. Lu Palmer, the popular radio commentator, had organized a group called Black Men's Forum that met at the Center of Inner City Studies. Lu Palmer said:

> While Jane Byrne was politically castigating the black community, the Black Men's Forum was thinking of ways to give her an early retirement. One evening the group was discussing the subject of who was making input on the new school board that Jane Byrne had been mandated to put together as part of the state's requirements in the Chicago Board of Education bail out agreement. To our surprise, we found that the only input coming from the black community was through the Chicago Urban League and Chicago United. Both groups are definitely stacked against any political activitists participating. Therefore, we decided that we were not going to let Jane Byrne get away without grass roots input. Therefore, we decided that we would call all of the black organizations together. We then went to Harold Washington and asked him to formally head the group. He was then in the

state senate. A meeting was called, and we met in the parish house of the Bethel A.M.E. Church at 4448 S. Michigan Avenue. We must have had representatives from twenty to twenty-five organizations. And we came out of that meeting with our list of nominees to the school board, which we took to Jane Byrne. It was the first time I had ever seen the woman. I don't think she selected more than one or two individuals from our list, and they were people who were on the Urban League's list. Therefore, I concluded that she took our two people simply because the Urban League had already selected them. Another decision that came out of that meeting was an agreement to become permanent and call ourselves the Chicago Black United Communities (CBUC). One of our first 1981 goals in the organization was to elect a black mayor in 1983. Hence, the slogan, 'We Shall See In '83.' However, 'We Shall See In '83' was more than a slogan, it was a theme upon which to build a political movement.

In the fall of 1981, CBUC started a political education clinic in the coach house located at 330 E. 37th Street, which is directly behind my home at 3656 S. Martin Luther King Drive.

Lu Palmer was in an excellent position to promote CBUC's educational program because he made radio commentaries on a show entitled *Lu's Notebook* twice a day over four black-oriented stations five days a week in addition to hosting a two-hour talk show called *On Target* one night a week on local radio station WVON (1450 AM). Palmer always ended each program with, "We Shall See In '83." Lu's objective in repeating the slogan was to change the mindset of black folk about the dream of having a black mayor to actually electing one.

Mayor Jane Byrne must have thought that Lu Palmer's "We Shall See In '83" was a Negro nursery rhyme and not a threat because she continued cannibalizing black folk. On April 15, 1981, Byrne's aldermanic appointee, Allan Streeter of the Seventeenth Ward met with Mayor Byrne and told her that the black community was opposed to his earlier vote in the Education Committee supporting the Bonow-Janus appointments. Therefore, he could not vote for those nominations when they came up before the full city council despite the continuing pressure from his ward committeeman, William Parker. Streeter stuck by his guns when the two women's appointments came before the council, and Mayor Byrne sharpened her political ax and went for Streeter's scalp. Streeter expressed his reaction to Byrne's vindictiveness, "When race is involved, the machine does not ask for a compromise. The party wants us (the blacks) to sell our souls and give up our self respect for what the white bosses want. I just can't take it."

In January, 1982, a federal court ruled that a special election had to be held in the Seventeenth Ward to fill the remainder of the four year term for which

Allan Streeter had been appointed as a result of the resignation of Tyrone McFolling. The ruling gave Mayor Byrne an opportunity to hold a public lynching with Allan Streeter as the lynchee, and thereby exhibiting him for other colored folk who might entertain any notions about wandering off the plantation. To make sure that Allan Streeter's political lynching took place after sundown on June 1, 1982 at the special election, Byrne sent in a patronage lynch mob from the Third, Ninth, Fifteenth, Sixteenth, Twenty-first and Thirty-fourth Wards to select the tree, the rope and witnesses for the hanging.

The Byrne mob did not succeed in the political lynching of Allan Streeter on June 1 because Streeter outran a field of nine political bloodhounds and put some daylight between himself and the howling pack with the blocking assistance of Lu Palmer and seven hundred of his trained Chicago Black United Communities workers (CBUC). A special run-off election was called for June 29 since Streeter did not get fifty percent of the votes on June 1. The day before the special run-off, Streeter held a press conference at City Hall and charged that Alderman Edward Vrdolyak and the political machine were offering a $3,000 reward to anyone who won their precinct away from Streeter. One June 29, the CBUC campaign workers for Streeter asked voters, "Would you take a few minutes to help the man who stood up to Jane Byrne?" The answer was loud and clear as Streeter ended the day with more than a two thousand vote lead and fifty-six percent of the total ballots cast.

A black majority in the Seventeenth Ward made Allan Streeter's victory possible. The 1980 population census data had shown that blacks were in the majority in nineteen wards. Therefore, to minimize future black insurrections, Mayor Jane Byrne's chairman of the Committee on Committees and Rules, Alderman Thomas Casey (37), called upon his old friend Thomas Keane, a

Former Alderman Thomas P. Keane was the number two man during the Daley administration, chairman of the Finance Committee and also mayor Daley's floor leader.

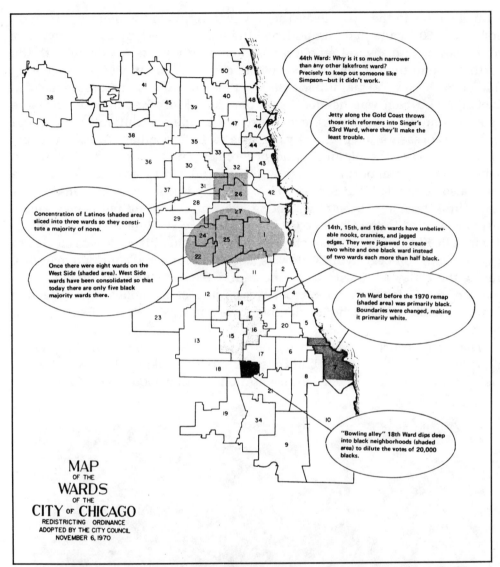

44th Ward: Why is it so much narrower than any other lakefront ward? Precisely to keep out someone like Simpson—but it didn't work.

Jetty along the Gold Coast throws those rich reformers into Singer's 43rd Ward, where they'll make the least trouble.

Concentration of Latinos (shaded area) sliced into three wards so they constitute a majority of none.

14th, 15th, and 16th wards have unbelievable nooks, crannies, and jagged edges. They were jigsawed to create two white and one black ward instead of two wards each more than half black.

Once there were eight wards on the West Side (shaded area). West Side wards have been consolidated so that today there are only five black majority wards there.

7th Ward before the 1970 remap (shaded area) was primarily black. Boundaries were changed, making it primarily white.

"Bowling alley" 18th Ward dips deep into black neighborhoods (shaded area) to dilute the votes of 20,000 blacks.

MAP
OF THE
WARDS
OF THE
CITY OF CHICAGO
REDISTRICTING ORDINANCE
ADOPTED BY THE CITY COUNCIL
NOVEMBER 6, 1970

A redistricting map, prepared and approved by the majority of both the black and white members of the city council. The map effectively diluted the black and hispanic communities of proper representation in the city council through gerrymandering.

brilliant former Chicago city alderman and lawyer who had recently been released from the federal penitentiary after serving a sentence for mail fraud, to design a map similar to the one that he had designed in 1970 that retrograded the black and hispanic voting power. Thomas Keane's new creation reduced the nineteen majority black wards to seventeen by extending the ward boundaries of the Fifteenth and Thirty-seventh Wards and adding enough whites to the two wards, thereby making them the majority. In addition, the 1980 Keane map "impotized" the hispanic vote by dispersing their voting power into several adjoining predominantly white wards on both the northwest and the southwest sides of the city. The remap was subsequently challenged by several plaintiffs, including the Political Action Conference of Illinois (PAC), which was headed by Al Johnson, Mars Ketchum, Charmaine Velaseo, and others. All were concerned about the dissolution of black and hispanic representation in the city of Chicago. In December of 1982, the court ruled in favor of the plaintiffs and ordered a new map drawn that would restore the black majorities in the Fifteenth and Thirty-seventh Wards. The court also demanded that four hispanic majority wards be created in the new map. Until the filing of the redistricting law suit, there had not been a single hispanic elected to the Chicago City Council since William Rodriquez left office in 1915. Fifty-one years had elapsed before another hispanic was elected to any municipal office. David Cerda was elected a municipal court judge in 1966 during the Daley administration, and Maria B. Cerda was appointed to the board of the Chicago Public School system in 1969 to replace Mrs. Wendell Green, a black woman who incidently like Maria was the wife of a municipal judge.

The remap court fight was long overdue because there was an abundance of evidence that showed how blatant white city council members had been in their efforts to limit black representation in that body. Dr. Charles R.

Maria B. Cerda, former member of the board of the Chicago Public School System and currently director of the Mayor's Office of Employment and Training.

Judson Miner, was one of the lead lawyers in the remap case, a former president of the Chicago Council of Lawyers and was appointed by Mayor Harold Washington in January 1986 as the Corporation Counsel for the city of Chicago.

Branham, a historian and expert witness for the remap plaintiffs, testified that the history of politics in Chicago had been characterized by a dominant-subordinate relationship between white and black politicians. His testimony also revealed a continuing pattern of white manipulation of the political process that deprived blacks of equal opportunity in both the public and private sectors. Judson Minor, one of several lawyers for the plaintifs, presented numerous exhibits showing evidence of retrogression of black voting strength in particular wards as well as citywide. Census data supported the fact that, in 1970, the Thirty-seventh, Fifteenth, Ninth and Seventh Wards had a majority white population, but in 1980 the majority had become black. However, the remap prepared by members of Jane Byrne's city council, with the assistance of Thomas Keane, showed that the black majority had been chipped away as revealed in the exhibit below.

Wards	% of Black Pop. '70	% of Black Pop. '80 old wards	% of Black Pop. '80 new remapped wards	Race of incumbent aldermen at time of redistricting
37th	12.5	76.3	36.8	White
15th	8.3	66.4	41.7	White
9th	28.3	49.3	46.4	White
7th	26.9	62.6	58.4	Black

The blatant racism employed by the city council and its lawyers in drawing the remap is obvious in the above chart.

The defendants in the redistricting litigation were the city council of the city of Chicago; the Board of Election commissioners of Chicago; Martin R.

Murphy, former commissioner of the city's Department of Planning; Thomas E. Keane and Mayor Jane N. Byrne. Byrne, Murphy and Keane were dismissed at the end of the plaintiff's case. However, the lawyers for the plaintiffs felt that the court's decision was erroneous, though the decision was not appealed.

Mayor Byrne burned the black community again in July 1982 when she made the decision to place three white individuals on the board of the Chicago Housing Authority, thus giving them the majority vote in matters that affected the ninety percent black majority of the 144,000 CHA residents. Mayor Byrne's decision showed an absolute and total disregard for the wishes, aspirations and feelings of the residents, and their leaders. Lu Palmer, Dorothy Tillman and Marion Stamps made immediate preparations to protest the Byrne appointment of Andrew J. Mooney, age 30, as the new chairman appointed to serve until July 14, 1987. Mooney was replacing the Housing and Urban Development Department (HUD) embattled Charles Swibel, a multi-millionaire real estate dealer and chief crony of Mayor Jane Byrne, who had come under a scathing attack by HUD in a report issued in April 1982. The report accused Swibel of making millions from awarding CHA contracts to certain companies he favored, depositing CHA money in interest-free accounts at local banks and paying exorbitant wages to workers in order to create "an army of patronage workers" for the mayor. Also appointed to the CHA board in addition to Mooney was Estelle S. Holzer, age 52, insurance executive for Prudential Life Insurance and wife of the politically connected Circuit Court Judge Reginald Holzer. She was to serve until July 14, 1986. The former interim general superintendent of schools, Angeline P. Caruso, age 59, was appointed to serve until January 8, 1986.

The three appointees were approved in a stormy Housing Committee meeting held in the city council's chambers on Wednesday, July 22, 1982. Alderman Terry M. Gabinski (32) chaired the meeting and frequently threatened to clear the room because of the audience's disturbances. Community leaders and activists said that they were angry about Byrne's three nominees because they were not representatives of the people who lived in the Chicago housing projects.

When asked why she wanted to serve on the CHA board and how she would qualify, Caruso said:

> Because the mayor asked me. And she (the mayor) felt concerned about the children, and she felt that I could help.
> Housing is nothing new to me. I serve on the Hellenic Foundation, which is a senior citizens' housing center, and I serve on my condominium association. I don't know how one can separate the impact on the quality of life in terms of the community from how children performed in school.

Holzer said, "I am a workaholic and organizer. The city has been very good to me, and I would like to give back something."

Alderman Larry Bloom (5) blasted Mooney on the CHA's inability to make changes based on the Oscar Newman housing report. Niles Sherman (21) said:

> The American dream is for everybody to share in the system. This is a rainbow.
>
> We (blacks) must be in these key positions. This is not sharing when only three of seven board members are black. Where's the rainbow? This is the storm that comes before the rainbow, and we've been in the storm before.

CHA Commissioner Renault Robinson said:

> This whole hearing is a sham. The chairman is a loyalist, and he's trying to exclude audience participation. This only shows that the Chicago city government is just as bad as (the CHA).
>
> They can play the game now, but they have to come before the voters. Every black alderman who participates in this should be looking for a new job in 1983.

The CHA nominees were scheduled to appear before the city council on Friday, July 24, 1982 to be confirmed. Residents organized by Dorothy Tillman, Marion Stamps and Lu Palmer were down at City Hall at 7 A.M. Friday morning, the 24th, to get ring side seats to witness the procedure of the racist confirmation in the city council, and of course, record notes on those black aldermen who voted to support the nominees. When Tillman's group arrived at City Hall at 7 A.M., the police held the black opponents in a holding pattern outside of the chamber door while white city workers who had been instructed to come to work early to support the appointments entered the darkened council chambers through a back entrance in order to fill all the seats before the chamber doors were open to the public. Apparently, the person who was directing the sleazy back door operation couldn't count because after all of the city employees were seated, there were still fifty seats vacant. Hence, when the chamber doors opened, fifty of the waiting four hundred demonstrators from the South Side entered the room and to their surprise found that the chamber was almost filled to capacity. Tillman's demonstrators chanted and sang during the two and a half hours they had to wait for the session to begin. The three white CHA appointees were confirmed. Black aldermen supporting the confirmation were Robert Shaw (9), Eloise Barden (16), William Carothers (28), Eugene Ray (27) and Wilson Frost (34). Frost was the only one of the five who was re-elected in 1983. Frost's opponent was U.S. Representative Gus Savage's son, Thomas Savage.

Reverend T.L. Barrett, a former member of the Chicago Housing Authority (CHA) Oversight Committee and pastor of the Life Center Church, located on East Garfield Blvd.

Referring to the black aldermen who voted with Mayor Byrne, Reverend Jesse Jackson said, "Your souls ought to be nonnegotiable."

Reverend T. L. Barrett, pastor of Life Center Church, held a press conference officially announcing his resignation from the CHA Oversight Committee. He said:

> My resignation was an act of protest to Mayor Byrne's recent CHA actions. It is a sign of dissatisfaction from someone who tried to work with her. I only tried to get something better for my people.
>
> It is true Mayor Byrne gave my church $8,000 three weeks before my appointment, but she didn't tell me she was going to do this. When she arrived with the check, I was just as surprised as anyone else. I accepted the money as a gift. I do feel since there was so much community protest perhaps she had a sign that I was in her corner. I have and never can be bought. Someone in the community has to make it clear to Mayor Byrne that we are dissatisfied. This should be the message to her.

Congressman Gus Savage called for a federal investigation into the appointment of Andrew Mooney, CHA's new chairman. Savage said, "It gravely troubles me that appointed to this monumental task of renovating the CHA is a 30-year-old man with less than fifteen months experience in the housing field, whose primary qualification appears to be that he was second in command to Charles Swibel."

Journalist Lu Palmer said, "When Byrne locked us out of the city council confirmation hearings, it was the straw that broke the camel's back. It was in

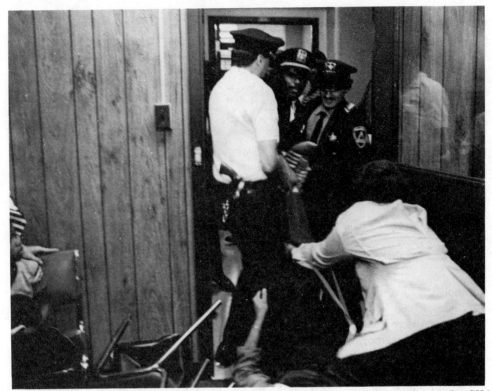

Three Chicago Housing Authority policemen drag an unidentified female tenant out of a CHA board meeting feet first. The woman in the white jacket, also a CHA tenant is attempting to impede the arrest of her friend. At the extreme left is a small boy observing the struggle.

fact the last nail in her (Byrne's) political coffin. We have had enough, and We Shall See In '83."

To help fulfill the black community's dream of a black mayor, Chicago Black United Communities (CBUC) sponsored a series of five week political training classes to educate and convert some brothers and sisters into deacons and deaconesses and purveyors of the underlying philosophy of "We Shall See In '83." CBUC graduated a new crop of trainees at the end of every fifth week. Lu Palmer recalls:

We held our first graduation on January 10, 1982, the coldest day in the history of Chicago. The wind chill factor was eighty-two degrees below zero. Congressman Harold Washington was our first graduation speaker. It was so cold in that room that he kept his coat and gloves on while he delivered the graduation address. The seventy-six graduates also kept on their hats, coats, scarfs and gloves, and you could literally see fog coming out of their

John H. Johnson, president of Johnson Publishing Company, publisher of Ebony *and* Jet Magazines, *chairman of the Supreme Life Insurance Company, chairman of radio station WJPC and also president of Fashion Fair Cosmetics.*

mouths. As a matter of fact, although there was a chill factor of eighty-two degrees below zero outside, I'm not so certain that it was equally as cold inside of the room.

The next morning following our first graduation, I called John H. Johnson, publisher of *Ebony* and *Jet* magazines, and I told him that I had to have some heat in the coach house for my students. He did not hesitate. He simply asked me how much money would I need to put heat in the building. I had gotten several estimates. I gave him the lowest bid which was $3500. Johnny came through without any fanfare and made it possible for our political education class to study in comfort.

Incidentally, our political education class was the only one blacks had on a sustaining basis other than those offered to blacks in the ward machine organizations. It was the people who we had trained in those classes that we put in the field to re-elect Allan Streeter in the Seventeenth Ward.

The politically-trained troops who came to the aid of Alderman Allan Streeter would not have been available had it not been for Lu Palmer and the Chicago Black United Communities Organization's early and invaluable educational programs that motivated and structured black thought on the real possibility of electing a black mayor in 1983. They were and are important segments of Chicago's new political mosaic which is supported by the fact that in April, 1980, the Political Action Committee of CBUC launched a black mayor's campaign entitled, "A Black Mayor? It's Up to You!" The background of the campaign was based on a survey that was taken by the women's auxiliary of the Lu Palmer Foundation and coordinated by Jorja Palmer, Lu's wife who conducted with a group of women a scientific survey to determine whether blacks wanted to see a black as mayor of Chicago, and if so, when. The survey was conducted by telephone and followed up with a mailing of 5,000 questionnaires, one to each person who had been interviewed.

On August 15, 1981, the Chicago Black United Communities organized a citywide political conference held at Malcolm X College located at 1900 W. Van Buren Street from 9 A.M. to 5 P.M. For a ten dollar registration fee, a light breakfast and a lunch were served to participants. In addition the conference materials were given without an additional charge. The purpose of the citywide conference was to examine old and new strategies that would enable black people to chart new paths toward full political representation and empowerment in black communities, in black wards, in black state legislative districts, in black congressional districts and in Chicago's City Hall.

On July 7, 1982, Lu Palmer called the ten top people on a list from the May 1982 CBUC political survey and asked them if there were any circumstances or conditions under which they would not run for mayor of Chicago. The persons called were Margaret Burroughs, Manford Byrd, Anna Langford, Renault Robinson, Lenora Cartwright, Jesse Jackson, Roland Burris, Danny Davis and Harold Washington. Lu Palmer's name was also included in that list of ten. Palmer recalls:

> Both Manford Byrd and Renault Robinson indicated they had no interest in running. Margaret Burroughs also said she wasn't interested in running, and I believe Lenora Cartwright did the same. So, we ultimately ended up with six people. Our keynote speaker at the plebiscite, which was held at the Bethel AME Church on July 26, was Congressman Harold Washington. And, of course, he was the runaway winner in votes like ten to one.
>
> Harold, the plebiscite favorite, disturbed me with the contents of his speech because he kept harping on the theme that it is the plan and not the man. I looked at some of the other organizers of the meeting and frowned. I did not know what he was talking about when he said, 'it was the plan and not the man,' because he was our man, and we wanted him right now.
>
> Directly after the meeting, we went to Harold to see if he would consider running for mayor. Congressman Harold Washington replied, 'There has to be a war chest of at least $250,000 to $500,000, and you have got to prove that you can get a number of people registered, at least fifty thousand.'

Two weeks after Congressman Harold Washington articulated the prerequisites that would have to be fulfilled before he would consider running for mayor, Lu Palmer, Tim Black, Zenobia Black, Connie Howard, Oscar Worrill and Nate Clay organized a group called, People's Movement for a Voter's Registration. It was launched with a big mass meeting at the Bethel AME Church in August 1982, and the keynote speaker was Harold Washington.

Bethel AME Church, 4448 S. Michigan Avenue, pastored by Reverend David C. Coleman. Bethel Church was the site of many of the "We Shall See In '83" rallies sponsored by Chicago Black United Communities (CBUC).

In the meantime, Slim Coleman, the Harvard trained leader of The Heart of Uptown Coalition, and Nancy Jefferson, executive director of The Midwest Community Council, through a coalition of community organizations called P.O.W.E.R. (People Organized for Welfare and Employment Rights) launched a citywide voters' registration campaign with the cooperation of election commissioners after the group threatened lawsuits. Organizational members of P.O.W.E.R. in addition to the Uptown Coalition and Midwest Community Council were the Southeast Welfare Concerned Recipient Organization, the Chicago Housing Tenants Organization, Operation PUSH, the South Austin Community Coalition, the Chicago Area Black Lung Association, the Chicago Welfare Rights Organization, the Pilsen Housing and Business Alliance, the Public Welfare Coalition, the Illinois Welfare Rights Coalition, the Parents Equalizer of Chicago, the Kenwood-Oakland Community Organization, the Chicago Gray Panthers, the Tranquility-Markman Memorial Organization, the Chicago Urban League and the All Peoples' Congress.

P.O.W.E.R. actually entered the voter registration campaign through the rear door because the group was originally formed in June 1982 to fight Governor James Thompson's reduction in general assistance grants from $162 to $144. The coalition was not getting any respect from state legislators for their efforts because most people on general assistance were not registered voters. Hence, Nancy Jefferson and Slim Coleman came up with the bright idea that they could get the public officials' attention if the 110,000 plus grant recipients were registered voters. Slim Coleman describes his experience and rationale for pursuing the voter registration route:

> We believed that if we got all our welfare people registered that elected officials would listen better. Moreover, we had a captured audience because we knew exactly where each one of these people would come every month to sign their general assistance checks. However, first we had to file a lawsuit to get the election commission's permission to register aid recipients at the various public aid offices. Then, we had to negotiate with the Board of Election Commissioners to put registrars at the sites since they initially would not deputize our people as registrars.
>
> The commissioners were stubborn, so I went to Joe Novak, who was running the campaign for Adlai Stevenson and said, 'Look, we can register a lot of voters for your campaign if you can get the Board of Election Commissioners to cooperate.' Joe Novak went to Edward Vrdolyak, and Vrdolyak got the commissioners to cooperate and agree to furnish two voter registrars outside of each public aid office providing we could furnish vans that would remain at every site all day. We did not have any money, so we got the radio people to give us some public service time to make our plea. Vans poured in from all over the city. We went back to Novak and told him we needed some money to keep the campaign going. He got Alfred G. Ronan (14th District), a state representative and north side committeeman, to give us $5,000. In the

Slim Coleman, editor and chief of All Chicago City News *and chairperson of the Heart of the Uptown Coalition, delivers a major address at the coalition's annual meeting as Congressman John Conyers (D-Mich), seated at Coleman's left, listens intently.*

George O'Hare, an Irish Catholic, leads a picket line near the gates of Navy Pier, the site of the Chicago Fest. O'Hare is carrying a sign that reads, "One term Byrne, never to return, boycott Chicago Fest." And third from the rear, also carrying a picket sign, is Santita Jackson, daughter of the Reverend Jesse L. Jackson.

last two weeks in August, and the first two weeks in September, we registered forty-seven thousand people. When Al Ronan learned about the success of our efforts, he said, 'The hell with Stevenson. Those votes could be used to elect Harold Washington the mayor of Chicago.'

The voters' registration campaign had not really caught fire in late July 1982. However, Mayor Byrne's CHA appointments and the City Hall lockout had raised the black community's body temperature to a boiling point. The only resolution that community leaders had offered for most of the dog days of July was hot rhetoric. However, early one Sunday morning a woman who identified herself as a Gary, Indiana resident called into Derrick Hill's *Sunday Morning Live* talk show on radio station WBMX, 107.5 FM, on July 24, 1982 and said, "If Mayor Jane Byrne can lock us out of City Hall, why can't we boycott her upcoming Chicago Fest?

The Reverend Jesse Jackson, who was the next guest on the *Sunday Morning Live* show, was asked what he thought about the Gary lady's idea. Jackson thought it was an excellent idea. As a matter of fact, the following Saturday at the regular Operation PUSH meeting, Reverend Jackson burned his Chicago

Fest tickets in the presence of two thousand supporters who had packed the PUSH auditorium at 930 E. 50th. Jackson said:

> We will begin boycotting Chicago Fest down at Navy Pier this Wednesday morning, August 3, at 10 A.M. This boycott is a religious rebellion. We must put dignity over dollars and emancipation over entertainment. It is better to boycott with dignity than to sing and dance in shame. We are not bound by Chicago plantation politics. We must aggressively and militantly use our dollars and our votes. We will win, not because we are the majority, but because we are the margin of profit. We will win because of black volume. . . . They can't do without us. We are necessary. The black dollar is the margin of failure or salvation. We are a wild card, not a discard. This is not a black only Chicago Fest boycott.

Standing with Reverend Jackson that morning on the podium, supporting the boycott, were Alderman Lawrence Bloom (5), Alderman Ivan M. Rittenberg (40), Alderman Martin J. Oberman (43), and a representative of the Independent Voters of Illinois (IVI). Also supporting the boycott were Alderman Danny K. Davis (29), Alderman Allan Streeter (17), Alderwoman Marian Humes (8), Alderman Niles Sherman (21), State Representative Larry Bullock (22-D), State Representative Carol Moseley Braun (24-D), State Senator Richard Newhouse (24-D), Commissioner John Stroger, Congressman Harold Washington (1-D) and Congressman Gus Savage (2-D). Alderman Clifford Kelly (20) said he would be leading the way.

Stevie Wonder, Motown's superstar, who was scheduled to perform at Chicago Fest on August 7, cancelled his engagement after learning of the

Left: Stevie Wonder, singer, musician and composer. He is America's most creative and prolific songwriter. He is definitely cast in the mold of his mentor, the late Duke Ellington, who wrote more than 3,000 songs in his lifetime. Right: Aretha Franklin, the Queen of Soul, said, "If I performed at Chicago Fest, I could never sing Respect again."

boycott of the festival. Stevie was the first of the main attractions to bow out of his contract following the suggestions of Reverend Jackson. Reverend Jackson blasted the white news media for saying that singer Aretha Franklin, known as the Queen of Soul, wanted to perform in Stevie Wonder's place.

Jackson said, "Aretha said to me, 'How can I sing *Respect* and do this to my brother? I never said that.'" Jackson said, "This is just a tool to divide the black community, but it won't work. Instead, it's bringing us closer together."

A political worker on the Byrne plantation who did not wish to be identified told Chinta Strausberg, a *Chicago Daily Defender* political reporter, the following: "I have never seen one issue (the mayor's recent confirmation of three controversial white CHA board members) unify the black community in my life. It is the most beautiful thing I have ever seen. I am surprised."

Roger Simon reported in his *Chicago Sun-Times* July 30 column:

> Jesse Jackson's planned boycott of Chicago Fest has already succeeded. Not because Stevie Wonder, probably the most popular black performer in America, has cancelled his appearance. Not because Jackson believes that large numbers of people will stay away. And not because he expects black vendors to pull out. He has succeeded because his goal was to engulf in controversy Jane Byrne's most popular event, to tarnish her image as a kindly provider of bread and circuses, and to turn up the heat on her summer. It has even led him to hint he may run for mayor in 1983.

Jackson said:

> I will not rule it out. I will not reject it with some public statement. I am eligible. I am qualified. I could gain a significant following, which I deserve.
>
> There are not just blacks, but hispanics and whites and elements in labor who would all vote for a credible black candidate. If I run, I would be a factor to be reckoned with. The polls show that.
>
> Chicago has become a coronation for Jane Byrne's queenship. Now, with this boycott, we are letting people know that those who choose to blatantly disrespect black persons must face the consequences.
>
> Jane Byrne is not my magnificent obsession. I don't want any anti-Byrne mania. She can organize that herself. In fact, she's the best organizer of that in the city.
>
> I don't think she can be elected without the black vote. So her actions are baffling. She assumes that blacks will not vote for her and she has written them off, or that we are so docile and stupid we will vote for her no matter what she does.

The antics of Jane Byrne and the need to add more thrust to the voter registration campaign were the main topics among persons walking the picket line at the Chicago Fest. It appears that the success of the Fest boycott was being translated into an escalating enthusiasm to get more people to register and vote. In absence of the smell of Leon's Bar-B-Que, there was a smell of victory. *(The Leon Finneys withdrew their Bar-B-Que concession from the Chicago Fest.)*

Renault Robinson drove north on the Dan Ryan Expressway thinking about the Chicago Fest victory and the potential for a very successful voter registration campaign when someone announced on the radio that Mr. Edward Gardner had made a contribution to some struggling charitable organization. Robinson immediately picked up his telephone, dialed information and got Mr. Gardner's telephone number. Robinson recalls:

Without giving it a second thought, I called Mr. Gardner's company cold. I had never met Mr. Gardner. Neither had I ever heard his name mentioned until I heard that radio announcement. However, I was able to get through to him immediately. I told him that I would like to see him.

He said, 'Come on.' I got off the northbound expressway and got back on the southbound and went directly to his office at 1000 East 87th Street.

I told Mr. Edward Gardner about my activities in the Afro-American Patrolman's League and some other activities in which I had been involved. I also told him that we wanted to do something about the voter registration campaign right now.

Mr. Gardner said, 'What difference will it make?'

I told him I thought it would make a significant difference in that there was a good possibility that we could put a black mayor in City Hall next year, one who would respond to the needs of all the citizens of Chicago. Mr.

Edward Gardner, chairman of the board of the Soft Sheen Products Co., Inc. is one of America's most successful businessmen. He and his wife, Bettiann Gardner, are two of Chicago's most sensitive philanthropists.

Gardner seemed to be very, very interested in what I was saying. As a matter of fact, he called his son Gary and his daughter Terri in to meet me and he also introduced me to his wife Mrs. Bettiann Gardner. And we all talked some more about the possibilities of a black mayor and the need to get a maximum number of people registered. I also told him that we had to have a media campaign and message that was more dynamic than our current street efforts because the street efforts in my opinion were not going to make it. It was not enough by itself. I further indicated that I thought that black people had to be educated politically. We discussed a media campaign a bit more and before I left Mr. Gardner put me in touch with some of the media people in his organization and gave me a check for $5,000, which was the first significant lump sum that I had received for the voter registration campaign.

Mr. Edward Gardner, chairman of the board of Soft Sheen Products, and one of America's most successful businessmen, remembers very vividly the first day Renault Robinson visited him. Renault was the first person who had ever approached Mr. Gardner in reference to participating in the voter registration campaign. Mr. Gardner summons these facts about his conversation with Renault Robinson:

I asked Renault how we could bring about a change in the political life and enable blacks to be more representative in the city council, have more voice and get their share of contracts and of business and so forth.

Robinson replied: 'Ed, you can't bring about any change unless we get more black people to register and vote. That's the problem. We can talk until we're blue in the face, but if they don't register, then you are not going to have the numbers to effect any kind of political change in the city where people can see that jobs are equally shared with all sectors of the city.'

I turned to my son Gary who is the president of the company and said, 'It's near the end of our advertising period, which is September and October. Why don't we allocate a certain amount of our advertising dollars and time to voter registration between now and October 5.' My son and I both agreed that that was a good idea. So we decided that we'd turn it over to 'Brainstorm' Communications which is our in-house advertising agency headed by my daughter Terri.

Terri's 'Brainstorm' people came up with some fantastic creative ideas and thoughts to make voter registration a significant thing in black Americans' lives here in the city of Chicago. Their idea was, 'Come Alive October 5.' Their 'Come Alive October 5' was a voter registration rallying call that caught on.

We at Soft Sheen became so wrapped up in the voter registration campaign that instead of using our dollars to advertise Soft Sheen we put them into the voter registration campaign. In fact, we continued to increase the number of dollars we put in the campaign. We did not say that the ads were sponsored by Soft Sheen. In fact, one of my sons said, 'Well, look daddy, we want to be sure we don't say this is being brought to you by Soft Sheen Products Company.' And we never did. On the sixty second commercials, nothing was ever said about Soft Sheen at all. And finally, Marty Faye, the WBEE (1570 AM) radio disc jockey, said, 'Damn, I'm going to tell the people who's behind all this.' And that's the only time it ever got out that we were paying for those commercials.

The big boys were in a quandary about who was paying for all of those sixty second spots. They wanted to know who was putting the money behind those thousands of sixty second 'Come Alive October 5' commercials. We weren't concerned because by the time Marty Faye went public, our program was in high gear. This campaign was not for any specific politician. It was primarily to improve the quality of life for black Chicagoans because our strength, growth and dollar capabilities are derived from the black Americans. If successful black businesses don't take steps to use their dollars in a constructive way to move black Americans forward, then we can not blame the major white companies who say we are not doing anything.

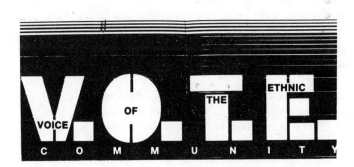

Poster

Bumper Sticker

Color became the key consideration in designing a "Come Alive" logo because it had to grab attention and leave an impression. Yellow is the hottest color and that color was used in variant hues against a blue and black background for buttons, V.O.T.E. posters, banners, bumper stickers and T-shirts.

Keep in mind that for every spot Soft Sheen Products ran on the radio, the radio people gave us a spot. And that was just beautiful. All of the major radio stations gave one spot for every spot that we purchased. We purchased thousands of spots, and they ran an equal number. And I'd say between print advertising, posters, window streamers and T-shirts, buttons and so forth, we spent over $350,000 in the voter registration campaign. And I am saying every dollar I think was well spent. It was not only exciting to Chicago, it has excited the black communities across the nation to realize the power and the strength within Black America.

After we got the advertising and promotional part of the voter registration program off the ground, the Soft Sheen community service people commenced inviting various community groups such as the Urban League and Operation PUSH to meetings at our 87th Street office. However, initially we had a meeting at the Reverend Jesse Jackson's home to make sure that they were with us in the voter registration drive. The Soft Sheen people had formulated a program and procedure that was strictly being orchestrated by the creative people at our company.

During our meeting with the Reverend Jesse Jackson, he inferred that he wanted our voter registration meetings held at Operation PUSH headquarters and become a part of Operation PUSH. I told the Reverend Jackson that 'Come Alive October 5' was a brainchild of the creative people at Soft Sheen and that the meetings were going to be held at the Soft Sheen Products headquarters, which is located at 1000 E. 87th Street.

It was our opinion that we could get more city organizations to meet on neutral ground and become united. As a matter of fact, we got organizations working together that had never worked together before. We had more than thirty organizations that met regularly at Soft Sheen and formulated citywide programs.

Many of the organizations such as the Citizens Committee, CBUC, Operation PUSH, People Organized for Welfare Rights (P.O.W.E.R.), the Chicago Urban League, People's Movement and others had already started serious plans for massive voter registration to support a black mayor prior to Robinson approaching Soft Sheen. However, out of the meetings at Soft Sheen, it was determined that: a) There were three hundred thousand unregistered black voters in Chicago; b) The objective was to register one hundred thousand new black voters in time for the mayoral primary and c) Soft Sheen's advertising and marketing department would prepare a marketing plan for a massive voter registration effort, which would be implemented following approval by the assembled body.

The assembled body, recognizing the need to work together, formed an umbrella organization known as VOICE OF THE ETHNIC COMMUNITIES. Hence, working as a unit under the umbrella of V.O.T.E. Communities; concerned citizens, grassroots organizations and businesses were able to pull together and draw from each other.

The goal of V.O.T.E. Communities was to expand the number of registered voters within the city of Chicago before the November 2 general election. The deadline for voters to be registered to vote in the election was October 5. Specifically, V.O.T.E. Communities' goal was to register 100,000 new minority voters on or before October 5, 1982, another 100,000 by January 25 for the mayoral primary on February 22, 1983, and an additional 100,000 by March 4, 1983 for the April 12, 1983 mayoral election.

October 5 was established as 'Precinct Registration Day'. This meant that regular voter registration sites would operate through September 25, 1982 and then on October 5 (one day only) three thousand additional registration sites would open throughout the city. This date was designed as the target around which all our efforts would revolve. Organizational members included the Afro-American Patrolman's League, the Black Illinois Legislative Lobby, Ethnic Communications Outlet, Chicago Urban League, the First Congressional District, Soft Sheen Products, Inc., People's Action Coalition, Inc. (PACI), People's Movement, the Woodlawn Organization, Leon's Bar-B-Que, Operation PUSH, Salter and Cater Advertising, Central Advisory Council—Chicago Housing Authority and the CAA Black Secondary Educators.

Chicago Black United Communities (CBUC) sponsors a reception to honor the Gardners for their efforts in the successful voter registration drive. (Left to right): Congressman Harold Washington, Lu Palmer, Mrs. Bettiann Gardner and Mr. Edward Gardner.

Soft Sheen's rapid growth was largely due to the effectiveness of the company's marketing and advertising strategies. Gary Gardner, my son, believed that perhaps those same concepts and strategies could be applied to marketing a black mayoral candidate.

I think that our success in having all of these groups working together resulted from the fact that this was the first time that they had a strong financial business organization as a supportive rallying point. They appeared to be proud to come out to Soft Sheen headquarters and meet and express themselves and not feel threatened, and also know that they were under the umbrella of a major financial source that would help them do what they wanted to do. Remember, most of these community organizations are perpetually strapped for dollars. Dollars were not their problem in this voter registration crusade because we had the dollars to fit their needs.

The role that Operation PUSH and the other organizations played in making the voter registration campaign an unqualified success was significant. However, I am still of the opinion that had we not been independent of the PUSH umbrella, that we would not have had the uniqueness and the freshness of what happened at Soft Sheen, which was considered neutral territory by all the groups that participated in the campaign.

The black churches were also instrumental in getting people to register in the 'Come Alive October 5' campaign. Father George Clements, pastor of the Holy Angels Church, made a dramatic move that caught the eyes and ears of the national media when he proclaimed, "I do not want any child attending classes at Holy Angels School whose parents are not registered to vote. And those parents who refuse to present their registration cards can simply take their child and go someplace else."

Although Father Clements received a lot of criticism from the general public and the media for making that demand, he took his proclamation a step higher and said, "Dr. Martin Luther King and others died for people to have the right to register and vote. And I am not going to let those deaths be in vain. Therefore, I do not want anyone to hold membership in the Holy Angels Church who does not have a voter registration card."

Pastor Joseph Wells of Mount Pisgah Baptist Church, at 4622 S. Dr. Martin Luther King Drive, announced that the church would no longer distribute free food to any person who could not present a registration card. In the meanwhile, the Reverend Jesse Jackson called a meeting of more than one hundred ministers at the Operation PUSH headquarters to discuss the voter registration campaign, and they all came away from that meeting agreeing to conduct a crusade for voter registration in their respective churches. In addition to the ministry, some black doctors and lawyers got on the band wagon and announced that they would not accept any patients or clients except on an emergency basis that did not have a registration card. The voter registration campaign had indeed taken hold from the depths of the grassroots to the peak of the mountain.

The voter registration campaign exceeded the expectations of even the most optimistic black leader's wildest dream. One hundred and thirty-five thousand people "came alive" on Tuesday, October 5 and registered to vote, whereas, seventy thousand people had registered during the months of August and September. Forty-two thousand of those registered in the July–August period were put on the registration rolls by P.O.W.E.R. at public aid and unemployment offices. In addition, there was another thirty-five thousand persons who had registered between January and July of 1982. Hence, there was a grand total of two hundred and thirty thousand spanking brand new registrants.

More people registered in the first nine months and five days of 1982 than had registered in the nine-year history of the Community Voters Registration Outreach Program that had been sponsored by the Board of Elections. According to the Board of Election officials, at least two times as many blacks as whites registered in '82. The black community was definitely on a political roll.

Another interesting sidelight in the registration crusade was the fact that the Forty-second and the Third Wards, which have the highest concentration of CHA housing in Chicago, were among the top five wards in voter registration on October 5. The high turnout in these wards was indicative of the involvement of grassroots organizations such as P.O.W.E.R. who were concerned about survival issues such as welfare, housing and education.

In mid-October, Congressman Harold Washington, in a speech at a banquet sponsored by the Concerned Young Adults (CYA) said, "The recent massive voter registration effort had created an almost certainty that there would be a black mayoral candidate in 1983 who would force a full discussion of the issues for a change in this city."

In less than thirty days after the "Come Alive October 5" registration victory, Congressman Harold Washington was re-elected to his congressional seat for a second term with the largest plurality of any congressman in the United States and with the largest number of votes that were ever cast in the history of the First Congressional District. On November 1, the eve of his congressional victory, U.S. Representative Harold Washington (D—Ill) predicted a black would challenge Mayor Byrne. Then, he said he would announce whether he wanted to be that challenger on November 10. However, prior to Representative Washington's November 1 statement, petitions were being circulated that would put him on the ballot for the February 22 mayoral primary.

David S. Canter, chairman of the Hyde Park–Kenwood chapters of the Independent Voters of Illinois–Independent Precinct Voters of Illinois–Independent Precinct Organization, said the Washington petitions were not authorized by the congressman. "It's a draft," said Canter. "We're attempting to force Washington to run."

Renault Robinson, a Washington disciple and a member of the board of the Chicago Housing Authority, said he thought the congressman would run for mayor, but the decision had not been made yet. On the other hand, a Washington top aide who requested anonymity, said the congressman had not made any preparations for organizing or financing a mayoral campaign.

Renault Robinson, in a state of extraordinary exuberance after the November 2 election votes were counted, bellowed, "We have proven that Washington has a lot of voting strength. Now, all we have to do is harness it and make it work." Making it work meant putting together a substantial financial war chest to comply with Washington's earlier mayoral prerequisites. Renault, acting as a committee of one, started making the rounds of black businesses in an effort to raise funds. Renault figured that the campaign needed at least $100,000 as a starter, fifty thousand to set up shop and another fifty thousand in cash for seed money. The amount was minuscule in comparison to that of "Jane of Arc," the incumbent mayor, who had a war chest of ten million dollars.

One of Robinson's first visits was with Al Boutte, chairman of the board of Independence Bank. After Robinson laid out his plans and his hopes, Al Boutte said, "Do you really think we can win?"

Robinson retorted, "The numbers are there. It's up to us to do the work and make it happen. It ain't going to happen automatically. But the potential is there."

Boutte then queried, "How much money do you need?"

Renault responded, "I have estimated that we need between $750,000 and one million dollars to make it a credible campaign."

Al Boutte then leaned back in his plush chair, put his right hand under his chin and looked out of the window in the easterly direction of 80th and Cottage Grove for a moment and then said, "Okay, I'll tell you what. I will try to commit my bank to raise $50,000. See if you can get Seaway National Bank to raise $50,000."

Robinson immediately arranged a meeting with Ernest Collins, chairman of the Seaway National Bank, and Al Johnson and Jacoby Dickens, who were both directors of the bank. They all agreed to match the other bank's dollar commitment. With those oral commitments under his belt, Robinson went back to U.S. Representative Harold Washington and reported his progress. Washington congratulated Renault for his efforts, then softly stated, "You know we can't go without the money. We've got to have the money."

Within forty-eight hours after the November 2 overwhelming re-election of Congressman Harold Washington, Robinson received a number of new promises of money from a variety of sources. However, it was not as much as they had wanted, but enough for Representative Washington to have Robinson set up a private luncheon meeting on Tuesday, November 9 at the Hyde Park Hilton and invite approximately forty people including Al Johnson, George Johnson, John H. Johnson, Edward Gardner, Bill Berry, Lu Palmer, Jesse Jackson, James Compton, Alvin Boutte, George Jones, Timuel Black, David Canter, former State Representative Robert E. Mann (D, Chgo) and Attorneys Thomas N. Todd and E. Duke McNeil in addition to twenty-five other movers and shakers. Harold Washington told those present at the close-to-the-press meeting that he did not want to run for mayor, but would bow to public pressure and wage a vigorous campaign. "To be blunt," Washington said, "I don't want to run for mayor. I like the Congress. Moreover, I have been trying to find a person to run, but unless that person appears within 24 hours, I will announce that I will run for mayor."

Two days prior to the November 9 meeting at the Hyde Park Hilton Hotel, Lu Palmer invited forty-five political activists to attend a meeting on Sunday, November 7 at the Roberts Motel in Room 101 to discuss options in the event Harold Washington did not declare. Lu Palmer had been bugging Harold on a nonstop basis to jump into the mayoral waters, and Harold refused because the congressman had always been a man who ran according to his own timetable. Lu felt that Harold should step out front because CBUC and other civil rights organizations had promised the people that they would have a major black candidate in the 1983 mayoral race. And if Harold didn't run, they'd look like fools. And if he did run, they needed time to put a mechanism in place to kick off the campaign. Prior to the meeting, Lu Palmer had sent Aldermen Allan Streeter, Danny Davis and Ed Smith to talk to Harold, but Harold didn't give them a clue. Lu found this frustrating and said, "We never know which way this guy is going to go, and we're only a few days away from November 10. Therefore, we're going to have to come out of this mini summit meeting with some sort of resolution."

There were several factions represented at the Roberts Motel summit meeting. Alderman Danny Davis represented one faction, Nancy Jefferson another, Lu Palmer a third and Anna Langford a fourth. Anna was mad because she had declared in mid October that she was willing to run for the mayoral chair. Anna stated in the meeting, "I feel like a fool. I said I would run, and nobody paid me any attention. I went and printed up all kinds of stuff and spent money. And now here you are begging Harold, and he won't run. It doesn't make any sense. Let's get another candidate." Alderman Clifford Kelly was singing an anti-Harold Washington chorus that was louder than Anna Langford's. The meeting got so steamy that Lu Palmer asked Tim Black to leave because he had not been invited.

Renault Robinson sat quietly in the midst of all this bickering and fighting knowing that an announcement of Congressman Harold Washington's willingness to run was imminent. As a matter of fact, as Robinson sat there mentally recording all of the activities, he was fearful that someone would show up at the meeting with an early copy of the Monday, November 8 *Chicago Tribune* which was carrying a front page headline story written by Monroe Anderson which read:

Washington in Mayor's Race

Bowing to a ground swell of public pressure and finding encouragement in the record number of blacks who registered and then voted in last week's election, U.S. Representative Harold Washington (D—Ill.) will announce Wednesday that he is entering the Chicago mayoral sweepstakes, the *Tribune* has learned.

Washington, an independent Democrat whose name has been mentioned frequently as a "unity" candidate in a bid to elect the city's first black mayor, will hold a news conference Wednesday morning to announce officially his entry into the February 22 Democratic primary, sources said.

Washington's campaign will be directed by Renault Robinson, a Jane Byrne-appointed board member and executive director of the Afro-American Patrolman's League, the *Tribune* has learned.

'Blacks have got the numbers. The only job we've got to do is convince black people that a black man can be the mayor of Chicago. We got a substantial war chest to mount the educational campaign,' Renault Robinson said.

Renault Robinson said that there are more than 600,000 registered black voters in Chicago. Because the average primary turnout has been 850,000 voters, if 80 percent of the registered blacks vote for Washington in February, he could easily win the race with Mayor Jane Byrne and State's Attorney Richard M. Daley splitting the white vote, Robinson said. Daley announced his candidacy last week.

'All of the other black elected officials will support him in making the race. We see it as a legitimate shot, and we're going to make it. Washington was legitimately drafted by the black community. He is the most logical candidate we got,' Robinson said.

The forthcoming mayoral announcement had been long anticipated by Lu Palmer. However, on the Tuesday evening before Congressman Washington was to announce his candidacy, Lu Palmer received two telephone calls, one asking him to be present at the Hyde Park Hilton for the Washington announcement, and another from the advertising agency for radio sponsors of *Lu's Notebook,* requesting that he presents himself at their North Michigan Avenue offices the first thing Wednesday morning, November 10, which coincidentally happened to be the same time that Washington was to announce. When Lu Palmer arrived at the agency office, he was told by the public relations officer for the sponsor, within two minutes after they had exchanged niceties, that he was through and hence forth would not represent them on the radio. In other words, he was fired.

Lu said, "Why are you knocking me off of the air?"

The sponsor's representative replied, "Your show has become too partisan."

Lu replied, "What do you mean too partisan? I talk about Democrats. I talk about Republicans. I talk about communism. I talk about all parties."

The sponsor's man replied, "Yes, Lu! But what it boils down to is your work with CBUC and your relationship to Harold Washington. We don't care if you support Mayor Byrne or (Cook County State's Attorney) Richard M. Daley. We bought a news commentary show, but quite often your show has been a platform for partisan political support. It undermines the advertising effectiveness of the program."

Within moments after leaving the meeting with his former sponsors, Lu Palmer proceeded to call his wife Jorja and Harold Washington to tell them what had happened. Lu indicated in his conversation with Washington that he didn't want to discuss it in any detail on the phone because he knew that Washington was rushing to the Hyde Park Hilton press conference.

When Lu Palmer reached the Hyde Park Hilton at 4900 S. Lake Shore Drive some twenty minutes later, the Outer Drive was packed with parked cars and a large crowd of people had gathered in front of the hotel because the room in which the press conference was held was jammed with humanity like sardines in a can. There were people present from all ethnic groups: black, brown, white, yellow, red and mixtures of all of them. However, Palmer muscled his way through the crowd and joined his wife Jorja and Jesse Jackson on the front row where the three of them shared two seats. Standing beside Washington on the small podium was his fiancee Mary Ella Smith. Directly behind Washington and Ms. Smith on the wall was a huge enlarged picture of the congressman with the inscription: Washington for Chicago! '83.

The emotionally-charged press conference started with a prayer by the Reverend John Porter of Christ United Methodist Church, "Lord, we thank you, for the man, the moment and the movement have come together."

Congressman Harold Washington delivered his statement of candidacy for mayor with gusto:

> Chicago is a divided city. Chicago is a city where citizens are treated unequally and unfairly. Chicago is a city in decline. Each year for the last decade, we have lost 11,500 jobs, 3,500 housing units and nearly 36,000 people.
>
> Since 1955, women, latinos, blacks, youth and progressive whites have been left out of the Chicago government. Since 1979, the business, labor and intellectual communities have been allowed but token involvement in Chicago government.
>
> Sadly we have learned what happens when there is no government stability—and when the few rule over us. The results are more people don't have jobs, more are out of food, out of their homes and out of hope.
>
> Our businesses are failing at the highest rate since the Depression, in part from high interest rates, and the only answer the city government provides is fat consultant contracts for a few politically-connected firms and jobs for a few patronage workers.
>
> We have a school system which does not educate, in which students continue to lag far behind the rest of the country in tests of reading and math ability.

At this point, Congressman Washington was interrupted by activist Marion Stamps, who shouted, "Harold, you are like the second coming."

Somebody else across the room yelled, "Tell 'em Mister Mayor."

And then, of course, there were those who were chanting, "We Shall See In '83."

After the applause and shouts subsided, Washington continued:

> We have a continuing crime problem in the city. Despite a drop in crime statistics, it's still not safe to walk the streets or run a business. Even at home, Chicagoans are robbed, mugged and beaten.
>
> We no longer have dependable housing in this city. There has been an epidemic of abandoned buildings, and rents have skyrocketed. Subsidized housing is no longer being built. And with interest rates as they are, no one can afford to buy their own home anymore.
>
> Finally, 'the city that works' doesn't work anymore. City services cost more than any other city in America, and yet they just aren't there—sewers

are in disrepair, streets are marred with giant pot holes. We have one of the highest infant mortality rates in the country, and traffic is snarled permanently.

We have these terrible problems in Chicago, partly because leadership has not striven for unity and pointed boldly to the new directions. Instead, it has perpetuated outdated politics and pie-in-the-sky financing.

I have a compassion for the terrible plight of our people and a vision for its future: I honestly believe that of those candidates mentioned, only I can rebuild Chicago by rallying Chicagoans to create a city in which every individual will receive his or her full measure of dignity. In the future, I see a Chicago of compassion; a city where no one has to live with rats, where the sick can be cured and where no one is over taxed by impossible property and other hidden taxes.

All candidates who have declared and who will be running for mayor would perpetuate politics as usual. All the candidates will continue the shell game of city financing at a time of crisis.

I would prefer not to run. But, there is a sense of urgency which moves me. Chicago can only be rebuilt if all the people of Chicago and her leaders work together. I was born, raised and educated in this city, and I have served it on three levels of government. I love representing Chicago in Washington, where we need courageous voices to speak out and act against (President Ronald) Reagan and Reaganomics. But I can't watch the city of Chicago be destroyed by petty politics and bad government. I have been urged by the earnest pleas of thousands of people to enter the race. Therefore, I declare that I am a candidate for mayor of Chicago. Not to do so would be a mockery of my long standing dedication to public service.

Again, U.S. Represenative Washington was interrupted by thunderous applause, stamping feet, shouts of joy and tears of happiness. Pandemonium reigned throughout the room. The uncontrolled jubilation of the crowd must have lasted at least five minutes before Congressman Washington could continue with his statement:

I see a Chicago that runs well, in which services are provided as a right, not as political favors.

I see a Chicago of education excellence and equality of treatment in which all children can learn to function in this ever more complex society, in which jobs and contracts are dispensed fairly to those that want and qualify for them, and in which justice rains down like water.

I see a Chicago in which the neighborhoods are once again the center of our city, in which businesses boom and provide neighborhood jobs, in which neighbors join together to help govern their neighborhood and their city. Some may say this is visionary—I say they lack vision.

Already, a new day is dawning. The unprecedented voter registration and voter turnout in Chicago in the last week's election is evidence of this new beginning. The people of Chicago who have been neglected by the political bosses have announced their willingness to become involved, to unify and to act. I invite them to join in support of my campaign. For if I'm to be mayor, it would be as the spokesperson of this new movement—not the mayor of just a political faction—but mayor of all Chicago. We devoutly search for unity.

As mayor of this city, I would so open the doors of City Hall. I shall dig into that untapped reservoir of talent of whites, latinos, women and blacks and unleash that ability for the benefit of this city. *Fairness* will be our standard. On my first day in office, I will sign a freedom of information order to open the secret files of City Hall to inspection by all citizens. We seek *accountability*. As mayor, I shall gather the best talent of the city to tackle the record of

Congressman Harold Washington's face reflects a look of relief and contentment as his constituents applaud him. (Left to right): Unidentified security person, Congressman Washington's fiancee Mary Ella Smith, the Congressman, Lu Palmer (head partially shown near white drape) and Renault Robinson.

problems I have outlined. We shall strive for excellence. Thousands of Chicagoans have beseeched me to undertake this task—their faith is not misplaced.

When the last word dripped from Congressman Washington's lips, the voices of the crowd went up in a chant, "We Shall See In '83." The pandemonium of joy permeated the walls of the Hyde Park Hilton. Everybody was rejoicing and congratulating each other. The only solemn face in the crowd besides Congressman Washington's was that of Lu Palmer, who was standing in the northwest corner of the room with his head slightly bowed. Lu had become the first political casualty in Chicago's crusade for a black mayor.

Congressman Harold Washington filed his mayoral petitions on December 6, 1982 with the city clerk. Directly behind Washington on his right is former State Representative Robert Mann.

Chapter *XXV*

Destination: Fifth Floor

But Jesus said unto them, They need not depart; give ye them to eat.

And they say unto him, We have here but five loaves, and two fishes.

He said, Bring them hither to me.

And he commanded the multitude to sit down on the grass, and took the five loaves, and the two fishes, and looking up to heaven, he blessed, and brake, and gave the loaves to his disciples, and the disciples to the multitude.

And they did all eat, and were filled: and they took up of the fragments that remained twelve baskets full.

And they that had eaten were about five thousand men, beside women and children.

Matthew 14:16–21

The event of Congressman Harold Washington's declaration to run for mayor on November 10, 1983 was God-inspired because the thought of a black man becoming the mayor of a city that had been labeled "the most racist municipality in America" was tantamount to one believing that Moses could have become a pharaoh in ancient Egypt. Harold Washington and his band of disciples were strong believers in the first Gospel of Saint Matthew and, hence, felt confident that they could overcome the political oppression of Chicago's pharaohs.

On Monday, December 6, 1982, Congressman Harold Washington filed a pile of nominating petitions that was taller than ten Bibles with the City Clerk's Office. Following the petition filing he stated:

We have just filed the nominating petitions for our candidacy in the Democratic primary.

This campaign is built on the premise that the citizens from every part of Chicago want and deserve fairness, excellence and accountability in city government.

Together we can move forward into the future with new vision and a new mutual respect among the fellowship of men and women throughout this great city.

Hurley Green, Sr., publisher of the *Chicago Independent Bulletin,* analyzed the petition filing in his column entitled "Shifting Scenes" on December 9, 1982. Green wrote:

The race is on. What race? The Chicago mayoral race, that's what race! As of Monday morning, those persons whose egos tell them that their destinies include leading the masses; have taken another step toward being included in Chicago's history books. They have filed petitions allegedly signed by eligible voters, attesting to a desire to have their candidate on the official ballot for mayor. Two of the most publicized candidates showed up at the City Clerk's Office with pages of signatures numbering in the thousands. (The mayor alleged fifty thousand signatures; Washington delivered twenty-five thousand, with another fifty thousand in his office; and a Daley aide had over ten thousand names.) Of course, these petitions/signatures can be challenged, but the script for this scenario has already been written. Mayor Jane Byrne and Richard M. Daley must convince the voters that, "Chicago ain't ready for a black mayor." Congressman Washington has to convince at least six hundred thousand black and white voters that he is better for Chicago. All along the way, Washington and his supporters will suffer from all the slings and arrows of an outraged and somewhat threatened white populous.

Congressman Harold Washington was not the cause but the conduit for a people's movement that had no campaign slogan, no money in a political war chest and no bank credit to enable it to rent office space to accommodate those who volunteered to become political mountain movers. Renault Robinson, one of the faithful disciples in the people's movement, volunteered the use of the Afro-American Patrolman's League's offices, which were located at 7801 South Cottage Grove. Robinson temporarily suspended all operations of the Afro-American Patrolman's League and had extra phones installed for the campaign volunteers in the name of the Patrolman's League because the $60,000 in commitments that had been promised for Washington's political war chest was still an unfulfilled promise. Therefore, initially, the Washington mayoral campaign was being held together by the glue of faith. Moreover, there was not a single piece of literature that read, "Vote for Harold

The blue and white "Harold Washington For Chicago" button, which became a symbol of pride for the wearer during both the primary and the mayoral campaigns.

Washington," except that which appeared in the *All Chicago City News,* the bimonthly newspaper of which Slim Coleman was editor and chief. In fact, Washington for Mayor stationery was not printed because there were no funds. The first ten thousand blue and white "Harold Washington For Chicago" campaign buttons were designed by Helen Schiller and paid for by an anonymous donor. Furthermore, Congressman Washington had to pay for the first campaign literature out of his own pockets, which were not too deep, because the disciples working in the trenches couldn't get anybody on the committee to move and approve any campaign literature. The refusal to act by some persons in authority on the "Washington for Mayor" committee was not intended to be obstructive. The committee members were simply too embarassed to admit that there was no bread in the campaign cupboard.

The money to build a political organization began to trickle in about mid-December. Approximately $30,000 of the $60,000 of the initial commitment had been honored and instantly spent. The monies enabled the committee for the mayoral campaign to start a search for larger offices. On Sunday, January 9, 1983, Congressman Washington announced the opening of six campaign sites at these locations: 109 N. Dearborn (5th floor), 22 E. Van Buren (4th floor), 215 S. Cicero, 4859 S. Wabash, the Fernwood United Methodist Church at 10057 S. Wallace and 2507 W. Fullerton.

The congressman gave short dedication speeches at each of the new offices that Sunday. As he toured his offices, he repeated the theme that the people of Chicago could not afford Jane Byrne as mayor. He also said that the opening of the six new campaign offices around the city stood as proof that he had put together "one of the most awesome independent organizations ever to set forth on this Earth." Washington told the audience at his new office at 4859 S. Wabash, "Don't let any one tell you that this campaign is not structurally well-directed." He also told the audience that he was critical of the news

Some members of the "Harold Washington For Mayor" Finance Committee. Seated left to right: the late Garland Grice, unidentified member, John Dobbs, Jr., Jacoby Dickens, chairman of the board of the Seaway National Bank, unidentified member, Bill Berry, the coordinator of the "Washington For Mayor" campaign. Standing left to right: Attorney Thomas Coffey, Attorney Robin Charleston, Earl Hord, president of the Independence Bank, Clarence Jenkin, Donald C. Walker, publisher and editor of Dollars and Sense *Magazine, Walter Clark, vice chairman of First Federal of Chicago and also co-chairman of the "Washington For Mayor" Finance Committee, the Reverend Jesse Cotton, Attorney Garland Watt, Odell Hicks, Jr., co-chairman, Ernest Bush, Sr., president of Bush Construction Co., John Swain, president of Swain Drugs, the Reverend Al Sampson, pastor of Fernwood Methodist Church, Mrs. Jolyn Robichaux, president of the Baldwin Ice Cream Co. and an unidentified member.*

coverage of his campaign, saying he was "sick and tired of being called the black candidate." They don't talk about Jane Byrne as the white candidate. I don't even want to be called intelligent. That's a put down. It's manifestly obvious I am intelligent," Washington said to loud applause. He continued:

> Nor is it necessary to constantly refer to me as articulate. Why don't they just come out and say I know what I'm talking about. Richard M. Daley believes he should be mayor simply because his father was. We don't have the divine right of kings in this country, I don't think.

Odell Hicks, Jr., the campaign treasurer and co-chairman with Walter Clark, of the finance committee, recalls that the organization was in a hand-to-mouth financial posture because the big boys downtown did not think that Congressman Washington had a ghost of a chance of winning. Odell Hicks states:

> The early financial integrity of the organization was heavily dependent upon the weekend fund-raising parties given in homes across the city by various "Washington for Mayor" volunteers. Some weekends, there would be as many as twenty fund-raisers. The members of the finance committee would always arrange to have someone from the committee present at each

party to bring the money directly back to the campaign headquarters. On Friday afternoon, the organization would usually be broke. However, by the time Monday morning rolled around, we might have as much as $15,000 or $20,000 in the treasure. We were averaging approximately $1,000 per fund-raiser. In some instances, we'd get a check as small as one dollar. On the other hand, we'd might get one for $500 or even $1,000. It was truly a peoples' movement. There's no other way I can describe it.

As a matter of fact, Bill Berry, who came aboard the Washington Express in early December with the blessings of George Johnson of Johnson Products, was somewhat distraught because the big time white folk downtown with whom he was associated at Chicago United and some others who had worked with him on the board of the Chicago Urban League turned deaf ears on him when he asked for money to support a campaign for a black mayoral candidate. Many of Bill's "big shot" white friends did not even give him the common courtesy of returning his calls. Bill Berry was so hurt about being rejected that he told his story to a reporter at the *Chicago Sun Times*.

Washington had relied on Bill Berry's ties to the white establishment to lure campaign funds and support, but Berry's hundreds of phone calls yielded little. The tradition in the city of Chicago is for the business community to hedge their bets with any serious mayoral candidate. That is give each candidate some money. But in the case of Washington, not even the most liberal among them were willing to hedge their bets with Washington.

"The largest individual white pre-primary contributors were former Cook County Hospital Administrator Dr. Quinton Young, author Studs Terkel and

George E. Johnson, president and chief executive officer of Johnson Products. Mr. Johnson loaned three key executives to the Washington campaign on a full-time basis to wit: Bill Berry, Grayson Mitchell and Attorney DeWayne Kyles.

United States Senator Alan Cranston of California," according to the mayoral campaign fund raiser Jay Doherty. The campaign had only one national major white political endorsement. That was from U.S. Senator Alan Cranston (D—Calif) because former Vice President Walter Mondale supported Richard M. Daley while Senator Ted Kennedy supported Jane Byrne in the mayoral primary. Locally, white support was also scarce because only State Representative Barbara Flynn Currie, Fifth Ward Alderman Lawrence S. Bloom and former Forty-fourth Ward Alderman Dick Simpson supported Washington in the primary. The only media to endorse the Washington candidacy were the *Chicago Defender, Dollars and Sense* Magazine and WBBM-Radio.

The amount of monies raised to finance the Washington mayoral campaign was so minuscule that State's Attorney Richard M. Daley and Mayor Jane Byrne literally dismissed Washington's effort as a flash in the pan that they hoped would disappear like a cheshire cat leaving only a smile behind.

The first big public rally for Mayor Washington's campaign was sponsored by the Women for Washington Committee. The women spearheading that group were Nancy Jefferson, Reverend Willie "Little Warrior" Barrow, Addie Wyatt and Rebecca Sive-Tomashefsky. The women's rally which was held at the Hilton Hotel on December 20, 1982, was attended by over three hundred women with only eight being identified as white.

Rebecca Sive-Tomashefsky recalls the following developments that came from the Hilton rally:

> We set a goal that night of $100,000. Reverend Willie Barrow went to Mr. Edward Gardner and asked him to give us some assistance. Mr. Gardner offered us a building near his Soft Sheen plant on East 87th Street, and he installed approximately thirty or forty phones that we could use in our campaign in soliciting other women and other individuals who would be interested in working in the Washington campaign. He also furnished Peggy Montez as the staff person for the Women for Washington campaign committee.

In the meantime, organizations such as Kenwood-Oakwood Community Organization, Midwest Council, Operation PUSH, the Heart of the Uptown Coalition, Fernwood Methodist Church and dozens of other grassroots institutions almost spontaneously converted their headquarters into "Washington for Mayor" satellite offices on their own turf. It was this kind of brush fire independent action that made Congressman Washington's mayoral crusade a movement as opposed to a campaign. In tandem with the satellite activities, Congressman Washington spoke at six to eight black churches throughout

Sponsors of the "Women for Harold Washington For Chicago" committee. (Left to right): Addie Wyatt, Reverend Willie "The Little Warrior" Barrow, Congressman Harold Washington, Rebecca Tomashefsky, and Nancy Jefferson, both co-chairpersons of the committee.

the city of Chicago every Sunday. Even more significant was the fact that he had maintained that kind of speaking itinerary for several years before he announced to run for mayor.

Out at the Soft Sheen campaign offices on East 87th Street, the Women for Washington Committee made plans for their January 16 rally at the Liberty Baptist Church. Nancy Jefferson, who was the co-chairperson with Rebecca Tomashefsky, said:

Our goal was to recruit ten thousand women volunteers. The strategy was to get every woman who had been present at the Hilton rally to bring ten to the Liberty rally. The press had ignored our December rally because they did not think that we had anything going. However, they showed up in full force at the Liberty Baptist Church rally because by that time they probably sensed that we were for real. What they found at 4:30 that Sunday afternoon was a large church that was packed to its rafters with thousands of women standing around the walls, in the lobby, and some outside on the street be-

Congressman Harold Washington addresses a Dr. Martin Luther King birthday rally at the Daley Center Plaza in Chicago. (Left to right): George O'Hare, the congressman and Alderman Allan Streeter (17). Note in the background, the signs that read: "Washington For Chicago," "Come Alive January 25," (the next registration date) and "Let's Bring the Dream to City Hall."

cause they could not get in. All these women had one common goal, and that was to elect Harold Washington mayor of the city of Chicago. Although there was no room in the temple, when Congressman Washington arrived the waters parted as he walked down the center aisle towards the dais. The Barrett sisters jumped up and started singing *I'm Looking for a Miracle,* and the walls of Liberty Baptist Church shook like the walls of Jericho.

The Women for Washington's activity would certainly have to be given a very high grade for the extra dimension that it brought to the Washington movement for mayor. If it was not the hub, it was a significant spoke in the wheel that was rolling Harold Washington toward his destination on the fifth floor in City Hall.

On Wednesday, January 12, 1983, four days before the Women for Washington's rally at Liberty Baptist Church, a group of one hundred and fifty black ministers met at the Hyde Park Hilton Hotel to endorse the candidacy of State's Attorney Richard M. Daley. This meeting was held despite the fact that Dr. Robert Starks and Reverend Al Sampson were leading twenty members of the Task Force for Black Empowerment in a picket line outside of the hotel and chanting, "Plantation politics must end" as the pro-Daley ministers entered the Hyde Park Hilton Hotel meeting. After Daley received a standing ovation from the black ministers, Daley told the group, "To me, each and every one of you has stood by his conviction. I need your help because this is a long and difficult election. We are up against a ten million dollar Byrne campaign fund."

Dr. Robert Starks asked Daley, "Have you spoken out against police brutality? Have you spoken out against abuses of blacks in your community?"

Daley replied, "We have," and then proceeded to talk with the black ministers who were present.

(Left to right) Michael Scott and State's Attorney Richard M. Daley are walking through a picket line in front of the Hyde Park Hilton Hotel where the picketers were shouting, "Plantation politics must go."

The Reverend Al Sampson, pastor of Fernwood United Methodist Church and political activist. Sampson was a member of the staff of Dr. Martin Luther King.

Reverend Al Sampson, pastor of the Fernwood Methodist Church, said he believed that "black ministers must support U.S. Representative Harold Washington, (D—Ill) in the February 22 Democratic mayoral primary." He further added, "What has Byrne done to buy her way into the black churches? What has Daley contributed to politic himself into black churches?"

Some ministers who attended the Daley endorsement rally asked *Chicago Defender* reporter Chinta Strausberg not to identify them whereas others didn't care who knew their beliefs about why Chicago was not ready for a black mayor. One such minister was Reverend O.D. White, pastor of the Spirit of Love Baptist Church, at 6035 S. Ashland. He said:

> If Harold Washington is elected, the city would go down the tubes . . . like Gary. We know what happened to Cleveland, Gary and Detroit. When Mayor Hatcher was elected, the white officials took all the money to Merrillville, Indiana. Gary is now a ghost town. Maybe with the name of Daley, this will not happen to Chicago. However, we're not banking on his name. He can motivate the businesses to produce the jobs.

Reverend E.J. Jones, pastor of the First Unity Baptist Church, 5129 S. Indiana, and an aldermanic candidate for the Third Ward announced his support at the meeting for Daley and hoped his parishioners would follow his suggestion. Jones said he should be able to support whomever he pleased.

> But I am not hung up on black. I'll look at the man. And with Daley, I like what I see. He's the right man for this time.

I know there will be a lot of friends lost in this election, but I'll stand by my convictions. My choice of mayoral candidacy puts me in a bind . . . running for alderman in an all black ward and supporting a white mayoral candidate. But I have to do what I think is right.

Jones added:

It is my spiritual insight and my better judgment that guided me to this decision. I am not an Uncle Tom, but I believe that homework should be done. We moved into this 'Harold Washington for Mayor' too rapidly. I guess we got excited with the extra few thousand registered voters.

Dr. Conrad Worrill, press secretary for the Task Force for Black Political Empowerment, after hearing Jones' remarks retorted:

They said blacks needed more time in 1977 (when Washington ran for mayor.) I think his (Jones) remarks are ludicrous and insane. Is he saying that if Washington is elected mayor, the Sears Tower and Prudential will leave because a black man is mayor?

We are not attacking the black church as an institution. We want spiritual reciprocity. We want Richard M. Daley and Jane Byrne to invite Father George Clements to churches in Bridgeport and in the white Forty-second Ward. We want an open door policy. Our position is that these black preachers can not eat in Bridgeport without being physically attacked. And Daley would never invite them to dinner in his home in Bridgeport. And yet these same preachers have allowed Daley to come into their pulpits. Many

Dr. Conrad Worrill, press secretary for the Task Force for Black Political Empowerment, and also a professor at the Center for Inner City Studies, a Northeastern University Branch, and a columnist for the Chicago Defender.

black churches have always been an appendage or parasite to the Democratic party in this town. I have always felt that that was a theological error. If God is who he says he is, then He ought to take care of you rather than the Democratic party. You never heard of Moses running with pharaoh and eating at pharaoh's table.

Two South Side ministers openly endorsed Jane Byrne, one believing Congressman Harold Washington couldn't win and the other because he did Byrne wrong four years ago.

Father Paul Smith, 52, principal of the Holy Angels Church for the past thirteen years, said he was endorsing Mayor Byrne because she had done a credible job. Smith said:

> Washington is an eloquent speaker and an excellent congressman who should be gunning for (Charles) Percy's seat. Harold Washington is the most outstanding, most articulate politician we have, and I believe Washington would serve himself and the black community better by remaining in Washington, D.C. My support of Mayor Byrne is in no way disparating to him.
>
> But I feel that a person should not run for office unless he is certain he will win, and I don't think he can. I don't think we should send our finest candidates down the drain.

Father Smith said his endorsement of Byrne "as a private citizen" was not connected in any way with Holy Angels Church, which was pastored by Father George Clements, a long time civil rights activist.

The Reverend Joseph Wells, pastor of Mount Pisgah Baptist Church, 4622 S. King Drive, said he was also supporting Byrne after he turned down her re-

Reverend Joseph Wells, pastor of Mount Pisgah Baptist Church. Reverend Wells felt that the people who were picketing in front his church because he supported Jane Byrne were "misguided."

Left: The Reverend Jesse W. Cotton, pastor of the Greater Institutional African Methodist Episcopal Church and the convener of Black Ministers for Harold Washington. Right: Reverend Harry B. Gibson, pastor of St. Mark United Methodist Church.

quest to speak at his church during her 1979 campaign. He explained, "I turned thumbs down on her. I criticized her, and I did not know her. I did the lady a wrong."

Reverend Wells said that when he was working with the African relief fund he decided to see Mayor Jane Byrne and ask her for a donation to the program. He said, "Byrne came through to the tune of $5,000."

"If she was that gracious," Wells added, "This time I owe her because she cared enough to help those black babies in Africa. I have no problems with people picketing my church. They are misguided. . . These things happen because we have no base, and before you can elect a black mayor, you have to get a base."

The Reverend Jesse W. Cotton, pastor of the Greater Institutional African Methodist Episcopal Church, was very disturbed when he read about the fact that the one hundred and fifty black ministers had endorsed Richard M. Daley, and another large group of black ministers had come out for Mayor Byrne, and yet no group of black clergy had endorsed Congressman Harold Washington. Therefore, Reverend Cotton convened a group of nine ministers from various denominations that included Reverends Gessel Berry Jr., A.I. Dunlap, Harry Gibson, Gregory Ingram, John W. Jackson, B. Herbert Martin, Al Sampson, Jeremiah Wright and Claude Wyatt. The group drafted a statement to support Harold Washington that was subsequently given to Reverend Jeremiah Wright to polish and refine. The Reverend Jesse W. Cotton said:

The Reverend Jeremiah Wright, pastor of Trinity United Church of Christ.

We made it known among the clergy that we were not interested in anyone who wanted to simply say 'I support Harold Washington' without putting his or her signature on the line in a full page ad endorsing the congressman for mayor. I realize that this was a hard pill to swallow for some of our members because they were already being hassled by Jane Byrne's City Hall. I believe Jeremiah Wright was one of them and Claude Wyatt was another who was attempting to build a new church on Stony Island and was left with a hole in the ground from some years because of his civil rights activity. Plus there was another minister in our group whose name escapes me now who was trying to get a simple permit to do some work in his church, which he never was able to get.

In spite of the political threats, harassments and hassles, two hundred and fifty ministers signed the "Washington for Mayor" statement that subsequently appeared in the *Chicago Defender* and also in the *Westside Journal.* The ad read:

THE BLACK CHURCH SUPPORTS HAROLD WASHINGTON FOR MAYOR

The black church which stands firmly in the tradition of Dr. Martin Luther King, Jr. (and not that splinter group which backs the "Daley Regime" who opposed Dr. King) . . .

The black church which stands firmly in the Afro-Christian tradition of Richard Allen, George Liele, Henry Highland Garnett, and Henry McNeal Turner—a tradition of liberation and self-determination (and not that other splinter group which rolls over and plays dead in the face of insult after insult to the black community from the "Byrne Regime") . . .

The black church which stands on the shoulders of those African slaves who sang "Before I'd be a slave, I'd be buried in my grave; and go home to my God and be free! . . .

Unashamedly black and unapologetically Christian, we—the undersigned 250 black ministers of the Chicago metropolitan area—put our full personal support behind Congressman Washington in his mayoral bid, and we urge our congregations to do the same.

The ministers listed below are affiliated with the following denominations:

United Methodist Church, African Methodist Episcopal Church, African Methodist Episcopal Zion Church, United Church of Christ, The Lutheran Church, The Presbyterian Church, Reformed Church, Advent Christian Church, Community Church, Christian Reformed Church, Catholic Church, Baptist Church, Church of God and the Christian Methodist Episcopal Church.

Odis Anderson	Alfloyd Butler	John Ferguson
Essex Alexander	Charlie Butler	Hugh Flemming, Sr.
Marvin Alexander	Walter Butts	Basil Foley
Andrew Allen	Steven Camp	Roosevelt Foster
Barbara Allen	Clarence Carr	W.H. Foster
N. Andrew Allen, Sr.	Sterling Cary	William F. Fristoe, Jr.
Nathaniel Allen	Darryl Chew	William F. Fristoe, Sr.
Paul Ayres	Edward Chew	Eugene L. Gibson, Sr.
Willie Barrow	Willie B. Clay	Harry B. Gibson, Jr.
James Bass	George Clements	Rozell Gilmore
Alonzo Bates	Frederick Cole II	Marty Goole
F. Bellman	Major Coleman	C. Jarrett Gray
William Bentley	James O. Conner	Eugene B. Green
Gessel Berry, Jr.	Wilfred Cornell	Betty Jane Greer
George L. Blackwell	Jesse Cotton	Andrew Griffin
D.L. Blakley	Tyron Crider	Arthur Griffin
Arthur Bodley	D.A. Crushon	William H. Griffin
Simon Bodley	George Cummings	Alvin J. Halthon
George Boler	J. Curington	Henry Hardy
Gerald Brantford	L.K. Curry	Ferdinand Hargrett
Kenneth Brigham	Wilson T. Daniel	Phillip A. Harley
Sylvester Brinson III	W.B. Daugherty	R.H. Harris
Curtis Brook	W.D. Davis	V.B. Harris
Earl Brooks	Vesta Dixon	Willie S. Harrison
Fred Brooks	P.D. Dixon	Cornelius Harvey
Melvin Brooks	Sidney Draper	J.H. Harvey
Aaugust Brown	A.I. Dunlap	Cornelius Hayes
Brenda Brown	Leon Edwards	George Henderson
Joseph Brown	Clara Epps	John Henderson
Norval Brown	Elmore Erving	Johnny Henderson
S.T. Brown	Emanuel Erving	Samuel C. Henderson
C.B. Burns	Clay Evans	Ralph G. Henley
Robert Burns	Donald Fairley	Thomas Henry
Eugene Burrage	C.E. Ferguson	William Hilleman

Clarence L. Hilliard
Phillip Hilliard
Larry Hopkins
J. Howard
Gregory Ingram
William Ivy
A.P. Jackson
Darryl Jackson
Frank Jackson
John C. Jackson, Jr.
Paul L. Jakes, Jr.
Paul L. Jakes, Sr.
S.L. Jamison, Jr.
Nathaniel Jarrett
Willie Jemison
William Jenkins, Jr.
William Jenkins, Sr.
Aaron Johnson
Walter B. Johnson
C.W. Jones
Joseph Jones
Mark Jones
Charles W. Jordan
Carl Kenard
Jonathan Keaton
H. Bernard King
Lenard Lane
Lafond Lapointe
Charles Larry
James Lawson, Jr.
James Lawson, Sr.
Christine B. Leak
Raymond Legania
E.M. Lesure
Lloyd C. Lindo
Elmer Lindsay
Abraham Linnear
James Mack
Clifford Mannis
Nelson Mariner
Lilton Marks, Sr.
Gordon Marshall
B. Herbert Martin
Joseph Massir
Donald Matthews
Alfred May
Myron F. McCoy
Ernest McDonald
John McGruder
Odies Mhoon

Michael Miller
R.L. Miller
John W. Moore
Douglas D. Moye, Sr.
Charlie Murray
Warren J. Myles
Joseph Napier, Sr.
Cedell Newsome
Wardell Newsome
Frazier Odom
Wilfred Oliney
Milton Oliver
James Owens
John Parker
Walter Parks
Donald Parson
Sylvia Pleas
Brenda W. Piper
Florezell Porter
John Porter
Reese Price
Ralph Ramey
Eugene Rawlings
Wilfred Reid
Heldia Richardson
George Riddick
Eddie Robinson
Foster Robinson
Wayne Robinson
James Rodgers
J.D. Rogers
Wilson Roman
Charles S. Rooks
Michael Rouse
Al Sampson
Leroy Sanders
Hazelia Savage
Andrew Seals
Leonard Sharbon
Donald Sharp
Levi Sharp
Albert Shears
Richard Shelton
Addison Shields
Dwight Shields
S.F. Simpson
B.T. Smith
Clifton Smith
Julius J. Smith

Kenneth Smith
Willie Smith
J. Smylie
Jesse Taylor
John Taylor
Leroy Taylor
Woodrow Taylor
Claude Tears
Charles Thomas
Darius Thomas
Eddie Thompkins, Jr.
P.W. Thompson
J.L. Thorn
Stephen Thurston
Julius Trimble
Oliver L. Trimiew
Larry Trotter
Edward Turner
Walter E. Turner
Walter P. Turner
Melvin Upchurch
Willie Upshire
William J. Vance
Robbie Wade
George Walker
William Watts
J.C. Weathers
A.H. Weaver
C.L. White
Bennie Whiten
Amos Williams
Charles B. Williams, Jr.
I.W. Williams
H.L. Williams
Jacon Williams, Jr.
Marvell Williams
R. Williams
Tallualaha F. Williams
Walter L. Williams
W.J. Williams
Nelson Willis
Karl Wilson
Napoleon Wordlaw
Donald Wright
Jeremiah A. Wright
Claude Wyatt
Leroy Yates
Henry Young
Alexander Yuille

**We urge you—especially in this month of Black Liberation—to do the same.
On February 22nd, strike a punch for freedom. Vote for Harold Washington
for Mayor of Chicago, and "Let us march on . . ."**

"TIL VICTORY IS WON!"

The DEBATERS.

The January debates were the turning points in Congressman Harold Washington's anemically funded mayoral campaign. Unlike the other two candidates, Richard M. Daley and Mayor Byrne, the debates gave him television exposure that he could not afford to buy, yet needed because he was not well-known outside of the black community except in political circles. Mayor Jane Byrne's offer to debate was one offer that Washington could not refuse. Byrne, the incumbent, made the unprecedented offer because she felt she could beat both candidates hands down with her scythe-sharp intelligence blended with killer instincts. Richard M. Daley, who had some doubts about his ability to beat her and Harold Washington, reacted like the sly old "Br' Rabbit" who asked not to be thrown in the briar patch. The language of Washington's January debate gave black folk a strong hook for his candidacy:

> There are some who believe that I should avoid the race issue, but I will not avoid it because it permeates our entire city and has devastating implications . . . I'm running to end Jane Byrne's four year effort to further institutionalized racial discrimination in this great city.

Washington was not shooting in the dark at Byrne in that final debate. He was reacting to some remarks she had made three days earlier to a group of DePaul University students. Mayor Jane Byrne, in itemizing her record of minority appointments, listed their names, cited their credentials and mentioned that the person happened to be black. When she got to Commissioner of Human Services Lenora Cartwright, Mayor Byrne said: "She happens to be black, but she's good." Again, when she came to Elmer Beard, Jr., the Chicago

Housing Authority executive director, she noted that he also "happened to be black, but (he) also happens to be good." The audience gasped audibly at both of these references; the mayor seemed to be saying that these appointments were good despite being black, implying that it was unusual for blacks to be qualified. Byrne's remarks incensed blacks generally and Washington specifically.

Washington's excellent showing in the first debate made people who did not know him begin to see him differently and look at him seriously as a mayoral candidate. In early February, a small trickle of money people began knocking at the doors of his various campaign offices.

In reference to the debates, Washington said, "Until then, I was practically an unknown quantity. The debates represented the only way for me to project myself as experienced and knowledgeable. It was my role to project that, and I think I did."

Alderwoman Marian Humes (8th) said the reaction she got from many of her fellow white aldermen who watched the debates was the acknowledgement that Harold Washington was the best of the three candidates. However, they also said that their constituents were actually frightened by Congressman Washington's competence and intelligence.

Vernon Jarrett made the following observations about Congressman Harold Washington's debating ability in his January 23, 1983 *Chicago Tribune* column:

> U.S. Representative Harold Washington registered one of the big gains during the first debate last week between the Democratic candidates for mayor of Chicago. It was the enhancement of his support among black people who already supported him.
>
> Washington made a fine impression among blacks throughout the city, including some of those who were beholding to Mayor Jane Byrne and State's Attorney Richard M. Daley. Regardless of how Washington impressed other voters, the First District congressman looked 'mighty good' to blacks in all sections of Chicago. His composure, display of knowledge, superior verbal skills and general stage presence evoked an understandable pride on the South and west sides.
>
> I've listened closely to comments from individuals from all levels of Chicago's black social and economic life for many hours since the debate. As of Thursday afternoon, I had not met a single black person who did not feel that Washington came across 'much better' than Byrne or Daley.
>
> One of the first individuals to praise Washington 'off the record' was one of the high profile black Regular Democrats to openly campaign for Daley.
>
> 'There's no doubt about it, Harold was better than the others,' he said as he left the auditorium of the First National Bank where the debate was held.

'Every black who tries to sell other blacks on supporting anybody but Harold will have to do a lot of explaining—if he can.'

Another 'neutral' (usually meaning an individual obligated to Byrne or Daley) said the following about the debates: 'Probably the greatest impact of Washington's television appeal will be felt in the black churches, particularly those who have pastors who support Byrne or Daley.

The more Washington is seen and heard by large audiences, the greater the gain in respect for his knowledge and forensic skills learned over many years in politics.'

'What I like about the brother is that he didn't have to think so hard to come up with the right answers,' said a black city employee. 'You could tell that he had been thinking about this city for a long time. The brother is smart with guts. I bet his I.Q. is higher than those other two.'

The general enthusiasm generated during the mayoral debates spilled over into the February 6 "Washington for Mayor" rally which was held at the cavernous University of Illinois Pavilion at Racine and Harrison. More than fifteen thousand high-spirited citizens braved Chicago's hawkish weather that Sunday afternoon. The sponsors of the event had feared that the weather would cause the rally to be a failure. Also, the weather forecast was dismal because low temperatures and more snow for the rest of the day were forecast. However, no one had measured the political temperature of the people's movement because at this point in the campaign, nothing could prevent the people from coming out to support their beloved Harold. Many persons arrived hours before the event was to begin at 4:00 P.M.

The people's session at the University of Illinois Pavilion had the flavor of a religious revival unlike Mayor Richard J. Daley's Democratic rallies of the old days. Reverend Henry O. Hardy, pastor of Cosmopolitan Church at 52nd and

Reverend Henry Hardy, pastor of Cosmopolitan Community Church, gave a rhythmic invocation at the Harold Washington For Mayor rally held at the University of Illinois Pavilion.

Wabash, gave a rhythmic invocation. The musical beat was furnished by the Barrett sisters and Curtis Mayfield rather than the Shannon Rovers. When Congressman Harold Washington entered the Illinois pavilion, he received a six minute standing ovation as thousands of balloons floated down from the ceiling, and people cheered and chanted, "Harold! Harold! Harold!" In addition to Washington, many other elected officials were present from all over the United States: Ronald Dellums from California, U.S. Senator Alan Cranston from California, U.S. Representative Gus Savage, Jesse Jackson, former New York mayoral candidate Herman Badillo and Representative Mervyn M. Dymally. Congressman John Conyers, Jr. (D—Mich) pledged that the appearance of the black congressmen was not just cosmetic. He further said, "As many of us who can will be here every day we can from now until February 21."

Father George Clements, pastor of Holy Angels, praised the national leaders for coming to Chicago to assist Washington's election bid. Slim Coleman, director of the Uptown Coalition, told the festive audience that, "When you're poor in Chicago, you know what you can afford. And you know you can't afford Jane Byrne for another four years."

State Senator Richard Newhouse said, "A Washington victory will be a boost to putting many of the unemployed persons here tonight back to work." Newhouse was indicating an end to Byrne's City Hall political patronage formula which excluded many blacks from city employment.

So many speakers and dignitaries were on the dais that Congressman Washington did not get an opportunity to address his followers until the third hour of the program. However, as always, he had a lot to say, and he said it.

Congressman Harold Washington on stage at the University of Illinois Pavilion rally with Reverend Jesse Jackson and U.S. Senator Alan Cranston on his left in a show of unity.

The excitement of the crowd at the Washington rally on February 6 is reflected in the faces of the individuals in the above picture. Note that Juanita Passmore, holding up the Washington sign, is wearing four Washington buttons. Also note that the lady in the aisle is wearing four Washington buttons. The religious fervor of the meeting could be felt but not fully described.

He started by announcing that Byrne was turning the board of education and the Chicago Housing Authority into a racial battleground. He added, "I pledge to you that I will take the Chicago Public Schools out of politics and put them back into the business of educating our children." Then he said he had made one other pledge, but before he could finish his sentence, the crowd anticipated his words and broke into a chant, "Fire Brzeczek! Fire Brzeczek! Fire Brzeczek!"

(Police Superintendent Richard Brzeczek campaigned for Mayor Jane Byrne and warned that the streets would not be safe if Washington were elected. "I guarantee that it (the police department) will be a circus," Brzeczek said. Washington's subsequent appointment of Fred Rice as superintendent has proven Brzeczek 200 percent wrong.)

Odell Hicks, the treasurer of the Harold Washington For Mayor campaign, made the following observations about the pavilion rally:

> I don't think anybody outside of the black community thought that the campaign was serious until the Illinois pavilion rally. Even the sponsors of the event thought that if we could raise enough money to simply pay for the rally expenses including printing tickets, circulars and rent, we would have done well. As a matter of fact, all we wanted to do was to break even and not end up in the hole. Fourteen thousand (dollars) was our break even point.

Left: Dr. Manford Byrd was appointed by Mayor Harold Washington to the position of superinten-dent of the public schools on March 25, 1985. As deputy superintendent, Dr. Byrd stood qualified and ready in the shadows of that job for two decades. Right: Fred Rice was appointed superinten-dent of the Chicago Police Department by Mayor Harold Washington on August 23, 1983. Rice rose through the ranks and is one of the mayor's most important appointees. Rice is the first superinten-dent, since O.W. Wilson was brought here in 1960 to clean up corruption in the police department, who can call his own shots.

My fear of not breaking even went out of the window when I saw that huge crowd. Particularly, after Reverend Jesse Jackson started his fund-raising ritual. The Reverend Jackson started calling on people to come down to the front of the auditorium who wanted to give one hundred dollars and so forth. And of course, as he developed the plea for funds, he continued to lower the dollar amount of the requested contribution. We had two large barrels at the foot of the podium where people could deposit their money. In addition, we had large collection buckets that were being passed up and down the aisles for those who couldn't come to the front or who didn't desire to come to the front.

About 7:30, I left the stage to go under the bleachers to see how the money counters were doing. To my surprise, there were dollar bills every-where, like that picture I saw in the *Sun-Times* where dollars were scattered all over the floor in the CTA office out on 78th Street. We started sorting and counting money about 8 P.M., and we did not finish until after midnight. We counted in excess of $40,000 in one dollar and five dollar contributions. I will never forget how nervous I was that night carrying two mail bags full of money with no police protection around in the trunk of my car. I certainly felt relieved when I was able to deposit the funds at the Independence Bank the next morning.

As the campaign became more visible and more viable, the racist hate mongers began to beat their drums louder and more consistently, thus, prompting the Reverend Jesse Jackson to make the following remarks to the Steering Committee of the Harold Washington for Mayor Campaign:

> The enemies of black emancipation will be unrelenting in attacks upon the candidates and people identified with the candidates the closer we get to February 22. I am convinced that volunteers must operate with the fervor of a crusade and not merely succumb to the mechanisms of a campaign. The will to be free can be neither bought with a big campaign chest nor sold. It was the fervor of the people that allowed Martin Luther King, Jr. to overthrow the southern military occupation forces without a standing army and allowed Jane Byrne to overthrow Bilandic with a $75,000 budget.
>
> The spirit of a crusade is children writing term papers, churches putting out bumper stickers with 'God Bless Harold Washington,' and various forms of freedom-code words and hand shakes.
>
> The thunderous motion of the ground swell among black voters will attract a significant number of whites who will not permit themselves to commit suicide by identifying with losers. The greater the unity among black voters, the more attractive a black candidate will be to the financial and judicial vested interests of the city, the state and the nation.

Congressman Washington is greeted by an admirer as he walks into one of his frequent Sunday services. Note that his admirer is wearing three "Harold Washington For Chicago" buttons.

The week following the "Washington for Mayor" rally at the University of Illinois Pavilion, the voter interest in the Washington election campaign became so strong that one could literally smell it and see it. The South Side and the west side of Chicago broke out with an epidemic of "blue measles." People wore blue and white buttons which read, "Washington For Chicago." For some people, one button was not enough because they had to have one on their caps, their jackets and overcoat. The author will never forget a seedily dressed black gentleman who was passing out literature for Mayor Byrne on the northeast corner of 79th and Stony Island Avenue in front of one of her South Side satellite offices. The gentleman stopped me on that corner and handed me a piece of the Byrne literature and said, "I bet you don't know who I'm going to vote for."

I replied, "Mayor Byrne."

He looked at me with a very hurt expression and threw back his overcoat to display ten Harold Washington blue buttons pinned to his jacket. This gentleman may have been an extremist. However, there were thousands of people infected with the blue measles. As a matter of fact, the epidemic got so bad that people were actually stealing the buttons off other people's garments a week or so before the primary election.

Zenobia Black, wife of Loop College Professor Timuel Black, was shocked when someone broke into her car window and stole one thousand "Harold Washington For Chicago" buttons. She issued a plea for their return saying, "They are really hot items. Everyone's not bad, but if you see somebody out there selling 'Harold Washington' buttons—they are not for sale."

The blue measles fervor of the streets pulled the purse strings of the black penthouse crowd. Al Johnson, the Cadillac dealer, gave a fund-raising party for Congressman Harold Washington on February 18, four days before the

Al Johnson, president of Johnson Cadillac, and Congressman Harold Washington. Johnson raised $60,000 at a single fund-raiser held in his home.

primary, in the penthouse of his North Lake Shore Drive condominium. He invited approximately sixty people. And they, in turn, contributed $60,000 to the Washington fund that night. Johnson's party was the most successful private fund-raiser given by an individual prior to Washington's winning the primary. Edward Gardner spent an additional $50,000 over the $350,000 he had spent earlier and also set up a new satellite office on 47th Street three weeks before the primary with a battery of telephones and volunteers to encourage the new registrants to come out and vote in the primary on February 22, 1983.

The weekend before the primary, the political pharaohs of Chicago declared full scale war by taking off their white robes and letting all of their bigotry hang out. Eddie Vrdolyak, the Cook County party chairman, addressed a northwest side rally and said very frankly:

> A vote for Daley is a vote for Washington. It's a two-person race. It would be the worse day in the history of Chicago if your candidate, the only viable candidate, was not elected. It's a racial thing. Don't kid yourself. I am calling on you to save your city, to save your precinct. We are fighting to keep the city the way it is.

Mayor Jane Byrne picked up on the theme and went to the southwest side, which was Daley territory, and said Daley was through and that the choice was her or Washington. It was the mayor's intention to strike fear in the hearts of those southwest side Gage Parkers and make them shake in their boots with the thought that a black man would be the mayor of Chicago. The blatant racism displayed by both Byrne and Vrdolyak made George Wallace of Alabama look like a pious Baptist Sunday School teacher.

On Tuesday, February 22, the rhetoric ceased, and the voting began. However, the southbound Dan Ryan El trains stopped running without any explanation. The voter turnout during the day in the black wards had been excellent, but at about 5 o'clock, just as people were getting off work to rush back home to vote, they were stranded in the Loop. Thousands of blacks could not get home in time to cast their ballots. How many votes were lost, why the lights went out, why the trains stopped running will never be known. Until this day, no one has given a satisfactory explanation. Could it have been political sabotage?

By 7 P.M. Tuesday night, February 22, the McCormick Inn had been invaded by thousands of Washington supporters. The hotel lobby was crushed tight with wall-to-wall people. The elevators to the upper floors were sardine tight when they reached the lobby. People walked up to the fourth and fifth floors to take the elevator down in order to go up to the very top floors of the

Support for Harold Washington came in many forms. Those who could not afford to buy signs painted them themselves.

hotel. If that sounds crazy, it was because the bedlam of victory reigned at the McCormick Inn on primary night. Outside the hotel, cars were parked bumper to bumper, double parked on the Outer Drive and on the north and south ramps exiting and entering the Drive. The closest legal parking space on the street or vacant lots was six to eight blocks from the McCormick Inn. A view of the parking from the mayor's suite on the penthouse floor of McCormick Inn reminded the author of a quilt patched by his grandmother with one thousand bits and pieces of scraps of material of various colors. There was no description for the parking, other than chaotic.

In the main ballroom on the second floor of the McCormick Inn where Sid Ordower was the master of ceremonies, people stood hip to hip and stomach to back with no breathing room in between.

The Reverend Jesse Jackson, who was accused by many who saw him on television that night of trying to take the limelight from Harold Washington, describes exactly what happened in the McCormick Inn Grand Ballroom on primary night. The author and many others who were there support Jackson's description of the event. Reverend Jackson explains:

> In the first place, the place was too small, just an explosion. It was predict-able. I came to McCormick Inn. I brought my son Yusef with me because I was going to leave for Dayton early the next morning. Harold was supposed to come down at 7 o'clock, then 8, then 9. Sid Ordower, who had been buying time trying to keep the people in order, introduced Lerone Bennett, Jr., who in turn, introduced some other people in an effort to try to keep some sort of order in the crowd. Then about ten minutes later, Lerone Bennett and I were

trying to get out of the crowd. And as I reached the door, Sid Ordower said, 'Ladies and gentlemen, here is Jesse Jackson.' People started screaming, 'Jesse! Jesse! Jesse!' So I went back to the stage. I could see people falling out and fainting from the pressure of the bodies and the extremely high temperature caused by such a large hunk of humanity crammed into such a small space. We discovered that there was a cube maker in the back of the stage. We sent for Dr. Andy Thomas and some nurses to set up a first aid station on the floor. And as people fell out, we brought them through the crowd and put ice packs on their heads in the makeshift medical station back stage. Meantime, it's 10 o'clock, then it's 11 o'clock, then it's 12 o'clock and Harold's still upstairs. People are still coming in, and everybody is asking when is Harold coming. Dr. Conrad Worrill was trying to get an elevator to go up to the penthouse floor to bring Harold down, but as you know, the elevators were jammed. In the meantime, I'm still standing up there doing everything from singing *We Shall Overcome* to telling jokes in an effort to buy time. I did not realize that the entire episode was being shown live on television. Blacks were celebrating; whites were upset because they lost. People who lose get upset. Somebody said Walter Jacobson, on one of his rare insightful moments, said, 'You know, part of the problem is us.'

And somebody said, 'What do you mean?'

He said, 'Look at us. Six white men sitting up here doing a group analysis about black people.'

Our friends felt good about what was happening for Harold Washington. Our enemies used it as a take-off point. A black had won and not the black of their choice. I just became a convenient diversion. That's what happened.

Sid Ordower announced at 12:40 A.M. that Jane Byrne had gone to bed. There was a loud "Boo" from the audience, who was disappointed that she retired without conceding. Ordower said, "Knowing that we are dealing with snakes, Harold Washington wants to know what the exact vote is. We are asking you, pleading with you, to be patient."

A parade of campaign officials continued to march across the podium to proclaim that victory was on the way. "No more Byrne! No more Byrne! No more Vrdolyak!," shouted a member of the crowd referring to Edward Vrdolyak, chairman of the Cook County Democratic party. "Ten million dollars down the drain, and with one million we made it," another Washington supporter yelled, referring to the ten million dollars that Byrne had collected and spent in her campaign to derail the Harold Washington movement.

Early Wednesday, shortly after 2 A.M., ninety-eight percent of the votes had been counted. The unofficial returns gave Congressman Harold Washington 410,780 to Mayor Jane Byrne's 380,840. State's Attorney Richard M. Daley trailed with 339,227 votes. For those who did not believe what they heard, the

Reverend Jesse Jackson and George O'Hare jubilantly displayed a large sheet of paper showing the final vote count which made Congressman Harold Washington the Democratic nominee for mayor of the city of Chicago. Sid Ordower is seen on the extreme right.

Reverend Jesse Jackson and George O'Hare jubilantly held up a large sheet of paper with the latest political score for the screaming crowd. Shortly thereafter, the first black Democratic nominee for mayor of Chicago appeared on the stage of McCormick Inn's Picasso Ballroom before the excited and joyous throng. Congressman Harold Washington said in a very hoarse voice, "I proudly and humbly accept on behalf of the people of the city of Chicago, the Democratic nomination for mayor of Chicago. Less than three months ago, we started out with no money, nothing more than a dream."

The crowd cheered and applauded as several people standing near the podium shouted, "Dr. King's dream lives."

After the cheering subsided, Washington continued. "By your vote, the Democratic party has been returned to the people. We shall have an open and fair government in which all people of all colors, races and creeds are treated fairly, equally and equitably."

The crowd continued cheering as Washington inched his way off the podium.

The majority of the crowd was black, reflecting the base upon which Washington had won. However, a large number of whites and hispanics were also present at the festivities, a reflection of the coalition that Congressman Harold Washington had put together. A large sign across one wall in the Picasso Ballroom echoed the congressman's philosophy. It read, "We have the voting power to heal this city and turn it around towards justice for all

Chicagoans." Sid Ordower closed out the evening shouting to the audience, "We still have another election, Tuesday, April 12. Don't forget now! We have a general election to win!"

The primary fight for Congressman Harold Washington had been relatively clean. Neither of his opponents attacked him personally because each was hopeful of getting some black votes. However, Bernard Epton, the Republican challenger, believed that he could break through the loyalty knot that held most blacks together politically and opted to go after the jugular vein in the general election campaign against Washington. Epton had known Washington for twenty years as a result of their both having served in the Illinois House of Representatives at the same time. Hence, Bernard Epton, James Fletcher, his general campaign manager and former manager for Governor James Thompson, in addition to John Deardourff, his media consultant, decided to use Epton's knowledge of the Democratic mayoral nominee to put some meat on the bones of the skeletons in Harold Washington's closet. Specifically, they decided to zero in on Washington's past legal problems, his jail term in 1972 for failing to file income tax returns, the suspension of his law license in 1970 for not performing work for which clients had paid him, and the failure by Washington to disclose that five legal actions were on record against him when he petitioned to regain his law license in 1975. Although Harold Washington had discussed, disclosed, aired and settled his past legal problems when he ran for mayor in 1977, Epton and his advisors felt that Washington's legal problems were his Achilles heel and their red, white and blue flag, one that they could wrap around their campaign and enable white

Congressman Harold Washington takes his mayoral campaign to Springfield, Illinois. (Left to right): Harold Washington, House Speaker Michael Madigan, State Representatives Carol Moseley Braun and Howard Brookins.

ethnic Democrats to vote Republican without having to feel any guilt feelings about their racial motives.

Epton's tactic of constantly bombarding the media almost daily with some new angle on Washington's past legal problems kept the congressman busy explaining the past as opposed to planning strategies for the future. Epton capitalized on Washington's vulnerability during their debates by using his caustic wit to plant seeds of doubt about the congressman's character. For example, when Washington promised to promote affirmative action at City Hall, Epton quipped, "I'm glad the congressman is going to follow the law. It would be refreshing." Epton twisted the American flag tightly around himself in projecting his image as a war hero while depicting Congressman Washington as a tax-fraud, a shady lawyer and an ex-convict in television commercials. Some television spots included a pitch aimed at countering the guilt Democrats might feel about voting Republican. Thus, one commercial quoted President John F. Kennedy saying, "Sometimes party loyalty asks too much. Surely, this is such a time."

Washington had anticipated such an attack from his opponent, but he had no notion that it would be so down right vicious. In January 1983, Washington felt that he had prepared himself for such an attack when he bared his "financial skeletons" before a Rotary Club luncheon. At that time, Washington showed three charts that disclosed his failure to file federal income tax returns for the years 1964 through 1969, the penalty, the reason the judge ordered a temporary suspension of his license to practice law, and copies of financial statements for the years 1964 through 1981.

"Everyone has skeletons," Washington said. "The only difference is that you may look at mine. This is not to say that I am proud of this, but I don't want a neon sign advertising it. I want to lay to rest rumors that I have been charged with fraud, that I have been disbarred and other untruths." According to Washington's official tax records, in 1964, his gross income was $8,899.92. Taxes withheld were $1,221.08, and taxes owed were $35.53. In 1965, his gross income was $15,370.83. Taxes withheld were $2,054.64, and taxes owed were $32.94. In 1967, he grossed $18,000. Taxes withheld were $2,452 and $0 taxes were owed. In 1969, his gross income was $24,000. Taxes withheld were $3,262, and $439.58 in taxes were owed, thus making the total tax amount for the entire period $508.05.

The IRS-invoked fine was forty days of imprisonment, three years probation and a fine of $1,036.68.

Washington's lawyer Elbert W. Washington felt that his client was being prosecuted for political purposes. And it appears that Honorable J. Sam Perry, judge of the Senior Court of the United States District Court, Northern District of Illinois, East Division, supported that implication he made in court on March 27, 1972 at 2 P.M. in the presence of:

Hon. James Thompson, United States Attorney, (currently governor of Illinois)
represented by
Attorney Howard Hoffman,
appearing on behalf of the plaintiff

and

Harold Washington
represented by
Attorney Elbert W. Washington,
appearing on behalf of the defendant.

On behalf of the defendant, Judge Perry made the following significant statement:

> I just want the record clear that this is not a fradulent case. This man is not charged with defrauding the government and filing false returns. It is a misdemeanor in each of the four years. It is not a felony . . .
>
> So this case is not the case of fraudulent taxes. This is not the case where a man has paid no taxes at all. He simply refused to file his return for these particular years . . .
>
> Mr. Washington, incidentally, the reports *(sic)* I get here is he is an excellent legislator, he has a high standing in this community and is well liked . . .
>
> So far as I know, a number of Democrats have been indicted within the last year or two, and I have yet to see a person affiliated with the *Republican party* who has been indicted for any of these charges . . .
>
> Moses had forty days when he refused to obey the laws that were handed down to him by the Almighty; and the Almighty sent him out forty days to meditate in the wilderness. We don't have any wilderness to send you to, but I think you need forty days' meditation on this matter. You are not a vicious person. You are just refusing to do what is required: namely file returns, and that is the action that I feel is proper.

The information in the United States District Court Case #71 CR 292, United States of America, plaintiff vs. Harold Washington and the judge's comments were never mentioned in the media. Therefore, Bernie Epton continued to drip his daily venom in the ears of anyone who would listen and anyone who was watching television. It appeared during the last weeks of the general election campaign that Bernie Epton was the only political voice in town. He had become Chicago's "last white hope." Life-long card carrying Democrats packed his political rallies, cheered his coded racist remarks and applauded his presence. The overwhelming abundance of racist sentiment that surfaced during Epton's campaign was not created by Bernie Epton; he

simply gave it a vehicle to express loudly and clearly the well-known fact that Chicago was the most racist city in America.

The volume of the racist tone in the Bernie Epton campaign became so loud on Palm Sunday, March 27 when Congressman Harold Washington and former Vice President Walter Mondale visited the St. Pascal's Church on the northwest side, that the national media became attentive. The congressman and the vice president were greeted by Epton demonstrators shouting, "Go home!" "Tax cheater!" "Carpetbagger!" "Epton!" "Epton!" "Epton!" The door that Mondale and Washington had to enter to get inside the church was freshly sprayed with the words, "Nigger, Nigger die!" The shouts and jeering of the Epton placard-waving supporters outside of the church was so disruptive to the church service that Mondale and Washington left the House of the Lord very shortly after they had been seated in deference to those who wanted to worship with their God in peace.

The Palm Sunday shame at St. Pascal's got national headlines. *Newsweek* did a four page cover story on "Chicago's Ugly Election" and *People's Magazine* carried a picture of a jeering mob and the headline "Hatred Walks The Street." *Esquire Magazine* warned that, "The campaign is disastrous for Chicago in terms of its own immediate future and certainly in terms of its national image. The image is taking. And the unfortunate thing is that part of the image is true." The *Boston Globe* said, "Obviously, there are people who are hyping the racial aspect of this campaign, but it can't be minimized. It is the overriding issue. Racial polarization tends to give the city a black eye that maybe is not fully deserved. But at the same time, there's a great deal of truth in it."

On Monday, March 28, Congressman Claude Pepper, the 80-year-old Floridian, came to Chicago to campaign for Congressman Harold Washington before an audience of senior citizens on the northwest side. The mention of Washington's name to the group evoked cat calls, boos and jeers. "This is America," Pepper exploded. "It isn't the color of a man's skin . . . it's his character and the spirit he possesses that determines excellence. I wouldn't be here if I didn't believe that Harold Washington would be a good mayor for every man, woman and child in this city."

The members of the Democratic party were too devious to jeer and boo Harold Washington. They simply switched their political allegiance overnight and began vigorously supporting the election of Bernie Epton. George Dunne was an exception. In the primary, Dunne had supported Richard Daley. And when Daley lost, he immediately switched his support to Washington. Dunne said:

> Some people were surprised that I switched to Washington so quickly. As
> far as I was concerned, the primary was over, and the numbers were in. I

Bernard Epton supporters shouting expletives at Vice President Walter Mondale and Congressman Harold Washington as they arrive at St. Pascal's Church on Palm Sunday, March 27, 1983.

Mondale and Washington leaving St. Pascal's Church through a throng of placard-waving and jeering Epton supporters.

Cook County President George Dunne and Harold Washington marching near the front of the St. Patrick's Day Parade. Comptroller Roland Burris can be seen at the extreme right.

believe in democracy, that the majority rules and the minority should be heard. And the majority said that Harold Washington was the Democratic candidate. There were a number of so called Democratic committeemen who worked against him. They sabotaged the party. I'm not cut out of that kind of cloth. I supported Jane Byrne when Jane Byrne won four years ago and beat the organization. Therefore, I'm going to support Washington. I called him up St. Patrick's Day and asked him if he was going to march in the parade and if he thought it would be alright if he walked with me.

He said, 'I'd love it George.'

We walked in that parade together near the front. He had been assigned a donkey drawn carriage in thirty-eighth place among the one hundred and thirty-one floats and bands. I am consistent. It's a matter of principles. Whoever wins the primary, I'm going to support. I have supported Washington since the day he got in office. And I will continue to do it until such time that something comes up and I feel that he isn't the guy. But I haven't seen that yet.

Washington wore a "McWashington" button, a green tie, green boutonniere, and he waved and blew kisses at the crowd as he marched. Marching with Washington, in addition to Dunne, were Attorney General Neal F. Hartigan, the Reverend George Clements, State Comptroller Roland W. Burris and Washington's pollster Patrick Caddell. Washington said he felt entitled to front rank because "I am the next mayor." He added, "My grandfather would be proud. Washington is an English name."

In the evening on St. Patrick's Day, Epton gave a speech dripping with sarcasm. Epton showed no mercy for liberal white voters and Washington's black supporters. He called them both "clowns." Epton said, "I am not ashamed of being white." He told an audience of about one hundred Republicans from the Forty-seventh Ward that "some of my great liberal friends feel they have to

State Comptroller Roland W. Burris is the first black official to be elected to a statewide position in Illinois' history.

prove they are liberal by voting for a black who was sentenced to jail and who's supposed to run a city budget of $2 billion plus. They call that liberalism. I call it sheer idiocy."

Many who knew Harold Washington as an even-tempered, cool-headed individual felt that Washington was being too much of a gentleman by not getting angry and fighting back at Epton on every street corner and on every rooftop. On Thursday, April 7, five days before the election, Bernie Epton's campaign reached such a low that Congressman Washington could no longer contain his fury. Comparing himself to fiery President Harry S. Truman, Washington angrily declared that night that he would fight "scurrilous" attacks on his candidacy. He was particularly irate about flyers that accused him of molesting a child. "That particular piece of literature happened to

On April 1, a fund-raiser for Harold Washington was hosted by Louis, Gerald and Kenneth Ritter and Jay Hergott in the penthouse of a condominium at 1110 N. Lake Shore Drive, where both Bernard Epton and Louis Ritter reside. (Left to right): Louis Ritter, Harold Washington, and Dempsey J. Travis.

*Mayoral candidate Harold Washington jubilantly greets a crowd of sup-
porters from lake front precincts at the Belmont Hotel on Saturday, April
9, 1983. Seen at the extreme left is County Commissioner of the
Metropolitan Sanitary District, Joanne Alter.*

describe me as a child molester," Washington shouted to a sympathetic,
stunned lakefront audience at Mundelein College.

"Here I am running a campaign in which little children all over my com-
munity are ecstatic . . . telling their mothers to vote for me . . ." he shouted.
"Why am I the victim of this scurrilous, incessant low life kind of attack? . . .
Well, I've had enough."

Contending that his character and manhood were at stake, Washington
launched into a five minute attack against what he said were other "lies"
about his taxes and bill payments.

"I say to you, Mr. Epton, if you want this job so badly that you will destroy
character . . . if the taste of power is so much in your veins . . . if that's the
kind of man you are . . . and these are the kinds of dogs of racism and scur-
rilism you are going to unleash, I say to you Mr. Epton I will fight you day and
night." The audience at the rally for the Forty-eighth and Forty-ninth Wards
responded wildly to Washington's remarks, repeatedly interrupting him with
chants of "We Want Harold."

In the opinion of some political pundits, when Harold Washington put on
his boxing gloves and came out in the middle of the ring fighting during the
last few days before the election, he picked up the extra margin that he needed
to win the fight! And win he did with 96.4 percent of the city's 21,914 precincts
counted. Washington had 640,738 votes or 51.5 percent of the vote to Epton's

599,144 or 48.2 percent of the vote. The Social Workers Party candidate, Ed Warren, had 3,613.

Shortly before midnight, Cook County Democratic Party Chairman Edward R. Vrdolyak predicted a victory of only 35,000 out of a record turnout of slightly more than 1.3 million. Vrdolyak said, "No one expected this kind of turnout." At the same time, a glum Epton rushed past reporters at the Palmer House and said, "This is certainly not conceding. But Washington got a surprising number of votes in the black area, more than enough to take over the lead I had." Minutes later, Governor Thompson left Epton's headquarters with a grim look. "There are some new numbers," Thompson said, explaining they "are Harold's."

Washington and his fiancee Mary Ella Smith left a north Michigan Avenue hotel about 12:45 A.M., where they had been watching the election returns with some friends. Enroute to the Donnelley Hall, they stopped by the Imperial Suite in the Hilton Hotel and Towers to greet about one hundred of his supporters who had gathered there at a victory party sponsored by Al Johnson. From the Hilton, a caravan of cars from the Hilton party followed the mayor to

Harold Washington and Senator Richard Newhouse arriving at the Donnelley Hall on 22nd and King Drive moments before Washington gave his victory speech.

Donnelley Hall at 22nd and King Drive, where he arrived at approximately 1:30 A.M. to be greeted by fifteen thousand supporters who had been screaming, "Harold! Harold!," throughout the evening as television sets flashed returns showing that Washington was in the lead.

The throng of people who had been waiting all evening cheered and chanted, "Harold! Harold!," when they got a glimpse of the mayor moving toward the podium with his arms raised in victory. After the applause, feet stomping and cheers subsided, the mayor-elect said:

> Tonight, we are here to celebrate a resounding victory. We have fought a good fight. We have finished our course, and we have kept the faith. We fought it with . . . a phalanx of people who had mostly never been involved in political campaigns before.
>
> This has truly been a pilgrimage. Our government will be moving forward, as well, including more people and more kinds of people than any government in the history of Chicago. Today, Chicago has seen the bright daybreak for this city and for perhaps the entire country. The whole nation is watching, and Chicago has sent a powerful message. Oh yeah!
>
> They are watching. They are watching out of the crucible of this city's most trying election, carried on in the tide of the most massive voter turnout in Chicago's history.
>
> Blacks, whites, hispanics, Jews, gentiles, protestants and Catholics of all stripes have joined hands to form a new Democratic coalition and to begin in this place a new Democratic movement. The talents and dreams of our citizens and neighborhoods will nourish our government the way tributaries feed into the moving river of mankind.
>
> We have kept the faith in ourselves as decent, caring people who gather together as part of something greater than themselves.
>
> We never stopped believing that we were a part of something, something good and something that has never happened before. We intend to revitalize and to rebuild this city, to open the doors and be certain that its babies are healthy and its old people are fed and well housed.
>
> We intend that our city will grow again and bring prosperity to all of its citizens.
>
> We have been victorious, but I am mindful that there were many other friends and neighbors who were not a part of our campaign. But that's alright. It's alright.
>
> We will never get them all. That's why we have a democracy because there are many opinions in a city as diverse and multi-ethnic as the city of Chicago.
>
> To those who supported me, I offer my deepest thanks. I will initiate your reforms, but challenge you. I challenge each and every one of you to rededicate your efforts to heal the divisions that have plagued us.

Reflecting the ecstasies of victory on election night: State Senator Richard Newhouse (center) raises the hands of Harold Washington, Chicago's first black mayor and his fiancee, Mary Ella Smith.

Each of us must reach out and open our arms. Together we will overcome our problems and restore Chicago to its proper position as one of the most dynamic cities in all the world.

To those of you, wherever you are, who opposed this election, I assure you I understand your needs and your desires. I know I can rely on you for your assistance and cooperation.

Chicago is one city. We must work as one people for our common good and our goals. Our politics are strong and vigorous and are on the verge of revibrant growth and development here. I want to reach out my hand in friendship and fellowship to every living soul in this city. The healing that we seek—the healing we are winning—is economic and social and more. And it includes justice and love, not just ourselves as individuals alone, but for all, all, all in this city.

Our most important concern at this moment is unity. Tomorrow, we'll begin with a prayer breakfast. It will be a symbol that our gathering together includes all Chicago. I intend to lead a prayer for our continued unity and great success as a great city. I can't tell you how happy I am. History—history was made tonight.

And this history has been coming on the horizon. It's been talked about in our streets and homes, but there's nothing like victory to make an old track man like me glad he dared to enter this race.

A great adventure has begun right here. I am proud to be a part of that

The day after at a post-election "unity" breakfast. (Left to right): Judge Saul Epton substituted for his brother, the defeated candidate Bernard, Mayor Jane Byrne, Mayor-elect Harold Washington and State's Attorney Richard M. Daley.

great adventure. I am so humble by the fact that you have seen fit to give me the responsibility to lead that adventure.

And, as I said before, I did nothing during the course of that campaign that would make it difficult to govern this city with fairness and justice to all.

And to all of you out there who worked so hard for this day but are not here and to all of you over this country who wished us well, sent us your honor, sent us some of your children to work with us, prayed for us and worked for us—God bless you all, and thank you from the bottom of my heart.

Earlier Tuesday evening, April 12, the Reverend Jesse L. Jackson saluted about eight hundred college students bussed in from seven colleges to help turnout the vote for Harold Washington. "You are Harold Washington's unpaid army, his silent force," Jackson told the students at the Operation PUSH headquarters at 930 E. 50th Street.

The reaction to Washington's election even among his supporters was as varied as there were people. For example, one woman struck a sour note when she murmured, "There are not enough (white people) who hate us enough to turn this Democratic stronghold over to the Republicans." Earlier in the evening, Jim Compton announced, "It's too early to shout because the numbers are not in." However, later he exclaimed, "I feel great. This is the most significant thing that's happened in Chicago." His voice was hardly audible over the clamor of the crowd in the background.

With tears in his eyes, Father George Clements, pastor of Holy Angels

James Compton, president of the Chicago Urban League.

Church, stated, "Never in my wildest dreams did I feel I would live to see the day my city would elect a black mayor. I am gratified for those fair-minded white people who voted for Harold Washington, because they proved that we do have a city where there can be love and brotherhood."

Despite the light, intermittent showers and chilly night air, an elderly woman uttered, "I may be sick in the bed with a cold tomorrow, but this miracle is what I've been waiting for all my life. I am not about to let the weather keep me from witnessing it."

Eighteen days after mayor-elect Harold Washington made his victory speech at Donnelley Hall, he was sworn in as the forty-second mayor of Chicago at an inauguration ceremony at Navy Pier that should have been called a coronation because of the splendor and grandeur of the occasion. All of the ladies were beautifully gowned, and the men were well groomed to the button. The pride of being present on such an occasion beamed through both the tear-filled eyes and broad smiles of both the sons and daughters of slaves and slave masters. Water welled in the eyes of many who had witnessed and heard Dr. Martin Luther King give his *I Have A Dream Speech* at the foot of the Lincoln Monument in Washington, D.C. twenty years earlier. Harold Washington was symbolic of that dream in that he was a descendent of slaves and also the keeper of the dream.

Harold Washington's inauguration was unique in that historically such ceremonies were held in the City Council Chambers and attended only by relatives and a very few close friends of the candidate. In contrast, Washington had a three-tier speaker's platform and four thousand invited guests representing every ethnic and political persuasion in the city. Even the music, furnished by the Morris Ellis Orchestra, gave each ethnic group a song

Judge Charles E. Freeman swears in Harold Washington as Chicago's forty-second mayor, as Cardinal Joseph Bernadin looks on.

After taking the oath of office, Mayor Washington is congratulated with a kiss by his fiancee, Chicago school teacher Mary Ella Smith. Also seen on the extreme left is City Treasurer Cecil Partee, County Clerk Walter J. Kozubowski, Studs Terkel, Judge Charles A. Freeman and Gwendolyn Brooks, Illinois Poet Laureate.

to remember. The band played *Hav'a Nagilla, Besame Mucho, "A" Train, Irish Eyes, Auf Wiedersehn, O Sol Mio, Fanfare for The Common Man*, and of course, *Illinois* and *Chicago, My Chicago* and closed out the entire ceremonies with *Oh Happy Day*. Prior to Ellis playing *Oh Happy Day*, Mayor Harold Washington's final inaugural remarks to the audience were:

> In our ethnic and racial diversity, we are all brothers and sisters in a quest for greatness. Our creativity and energy are unequaled by any city anywhere. We will not rest until renewal of our city is done . . . I reach out my hand and ask for your help. With the same adventurous spirit of Jean Baptiste DuSable when he founded Chicago, we're going to do some great deeds here together. In the beginning, there was the Word. Throughout this campaign, you have given me the word. The word is over. Let's go to work!

Bibliography

CHAPTER I
SOURCES

BOOKS:

Andreas, A. T., *History of Chicago From the Earliest Period To The Present Time, Volume I, 1670 to 1857*, Chicago: A. T. Andreas, 1884.
_____, *History of Chicago From The Earliest Period To The Present Time, Volume II, 1857 to 1871*. Chicago: A. T. Andreas, 1885.
_____, *History of Chicago From The Earliest Period To The Present Time, Volume III, 1872 to 1885*, Chicago: A. T. Andreas, 1886.
Harris, Norman Dwight, *The History of Negro Servitude In Illinois and of the Slavery Agitation In That State, 1719 to 1864*, Chicago: A. C. McClurg and Co., 1904.
Pierce, Bessie Louise, *A History of Chicago, Volume I The Beginning of a City: 1673-1848*, New York: Alfred A. Knopf, 1937.
_____, *A History of Chicago, Volume II From Town To City, 1848-1871*, New York: Alfred A. Knopf, 1940.
Scammon, Jonathan Young, William B. Ogden *(Ferguson Historical Series Number 17)*, Chicago: Ferguson Printing Company, 1882.

NEWSPAPERS:

Chicago Democrat, 26 November 1833, (First Newspaper Printed In Chicago)
Chicago American, 8 May 1835
The Daily Chicago American, 9 April 1839
The Chicago Morning Democrat, 27 February 1840
Chicago Tribune, 10 October 1840
Western Citizen, (Anti-Slavery Anterperance Weekly, 1842-53)
The Chicago Express, 21 October 1843
The Chicago Daily Journal, 3 September 1844
Chicago Tribune Morning Edition, 28 December 1850

DIRECTORIES:

Ferguson, Robert, *Directory of the City of Chicago,* 1839
Norris, James W., *Business Directory and Statistics of the City of Chicago*, Eastman and Davidson, 1846.
Hall and Smith, *Chicago City Directory*, 1853-54, Chicago: Robert Ferguson, 1863.
The City of Chicago Directory, 1850

City of Chicago Directory, 1860
City of Chicago Directory, 1870
The Colored Men's Professional and Business Directory of Chicago, Chicago: I. C. Harris Publisher, 1865.

OFFICIAL DOCUMENTS:

"An Act To Incorporate The City of Chicago Was Passed", 4 March 1837, *Chicago Democrats,*Chicago 1837.
Sixth Census of the United States, 1840 p. 221.

REPORTS

Vital Statistics, 1850, U.S. Census Report
U.S. Census Report, 1860
U.S. Census Report, 1970

CHAPTER II
SOURCES

BOOKS:

Historic City: *The Settlement of Chicago, Chicago: The City of Chicago, Department of Development and Planning,* 1976.
Drake, St. Clair, Horace R. Cayton, *Black Metropolis, A Study of Negro Life In The Northern City, Volume I & II,* New York, Harper and Row, 1945.
Hammurabis, F. H., *The Negro In Chicago: 1779-1929, Volumes I & II,* Washington Intercollegiate Club of Chicago, Inc. Chicago, 1929.
Holli, Melvin G., Peter., d' A. Jones, editors, *The Ethnic Frontiers,* Grand Rapids, Michigan: William B. Eerdmans Publishing Company, 1977.
Quarles, Benjamin, *Black Abolitionist,* Oxford University Press, New York, 1969.
Travis, Dempsey J., *An Autobiography of Black Chicago,* Urban Research Institute, Inc., Chicago, 1981.

PAMPHLETS:

"Chicago Negroes and the Reformer, 1847-1853" *The Negro History Bulletin, 1 April 1958*
John Jones, *The Black Laws of Illinois and a Few Reasons Why They Should be Repealed* (Chicago, 1864)
Rose E. Vaughn, "Black Codes" 10 October 1946
The Negro History Bulletin, 1 April 1958

JOURNALS:

Illinois Journal of the Senate, 3 January 1864
Illinois Journal of the House of Representatives, 4 January 1864.
Illinois Journal of the House of Representatives, 2 January 1865.

LETTERS:

Mrs. John Jones, 43 Race Street To Albert Hagen, Chicago Historical Society, 29 July 1879.
From Theodora Lee Purnell, Granddaughter of John Jones to H. Maxon Holloway, Assistant Director of Chicago Historical Society, 24 October 1955.

DOCUMENTS:

Certificates of Freedom For John Jones and Mary Jones

NEWSPAPERS:

The Watchman of the Prairies 11 January 1853
Northwestern Christian Advocate 16 March 1853
The Christian Times 31 August 1853
Chicago Tribune 26 October 1864
Chicago Evening Journal 19 November 1864
Chicago Tribune 20 January 1865
Chicago Evening Journal 11 March 1875
Chicago Tribune 22 May 1879
Chicago Defender 21 July 1951

CHAPTER III
SOURCES

BOOKS:

DuBois, W.E.B. *Black Reconstruction,* Philadelphia, PA.: Abbott Saifer, 1935.
Gosnell, Harold F. *Negro Politicians: The Rise of Negro Politics in Chicago,* Chicago: University of Chicago Press, 1935.
Holli, Melvin G. and Peter d' A. Jones, *The Ethnic Frontier,* Grand Rapids, Michigan: William B. Eerdmans, 1972.
Norton, Mary Beth, et al. *A People And A Nation: A History of the United States,* Boston, MA: Houghton Mifflin Company, 1982.
Robb, Frederic H. *The Negro in Chicago: 1779–1929.* Volume One, Chicago: Washington Intercollegiate Club of Chicago, Inc., 1929.

NEWSPAPERS:

Inter Ocean, 16 October 1876
Inter Ocean, 6 November 1876
Inter Ocean, 30 September 1878
Inter Ocean, 7 October 1878
Chicago Tribune, 14 September 1880
State Capital, 27 February 1892
Chicago Tribune, 16 September 1884
Chicago Tribune, 20 September 1884
Chicago Tribune, 21 September 1884

Chicago Tribune, 24 September 1884
Cleveland Gazette, 22 November 1884
Cleveland Gazette, 21 February 1885
Cleveland Gazette, 28 March 1885
Cleveland Gazette, 29 August 1885
Cleveland Gazette, 5 September 1885
Champaign-Urbana News Gazette, 14 December 1981
Chicago Tribune, 19 December 1899; 20 December 1981
Chicago Tribune, 19 December 1899; 20 December 1981
Inter Ocean, 19 December 1899
Chicago Legal News, 19 December 1899

JOURNALS:

The Journal of Negro History, Autumn, 1932
The Journal of the Illinois State Historical Society, Summer 1981

UNPUBLISHED DOCUMENTS:

Branham, Charles Russell, "A Transformation of Black Political Leadership
    In Chicago", 1864–1942. Doctoral Dissertation, University of Chicago, 1981.

NOTES, MINUTES AND LETTERS:

*Minutes of the 34th Annual Meeting of the Wood River Baptist Association and
    Sunday School Convention held with the Olivet Baptist Church.* Chicago:
    Olivet Baptist Church, 29, 30 and 31 August 1872.
Thomas, John W. E. "Letter to the Republicans of the Second Senatorial Dis-
    trict." 8 October 1978
Jones, Roma. "A Note on the John W. E. Thomas Family." Chicago: Chicago
    Historical Society

DIRECTORIES AND REFERENCE BOOKS:

Chicago City Directory for the Years 1860–1870, 1871 and 1890–91
Illinois Legislative Manual, 30th General Assembly, 1877–1878
The Colored Men's Professional and Business Directory of Chicago, Chicago:
    I. C. Harris, 1885.
Chicago City Directory, 1886
Lakeside Business Directory, 1890
United States Biographical Dictionary
Champaign-Urbana News Gazette, 14 December 1981
Municipal Reference Street Guide, 1900

CHAPTER IV
SOURCES

BOOKS:

Dedmon, Emmett, *Fabulous Chicago*. New York: Atheneum, 1981

Drake, St. Clair and Horace R. Cayton. *Black Metropolis: A Study of Negro Life In A Northern City*. Volume One. New York: Harper and Row, Inc., 1945.

Duster, Alfreda M. ed. *Crusade For Justice: The Autobiography of Ida B. Wells*, Chicago: University of Chicago Press, 1970.

Gosnell, Harold F. *Negro Politicians: The Rise of the Negro Politics in Chicago*. Chicago: University of Chicago Press, 1935.

Harrison, Carter H. *Stormy Years*. New York: Bobbs-Merrill, 1935.

Johnson, Claudius O. and Carter H. Harrison, *Social Science Studies*, Chicago: University of Chicago Press, 1928

Norton, Mary Beth, et al. *A People and A Nation: A History of the United States*. Boston: Houghton-Mifflin, 1982

Ransom, Reverdy C. *Pilgrimage of Harriet Ransom's Son*. Nashville, Tennessee: Sunday School Union, 1946.

_____, *The Negro*. Boston: Ruth Hill Publisher, 1935.

Robb, Frederic, *The Negro In Chicago: 1779–1927*. Volume One. Chicago: The Washington Intercollegiate Club of Chicago, Inc., 1927.

Spear, Allan H. *Black Chicago: The Making of a Negro Ghetto*. 1890–1920. Chicago: University of Chicago Press, 1967.

Travis, Dempsey J., *An Autobiography of Black Chicago*, Chicago: Urban Research Institute, Inc., 1981.

Wendt, Lloyd and Herman Kogan. *Lords of the Levee*. New York: Bobbs-Merrill, 1943.

MANUSCRIPTS AND THESES:

Monroe Nathan Work. Negro Real Estate Holders of Chicago. M.A. Thesis, University of Chicago, 1903.

PERIODICALS:

"The South Loop Legacy". *Chicago Magazine*. September 1978

DIRECTORIES AND REFERENCES:

The Colored Men's Professional and Business Directory of Chicago, Chicago: I.C. Harris, 1885.

CHAPTER V
SOURCES

BOOKS:

Clayton, Edward T., *The Negro Politician, His Success and Failure*, Chicago: Johnson Publishing Company, 1964.

Duster, Alfreda M., ed. *Crusade For Justice: The Autobiography of Ida B. Wells*, Chicago: University of Chicago Press, 1935.

Gosnell, Harold F., *Negro Politicians: The Rise of the Negro Politics in Chicago*, Chicago: University of Chicago Press, 1935.

Harrison, Carter H., *Stormy Years*, New York: Bobbs-Merrill, 1935.

Robb, Frederic H., *The Negro in Chicago, 1779-1927*, Volume One. Chicago: The Washington Intercollegiate Club of Chicago, Inc., 1927.

Stone, Chuck, *Black Political Power In America*, New York: Delta Publishing Co., 1968.

Travis, Dempsey J., *An Autobiography of Black Chicago*, Chicago: Urban Research Institute, Inc., 1981.

Wendt, Lloyd & Herman Kogan, *Big Bill of Chicago*, New York: Bobbs-Merrill Company, Inc., 1953.

NEWSPAPERS:

Broad Ax 10 February 1900
Broad Ax 7 December 1900
Broad Ax 4 May 1907
Broad Ax 26 March 1910
Daily News 2 April 1910
Chicago Defender 15 June 1912
Chicago Defender 17 April 1915
Chicago Daily News 21 July 1915
Broad Ax 15 January 1916
Broad Ax 9 April 1919

OFFICIAL RECORDS:

Board of Cook County Commissioner's Official Proceedings, 10 September 1900, p. 793.

UNPUBLISHED PAPERS:

Branham, Charles Russell, "A Transformation of Black Political Leadership in Chicago 1864-1942" Doctoral Dissertation, University of Chicago, 1981.

INTERVIEWS:

Evans, Lovelyn, Former Personnel Director, Campbell Soup Company, Personal Interview, Chicago, 3 June 1985.

Harewood, Richard A., Municipal Judge, Personal Interview, Chicago, 2 January 1985.

Jones, Sidney, Judge, Personal Interview, Chicago, 20 December 1984.
Payne, Aaron, Attorney, Personal Interview, Chicago, 5 September 1984, 15 October 1984.

CHAPTER VI
SOURCES

BOOKS:

The Negro In Chicago, *A Study of Race Relations and Race Riots of 1919,* New York: Arno Press, 1968.
Biles, Roger, *Big City Boss,* DeKalb, Illinois: Northern Illinois University, 1984.
Brashler, William, *The Don, The Life and Death of Sam Giancana,* New York: Harper and Row, 1977.
Clayton, Edward T., *The Negro Politician, His Success and Failures,* Chicago: Johnson Publishing Company, 1964.
Demaris, Ovid, *Captive City,* New York: Lyle Stuart, Inc., 1969.
Duster, Alfreda M., ed, *Crusade For Justice, An Autobiography of Ida B. Wells,* Chicago: University of Chicago Press, 1970.
Gosnell, Harold F., *The Negro Politicians,* Chicago: University of Chicago Press, 1937.
―――――――, *Machine Politics: Chicago Medal,* Chicago: University of Chicago Press, 1937.
Gottfried, Alex, *Boss Cermak of Chicago,* Seattle: University of Washington Press, 1962.
Kobler, John, *Capone, The Life and World of Al Capone,* New York: G. P. Putnam's Sons, 1971.
Lewis, Lloyd, Jesse Henry, Justin Smith, *New York: The History of its Reputation,* New York: Harcourt Brace & Company, 1929.
McDonald, Forrest, *Insull,* Chicago: University of Chicago Press, 1962.
Ottley, Roi, *The Lonely Warrior: The Life and Times of Robert S. Abbott,* Chicago: The Henry Regnery Company, 1955.
Royko, Mike, *Boss, Richard J. Daley of Chicago,* New York: E. P. Dutton & Co., Inc., 1971.
Spear, Allan H., *Black Chicago: The Making of a Negro Ghetto,* 1890–1920, Chicago: University of Chicago Press, 1970.
Tuttle, William M., Jr., *Race Riot, Chicago In The Red Summer of 1919.* New York: Atheneum, 1970.
Wendt, Lloyd and Herman Kogan, *Big Bill of Chicago,* Chicago: Bobbs-Merrill Company, Inc., 1953.

NEWSPAPERS:

"What Will He Do If Chosen Mayor." *Chicago Daily Tribune,* 14 March 1915.
"Entire City Turns Out To Welcome Mayor Thompson" *Chicago Defender,* 1 May 1915.
"Hardings (Blacks) Heroes Fill 20 Automobiles, *Chicago Defender,* 1 May 1915.

"Alderman DePriest of the 2nd Ward Orders Motion to Make August 23, 1915 A Legal Holiday Commemorating The Emancipation of the Race.", *Chicago Defender,* 23 August 1915.

"House Passes Bill by 111 to 2 Supporting Thompson Who Refused a Permit to Birth of a Nation Exhibitors.", *Chicago Defender,* 22 May 1915.

"Thompson Refuses to Close Saloons.", *Chicago Defender,* 16 October 1915.

"Charles E. Morrison Appointed Special Messenger to His Honor William Hale Thompson.", *Broad Ax* 2 October 1915.

"Mayor William H. Thompson Closes Saloons For The Weekend." *Broad Ax* 9 October 1915.

"Blacks Still Loyal To Thompson" *Norfolk News* 15 April 1916.

"William H. Thompson Still On Warpath After Alderman He Cannot Control.", *Broad Ax* 26 October 1916.

"City Hall Forces Show Real Democracy Slatmaking" *Chicago Defender* 6 July 1919.

"Second Ward Votes Decides Battle" *Chicago Defender* 5 April 1919.

"Chicago Police Deliver Rum In Patrol Wagon" *New York Times,* 27 September 1921.

"Big Screen of Votes To Denver" *Chicago Daily Tribune,* 4 April 1927.

"Honorable William Hale Thompson Elected Mayor of Chicago by 512,740 Votes" *Broad Ax* 9 April 1927.

INTERVIEWS:

Dickerson, Earl B., Attorney, Personal Interviews, Chicago, 25 February 1982, 5 September 1984, 7 September 1984, 28 June 1985.

Harris, George S., President, Metropolitan Mutual Assurance Company, Personal Interview, Chicago, 17 September 1965.

Hill, Richard C., Attorney, President of Douglas National Bank, Personal Interview, Chicago, 11 June 1968.

Lewis, Julian, Dr., Personal Interview, Chicago, 16 September 1984.

CHAPTER VII
SOURCES

BOOKS:

Banfield, Edward C., *Political Influence,* New York: The Free Press, 1961.

Bontemps, Arna and Jack Conroy, *They Seek A New City,* New York: Doubleday, Inc., 1945.

Clayton, Edward T., *The Negro Politician: His Success and Failure.* Chicago: Johnson Publishing Co., 1965.

Drake, St. Clair and Horace R. Cayton, *Black Metropolis: A Study of Negro Life in a Northern City,* Volume One, New York: Harper and Row, 1945.

Strickland, Arvarh E., *A History of the Chicago Urban League,* Urbana, IL: University of Illinois Press, 1966.

Travis, Dempsey J., *An Autobiography of Black Chicago*, Chicago: Urban Research Institute, Inc., 1981.

Tuttle, William M., Jr., *Race Riot: Chicago in the Red Summer of 1919*. New York: Atheneum, 1977.

Weaver, Robert C. *The Negro Labor: A National Problem*, New York: Harcourt, Brace and Company, 1946.

——————————, *The Negro Ghetto*, New York: Harcourt, Brace and Company, 1948.

Wendt, Lloyd and Herman Kogan, *Big Bill of Chicago*, New York: Bobbs-Merrill Company, Inc., 1953.

THESES AND DISSERTATIONS:

Branham, Charles Russell, "The Transformation of Black Political Leadership in Chicago: 1864–1942." Doctoral Dissertation, University of Chicago, 1981.

NEWSPAPERS:

"Mayor Regrets Race Riots and Hopes Child Slayer Will be Punished Swiftly." *The Chicago Daily Journal*, 28 July 1919.

"Blacks' Condition Caused Race Riot." *Chicago Daily News, Journal*, 28 July 1919.

"Drain Reserves To Curb Black Belt Tonight." *Chicago Daily Journal*, 28 July 1919.

"Crowd Courts With Rioters." *Chicago Daily Journal*, 31 July 1919.

"Mayor Asks For 2,000 More Police." *Chicago Daily Journal*, 31 July 1919.

"Negro Rioters Draw Heavy Fines In Court." *Chicago Daily News*, 31 July 1919.

"Joe Stauber Is Accused As Negro Slayer." *Chicago Journal*, 1 August 1919.

"Devastation Wrought By Race Riots." *"Chicago Daily Journal*, 1 August 1919.

"Drowning Not Stones Killed Negro Whose Death Started Riot." *Chicago Daily Journal*, 2 August 1919.

"Four Thousand Troops Held Under Arms to Put Down Riots." *Chicago Daily Journal*, 28 July 1919.

"Troops Move on Chicago As Negroes Shoot Into Crowds." *Chicago Daily News*, 29 July 1919.

"Two Negroes Slain by Mob In Loop." *Chicago Daily Journal*, July 1919.

"Order Troops To Quit Zone of Race Riot." *Chicago Daily Journal*, 8 August 1919.

"Death To Rioters Court Says." *Chicago Daily Journal*, 8 August 1919.

"Representative of Urban League Give Observations of Race Riots In Chicago." *New York Age*, 16 August 1919.

"Citizens Ask Removal Of The State's Attorney." *Chicago Defender*, 6 September 1919.

MAGAZINES:

"Chicago Rebellion Free Black Men Fight Free White Men." *The Messenger*, September 1919.

"The KKK in Chicago." *The Messenger,* December 1919.
"A Report on Chicago Riot By An Eyewitness." *The Messenger,* December 1919.

CHAPTER VIII
SOURCES

BOOKS:

Clayton, Edward T., *The Negro Politician,* Chicago: Johnson Publishing Co., Inc., 1965.

Drake, St. Clair and Horace R. Cayton, *Black Metropolis,* Volume One. New York: Harper and Row, 1945.

Duster, Alfreda M. ed. *Crusade For Justice: The Autobiography of Ida B. Wells.* Chicago: University of Chicago Press, 1970.

Gosnell, Harold F. *Negro Politicians.* Chicago: University of Chicago Press, 1968.

Robb, Frederic H. ed. *The Negro in Chicago: 1779-1927.* Volume One. Chicago: Washington Intercollegiate Club of Chicago, 1927.

Stone, Chuck, *Black Political Power In America.* New York: Delta Books, 1968.

Wendt, Lloyd and Herman Kogan, *Big Bill of Chicago,* New York: Bobbs-Merrill Co., Inc. 1953.

DISSERTATIONS:

Branham, Charles Russell, "The Transformation of Black Political Leadership in Chicago: 1864-1942." Doctoral Dissertation University of Chicago 1981.

NEWSPAPERS:
Chicago Defender
"Wright The Mayor's Candidate." 10 April 1920.
"Ed Wright Sought To Be Bomb Target." 15 April 1924.
"Addison and Jackson Re-Elected — Ed Wright Victor Over DePriest." 28 February 1925.
"Edward H. Wright Dead." 9 August 1930.
"Edward H. Wright Leaves $10,000 to Ms. McCoo." 9 August 1930.

INTERVIEWS:

Dickerson, Earl B., Attorney, Personal Interview, Chicago, 21 August 1977. Various dates in 1978, 1979, 1980, 1981; 5 September 1984; 7 September 1984.

Davis, Corneal, Commissioner of Voter Registration, city of Chicago, Personal Interview, Chicago, 30 July 1984, 19 August 1984, 14 November 1984, 4 December 1984, 5 January 1985.

Payne, Aaron, Attorney, Personal Interview, Chicago, 5 September 1984, 14 October 1984.

Harewood, Richard A., Municipal Judge, Personal Interview, Chicago, 2 January 1985.

Jones, Sadie Waterford, Widow of State Representative, Warner B. Douglas, Personal Interview, Chicago, 22 April 1985.

CHAPTER IX
SOURCES

BOOKS:

Clayton, Edward T., *The Negro Politician: His Success and Failure.* Chicago: Johnson Publishing Co., Inc., 1964.

Drake St. Clair and Horace R. Cayton, *Black Metropolis: A Study of Negro Life in a Northern City.* Volumes One and Two. New York: Harper and Row, 1945.

Duster, Alfreda M., ed. *Crusade For Justice: The Autobiography of Ida B. Wells.* Chicago: University of Chicago Press, 1970.

Forrest, McDonald, *Insull,* Chicago: University of Chicago Press, 1962.

Gosnell, Harold F. *Negro Politicians: The Rise of the Negro In Politics in Chicago.* Chicago: University of Chicago Press, 1935.

Ottley, Roi, *The Lonely Warrior: The Life and Times of Robert S. Abbott.* Chicago: Henry Regnery Co., 1955.

Stone, Chuck, *Black Political Power in America.* New York: Delta Books, 1970.

Travis, Dempsey J., *An Autobiography of Black Chicago.* Chicago: Urban Research Institute, Inc. 1981.

PERIODICALS:

"Oscar DePriest and the Jim Crow Restaurants In The U.S. House of Representatives." *Journal of Negro Education,* 15 (1966): 77–83

NEWSPAPERS:

Chicago Defender
"DePriest Is Named To Go To Congress." 5 May 1928.
"DePriest Elected: Foul Count Upset Ballot Dope." 19 November 1928.
"William Hale Thompson Is The Greatest Friend For The Colored Race Since The Days of Abraham Lincoln." 1 November 1930.
"DePriest Re-elected Judge, George Beaten As Democrats Win." 8 November 1930.
"DePriest Asks Law Changes To Seek Fair Trials." 13 November 1933.
"Congressman Unable to Reconcile King and Alderman Dawson." 13 January 1934.

"DePriest Puts Jim Crow Order Up To Congress." 27 January 1934.
"DePriest's Resolution To Get Hearing On House On Jim Crow Barrier In Cafe." 28 April 1934.

Baltimore Afro-American:
"Congressman Who Signed The DePriest Resolution To Probe Jim Crow Cafes." 31 March 1934.
"House To Head Two Reports On Restaurant Jim Crow." 16 June 1934.

UNPUBLISHED MATERIAL:

Branham, Charles Russell. The Transformation of Black Political Leadership in Chicago, 1864–1942. Dissertation University of Chicago, 1981.
"House To Head Two Reports On Restaurant Jim Crow." Washington, DC: *Congressional Record,* 16 June 1934.

DOCUMENTS:

"Judgment Search On Oscar DePriest." *Metropolitan Title Report Company.* 8 December 1933.

INTERVIEWS:

Davis, Corneal, Commissioner of Voter Registration, City of Chicago, Personal Interview, Chicago, 30 July 1984, 19 August 1984, 14 November 1984, 4 December 1984, 5 January 1984.
Dickenson, Earl B., Attorney, Personal Interview, Chicago, 5 September 1984, 7 September 1984.
Duster, Alfreda M. Barnett, Retired Social Worker, Personal Interview, Chicago, 10 July 1977.
Evans, Lovelyn, Former Personnel Director, Campbell Soup Company, Personal Interview, Chicago, 3 June 1985.
Gibson, T.K., Sr., President, Supreme Liberty Life Insurance Co., Personal Interview, Chicago, 10 September 1965.
Harris, George S., President, Metropolitan Mutual Assurance Company, Personal Interview, Chicago, 17 September 1965.
Jones, John, Attorney, Personal Interview, Chicago, 20 December 1984.
Mead, Ripley B., Sr., Real Estate Broker, Personal Interview, Chicago, 10 June 1969.
Smith, Reginald, M.D. Ophthalmologist, Personal Interview, Chicago, 15 June 1969.

CHAPTER X
SOURCES

BOOKS:

Allswang, John W., *A House For All People, Ethnic Politics In Chicago, 1890–1936*, Lexington Kentucky: University of Kentucky Press, 1971.

Biles, Roger, *Chicago City Boss*, DeKalb, Illinois: Northern Illinois University Press, 1984.

Brashler, William, *The Don: The Life and Death of Sam Giancana*, New York: Harber and Row, 1977.

DeMaris, Ovid, *Captive City*, New York City: Lyle Stuart, Inc., 1969.

Gosnell, Harold F., *The Negro Politicians, The Rise of Negro Politics In Chicago*, Chicago: University of Chicago Press, 1935.

Gottfried, Alex, *Boss Cermak of Chicago, A Study of Political Leadership*, Seattle: University of Washington Press, 1962.

Kantowitz, Edward R., *Polish-American Politics in Chicago 1888–1940*, Chicago: University of Chicago Press, 1975.

Kobler, John, *Capone, The Life and World of Al Capone*, New York: G. P. Putnam's Sons, 1971.

Lindell, Arthur G., *City Hall: Chicago's Corporate History, 1966*, Chicago Municipal Reference Library, 1966.

Peterson, Virgil W., *Barbarians in our Midst; A History of Chicago Crime and Politics*, Boston, Massachusetts: Little Brown and Company, 1952.

Rakove, Milton, *We Don't Want Nobody, Nobody Sent: An Oral History of the Daley Years*, Bloomington, Indiana: Indiana University Press, 1979.

Wendt, Lloyd, Herman Kogan, *Big Bill of Chicago*, New York: Bobbs-Merrill Co., Inc., 1953.

Williams, Elmer Lynn, *The Fix It Boys: The Inside Story of the Kelly-Nash Machine*, Chicago, Illinois: Elmer Lynn Williams, 1940.

Wilson, James Q., *Negro Politics, The Search for Leadership*, Glencoe, Illinois: Free Press, 1960.

NEWSPAPERS:

"Thousands Attend Mayor Cermak's Funeral", *Chicago Defender*, 11 March 1933.

"Republicans Fired by New Mayor, South Side is Affected," *Chicago Defender*, 11 April 1931.

"As Thousands Bow and Grief for Bier of A.J. Cermak," *Chicago Defender*, 11 March 1933.

"Legislators Give Wide Power to City Council," *Chicago Defender*, 1 April 1933.

"New Elected Council Rushes Re-organization Vote on May Soon," *Chicago Daily News*, 5 April 1933.

"Mayor Corr Returns Home," *Chicago Daily News*, 11 April 1933.

"Kelly Pledges Energy to City as He Accepts," *Chicago Daily News*, 13 April 1933.

"Handpicked Audience Crowds Council Chambers to Witness Election of New Mayor," *Chicago Daily News,* 13 April 1933.

"Party Caucus is Unanimous for Park Chief," *Chicago Daily News,* 13 April 1933.

"Democratic Caucus Agreed On Edward J. Kelly As Marty's Choice for Mayor," *Chicago Daily News,* 13 April 1933.

"Police Say 'Yes We Beat Niggers' ", *Chicago Defender,* 19 May 1934

UNPUBLISHED MATERIAL:

Branham, Charles Russell, "The Transformation of Black Political Leadership in Chicago: 1864–1942." Dissertation. University of Chicago, 1981.

INTERVIEWS:

Davis Corneal, Commissioner of Voter Registration, City of Chicago, Personal Interview, Chicago, 5 January 1984, 30 July 1984, August 1984, 14 November 1984, 4 December 1984.

Dickerson, Earl B., Attorney, Personal Interview, Chicago, 2 February 1982, 5 September 1984, 7 September 1984, 28 June 1985.

Duster, Alfreda M. Barnett, Retired Social Worker, Personal Interview, Chicago, 10 July 1977.

Jones, John, Attorney, Personal Interview, Chicago, 27 March 1985.

Smith, Reginald, M. D. Ophthalmologist, Personal Interview, Chicago, 15 June 1969.

CHAPTER XI
SOURCES

BOOKS:

Biles, Roger, *Big City Boss, In Depression and War: Mayor Edward J. Kelly of Chicago,* DeKalb, IL: The Northern Illinois University Press, 1984.

Clayton, Edward T., *The Negro Politician, His Success and Failure,* Chicago: Johnson Publishing Co., Inc., 1964.

Daylie, Daddy'O, *You're On The Air,* Chicago: Children's Press, 1969.

Dedmon, Emmett, *Fabulous Chicago,* New York: Atheneum Press, 1981.

Degregorio, William A., *The Complete Book of U.S. Presidents,* New York: Dembner Books, 1950.

Demaris, Ovid, *Captive City,* New York: Lyle Stuart, 1969.

Drake, St. Clair, Horace R. Cayton, *Black Metropolis, A Study of Negro Life In A Northern City,* Volume I and Volume II, New York: Harper & Row 1945.

DuBois, W. E. Burghardt, *Black Reconstruction 1860–1880,* Philadelphia: Albert Saifer Publisher, 1935.

Gosnell, Harold F., *The Negro Politician, The Rise of Negro Politics In Chicago,* Chicago: University of Chicago Press, 1935.

Gottfried, Alex, *Boss Cermak of Chicago,* Seattle, WA: University of Washington Press, 1962.

Herrick, Mary J., *The Chicago Schools — A Social and Political History,* Beverly Hills, California: Sage Publication, 1971.

Kane, Joseph Nathan, *Facts About the President,* New York: H.W. Wilson Company, 1981.

McKissick, Floyd, *Three-Fifths Of A Man,* London: MacMillan, Company, 1969.

Ottley, Roi, *The Lonely Warrior: The Life and Times of Robert S. Abbott,* Chicago: Henry Regnery Company, 1955.

Royko, Mike, *Boss: Richard J. Daley of Chicago,* New York: E.P. Dutton and Company, Inc., 1971.

Travis, Dempsey J., *An Autobiography of Black Chicago,* Chicago: Urban Research Institute, 1981.

Wendt, Lloyd and Herman Kogan, *Big Bill of Chicago,* New York: Bobbs-Merrill Co., Inc., 1935.

Who's Who In Chicago and Vicinity, The Book of Chicagoans, Chicago: N.A. Marquis Co., 1931.

Who's Who In Chicago Illinois, Ninth Edition, Chicago: N.A. Marquis, 1950.

NEWSPAPERS:

"Mayor Kelly to Carry Out Cermak's Policies," *Chicago Daily News,* 14 April 1933

"Advance of Social Work To Be Illustrated At Fair," *Chicago Daily News,* 24 April 1933

"Bill to Force Payment of Tax to Help Chicago is Approved by House," *Chicago Daily News,* 26 April 1933

"Loop Bankers Ready to Adopt Kelly Plan for Paying Teachers," *Chicago Daily News,* 1 May 1933

"Mark Out Site for Memorial to Pointe DuSable," *Chicago Daily News,* 17 May 1933

"World's Fair Ready For Huge Crowd at Opening Tomorrow," *Daily News,* 26 May 1933

"Race Get's Honored Spot in Chicago Pageant," *Chicago Defender,* 22 September 1934

"Mayor Kelly Balks Jim Crow In Morgan Park," *Chicago Defender,* 13 October 1934

"Mayor Kelly Stands Up for Principles in Morgan Park Affair," *Chicago Defender,* 13 October 1934

"The Representative DePriest Defeated by A. W. Mitchell," *Chicago Herald Examiner,* 8 November 1934

"Jim Crow Move Hits Snag at Springfield," *Chicago Defender,* 17 November 1934

LETTERS:

From Arthur W. Mitchell to Mayor Edward J. Kelly, Mitchell Papers, Chicago Historical Society Files, 15 April 1933

From Alain Locke to Arthur W. Mitchell, Mitchell Papers, Chicago Historical Society Files, 8 November 1934

From A. L. Foster, Executive Secretary of the Chicago Urban League, to Honorable Arthur W. Mitchell, Mitchell Papers, Chicago Historical Society, 14 November 1934

From Arthur W. Mitchell to Mayor Edward J. Kelly, Mitchell Papers, Chicago Historical Society Files, 22 November 1934

From Attorney C. Francis Stradford to Congressman Arthur W. Mitchell, Mitchell Papers, Chicago Historical Society

From Alfred T. Lucas to Honorable Arthur W. Mitchell, Mitchell Papers, Chicago Historical Society Files, 5 January 1935

TELEGRAM:

From Oscar DePriest to Congressman-elect Arthur W. Mitchell, Mitchell Papers, Chicago Historical Society

DIRECTORIES:

Business Directory of Chicago, 1907 Publisher unknown

DOCUMENT:

List of Contributors to the Arthur W. Mitchell Campaign, Mitchell Papers, Chicago Historical Society, 3 December 1934

PERIODICALS:

Bristol-Cochran, Margaret, "Changes In Work Relief In Chicago," *Social Service Review* (June 1955): 243–55

Bristol-Cochran, Margaret, "WPA In Chicago, Summer 1936," *Social Service Review* (September 1937): 372–394

Gordon, Rita, "The Change in the Political Alignment of Chicago Negroes During The New Deal," *Journal of American History* (December 1969): 584–603

Gosnell, Harold F., "The Chicago Black Belt, Black Belt As A Political Background" *American Journal of Sociology* 39 (November 1933): 324–41

UNPUBLISHED AND ARCHIVAL MATERIALS:

Branham, Charles, The Transformation of Black Political Leadership in Chicago, 1865–1942, Doctoral Dissertation, University of Chicago, 1981

Hirsch, Arnold R., *Politics and the Interracial Struggle for Living Space in Chicago, After World War II,* Department of History and School of Urban and Regional Studies, University of New Orleans, 1984

INTERVIEWS:

Davis, Corneal, Former State Representative, and currently Commissioner of Voter Registration, City of Chicago, Personal Interview, Chicago, 19 August 1984.

Herrick, Mary, School Teacher, Organizer and Civic Leader Author, Personal Interview, Chicago, 17 October 1979.

Todd, Thomas N., Attorney, Former Professor of Constitutional Law at Northwestern University, Personal Interview, Chicago, 15 August 1985.

Wheeler, Lloyd, The President of Supreme Life Insurance Company, Personal Interview, Chicago, 25 July 1985.

Young, Dave, Advertising Manager, *Chicago Defender*, Personal Interview, Chicago, 25 July 1985.

CHAPTER XII
SOURCES

BOOKS:

Banfield, Edward C. and Martin Meyerson, *Politics, Planning, and the Public Interest, The Case Of Public Housing In Chicago*, New York: First Press, 1935.

Biles, Roger, *Big City Boss, In Depression Year and War:* Mayor Edward J. Kelly of Chicago, DeKalb, Illinois: The Northern Illinois University Press, 1984.

Clayton, Edward T., *The Negro Politician, His Success and Failures*, Chicago: Johnson Publishing Company, Inc., 1964.

Drake, St. Clair, Horace R. Cayton, *Black Metropolis, A Study of Negro Life In A Northern City*, Volume I & II, New York: Harper & Row, 1962.

Ottley, Roi, *The Lonely Warrior: The Life and Times of Robert S. Abbott*, Chicago: Henry Regnery Company, 1955.

Holli, Melvin J. and Peter J. d'A. Jones, *The Ethnic Pioneer*, Grand Rapids, Michigan: William B. Eerdmans Publishing Company, 1977.

NEWSPAPERS:

"Mayor Edward Kelly Names His Choice For Alderman," *Chicago Defender*, 23 February 1935

"Second Ward Republicans Push Fight For Kelly," *Chicago Defender*, 28 March 1935

"Mayor Kelly Rips Into Governor Horner, *Pittsburgh Courier*," 11 April 1935

"Chicago Wards Go Democratic," *Pittsburgh Courier*, 13 April 1935

"Roosevelt Reveals Outline of Work-Relief Program," *Chicago Daily News*, 17 April 1935

"United States Government Buys Property For Housing Project," *Chicago Defender*, 11 July 1935

"Editor Abbott Picks Colonel McCormick For U.S. Senate," *Chicago Defender*, 5 October 1935

"Joe Louis Rules Ten Minutes," *Chicago Defender*, 5 October 1935 January 1935

"State Relief Bill Due To Become Law Today," *Chicago Daily News*, 15 January 1935

"12,000 Chicago Home Owners On Relief List," *Chicago Daily News*, 18 January 1935

"Mayor Kelly Has Plans to Hire 50,000 on PWA Program," *Chicago Defender*, 19 January 1935

"Third Ward Democrats Plan Roosevelt Party On January 3rd," *Chicago Defender*, 26 January 1935

"Former Alderman Endorses Dawson For Re-Election," *Chicago Defender*, 26 January 1935

"Make Plea For Moratorium In Eviction Drive," *Chicago Defender* 26 September 1936

"Real Estate Men Fight New Hyde Park Bar," *Chicago Defender*, 26 September 1936

"U.S. Buys More Land For South Side Project," *Chicago Defender* 3 October 1936

"DePriest Crushed By Avalanche Of Votes," *Chicago Defender* 7 November 1936

"State Fails To Pay Widow of Warren B. Douglas," *Chicago Defender*, 28 March 1936

"Anderson and Dawson Expect Primary Win," *Chicago Defender*, 28 March 1936

"Tenants Threaten Rent Strike, Join Force To Put Halt To Gouging," *Chicago Defender*, 27 March 1937

"GOP Dawson To Oppose Mitchell," *Washington Afro-American*, 15 January 1938

"Mitchell Safe: DePriest Likely to Get GOP Bid," *Washington Afro-American*, 3 April 1938

"South Side Kelly Committee Tells of Improvements," *Chicago Defender*, 11 February 1939

"Douglas Gets Mayor Kelly's Endorsement," *Chicago Defender* 25 February 1939

"Joe Louis is Rated Third by NBA Group," *Chicago Defender*, 27 March 1937

PERIODICALS:

Allswang, John M., "The Negro Voter And A Democratic Consensus: A Case Study, 1918–1936," *Journal of Illinois State Historical Society* (Summer, 1967): pp. 145–75.

Homel, Michael W., "Lilydale School Campaign of 1936: Direct Action In The Verbal Protest Era," *Journal of Negro History* (July 1974): pp. 228–241.

Bristol, Margaret C., "W.P.A. In Chicago, Summer, 1936: A Study of 550 Cases Assigned to W.P.A. Now Under Care By The Chicago Relief Administration," *A Social Service Review* (June 1937): pp. 372–394.

Gordon, Rita Werner, "The Changes In The Political Alignment Of Chicago Negroes During The New Deal," *Journal of American History* (December, 1969): pp. 584–603.

POLITICAL PAMPHLETS:

"Franklin D. Roosevelt: A Leader In Progressive Democracy," Issued by The National Coloured Citizens, Roosevelt Committee, 331 Madison Avenue, New York City

"Tenants' War Cry," Issued by Consolidated Tenants Association, 3507 South Parkway, Suite 6, Chicago, Illinois

INTERVIEWS:

Davis, Corneal, Commissioner of Voter Registration, City of Chicago, Personal Interview, Chicago, 30 July 1984, 19 August 1984, 14 November 1984, 4 December 1984, 5 January 1985.

Dickerson, Earl B., Attorney, Personal Interview, Chicago, 21 August 1977. Various dates in 1978, 1979, 1980, 1981; 5 September 1984; 7 September 1984.

Harewood, Richard A., Municipal Judge, Personal Interview, Chicago, 2 January 1985.

Herrick, Mary, School Teacher Organizer and Civil Leader Author, Personal Interview, Chicago, 17 October 1979.

Jones, Sadie Waterford, Widow of State Representative, Warren B. Douglas, Personal Interview, Chicago, 22 April 1985.

Payne, Aaron, Attorney, Personal Interview, Chicago, 5 September 1984, 14 October 1984.

Wheeler, Lloyd, The President of Supreme Life Insurance Company, Personal Interview, Chicago, 25 July 1985.

CHAPTER XIII
SOURCES

BOOKS:

Clayton, Edward T., *The Negro Politician: His Success and Failures,* Chicago: Johnson Publishing Company, Inc., 1964

Forrest, McDonald, *Insull,* Chicago: University of Chicago Press, 1962.

Stone, Chuck, *Black Political Power in America,* New York: Delta Books, 1970.

Travis, Dempsey J., *An Autobiography of Black Chicago,* Chicago: Urban Research Institute, Inc., 1981.

NEWSPAPERS:

"Mitchell Files Jim Crow's Suit Against Railroad," *Chicago Defender,* 19 March 1938.

"Dawson Beats Anderson," *Chicago Defender,* 16 April 1938.

"DePriest Loses In Chicago Primary," *Chicago Defender,* 23 April 1938

"A Negro Charged First Class For Jim Crow Ride, A Suit Says," *Pittsburgh Courier,* 30 April 1938.

"DePriest, Simmon Action Again," *Pittsburgh Courier,* 22 January 1938.

"Marjorie S. Joyner Forced To Ride In Baggage Car With Corpse," *Pittsburgh Courier,* 29 January 1938.

"Dickerson Is Right Man For Second Ward Alderman," *Chicago Defender,* 25 February 1939.

"Dickerson Endorsed By Dawson," *Chicago Defender,* 25 March 1939.

"Green Vote 640,000 GOPs Record Since 1932," *Herald Examiner,* 5 April 1939.

"Grant Happy Over Aldermanic History," *Chicago Defender,* 8 April 1939.

"Whites Back Moves To Shift Black Group," *Chicago Defender,* 13 May 1939.

"Tittinger's Captain In Open Revolt," *Chicago Defender,* 17 June 1939.

"Dawson Opens Campaign For Re-Election," *Chicago Defender,* 28 January 1939.

"William E. King, Loser of Many Tilts, Lead Political War?" *Chicago Defender,* 6 April 1940.

"Dickerson and Dawson Fight For Mitchell's Seat," *Chicago Defender,* 7 February 1942.

"Dawson Ran Over Alderman Earl Dickerson New Crowd," *Chicago Defender,* 18 April 1942.

"Holds Final Rites For R.R. Jackson," *Chicago Defender,* 20 June 1942.

"Chicago Defender Endorses William L. Dawson, Representative of the First Congressional District and William G. Straten for State Treasurer," *Chicago Defender,* 31 October 1942.

"William E. King Congressional Nominee For First Distrct," *Chicago Tribune,* 1 November 1942.

"Negroes Swing Back To GOP, Praise Brooks," *Chicago Tribune,* 1 November 1942.

"Dawson Sees Victory Sign of Loyalty," *Chicago Defender,* 6 November 1942.

"Where Was Mitchell?" *Chicago Defender,* 7 November 1942.

"Here Is What Dawson Gets As New Congressman," *Chicago Defender,* 2 December 1942.

"Dickerson Enters Race for Congress, *Chicago Defender,* 31 January 1942.

LOCAL GOVERNMENT DOCUMENTS:

Minutes of the City Council, 6 July 1938, 24 March 1939, 13 September 1939, 10 May 1939, 14 June 1939.

Minutes of the City Council Proceedings, 8 March 1940.

MAGAZINE ARTICLES AND SPEECHES:

Sullivan, Louis, "The Negro Vote," Atlantic Monthly, October 1940 pp. 477–84.

Speech by Earl Dickerson, "Occasion of the Celebration of Black History Month," Chicago Historical Society, 20 February 1983.

Remarks by Earl B. Dickerson on "Occasion Of The Hyde Park Career Academy Third Annual Heroes' Day," Chicago, IL., 18 March 1983.

PAMPHLETS:

"News from Labor Non-Partisan," *Native Cook County,* 17 April 1939.

INTERVIEWS:

Dickerson, Earl B., Attorney, Personal Interview, Chicago, 25 February 1982, 5 September 1984, 7 September 1984, 28 June 1985.

Davis, Corneal, Commissioner of Voter Registration, City of Chicago, Personal Interview, Chicago, 30 July 1984, 19 August 1984, 14 November 1984, 4 December 1984, 5 January 1985.

Harewood, Richard A., Municipal Judge, Personal Interview, Chicago, 2 January 1985.

Jones, Sadie Waterford, Widow of State Representative, Warren T. Douglas, Personal Interview, Chicago, 22 April 1985.

Payne, Aaron, Attorney, Personal Interview, Chicago, 5 September 1984, 14 October 1984.

Harris, George S., President, Metropolitan Mutual Assurance Company, Personal Interview, Chicago, 17 September 1965.

CHAPTER XIV
SOURCES

BOOKS:

Biles, Roger, *Big City Boss In Depression and War:* Mayor Edward J. Kelly of Chicago, DeKalb, Illinois: Northern Illinois University Press, 1984.

Drake, St. Clair and Horace R. Cayton, *Black Metropolis: A Study of Negro Life In A Northern City,* Volume I & II, New York: Harper & Row, 1945.

Meyerson, Martin, and Edward C. Banfield, *Politics, Planning, In The Public Interest,* New York: Free Press, 1955.

Norton, Mary Beth, David M. Katzman, William M. Tuttle, Jr., *A People and A Nation,* Boston: Houghton Mifflin Company, 1982.

Ottley, Roi, *The Lonely Warrior: The Life and Times of Robert S. Abbott,* Chicago: Henry Regnery Company, 1955.

Stone, Chuck, *Black Political Power in America,* New York: Delta Books Company, 1968.

Travis, Dempsey J., *An Autobiography of Black Chicago,* Chicago: Urban Research Institute, Inc., 1981.

Truman, Margaret, *Harry S. Truman,* New York: William Morrow & Company, Inc., 1973.

Truman, Harry S., *Memoirs By Harry S. Truman: Volume I, Years of Decision,* New York: Double Day & Co., Inc., 1955.

_____., *Memoirs By Harry S. Truman: Volume II, Years of Trials and Hope,* New York: Double Day & Company, Inc., 1956.

Wilson, James Q., *Negro Politics: The Search for Leadership,* Glencoe, Illinois: Free Press, 1960.

NEWSPAPERS:

"Skidmore Quiz To Jar Gamblers," *Herald Examiner,* 3 February 1939.

"State Asks To Halt Vice Near U. of I," *Herald Examiner,* 18 February 1939.

"Grand Jury Called Commissioner Allman On Gambling," *Chicago Herald American,* 21 September 1939.

"Federal Agents Hunt Skidmore's Racket Partners," *Chicago Daily News,* 1 November 1939.

"Charles Kelly Is Responsible For Gambling," *Chicago Daily News,* 13 November 1939.

"Policy King Shot Dead In Car On Michigan Avenue," *Herald American,* 9 January 1939.

"Policy-King Killing Lead to Capone Ring," *Herald Examiner,* 11 January 1939.

"A Capone Policy Grab Is Seen Only As A Dream," *Chicago Defender,* 6 June 1942.

"Roosevelt and Wallace Here For Big Rally," *Chicago Defender,* 28 October 1944.

"Roosevelt Leads Dewey By 4-1 Vote In Harlem," *Chicago Defender,* 11 November 1944.

"Dawson Wins By 14,000 Vote Edge Over King," *Chicago Defender,* 11 November 1944.

"President Gets Record Margin On South Side," *Chicago Defender,* 11 November 1944.

"Dawson, Powell Take Seats in New Congress," *Chicago Defender,* 6 January 1945.

"Jim Crow At Y Pool Hit Negro Girl, Polio Victim," *Chicago Defender,* 17 February 1945.

"U.S. Asked to Oust Racism at Hein Hospital," *Chicago Defender,* 17 February 1945.

"Bar Negro Vets From Training at Trade School," *Chicago Defender,* 12 May 1945.

"Alliance Wants Showdown on Post Office Jim Crow," *Chicago Defender,* 12 May 1945.

"House Panel Proposes Legalizing Policy Game," *Chicago Tribune,* 28 June 1975.

"A Policy of Fortune Wheels Met Big Profits," *Chicago Tribune,* 22 June 1975.

MAGAZINES:

"The Day Dawson Saved America From A Racist President," *Ebony,* (July 1972) pp. 42–45, 48–50.

SPEECHES AND LETTERS:

Letter From State Representative Lewis A. H. Caldwell To The Honorable Michael J. Hartigan, Secretary of State, Dated April 29, 1975.

Speech Delivered By Lewis A. H. Caldwell Before The House Of Representatives in June, 1975.

Speech Delivered By Congressman Dawson at the Golden Gate Ballroom in New York City on October 1, 1944.

Letter to Lewis A. H. Caldwell, Cook County Bureau of Public Welfare, Chicago 6 July 1937, From The President of Chicago Northern District Association of Coloured Women.

Letter to Margaret Aldredge, 4 April 1975, from Samuel H. Young, Subject: Policy Wheels.

DISSERTATION:

Fifteen Page written dissertation by Lewis Caldwell on his memories of William L. Dawson.

GOVERNMENT PAPERS:

Copy of House Bill 3123, introduced June 27, 1975.
Copy of House Bill 41, introduced February 4, 1977.

UPDATED PAPERS:

WPA paper titled "Local Policy Barons"
WPA paper titled "The Negro in Illinois, Subject: Policy."

INTERVIEWS:

Caldwell, Lewis A. H., The Former State Representative, Personal Interviews, Chicago, 23 June 1984, 22 April 1985.
Davis, Corneal, Commissioner of Voter Registration, City of Chicago, Personal Interviews, Chicago, 30 July 1984, 19 August 1984, 4 November 1984, 4 December 1984, 1 October 1984, 6 October 1985, 10 October 1985, 26 October 1985, 5 January 1985.
Dawson, William L., Congressman, Personal Interview, Chicago, 30 August 1959.
Dickerson, Earl B., Attorney, Personal Interview, Chicago, 25 February 1982, 5 September 1984, 7 September 1984, 28 June 1985.
Jones, Sadie Waterford, Widow of State Representative, Warren B. Douglas, Personal Interview, Chicago, 22 April 1985.
Payne, Aaron, Attorney, Personal Interview, Chicago, 5 September 1984.
Sengstacke, John, Publisher, Chicago Defender, Personal Interview, Chicago, 16 May 1985.

CHAPTER XV
SOURCES

BOOKS:

Banfield, Edward C., *Political Influence,* New York: The Free Press, 1961.
Demaris, Ovid, *Captive City,* New York: Lyle Stuart, 1969.
Hirsch, Arnold R., *Making The Second Ghetto: Race and Housing in Chicago, 1940–1960,* New York: Cambridge University Press, 1983.
Herrick, Mary J., *The Chicago School: A Social and Political History,* Beverly Hills, California: Sage Publication, 1971.

Kennedy, Eugene. *Himself: The Life and Times of Mayor Richard J. Daley,* New York: The Viking Press, 1978.

O'Connor, Len, *Clout: Mayor Daley and His City,* Chicago: Contemporary Books: 1975.

Rakove, Milton L., *We Don't Want Nobody Sent: An Oral History of the Daley Years,* Bloomington, Indiana: Indiana University Press, 1979.

Royko, Mike, *Boss: Richard Daley of Chicago,* New York: E.P. Dutton & Co. 1971.

Stone, Chuck, *Black Political Power in America,* New York: Delta Book, 1968.

NEWSPAPERS:

"West Side Tenants' Owners Triples Rent On Flat Without Water or Heat," *Chicago Defender,* 5 April 1947

"Experts Clash on Housing And City Council Hearings," *Chicago Defender,* 12 April 1947

"Martin H. Kennelly Takes Oath of Office," *Chicago Defender,* 19 April 1947

"Racial Restrictive Covenant Boundaries in Chicago," *Chicago Defender,* 2 August 1947

"Mayor Demands Cops Make Arrest In Troubled Areas," *Chicago Defender,* 16 August 1947

"Gory Hand of Covenant Evidence in Fire Desk," *Chicago Defender,* 18 October 1947

"Sue I.C. For Travel Bias," *Chicago Defender,* 25 October 1947

"Governor's Area Advisor Board Wants to Raise Chicago's Rents" *Chicago Defender,* 8 November 1947

"Wendell E. Green First Choice Bar Association," *Chicago Defender,* 18 November 1947

"William Dawson Defeats Jim Crow Draft," *Chicago Defender,* 21 April 1951

"Sidney Jones, Sixth Ward Candidate," *Chicago Defender,* 8 January 1955

"Gambling Raiders Hit Dawson's Bailiwick Again," *Chicago Sun Times,* 14 January 1955

"Congressman Note Target of Probe," *Chicago Defender,* 15 January 1955

"Ex-Policy Man Charges Payoff to Congressman'" *Chicago Sun Times,* 21 January 1955

"Stevenson Endorses Daley in Mayoral Race," *Chicago Sun Times,* 1 February 1955

"Kennelly Says Dawson Dumped Him," *Chicago Defender,* 5 February 1955

"We Recommend Daley, Merriam: An Editorial," *Chicago Defender,* 19 February 1955

"Voters Really Dump Kennelly," *Chicago Defender,* 26 February 1955

"Metcalfe Winner," *Chicago Defender,* 26 February 1955

"Elect Mayor Daley: An Editorial," *Chicago Defender,* 2 April 1955

"Leon Depres Is Rights' Advocate," *Chicago Defender,* 2 April 1955

"Voters Decide Tuesday Between Daley And Merriam," *Chicago Defender,* 2 April 1955

"Stevenson Top Leaders Supporting Dick Daley," *Chicago Defender,* 3 April 1955

"Negro Vote Is 77% Of Daley's Edge," *Chicago Defender,* 9 April 1955

MAGAZINES:

"Report From Chicago," *New Republic*, 14 April 1947
"Chicago: Mayor's Example," *Newsweek*, 12 May 1947
"Political Notes: Twenty-four Years After Big Bill," *Time Magazine*, 3 January 1955
"Paddy's Triumph," *Newsweek*, 7 March 1955
"Who's for Whom," *Newsweek*, 4 April 1955
"Chicago Ain't Ready Yet," *Newsweek*, 18 April 1955
"Democrats Running Scared," *Newsweek*, 21 April 1955

INTERVIEWS:

Caldwell, Lewis A.H., Former State Representative, Personal Interviews, Chicago, 23 June 1984, 22 April 1985, 16 November 1985.
Davis, Corneal, Commissioner of Voter Registration, City of Chicago, Personal Interviews, Chicago, 30 July 1984, 19 August 1984, 14 November 1984, 4 December 1984, 5 January 1985, 16 November 1985.
Dickerson, Attorney Earl B., Personal Interviews, Chicago, 25 February 1982, 5 September 1985, 7 September 1984, 28 June 1985.
Harewood, Richard A., Former Municipal Judge, Personal Interviews, Chicago, 2 January 1985, 10 February 1985.
Harris, George S., President of the Metropolitan Mutual Assurance Company, Personal Interview, Chicago, 17 September 1965.
Payne, Attorney Aaron, Personal Interviews, Chicago, 5 September 1984, 4 October 1984.
Sengstacke, John H., Publisher of the *Chicago Defender* Chain, Personal Interview, Chicago, 16 May 1985.

CHAPTER XVI
SOURCES

BOOKS:

Davis, Corneal A., *Corneal A. Davis Memoirs, Volume I & II,* Springfield, Illinois: Oral History Office, Legislative Studies Center of Sangamon State University, 1984
Partee, Cecil, *Cecil A. Partee's Memoirs, Volume I & II,* Springfield, Illinois: Oral History Office, Legislative Studies Center of Sangamon State University, 1982.

NEWSPAPERS:

"Congressman Dawson: Chicago Democrat With Clout," *Chicago Sunday Tribune,* 6 February 1955.
"Mayor at Rites For General Dawson," *Chicago Daily Defender,* 14 May 1955.
"Near Split In Democratic Unit," *Chicago Daily Defender,* 20 June 1960.
"Leon Despres in Fifth Ward," *Chicago Daily Tribune,* 11 February 1963.

"Chew Backers Find Seventeenth Ward Alderman Unknown," *Chicago Daily Defender,* 14 February 1963.

"Seventeenth Ward Incumbent Caught In Squeeze of Racial Change," *Chicago Sun Times,* 25 March 1963.

"Chew Attributes His Victory To Children," *Chicago Daily Defender,* 3 April 1963.

"Seventeenth Ward Revolt Knocks Out Slight," *Chicago Daily News,* 3 April 1963.

"Campbell Leans As Top Negro Leader In City Council," *Chicago Daily News,* 3 April 1963.

"There Is A Scrapper In City Council Now," *Chicago Daily News,* 5 April 1963.

"Chicago Negro Alderman Stun By Criticism of Rights' Failures, Blast Illinois NAACP Official," *Associated Negro Press,* 10 July 1963.

"Robichaux Wins Nod In 21st; Changes Fly," *Chicago Daily Defender,* 14 November 1963.

"Shannon Out In The Seventeenth Ward," *Chicago Daily Defender,* 11 February 1964.

"Chew Joins Democrats," *Bulletin,* 17 September 1964.

"Despres, TWO Questioning Poverty Petition," *Chicago Daily Defender,* 13 February 1966.

"Chew To Run For State Senate," *Chicago Daily News,* 15 February 1966.

"Chew's Assembly Bid Faces Daley Hurdle," *Chicago Daily News,* 16 February 1966.

"Mikva Puts Emphasis On People, Issues," *Chicago Daily News,* 11 June 1966.

"Times Change, But Dawson Goes Right On Winning," *Chicago Daily News,* 15 June 1966.

"Carey Runs For First Office as Democrat," *Chicago Daily Defender,* 7 November 1966.

"Logan Quits in Twenty-first Ward Race: Backs Frost," *Chicago Daily Defender,* 7 February 1967.

"Montgomery Fights to Win." *Chicago Daily Defender,* 16 February 1967.

"Ward Contest Reflects City's Racial Change: Negroes to Gain," *Chicago Daily News,* 16 February 1967.

"Savage, Rayner In South Side Aldermanic Races," *Chicago Daily Defender,* 28 February 1967.

"Five Council Choices," *Chicago Daily News,* 28 February 1967.

"Representative William L. Dawson Dies: Served Chicago Area Since 1942," *New York Times,* 10 November 1970.

"Six-five from U.S. House Due For Dawson's Rites Thursday," *Sun-Times,* 11 November 1970.

"Two Thousand Lead By Daley Attend Representative Dawson's Funeral," *Chicago Tribune,* 13 November 1970.

"Charlie Chew," *Reader,* 9 April 1982.

MAGAZINES:

"Negro Americans' Top Politician," *Ebony,* January 1955.

"Lone Negro Spokesman In Chicago City Council," *Negro Digest,* (December 1966)

UNPUBLISHED MATERIAL:

Hirsch, Arnold R., *Politics And The Interracial Struggle For Living Space In Chicago After World War II,* New Orleans: Department of History in School of Urban and Regional Studies, University of New Orleans, 1984.

INTERVIEWS:

Black Jr., Timuel, Professor, Personal Interview, Chicago, 24 November 1984, 28 April 1984.

Caldwell, Lewis A. H., Former State Representative, Personal Interviews, Chicago, 23 June 1984, 22 April 1985, 16 November 1985.

Campbell, Kenneth, Alderman, Personal Interview, Chicago, 23 May 1967

Chew, Jr., Charles, State Senator, Personal Interview, Chicago, 10 October 1984.

Davis, Corneal, Former State Representative and current Commissioner of Voter Registration, City of Chicago, Personal Interview, Chicago, 30 July 1984, 19 August 1984, 14 November 1984, 4 December 1984, 5 January 1985, 16 November 1985.

Dawson, Ira, Attorney and nephew of Congressman William L. Dawson, Personal Interviews, Chicago, 12 January 1985, 25 November 1985.

Despres, Leon, Former Alderman and current Parliamentarian to the Mayor, Personal Interviews, Chicago, 30 May 1984, 28 July 1984, 13 December 1985.

Eskridge, Chauncey, Attorney, Personal Interview, Chicago, 7 January 1985.

Frost, Wilson, Alderman, Personal Interview, Chicago, 21 September 1985, 7 January 1986.

Gilbert, Herman, Executive Vice President and Editorial Director of Path Press, Personal Interviews, Chicago, 24 November 1984, 28 April 1984, 19 December 1985.

Harris, William F., Commissioner of Building and Zoning in Cook County, Personal Interviews, Chicago, 13 August 1984, 10 November 1985, 5 December 1985, 15 December 1985

Johnson, Bennett, President of Path Press, Personal Interview, Chicago, 20 March 1985.

Korshak, Marshall, State Senator, Personal Interview, Chicago, 12 December 1985.

Montgomery, James D., Corporation Counsel, Personal Interview, Chicago, 28 December 1985.

Neal, Earl L., Personal Interview, Chicago, 19 January 1985.

Newhouse, Richard, State Senator, Personal Interviews, Chicago 23 October 1984, 20 December 1985.

Partee, Cecil, City Treasurer and former President of State Senate, Personal Interviews, Chicago, 28 December 1984, 14 December 1985, 21 December 1985.

Rayner Jr., A. A. (Sammy), Former Alderman, Personal Interview, Chicago, 23 October 1984.

Savage, Augustus A., Congressman, Personal Interview, Chicago, 22 April 1984, 13 December 1985.

Stroger Jr., John H., County Commissioner, Eighth Ward Committeeman, Personal Interview, Chicago, 20 June 1984.

Washington, Harold, Mayor of the City of Chicago, Personal Interviews, Chicago, 23 April 1983, 31 April 1983, 31 May 1983, 16 April 1984, 22 January 1984, 12 May 1984, 19 May 1984, 17 July 1984, 24 April 1985, 11 August 1985, 24 August 1985.

AUDIO & VIDEO TRANSCRIPTIONS:

Newsmakers—CBS, Mayor Harold Washington, 24 July 1983.
Vernon Jarrett Show—ABC, Mayor Harold Washington, 22 January 1984.
Vernon Jarrett Show—ABC, Mayor Harold Washington, 22 April 1984.
City Desk—NBC, Mayor Harold Washington, 28 May 1984.
Vernon Jarrett Show—ABC, Mayor Harold Washington, 8 July 1984.
Warner Saunders TV Show—NBC, State Senator Charles Chew, 5 May 1985.
Eyewitness Forum—ABC, Mayor Harold Washington, 26 May 1985.
Radio Station WJPC—AM 95, Mayor Harold Washington, 26 May 1985.

CHAPTER XVII
SOURCES

BOOKS:

Anderson, Jervis, *A. Phillip Randolph: A Biographic Portrait,* New York: Harcourt, Brace, Jovanovich, Inc., 1972.
Clayton, Edward T., *The Negro Politician: His Success and Failure,* Chicago: Johnson Publishing Co., Inc., 1964.
Ebony Editors, *Ebony Hand Book,* Chicago: Johnson Publishing Co., Inc., 1974.
McClory, Robert, *The Man Who Beat Clout City,* Chicago: The Swallow Press, Inc., 1977.
Rather, Earnest R., *The Chicago Negro Almanac And Reference Book,* Chicago: Chicago Negro Almanac Publishing Co., Inc., 1972.
Reddick, Arthur Lawrence Dunbar, *Crusader Without Violence: A Biography of Martin Luther King, Jr.,* New York: Harper and Brothers Publisher, 1959.
Stone, Chuck, *Black Political Power In America,* New York: Delta Books Company, 1968.
Travis, Dempsey J., *An Autobiography of Black Chicago,* Chicago: Urban Research Institute, Inc., 1981.
Wilson, James Q., *Negro Politics: The Search For Leadership,* Glencoe, Illinois: Free Press, 1960.

NEWSPAPERS:

"Abner vs. Jones For NAACP Head," *Chicago Daily Defender,* 14 December 1937.
"NAACP Survey Shows Bias In City Schools," *Chicago Daily Defender,* 5 January 1957.
"School Issue Major Project," *Chicago Daily Defender,* 2 February 1957.
"Roy Wilkins Hits Little Rock Racist," *Chicago Daily Defender,* 12 October 1957.

"Ted Jones Bids For NAACP Prexy," *Chicago Daily Defender*, 14 December 1957.

"Fight Looms In NAACP Election," *Chicago Daily Defender*, 5 December 1959.

"Negro Finds Segregation In The Loop," *Chicago Daily News*, 27 January 1960.

"Chicagoans Live Behind Ebony Curtain," *Chicago Daily News*, 30 January 1960.

"Deerfield Integration Foes To Abide By Judge's Ruling," *Chicago Daily News*, 1 February 1960.

"Negroes Battle For Civil Right," *Pittsburgh Courier*, 16 July 1960.

"Kennedy Backs Full Rights," *Pittsburgh Courier*, 16 July 1960.

"Dawson's Power As Success Key," *Chicago Daily Defender*, 19 July 1960.

"Elect Dawson One Of Six Democratic Chairmen," *Chicago Daily Defender*, 19 July 1960.

"NAACP Demands That GOP Match Democratic Rights Plank," *Chicago Sun-Times*. 21 July 1960.

"Leaders, NAACP, 7,000 Picket For Civil Rights Plank," *Pittsburgh Courier*, 23 July 1960.

"Rally Demands Strong On Civil Rights," *Chicago Daily Defender*, 25 July 1960.

"March of 10,000 Negroes Is Led By Boy, Nine," *Chicago Sun-Times*, 26 July 1960.

"Negroes Will March On Convention Hall," *Chicago Sun-Times*, 29 July 1960.

"Rights Planks Only Promises," *Chicago Daily Defender*, 30 July 1960

"Swimming Pool Causes Chicago Racial Flair Up," *Pittsburgh Courier*, 6 August 1960.

"King Opens New Integration Fight," *Chicago Daily Defender*, 28 October 1960.

"Rev. King Helped By Kennedy, Silent On Nominee Choice," *Chicago Tribune*, 2 November 1960.

"NAACP Sets Rally For Rev. Dr. Martin Luther King," *Chicago Daily Defender*, 4 November 1960.

"Release King From Georgia Jail," *Chicago Daily Defender*, 4 November 1960.

"Dawson Rejects Cabinet Post," *Chicago Daily Defender*, 17 December 1960.

"Claim Dawson Making NAACP Harmless Body," *Amsterdam News*, 7 January 1961.

"George T. Sims Takes A Giant Step," *Chicago Daily Defender*, 6 May 1968.

"Dawson: Master, Quiet Politician," *Chicago Daily Defender*, 14 November 1970.

"Metcalfe Issues Ultimatum: Conlisk Considers Sixth Demands," *Chicago Daily Defender*, 25 April 1972.

MAGAZINE ARTICLES AND SPEECHES:

"Eight Days In Georgia's Jail Leaves Rev. King Unbowed," *Jet* 10 November 1960.

"Negro Advisors Help Candidate End Drives," *Jet* 3 November 1960.

"Why Nixon Lost The Negro Vote," *The Crisis*, January, 1961.

"Why Dawson Refused Post Office-General's Post," *Jet*, 31 November 1960.

PAMPHLETS:

"From The Alley To The Hall," Afro-American Police League, 19 August 1983.

INTERVIEWS:

Clements, George, Father, Personal Interview, Chicago, 18 October 1984, 14 February 1986.

Davis, Corneal, Commissioner of Voter Registration, City of Chicago, Personal Interview, Chicago, 30 July 1984, 19 August 1984, 14 November 1984, 4 December 1984, 5 January 1985, 16 November 1985, 20 February 1986.

Deas, Milton, Former Commander, Chicago Police Department, 11 February 1986.

Ewing, Russ, Investigative Reporter, ABC Channel 7, 13 February 1986, 14 February 1986, 18 February 1986.

Hayes, Charles, Congressman, Personal Interview, Chicago, 5 June 1984.

Morgan, Fred, Retired District Chief, Chicago Fire Department, Personal Interview, Chicago, 8 May 1985, 12 February 1986.

Savage, Augustus A., Congressman, Personal Interview, Chicago, 22 April 1984, 13 December 1985, 14 January 1986.

Sims, George, Commander, Chicago Police Department, Personal Interview, Chicago, 13 July 1985.

CHAPTER XVIII
SOURCES

BOOKS:

Farmer, James, *Lay Bare the Heart: An Autobiography of the Civil Rights Movement,* New York, New York: Arbor House, 1985.

Gregory, Dick and Robert Lipsyte, *Nigger,* New York, New York: E.P. Dutton & Company, Inc., 1964.

Herrick, Mary J., *The Chicago Schools: A Social and Political History,* Beverly Hills, California: Sage Publications, 1971.

Meier, August and Elliott Rudwick, CORE: *A Study in the Civil Rights Movement, 1942–1968,* New York, New York: Oxford University Press, 1973.

O'Connor, Len, *Clout: Mayor Daley and His City,* Chicago, Illinois: Henry Regnery Co., 1975.

Travis, Dempsey, *An Autobiography of Black Chicago,* Chicago, Illinois: Urban Research Institute, 1981.

NEWSPAPERS:

"Interracial Committee Pickets Six Restaurants: Dickerson Pledges Aid," *Chicago Daily News,* 10 April 1942.

"CORE Group Forms National Federation," *Chicago Daily Defender,* 12 June 1943.

"Blood Bank Jim Crow Being Fought at Red Cross," *Chicago Daily Defender,* 14 August 1943.

"Plan $100,000 Suit Against Northwestern University," *Chicago Daily Defender,* 14 August 1943.

"Loop Hotels Ban Negro History Week Banquet," *Chicago Daily Defender*, 2 February 1946.

"Negro Doctors Sue Hospitals", *Chicago Daily News*, 10 February 1961.

"School Bias Hit by 800 NAACP Pickets", *Chicago Daily Defender*, 3 July 1963.

"Chicago Negro Alderman Stung by Criticism of Rights Failures, Blast Illinois NAACP Official", *American Negro Press*, 10 July 1963.

"Chicago Schools Open to a Jim Crow Tune", 3 September 1963.

"Chicago's Schools Seen Teaching Negroes to be Second-Class People", *Chicago Daily Defender*, 19 September 1963.

"October 22nd School Boycott Planned as Protest Against Ben Willis", *Chicago Daily Defender*, 14 October 1963.

"Fear Teachers' Reprisal Against Students in October 22nd Boycott", *Chicago Daily Defender*, 16 October 1963.

"Negro Aldermen Disagree With Daley in Willis Role", *Chicago Daily Defender*, 16 October 1963.

"Anti-Willis 'Freedom Day' Tuesday October 22nd: No School", *Chicago Daily Defender*, 17 October 1963.

"Second Boycott May be Held in November", *Chicago Daily Defender*, 21 October 1963.

"Democratic Party in Chicago — Except Daley — Backing Boycott', *Chicago Daily Defender*, 21 October 1963.

"School Boycott Success; 224,770 Pupils Agsent", *Chicago Daily Defender*, 23 October 1963.

"CCCO Selects Landry as Group's Spokesman", *Chicago Daily Defender*, 4 November 1963.

"Willis' New Integration Plan Comes Under Attack From Leaders", *Chicago Daily Defender*, 13 November 1963.

"Is Disobeying An Unjust Law?: A Dilemma to the Chicago NAACP?", *Chicago Daily Defender*, 2 January 1964.

"Second Boycott Possible Because of Council's 13-1 Vote", *Chicago Daily Defender*, 2 January 1964.

"Boycott Mustn't Fail"—Despres, *Chicago Daily Defender*, 18 February 1964.

"Boycott Friends and Foes Press for School Decision", *Chicago Sun-Times*, 24 February 1964.

"Warning Issued by O.W. Wilson", *Chicago Daily News*, 24 February 1964.

"Majority of Negroes Cut Class", *Chicago Daily News*, 25 February 1964.

"School Boycott Effective," *Chicago Sun-Times*, 26 February 1964.

"Boycott A Surprise, 172,350 Absent", *Chicago Daily News*, 26 February 1964.

"CCCO Ignores Threats, Plans Further Action", *Chicago Daily Defender*, 2 March 1964.

"If Negro Boycott Meant Ballots", *Chicago Daily News*, 19 March 1964.

"Top Negroes All Agree Mrs. Green's Got to Go", *Chicago Daily Defender*, 23 March 1964.

LETTERS:

Letter from Gordon R. Carey, Field Secretary to Ms. Chomingwen Pond, Garrett Biblical Institute, Evanston, Illinois, discussing CORE's picket line against a Woolworth Store in the Loop, February 25, 1960.

INTERVIEWS:

Brazier, Reverend Arthur, Former President of the Woodlawn Organization and original convener of the Coordinating Council of Community Organizations, Personal Interview, Chicago, 14 March 1986.

Davis, Bessie, Retired Chicago School Teacher and Civil Rights Activist, Personal Interview, Chicago, Illinois, 12 March 1986.

Hutchinson, Elson, Former Campaign Manager for James Montgomery and representative of the Greater Roseland Community on the Coordinating Council of Community Organizations, Personal Interview, Chicago, 26 February 1986.

Lafontant, Attorney Jewel, Former member of CORE, Personal Interview, Chicago, Illinois, 23 July 1981.

Lucas, Robert, Executive Director of KOCO and Former Chairman of Chicago CORE, Personal Interview, Chicago, Illinois, 9 July 1981.

CHAPTER XIX
SOURCES

BOOKS:

Carmichael, Stokely and Charles V. Hamilton, *Black Power: The Politics of Liberation in America,* New York: A Vantage Book, 1969.

Hannah, Hilton E. and Joseph Belsky, *Picket and the Pen,* Yonkers, New York: American Institute of Social Science, Inc., 1960.

Herrick, Mary J., *The Chicago Schools: A Social and Political History,* Beverly Hills, California: Sage Publications, 1971.

MacDonald, J. Fred, *Black and White T.V.: Afro-American's In Television Since 1948,* Chicago: Nelson-Hall, 1983.

Oates, Stephen B., *Let The Trumpet Sound: The Life of Martin Luther King Jr.,* New York: New American Library, 1983.

O'Connor, Len, *Clout: Mayor Daley and His City,* Chicago: Henry Regnery Co. 1975.

Reynolds, Barbara A., *Jesse Jackson: The Man, The Movement, The Myth,* Chicago: Nelson-Hall, 1975.

Royko, Mike, *Boss: Richard J. Daley of Chicago,* New York: E.P. Dutton & Company, Inc., 1971.

Tweedle, John, Edited by Hermene D. Hartman, *A Lasting Impression: A Collection of Photographs of Martin Luther King Jr.,* Columbia, South Carolina: University of South Carolina Press, 1983.

NEWSPAPERS:

"Church, Civil Groups Support School Boycott, Blast Willis" *Chicago Defender,* 21 October 1963.

"Don't Blame Willis, Blame Mayor Daley", *Chicago Defender,* 2 April 1964.

"Daniel Unafraid of Dawson's Lion's Den", *Chicago Defender,* 16 April 1964.

"Arrest Gregory, Raby At 'Visual' ", *Chicago Tribune*, 8 June 1965.

"NAACP Boycott Plan Opposition to Superintendent Willis", *Chicago Defender*, 8 June 1965.

"Boycott Banned", *Chicago Defender*, 9 June 1965.

"Issue Orders Restraining Rights Units", *Chicago Tribune*, 9 June 1965.

"Ban On School Boycott', *Chicago Tribune*, 10 June 1965.

"Willis March Jams Traffic", *Chicago Tribune*, 11 June 1965.

"Willis Foes March To City Hall", *Chicago Tribune*, 11 June 1965.

"Arrest Two-Hundred Twenty Eight Protestors Sitting Down In Park Drive", *Chicago Tribune*, 12 June 1965.

"Two-Hundred Sixty Two Protestors Held In Chicago: School Demonstration Ends In Dispute With Police", *New York Times*, 12 June 1965.

"Pickets Jam Loop, Jail One Hundred-Ninety Six", *Chicago Tribune*, 13 June 1965.

"One Hundred-Fifty Jailed in Chicago Sit-Down Over Hiring Of School Chief", *New York Times*, 13 June 1965.

"U.S. Steps Into Controversy Over Willis", *Chicago Tribune*, 15 June 1965.

"Present Demands To Daley", *Chicago Defender*, 16 June 1965.

"Willis Foes March Again, Meet Daley", *Chicago Tribune*, 17 June 1965.

"Demonstrators Stage Lie-Down on LaSalle Street", *Chicago Defender*, 29 June 1965.

"The Chicago in King's Sight", *Chicago Defender*, 8 July 1965.

"Dr. King Rallies Forces To March On City Hall", *Chicago Tribune*, 25 July 1965.

"Thirty-Thousand March With King In Mighty Rally", *Chicago Defender*, 27 July 1965.

"Chicago No Promised Land Says King", *Chicago Defender*, 27 July 1965.

"Priests Fined One Hundred Twenty-Five Dollars Each For Sit-Down", *Chicago Tribune*, 27 July 1965.

"Dr. King's Flat, Although Painted, Is Very Dismal", *Chicago Tribune*, 26 January 1966.

"King and Wife Move Into Slum", *Chicago Defender*, 27 January 1966.

"Forbids King Group To Recruit In Schools," *Chicago Tribune*, 27 January 1966.

"King Return; Sets Protest Over School", *Chicago Tribune*, 3 February 1966.

"King Assails Board On New Kenwood High", *Chicago Tribune*, 4 February 1966.

"Cody Sees Hope In Racial Work", *Chicago Tribune*, 5 February 1966.

"Negroes Hear King Urge; Be Dissatisfied", *Chicago Tribune*, 6 February 1966.

"Dr. King Tells Plans For Negro Boycott, *Chicago Tribune*, 12 February 1966.

"Thirteen Thousand Filled A Jam Packed Chicago Freedom Festival", *Chicago Defender*, 14 March 1966.

"Willis Quitting His School Post Ahead of Time", *Chicago Defender*, 24 May 1966.

"Willis Stuns Board With Resignation", *Chicago Tribune*, 24 May 1966.

"Superintendent Willis Sets Early Date for Resignation to Aid Successor", *Chicago Tribune*, 24 May 1966.

"Archbishop Supports Rally", *Chicago Tribune*, 10 July 1966.
"King Post's Fourteen Demands for Daley on Door", *Chicago Tribune*, 11 July 1966.

INTERVIEWS:

Hayes, Congressman Charles, Personal Interview, Chicago, 16 April 1984, 5 June 1984.

Jackson, Rev. Jesse L., Former Staff Member of the Southern Christian Leadership Conference, President of Operation Breadbasket, President of Operation Push, 1984 Presidential Candidate, An International Civil Rights Leader, Personal Interview, Chicago, 30 November 1984.

Savage, Congressman Augustus A., Personal Interview, Chicago, 22 April 1984, 13 December 1985, 14 January 1986.

Johnson, Bennett, Publisher and Civil Rights' Activist, Personal Interview, Chicago, 20 March 1985.

Tillman, Dorothy, Alderman, Third Ward and Former Staff Member of Dr. Martin Luther King's Southern Christian Leadership Conference, Personal Interview, Chicago, 31 May 1985.

Bevel, Rev. James L., A Dr. Martin Luther King Missionary and Organizer for the Southern Christian Leadership Conference on the Westside, Chicago, Personal Interview, 2 July 1985.

Davis, Theodore, Chicago Police Officer, A DuSable grad who served with Mayor Harold Washington in the South Pacific during World War II, Personal Interview, Chicago, 11 November 1985.

Hutchinson, Elson, Campaign Manager for James Montgomery and Representative of the Greater Roseland Community in the Coordinating Council Community Organizations, Personal Interview, Chicago, 26 February 1986.

Davis, Bessie, Retired Schoolteacher and Civil Rights Activist, Personal Interview, Chicago, 12 March 1986.

Brazier, Rev. Arthur, Former President of the Woodlawn Organization and Original Convener of the Coordinating Council of Community Organizations, Personal Interview, Chicago, 14 March 1986.

CHAPTER XX
SOURCES

BOOKS:

Carmichael, Stokely, and Charles V. Hamilton, *Black Power: The Politics of Liberation in America*, New York: A Vantage Book, 1969.

Herrick, Mary J. *The Chicago Schools: A Social and Political History,* Beverly Hills, CA: Sage Publications, 1971.

MacDonald, J. Fred, *Black and White Television: Afro-American's In Television Since 1948,* Chicago: Nelson-Hall, 1983.

Oates, Stephen B., *Let the Trumpet Sound: The Life of Martin Luther King Jr.,* New York: New American Library, 1983.

O'Connor, Len, Clout: *Mayor Daley and His City,* Chicago: Contemporary Books, Inc., 1975.

Reynolds, Barbara A., *Jesse Jackson: The Man, The Movement, The Myth,* Chicago: Nelson Hall Publishing Company, 1975.

Royko, Mike, *Boss: Richard J. Daley of Chicago,* New York: E.P. Dutton & Company, Inc., 1971.

Travis, Dempsey J., *An Autobiography of Black Chicago,* Chicago: Urban Research Institute, Inc., 1981.

NEWSPAPERS:

"Operation Breadbasket Campaign Nets Negro Jobs Here", *Chicago Daily News,* 8 June 1966.

"Puerto Rican Riot: Thirty-five Hurt", *Chicago Tribune,* 13 June 1966.

"King Calls For A Puerto Rican Meet", *Daily Defender,* 15 June 1966.

"Westside Riots Parallel Earlier Outbreaks", *Chicago Defender,* 18 June 1966.

"Two Sides 'Wooing' Puerto Ricans", *Chicago Defender,*20 June 1966.

"First Puerto Rican Protest March, Rally Set Today", 28 June 1966.

"Puerto Ricans March, Present Demands", *Daily Defender,* 29 June 1966.

"Gage Park Area Racial Incident Spurs Patrolling", *Chicago Sun-Times,* 8 July 1986.

"Daley Links Outsiders To Lawlessness, *Chicago Tribune,* 16 July 1966.

"Puerto Rican Grievances Heard By City", *Chicago Tribune,* 16 July 1966.

"Call Seventeen Guard Units To Reinforce Police", *Chicago Tribune,* 16 July 1966.

"Leaders Voice Ideas On Riots", *Chicago Defender,* 18 July 1966.

"An Editorial: Let's Face Facts", *Chicago Defender,* 18 July 1966.

"Fifty-four Hurt As Whites In Chicago Hurl Bricks At Rights' Marchers", *New York Times,* 1 August 1966.

"Police Did Not Protect Marchers—King, Raby", *Chicago Daily News,* 1 August 1966.

"Dr. King, Realtors Agreed To Meeting", *Chicago Defender,* 14 August, 1966

"Can't Force Sales, The Realtors Replied to Negro Protestors", *Chicago Daily News,* 16 August 1966.

"Rights' Marchers Take Aim At Six Targets", *Chicago Daily News,* 16 August 1966.

"Housing Boss Admits U.S. Aids Slums", *Chicago Tribune,* 17 August 1966.

"City Leaders Meet On Racial Turmoil", *Chicago Daily News,* 17 August 1966.

"Marches and Motives", *Chicago Daily News,* 17 August 1966.

"Cops, Rights Aides At Odds Over Notice Of Marches", *Chicago Daily News,* 17 August 1966.

"March Meets Ire But Little Violence", *Chicago Daily News,*17 August 1966.

"Bargaining Strategy: Behind Rights Aides Holdout", *Chicago Daily News,* 17 August 1966.

"City Leaders Meet On Racial Turmoil", *Chicago Daily News,* 17 August 1966.

"Marches To Continue: How 'Fruitful Summit' Left Daley On The Hook", *Chicago Daily News,* 18 August 1966.

"King Reports No Chicago Truce", *New York Times,* 18 August 1966.

"King Rejects Plea To End City Marches", *Chicago Tribune,* 18 August 1966.

"Rights Leaders Weigh Next Occupancy", *Chicago Daily News,* 18 August 1966.

"Katzenbach Warns of New City Riots", *New York Times,* 18 August 1966.

"Daley Makes Plea To City: Demands Order, Tells Why He Asked To Enjoin Marchers", *Chicago Tribune,* 20 August 1966.

"Daley's Life Is Threatened After Speech", *Chicago Tribune,* 20 August 1966.

"King Orders New March Held Today", *Chicago Tribune,* 21 August 1966.

"Two Marchers Greeted By Bricks", *Chicago Defender,* 22 August 1966.

"Outsiders Stir Hate", *Chicago Daily News,* 22 August 1966.

"Marches Rocky Road: The Ewing Avenue Route to "Freedom Land", *Chicago Daily News,* 22 August 1966.

"Ogilvie Out to Bar Cicero Trek", *Chicago Daily News,* 22 August 1966.

"A. Phillip Randolph Favors March Moratorium", *Chicago Daily News,* 22 August 1966.

"Excerpts From Interviews With Six Civil Rights Leaders On Race", *New York Times,* 22 August 1966.

"Dr. King and Five-Hundred Jeered In Five Mile Chicago March", *New York Times,* 22 August 1966.

"New March In South Deering Set For Today", *Chicago Defender,* 23 August 1966.

"Sheriff Asks Dr. King to Call Off Cicero March", *New York Times,* 23 August 1966.

"Kerner Ponders Calling Guards Into Cicero", *Chicago Defender,* 24 August 1966.

"Cicero Fears Violence At Rights March", *Chicago Tribune,* 24 August 1966.

"Confusion on March Plan Holds Up Cicero Permit O.K.", *Chicago Sun-Times,* 1 September 1966.

"King Prevails Over Cry of Black Power", *Chicago Sun-Times,* 1 September, 1966.

"Six Bayoneted, Forty-two Arrested In Cicero", *Chicago Sun-Times,* 5 September 1966.

"The Big March: Two-Hundred Venture Into Cicero, *Daily Defender,* 6 September 1966.

"Lucas Could Start A Race War: O.W.", *Chicago Defender,* 7 September 1966.

"Briscoe Supports Jackson In Opposition to Dr. King", *Chicago Defender,* 13 September 1966.

"Dr. King Tells News Slum Housing Plan", *Chicago Tribune,* 21 December 1966.

MAGAZINES:

"Poor Chicago: Down and Out With Daley", *New Republic,* 15 May 1965.

"Chicago A Racial Battleground: What The Fight Is About", *U.S. News and World Report*, 2 August 1965.

"Why A Big City Faces A Crisis In Schools", *U.S. News and World Report*, 9 August 1965.

"Chicago: Gamble In The Ghetto", *Newsweek*, 31 January 1966.

"A Beach Head In The North: King In Chicago", *Commonwealth*, 29 April 1966.

"A Requiem Or Revival", *Look Magazine*, 14 June 1966.

"Focus In Chicago: The New Gerico", *Look Magazine*, 14 June 1966.

"One Last Chance", *Christian Century*, 22 June 1966.

"Victory In The North", *Newsweek*, 5 September 1966.

"Steal King", *Christian Century*, 7 September 1966.

"Open City", *New Republic*, 17 September 1966.

"Chicago Summer: Bossism, Racism, and King", *Nation*, 19 September 1966.

INTERVIEWS:

Bevel, Rev. James, Leader of Dr. Martin Luther King Chicago Project, Chicago, Personal Interviews, 2 July 1985, 22 July 1986.

Brazier, Rev. Arthur, Former President of the Woodlawn Organization and Original Convener of the Coordinating Council of Community Organizations, Personal Interview, Chicago, 14 March 1986.

Davis, Bessie, Retired Schoolteacher and Civil Rights Activist, Personal Interview, Chicago, 12 March 1986.

Despres, Alderman Leon, Personal Interviews, 29 July 1984, 15 July 1986.

Hayes, Charles, Member of U.S. House of Representatives, Personal Interviews, Chicago, 16 April 1984, 5 June 1984.

Hutchinson, Elson, Campaign Manager for James Montgomery and Representative of the Greater Roseland Community in the Coordinating Council Community Organizations, Personal Interview, Chicago, 26 February 1986.

Jackson, Rev. Jesse L., Former Staff Member of the Southern Christian Leadership Conference, President of Operation Breadbasket, President of Operation Push, 1984 Presidential Candidate, An International Civil Rights' Leader, Personal Interview, Chicago, 30 November 1984.

Johnson, Bennett, Publisher and Civil Rights Activist, Personal Interview, Chicago, 20 March 1985, 13 August 1986.

Sampson, Rev. Al, Former top organizer for Dr. Martin Luther King's Chicago Project and Currently Pastor of Fernwood United Methodist Church, Chicago.

Savage, Augustus A., Member of U.S. House of Representatives, Personal Interviews, Chicago, 22 April 1984, 13 December 1985, 14 January 1986.

Tillman, Dorothy, Alderman Third Ward and Former Staff Member of Dr. Martin Luther King's Southern Christian Leadership Conference, Personal Interview, Chicago, 31 May 1985.

Williams, Kale, Staff director of the Leadership Council For Open Communities, Chicago, Personal Interview, 24 July 1986.

CHAPTER XXI
SOURCES

BOOKS:

Allen, Robert L. *Black Awakening in Capitalist America,* New York, Doubleday & Company, Inc., 1969.

Arlen, Michael J. *An American Verdict,* New York: Doubleday & Company, Inc., 1973.

Demaris, Ovid. *A Captive City,* New York: Lyle Stuart, 1969.

Major, Reginald. *A Panther Is A Black Cat,* New York: William Morrow & Company, Inc., 1971.

McClory, Robert. *The Man Who Beat Clout City,* Chicago: Swallow Press, 1977.

O'Connor, Len. *Clout: Mayor Daley And His City,* Chicago: Contemporary Books, Inc., 1975.

Reynolds, Barbara A. *Jesse Jackson: The Man, The Movement, The Myth,* Chicago: Nelson-Hall, 1975.

Rice, J. F. *Up On Madison, Down On 75th Street: A History of the Illinois Black Panther Party Part 1,* Evanston, Illinois: The Committee Publishers 1983.

Robinson, Stanley. *The Badge They're Trying to Bury,* Bluff, Utah: Simon Belt Publishing, 1975.

Royko, Mike. *Boss: Richard J. Daley of Chicago,* New York: E. P. Dutton & Company, Inc., 1971.

Zimroth, Peter L. *Perversion of Justice,* New York: The Viking Press, 1974.

NEWSPAPERS:

"U.S. Probers Find Only One Shot Fired AT Policemen in Raid," *Chicago Tribune,* 31 December 1969.

"Lawyer On Stand In Panther Raid Case," *Chicago Tribune,* 12 September 1972.

"Panther Raiders Change View On Who Fired First," *Chicago Sun-Times,* 13 January 1970.

"Thousands Flock To Hampton Rallies," *Chicago Sun-Times,* 7 December 1969.

"Black Groups Begin Two Days of Mourning," *Chicago Sun-Times,* 7 December 1969.

"Rush Stirs 3,000 At Church Rally For Hampton," *Chicago Sun-Times,* 7 December 1969.

"See Plot To Get Alderman Rayner," *Chicago Defender,* 8 December 1969.

"Hampton's Brother Tells Audience, Maintain Peace," *Daily Defender,* 9 December 1969.

"Hanrahan, Internal Investigation Division Clash On Probe," *Chicago Defender,* 9 December 1969.

"Man On The Streets Reacts," *Daily Defender,* 9 December 1969.

"Rights Groups Unite In Probe Demand," *Daily Defender,* 9 December 1969.

"Autopsy Refutes Slaying Reports," *Daily Defender,* 9 December 1969.

"Reps Sets Probe Here," *Chicago Defender,* 11 December 1969.

"Cops Altering Evidence," *Daily Defender*, 18 December 1969.

"Black Students Assail Police State," *Chicago Defender*, 23 December 1969.

"Panther Attorney Balks, Sentence," *Chicago Sun-Times*, 17 December 1970.

"Six of 7 Panthers Will Boycott Public Inquest," *Chicago Sun-Times*, 7 January 1970.

"Hatcher To Join In Panther Case Probe," *Chicago Sun-Times*, 18 December 1969.

"U.S. Asks Slain Panther's Grave Open For Jury," *Chicago Defender*, 10 February 1970.

"Black Probe Sparks U.S. Inquiry: Solons," *Chicago Defender*, 23 December 1969.

"Panther Hearing," *Chicago Defender*, 22 December 1969.

"Panther Slaying Split The City Into Name Calling Factions," *Chicago Tribune*, 14 December 1969.

"Didn't Fire Weapons At Police In Panther Raid, Another Survivor Said," *Chicago Tribune*, 11 August 1972.

"Negro Judge Rips Action Of Panthers," *Chicago Tribune*, 5 December 1969.

"Attempted Murder Charges Eyed In Panther Gun Fight," *Chicago Tribune*, 5 December 1969.

"Police Say Prints Weren't Sought On Panther Guns," *New York Times*, 9 January 1970.

"Second Panther Chief's Flat Raided Here," *Chicago Today*, 5 December 1969.

"Hampton's Paradox: Achiever To Radical," *Chicago Today*, 5 December 1969.

"How Two Panthers Died In Gun Battle During Police Raid," *Chicago Sun-Times*, 5 December 1969.

"Cops Kill Panther Leader," *Chicago Today*, 4 December 1969.

"U.S. Legal Task Force Studies Activities Of Black Panthers," *Chicago Sun-Times*, 15 December 1969.

"Black Chicago Demands Truth," *Chicago Defender*, 8 December 1969.

"Bobby Rush's Flat Searched: New Raid On Panthers," *Chicago Daily News*, 5 December 1969.

"Coroner's Report On Fred Hampton-Overdose of 'Law and Order'," *Muhammed Speaks*, 9 December 1969.

" 'News Distortion', A Threat To Enforcing The Law: Hanrahan," *Chicago Daily News*, 14 December 1971.

"Panthers Show Visitors Through Apartment Of Death," *Chicago Sun-Times*, 5 December 1969.

"Door Exploded Out: Panther Raider," *Chicago Sun-Times*, 16 January 1970.

"New Autopsy On Slain Panther Sought By Justice Department," *New York Times*, 6 February 1970.

"Black Lawyers' Association Raps Panther Inquest Jury," *Chicago Tribune*, 31 December 1969.

"American ACLU Rips Police On Panthers," *Chicago Sun-Times*, 30 December 1969.

"U.S. Jury Assails Police In Chicago On Panther Raid," *New York Times*, 16 May 1970.

"Seven Panthers Freed In Chicago Clash," *New York Times*, 9 May 1970.

"Panther Raiders Broke Rules: Lab Aide," *Chicago Tribune*, 19 July 1972.

"FBI Provided Tip For Raid—Hanrahan," *Chicago Tribune,* 15 February 1977.

"See Plot To Get Alderman Rayner," *Daily Defender,* 8 December 1969.

"Coroner Challenges Conflict On Panther Autopsy," *Sun-Times,* 9 December 1969.

MAGAZINES:

"Police And Panthers At War," *Time, Inc.,* 12 December 1969.

"Chicago: Organization Men," *Newsweek,* 5 June 1967.

" 'Crazy Niggers' Then And Now," *Ebony,* August 1972.

"Clearing The Slate," *Newsweek,* 3 January 1972.

"Out To Get The Panthers," *The Nation,* 28 July 1969.

"Myth vs. Method: The Cracks In Daley," *The Nation,* 22 March 1971.

"The FBI Trial: Was Fred Hampton Executed?," *The Nation,* 25 December 1976.

"The Grand Jury On Trial: Mayor Daley's Way With Justice, *The Nation,* 8 November 1971.

"Black Panthers," *The Chicago Journalism Review,* December 1969.

"The Secret Police in Chicago," *The Chicago Journalism Review,* February 1969

DOCUMENTS:

94th Congress Second Session Senate Report 94-755, *Intelligence Activities and the Rights of Americans,"* Book Two Senator Frank Church, Chairman.

94th Congress Second Session Senate Report 94-755, *Supplementary Detailed Staff Reports On Intelligence Activities and The Rights of Americans,* Book Three.

Senate Select Committee To Study Governmental Operations With Respect To Intelligence Activity, Frank Church, Idaho Chairman, U.S. Government Printing Office, Washington DC 1976.

The People of the State of Illinois Appellee vs. Barnabas F. Sears Appellant and the People Exreal. Barnabas F. Sears et al. Petitioner vs. Joseph A. Power, Judge et al. Respondent 44287, 44288, 44299 and 44348. Supreme Court of Illinois, June 23, 1971. Found in 273 Northeastern Reporter, Second Series.

INTERVIEWS:

Anderson, Cynthia T., M.D., Personal Interview, Chicago, 6 August 1986.

Bevel, Rev. James, Personal Interview, Chicago, 2 July 1985, 5 August 1986.

Evans, Rev. Clay, Pastor of Friendship Baptist Church, Personal Interview, Chicago, 2 September 1986.

Johnson, Bennett, Publisher and Civil Rights Activist, Personal Interview, 20, March 1985 13, August 1986.

Jones, Sidney, Personal Interview, Chicago, 20 December 1984.

Madhubuti, Haki R., University English Professor, Noted National Writer and Poet, Personal Interview, Chicago, 13 August 1986.

Montgomery, James, Attorney, Personal Interview, Chicago, 28 December 1985, 4 August 1986.

Pincham, R. Eugene, Appellate Court Judge in the First District of Illinois, Personal Interview, Chicago, 31 July 1986, 5 August 1986.

Rayner, A.A. (Sammy), Former Alderman, Personal Interview, Chicago, 23 October 1984, 19 August 1986.

Saffold, Howard, Chief of Security for Mayor Harold Washington, Personal Interview, Chicago, 28 July 1986.

Savage, Howard T., Circuit Court Judge in Cook County, Illinois, Personal Interview, Chicago, 2 August 1986.

Sims, George, Commander, Chicago Police Department, Personal Interview, Chicago, 13 July 1985, 14 August 1986.

Smith, Phil, Political Editor for *Dollars and Sense Magazine,* Personal Interview, Chicago, 6 August 1986.

Todd, Thomas N., Attorney, Personal Interview, Chicago, 15 August 1985, 6 June 1986, 29 July 1986.

CHAPTER XXII
SOURCES

BOOKS:

Holli, Melvin G. and Paul M. Green, *The Making of a Mayor:* Chicago, 1983, Grand Rapids, Michigan: William B. Eerdmans Publishing Company, 1984.

Levinson, Florence Humlish, *Harold Washington: A Political Biography,* Chicago: Chicago Review Press, 1983.

Travis, Dempsey J., *An Autobiography of Black Chicago,* Chicago: Urban Research Institute, Inc., 1981.

_____, *An Autobiography of Black Jazz,* Chicago: Urban Research Institute, Inc., 1983.

NEWSPAPERS:

"Mayor Yule Rooted An Old Time Religion", *Chicago Sun-Times,* 25 December 1983.

"A Walk Down Memory Lane", *Chicago Daily Defender,* 18 September 1984.

"The Mayor's Dad, His Only Hero", *Chicago Daily Defender,* 19 September 1984.

"Harold The Man, Politician and Mayor", *Chicago Daily Defender,* 22 September 1984.

"A Bitter Showdown", *Chicago Sun-Times,* 19 January 1986.

"Cities Stand Out Credits of Good Start", *Chicago Sun-Times,* 27 March 1986.

MAGAZINES:

"Mayor Harold Washington's Commemorative Issue", *Dollars and Sense,* June 1983.

"Black Politics: The New Road to Freedom" *Ebony,* August 1984.

INTERVIEWS:

Herrick, Mary, DuSable School teacher, Personal Interviews, Chicago, Various Dates: 1979, 1980, 1981, 1982 and 1983.

Washington, Harold, Mayor of Chicago, Personal Interviews, Chicago, 23 April 1983, 31 April 1983, 31 May 1983, 22 January 1984, 16 April 1984, 12 May 1984, 19 May 1984, 17 July 1984, 24 April 1985, 11 August 1985, 24 August 1985.

Plique, Eddie, Boxing and Sports Promoter, Personal Interview, Chicago, 13 September 1983.

Washington, Roy Lee Jr., Brother of Mayor Washington, Personal Interviews, Chicago, 5 May 1984, 20 May 1984.

Brown, Albert, A Track Teammate of Mayor Washington at DuSable High School, Personal Interview, Chicago, 6 August 1984.

Cheefus, John, Boyhood Friend of Mayor Washington, Personal Interview, Chicago, 11 September 1984.

Harewood, Richard A., Former Municipal Judge, Personal Interviews, Chicago, 2 January 1985, 10 February 1985.

NOTES:

Notes from the Personal Diary of Dempsey J. Travis for the years between 1937 and 1985.

CHAPTER XXIII
SOURCES

BOOKS:

The Negro Handbook, Chicago: Johnson Publishing Co., Inc., 1966.

Rod Bush, editors, *The New Black Vote: Politics and Power in Four American Cities,* San Francisco: Synthesis Publication, 1984.

The Ebony Handbook, Chicago: Johnson Publishing Co., Inc., 1974.

Melvin G. Holli and Paul M. Green, editors, *The Making of a Mayor: Chicago, 1983,* Grand Rapids, Michigan: William B. Eerdmans Publishing Co., 1984.

Paul Howell, editors, *The 1965–66 Illinois Blue Book,* Springfield, Ill: State of Illinois, 1966.

Illinois General Assembly Oral History Program, *Cecil A. Partee Memoir Vol. 1,* Springfield, Ill: State of Illinois, 1982.

Levinsohn, Florence Hamlish, *Harold Washington: A Political Biography,* Chicago Review Press, 1983.

McClory, Robert, *The Man Who Beat Clout City,* Chicago: Swallow Press, Inc., 1977.

Rakove, Milton L., *We Don't Want Nobody Sent,* Bloomington, Indiana: Indiana University Press, 1979.

Travis, Dempsey J., *An Autobiography of Black Chicago*, Chicago: Urban Research Press, 1981.

NEWSPAPERS:

"King's Birthday to be Marked in Schools," *Chicago Defender*, 5 January 1970.

"Rep. Harold Washington Tells Saga of King's Birthday Bill," *Chicago Defender*, 25 July 1973.

"Frost Ducks Mayor Issue," *Chicago Defender*, 15 May 1974.

"Metcalfe Won't be a Candidate for Mayor in '75," *Chicago Sun-Times*, 4 December 1974.

"Metcalfe Sees a Black Well Spring of Discontent," *Chicago Sun-Times*, 7 December 1974.

"Metcalfe About to Jump into Race," *Chicago Tribune*, 10 December 1974.

"How Richard Newhouse Became Mayor," *Chicago Defender*, 4 January 1975.

"Newhouse Nickels Help Keep Campaign Alive," *Chicago Defender*, 13 January 1975.

"McNeil Needs 50,000 Names," *Chicago Defender*, 14 January 1975.

"Charge Mayoral Sellout: Row Splits Top Leaders," *Chicago Defender*, 16 January 1975.

"72 Dems Fight, Jesse, Singer Win Suit," *Chicago Defender*, 16 January 1975.

"More Votes in Line Despite Defections," *Chicago Defender*, 20 January 1975.

"Newhouse Gains As McNeil Slips," *Chicago Defender*, 22 January 1975.

"Metcalfe Severs Daley Ties, Backs Singer for Mayor," *Chicago Tribune*, 26 January 1975.

"Newhouse: Calls Foe Faithless," *Chicago Defender*, 27 January 1975.

"18th Ward Hopeful Backs Newhouse," *Chicago Defender*, 28 January 1975.

"McNeil Backs Newhouse," *Chicago Defender*, 29 January 1975.

"McNeil Blasts Metcalfe," *Chicago Defender*, 30 January 1975.

"Anna Langford Sees Win," *Chicago Defender*, 30 January 1975.

"Newhouse Vote Dispute Has Been Damaged in Court," *Chicago Defender*, 4 February 1975.

"West Side Clerics Again Back Daley," *Chicago Defender*, 24 February 1975.

"Jesse Says Newhouse is Our Aspiration," *Chicago Defender*, 24 February 1975.

"See Record Black Vote, *Chicago Defender*, 24 February 1975.

"Mayor Win: Three Wards Upset," *Chicago Defender*, 26 February 1975.

"Moral Victory for Newhouse," *Chicago Defender*, 27 February 1975.

"Newhouse Charges: 'Remap Hurts Blacks'," *Chicago Defender*, 19 April 1975.

"Newhouse Map Adds Black Rep," *Chicago Defender*, 17 May 1975.

"Metcalfe-France Duel Takes Shape," *Chicago Tribune*, 7 January 1976.

"Metcalfe Allies Become Turncoats," *Chicago Tribune*, 16 January 1976.

"Campaign Brings France out of Shell," *Chicago Tribune*, 18 January 1976.

"Ralph Metcalfe Comes out Fighting," *Chicago Tribune*, 22 January 1976.

"Metcalfe Winner by a Landslide," *Chicago Sun-Times*, 17 March 1976.

"Metcalfe A Dream Win: France Loses in a Landslide," *Chicago Daily News*, 17 March 1976.

"Metcalfe Victory-Is it Black Omen for Daley?," *Chicago Tribune*, 21 March 1976.

"Metcalfe Rips Daley After Win in Ward," *Chicago Tribune,* 28 March 1976.
"Getting Metcalfe's Identity Straight," *Chicago Tribune,* 9 July 1976.
"Pick Mayor Today: Will Frost Run?" *Chicago Tribune,* 20 December 1976.
"Battle to Succeed Daley," *Chicago Tribune,* 24 December 1976.
"Police Guard Frost, Quinlan Homes," *Chicago Defender,* 27 December 1976.
"Bilandic Will be Interim Mayor," *Chicago Tribune,* 27 December 1976.
"Frost Declares He's Still In Race for Acting Mayor," *Chicago Sun-Times* 28 December 1976.
"Frost: 'No Deals': Seek Court Action," *Chicago Defender,* 28 December 1976.
"Frost Now Says He's Back in Mayor Race," *Chicago Sun-Times,* 28 December 1976.
"The Opportunity That Slipped Away," *Chicago Tribune,* 29 December 1976.
"Realism Carries the Day," Editorial *Chicago Daily News,* 29 December 1976.
"Wilson Frost Winner in City Hall (Non-Fight)," *Chicago Independent Bulletin,* 30 December 1976.
"Black Mayor Called on by Blacks," *Citizen Newspaper,* 31 December 1976.
"The Culprit is Racism," *Citizen Newspaper,* 31 December 1976.
"Fifty to Recommend Black Candidate," *Chicago Defender,* 5 January 1977.
"Leaders Push for Mayor," *Chicago Defender,* 6 January 1977.
"Group Will Insist on a Black Mayor," *Chicago Tribune,* 7 January 1977.
"Who Should Select a Black Mayor," *Chicago Tribune,* 9 January 1977.
"Renault Explains Mayoral Moves," *Chicago Defender,* 10 January 1977.
"Mayoral Search Group Multiply," *Chicago Defender,* 12 January 1977.
"Gaines Bids for Black GOP Ties in Mayor Hunt," *Chicago Defender,* 13 January 1977.
"Newhouse is Willing," *Chicago Defender,* 18 January 1977.
"Black Candidate Found But," *Chicago Defender,* 18 January 1977.
"Have Mayoral Backing, Senator Washington Says," *Chicago Daily News,* 19 January 1977.
"Blacks Favor Mayor Bid by Washington," *Chicago Tribune,* 20 January 1977.
"Washington Quits Race After a Metcalfe 'No'," *Chicago Sun-Times,* 22 January 1977.
"Hint Washington 'Reconsidering'," *Chicago Tribune,* 24 January 1977.
"Representative Washington Bows Out, New Candidate 'Emerges'," *Chicago Defender,* 24 January 1977.
"What to Talk About During a Long Ride," *Chicago Tribune,* 26 January 1977.
"Newhouse Wins Defender Poll," *Chicago Defender,* 31 January 1977.
"Blacks Square Off in Mayoral Contest," *Chicago Defender,* 31 January 1977.
"Why Black Leaders Snub Newhouse," *Chicago Defender,* 1 February 1977.
"Washington Shafted, Savage Says," *Chicago Defender,* 8 February 1977.
"Tucker Denies Misuse of Merit Funds," *Chicago Defender,* 8 February 1977.
"Washington Changes Mind, Will Run in Mayoral Primary," *Chicago Tribune,* 19 February 1977.
"Senator Washington Enters Mayoral Race After 'Draft'," *Chicago Tribune,* 20 February 1977.
"Senator in Switch on Mayoralty," *Chicago Defender,* 21 February 1977.
"Washington Vows Candid Campaign," *Chicago Defender,* 22 February 1977.
"Washington's Mini-Machine in the Works," *Chicago Defender,* 7 March 1977.

"Washington Train Picking Up Steam," *Chicago Tribune,* 9 March 1977.
"Bacon, Boutte to Back Washington," *Chicago Defender,* 21 March 1977.
"Cardiss, Rhodes in Row Over Mayor," *Chicago Defender,* 22 March 1977.
"IRS Says Washington File is Ready," *Chicago Defender,* 29 March 1977.
"Washington Reveals Plan, Blast Media," *Chicago Defender,* 5 April 1977.
"Washington See Win by His Poll," *Chicago Defender,* 19 April 1977.
"Washington Threatens Vote Suit, It's Bilandic by a Landslide," *Chicago Defender,* 20 April 1977.
"Washington Vows to Challenge Vote," *Chicago Defender,* 29 April 1977.
"Bilandic Strolls to Mayoral Victory," *Chicago Defender,* 29 April 1977.
"Harold Washington: I'll Be a Candidate for Mayor in '79," *Chicago Defender,* 2 May 1977.
"Metcalfe Dead," *Chicago Defender,* 11 October 1978.
"Dems Name Alderman Stewart to Replace Metcalfe on Ballot," *Chicago Tribune,* 17 October 1978.
"Stewart Will Replace Metcalfe on November Ballot," *Chicago Sun-Times,* 17 October 1978.
"Ralph Mecalfe's Replacement," Editorial *Chicago Tribune,* 18 October 1978.

MAGAZINES:

"Currency Exchanges Ripoffs," *Dollars and Sense*, August-September 1979.
"Congressman Ralph Metcalfe: A No Vote for the Daley Machine," *Chicago Tribune Magazine*, November 28, 1976.

INTERVIEWS:

Despres, Leon, Former Alderman and Current Parliamentary to the Mayor, Personal Interview, Chicago, 30 May 1984, 28 July 1984, 13 December 1985, 15 July 1986.
Frost, Wilson, Alderman, Personal Interview, Chicago, 21 September 1985, 7 January 1986.
Hayes, Charles, Member of U.S. House of Representatives, Personal Interview, Chicago, 16 April 1984, 5 June 1984.
Johnson, Bennett, Publisher and Civil Rights Activist, Personal Interview, Chicago, 20 March 1985, 13 August 1986, 24 September 1986.
Metcalfe, Fay, Widow of Congressman Ralph Metcalfe, Personal Interview, 1 August 1984.
Ordower, Sid, Civil rights activist, Personal Interview, Chicago, 24 April 1984.
Neal, Earl L., Attorney, Personal Interview, Chicago, 19 January 1985.
Savage, Gus, Member of U.S. House of Representatives, Personal Interview, Chicago, 22 April 1984, 13 December 1985, 14 January 1986.
Washington, Harold, Mayor of Chicago, Personal Interview, Chicago, 23 April 1983, 31 April 1983, 31 May 1983, 22 January 1984, 16 April 1984, 12 May 1984, 19 May 1984, 17 July 1984, 24 April 1985, 11 August 1985, 24 August 1985, 7 July 1986, 22 September 1986.

LETTERS AND MAILGRAMS:

Letters from Charles Hayes, chairman of the Committee for a Black Mayor, to the following persons, dated September 6, 1974. To Wit: Mayor Harold Washington, Congressman Ralph Metcalfe, A.A. Rayner, Richard H. Newhouse, Roland Burris, Josephy Bertrand, Honorable Cecil Partee, Honorable Wilson Frost, Attorney Thomas N. Todd, Edward Allen and Attorney E. Duke McNeil.

Letters from Charles Hayes, chairman of the Committee for a Black Mayor, to the following persons, dated February 5, 1975. To wit: Dr. Perry English Daryl Grisham, George Johnson, Dr. T.R.M. Howard, Harvey Collins, John H. Johnson, Elijah Muhammad, Earl Dickerson, and Dempsey J. Travis.

Mailgram from Charles Hayes and Al Boutte to Dempsey J. Travis dated January 11, 1977.

Letter from Charles Hayes to members of the Committee for a Black Mayor, dated January 11, 1977.

Mailgram from Alvin J. Boutte and Charles Hayes to Dempsey J. Travis, dated January 19, 1977.

Letter from Charles Hayes to Committee for a Black Mayor, dated February 25, 1977.

DOCUMENTS AND MEMORANDA

Statement outlining the criteria for a black mayor delivered before the Committee for a Black Mayor by State Representative Washington, dated September 14, 1974.

Pamphlet prepared by the Chicago League of Negro Voters, dated June 1962.

Sample ballot for a black mayor prepared by Dr. T.R.M. Howard, date August 14, 1974.

Criteria for a Black Mayor prepared by the Committee for a Black Mayor, undated.

Press statement by Charles A. Hayes, delivered on Tuesday, July 9, 1974.

List of leaders who attended the first black mayor's meeting in June 1974.

Memorandum from Edward C. "Bell" Berry to Congressman Ralph H. Metcalfe, dated January 8, 1975.

Ten page questionnaire for mayoral candidates for a black mayor prepared by the Committee for a Black Mayor.

Position paper, prepared by the Committee for a Black Mayor, undated.

Working paper, Committee for a Black Mayor, undated, prepared by Committee on Agenda and Platform: chairman-Thomas Todd, ex-officio-Charles Hayes, Larry Bullock, Tim Black, Lenora Cartwright, William Cousins, James Montgomery, Bill Smith.

Election schedule for mayoral and aldermanic races.

Suggested names to be called for mayoral interviews.

CHAPTER XXIV
SOURCES

BOOKS:

Black Power in Chicago, A Documentary Survey of the 1983 Mayoral Democratic Primary, Chicago: People's College Press, 1983.

Bush, Rod, editor, *The New Vote, Politics and Power in Four American Cities,* San Francisco: Syntesis Publication, 1984.

Fitzgerald, Kathleen Whalan, *Brass, Jane Byrne and the Pursuit of Power,* Chicago: Contemporary Books, Inc., 1981.

Granger, Bill and Lori, *Fighting Jane, Mayor Jane and the Chicago Machine,* New York: Dial Press, 1980.

Holli, Melvin G. and Paul M. Green, editors, *The Making of a Mayor: Chicago 1983,* Grand Rapids, Mich.: William B. Eerdmans Publishing Co., 1984.

Kleppner, Paul, *Chicago Divided: The Making of a Black Mayor,* Dekalb, Ill: Northern Illinois University Press, 1985.

Levinsohn, Florence Hamlish, *Harold Washington, A Political Biography,* Chicago: Chicago Review Press, 1983.

Powell, Paul, editor, *Illinois Blue Book 1965–1966,* Authority of State of Illinois.

Worrill, Conrad, *Worrill's World,* Chicago, Ill: National Black United Front, 1986.

NEWSPAPERS:

"Why Washington is Running," *Chicago Sun-Times,* 18 March 1971.

"Ready for a Black Mayor," *Chicago Defender,* 4 May 1977.

"Two Politicians Buried in Snow," *Chicago Tribune,* 21 January 1979.

"Chicagoans Now Fight Bitter Cold, 'Cabin Fever'," *Chicago Defender,* 27 January 1979.

"Byrne Expects Resignation," *Chicago Defender,* 3 March 1979.

"Exec's Host Gives Bilandic the Business About Snow," *Chicago Tribune,* 3 March 1979.

"Black Wards Break Binds," *Chicago Defender,* 3 March 1979.

"Official Tally—Byrne Wins by 16,775 Votes," *Chicago Tribune,* 3 March 1979.

"It Took Jane To Do It," *Chicago Defender,* 3 March 1979.

"Daley's Shoes Too Big for Bilandic," *Chicago Tribune,* 4 March 1979.

"Chicago Blacks Need A Lesson," *Chicago Tribune,* 4 March 1979.

"Slurs on Ayers, Urban League Outrageous," *Chicago Sun-Times,* 25 April 1980.

"The High Cost of a Senator," *Chicago Tribune,* 31 December 1980.

"Three Chicagoans Take Oath of Office," *Chicago Defender,* 6 January 1981.

"Alderman Tyrone F. McFolling (17) Resigns Because of Back Ailment," *Chicago Tribune,* 9 January 1981.

"Washington Gives Up State Post," *Chicago Defender,* 20 January 1981.

"Blacks File to Fight Racial Gerrymandering," *Chicago Defender*, 22 January, 1981.

"Washington Denies Plot," *Chicago Defender*, 27 January 1981.

"Congressmen Boycott Reagan," *Chicago Defender*, 4 February 1981.

"Blacks Dropped From School Board," *Chicago Defender*, 12 February 1981.

"Byrne Bumps Two Blacks," *Chicago Defender*, 12 February 1981.

"Senator Washington Seeks Police Protection After Death Threats," *Chicago Defender*, 12 February 1981.

"Out Flanked Us in School Picks: Lipinski," *Chicago Tribune*, 13 February, 1981.

"Byrne's School Move Called Political Blunder," *Chicago Defender*, 14 February 1981.

"Washington and Chew: Fighting the 'Reaper'," *Chicago Defender*, 23 February 1981.

"Congressman Washington Holds Accountability Session," *Chicago Defender*, 16 March 1981.

"School Nominee Hits Busing," *Chicago Tribune*, 21 March 1981.

"New School Board Member on Hot Seat," *Chicago Defender*, 23 March 1981.

"Community Activists Speak Up on Two New School Board Members," *Chicago Defender*, 23 March 1981.

"City Council Tables School Board Vote," *Chicago Defender*, 31 March 1981.

"Byrne-Cabrini Duet an Indictment of the City," *Chicago Defender*, 31 March 1981.

"Washington-Ewell Press Representative Scott in 26th District," *Chicago Defender*, 12 January 1982.

"Aldermen Accuse Byrne of Political Misuse," *Chicago Defender*, 10 April 1982.

"Byrne Vs Daley: How They Compare," *Chicago Sun-Times*, 7 May 1982.

"Washington a Shoe-In," *Chicago Defender*, 6 July 1982.

"October Target Date for Panhellenic Voter Registration Drive," *All Chicago City News*, 6 July 1982.

"CHA Board Member Responds to Plan to Ouster of Chairman," *Chicago Defender*, 7 July 1982.

"Streeter Wins 17th Ward Special Election," *All Chicago City News*, 9 July 1982.

"Unemployment Legislation Considered by Washington," *Chicago Defender*, 12 July 1982.

"Rap Win In CHA Action," *Chicago Defender*, 15 July 1982.

"Sweeping Changes in CHA Urged," *Chicago Defender*, 15 July 1982.

"Renault Robinson Calls CHA Battle 'A Critical Test'," *Chicago Defender*, 19 July 1982.

"Committee Approves CHA Nominees," *Chicago Defender*, 22 July 1982.

"Swiebel Resigns," *All Chicago City News*, 23 July 1982.

"Commissioners Agree to Support Voter Registration," *All Chicago City News* 23 July 1982.

"Suit Filed Against City Ward Map," *All Chicago City News*, 23 July 1982.

"Council Approves CHA Appointments in Ruckus Session," *Chicago Tribune*, 24 July 1982.

"Protestors Express Anger Over CHA Action," *Chicago Defender*, 26 July 1982.

"Washington Keys Black-Mayor's Hopes," *Chicago Tribune,* 26 July 1982.

"Washington Key Black in Mayor Race," *Chicago Tribune,* 26 July 1982.

"Threaten Boycott of Chicago Fest," *Chicago Defender,* 27 July 1982.

"CHA Protest Gains Steam as Cleric Pledges His Resignation," *Chicago Defender,* 28 July 1982.

"Stevie Wonder First To Cancel in Fest Boycott," *Chicago Defender,* 29 July 1982.

"Jackson Praises Stevie's Decision," *Chicago Defender,* 29 July 1982.

"Black Picketing Predicted at Chicago Fest," *Chicago Tribune,* 30 July 1982.

"Split in Legislative Confab," *Chicago Defender,* 2 August 1982.

"West Side G.A. Recipients Organize," *All Chicago City News,* 6 August 1982.

"Stormy Protest Against Byrne," *All Chicago City News,* 6 August 1982.

"Robinson Fights CHA 'Power Play'," *Chicago Defender,* 10 August 1982.

"Arrest Seven at CHA Meeting," *Chicago Defender,* 11 August 1982.

"P.O.W.E.R. Wins Special Voter Registration—Will Create 51st Ward, *All Chicago City News,* 20 August 1982.

"Voter Fever—Registration Theme," *Chicago Defender,* 1 September 1982.

" 'P.O.W.E.R.' Drive Nets 12,500 Registered," *Chicago Defender,* 8 September 1982.

"Charge Mayor Cut Community Funds," *Chicago Defender,* 15 September 1982.

"Sam Nolan Confesses 'Love for Police Work'," *Chicago Defender,* 20 September 1982.

"Mayoral Race Jockeying Begins," *Chicago Sun-Times,* 2 November 1982.

"Power-Full Mayor Race," *Chicago Sun-Times,* 3 November 1982.

"Daley Opens Race Today," *Chicago Sun-Times,* 4 November 1982.

"Rich Daley In Mayor's Race," *Chicago Defender,* 6 November 1982.

"Jane Byrne: Displaying A New Maturity," *Chicago Sun-Times,* 7 November 1982.

"Washington Mayoral Bid is Expected," *Chicago Sun-Times,* 8 November 1982.

"A New Political Factor: A Black With a Chance," *Chicago Tribune,* 8 November 1982.

"Washington in Mayor Race," *Chicago Tribune,* 8 November 1982.

"Blacks May Review Mayor Script," *Chicago Tribune,* 8 November 1982.

"Expect Washington to Say 'Yes' Wednesday," *Chicago Defender,* 9 November 1982.

"Washington is Reluctant But Ready," *Chicago Sun-Times,* 9 November 1982.

"Washington Leaps into Race for Mayor," *Chicago Sun-Times,* 11 November 1982.

"Lu Palmer Loses Radio Show," *Chicago Sun-Times,* 11 November 1982.

"A Machine Creature Turned Maverick Keeps Going His Own Way," *Chicago Tribune,* 11 November 1982.

"Washington in Race for Mayor," *Chicago Tribune,* 11 November 1982.

"Washington Joins the Race," *Chicago Sun-Times,* 12 November 1982.

"Washington Declares A Candidacy for All," *Chicago Metro News,* 13 November 1982.

"Byrne Announcing Candidacy With Vows, Her List of Credentials," *Chicago Sun-Times,* 22 November 1982.

"Byrne Gets Right to Campaigning," *Chicago Sun-Times*, 23 November 1982.
"And The Race Begins," *Chicago Defender*, 24 November 1982.
"Griffin To Run Byrne Election Drive," *Chicago Sun-Times*, 26 November 1982.
"Fee Fight Reopening Remap Scar," *Chicago Tribune*, 5 May 1986.

MAGAZINES:

"The Machine is not dead. It is waiting for Richie Daley," *Illinois Issues*, February 18, 1981.
"Bilandic: How did you get the mayor's job?," *Illinois Issues*, July 30, 1977.
"A transfer of power," *Chicago Magazine*, May 1979.

INTERVIEWS:

Braun, Carol Moseley, State Representative, Personal Interview, 4 March, 1985.
Brown, Bob, Political Activist and Organizer, Personal Interview, 18 October 1984.
Cerda, Maria B., Director, Mayor's Office of Employment and Training, Personal Interview, 25 October 1985.
Clements, George, Father of Holy Angels Church, Personal Interview, 18 October 1984, 14 February 1986.
Coleman, Slim, Editor and Chief of *All Chicago City News* and Chairperson of the Heart of Uptown Coalition, Personal Interview, 16 June 1984, 17 October 1986.
Gardner, Edward, Chairman of the Board of Soft Sheen Products Co., Inc., Personal Interview, 17 July 1984.
Hayes, Charles, Member of U.S. House of Representatives, Personal Interview, 16 April 1984, 5 June 1984, 8 June 1984.
Jackson, Reverend Jesse L., Former Staff Member of the Southern Christian Leadership Conference, President of Operation Breadbasket, 1984 Presidential Candidate, An International Civil Rights Leader, and Founder and Past President of Operation PUSH, Personal Interview, 30 November 1984.
Johnson, Al, President of both Johnson Cadillac the Political Action Conference of Illinois (PACI), and Dollar-A-Year-Man for Mayor Washington, Personal Interview, 25 July 1984.
Johnson, Bennett, Executive of Pathe Press and Political Activist, Personal Interview, 20 March 1985, 13 August 1986, September 24 1986.
Minor, Judson, Corporation Counsel for the city of Chicago, Personal Interview, 16 January 1986.
Newhouse, Richard, State Senator, Personal Interview, 23 October 1984, 20 December 1985.
O'Hare, George, Former Executive of Sears, Roebuck and Co., Radio Host of *Accent the Positive* and early volunteer in the Washington Campaign, Personal Interview, 17 May 1985, 31 May 1985, 18 October 1986.
Palmer, Lu, Journalist, Radio Host and Political Activist, Personal Interview, 13 March 1985.
Robinson, Renault, Former President of the Afro-American Patrolman's League and Currently a Member of the Board of Directors of the Chicago Housing Authority, Personal Interview, 6 June 1984, 6 July 1984.

Sampson, Reverend Al, Pastor of Fernwood Methodist Church, Personal Interview, 17 August 1984, 23 August 1984, 19 October 1986.

Washington, Harold, Mayor of the city of Chicago, 23 April 1983, 31 April 1983, 31 May 1983, 22 January 1984, 16 April 1984, 12 May 1984, 19 May 1984, 17 July 1984, 24 August 1984, 24 August 1985, 22 September 1986, 15 October 1986.

Worrill, Conrad W., Professor at Northeastern University, Personal Interview, 18 October 1984.

Wyatt Jr., Reverend Claude, Pastor of Vernon Park Church of God, Personal Interview, 4 August 1984, 28 August 1984.

Wyatt, Addie, Union Executive, Personal Interview, 4 August 1984.

DOCUMENTS:

Joint brief for plaintiffs-appellants in the United States Court of Appeals for the Seventh District, Cases #83-1044, #83-2065 and #63-2126.

Appeals from the United States District Court for Northern Illinois of Illinois Eastern Division:

Case #82 C 4085 Mars Ketchum-et al., plaintiff-appellants vs Jane M. Byrne-et al., defendants-appellees;

Case #82 C 4820 Political Action Conference of Illinois-et al., plaintiffs-appellants vs City Council, City of Chicago-et al., defendants-appellees;

Case #82 C 44231 Charmaine Velasco-et al., plaintiffs-appellants vs Jane M. Byrne-et al., defendants-appellees.

Voter registration manual prepared by Soft Sheen Products, Inc.

CHAPTER XXV
SOURCES

BOOKS:

Black Power in Chicago, A Documentary Survey of the 1983 Mayoral Democratic Primary, Chicago: People's College Press, 1983.

Bush, Rod, editor, *The New Vote, Politics and Power in Four American Cities,* San Francisco: Syntesis Publication, 1984.

Holli, Melvin G. and Paul M. Green, editors, *The Making of a Mayor: Chicago 1983,* Grand Rapids, Mich: William Eerdmans Publishing Co., 1984.

Kleppner, Paul, *Chicago Divided: The Making of a Black Mayor,* Dekalb, Ill: Northern Illinois University Press, 1985.

Levinsohn, Florence Hamlish, *Harold Washington, A Political Biography,* Chicago: Chicago Review Press, 1983.

Worrill, Conrad, *Worrill's World,* Chicago, Ill: National Black United Front, 1986.

NEWSPAPERS

"The Chicago Mayoral Race," *Chicago Independent Bulletin,* 9 December 1982.

"Fifteen Thousand at Rally for Washington," *Chicago Defender,* 7 February 1983.

"Fifteen Thousand Means Momentum in Mayoral Marathon," *Chicago Observer,* 12 February 1983.

"Washington Wins, Heavy Black Turnout Key to Victory," *Chicago Tribune,* 23 February 1983.

"Representative Washington, Chicago Victor, Sets Ambitious City Hall Agenda," *New York Times,* 24 February 1983.

"Epton, Washington Trade Charges," *Chicago Sun-Times,* 26 February 1983.

"Washington Can Help Chicago's Racial Mood," *USA Today,* 11 March 1983.

"US Representative Washington for Mayor," *Chicago Tribune,* 13 March 1983.

"Committeemen Gum Up Machine," *Chicago Tribune,* 13 March 1983.

"Tribune, IVI Unit, Endorse Washington," *Chicago Defender,* 14 March 1983.

"Charge Epton's Aide in 'Theft'," *Chicago Defender,* 16 March 1983.

"Mayoral Rivals Rip One Another," *Chicago Sun-Times,* 18 March 1983.

"It's Politics On Parade at St. Pat's," *Chicago Tribune,* 18 March 1983.

"Won't Tell All Details of Health—Epton," *Chicago Sun-Times,* 2 April 1983.

"Washington Debate Bid Rejected by Epton," *Chicago Sun-Times,* 2 April 1983.

Racist Plot Underway in Cop Area I Division," *Chicago Defender,* 6 April 1983.

"Chicago Candidates' Advisors Clash as Showdown Nears," *Washington Post,* 7 April 1983.

"Racial Issue Puts City in US Spotlight," *Chicago Tribune,* 7 April 1983.

"Angry Washington Vows to Fight 'Lies,'," *Chicago Sun-Times,* 8 April 1983.

"Irate Washington Retaliates," *Chicago Tribune,* 8 April 1983.

"Washington Elected: City's First Black Mayor," *Chicago Tribune,* 13 April 1983.

"Tension Rules at 'Victory Parties'," *Chicago Sun-Times,* 13 April 1983.

"Washington Fans Watch History in Making," *Chicago Tribune,* 13 April 1983.

"Throng Jams Victory Site," *Chicago Defender,* 13 April 1983.

"It's Washington, Huge Voters Key, Epton Exits on Bitter Note," *Chicago Sun-Times,* 13 April 1983.

"It's Washington's Day, But Battle for Power Looms," *Chicago Tribune,* 29 April 1983.

"Washington Takes Office; Vows Layoffs, Pay Slashes," *Chicago Sun-Times,* 30 April 1983.

"Emotion Gripped Washington's Audience," *Chicago Sun-Times,* 30 April 1983.

"Inaugural Surprises Some, Please Others," *Chicago Tribune,* 30 April 1983.

"Mayor Comes In Fine," *Chicago Tribune,* 30 April 1983.

MAGAZINES:

"Race in the Race: The Candidates and Their Strategies," *Chicago Reporter,* March 1983.

"Chicago: A Dream Come True," *Newsweek,* March 7, 1983.

"Mayor Jane Byrne, Bad Sport," *Newsweek,* March 28, 1983.

"Chicago's Ugly Election," *Newsweek,* 11 April 1983.

"The New Black Politics," *Newsweek,* 11 April 1983.

"Harold Washington Wins Hot Race To Become First Black Mayor of Chicago," *Jet,* May 2, 1983.

"Harold Washington's Muted Victory," *New Republic,* May 2, 1983.

"The Winds Shift in Chicago," *The Progressive,* June 1983.

"Mayor Harold Washington: Changing of the Guard in Chicago," *Ebony,* July 1983.

"Black Politics New Road to Freedom," *Ebony,* August 1984.

DOCUMENTS:

United States of America, plaintiff vs. Harold Washington, defendant Case #71 CR 292 Transcript for proceedings before Honorable Joseph Sam Perry, judge. United States of America, Northern District of Illinois, Eastern Division.

INTERVIEWS:

Alter, Joanne, Commissioner of the Metropolitan Sanitary District, Personal Interview, 2 October 1985.

Black, Timuel, Professor at Loop College, Personal Interview, 18 April 1984.

Braun, Carol Moseley, State Representative, Personal Interview, 4 March 1985.

Brookins, Howard, State Representative, Personal Interview, 3 April 1986.

Brown, Bob, Civil Rights Activist, Personal Interview, 18 October 1984.

Cerda, Maria B., Director, Mayor's Office on Employment and Training, Personal Interview, 25 October 1985.

Clements, George, Father of Holy Angels Church, 18 October 1984, 14 February 1986.

Coleman, Slim, Editor and Chief of *All Chicago City News* and Chairperson of the Heart of Uptown Coalition, Personal Interview, 16 June 1984, 17 October 1986.

Cotton, Jesse, Pastor of Greater Institutional AME Church, Personal Interview, 31 August 1984.

Davis, Danny, Alderman, Personal Interview, 6 October 1984.

Dunne, George W., President of the Cook County Board, Personal Interview, 14 August 1985.

Ellis, Morris, Musician and Orchestra Leader, Personal Interview, 18 February 1986.

Gardner, Edward, Chairman of the Board of Soft Sheen Products, Inc., Personal Interview, 17 July 1984.

Gilbert, Herman, Publisher, Personal Interview, 28 April 1984.

Hayes, Charles, Member of US House of Representatives, Personal Interview, 16 April 1984, 5 June 1984, 8 June 1984.

Hicks Jr., Odell, Certified Public Accountant, Personal Interview, 19 January 1985.

Jackson, Jesse L., Former Staff Member of the Southern Christian Leadership Conference, President of Operation Breadbasket, 1984 Presidential Candidate, An International Civil Rights Leader, and Founder and Past President of Operation PUSH, Personal Interview, 30 November 1984.

Jefferson, Nancy, Executive Secretary for the Midwest Community Council, Personal Interview, 3 July 1984.

Johnson, Al, President of Johnson Cadillac, the Political Action Conference of Illinois (PACI), and Dollar-A-Year-Man for Mayor Washington, Personal Interview, 25 July 1984.

Johnson, George, President and Chief Executive Officer of Johnson Products, Personal Interview, 7 December 1984.

Kennon, Lawrence, Attorney, Personal Interview, 20 June 1984.

McKeever, Lester, Attorney and Certified Public Accountant, Personal Interview, 7 January 1985.

Minor, Judson, Corporation Counsel for the city of Chicago, Personal Interview, 16 January 1986.

Newhouse, Richard, State Senator, Personal Interview, 23 October 1984, 20 December 1985.

O'Hare, George, Public Relations Consultant, Radio Host and Civil Rights Activist, Personal Interview, 17 May 1985, 31 May 1985, 18 October 1986.

Palmer, Lu, Radio Host, Journalist and Civil Rights Activist, 13 March 1985.

Robinson, Renault, Chairman of the Chicago Housing Authority, Former President of the Afro-American Patrolman's League, Personal Interview, 6 June 1984, 6 July 1984, 6 August 1984.

Sampson, Al, Pastor of Fernwood Methodist Church, Personal Interview, 17 August 1984, 23 August 1984, 19 October 1986.

Savage, Gus, Congressman, Personal Interview.

Sive-Tomashefsky, Rebecca, Public Relations Director and Member of Board of Directors of Chicago Park District, Personal Interview, 12 September 1984.

Washington, Harold, Mayor of the city of Chicago, Personal Interview, 23 April 1983, 31 April 1983, 31 May 1983, 22 January 1984, 16 April 1984, 12 May 1984, 19 May 1984, 17 July 1984, 24 August 1984, 24 August 1985, 22 September 1986, 15 October 1986.

Worrill, Conrad, Professor at Northeastern University, Personal Interview, 18 October 1984.

Wyatt, Claude, Pastor of Vernon Park Church of God, Personal Interview, 4 August 1984.

Wyatt, Addie, Union Executive, Personal Interview, 4 August 1984.

Index